NEW X MEN

WRITER: *Grant Morrison*

PENCILERS: *John Paul Leon, Igor Kordey, Phil Jimenez, Ethan Van Sciver, Keron Grant & Frank Quitely*

INKERS: *Bill Sienkiewicz, Igor Kordey, Andy Lanning, Norm Rapmund, Tim Townsend & Avalon Studios*

COLORISTS: *Hi-Fi Design, Dave McCaig & Chris Chuckry*

LETTERERS: *RS & Comicraft's Saida, Jimmy, Wes & Albert! and Virtual Calligraphy's Chris Eliopoulos*

COVER ARTISTS: *Frank Quitely, Ethan Van Sciver, Igor Kordey & Phil Jimenez*

ASSISTANT EDITOR: *Nova Ren Suma*

ASSOCIATE EDITOR: *Mike Raicht*

EDITOR: *Mike Marts*

COLLECTION EDITOR: *Jennifer Grünwald*
EDITORIAL ASSISTANTS: *James Emmett & Joe Hochstein*
ASSISTANT EDITORS: *Alex Starbuck & Nelson Ribeiro*
EDITOR, SPECIAL PROJECTS: *Mark D. Beazley*
SENIOR EDITOR, SPECIAL PROJECTS: *Jeff Youngquist*
SENIOR VICE PRESIDENT OF SALES: *David Gabriel*
BOOK DESIGNER: *Patrick McGrath*

EDITOR IN CHIEF: *Joe Quesada*
PUBLISHER: *Dan Buckley*
EXECUTIVE PRODUCER: *Alan Fine*

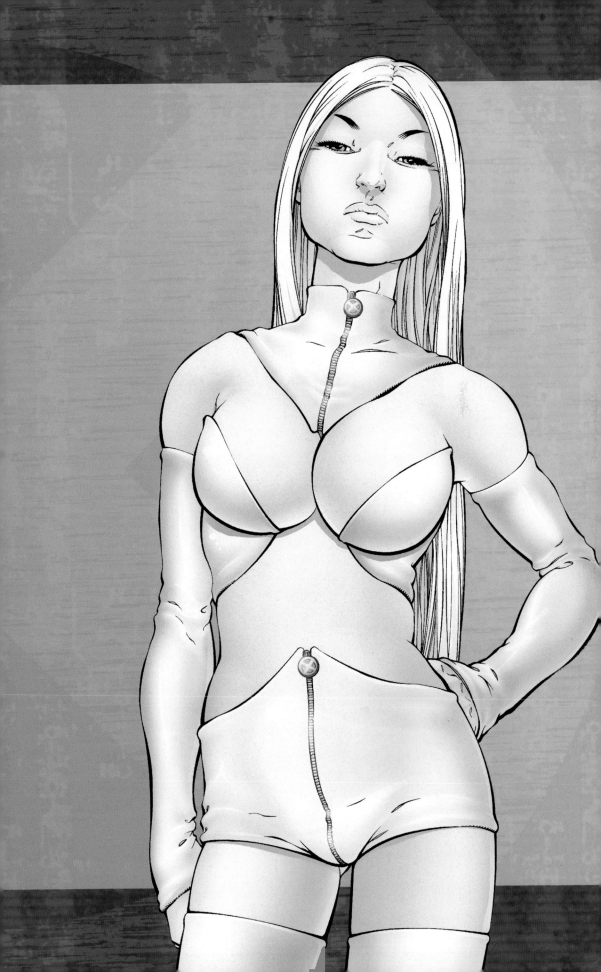

#127

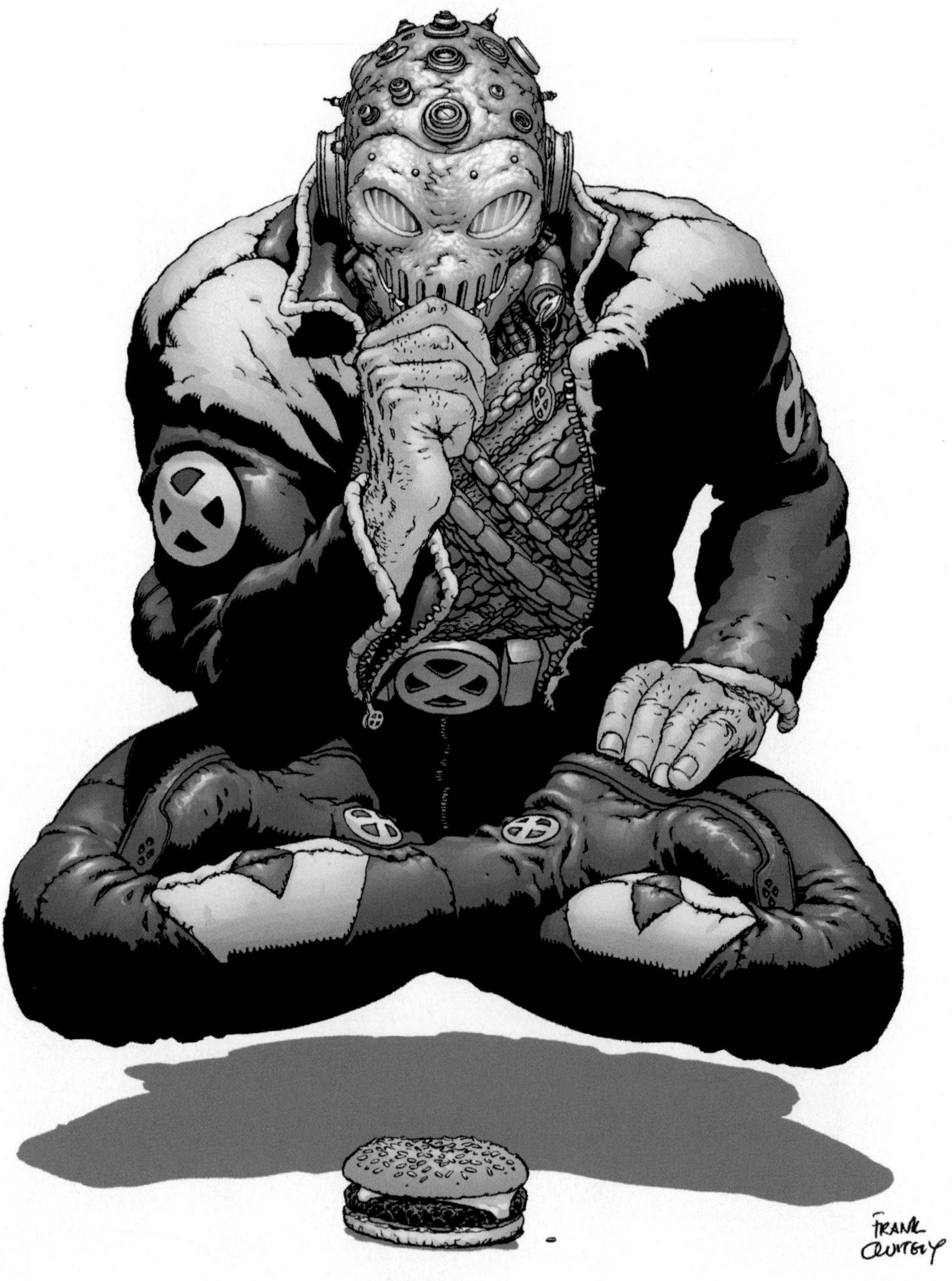
FRANK
QUITELY

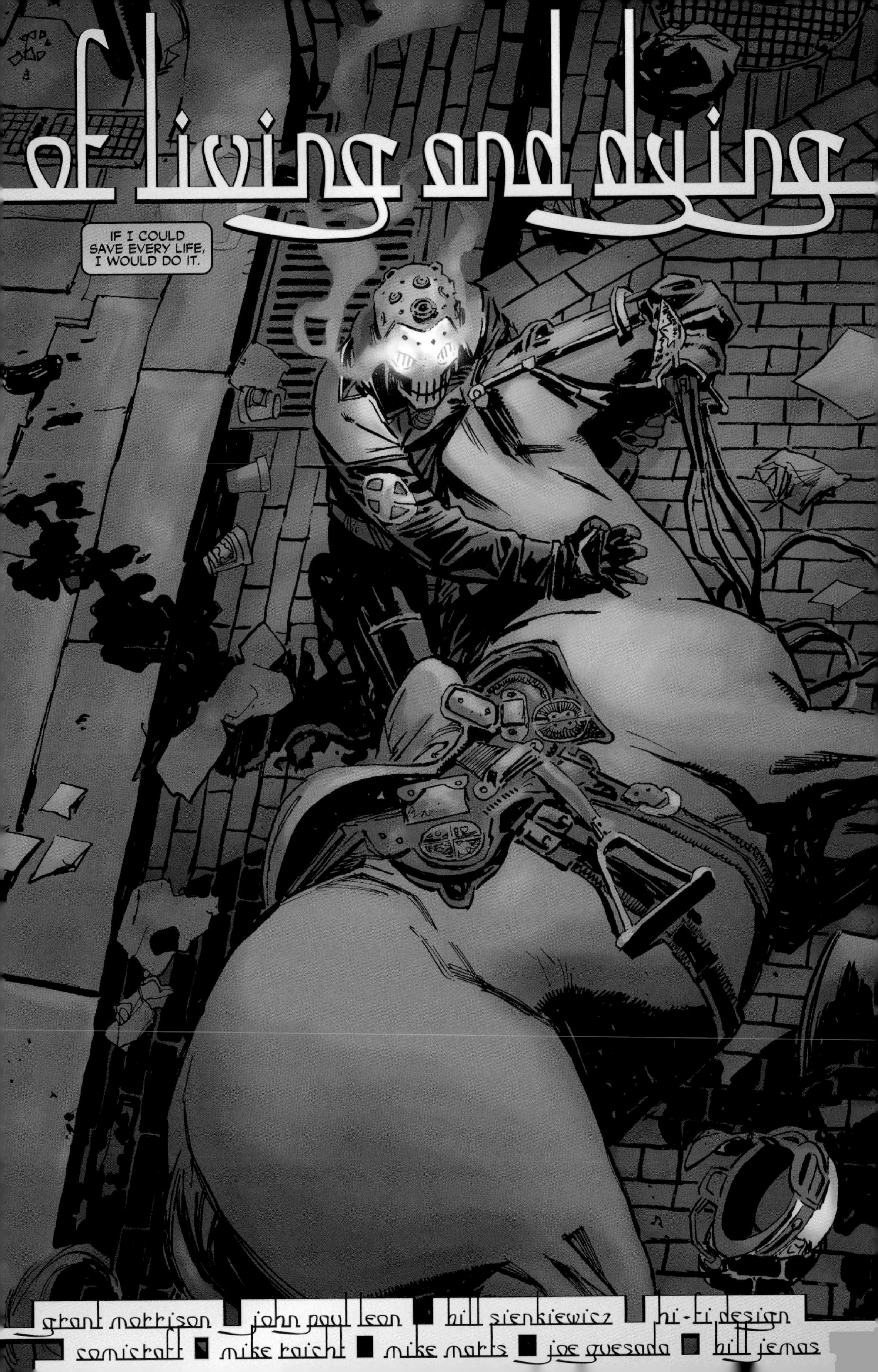

of living and dying
IF I COULD SAVE EVERY LIFE, I WOULD DO IT.
grant morrison
john paul leon
bill sienkiewicz
hi-fi design
comicraft
mike raicht
mike marts
joe quesada
bill jemas

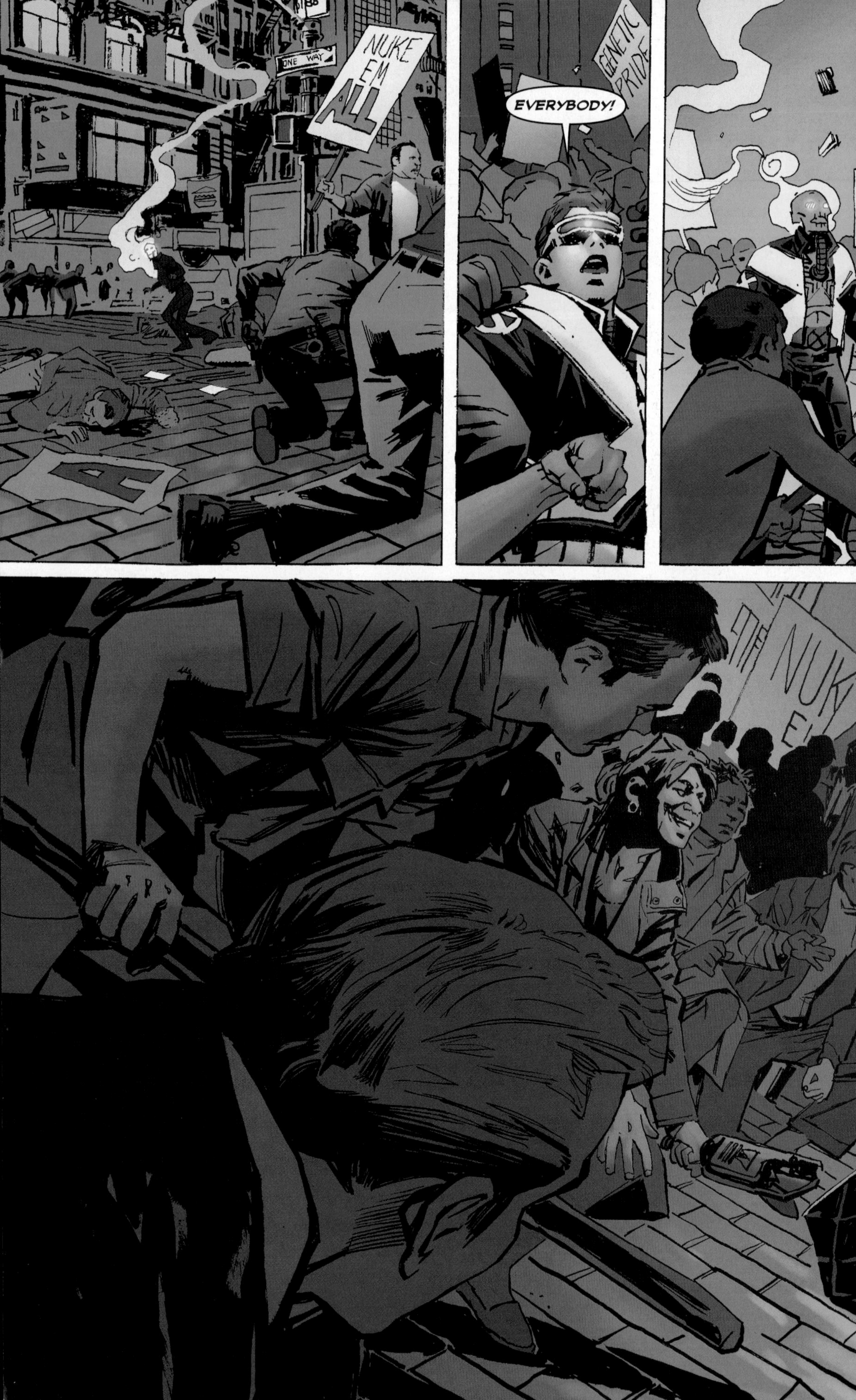
ONE WAY
NUKE EM ALL
GENETIC PRIDE
EVERYBODY!

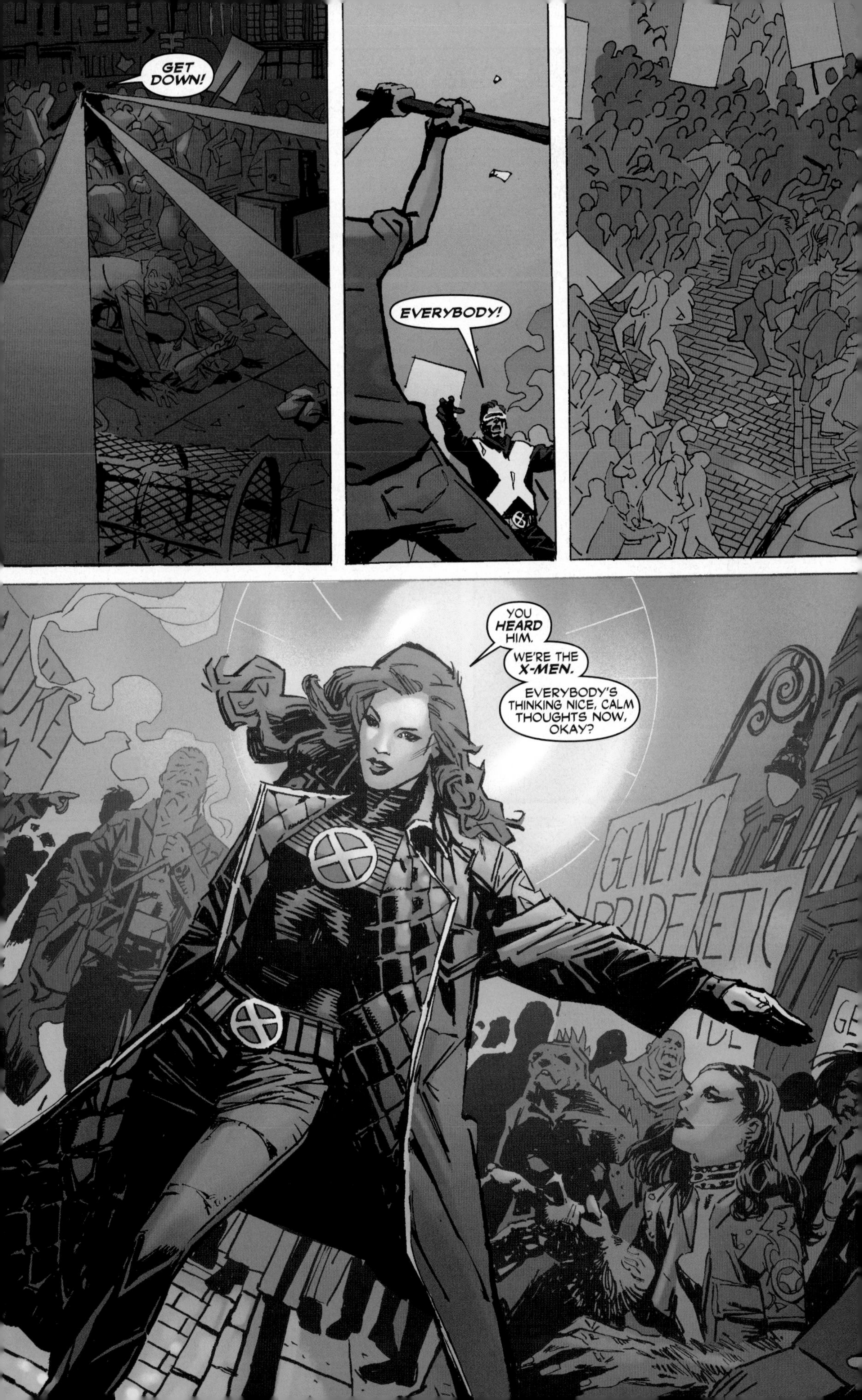
GET DOWN!
EVERYBODY!
YOU HEARD HIM.
WE'RE THE X-MEN.
EVERYBODY'S THINKING NICE, CALM THOUGHTS NOW, OKAY?
GENETIC PRIDE
GENETIC

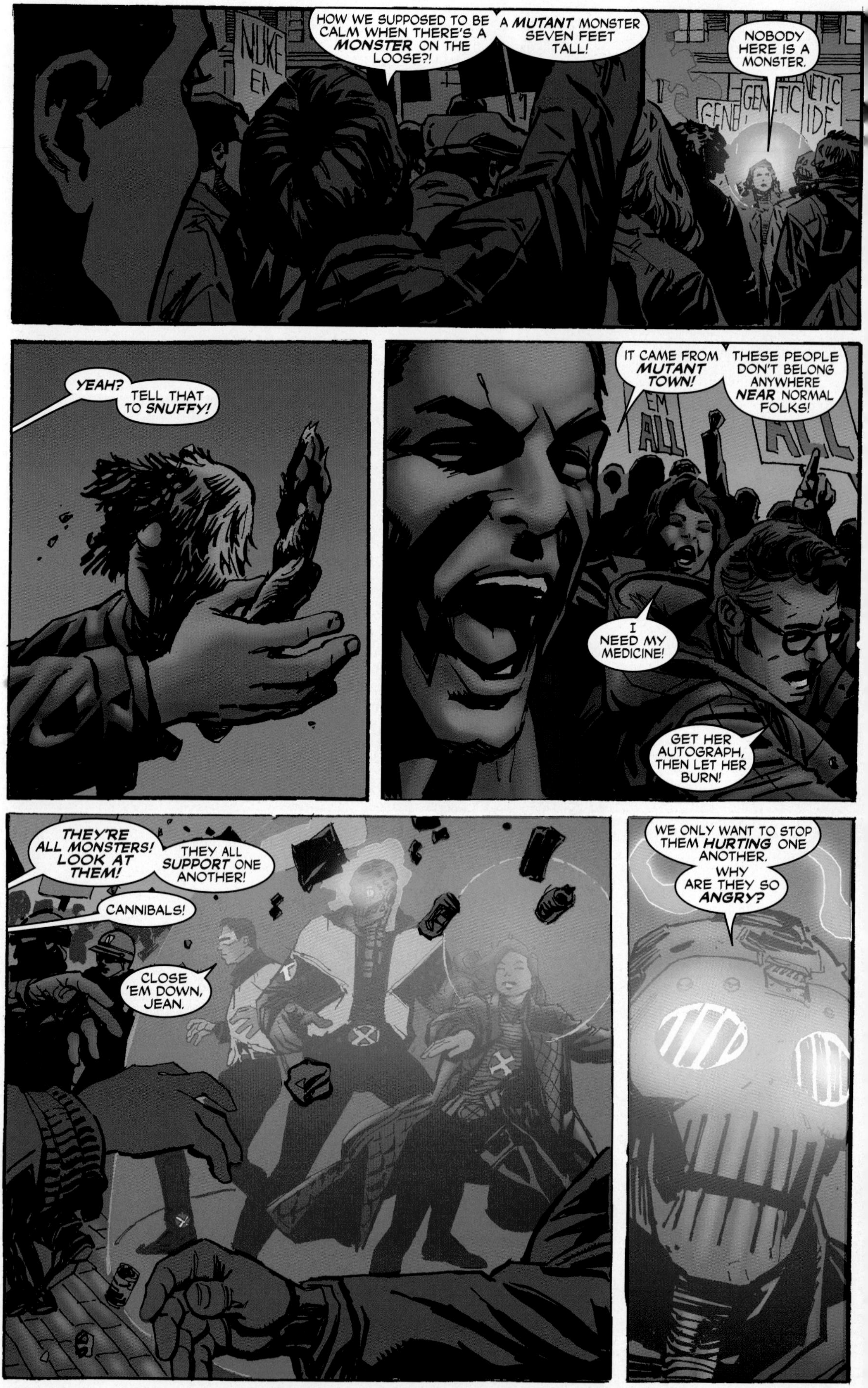
HOW WE SUPPOSED TO BE CALM WHEN THERE'S A MONSTER ON THE LOOSE?!
A MUTANT MONSTER SEVEN FEET TALL!
NOBODY HERE IS A MONSTER.
YEAH? TELL THAT TO SNUFFY!
IT CAME FROM MUTANT TOWN!
THESE PEOPLE DON'T BELONG ANYWHERE NEAR NORMAL FOLKS!
I NEED MY MEDICINE!
GET HER AUTOGRAPH, THEN LET HER BURN!
THEY'RE ALL MONSTERS! LOOK AT THEM!
THEY ALL SUPPORT ONE ANOTHER!
CANNIBALS!
CLOSE 'EM DOWN, JEAN.
WE ONLY WANT TO STOP THEM HURTING ONE ANOTHER. WHY ARE THEY SO ANGRY?

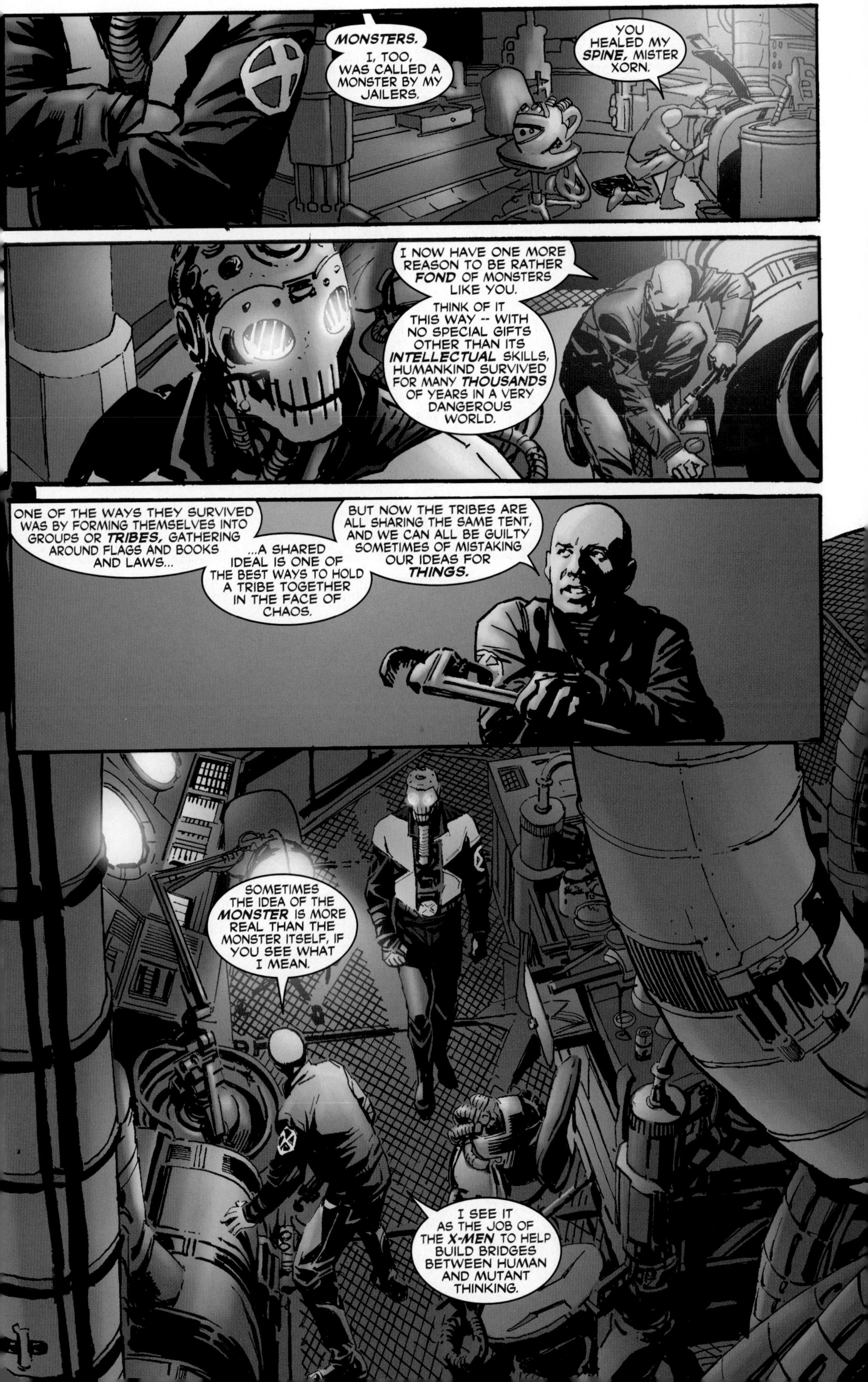
MONSTERS.
I, TOO, WAS CALLED A MONSTER BY MY JAILERS.
YOU HEALED MY SPINE, MISTER XORN.
I NOW HAVE ONE MORE REASON TO BE RATHER FOND OF MONSTERS LIKE YOU.
THINK OF IT THIS WAY -- WITH NO SPECIAL GIFTS OTHER THAN ITS INTELLECTUAL SKILLS, HUMANKIND SURVIVED FOR MANY THOUSANDS OF YEARS IN A VERY DANGEROUS WORLD.
ONE OF THE WAYS THEY SURVIVED WAS BY FORMING THEMSELVES INTO GROUPS OR TRIBES, GATHERING AROUND FLAGS AND BOOKS AND LAWS...
...A SHARED IDEAL IS ONE OF THE BEST WAYS TO HOLD A TRIBE TOGETHER IN THE FACE OF CHAOS.
BUT NOW THE TRIBES ARE ALL SHARING THE SAME TENT, AND WE CAN ALL BE GUILTY SOMETIMES OF MISTAKING OUR IDEAS FOR THINGS.
SOMETIMES THE IDEA OF THE MONSTER IS MORE REAL THAN THE MONSTER ITSELF, IF YOU SEE WHAT I MEAN.
I SEE IT AS THE JOB OF THE X-MEN TO HELP BUILD BRIDGES BETWEEN HUMAN AND MUTANT THINKING.

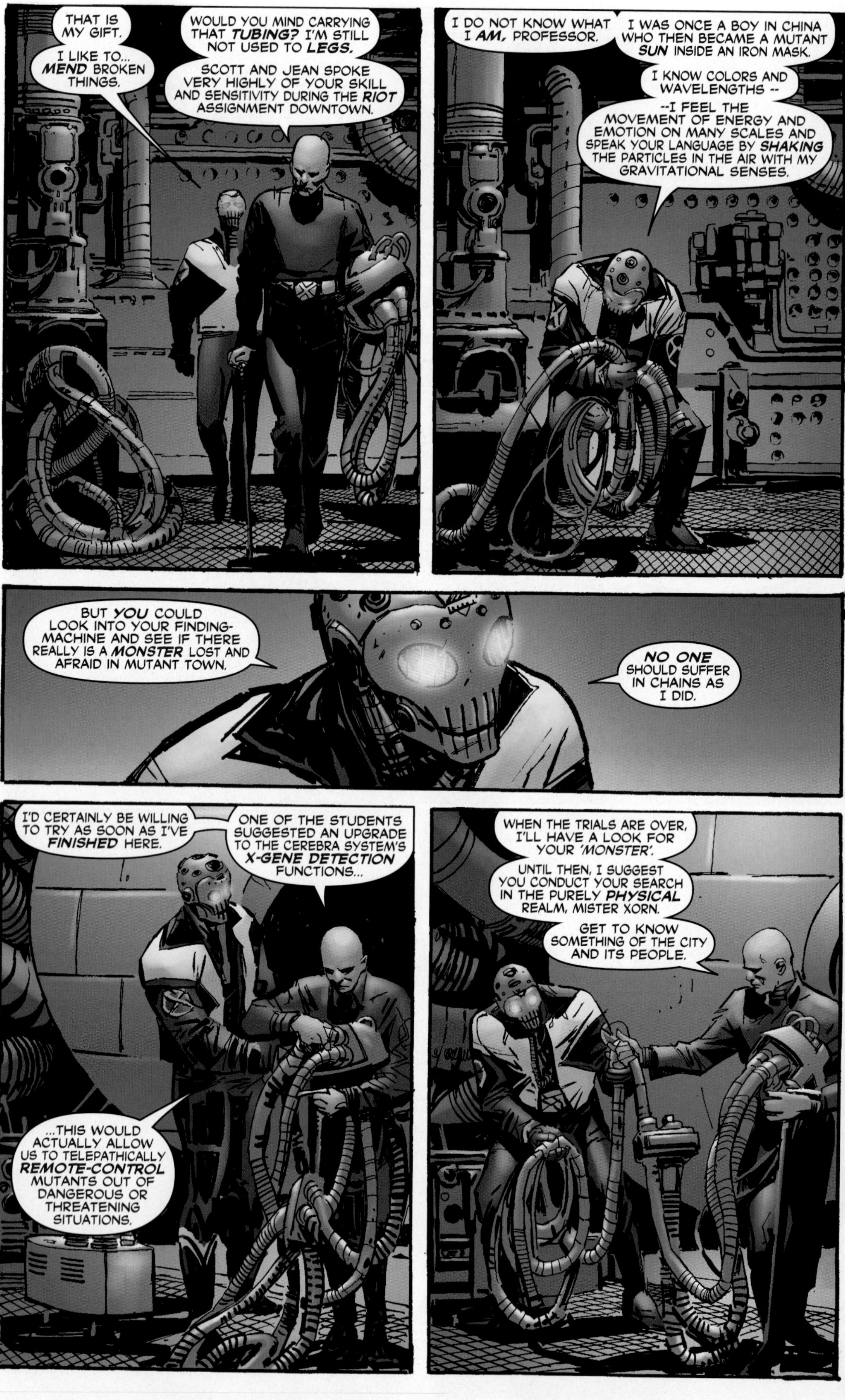
THAT IS MY GIFT.
I LIKE TO... MEND BROKEN THINGS.
WOULD YOU MIND CARRYING THAT TUBING? I'M STILL NOT USED TO LEGS.
SCOTT AND JEAN SPOKE VERY HIGHLY OF YOUR SKILL AND SENSITIVITY DURING THE RIOT ASSIGNMENT DOWNTOWN.
I DO NOT KNOW WHAT I AM, PROFESSOR.
I WAS ONCE A BOY IN CHINA WHO THEN BECAME A MUTANT SUN INSIDE AN IRON MASK.
I KNOW COLORS AND WAVELENGTHS --
--I FEEL THE MOVEMENT OF ENERGY AND EMOTION ON MANY SCALES AND SPEAK YOUR LANGUAGE BY SHAKING THE PARTICLES IN THE AIR WITH MY GRAVITATIONAL SENSES.
BUT YOU COULD LOOK INTO YOUR FINDING-MACHINE AND SEE IF THERE REALLY IS A MONSTER LOST AND AFRAID IN MUTANT TOWN.
NO ONE SHOULD SUFFER IN CHAINS AS I DID.
I'D CERTAINLY BE WILLING TO TRY AS SOON AS I'VE FINISHED HERE.
ONE OF THE STUDENTS SUGGESTED AN UPGRADE TO THE CEREBRA SYSTEM'S X-GENE DETECTION FUNCTIONS...
...THIS WOULD ACTUALLY ALLOW US TO TELEPATHICALLY REMOTE-CONTROL MUTANTS OUT OF DANGEROUS OR THREATENING SITUATIONS.
WHEN THE TRIALS ARE OVER, I'LL HAVE A LOOK FOR YOUR 'MONSTER'.
UNTIL THEN, I SUGGEST YOU CONDUCT YOUR SEARCH IN THE PURELY PHYSICAL REALM, MISTER XORN.
GET TO KNOW SOMETHING OF THE CITY AND ITS PEOPLE.

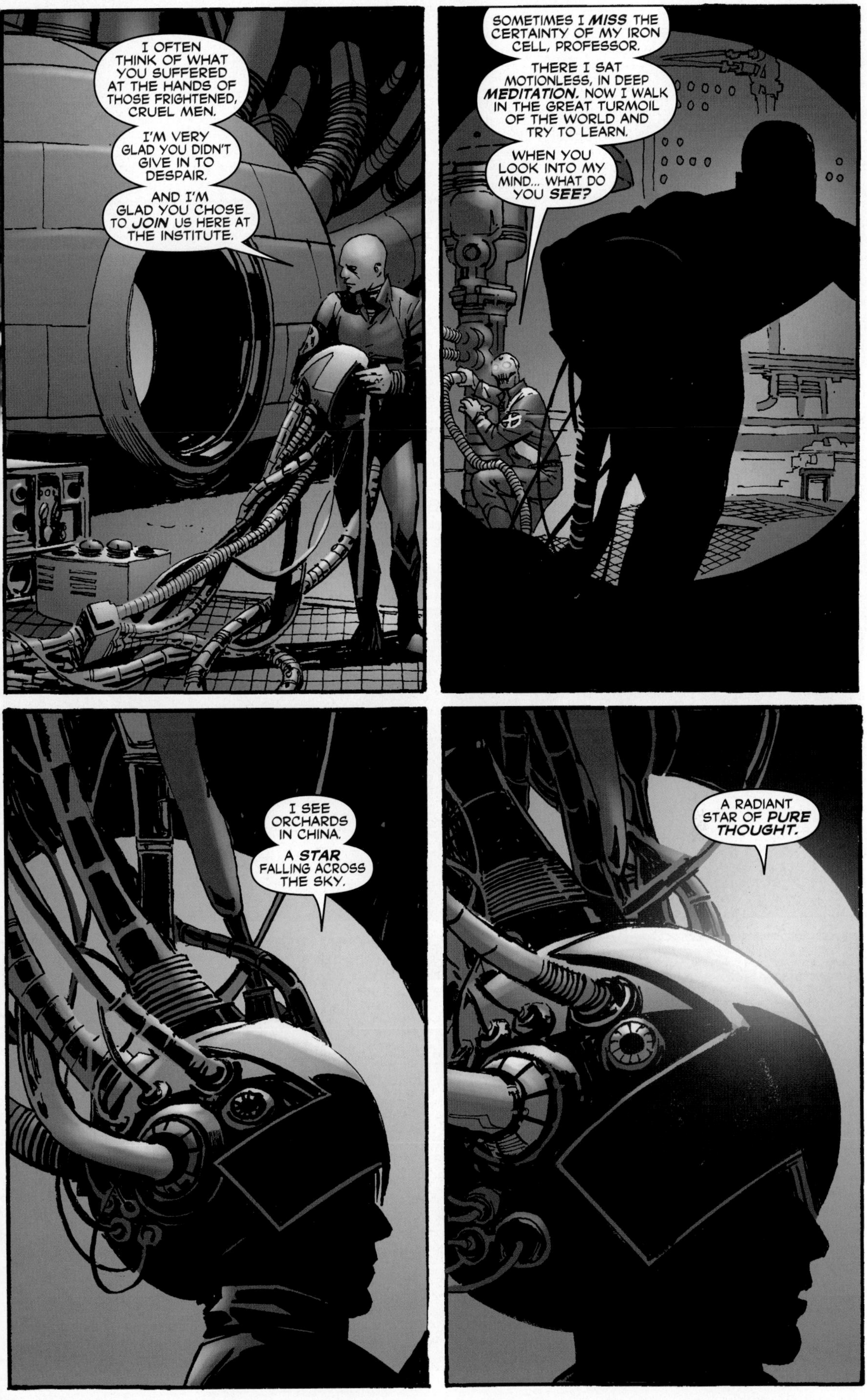
I OFTEN THINK OF WHAT YOU SUFFERED AT THE HANDS OF THOSE FRIGHTENED, CRUEL MEN.
I'M VERY GLAD YOU DIDN'T GIVE IN TO DESPAIR.
AND I'M GLAD YOU CHOSE TO JOIN US HERE AT THE INSTITUTE.
SOMETIMES I MISS THE CERTAINTY OF MY IRON CELL, PROFESSOR.
THERE I SAT MOTIONLESS, IN DEEP MEDITATION. NOW I WALK IN THE GREAT TURMOIL OF THE WORLD AND TRY TO LEARN.
WHEN YOU LOOK INTO MY MIND... WHAT DO YOU SEE?
I SEE ORCHARDS IN CHINA.
A STAR FALLING ACROSS THE SKY.
A RADIANT STAR OF PURE THOUGHT.

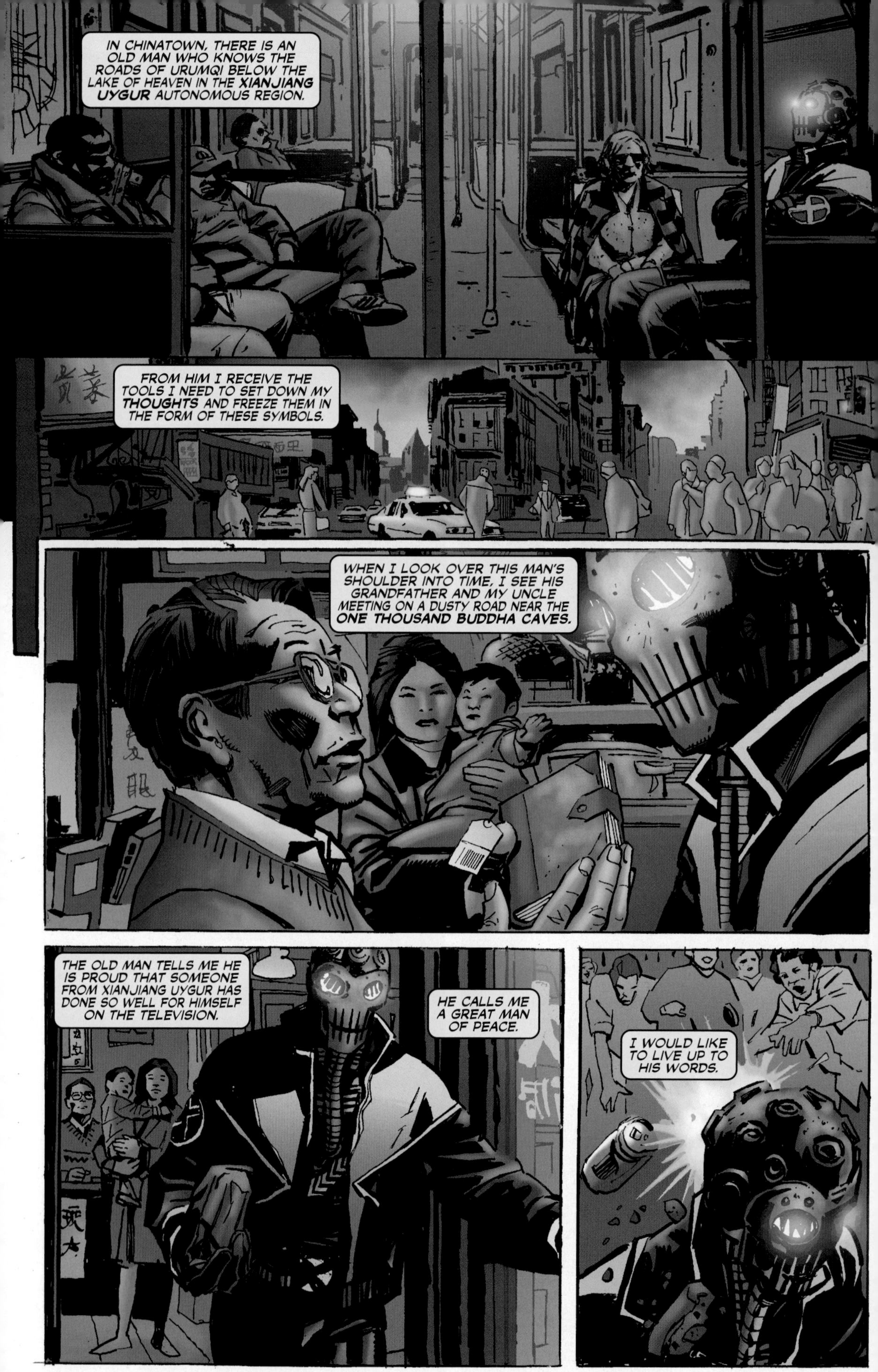
IN CHINATOWN, THERE IS AN OLD MAN WHO KNOWS THE ROADS OF URUMQI BELOW THE LAKE OF HEAVEN IN THE XIANJIANG UYGUR AUTONOMOUS REGION.
FROM HIM I RECEIVE THE TOOLS I NEED TO SET DOWN MY THOUGHTS AND FREEZE THEM IN THE FORM OF THESE SYMBOLS.
WHEN I LOOK OVER THIS MAN'S SHOULDER INTO TIME, I SEE HIS GRANDFATHER AND MY UNCLE MEETING ON A DUSTY ROAD NEAR THE ONE THOUSAND BUDDHA CAVES.
THE OLD MAN TELLS ME HE IS PROUD THAT SOMEONE FROM XIANJIANG UYGUR HAS DONE SO WELL FOR HIMSELF ON THE TELEVISION.
HE CALLS ME A GREAT MAN OF PEACE.
I WOULD LIKE TO LIVE UP TO HIS WORDS.

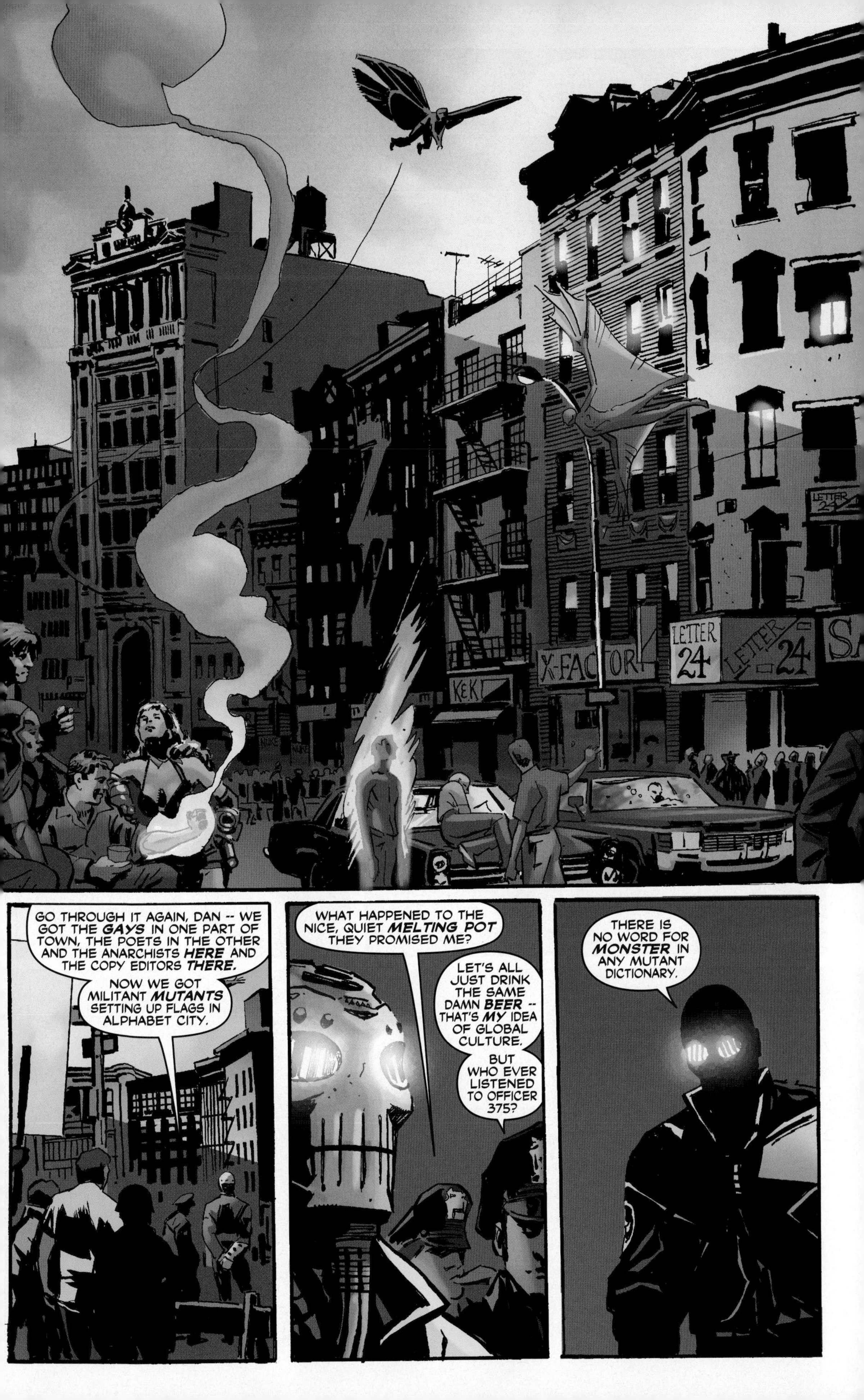
LETTER 24
LETTER 24
X-FACTOR
GO THROUGH IT AGAIN, DAN -- WE GOT THE GAYS IN ONE PART OF TOWN, THE POETS IN THE OTHER AND THE ANARCHISTS HERE AND THE COPY EDITORS THERE.
NOW WE GOT MILITANT MUTANTS SETTING UP FLAGS IN ALPHABET CITY.
WHAT HAPPENED TO THE NICE, QUIET MELTING POT THEY PROMISED ME?
LET'S ALL JUST DRINK THE SAME DAMN BEER -- THAT'S MY IDEA OF GLOBAL CULTURE.
BUT WHO EVER LISTENED TO OFFICER 375?
THERE IS NO WORD FOR MONSTER IN ANY MUTANT DICTIONARY.

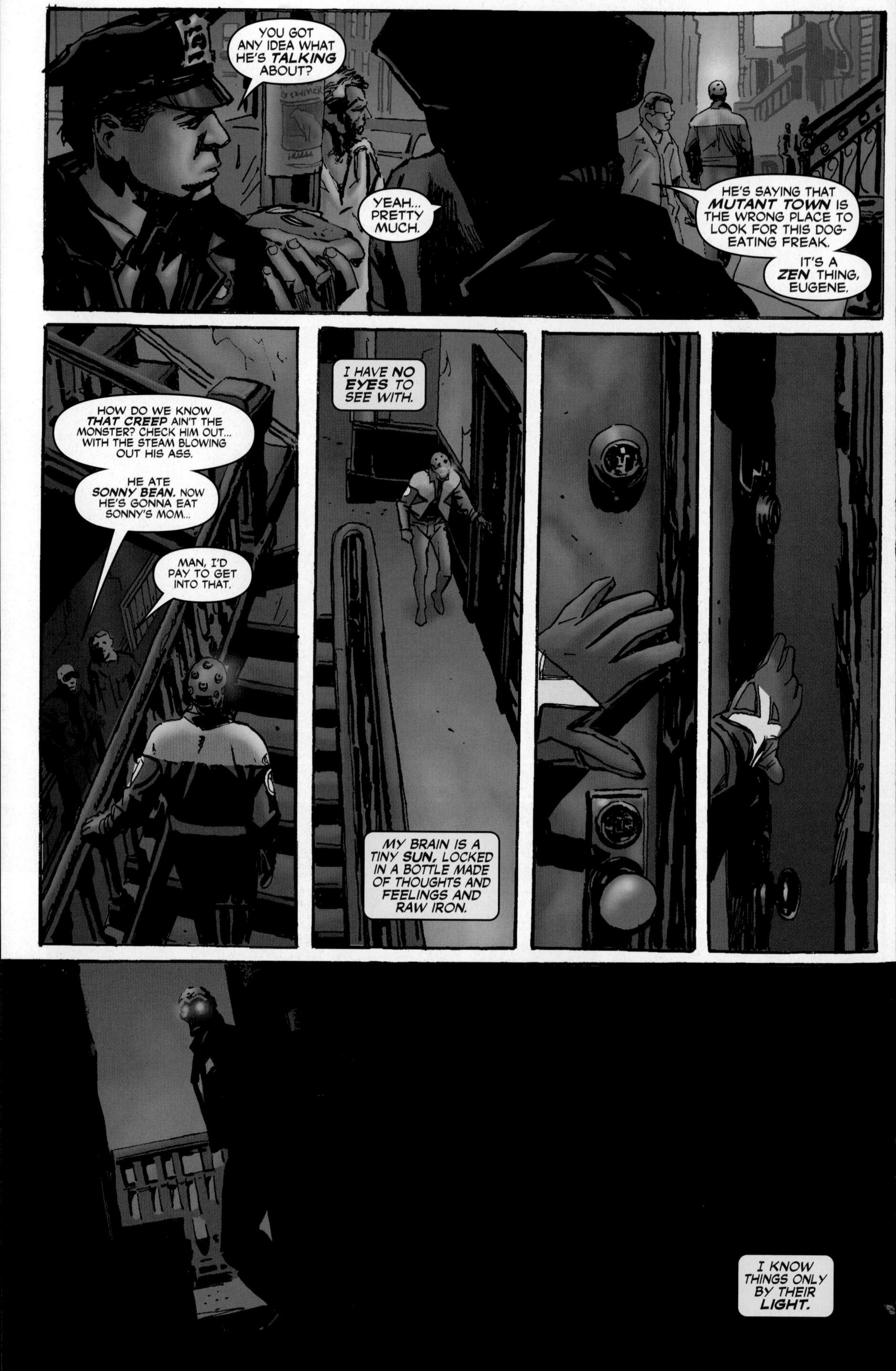
YOU GOT ANY IDEA WHAT HE'S TALKING ABOUT?
YEAH... PRETTY MUCH.
HE'S SAYING THAT MUTANT TOWN IS THE WRONG PLACE TO LOOK FOR THIS DOG-EATING FREAK.
IT'S A ZEN THING, EUGENE.
HOW DO WE KNOW THAT CREEP AIN'T THE MONSTER? CHECK HIM OUT... WITH THE STEAM BLOWING OUT HIS ASS.
HE ATE SONNY BEAN. NOW HE'S GONNA EAT SONNY'S MOM...
MAN, I'D PAY TO GET INTO THAT.
I HAVE NO EYES TO SEE WITH.
MY BRAIN IS A TINY SUN, LOCKED IN A BOTTLE MADE OF THOUGHTS AND FEELINGS AND RAW IRON.
I KNOW THINGS ONLY BY THEIR LIGHT.

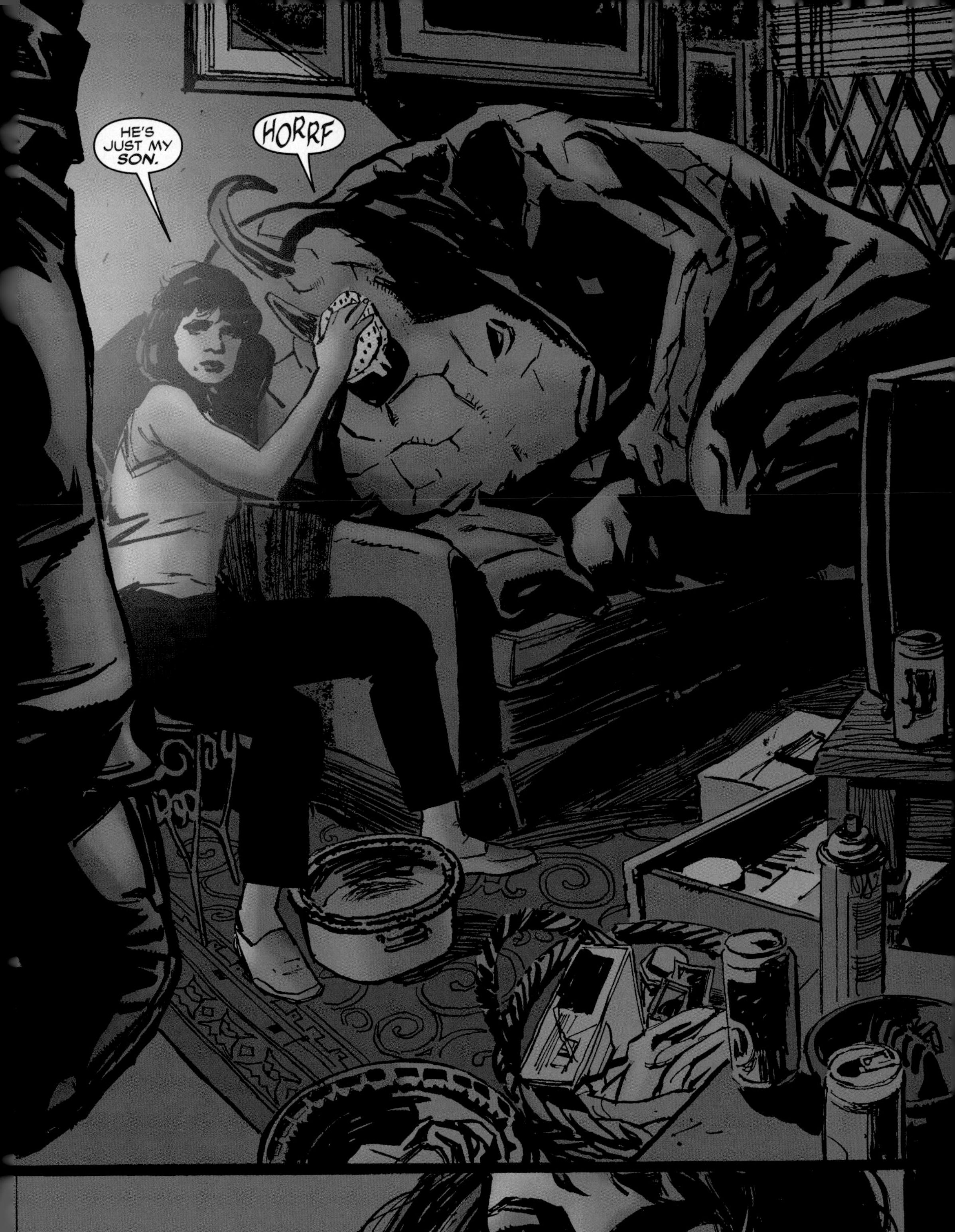
HE'S JUST MY SON.
HORRF
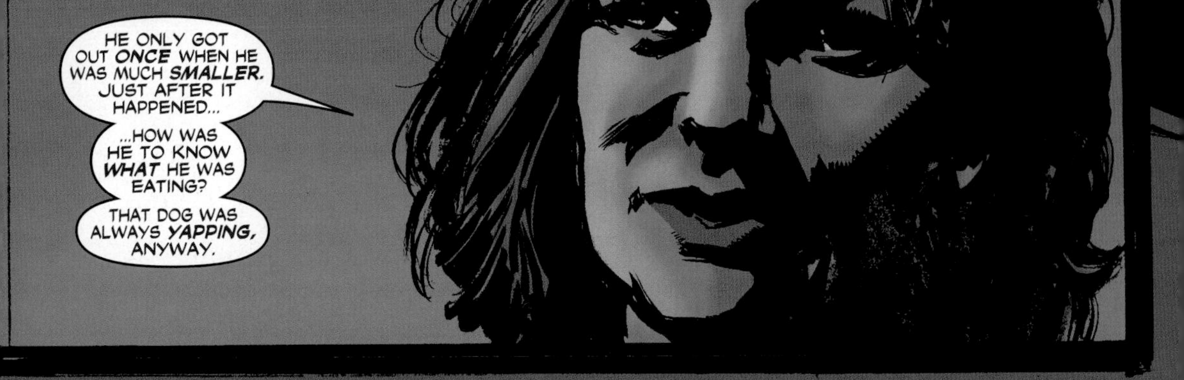
HE ONLY GOT OUT ONCE WHEN HE WAS MUCH SMALLER. JUST AFTER IT HAPPENED...
...HOW WAS HE TO KNOW WHAT HE WAS EATING?
THAT DOG WAS ALWAYS YAPPING, ANYWAY.

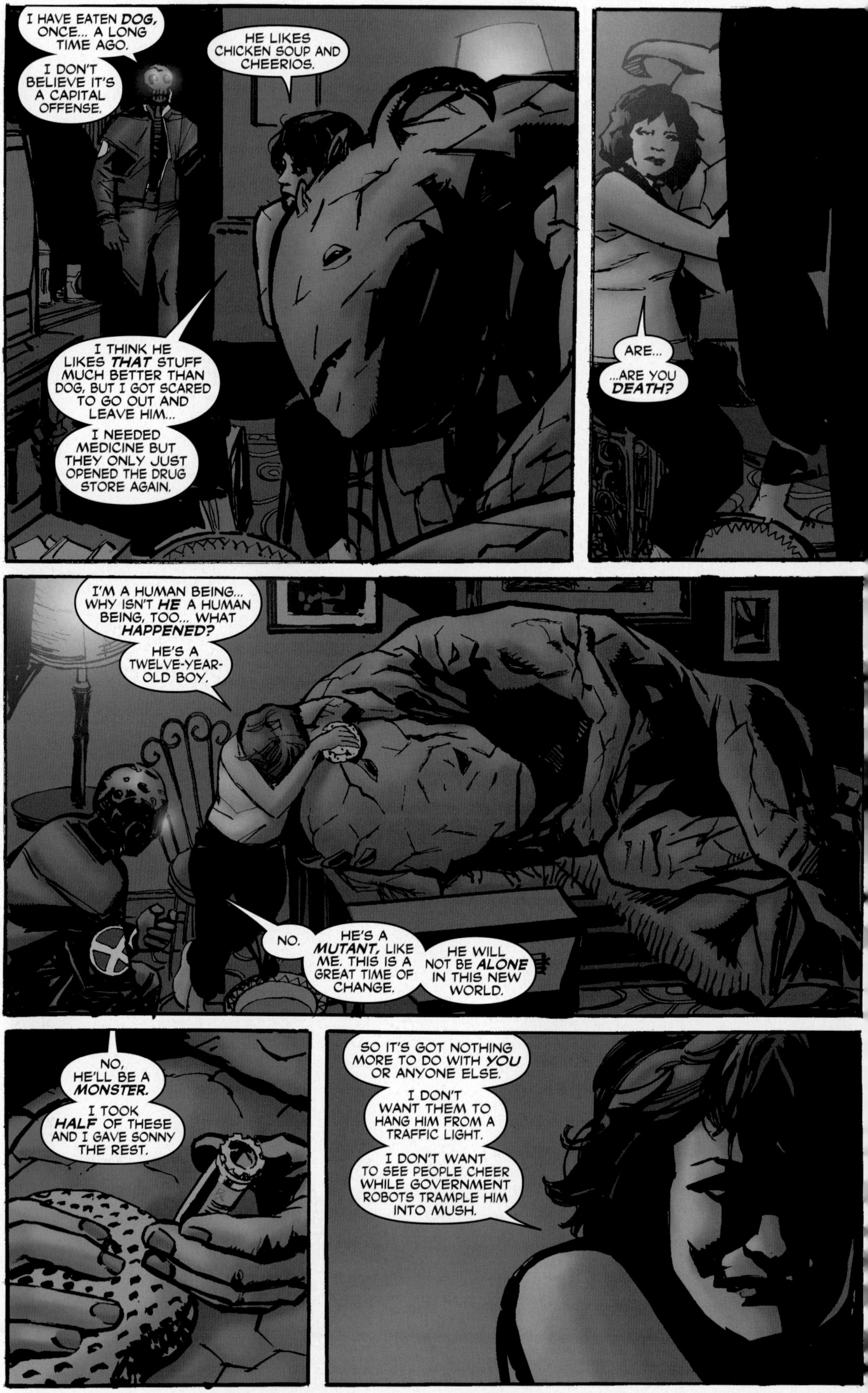
I HAVE EATEN DOG, ONCE... A LONG TIME AGO.
I DON'T BELIEVE IT'S A CAPITAL OFFENSE.
HE LIKES CHICKEN SOUP AND CHEERIOS.
I THINK HE LIKES THAT STUFF MUCH BETTER THAN DOG, BUT I GOT SCARED TO GO OUT AND LEAVE HIM...
I NEEDED MEDICINE BUT THEY ONLY JUST OPENED THE DRUG STORE AGAIN.
ARE...
...ARE YOU DEATH?
I'M A HUMAN BEING... WHY ISN'T HE A HUMAN BEING, TOO... WHAT HAPPENED?
HE'S A TWELVE-YEAR-OLD BOY.
NO.
HE'S A MUTANT, LIKE ME. THIS IS A GREAT TIME OF CHANGE.
HE WILL NOT BE ALONE IN THIS NEW WORLD.
NO, HE'LL BE A MONSTER.
I TOOK HALF OF THESE AND I GAVE SONNY THE REST.
SO IT'S GOT NOTHING MORE TO DO WITH YOU OR ANYONE ELSE.
I DON'T WANT THEM TO HANG HIM FROM A TRAFFIC LIGHT.
I DON'T WANT TO SEE PEOPLE CHEER WHILE GOVERNMENT ROBOTS TRAMPLE HIM INTO MUSH.

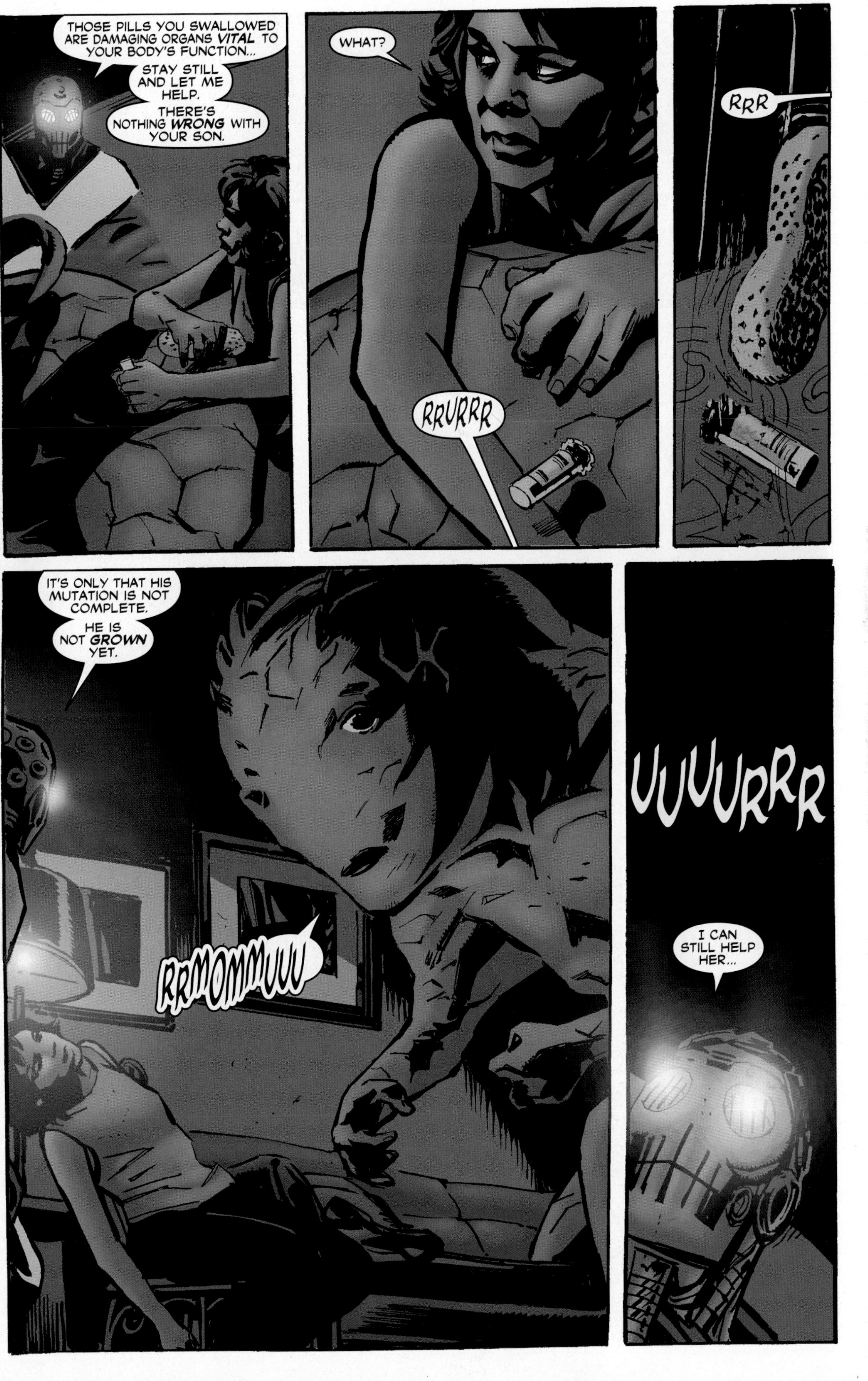
THOSE PILLS YOU SWALLOWED ARE DAMAGING ORGANS VITAL TO YOUR BODY'S FUNCTION...
STAY STILL AND LET ME HELP.
THERE'S NOTHING WRONG WITH YOUR SON.
WHAT?
RRURRR
RRR
IT'S ONLY THAT HIS MUTATION IS NOT COMPLETE.
HE IS NOT GROWN YET.
RRMOMMUUU
UUUURRRR
I CAN STILL HELP HER...

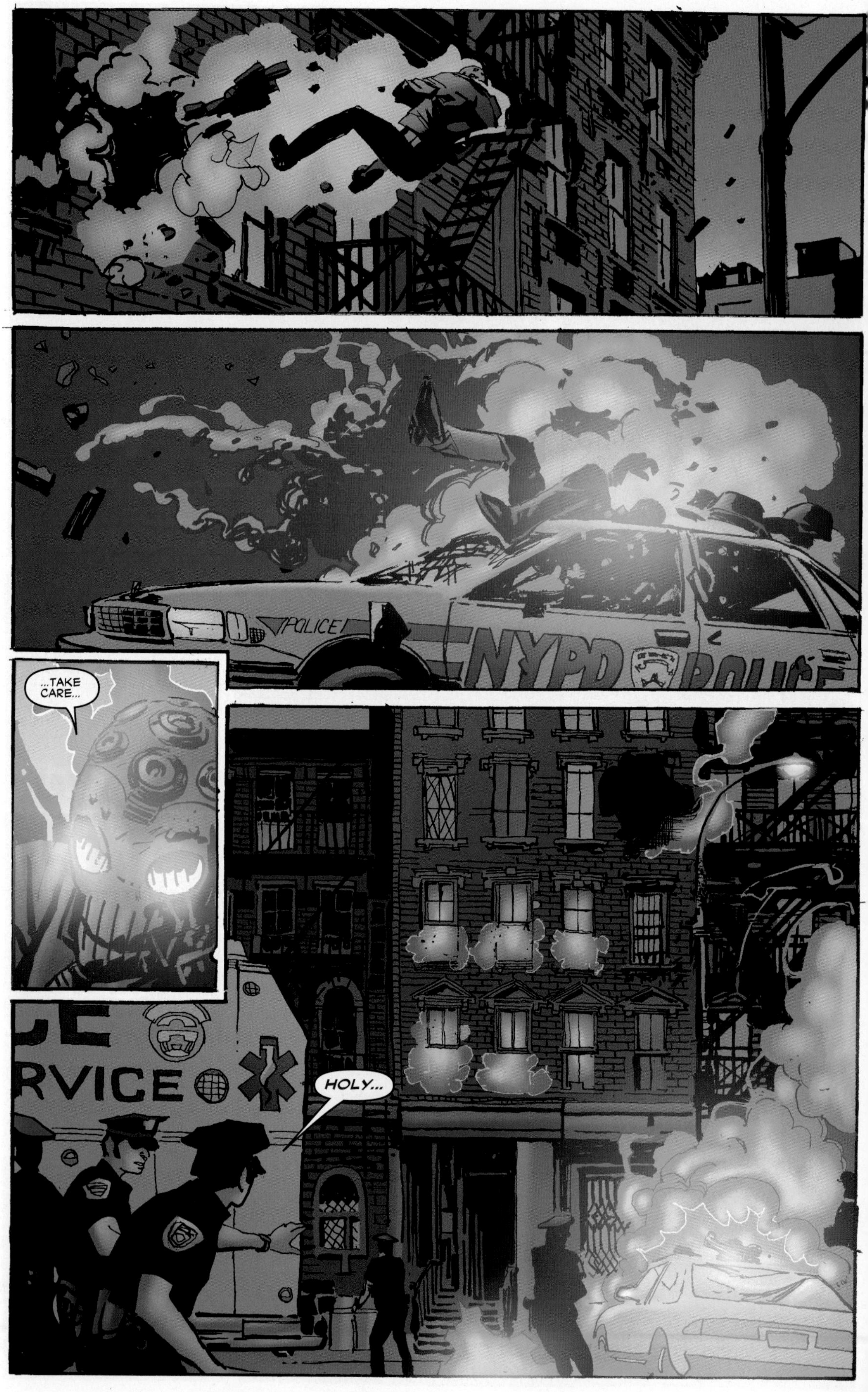
POLICE
NYPD
POLICE
...TAKE CARE...
RVICE
HOLY...

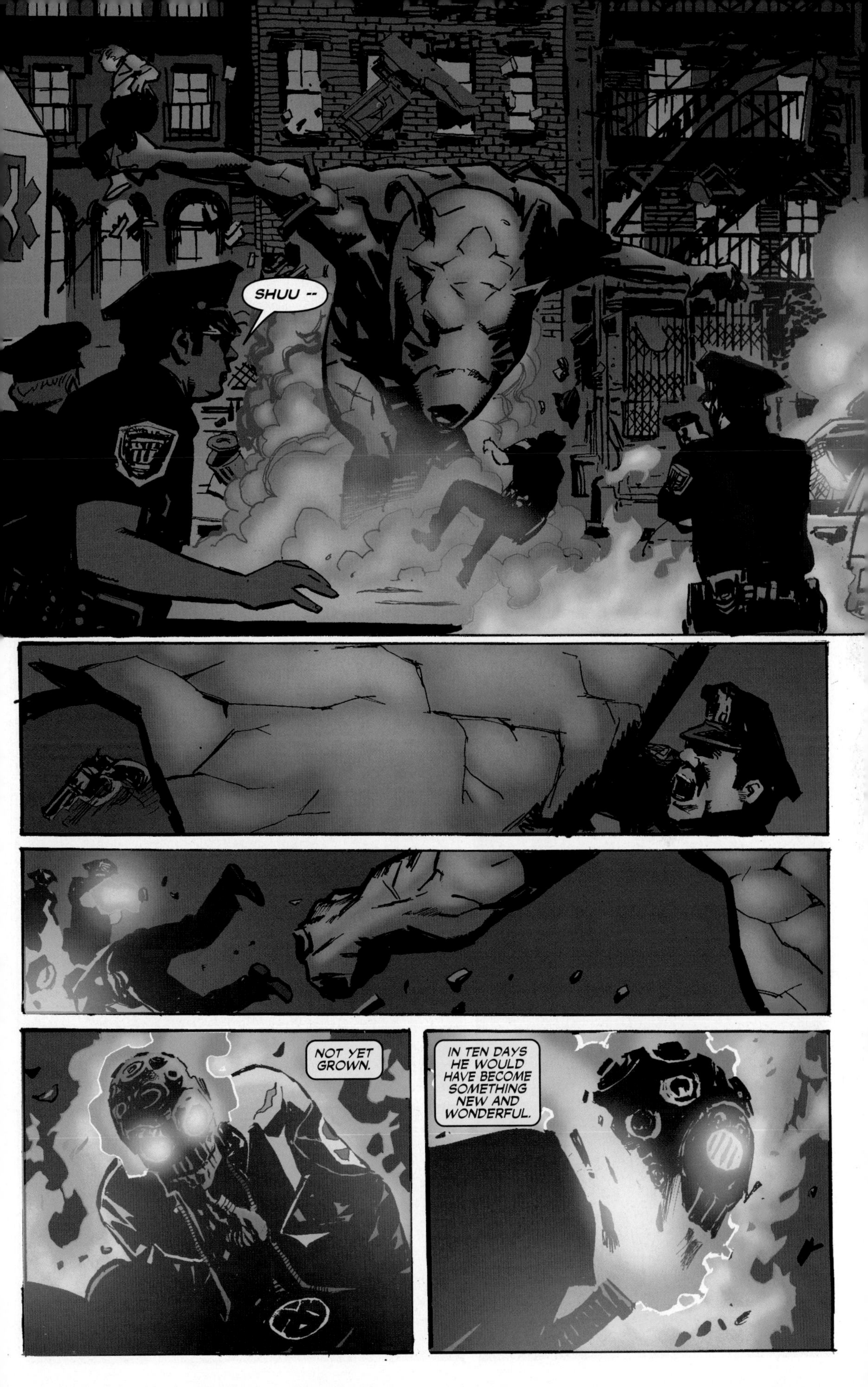
SHUU --
NOT YET GROWN.
IN TEN DAYS HE WOULD HAVE BECOME SOMETHING NEW AND WONDERFUL.

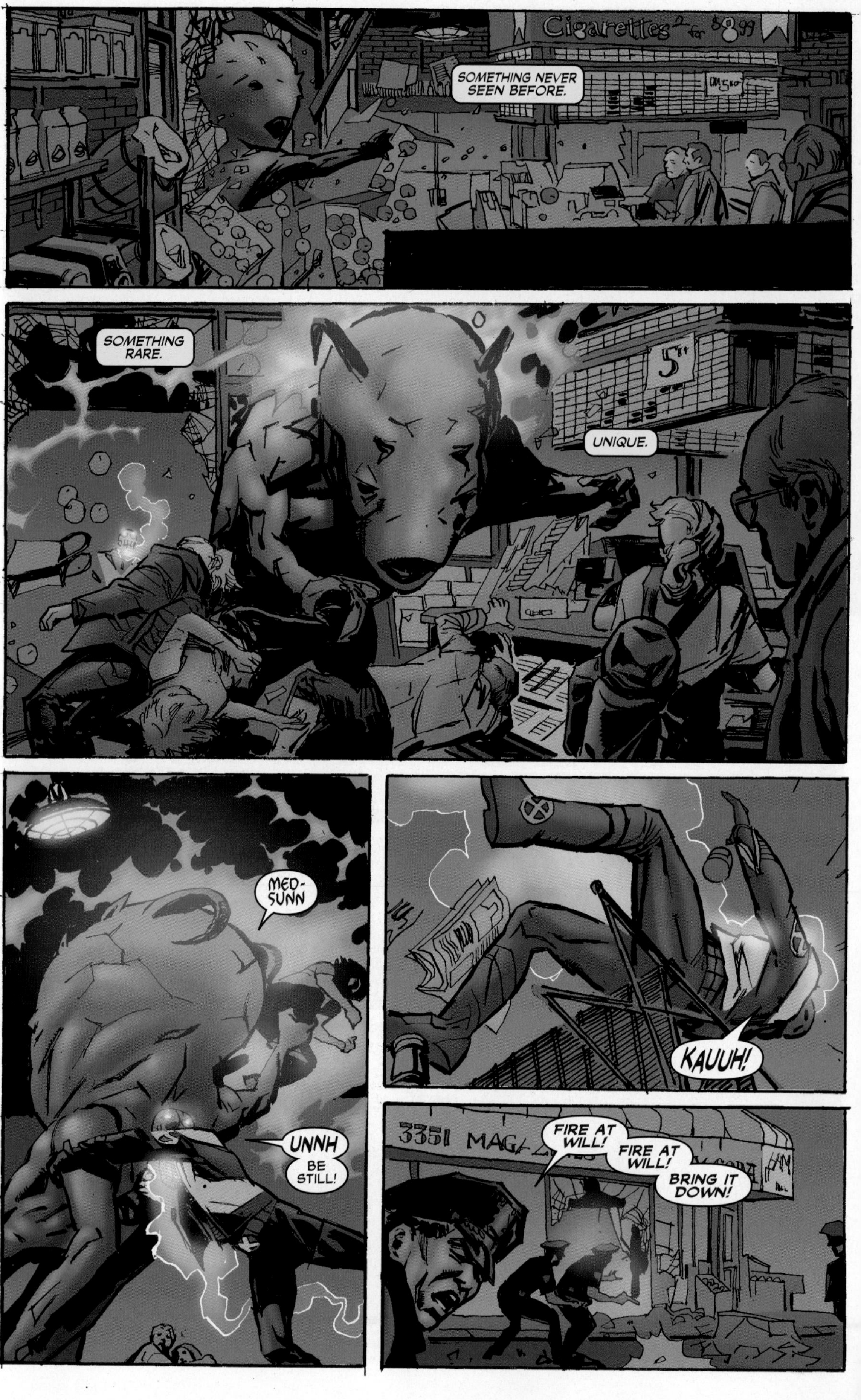
Cigarettes 2 for $8.99
SOMETHING NEVER SEEN BEFORE.
SOMETHING RARE.
UNIQUE.
MED-SUNN
UNNH
BE STILL!
KAUUH!
3351 MAG
FIRE AT WILL!
FIRE AT WILL!
BRING IT DOWN!

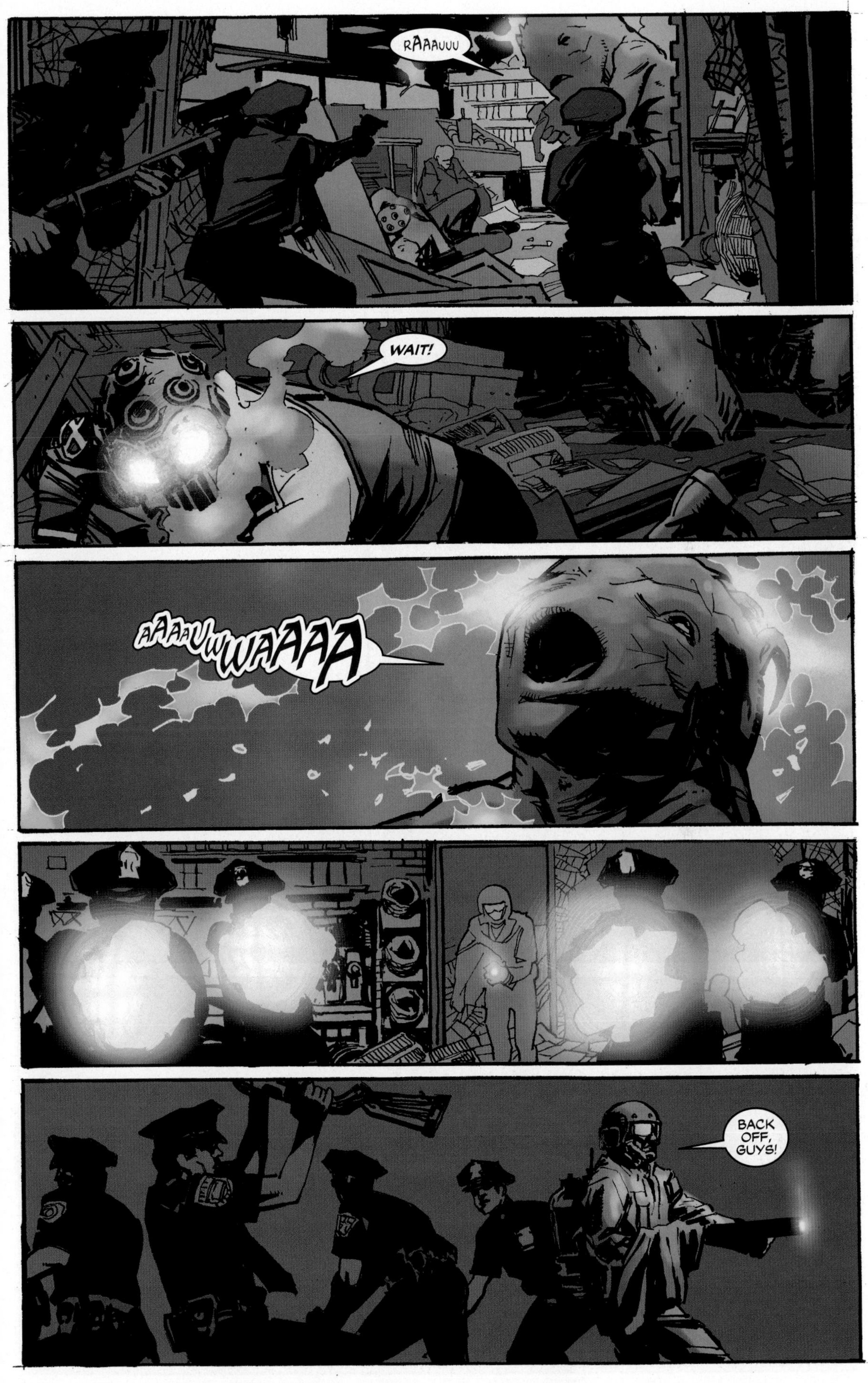
RAAAUUU
WAIT!
AAAAUWWAAAAA
BACK OFF, GUYS!

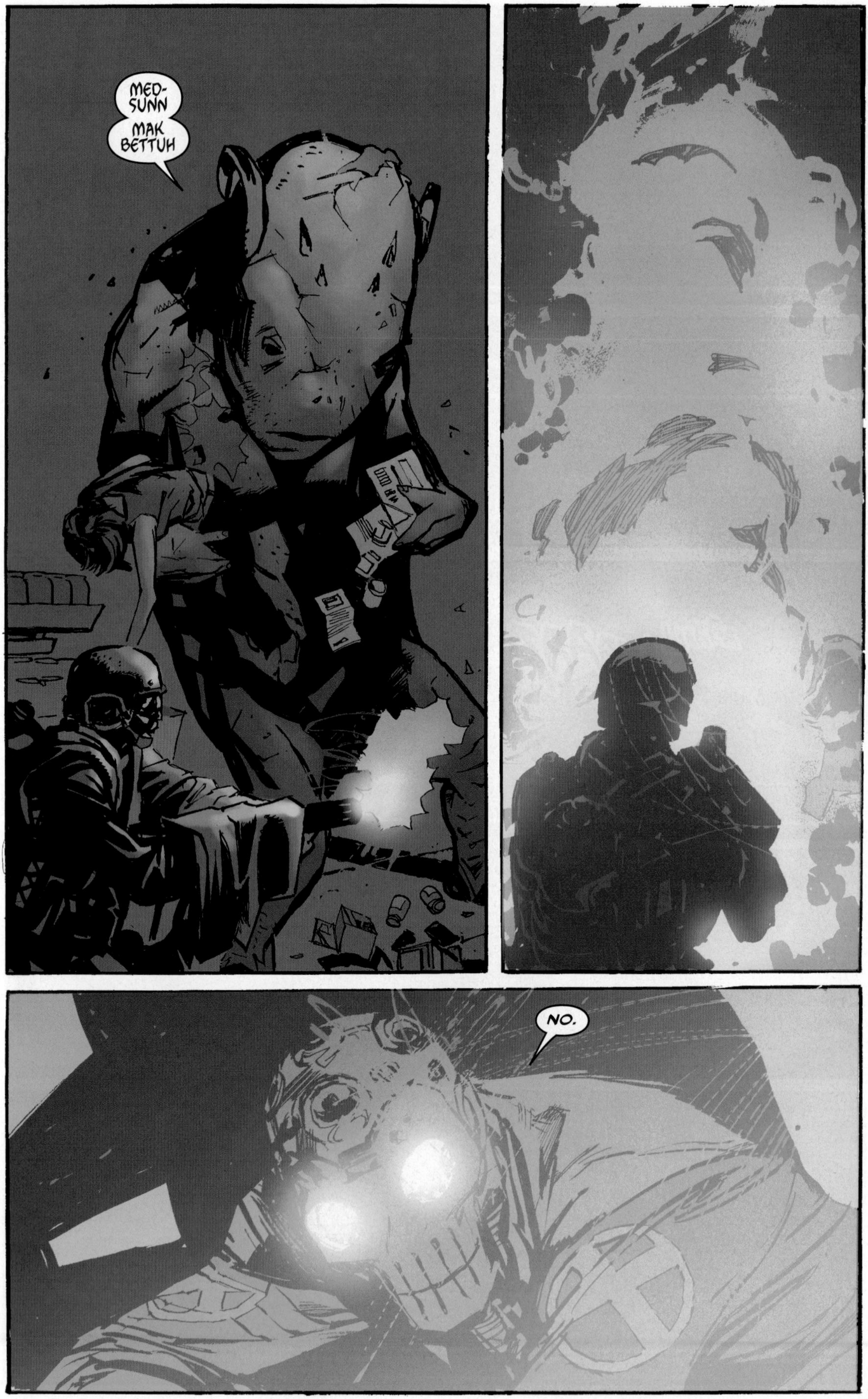
MED-SUNN MAK BETTUH
NO.

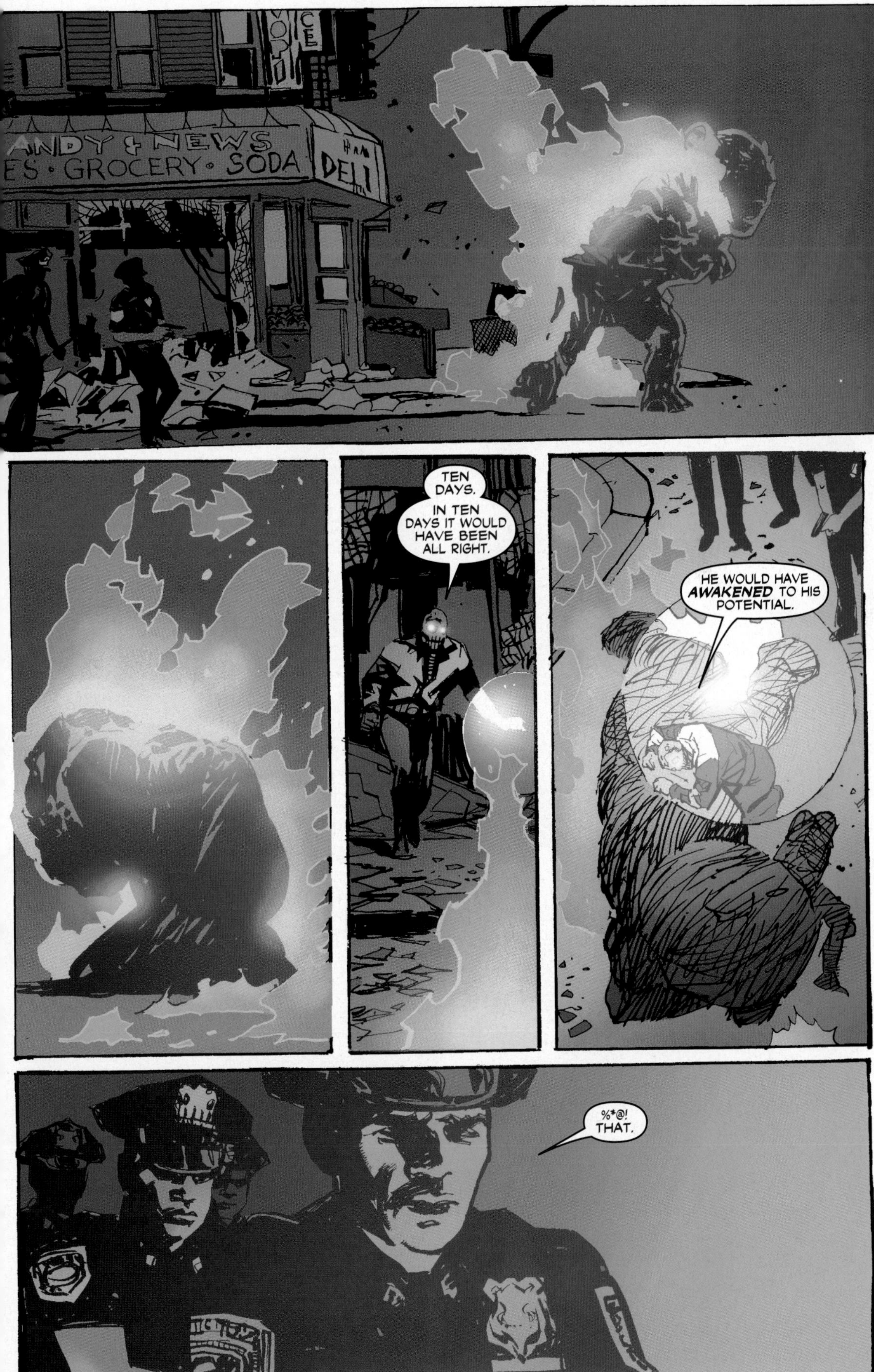
ANDY & NEWS
ES • GROCERY • SODA
DELI
TEN DAYS.
IN TEN DAYS IT WOULD HAVE BEEN ALL RIGHT.
HE WOULD HAVE AWAKENED TO HIS POTENTIAL.
%*@! THAT.

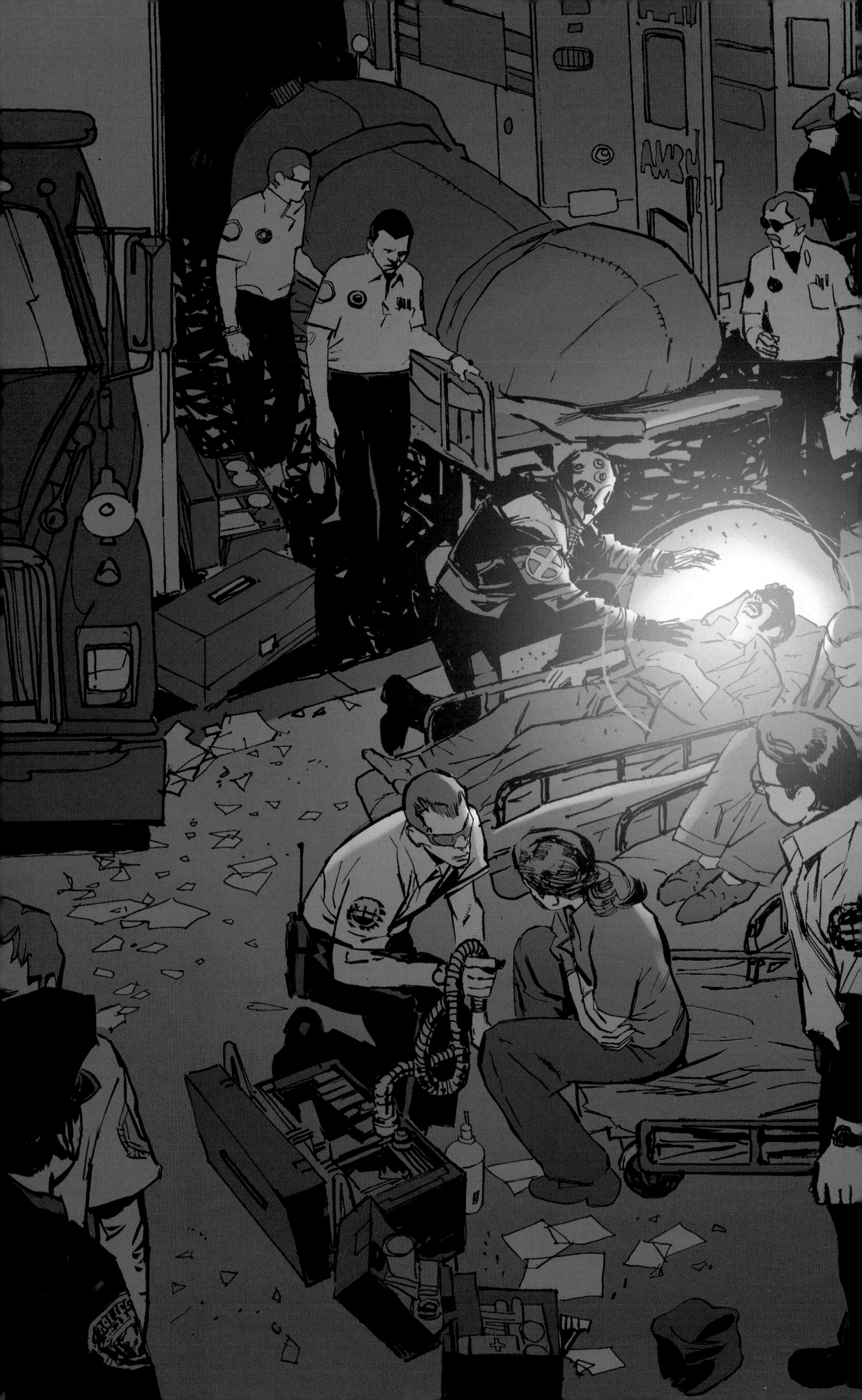

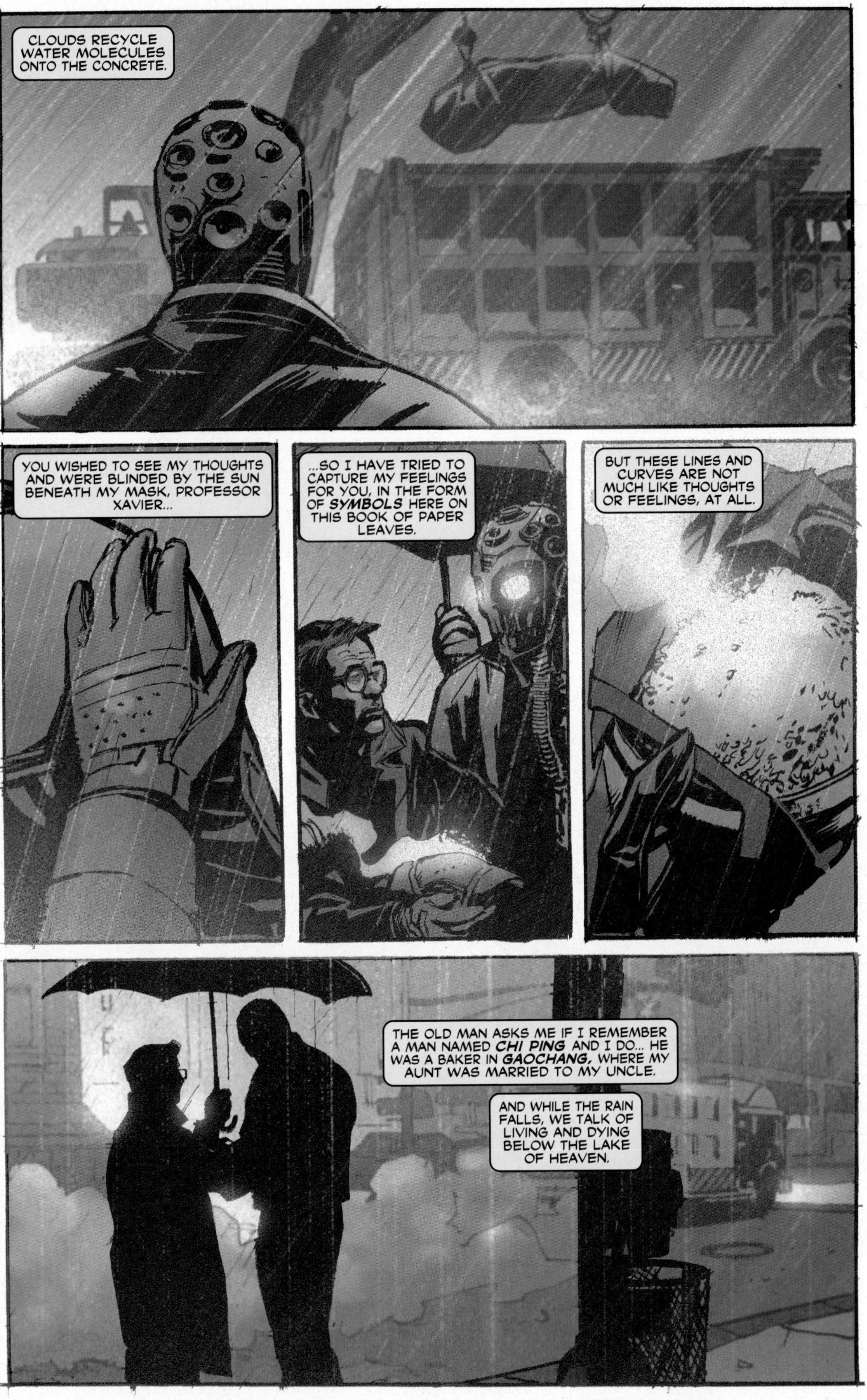
CLOUDS RECYCLE WATER MOLECULES ONTO THE CONCRETE.
YOU WISHED TO SEE MY THOUGHTS AND WERE BLINDED BY THE SUN BENEATH MY MASK, PROFESSOR XAVIER...
...SO I HAVE TRIED TO CAPTURE MY FEELINGS FOR YOU, IN THE FORM OF SYMBOLS HERE ON THIS BOOK OF PAPER LEAVES.
BUT THESE LINES AND CURVES ARE NOT MUCH LIKE THOUGHTS OR FEELINGS, AT ALL.
THE OLD MAN ASKS ME IF I REMEMBER A MAN NAMED CHI PING AND I DO... HE WAS A BAKER IN GAOCHANG, WHERE MY AUNT WAS MARRIED TO MY UNCLE.
AND WHILE THE RAIN FALLS, WE TALK OF LIVING AND DYING BELOW THE LAKE OF HEAVEN.

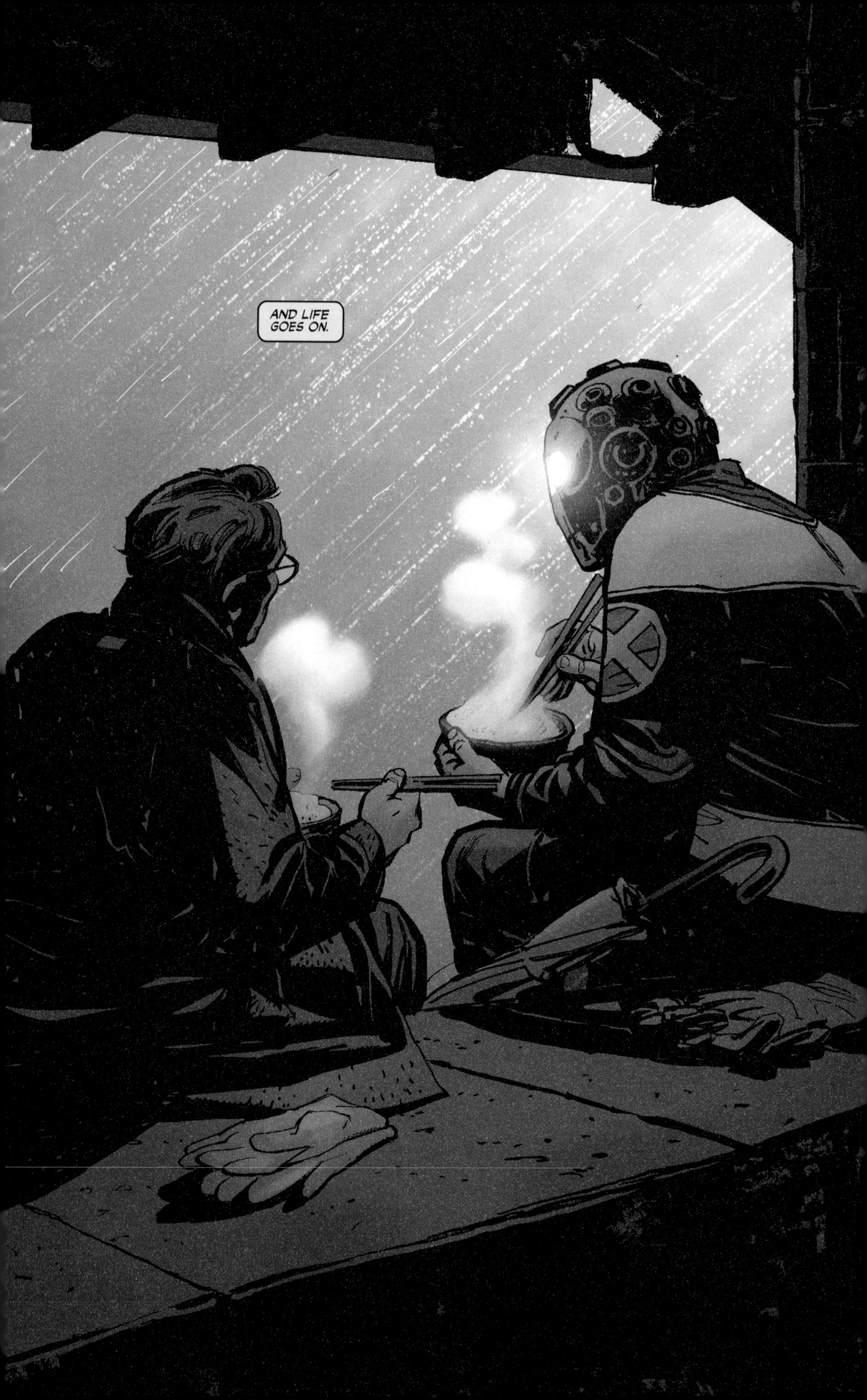
AND LIFE GOES ON.

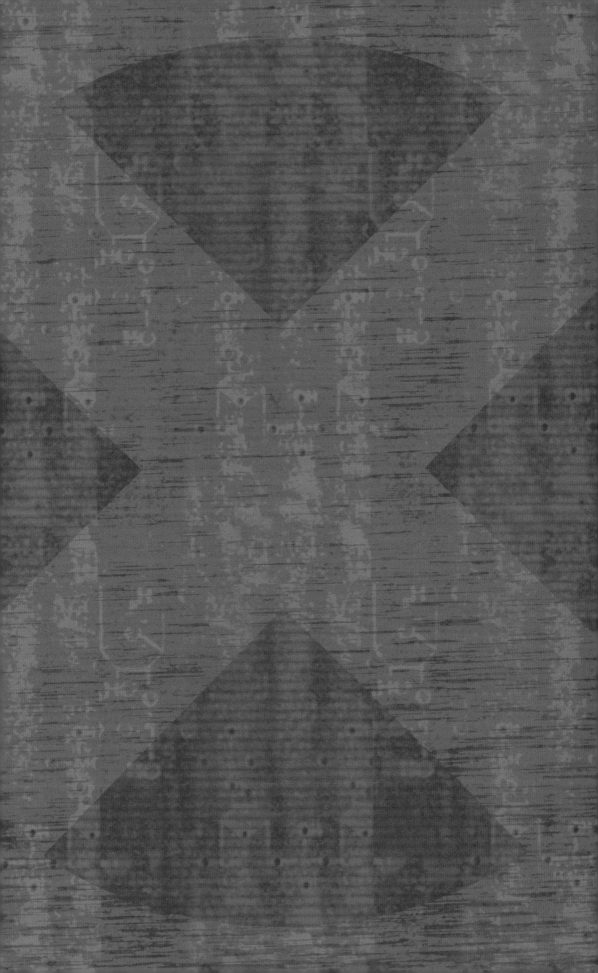

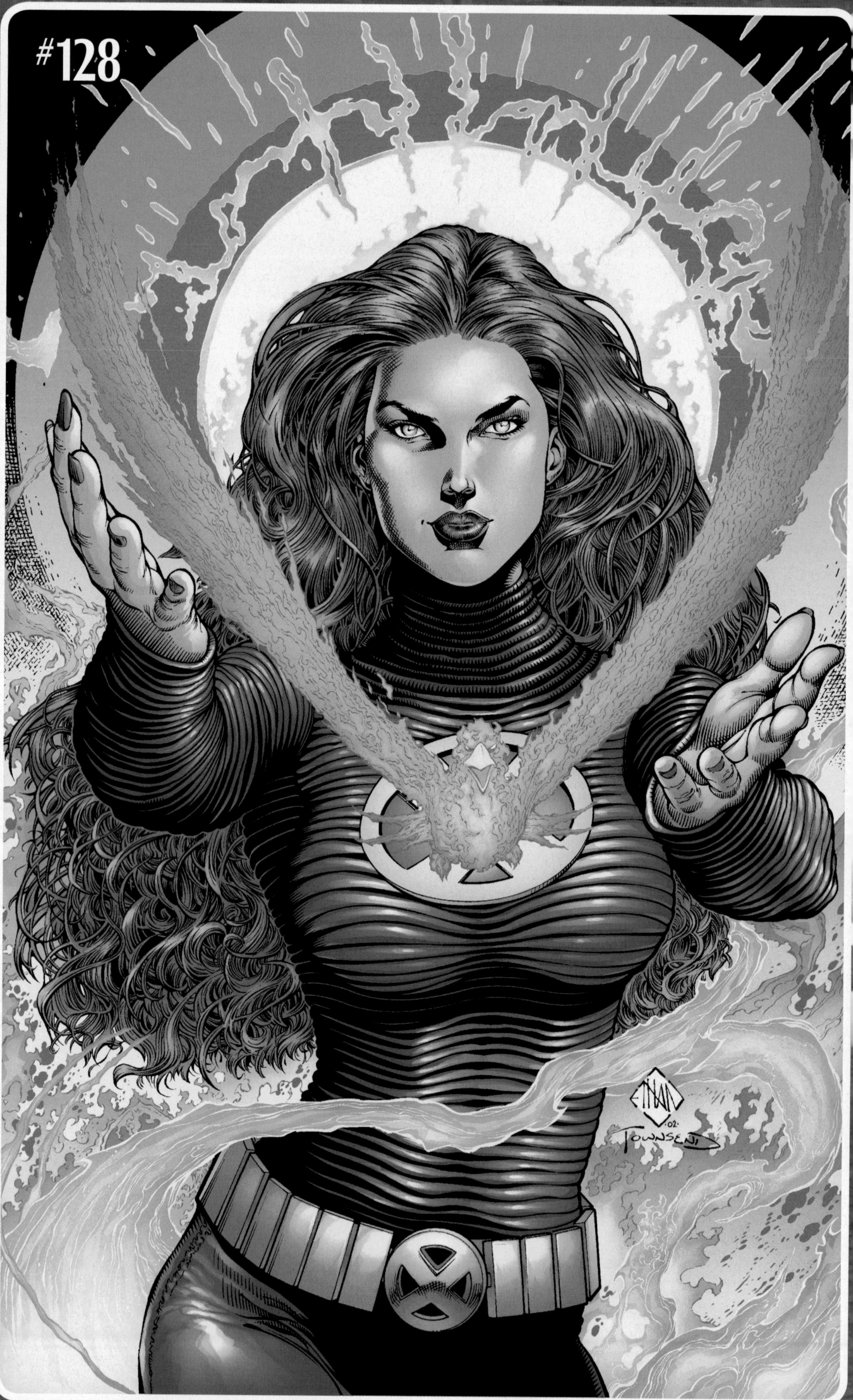
#128
TOWNSEND

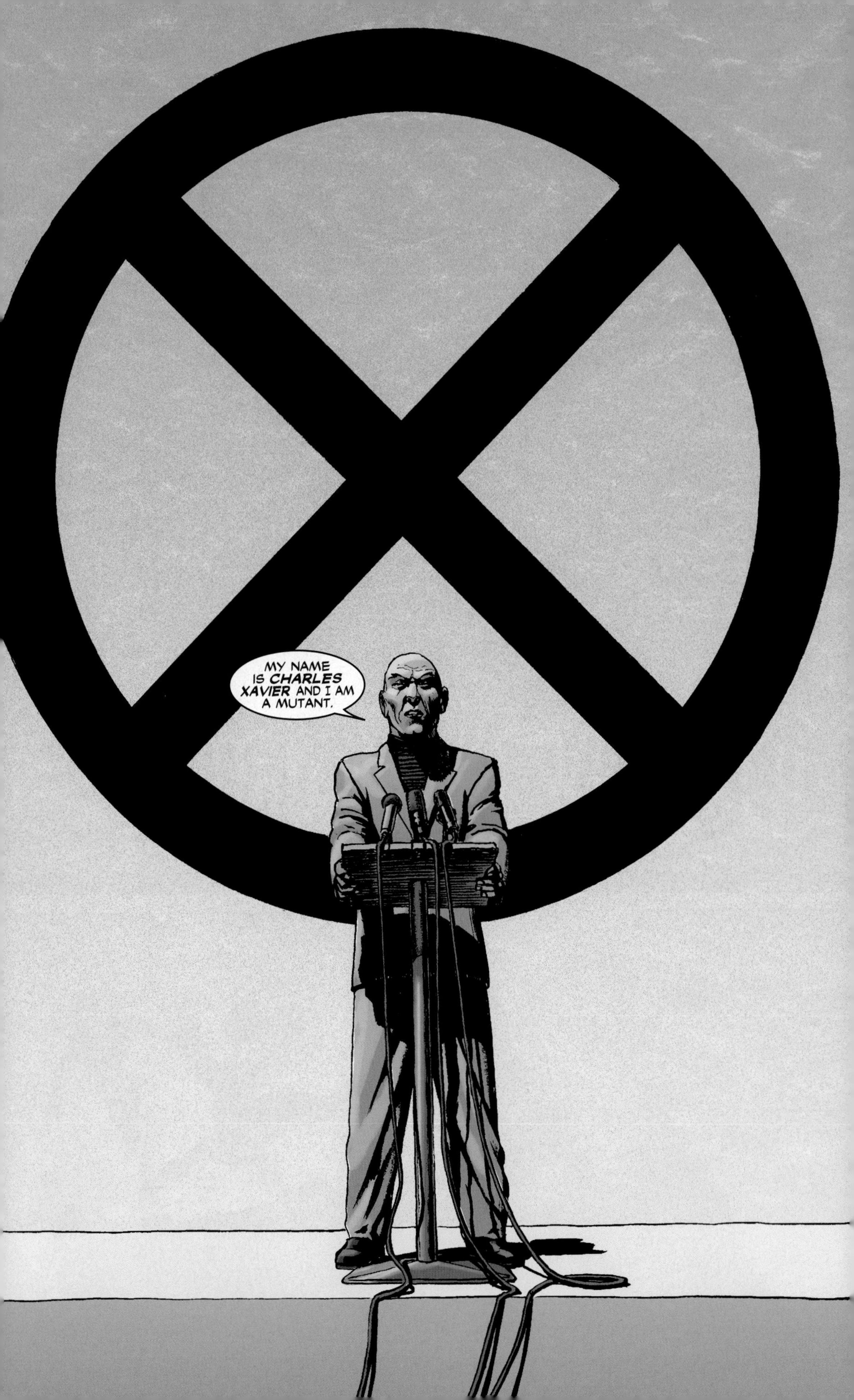
MY NAME IS CHARLES XAVIER AND I AM A MUTANT.

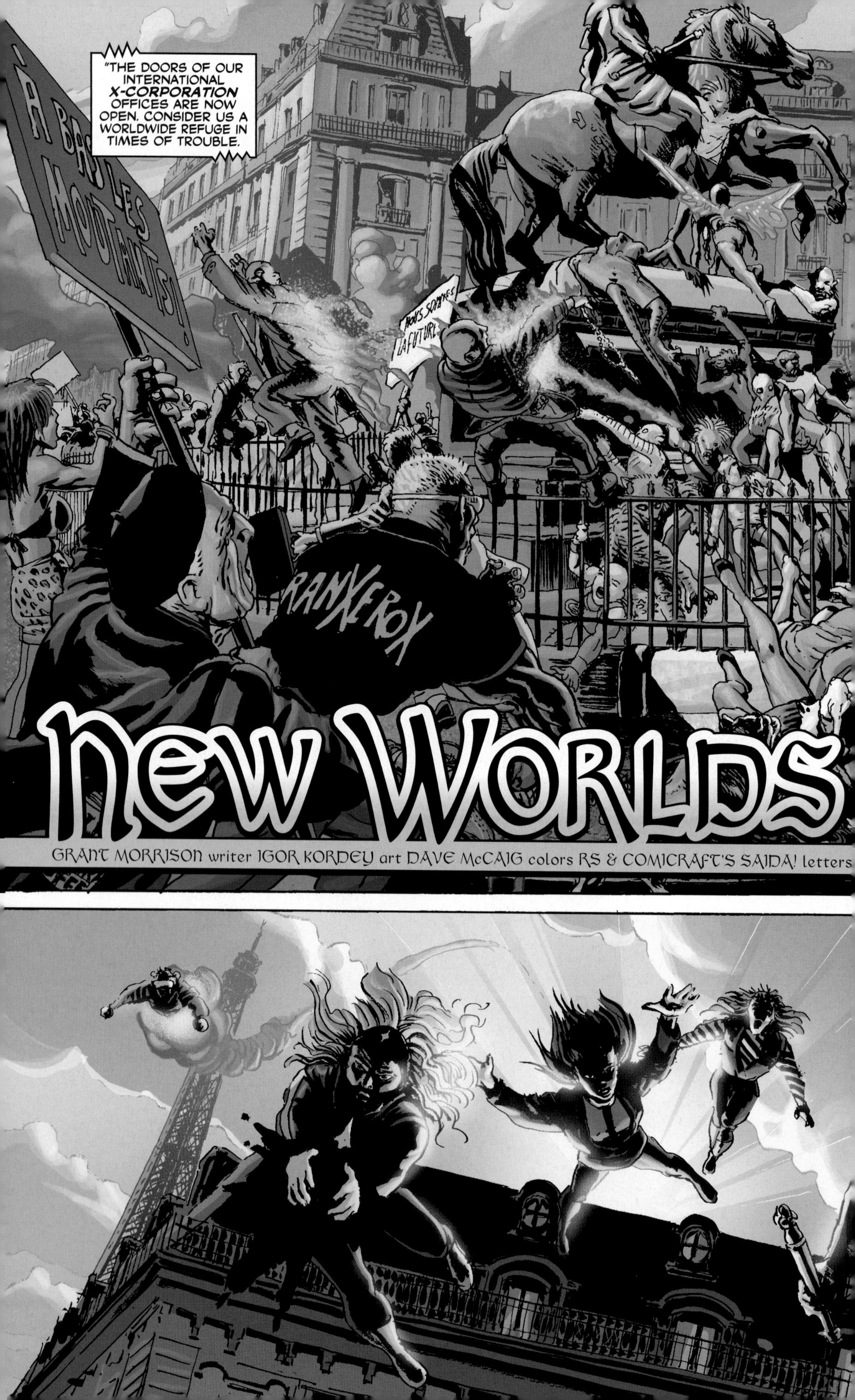
"THE DOORS OF OUR INTERNATIONAL X-CORPORATION OFFICES ARE NOW OPEN. CONSIDER US A WORLDWIDE REFUGE IN TIMES OF TROUBLE.
RANXEROX
new WORLDS
GRANT MORRISON writer IGOR KORDEY art DAVE McCAIG colors RS & COMICRAFT'S SAIDA! letters

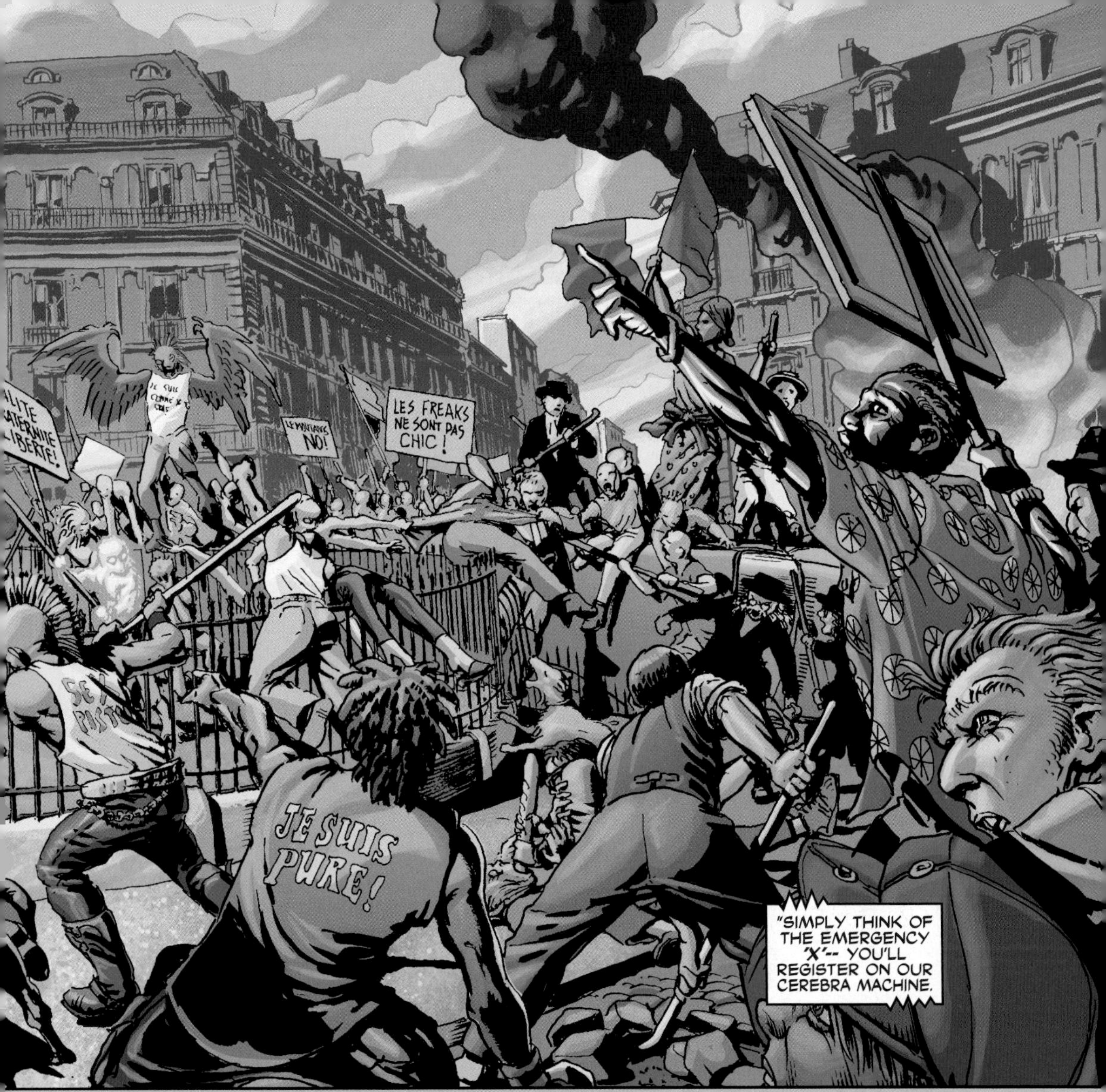
LES FREAKS NE SONT PAS CHIC !
JE SUIS PURE!
"SIMPLY THINK OF THE EMERGENCY 'X'-- YOU'LL REGISTER ON OUR CEREBRA MACHINE.

ETHAN VAN SCIVER cover MIKE RAICHT assistant editor MIKE MARTS editor JOE QUESADA chief BILL JEMAS president

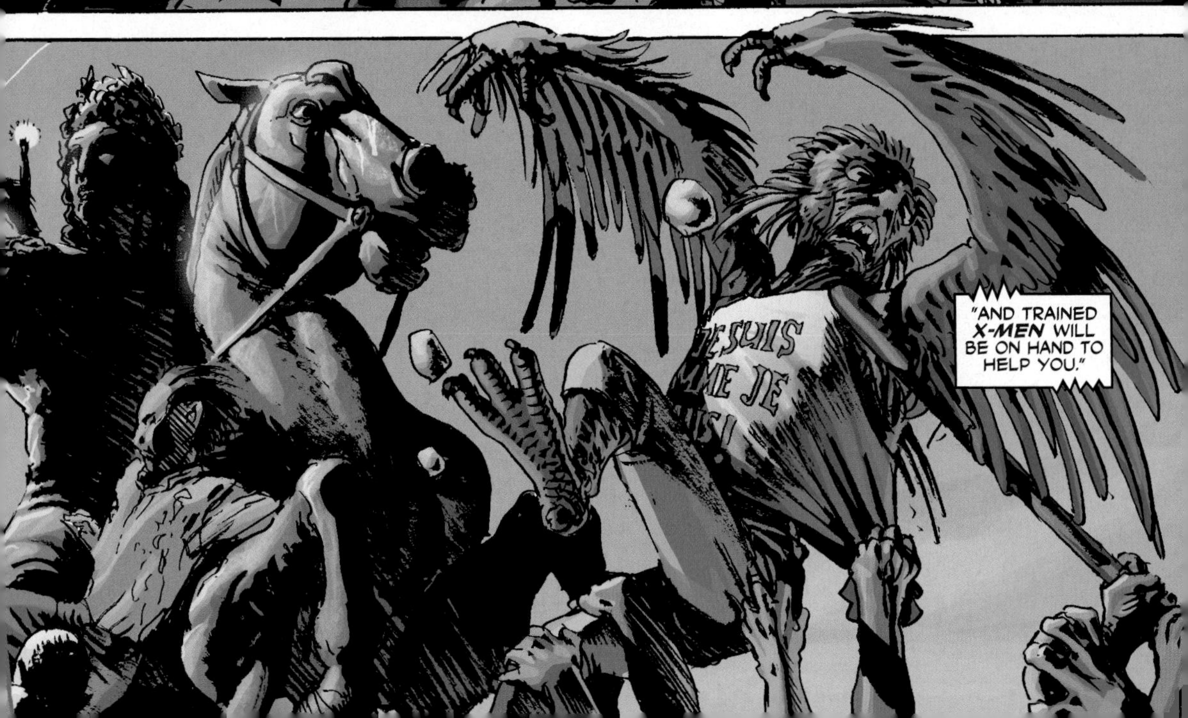
"AND TRAINED X-MEN WILL BE ON HAND TO HELP YOU."

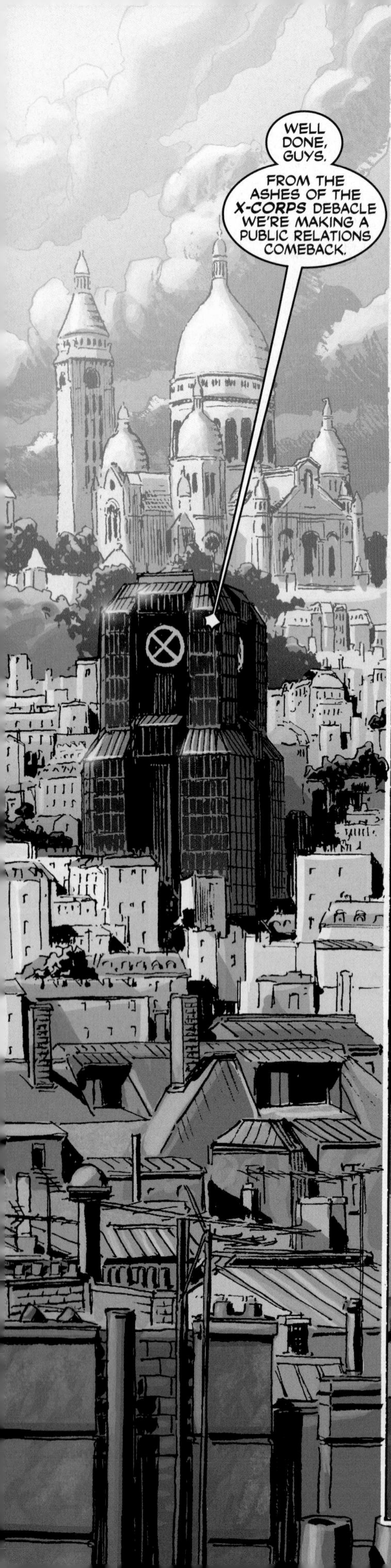
WELL DONE, GUYS.
FROM THE ASHES OF THE X-CORPS DEBACLE WE'RE MAKING A PUBLIC RELATIONS COMEBACK.

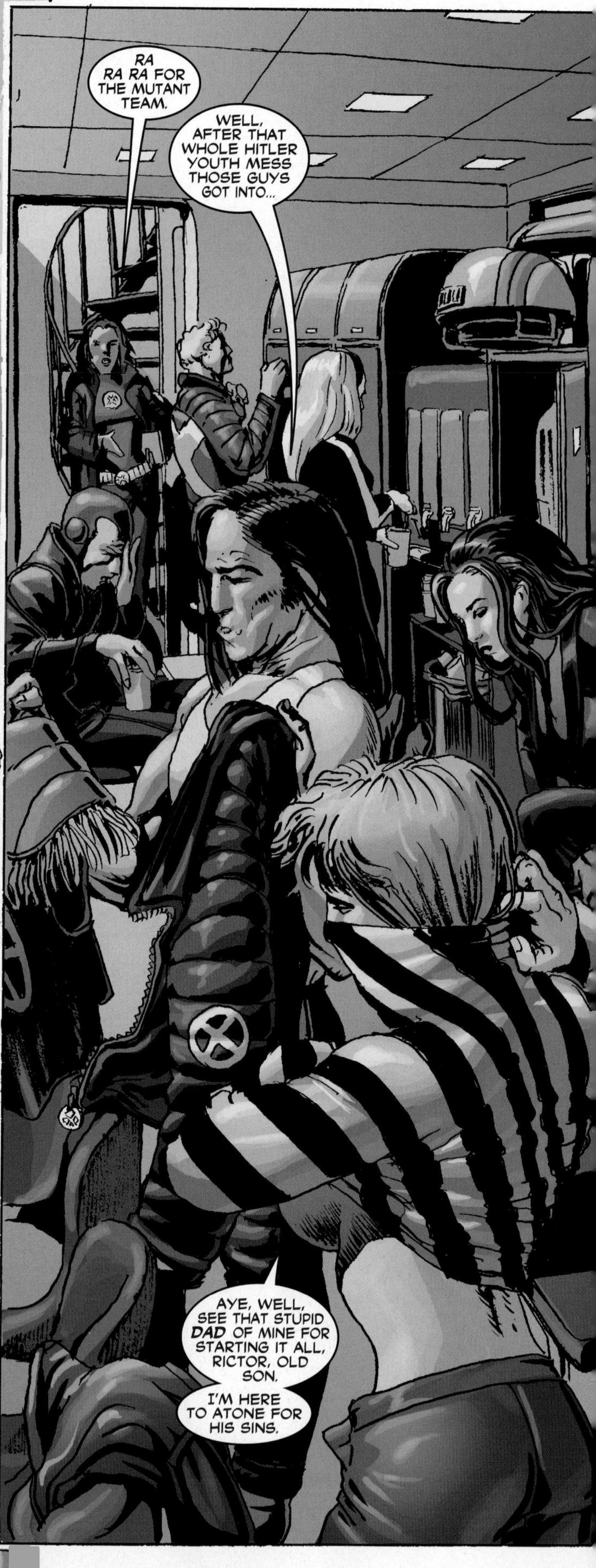
RA RA RA FOR THE MUTANT TEAM.
WELL, AFTER THAT WHOLE HITLER YOUTH MESS THOSE GUYS GOT INTO...
AYE, WELL, SEE THAT STUPID DAD OF MINE FOR STARTING IT ALL, RICTOR, OLD SON.
I'M HERE TO ATONE FOR HIS SINS.

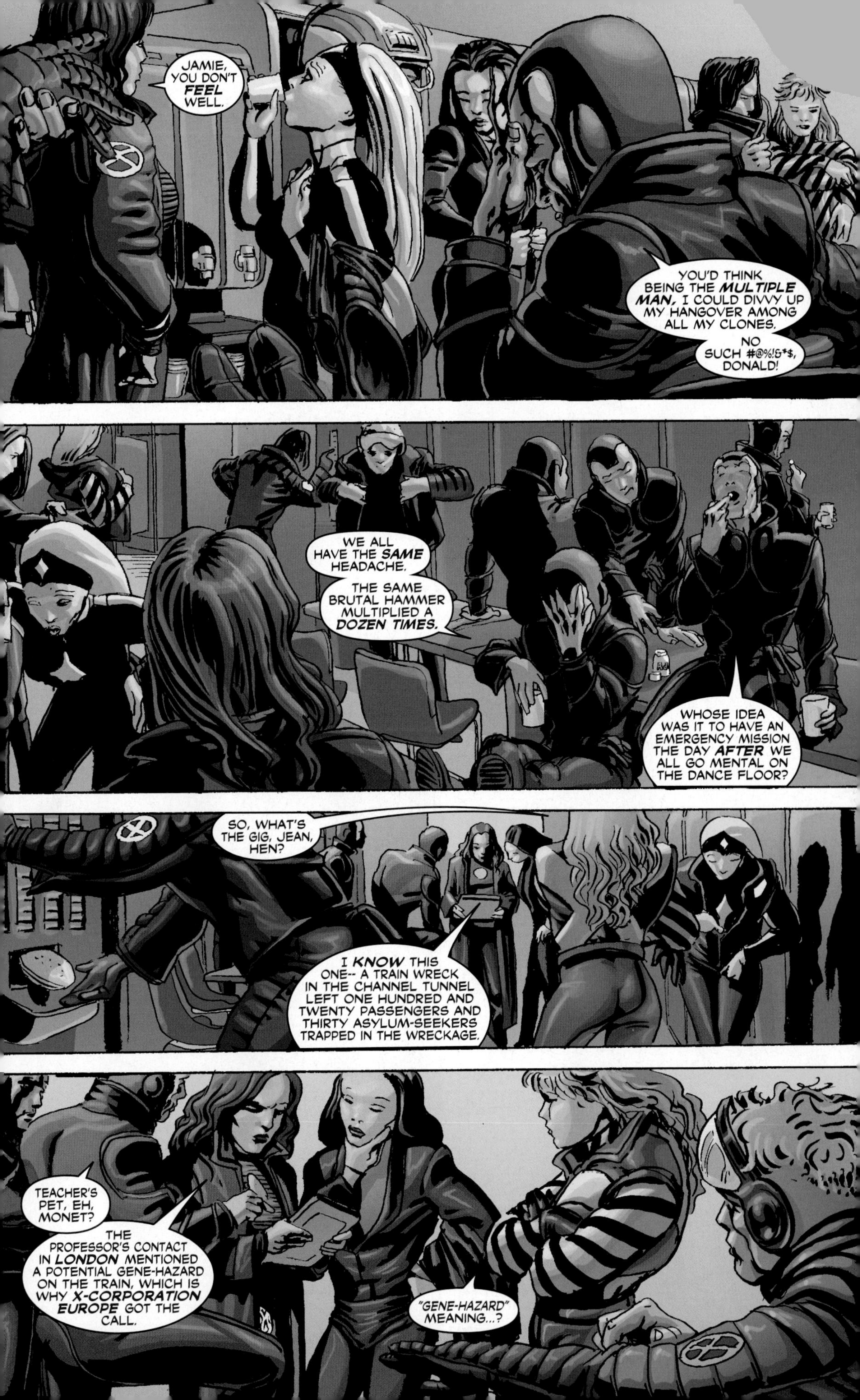
JAMIE, YOU DON'T FEEL WELL.
YOU'D THINK BEING THE MULTIPLE MAN, I COULD DIVVY UP MY HANGOVER AMONG ALL MY CLONES.
NO SUCH #@%!&*$, DONALD!
WE ALL HAVE THE SAME HEADACHE.
THE SAME BRUTAL HAMMER MULTIPLIED A DOZEN TIMES.
WHOSE IDEA WAS IT TO HAVE AN EMERGENCY MISSION THE DAY AFTER WE ALL GO MENTAL ON THE DANCE FLOOR?
SO, WHAT'S THE GIG, JEAN, HEN?
I KNOW THIS ONE-- A TRAIN WRECK IN THE CHANNEL TUNNEL LEFT ONE HUNDRED AND TWENTY PASSENGERS AND THIRTY ASYLUM-SEEKERS TRAPPED IN THE WRECKAGE.
TEACHER'S PET, EH, MONET?
THE PROFESSOR'S CONTACT IN LONDON MENTIONED A POTENTIAL GENE-HAZARD ON THE TRAIN, WHICH IS WHY X-CORPORATION EUROPE GOT THE CALL.
"GENE-HAZARD" MEANING...?

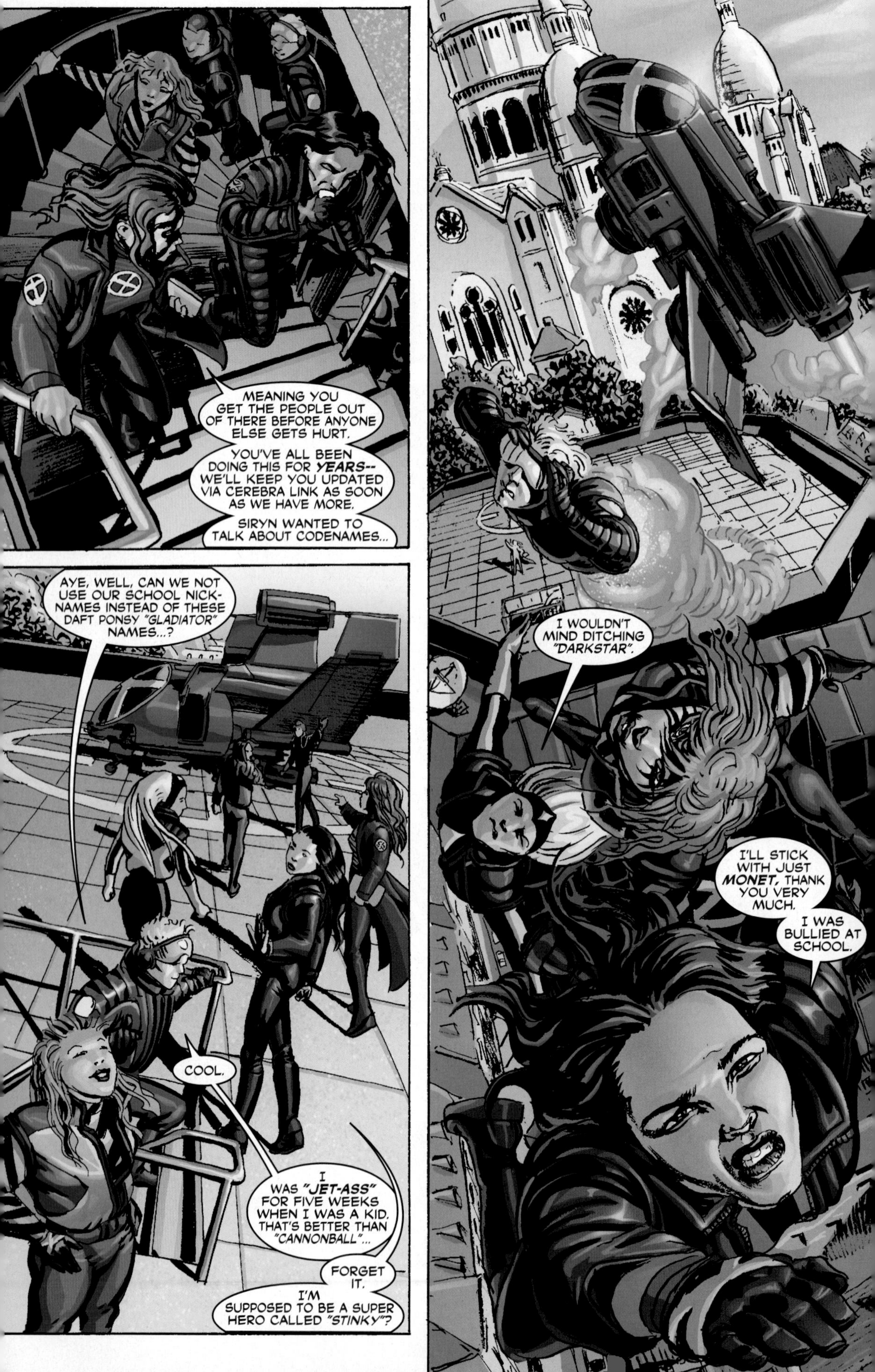
MEANING YOU GET THE PEOPLE OUT OF THERE BEFORE ANYONE ELSE GETS HURT.
YOU'VE ALL BEEN DOING THIS FOR YEARS-- WE'LL KEEP YOU UPDATED VIA CEREBRA LINK AS SOON AS WE HAVE MORE.
SIRYN WANTED TO TALK ABOUT CODENAMES...
AYE, WELL, CAN WE NOT USE OUR SCHOOL NICK-NAMES INSTEAD OF THESE DAFT PONSY "GLADIATOR" NAMES...?
COOL.
I WAS "JET-ASS" FOR FIVE WEEKS WHEN I WAS A KID. THAT'S BETTER THAN "CANNONBALL"...
FORGET IT.
I'M SUPPOSED TO BE A SUPER HERO CALLED "STINKY"?
I WOULDN'T MIND DITCHING "DARKSTAR".
I'LL STICK WITH JUST MONET, THANK YOU VERY MUCH.
I WAS BULLIED AT SCHOOL.

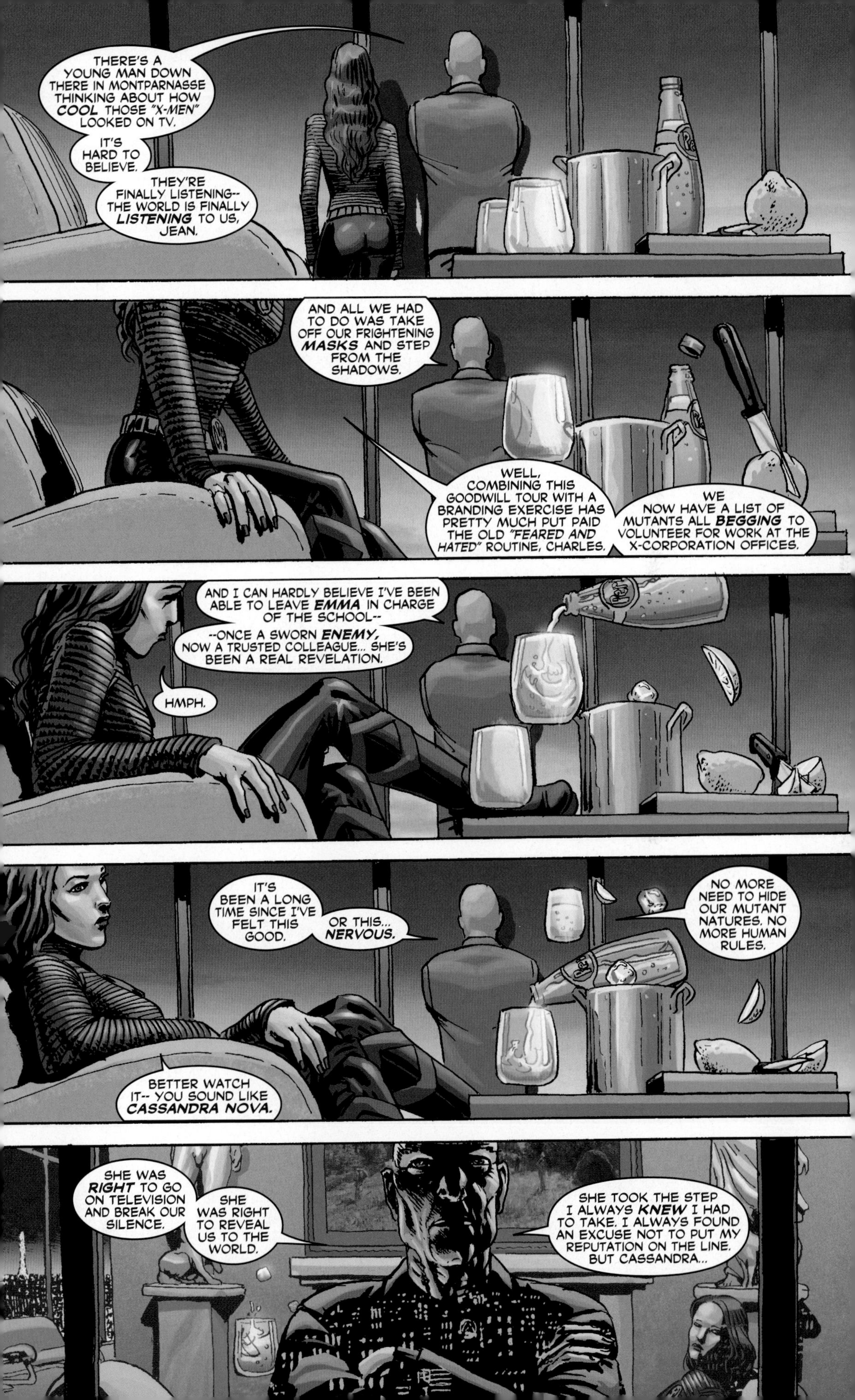
THERE'S A YOUNG MAN DOWN THERE IN MONTPARNASSE THINKING ABOUT HOW COOL THOSE "X-MEN" LOOKED ON TV.
IT'S HARD TO BELIEVE.
THEY'RE FINALLY LISTENING-- THE WORLD IS FINALLY LISTENING TO US, JEAN.
AND ALL WE HAD TO DO WAS TAKE OFF OUR FRIGHTENING MASKS AND STEP FROM THE SHADOWS.
WELL, COMBINING THIS GOODWILL TOUR WITH A BRANDING EXERCISE HAS PRETTY MUCH PUT PAID THE OLD "FEARED AND HATED" ROUTINE, CHARLES.
WE NOW HAVE A LIST OF MUTANTS ALL BEGGING TO VOLUNTEER FOR WORK AT THE X-CORPORATION OFFICES.
AND I CAN HARDLY BELIEVE I'VE BEEN ABLE TO LEAVE EMMA IN CHARGE OF THE SCHOOL--
--ONCE A SWORN ENEMY, NOW A TRUSTED COLLEAGUE... SHE'S BEEN A REAL REVELATION.
HMPH.
IT'S BEEN A LONG TIME SINCE I'VE FELT THIS GOOD.
OR THIS... NERVOUS.
NO MORE NEED TO HIDE OUR MUTANT NATURES. NO MORE HUMAN RULES.
BETTER WATCH IT-- YOU SOUND LIKE CASSANDRA NOVA.
SHE WAS RIGHT TO GO ON TELEVISION AND BREAK OUR SILENCE.
SHE WAS RIGHT TO REVEAL US TO THE WORLD.
SHE TOOK THE STEP I ALWAYS KNEW I HAD TO TAKE. I ALWAYS FOUND AN EXCUSE NOT TO PUT MY REPUTATION ON THE LINE. BUT CASSANDRA...

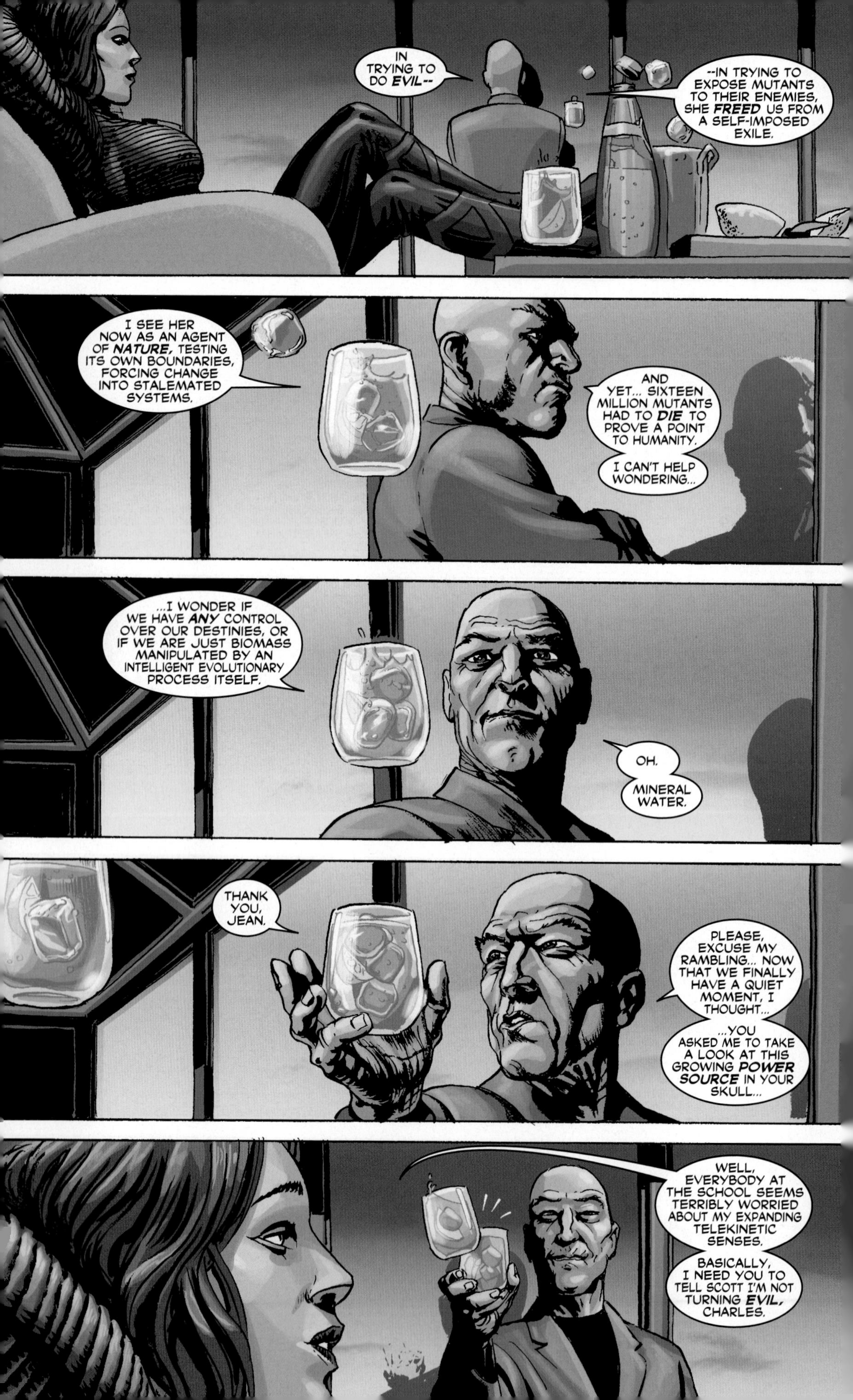
IN TRYING TO DO EVIL--
--IN TRYING TO EXPOSE MUTANTS TO THEIR ENEMIES, SHE FREED US FROM A SELF-IMPOSED EXILE.
I SEE HER NOW AS AN AGENT OF NATURE, TESTING ITS OWN BOUNDARIES, FORCING CHANGE INTO STALEMATED SYSTEMS.
AND YET... SIXTEEN MILLION MUTANTS HAD TO DIE TO PROVE A POINT TO HUMANITY.
I CAN'T HELP WONDERING...
...I WONDER IF WE HAVE ANY CONTROL OVER OUR DESTINIES, OR IF WE ARE JUST BIOMASS MANIPULATED BY AN INTELLIGENT EVOLUTIONARY PROCESS ITSELF.
OH.
MINERAL WATER.
THANK YOU, JEAN.
PLEASE, EXCUSE MY RAMBLING... NOW THAT WE FINALLY HAVE A QUIET MOMENT, I THOUGHT...
...YOU ASKED ME TO TAKE A LOOK AT THIS GROWING POWER SOURCE IN YOUR SKULL...
WELL, EVERYBODY AT THE SCHOOL SEEMS TERRIBLY WORRIED ABOUT MY EXPANDING TELEKINETIC SENSES.
BASICALLY, I NEED YOU TO TELL SCOTT I'M NOT TURNING EVIL, CHARLES.

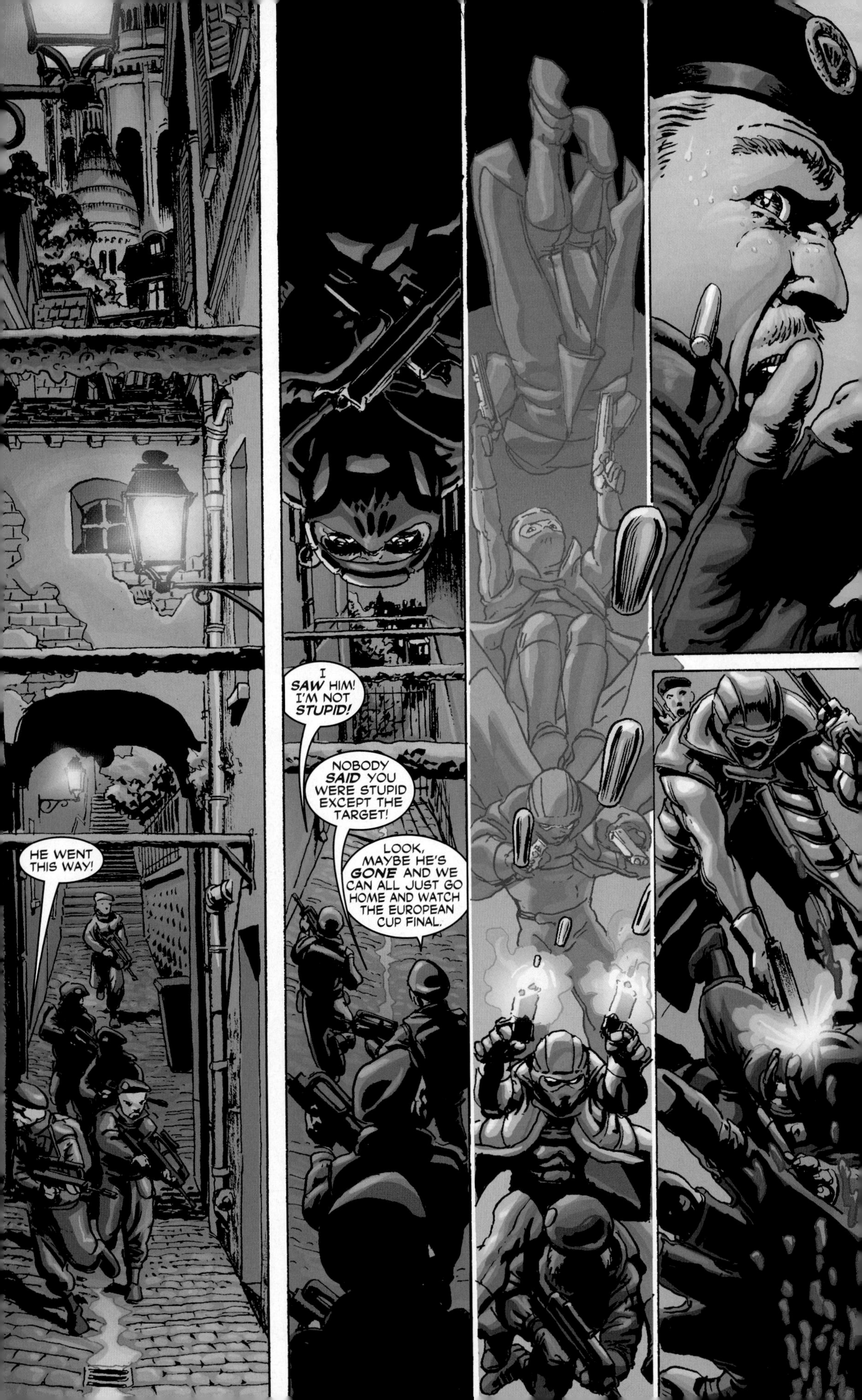
HE WENT THIS WAY!
I SAW HIM! I'M NOT STUPID!
NOBODY SAID YOU WERE STUPID EXCEPT THE TARGET!
LOOK, MAYBE HE'S GONE AND WE CAN ALL JUST GO HOME AND WATCH THE EUROPEAN CUP FINAL.

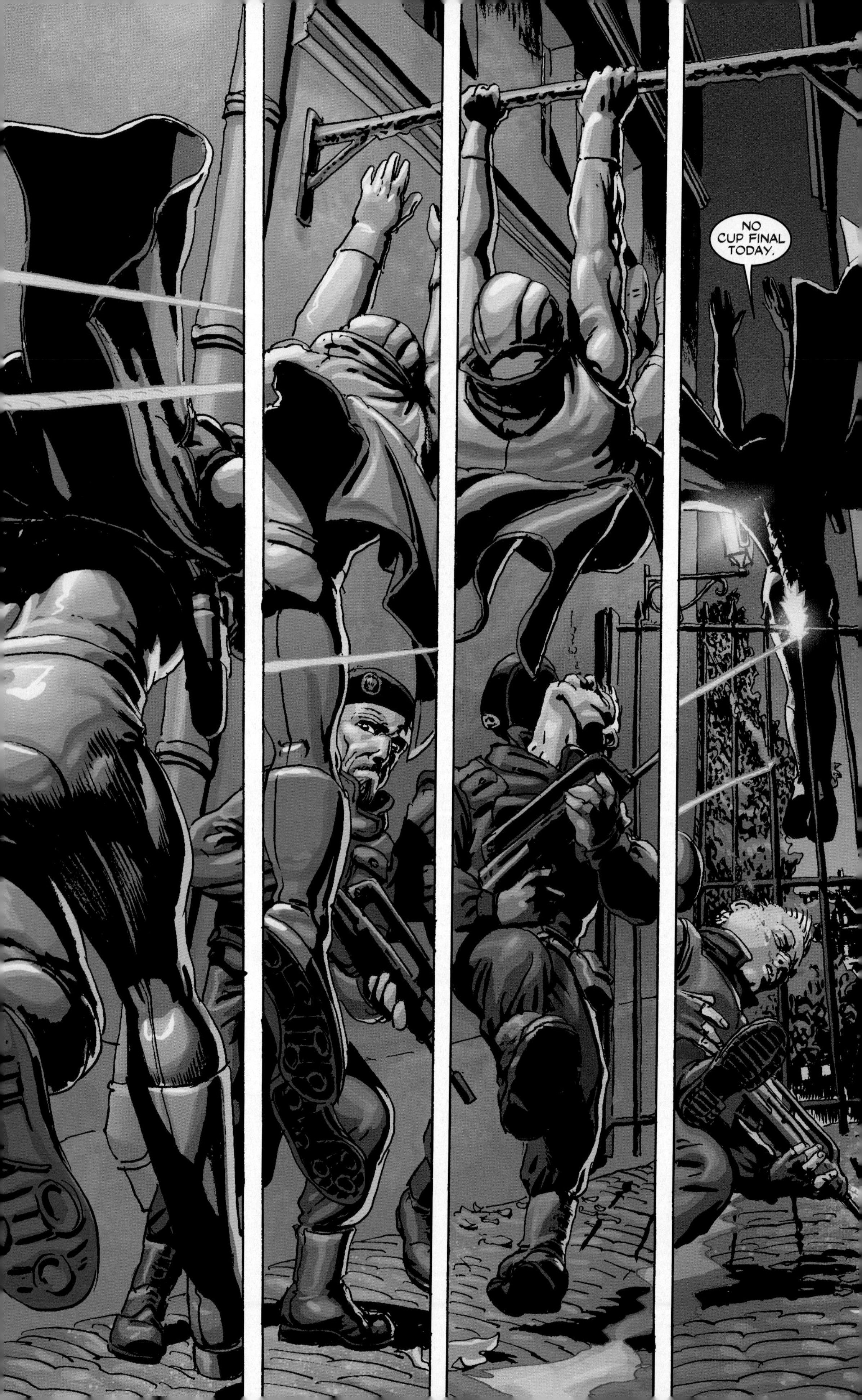
NO CUP FINAL TODAY.

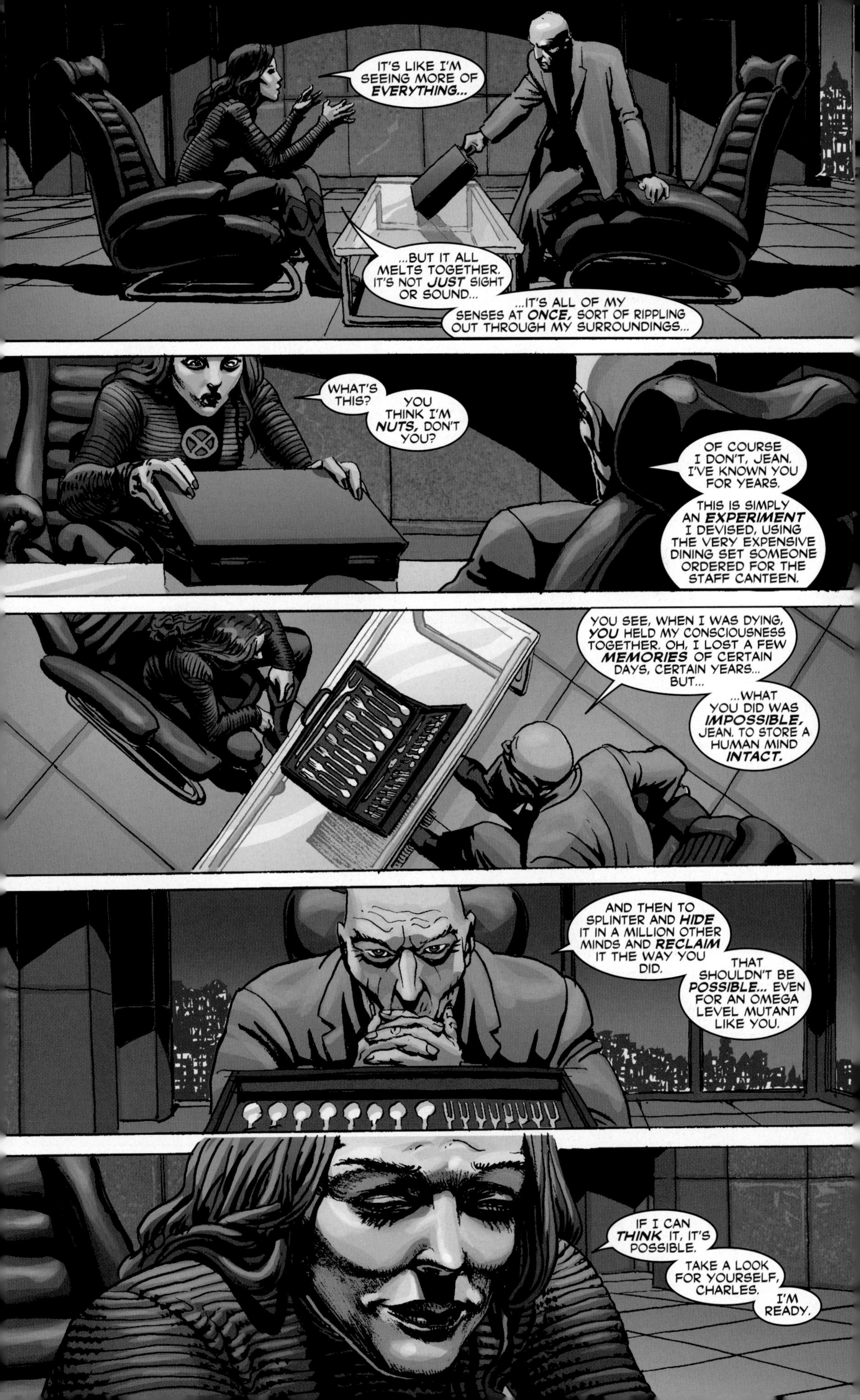
IT'S LIKE I'M SEEING MORE OF EVERYTHING...
...BUT IT ALL MELTS TOGETHER. IT'S NOT JUST SIGHT OR SOUND...
...IT'S ALL OF MY SENSES AT ONCE, SORT OF RIPPLING OUT THROUGH MY SURROUNDINGS...
WHAT'S THIS?
YOU THINK I'M NUTS, DON'T YOU?
OF COURSE I DON'T, JEAN. I'VE KNOWN YOU FOR YEARS.
THIS IS SIMPLY AN EXPERIMENT I DEVISED, USING THE VERY EXPENSIVE DINING SET SOMEONE ORDERED FOR THE STAFF CANTEEN.
YOU SEE, WHEN I WAS DYING, YOU HELD MY CONSCIOUSNESS TOGETHER. OH, I LOST A FEW MEMORIES OF CERTAIN DAYS, CERTAIN YEARS... BUT...
...WHAT YOU DID WAS IMPOSSIBLE, JEAN, TO STORE A HUMAN MIND INTACT.
AND THEN TO SPLINTER AND HIDE IT IN A MILLION OTHER MINDS AND RECLAIM IT THE WAY YOU DID.
THAT SHOULDN'T BE POSSIBLE... EVEN FOR AN OMEGA LEVEL MUTANT LIKE YOU.
IF I CAN THINK IT, IT'S POSSIBLE.
TAKE A LOOK FOR YOURSELF, CHARLES.
I'M READY.

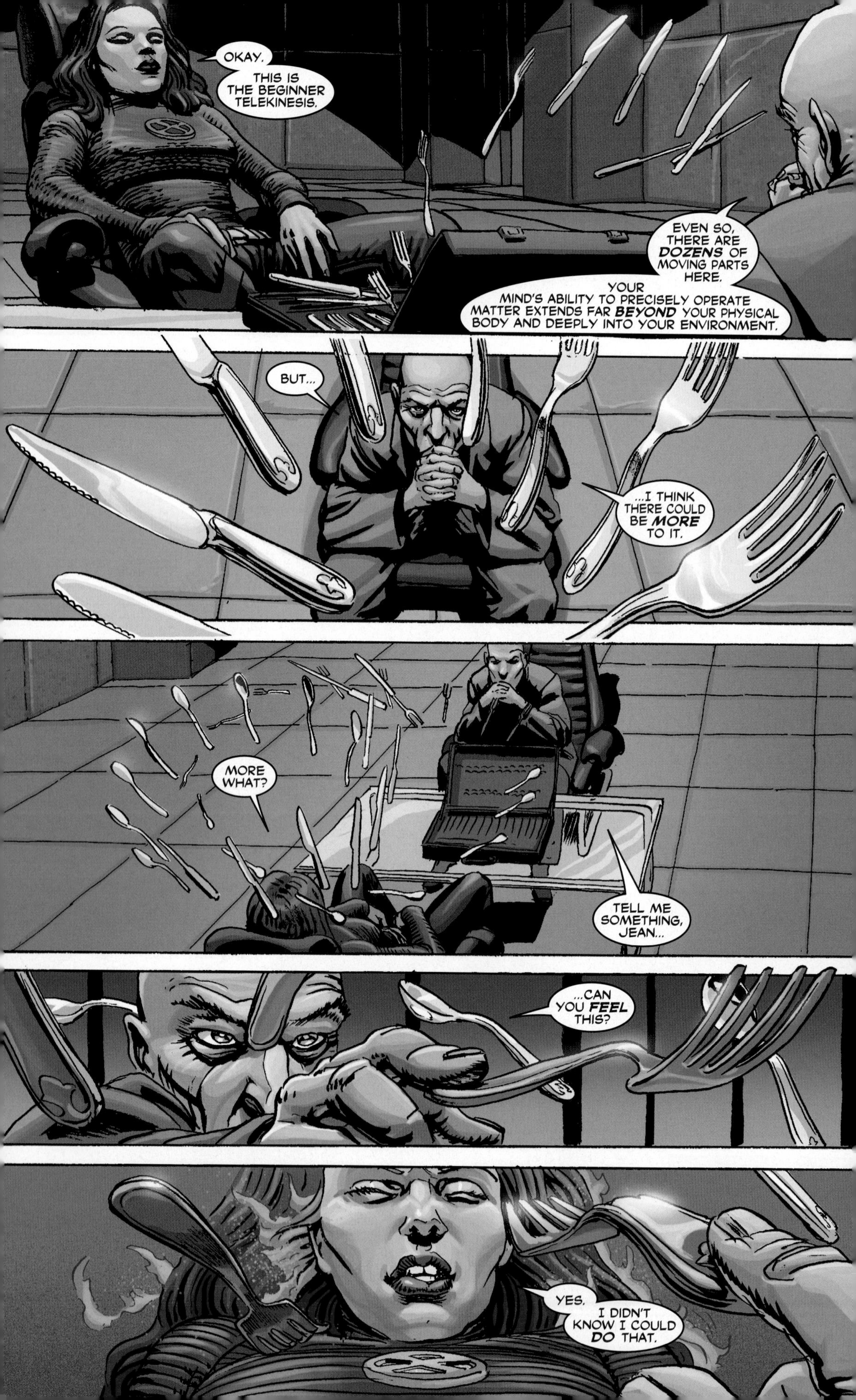
OKAY. THIS IS THE BEGINNER TELEKINESIS.
EVEN SO, THERE ARE DOZENS OF MOVING PARTS HERE.
YOUR MIND'S ABILITY TO PRECISELY OPERATE MATTER EXTENDS FAR BEYOND YOUR PHYSICAL BODY AND DEEPLY INTO YOUR ENVIRONMENT.
BUT...
...I THINK THERE COULD BE MORE TO IT.
MORE WHAT?
TELL ME SOMETHING, JEAN...
...CAN YOU FEEL THIS?
YES. I DIDN'T KNOW I COULD DO THAT.

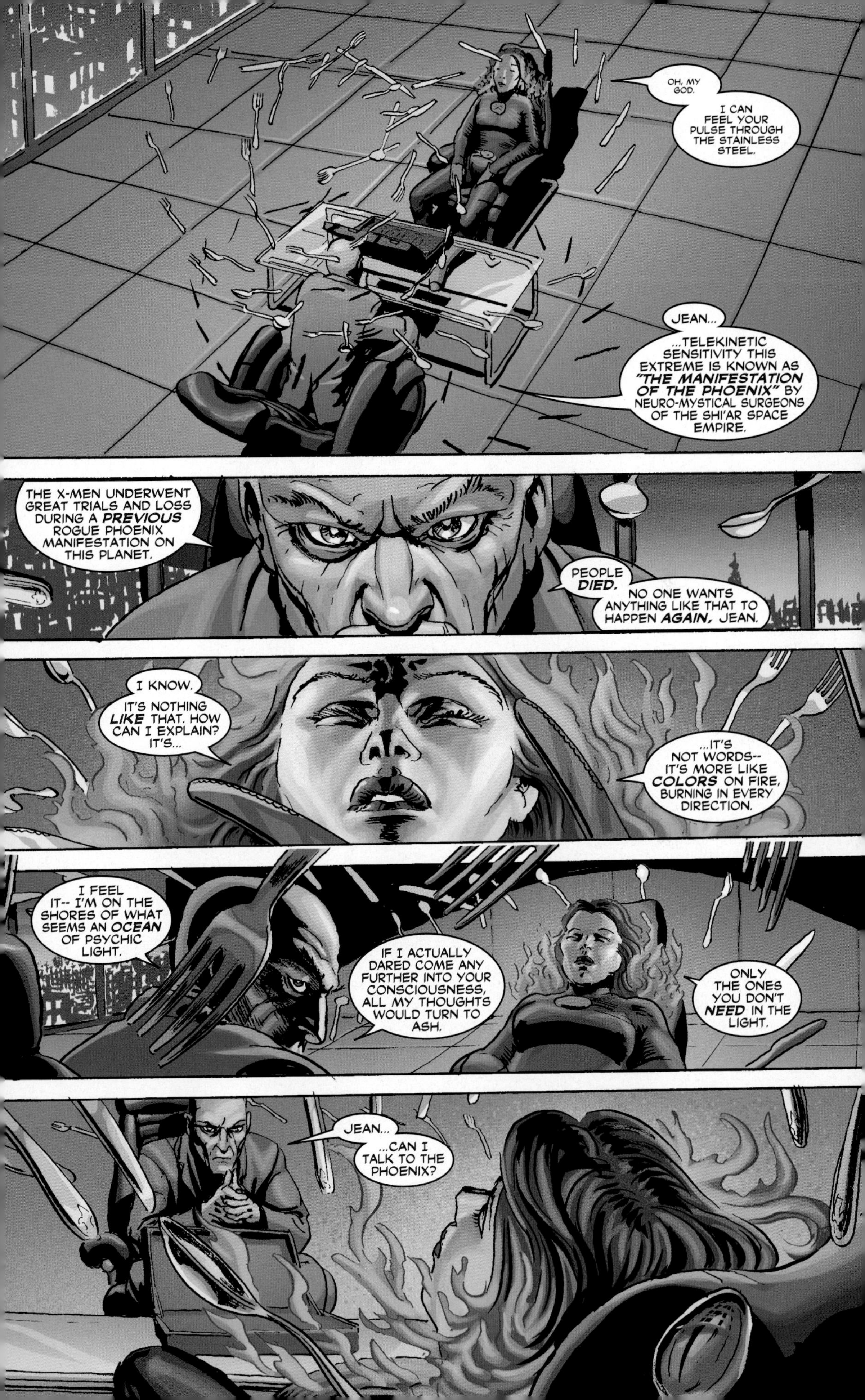
OH, MY GOD.
I CAN FEEL YOUR PULSE THROUGH THE STAINLESS STEEL.
JEAN...
...TELEKINETIC SENSITIVITY THIS EXTREME IS KNOWN AS "THE MANIFESTATION OF THE PHOENIX" BY NEURO-MYSTICAL SURGEONS OF THE SHI'AR SPACE EMPIRE.
THE X-MEN UNDERWENT GREAT TRIALS AND LOSS DURING A PREVIOUS ROGUE PHOENIX MANIFESTATION ON THIS PLANET.
PEOPLE DIED.
NO ONE WANTS ANYTHING LIKE THAT TO HAPPEN AGAIN, JEAN.
I KNOW.
IT'S NOTHING LIKE THAT. HOW CAN I EXPLAIN? IT'S...
...IT'S NOT WORDS-- IT'S MORE LIKE COLORS ON FIRE, BURNING IN EVERY DIRECTION.
I FEEL IT-- I'M ON THE SHORES OF WHAT SEEMS AN OCEAN OF PSYCHIC LIGHT.
IF I ACTUALLY DARED COME ANY FURTHER INTO YOUR CONSCIOUSNESS, ALL MY THOUGHTS WOULD TURN TO ASH.
ONLY THE ONES YOU DON'T NEED IN THE LIGHT.
JEAN...
...CAN I TALK TO THE PHOENIX?

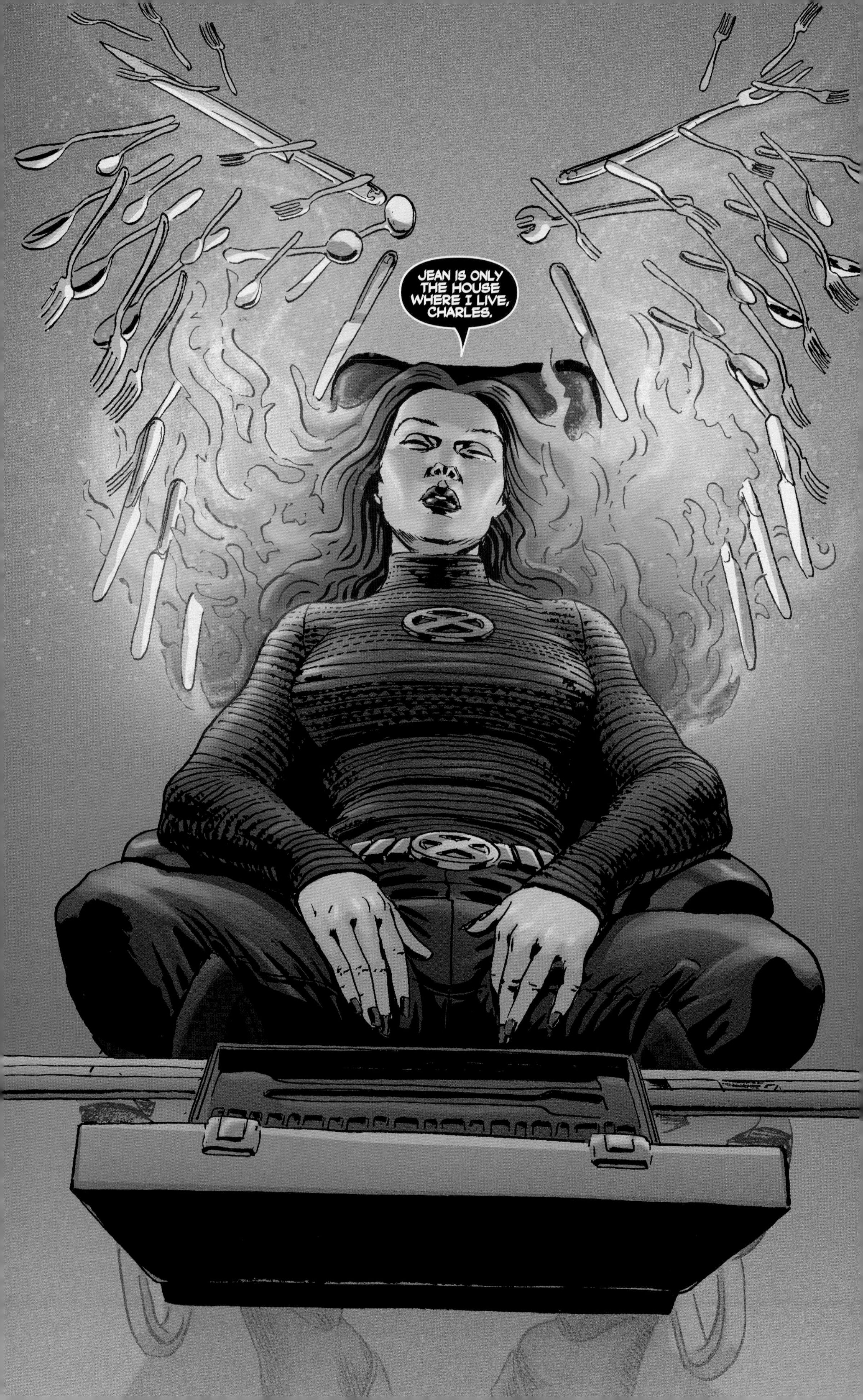
JEAN IS ONLY THE HOUSE WHERE I LIVE, CHARLES.

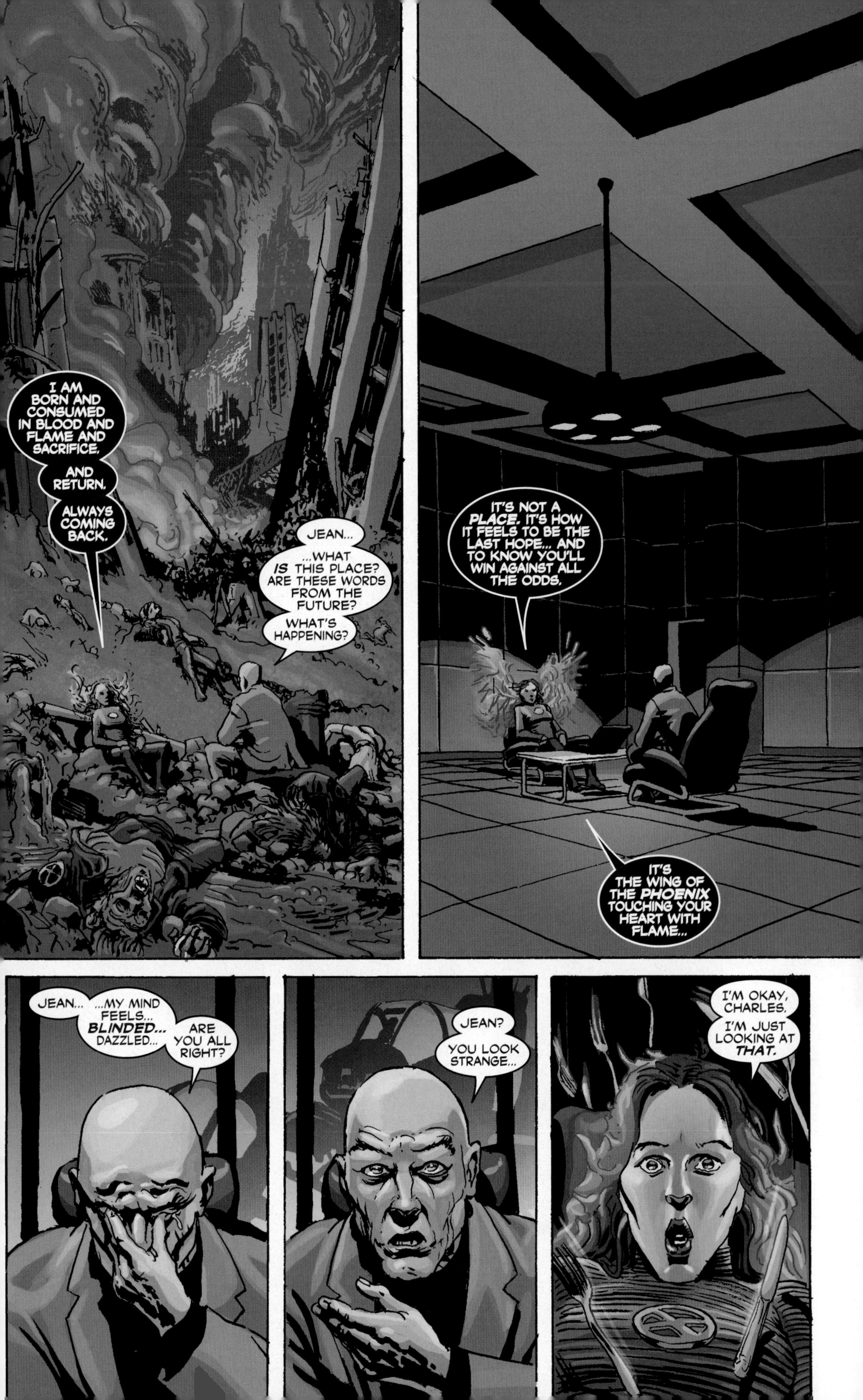
I AM BORN AND CONSUMED IN BLOOD AND FLAME AND SACRIFICE.
AND RETURN.
ALWAYS COMING BACK.
JEAN...
...WHAT *IS* THIS PLACE? ARE THESE WORDS FROM THE FUTURE?
WHAT'S HAPPENING?
IT'S NOT A *PLACE*. IT'S HOW IT FEELS TO BE THE LAST HOPE... AND TO KNOW YOU'LL WIN AGAINST ALL THE ODDS.
IT'S THE WING OF THE *PHOENIX* TOUCHING YOUR HEART WITH FLAME...
JEAN...
...MY MIND FEELS... *BLINDED...* DAZZLED...
ARE YOU ALL RIGHT?
JEAN?
YOU LOOK STRANGE...
I'M OKAY, CHARLES. I'M JUST LOOKING AT *THAT*.

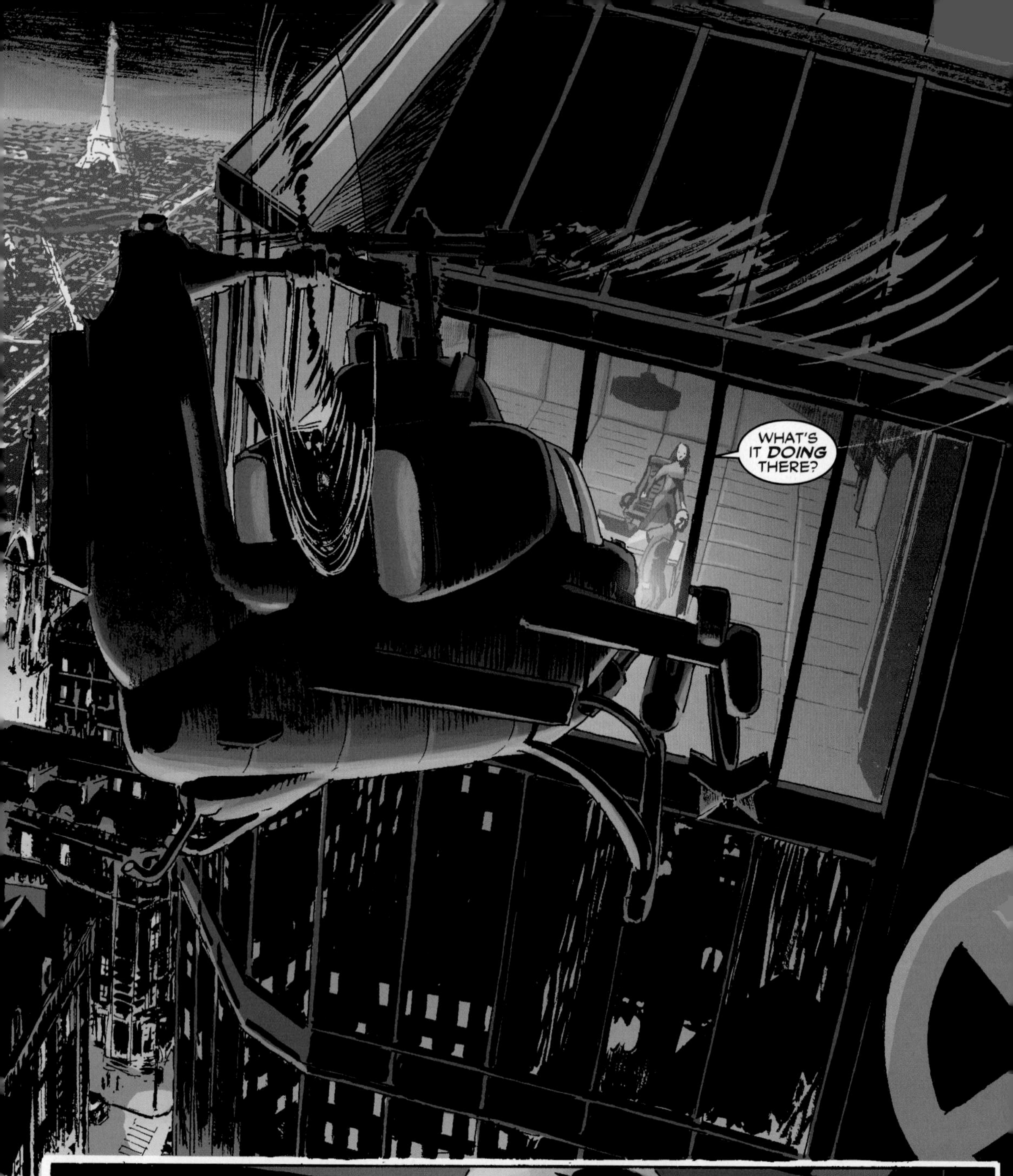
WHAT'S IT DOING THERE?

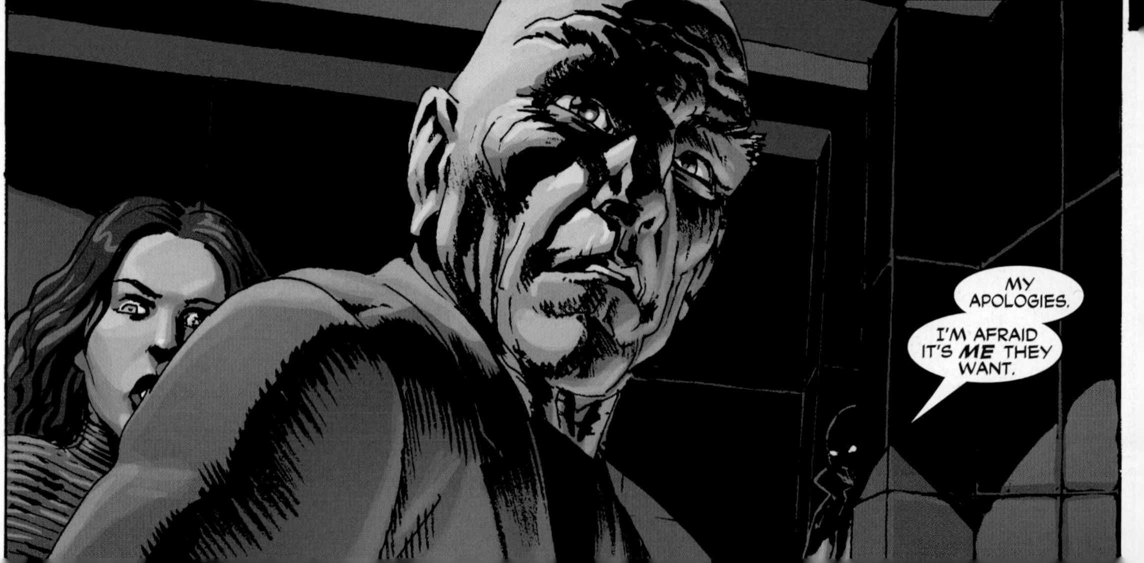
MY APOLOGIES.
I'M AFRAID IT'S ME THEY WANT.

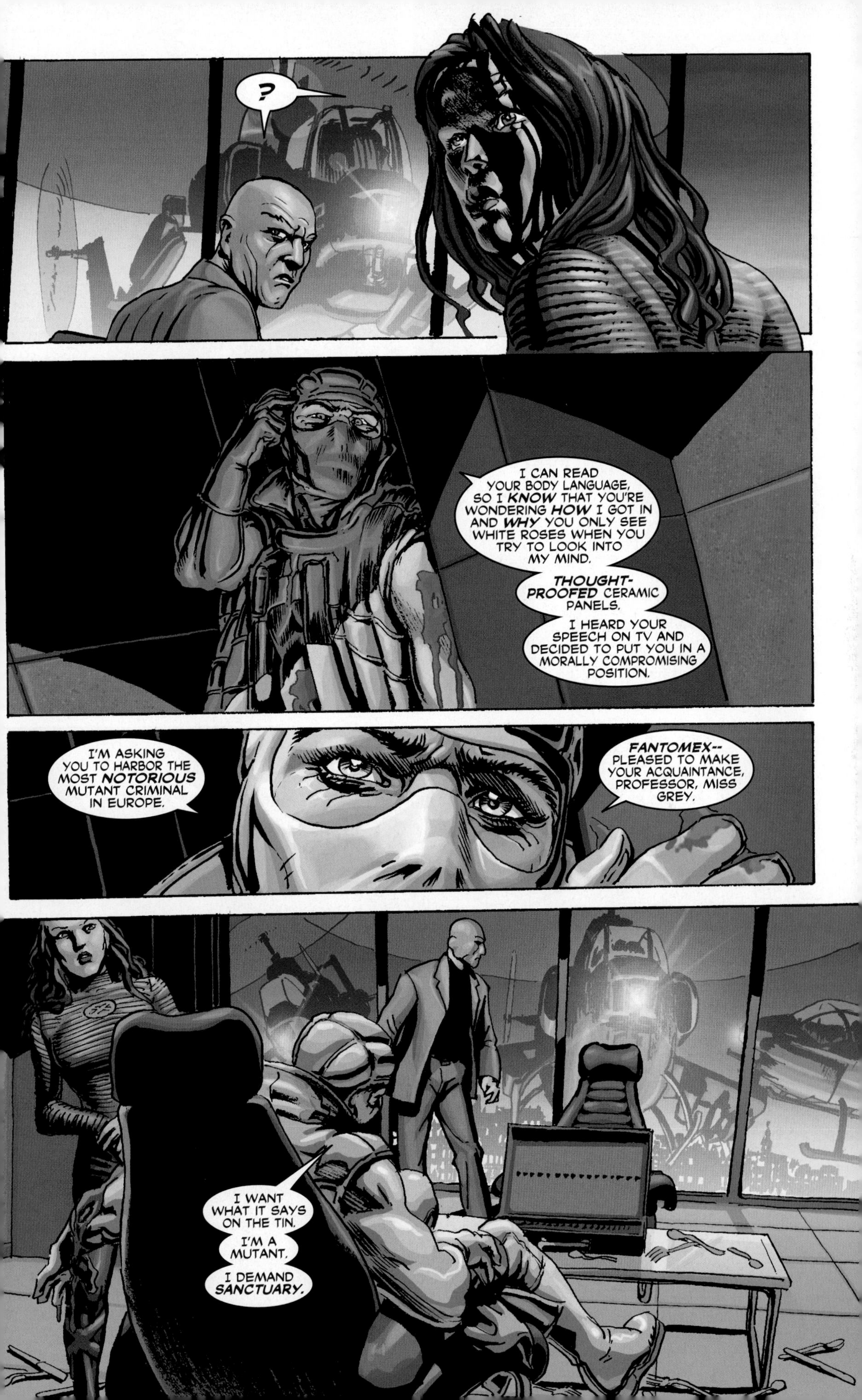
?
I CAN READ YOUR BODY LANGUAGE, SO I KNOW THAT YOU'RE WONDERING HOW I GOT IN AND WHY YOU ONLY SEE WHITE ROSES WHEN YOU TRY TO LOOK INTO MY MIND.
THOUGHT-PROOFED CERAMIC PANELS.
I HEARD YOUR SPEECH ON TV AND DECIDED TO PUT YOU IN A MORALLY COMPROMISING POSITION.
I'M ASKING YOU TO HARBOR THE MOST NOTORIOUS MUTANT CRIMINAL IN EUROPE.
FANTOMEX--PLEASED TO MAKE YOUR ACQUAINTANCE, PROFESSOR, MISS GREY.
I WANT WHAT IT SAYS ON THE TIN.
I'M A MUTANT.
I DEMAND SANCTUARY.

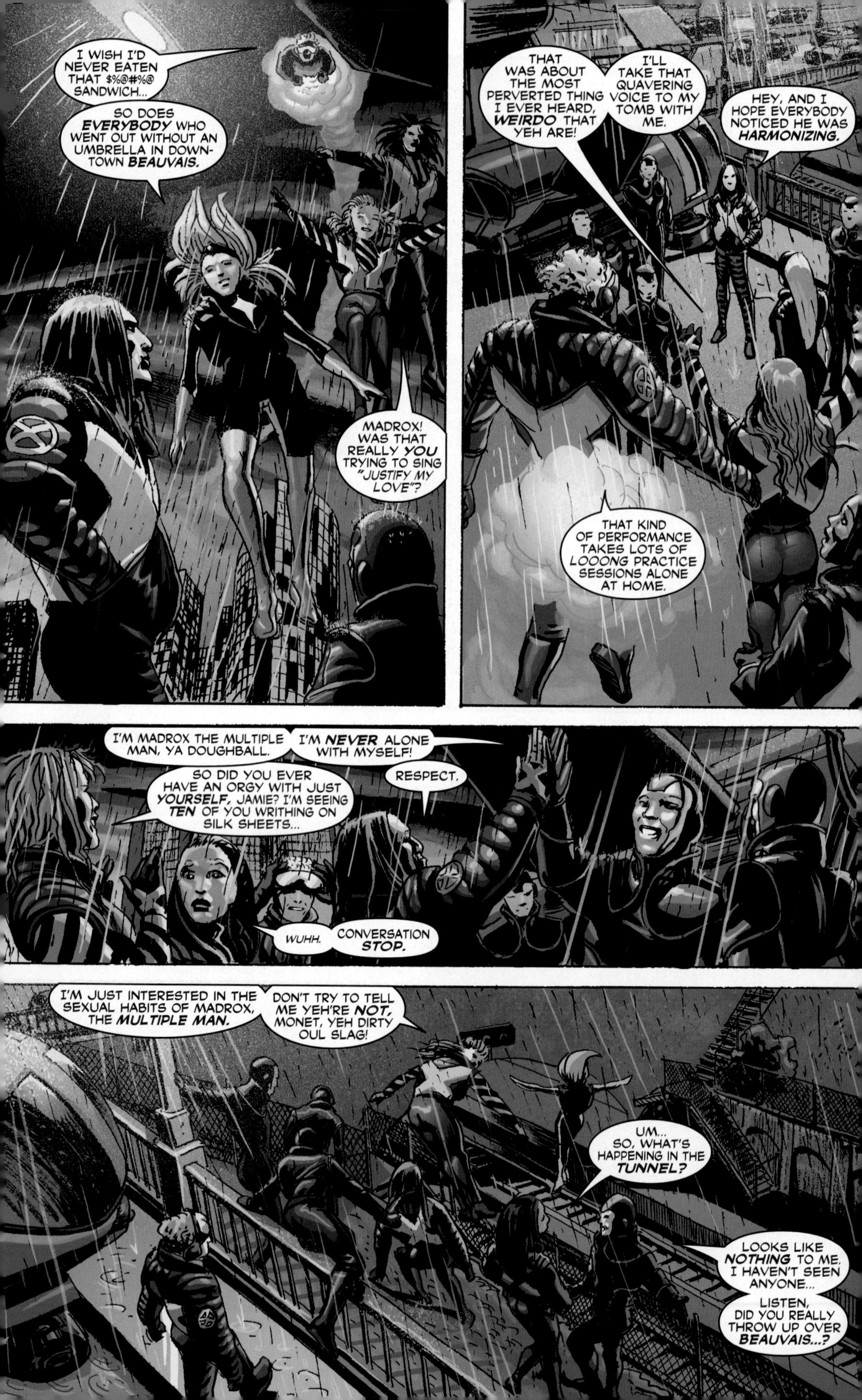
I WISH I'D NEVER EATEN THAT $%@#%@ SANDWICH...
SO DOES EVERYBODY WHO WENT OUT WITHOUT AN UMBRELLA IN DOWN-TOWN BEAUVAIS.
MADROX! WAS THAT REALLY YOU TRYING TO SING "JUSTIFY MY LOVE"?
THAT WAS ABOUT THE MOST PERVERTED THING I EVER HEARD, WEIRDO THAT YEH ARE!
I'LL TAKE THAT QUAVERING VOICE TO MY TOMB WITH ME.
HEY, AND I HOPE EVERYBODY NOTICED HE WAS HARMONIZING.
THAT KIND OF PERFORMANCE TAKES LOTS OF LOOONG PRACTICE SESSIONS ALONE AT HOME.
I'M MADROX THE MULTIPLE MAN, YA DOUGHBALL.
I'M NEVER ALONE WITH MYSELF!
SO DID YOU EVER HAVE AN ORGY WITH JUST YOURSELF, JAMIE? I'M SEEING TEN OF YOU WRITHING ON SILK SHEETS...
RESPECT.
WUHH.
CONVERSATION STOP.
I'M JUST INTERESTED IN THE SEXUAL HABITS OF MADROX, THE MULTIPLE MAN.
DON'T TRY TO TELL ME YEH'RE NOT, MONET, YEH DIRTY OUL SLAG!
UM... SO, WHAT'S HAPPENING IN THE TUNNEL?
LOOKS LIKE NOTHING TO ME. I HAVEN'T SEEN ANYONE...
LISTEN, DID YOU REALLY THROW UP OVER BEAUVAIS...?

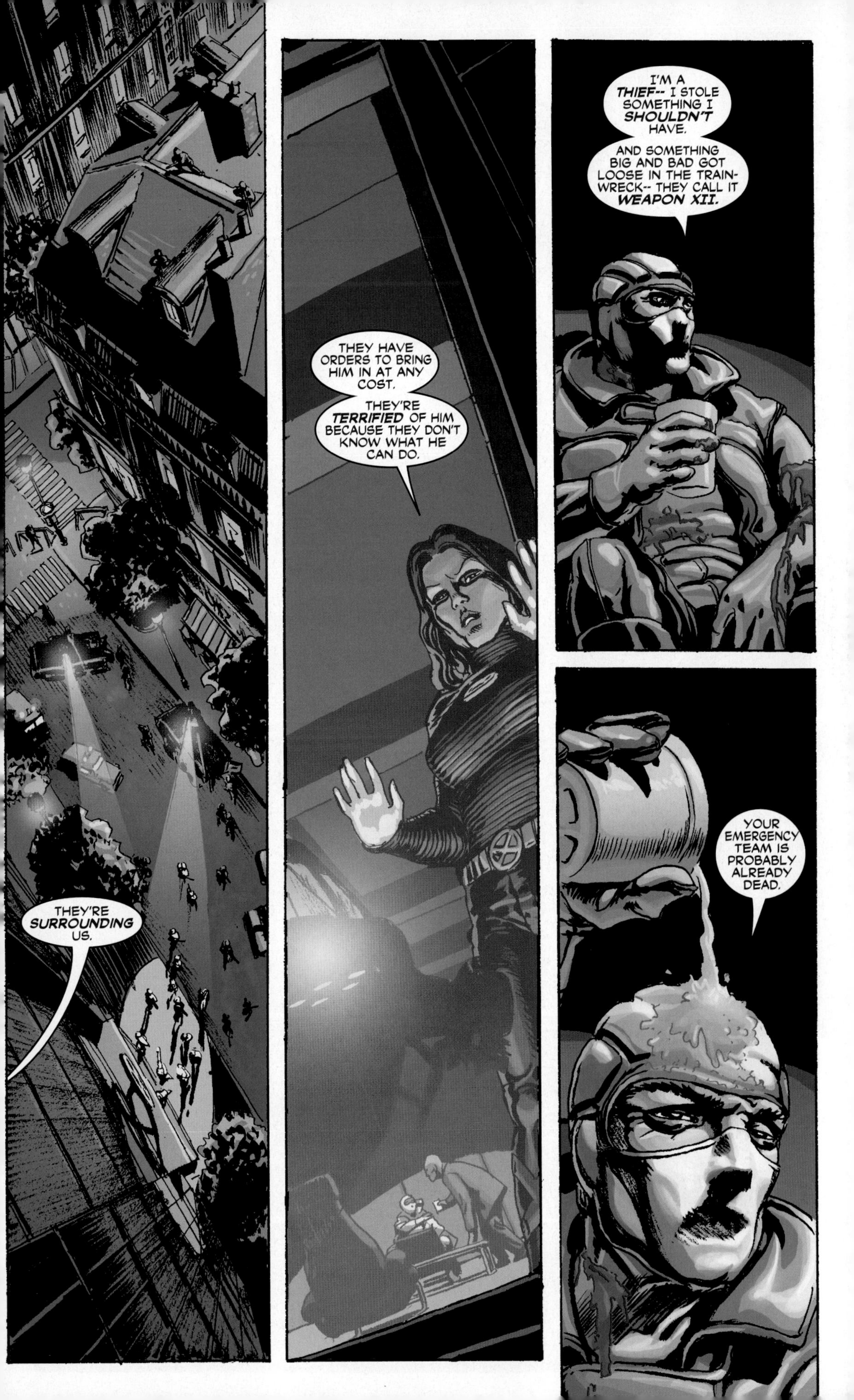
THEY'RE SURROUNDING US.
THEY HAVE ORDERS TO BRING HIM IN AT ANY COST.
THEY'RE TERRIFIED OF HIM BECAUSE THEY DON'T KNOW WHAT HE CAN DO.
I'M A THIEF-- I STOLE SOMETHING I SHOULDN'T HAVE.
AND SOMETHING BIG AND BAD GOT LOOSE IN THE TRAIN-WRECK-- THEY CALL IT WEAPON XII.
YOUR EMERGENCY TEAM IS PROBABLY ALREADY DEAD.

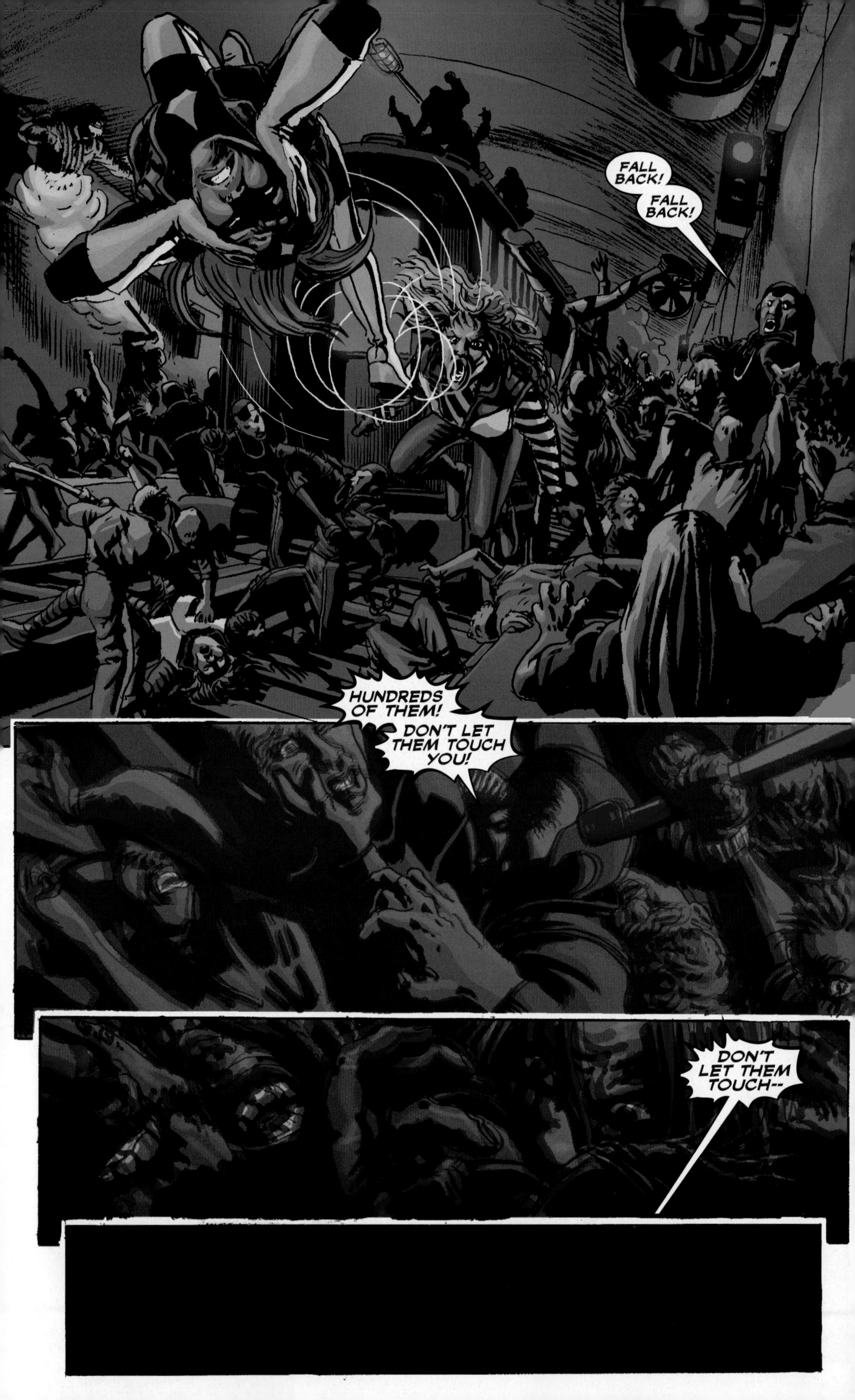
FALL BACK!
FALL BACK!
HUNDREDS OF THEM!
DON'T LET THEM TOUCH YOU!
DON'T LET THEM TOUCH--

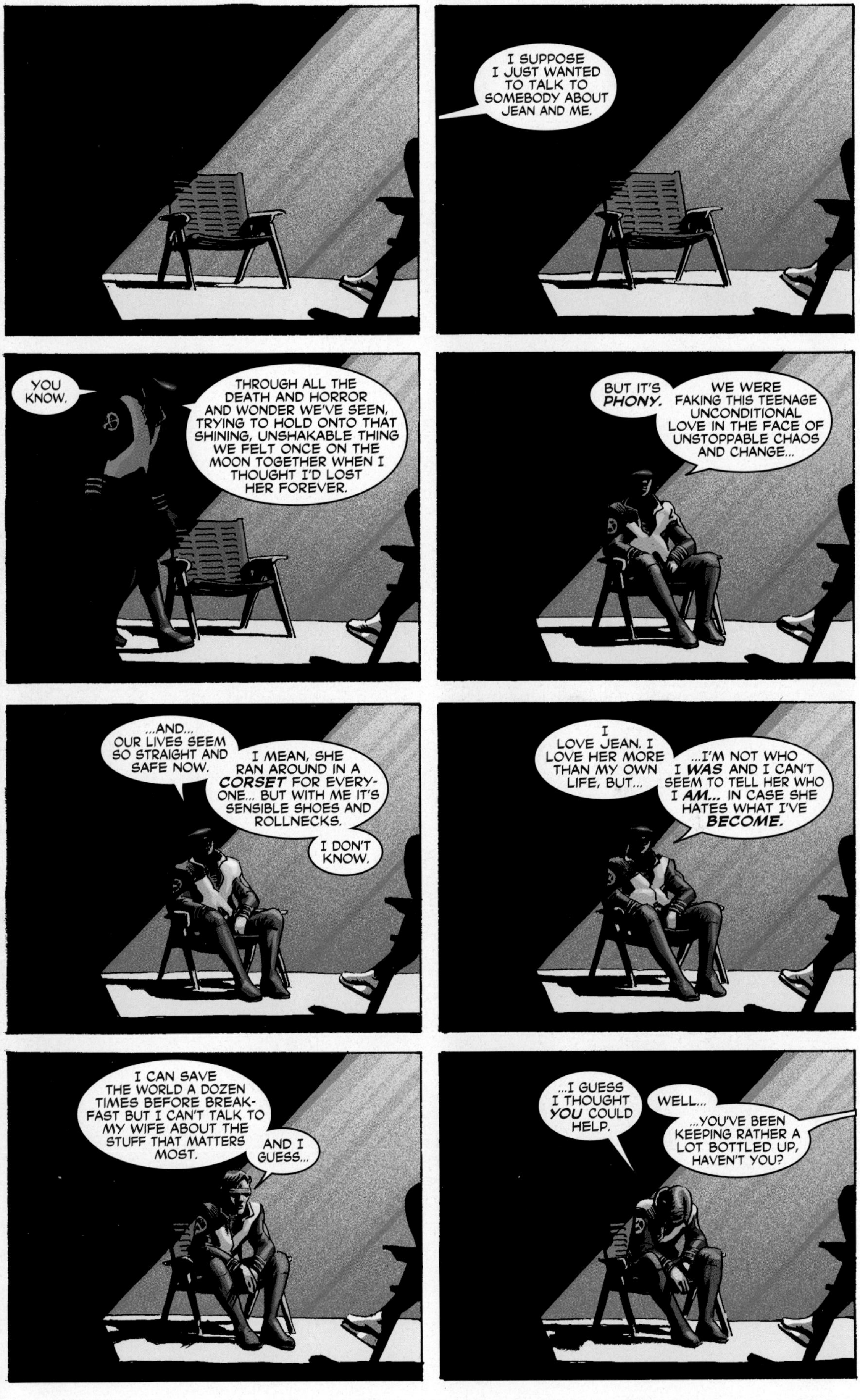
I SUPPOSE I JUST WANTED TO TALK TO SOMEBODY ABOUT JEAN AND ME.
YOU KNOW.
THROUGH ALL THE DEATH AND HORROR AND WONDER WE'VE SEEN, TRYING TO HOLD ONTO THAT SHINING, UNSHAKABLE THING WE FELT ONCE ON THE MOON TOGETHER WHEN I THOUGHT I'D LOST HER FOREVER.
BUT IT'S PHONY.
WE WERE FAKING THIS TEENAGE UNCONDITIONAL LOVE IN THE FACE OF UNSTOPPABLE CHAOS AND CHANGE...
...AND... OUR LIVES SEEM SO STRAIGHT AND SAFE NOW.
I MEAN, SHE RAN AROUND IN A CORSET FOR EVERYONE... BUT WITH ME IT'S SENSIBLE SHOES AND ROLLNECKS.
I DON'T KNOW.
I LOVE JEAN. I LOVE HER MORE THAN MY OWN LIFE, BUT...
...I'M NOT WHO I WAS AND I CAN'T SEEM TO TELL HER WHO I AM... IN CASE SHE HATES WHAT I'VE BECOME.
I CAN SAVE THE WORLD A DOZEN TIMES BEFORE BREAKFAST BUT I CAN'T TALK TO MY WIFE ABOUT THE STUFF THAT MATTERS MOST.
AND I GUESS...
...I GUESS I THOUGHT YOU COULD HELP.
WELL...
...YOU'VE BEEN KEEPING RATHER A LOT BOTTLED UP, HAVEN'T YOU?

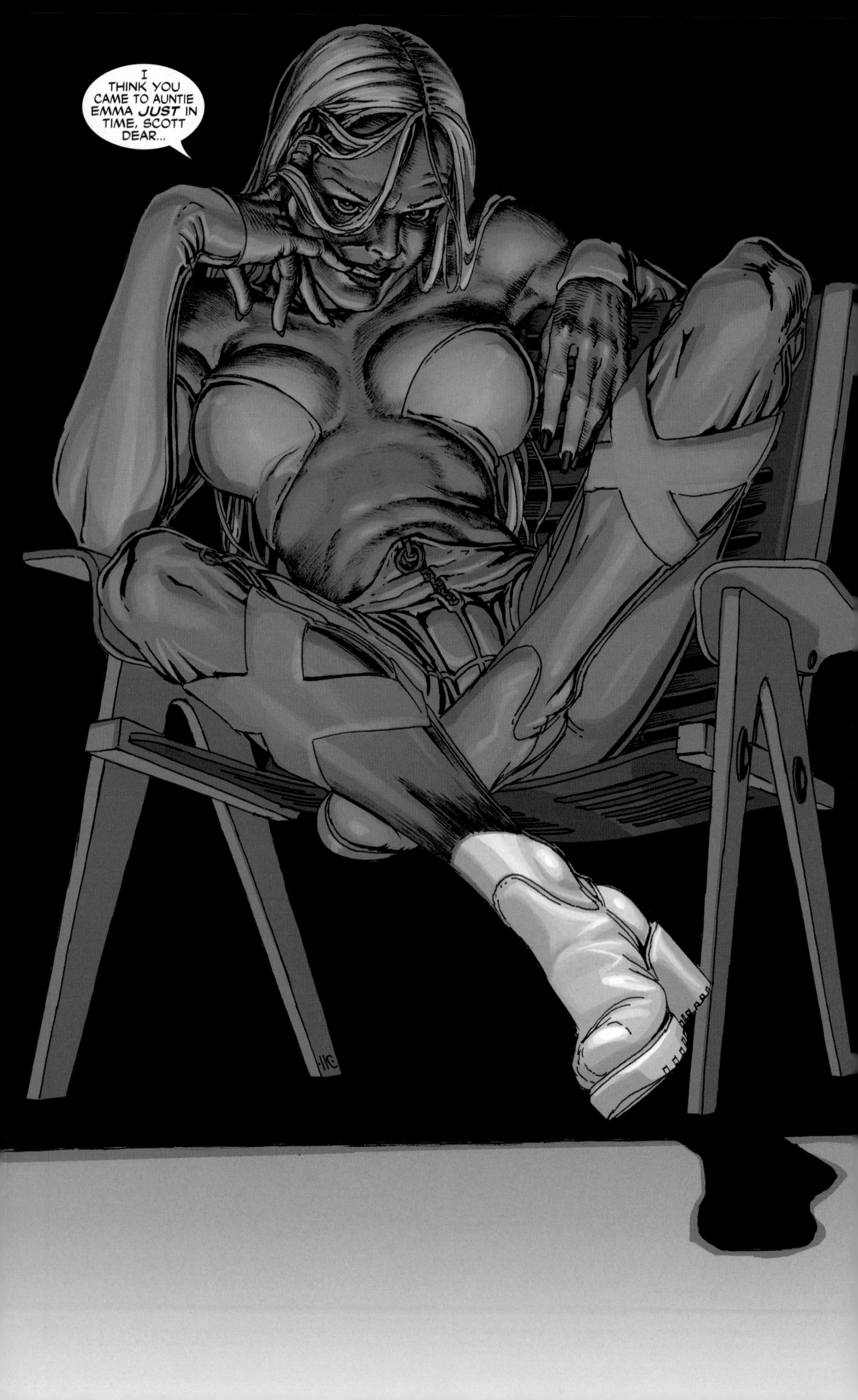
I THINK YOU CAME TO AUNTIE EMMA *JUST* IN TIME, SCOTT DEAR...

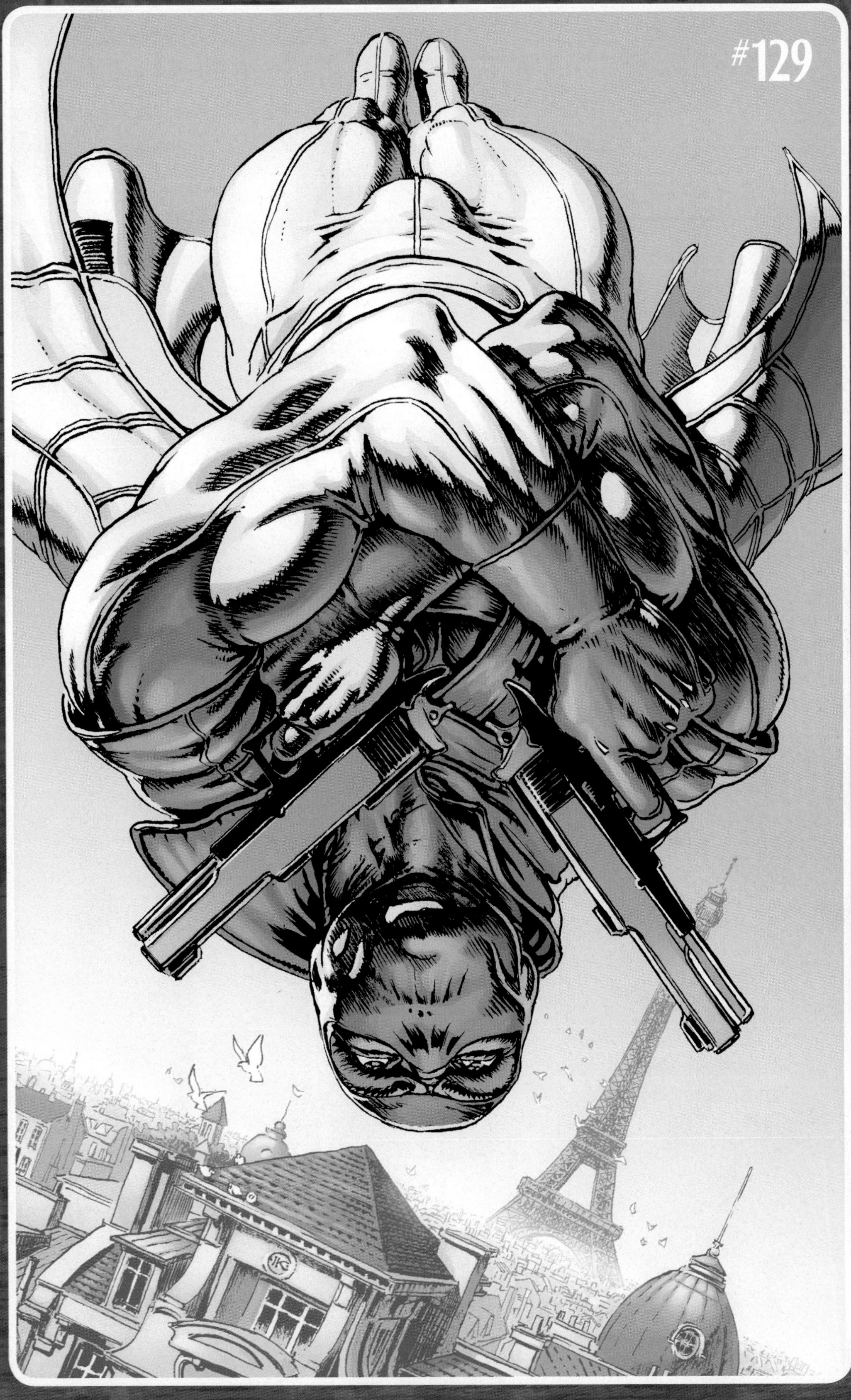
#129

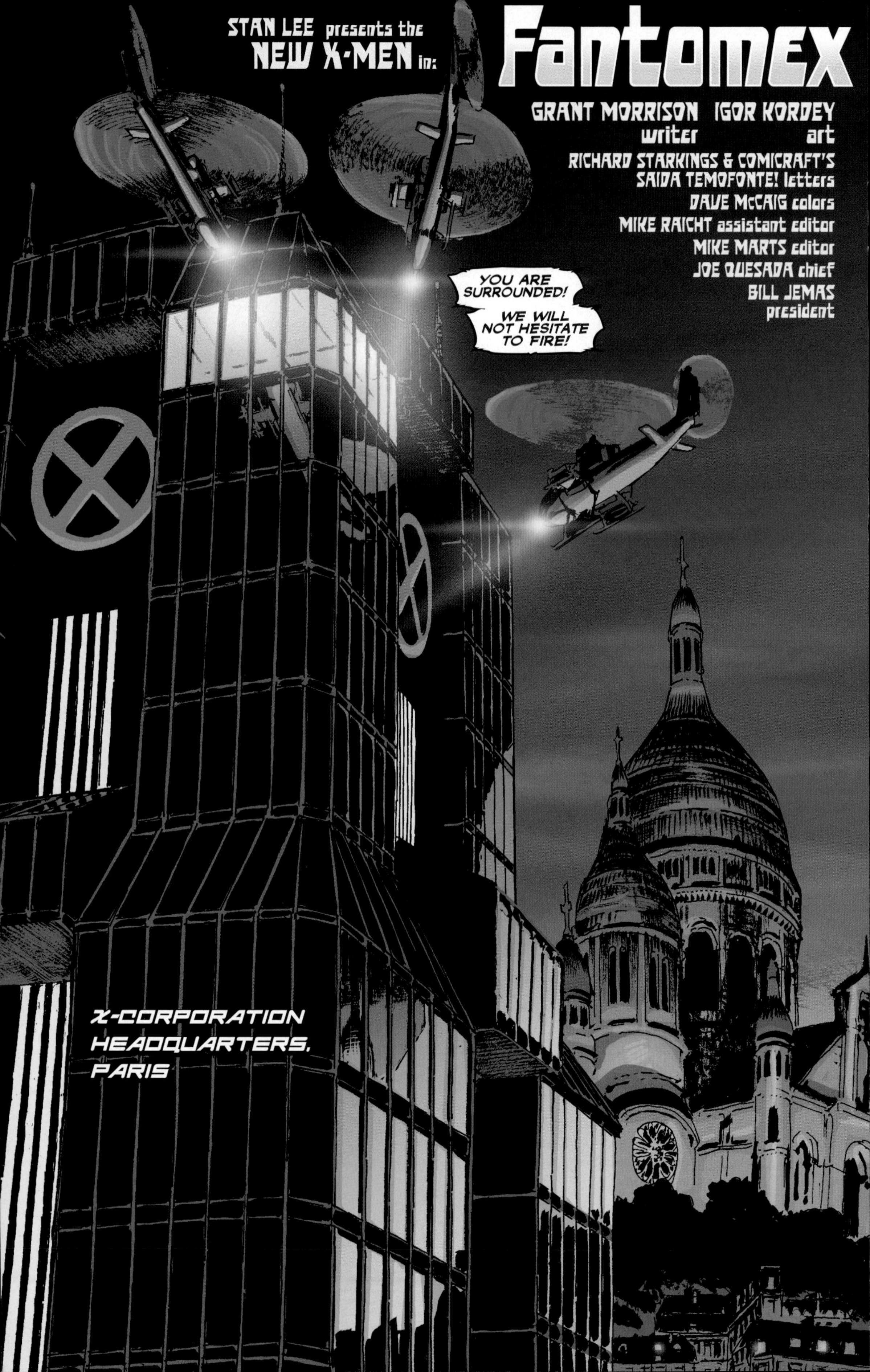
STAN LEE presents the NEW X-MEN in:
Fantomex
GRANT MORRISON writer
IGOR KORDEY art
RICHARD STARKINGS & COMICRAFT'S SAIDA TEMOFONTE! letters
DAVE McCAIG colors
MIKE RAICHT assistant editor
MIKE MARTS editor
JOE QUESADA chief
BILL JEMAS president
YOU ARE SURROUNDED! WE WILL NOT HESITATE TO FIRE!
X-CORPORATION HEADQUARTERS, PARIS

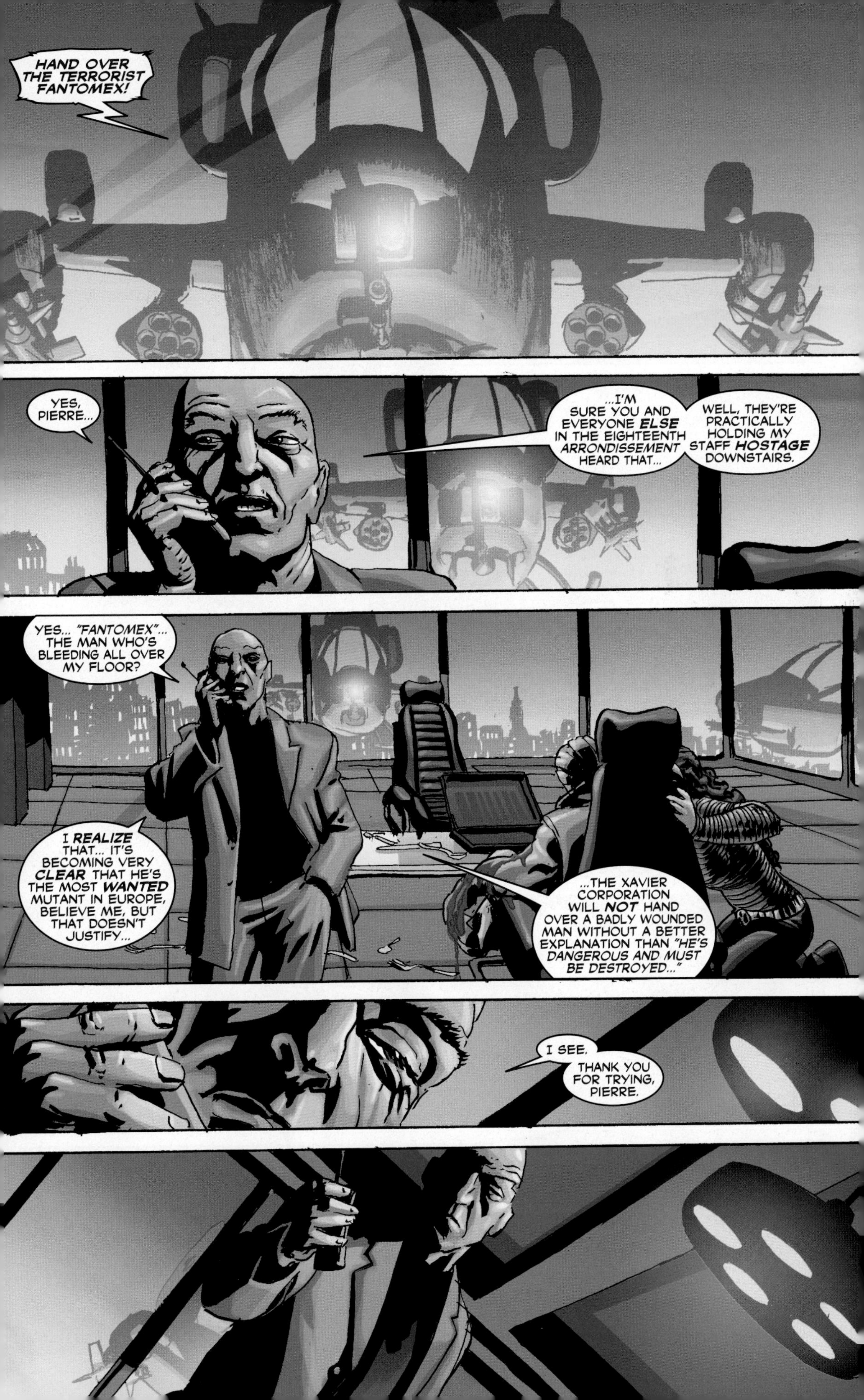
HAND OVER THE TERRORIST FANTOMEX!
YES, PIERRE...
...I'M SURE YOU AND EVERYONE ELSE IN THE EIGHTEENTH ARRONDISSEMENT HEARD THAT...
WELL, THEY'RE PRACTICALLY HOLDING MY STAFF HOSTAGE DOWNSTAIRS.
YES... "FANTOMEX"... THE MAN WHO'S BLEEDING ALL OVER MY FLOOR?
I REALIZE THAT... IT'S BECOMING VERY CLEAR THAT HE'S THE MOST WANTED MUTANT IN EUROPE, BELIEVE ME, BUT THAT DOESN'T JUSTIFY...
...THE XAVIER CORPORATION WILL NOT HAND OVER A BADLY WOUNDED MAN WITHOUT A BETTER EXPLANATION THAN "HE'S DANGEROUS AND MUST BE DESTROYED..."
I SEE.
THANK YOU FOR TRYING, PIERRE.

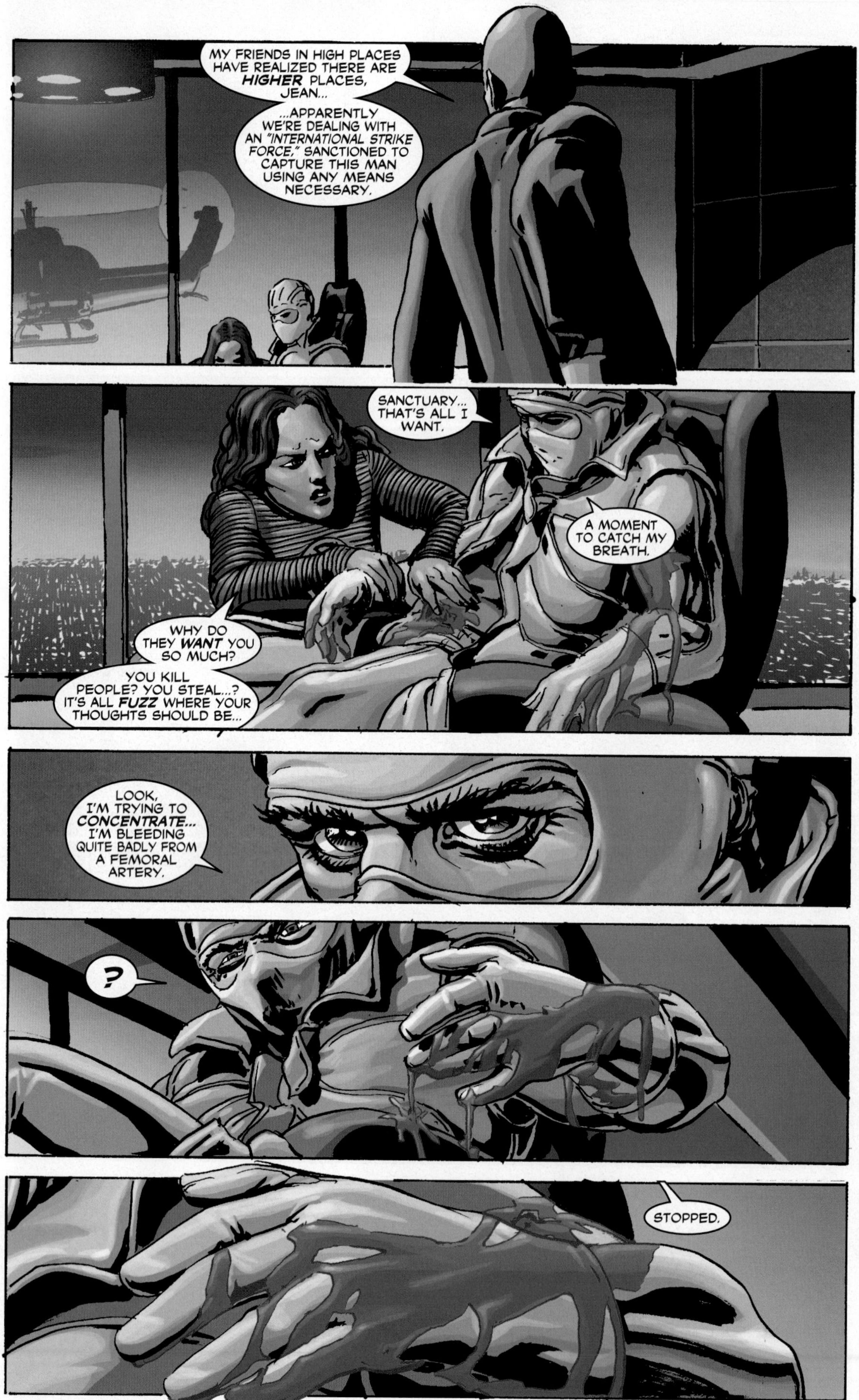

MY FRIENDS IN HIGH PLACES HAVE REALIZED THERE ARE HIGHER PLACES, JEAN...
...APPARENTLY WE'RE DEALING WITH AN "INTERNATIONAL STRIKE FORCE," SANCTIONED TO CAPTURE THIS MAN USING ANY MEANS NECESSARY.
SANCTUARY... THAT'S ALL I WANT.
A MOMENT TO CATCH MY BREATH.
WHY DO THEY WANT YOU SO MUCH?
YOU KILL PEOPLE? YOU STEAL...? IT'S ALL FUZZ WHERE YOUR THOUGHTS SHOULD BE...
LOOK, I'M TRYING TO CONCENTRATE... I'M BLEEDING QUITE BADLY FROM A FEMORAL ARTERY.
?
STOPPED.

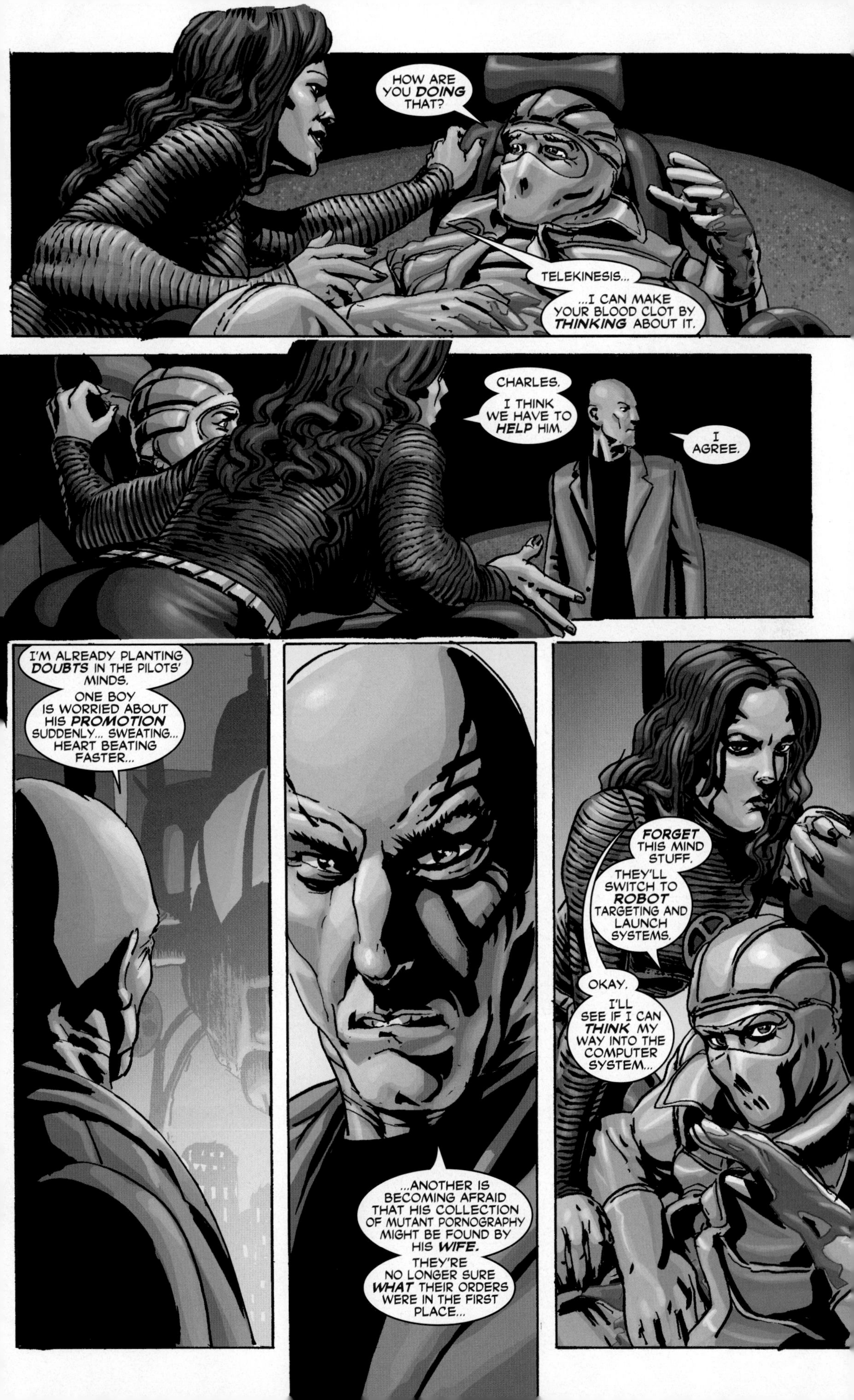
HOW ARE YOU *DOING* THAT?
TELEKINESIS...
...I CAN MAKE YOUR BLOOD CLOT BY *THINKING* ABOUT IT.
CHARLES.
I THINK WE HAVE TO *HELP* HIM.
I AGREE.
I'M ALREADY PLANTING *DOUBTS* IN THE PILOTS' MINDS.
ONE BOY IS WORRIED ABOUT HIS *PROMOTION* SUDDENLY... SWEATING... HEART BEATING FASTER...
...ANOTHER IS BECOMING AFRAID THAT HIS COLLECTION OF MUTANT PORNOGRAPHY MIGHT BE FOUND BY HIS *WIFE*.
THEY'RE NO LONGER SURE *WHAT* THEIR ORDERS WERE IN THE FIRST PLACE...
FORGET THIS MIND STUFF.
THEY'LL SWITCH TO *ROBOT* TARGETING AND LAUNCH SYSTEMS.
OKAY.
I'LL SEE IF I CAN *THINK* MY WAY INTO THE COMPUTER SYSTEM...

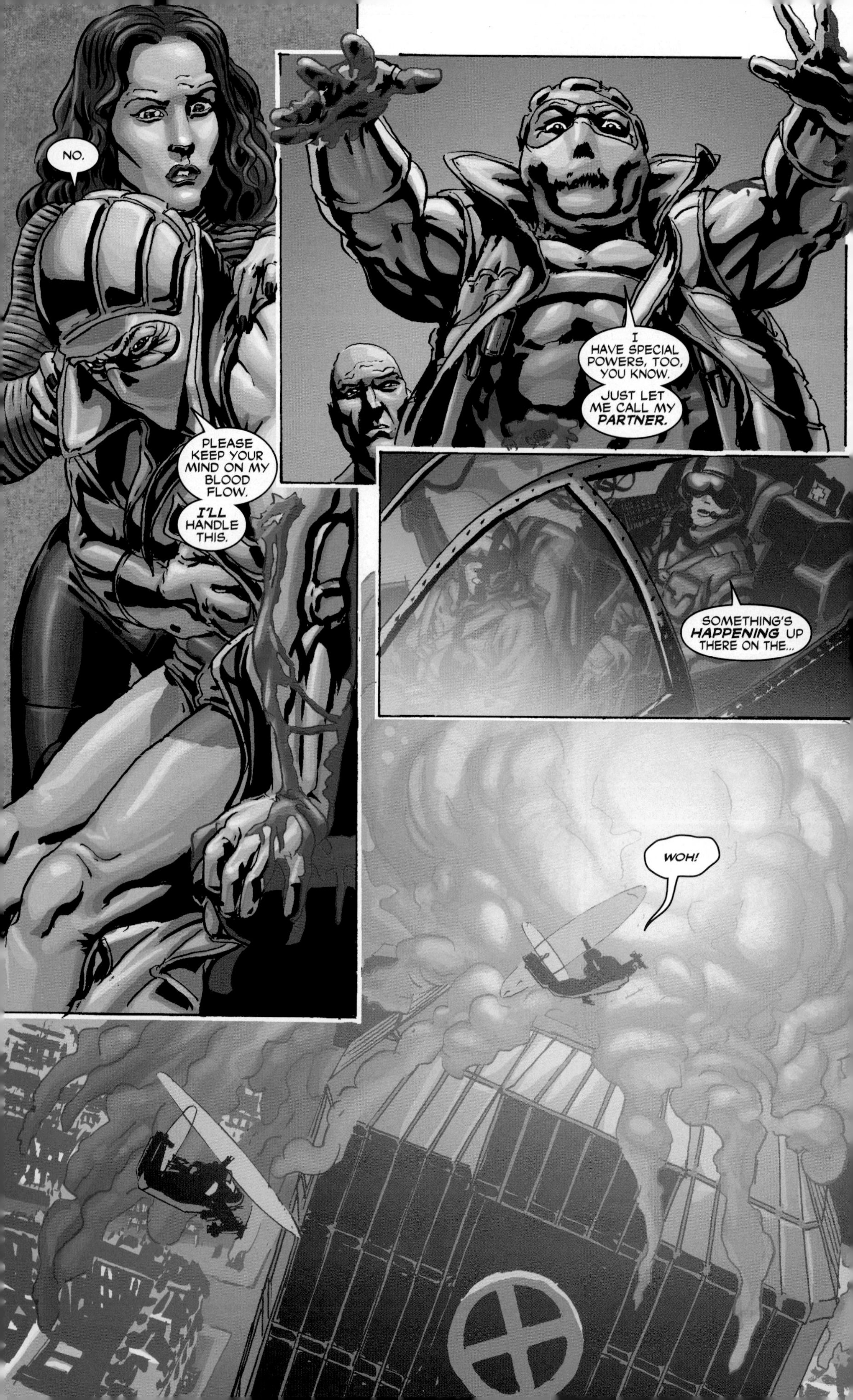
NO.
I HAVE SPECIAL POWERS, TOO, YOU KNOW.
JUST LET ME CALL MY PARTNER.
PLEASE KEEP YOUR MIND ON MY BLOOD FLOW.
I'LL HANDLE THIS.
SOMETHING'S HAPPENING UP THERE ON THE...
WOH!

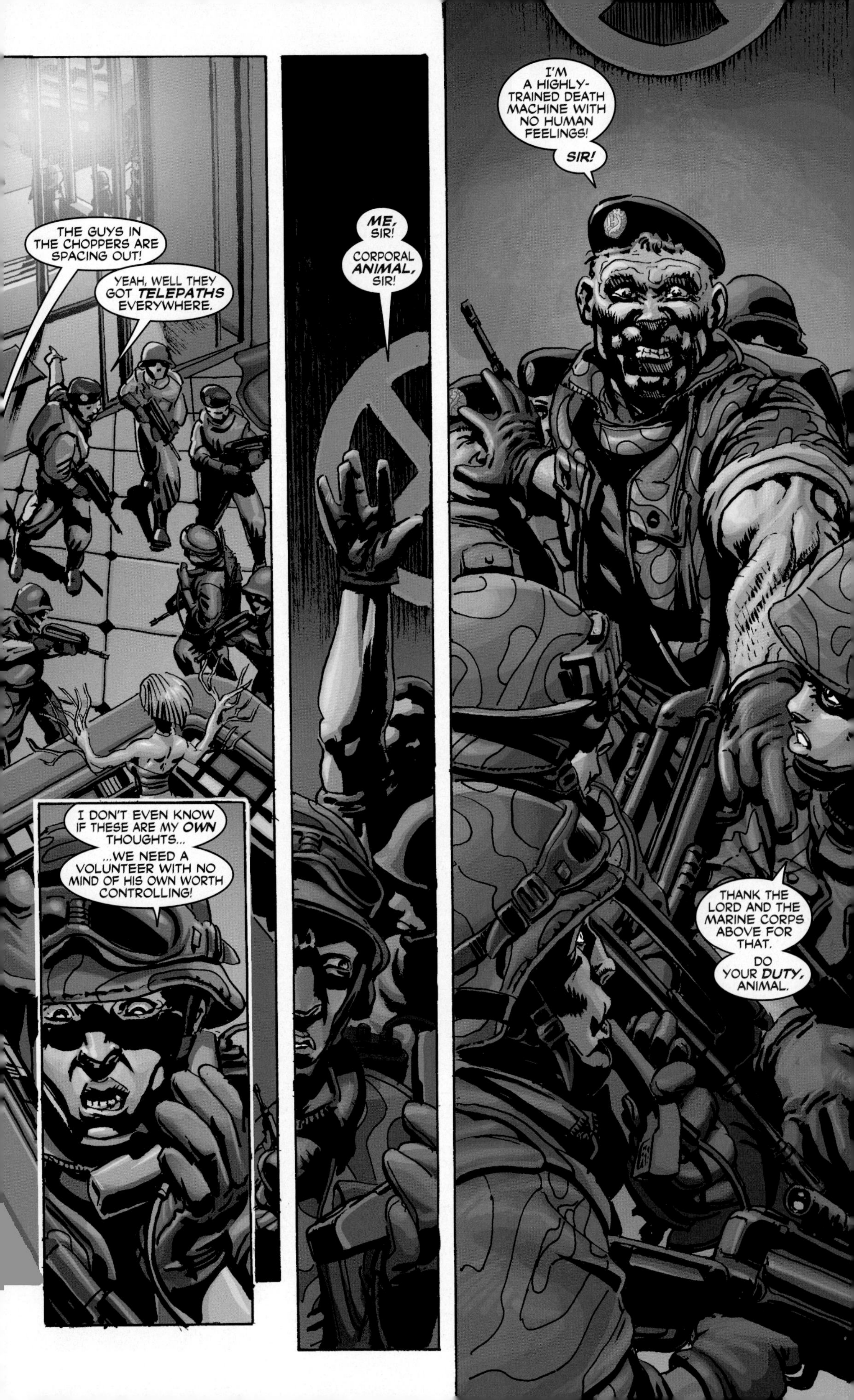
THE GUYS IN THE CHOPPERS ARE SPACING OUT!
YEAH, WELL THEY GOT **TELEPATHS** EVERYWHERE.
I DON'T EVEN KNOW IF THESE ARE MY **OWN** THOUGHTS...
...WE NEED A VOLUNTEER WITH NO MIND OF HIS OWN WORTH CONTROLLING!
ME, SIR!
CORPORAL **ANIMAL,** SIR!
I'M A HIGHLY-TRAINED DEATH MACHINE WITH NO HUMAN FEELINGS!
SIR!
THANK THE LORD AND THE MARINE CORPS ABOVE FOR THAT.
DO YOUR **DUTY,** ANIMAL.

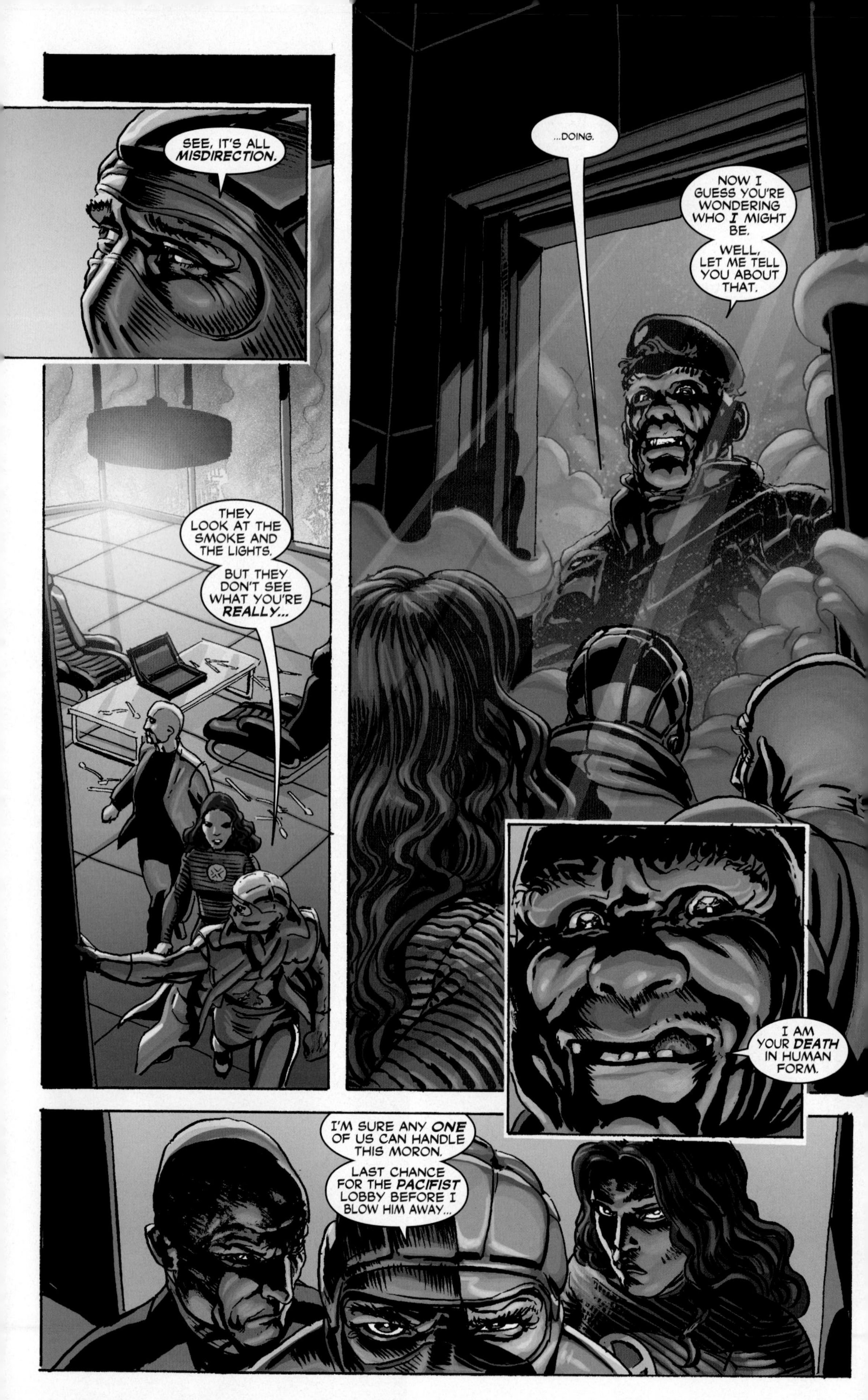
SEE, IT'S ALL MISDIRECTION.
THEY LOOK AT THE SMOKE AND THE LIGHTS.
BUT THEY DON'T SEE WHAT YOU'RE REALLY...
...DOING.
NOW I GUESS YOU'RE WONDERING WHO I MIGHT BE.
WELL, LET ME TELL YOU ABOUT THAT.
I AM YOUR DEATH IN HUMAN FORM.
I'M SURE ANY ONE OF US CAN HANDLE THIS MORON.
LAST CHANCE FOR THE PACIFIST LOBBY BEFORE I BLOW HIM AWAY...

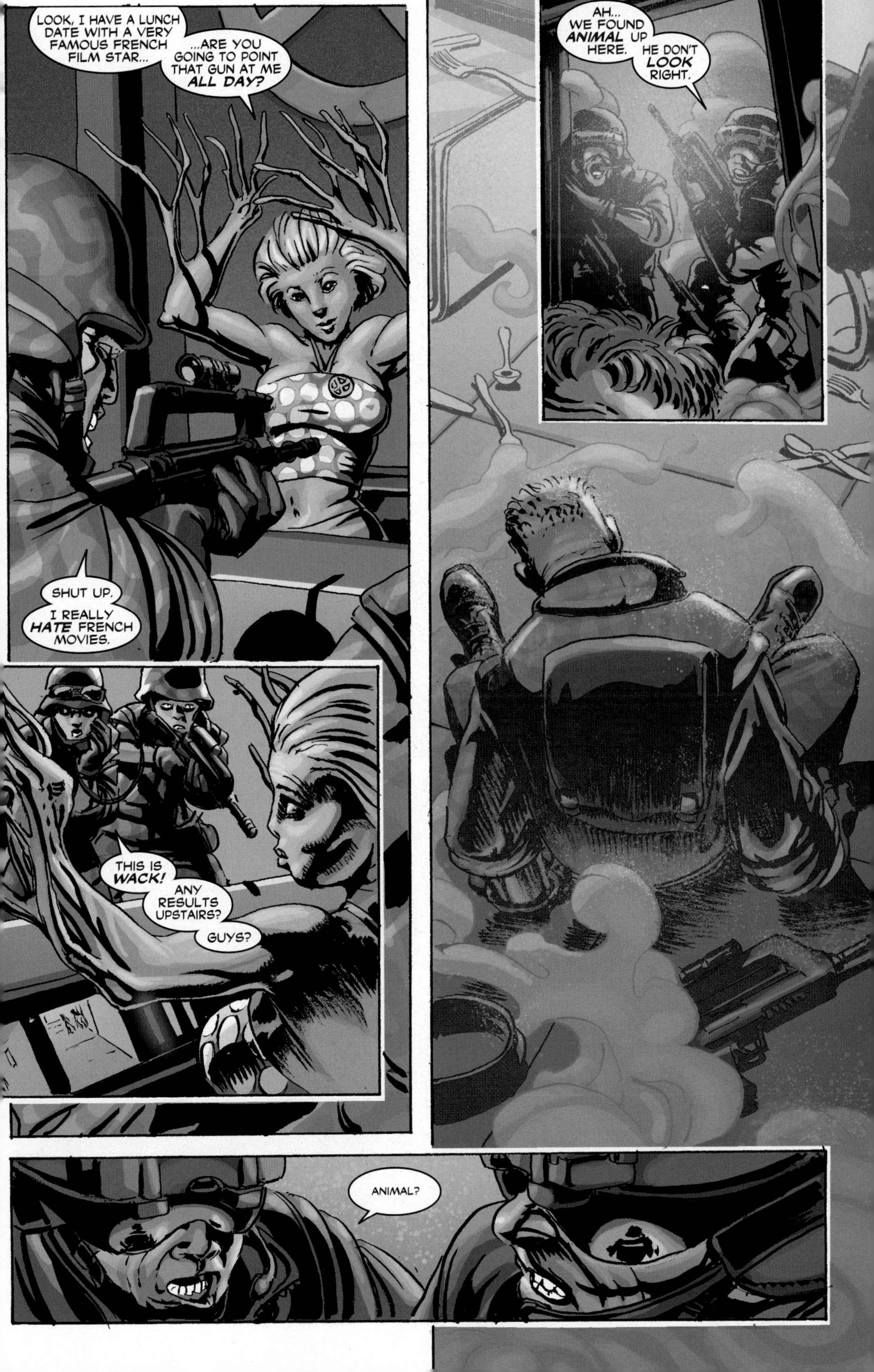
LOOK, I HAVE A LUNCH DATE WITH A VERY FAMOUS FRENCH FILM STAR...
...ARE YOU GOING TO POINT THAT GUN AT ME ALL DAY?
SHUT UP. I REALLY HATE FRENCH MOVIES.
AH... WE FOUND ANIMAL UP HERE.
HE DON'T LOOK RIGHT.
THIS IS WACK!
ANY RESULTS UPSTAIRS?
GUYS?
ANIMAL?

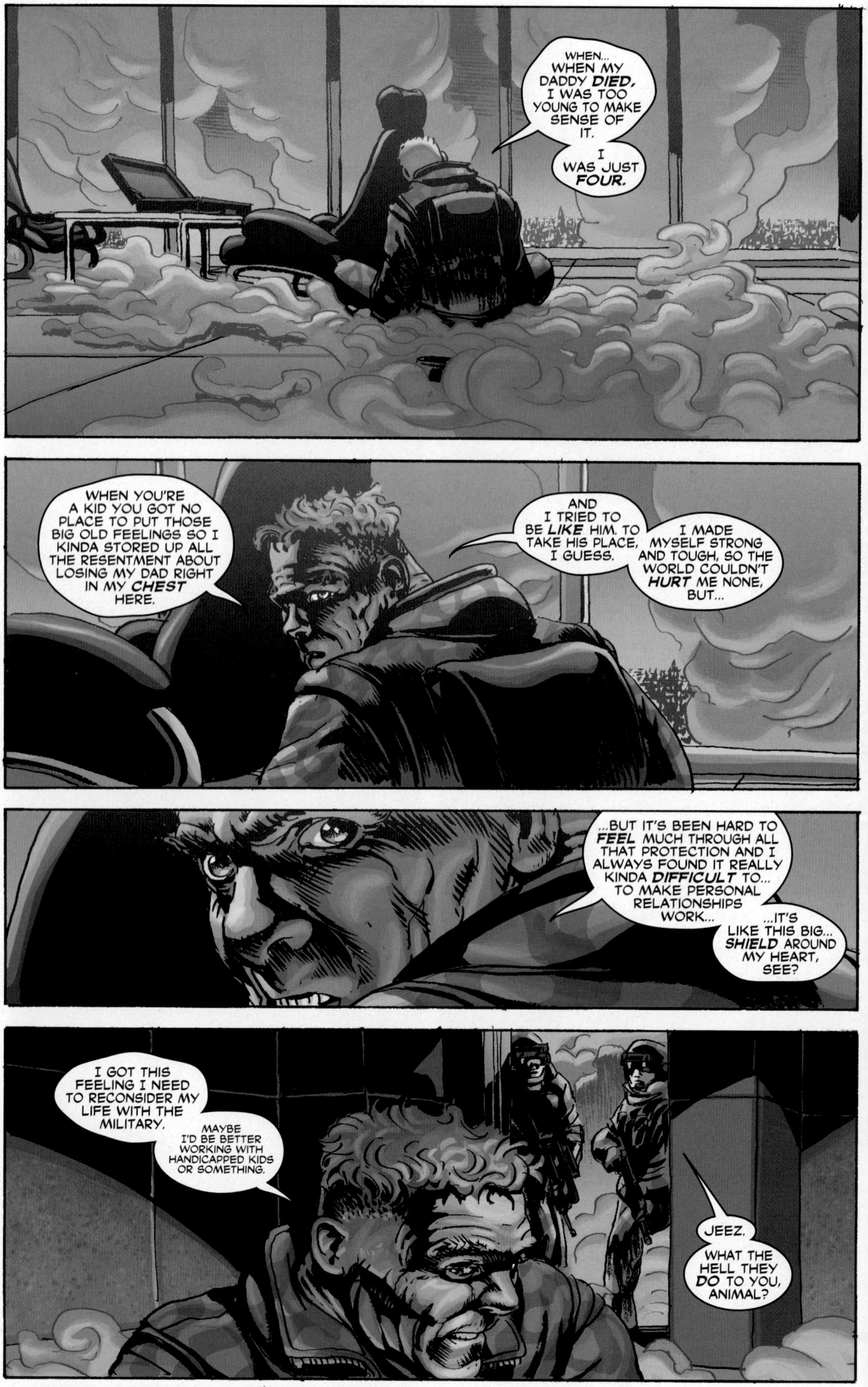
WHEN... WHEN MY DADDY DIED, I WAS TOO YOUNG TO MAKE SENSE OF IT.
I WAS JUST FOUR.
WHEN YOU'RE A KID YOU GOT NO PLACE TO PUT THOSE BIG OLD FEELINGS SO I KINDA STORED UP ALL THE RESENTMENT ABOUT LOSING MY DAD RIGHT IN MY CHEST HERE.
AND I TRIED TO BE LIKE HIM. TO TAKE HIS PLACE, I GUESS.
I MADE MYSELF STRONG AND TOUGH, SO THE WORLD COULDN'T HURT ME NONE, BUT...
...BUT IT'S BEEN HARD TO FEEL MUCH THROUGH ALL THAT PROTECTION AND I ALWAYS FOUND IT REALLY KINDA DIFFICULT TO... TO MAKE PERSONAL RELATIONSHIPS WORK...
...IT'S LIKE THIS BIG... SHIELD AROUND MY HEART, SEE?
I GOT THIS FEELING I NEED TO RECONSIDER MY LIFE WITH THE MILITARY.
MAYBE I'D BE BETTER WORKING WITH HANDICAPPED KIDS OR SOMETHING.
JEEZ.
WHAT THE HELL THEY DO TO YOU, ANIMAL?

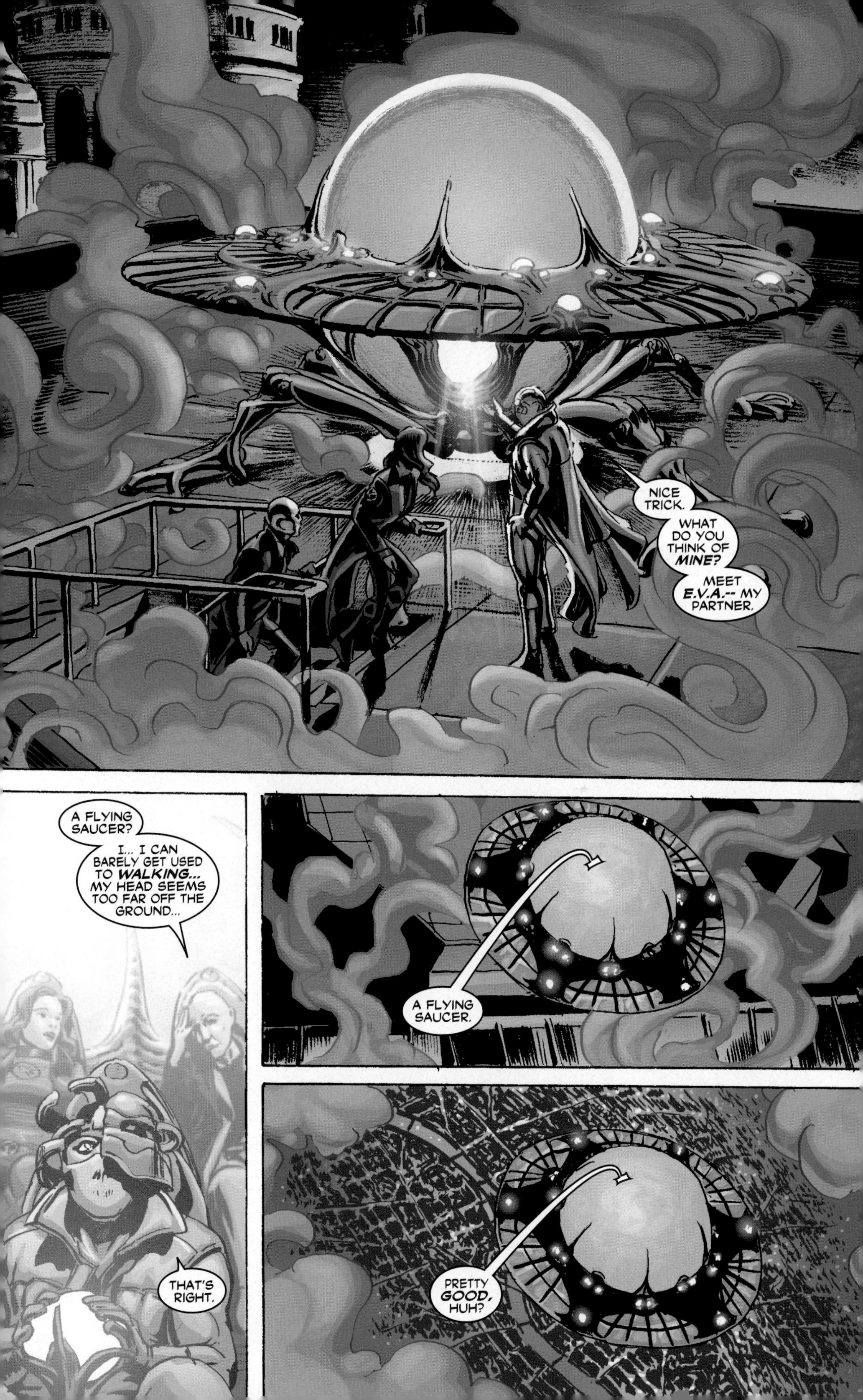

NICE TRICK.
WHAT DO YOU THINK OF MINE?
MEET E.V.A.-- MY PARTNER.
A FLYING SAUCER?
I... I CAN BARELY GET USED TO WALKING... MY HEAD SEEMS TOO FAR OFF THE GROUND...
A FLYING SAUCER.
THAT'S RIGHT.
PRETTY GOOD, HUH?

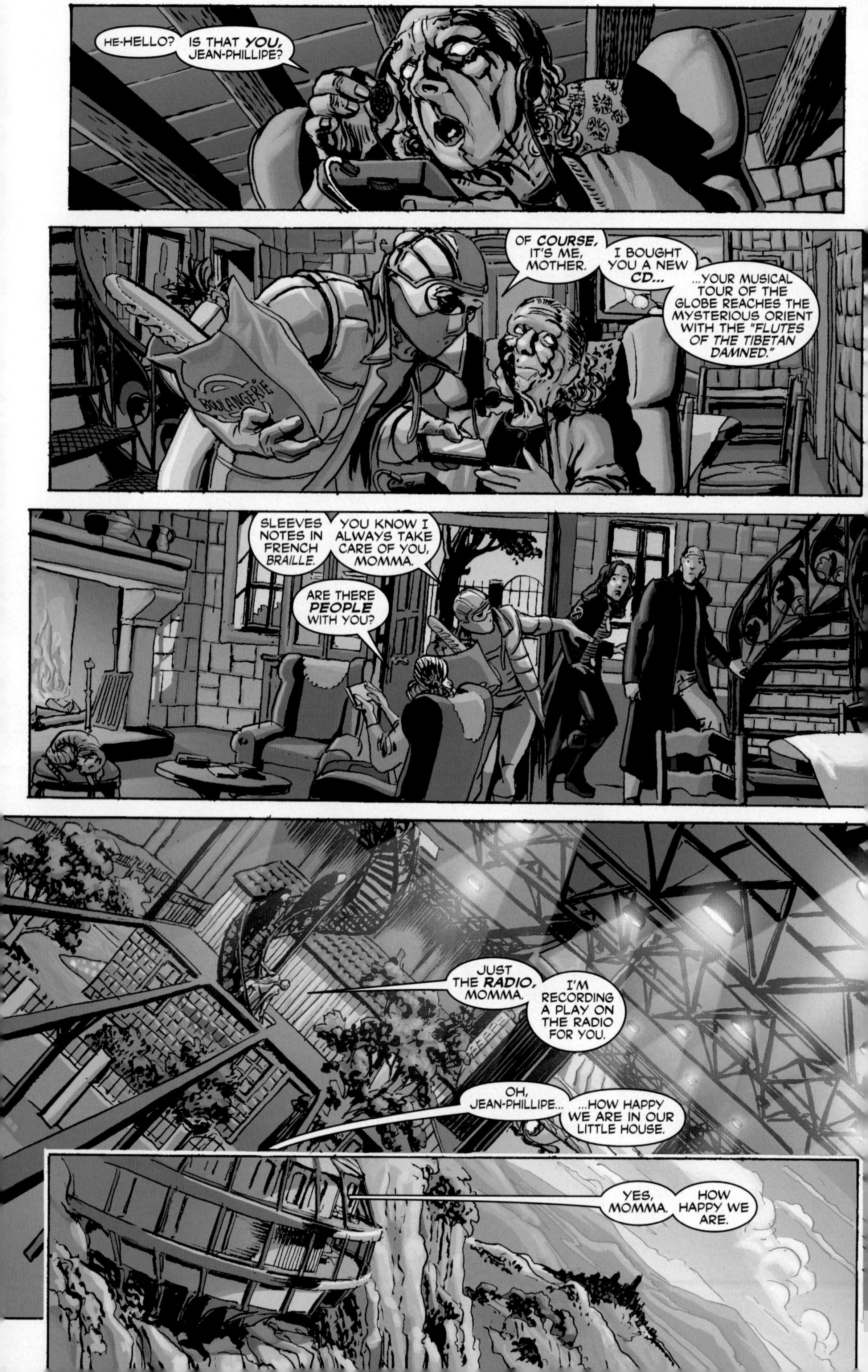
HE-HELLO?
IS THAT YOU, JEAN-PHILLIPE?
OF COURSE, IT'S ME, MOTHER.
I BOUGHT YOU A NEW CD...
...YOUR MUSICAL TOUR OF THE GLOBE REACHES THE MYSTERIOUS ORIENT WITH THE "FLUTES OF THE TIBETAN DAMNED."
SLEEVES NOTES IN FRENCH BRAILLE.
YOU KNOW I ALWAYS TAKE CARE OF YOU, MOMMA.
ARE THERE PEOPLE WITH YOU?
JUST THE RADIO, MOMMA.
I'M RECORDING A PLAY ON THE RADIO FOR YOU.
OH, JEAN-PHILLIPE...
...HOW HAPPY WE ARE IN OUR LITTLE HOUSE.
YES, MOMMA.
HOW HAPPY WE ARE.

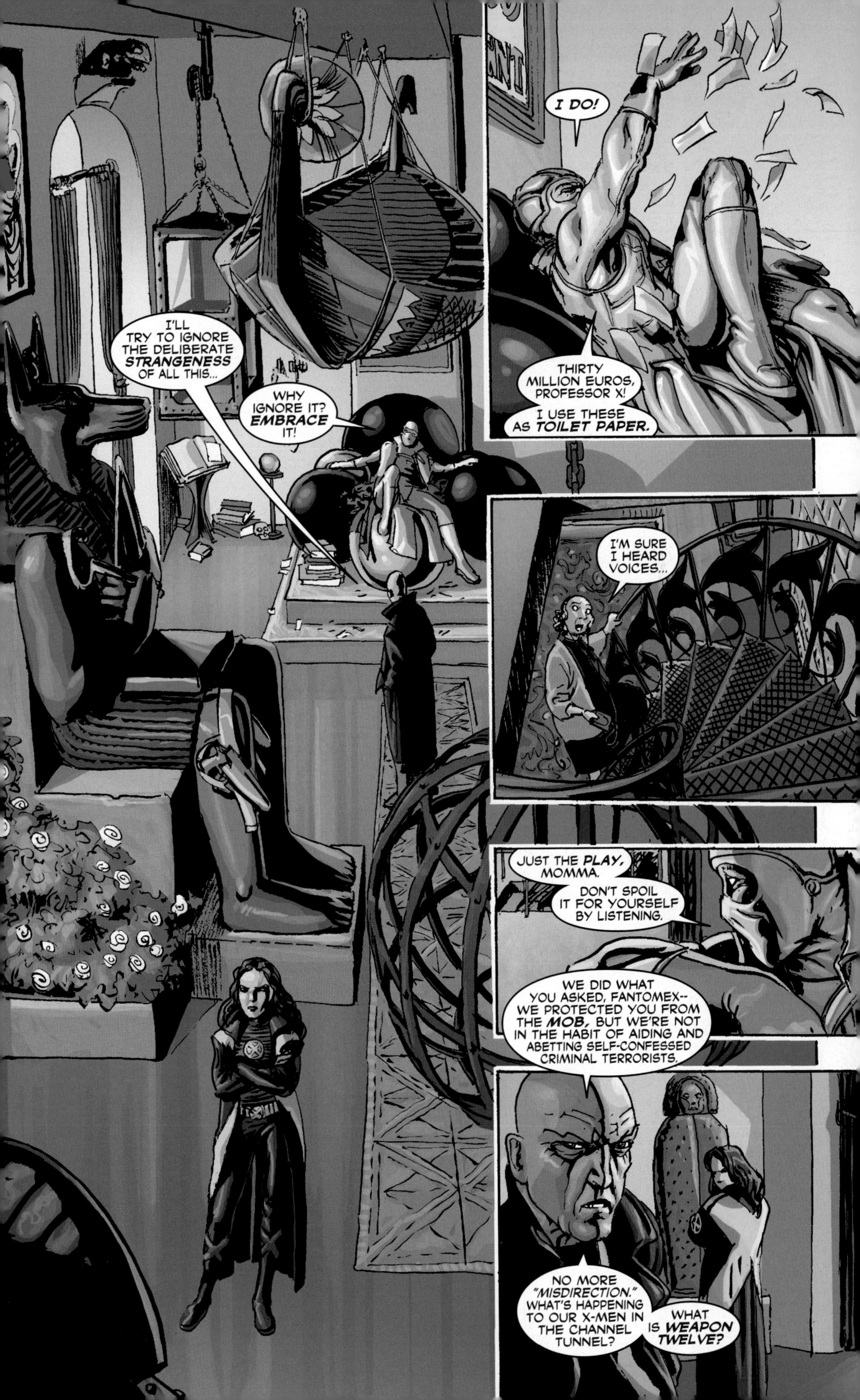

I'LL TRY TO IGNORE THE DELIBERATE STRANGENESS OF ALL THIS...
WHY IGNORE IT? EMBRACE IT!
I DO!
THIRTY MILLION EUROS, PROFESSOR X!
I USE THESE AS TOILET PAPER.
I'M SURE I HEARD VOICES...
JUST THE PLAY, MOMMA.
DON'T SPOIL IT FOR YOURSELF BY LISTENING.
WE DID WHAT YOU ASKED, FANTOMEX-- WE PROTECTED YOU FROM THE MOB, BUT WE'RE NOT IN THE HABIT OF AIDING AND ABETTING SELF-CONFESSED CRIMINAL TERRORISTS.
NO MORE "MISDIRECTION." WHAT'S HAPPENING TO OUR X-MEN IN THE CHANNEL TUNNEL?
WHAT IS WEAPON TWELVE?

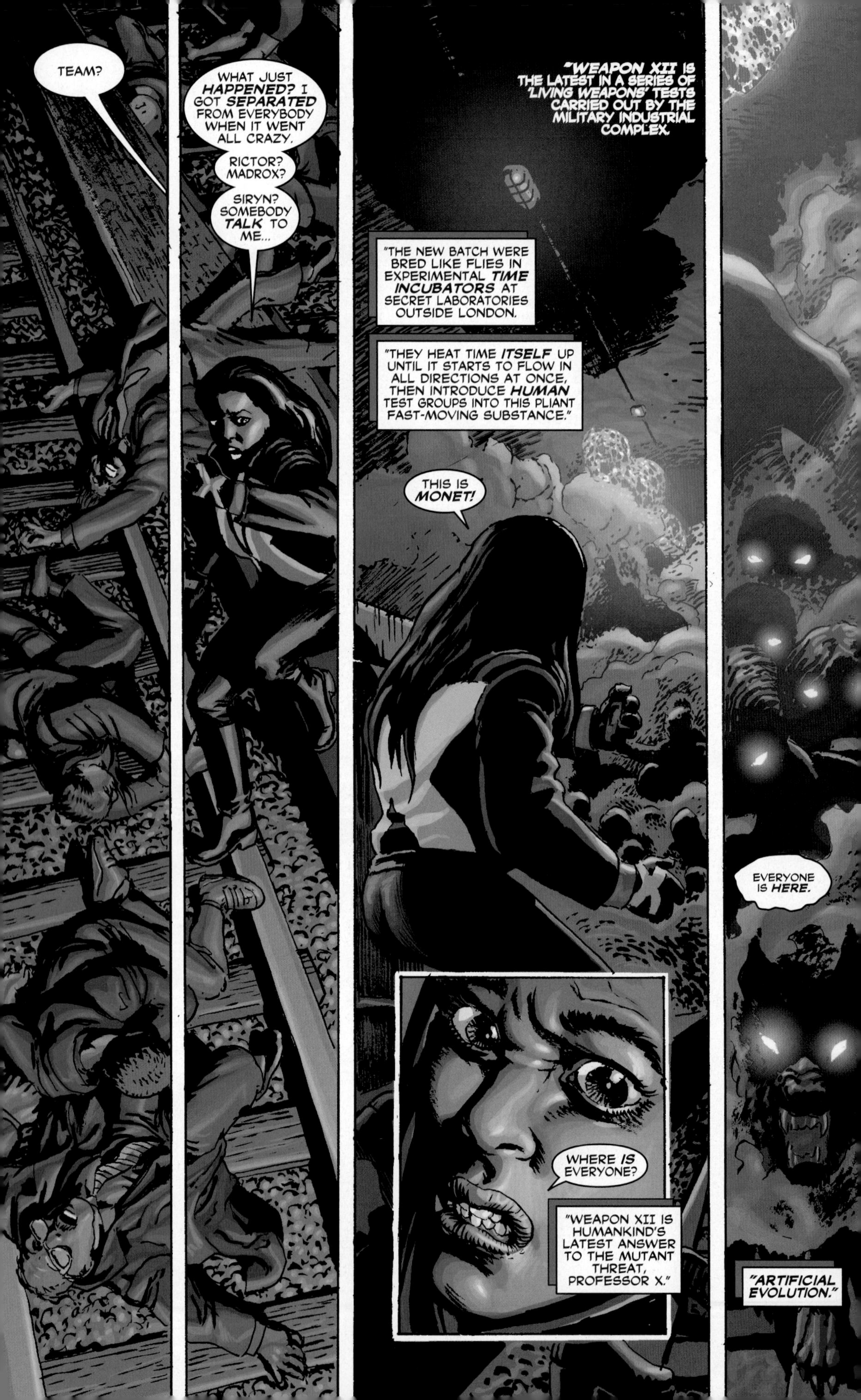
TEAM?
WHAT JUST HAPPENED? I GOT SEPARATED FROM EVERYBODY WHEN IT WENT ALL CRAZY.
RICTOR? MADROX?
SIRYN? SOMEBODY TALK TO ME...
"WEAPON XII IS THE LATEST IN A SERIES OF 'LIVING WEAPONS' TESTS CARRIED OUT BY THE MILITARY INDUSTRIAL COMPLEX.
"THE NEW BATCH WERE BRED LIKE FLIES IN EXPERIMENTAL TIME INCUBATORS AT SECRET LABORATORIES OUTSIDE LONDON.
"THEY HEAT TIME ITSELF UP UNTIL IT STARTS TO FLOW IN ALL DIRECTIONS AT ONCE, THEN INTRODUCE HUMAN TEST GROUPS INTO THIS PLIANT FAST-MOVING SUBSTANCE."
THIS IS MONET!
WHERE IS EVERYONE?
"WEAPON XII IS HUMANKIND'S LATEST ANSWER TO THE MUTANT THREAT, PROFESSOR X."
EVERYONE IS HERE.
"ARTIFICIAL EVOLUTION."

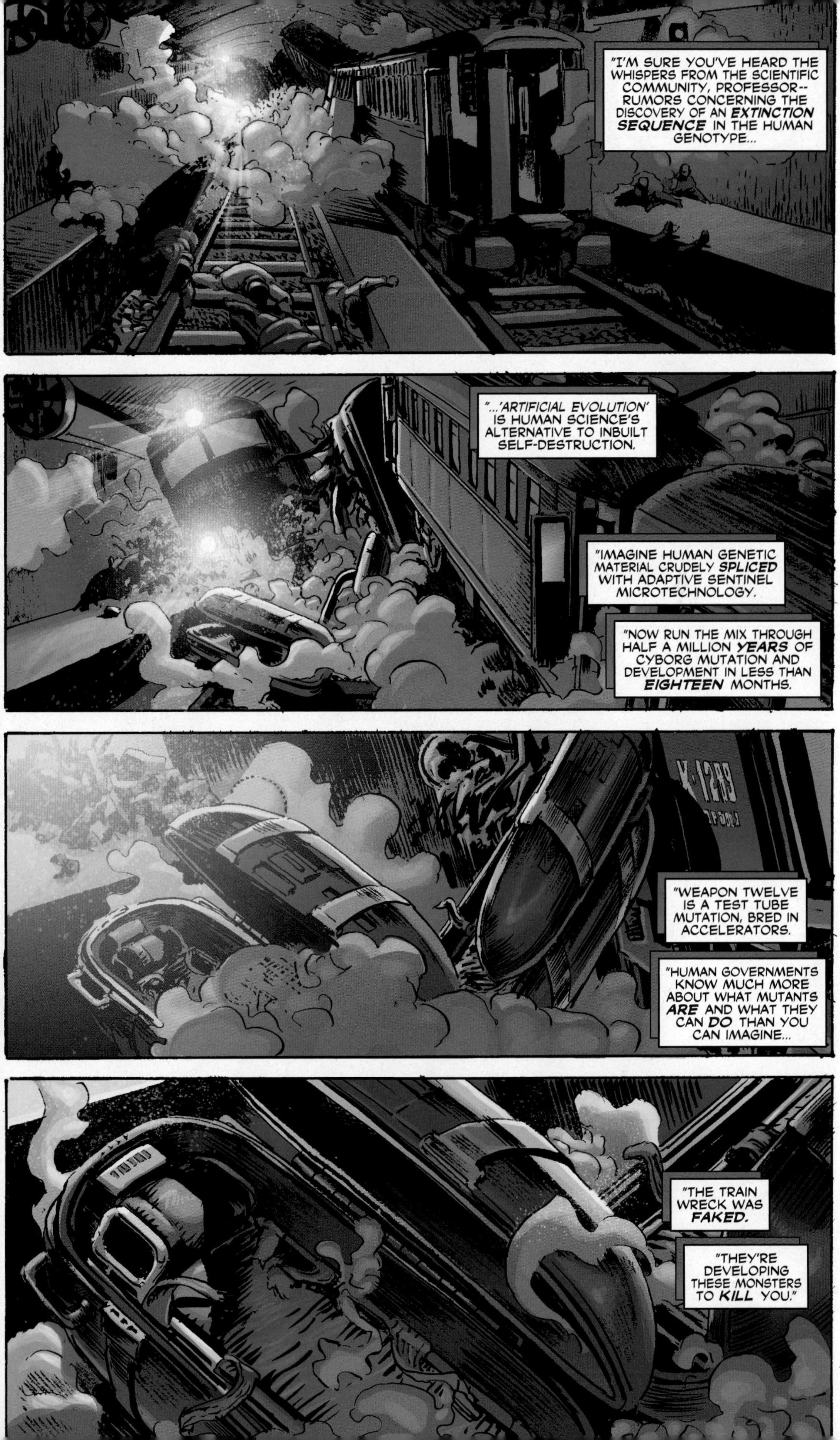
"I'M SURE YOU'VE HEARD THE WHISPERS FROM THE SCIENTIFIC COMMUNITY, PROFESSOR-- RUMORS CONCERNING THE DISCOVERY OF AN EXTINCTION SEQUENCE IN THE HUMAN GENOTYPE...
"...'ARTIFICIAL EVOLUTION' IS HUMAN SCIENCE'S ALTERNATIVE TO INBUILT SELF-DESTRUCTION.
"IMAGINE HUMAN GENETIC MATERIAL CRUDELY SPLICED WITH ADAPTIVE SENTINEL MICROTECHNOLOGY.
"NOW RUN THE MIX THROUGH HALF A MILLION YEARS OF CYBORG MUTATION AND DEVELOPMENT IN LESS THAN EIGHTEEN MONTHS.
K-1289
"WEAPON TWELVE IS A TEST TUBE MUTATION, BRED IN ACCELERATORS.
"HUMAN GOVERNMENTS KNOW MUCH MORE ABOUT WHAT MUTANTS ARE AND WHAT THEY CAN DO THAN YOU CAN IMAGINE...
"THE TRAIN WRECK WAS FAKED.
"THEY'RE DEVELOPING THESE MONSTERS TO KILL YOU."

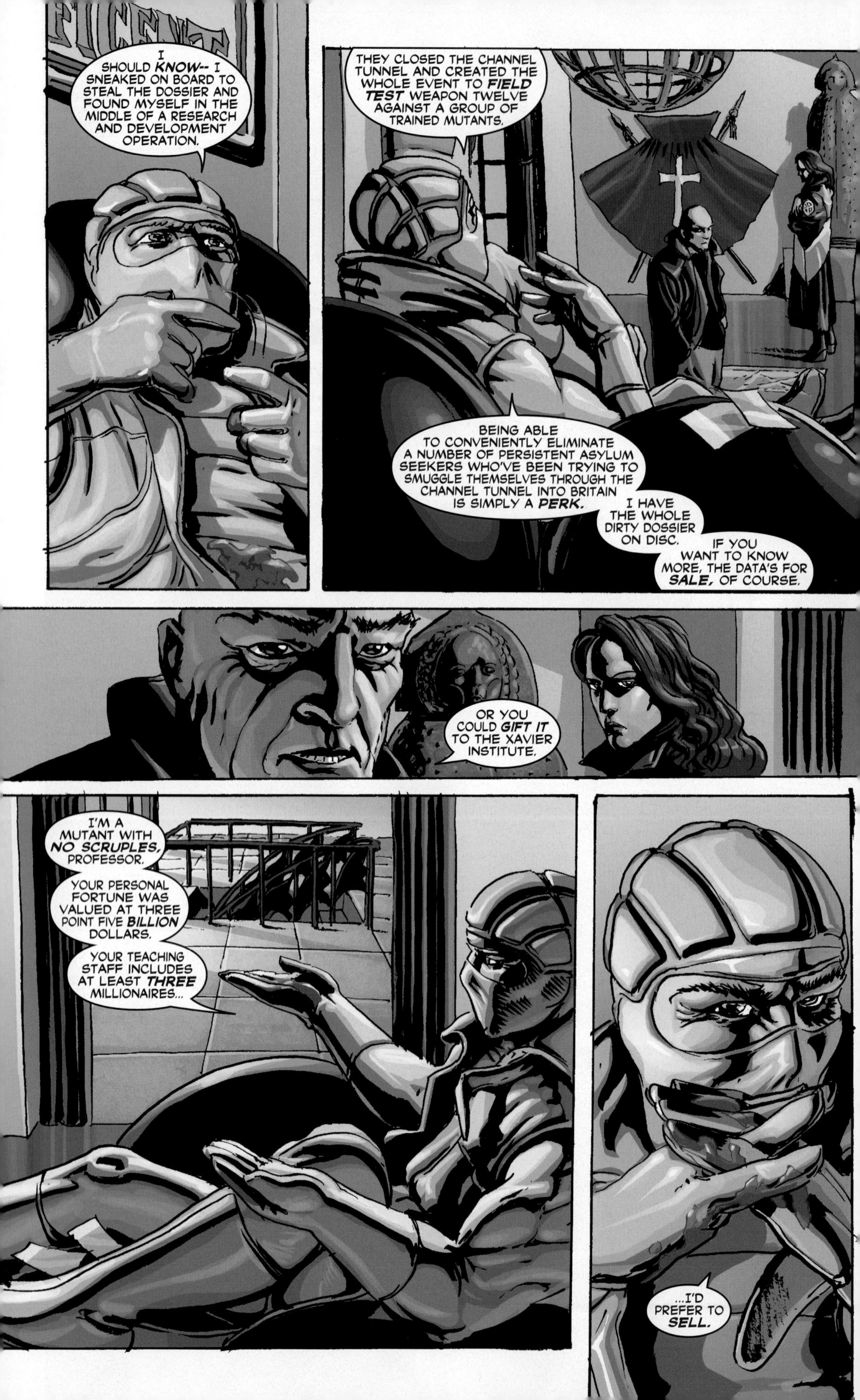
I SHOULD KNOW-- I SNEAKED ON BOARD TO STEAL THE DOSSIER AND FOUND MYSELF IN THE MIDDLE OF A RESEARCH AND DEVELOPMENT OPERATION.
THEY CLOSED THE CHANNEL TUNNEL AND CREATED THE WHOLE EVENT TO FIELD TEST WEAPON TWELVE AGAINST A GROUP OF TRAINED MUTANTS.
BEING ABLE TO CONVENIENTLY ELIMINATE A NUMBER OF PERSISTENT ASYLUM SEEKERS WHO'VE BEEN TRYING TO SMUGGLE THEMSELVES THROUGH THE CHANNEL TUNNEL INTO BRITAIN IS SIMPLY A PERK.
I HAVE THE WHOLE DIRTY DOSSIER ON DISC.
IF YOU WANT TO KNOW MORE, THE DATA'S FOR SALE, OF COURSE.
OR YOU COULD GIFT IT TO THE XAVIER INSTITUTE.
I'M A MUTANT WITH NO SCRUPLES, PROFESSOR.
YOUR PERSONAL FORTUNE WAS VALUED AT THREE POINT FIVE BILLION DOLLARS.
YOUR TEACHING STAFF INCLUDES AT LEAST THREE MILLIONAIRES...
...I'D PREFER TO SELL.

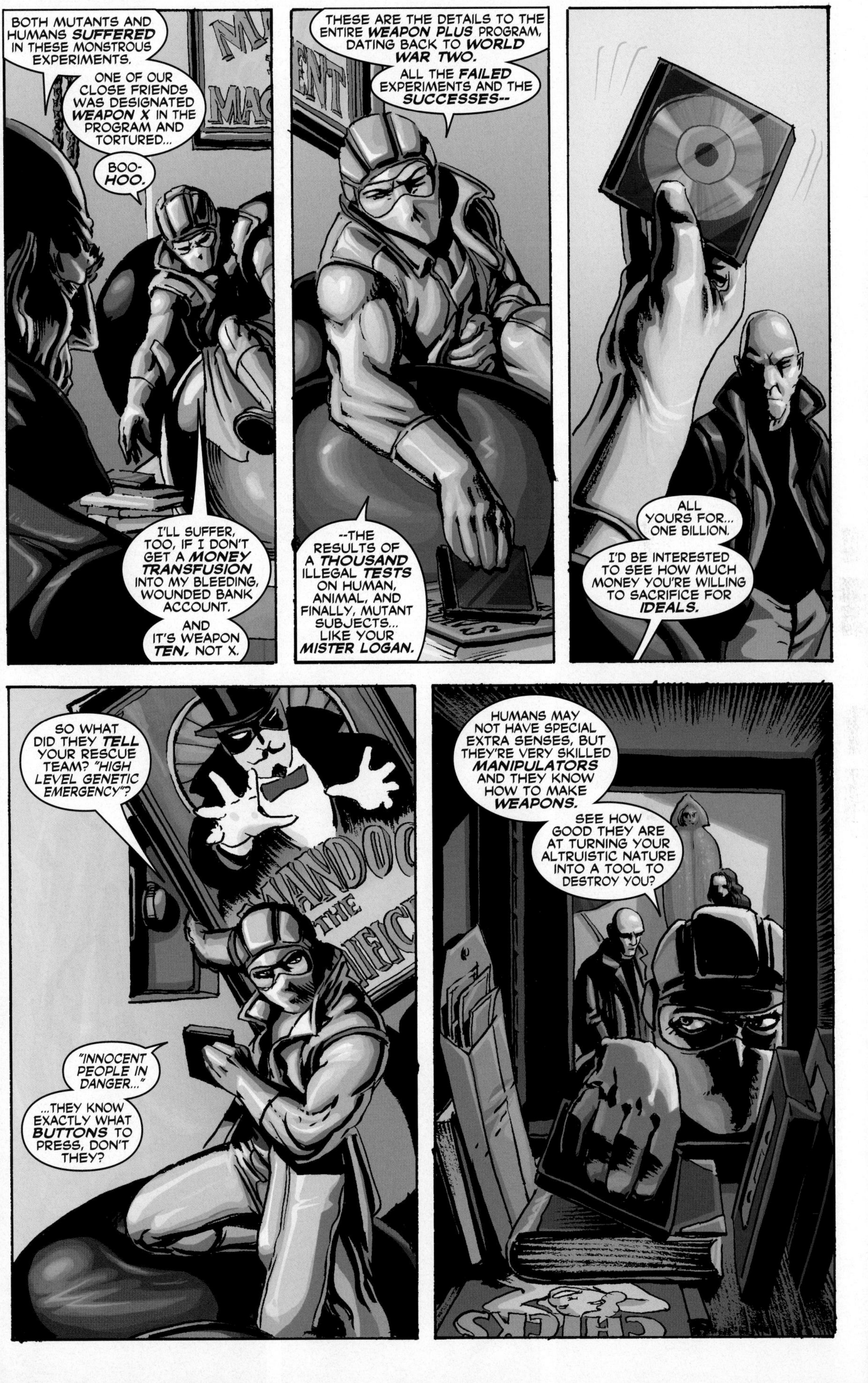
BOTH MUTANTS AND HUMANS SUFFERED IN THESE MONSTROUS EXPERIMENTS.
ONE OF OUR CLOSE FRIENDS WAS DESIGNATED WEAPON X IN THE PROGRAM AND TORTURED...
BOO-HOO.
I'LL SUFFER, TOO, IF I DON'T GET A MONEY TRANSFUSION INTO MY BLEEDING, WOUNDED BANK ACCOUNT.
AND IT'S WEAPON TEN, NOT X.
THESE ARE THE DETAILS TO THE ENTIRE WEAPON PLUS PROGRAM, DATING BACK TO WORLD WAR TWO.
ALL THE FAILED EXPERIMENTS AND THE SUCCESSES--
--THE RESULTS OF A THOUSAND ILLEGAL TESTS ON HUMAN, ANIMAL, AND FINALLY, MUTANT SUBJECTS... LIKE YOUR MISTER LOGAN.
ALL YOURS FOR... ONE BILLION.
I'D BE INTERESTED TO SEE HOW MUCH MONEY YOU'RE WILLING TO SACRIFICE FOR IDEALS.
SO WHAT DID THEY TELL YOUR RESCUE TEAM? "HIGH LEVEL GENETIC EMERGENCY"?
"INNOCENT PEOPLE IN DANGER..."
...THEY KNOW EXACTLY WHAT BUTTONS TO PRESS, DON'T THEY?
HUMANS MAY NOT HAVE SPECIAL EXTRA SENSES, BUT THEY'RE VERY SKILLED MANIPULATORS AND THEY KNOW HOW TO MAKE WEAPONS.
SEE HOW GOOD THEY ARE AT TURNING YOUR ALTRUISTIC NATURE INTO A TOOL TO DESTROY YOU?

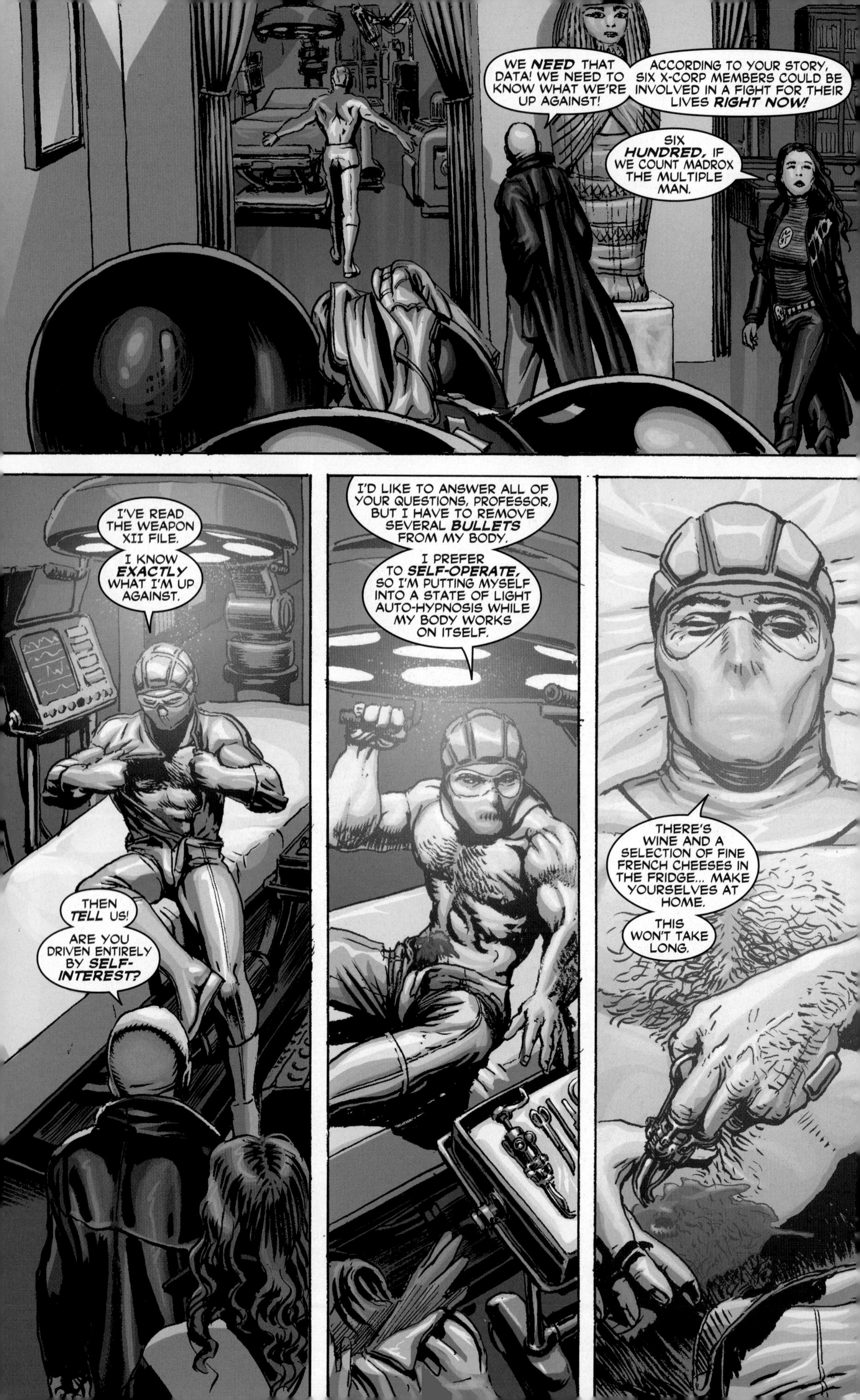

WE **NEED** THAT DATA! WE NEED TO KNOW WHAT WE'RE UP AGAINST!
ACCORDING TO YOUR STORY, SIX X-CORP MEMBERS COULD BE INVOLVED IN A FIGHT FOR THEIR LIVES ***RIGHT NOW!***
SIX ***HUNDRED,*** IF WE COUNT MADROX THE MULTIPLE MAN.
I'VE READ THE WEAPON XII FILE.
I KNOW ***EXACTLY*** WHAT I'M UP AGAINST.
THEN ***TELL*** US!
ARE YOU DRIVEN ENTIRELY BY ***SELF-INTEREST?***
I'D LIKE TO ANSWER ALL OF YOUR QUESTIONS, PROFESSOR, BUT I HAVE TO REMOVE SEVERAL ***BULLETS*** FROM MY BODY.
I PREFER TO ***SELF-OPERATE,*** SO I'M PUTTING MYSELF INTO A STATE OF LIGHT AUTO-HYPNOSIS WHILE MY BODY WORKS ON ITSELF.
THERE'S WINE AND A SELECTION OF FINE FRENCH CHEESES IN THE FRIDGE... MAKE YOURSELVES AT HOME.
THIS WON'T TAKE LONG.

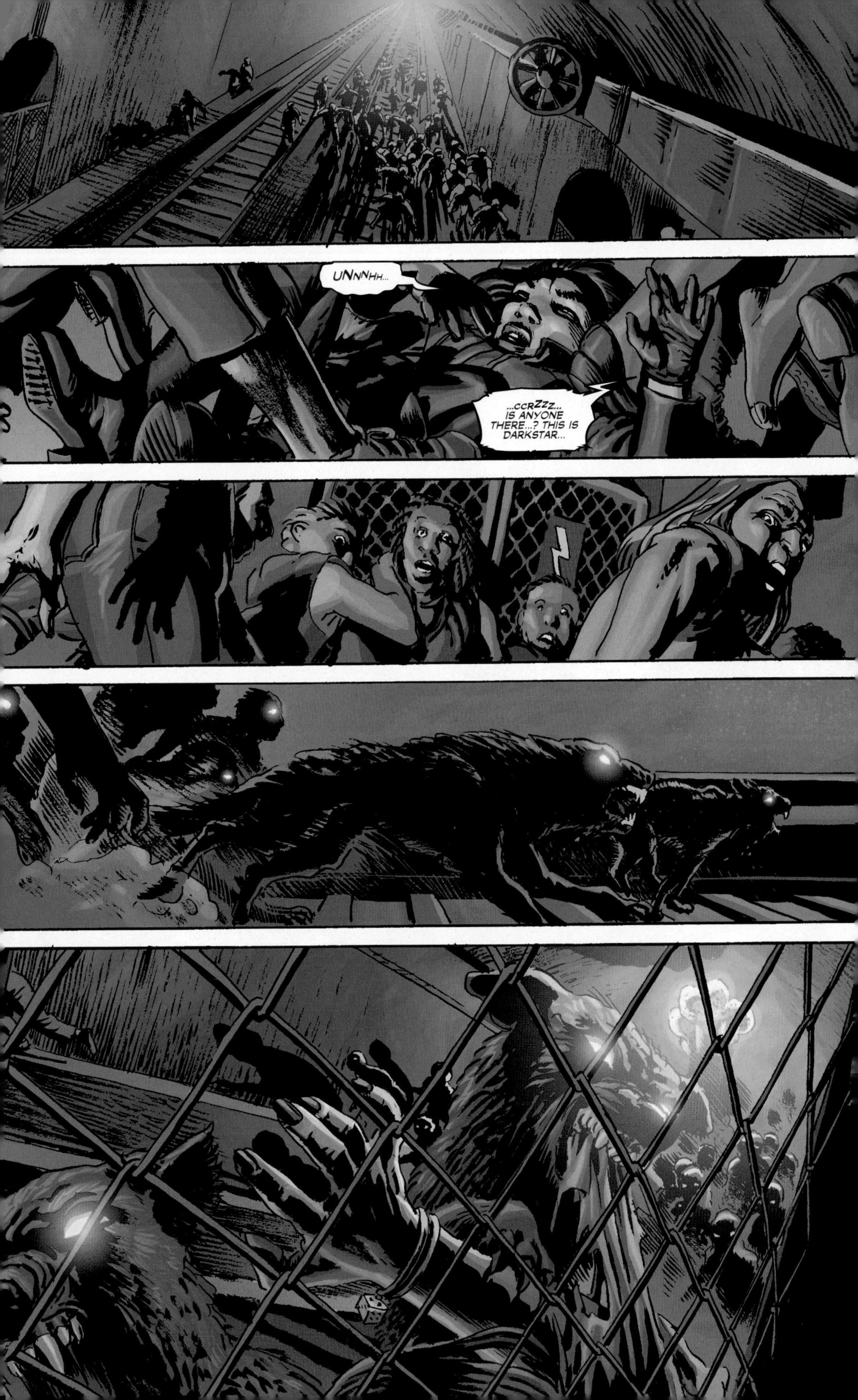
UNNNHH...
...CCRZZZ... IS ANYONE THERE...? THIS IS DARKSTAR...

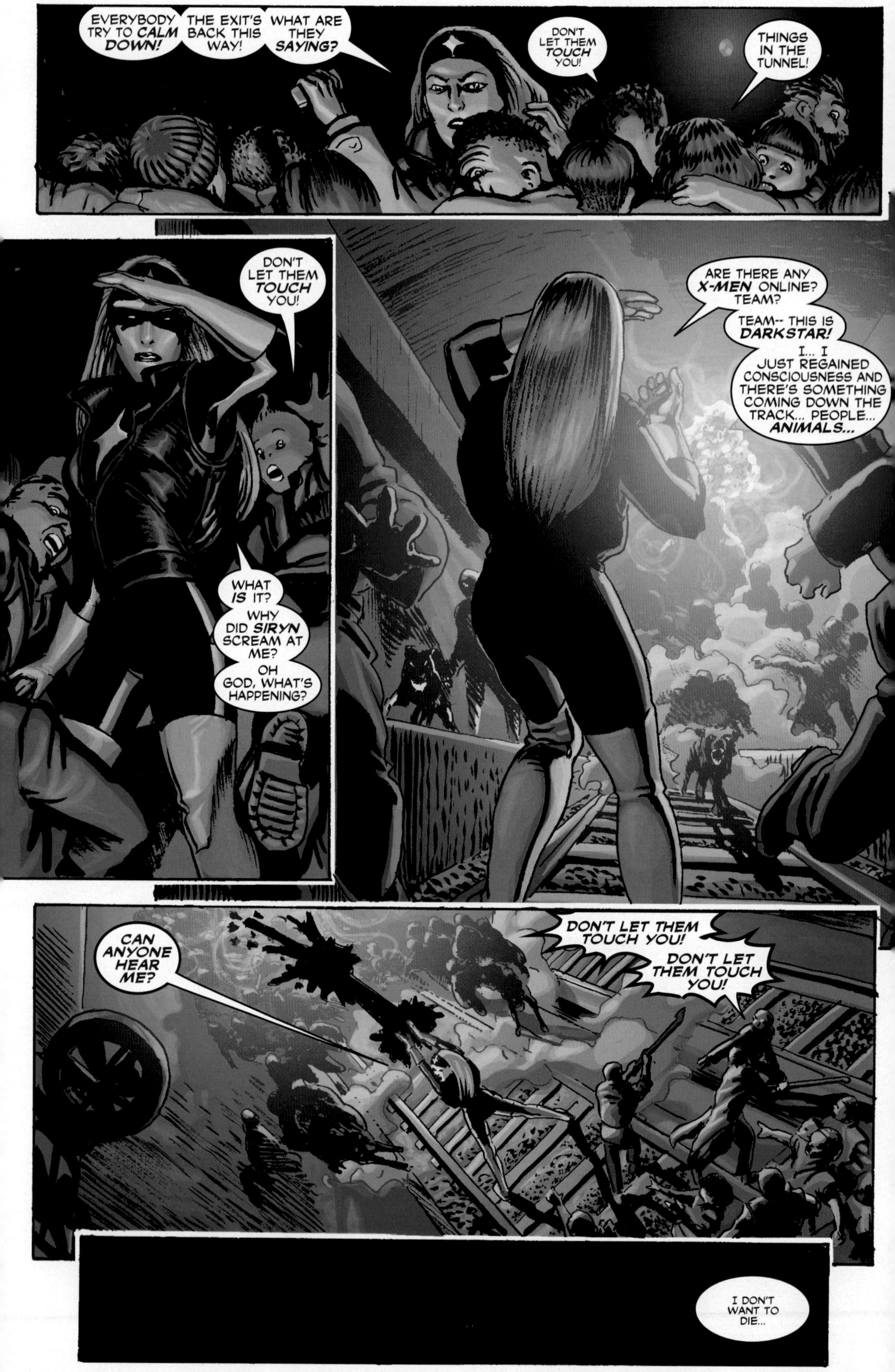
EVERYBODY TRY TO CALM DOWN!
THE EXIT'S BACK THIS WAY!
WHAT ARE THEY SAYING?
DON'T LET THEM TOUCH YOU!
THINGS IN THE TUNNEL!
DON'T LET THEM TOUCH YOU!
WHAT IS IT?
WHY DID SIRYN SCREAM AT ME?
OH GOD, WHAT'S HAPPENING?
ARE THERE ANY X-MEN ONLINE? TEAM?
TEAM-- THIS IS DARKSTAR!
I... I JUST REGAINED CONSCIOUSNESS AND THERE'S SOMETHING COMING DOWN THE TRACK... PEOPLE... ANIMALS...
CAN ANYONE HEAR ME?
DON'T LET THEM TOUCH YOU!
DON'T LET THEM TOUCH YOU!
I DON'T WANT TO DIE...

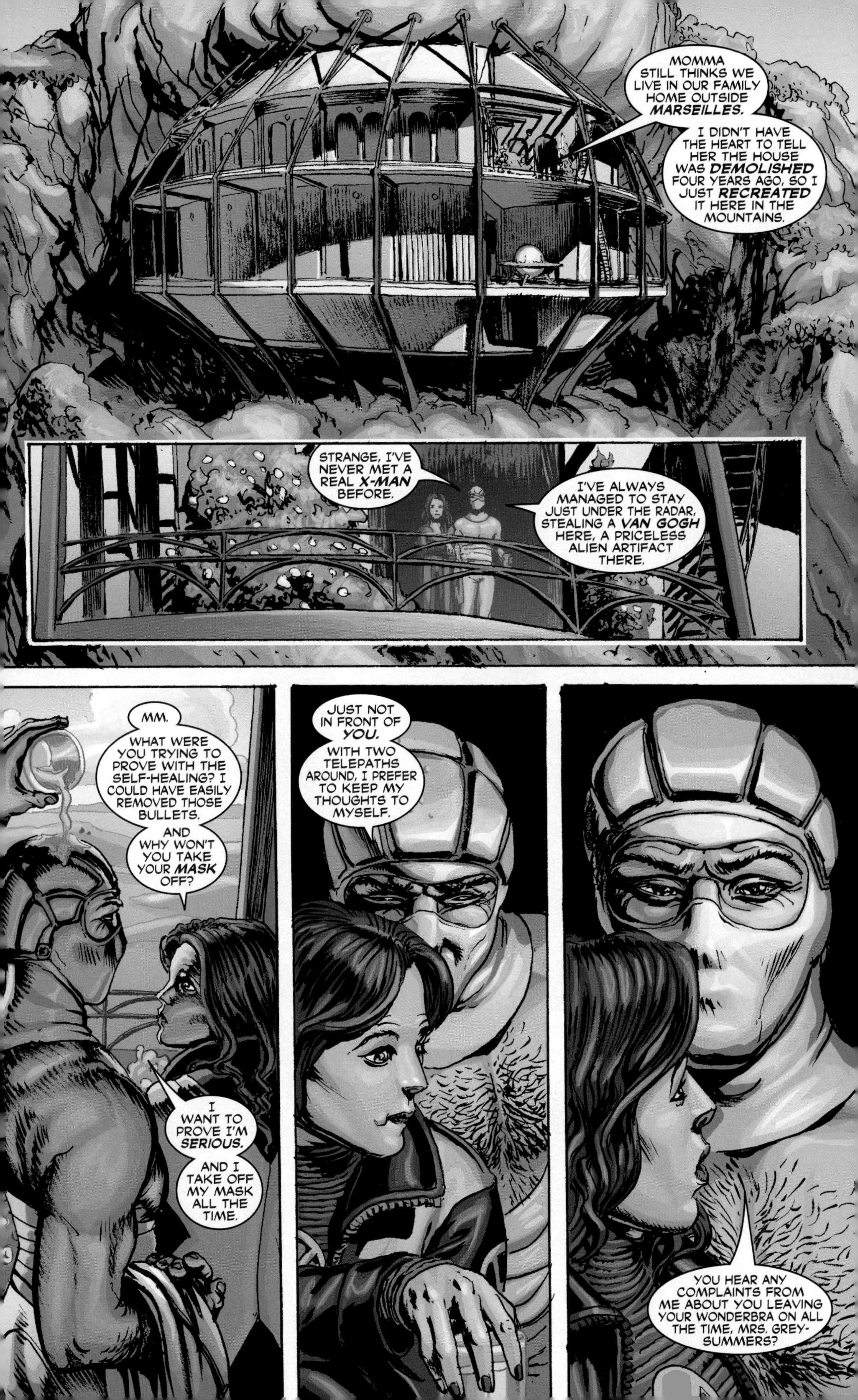
MOMMA STILL THINKS WE LIVE IN OUR FAMILY HOME OUTSIDE MARSEILLES.
I DIDN'T HAVE THE HEART TO TELL HER THE HOUSE WAS DEMOLISHED FOUR YEARS AGO, SO I JUST RECREATED IT HERE IN THE MOUNTAINS.
STRANGE, I'VE NEVER MET A REAL X-MAN BEFORE.
I'VE ALWAYS MANAGED TO STAY JUST UNDER THE RADAR, STEALING A VAN GOGH HERE, A PRICELESS ALIEN ARTIFACT THERE.
MM.
WHAT WERE YOU TRYING TO PROVE WITH THE SELF-HEALING? I COULD HAVE EASILY REMOVED THOSE BULLETS.
AND WHY WON'T YOU TAKE YOUR MASK OFF?
I WANT TO PROVE I'M SERIOUS.
AND I TAKE OFF MY MASK ALL THE TIME.
JUST NOT IN FRONT OF YOU.
WITH TWO TELEPATHS AROUND, I PREFER TO KEEP MY THOUGHTS TO MYSELF.
YOU HEAR ANY COMPLAINTS FROM ME ABOUT YOU LEAVING YOUR WONDERBRA ON ALL THE TIME, MRS. GREY-SUMMERS?

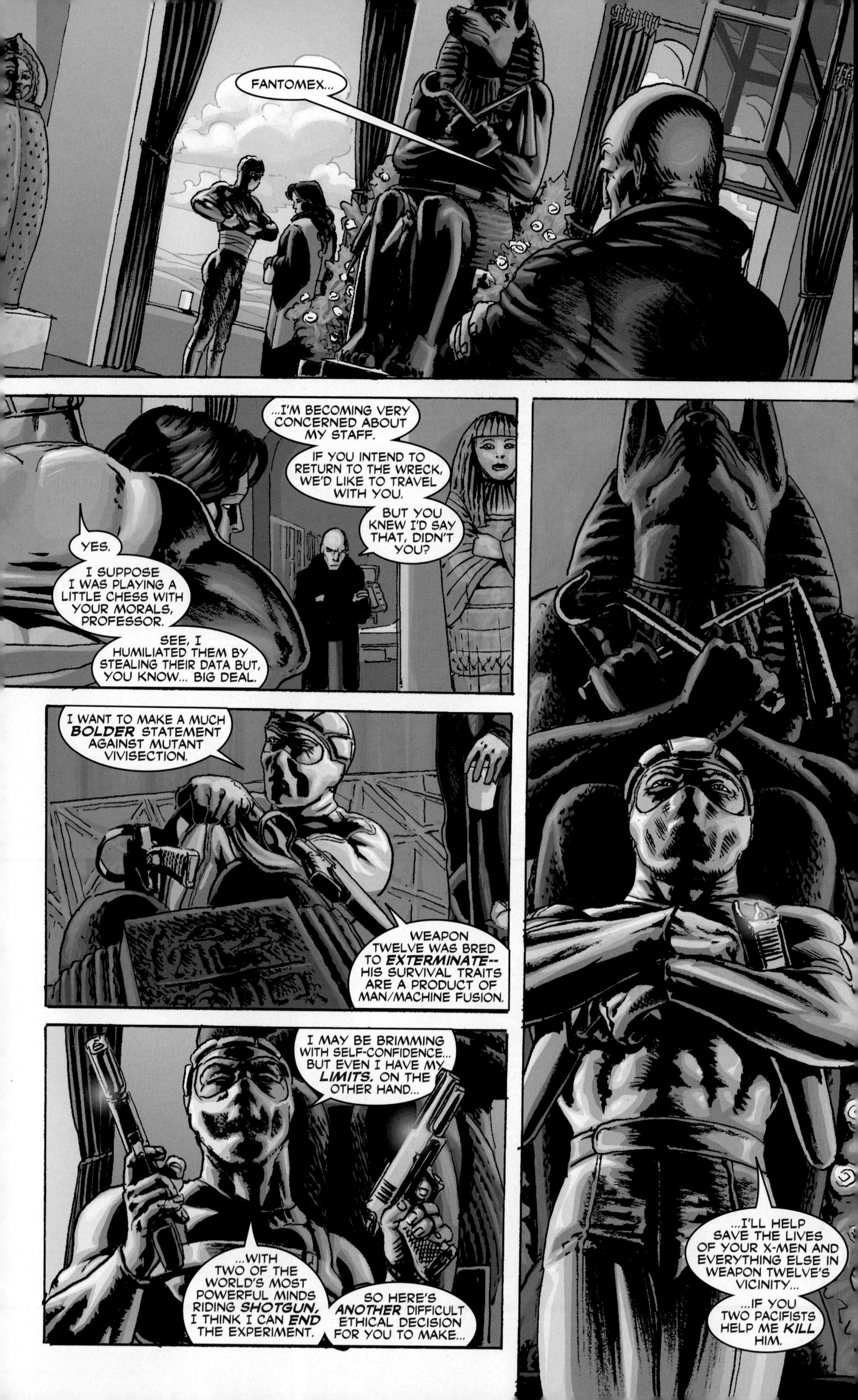
FANTOMEX...
...I'M BECOMING VERY CONCERNED ABOUT MY STAFF.
IF YOU INTEND TO RETURN TO THE WRECK, WE'D LIKE TO TRAVEL WITH YOU.
BUT YOU KNEW I'D SAY THAT, DIDN'T YOU?
YES.
I SUPPOSE I WAS PLAYING A LITTLE CHESS WITH YOUR MORALS, PROFESSOR.
SEE, I HUMILIATED THEM BY STEALING THEIR DATA BUT, YOU KNOW... BIG DEAL.
I WANT TO MAKE A MUCH BOLDER STATEMENT AGAINST MUTANT VIVISECTION.
WEAPON TWELVE WAS BRED TO EXTERMINATE-- HIS SURVIVAL TRAITS ARE A PRODUCT OF MAN/MACHINE FUSION.
I MAY BE BRIMMING WITH SELF-CONFIDENCE... BUT EVEN I HAVE MY LIMITS. ON THE OTHER HAND...
...WITH TWO OF THE WORLD'S MOST POWERFUL MINDS RIDING SHOTGUN, I THINK I CAN END THE EXPERIMENT.
SO HERE'S ANOTHER DIFFICULT ETHICAL DECISION FOR YOU TO MAKE...
...I'LL HELP SAVE THE LIVES OF YOUR X-MEN AND EVERYTHING ELSE IN WEAPON TWELVE'S VICINITY...
...IF YOU TWO PACIFISTS HELP ME KILL HIM.

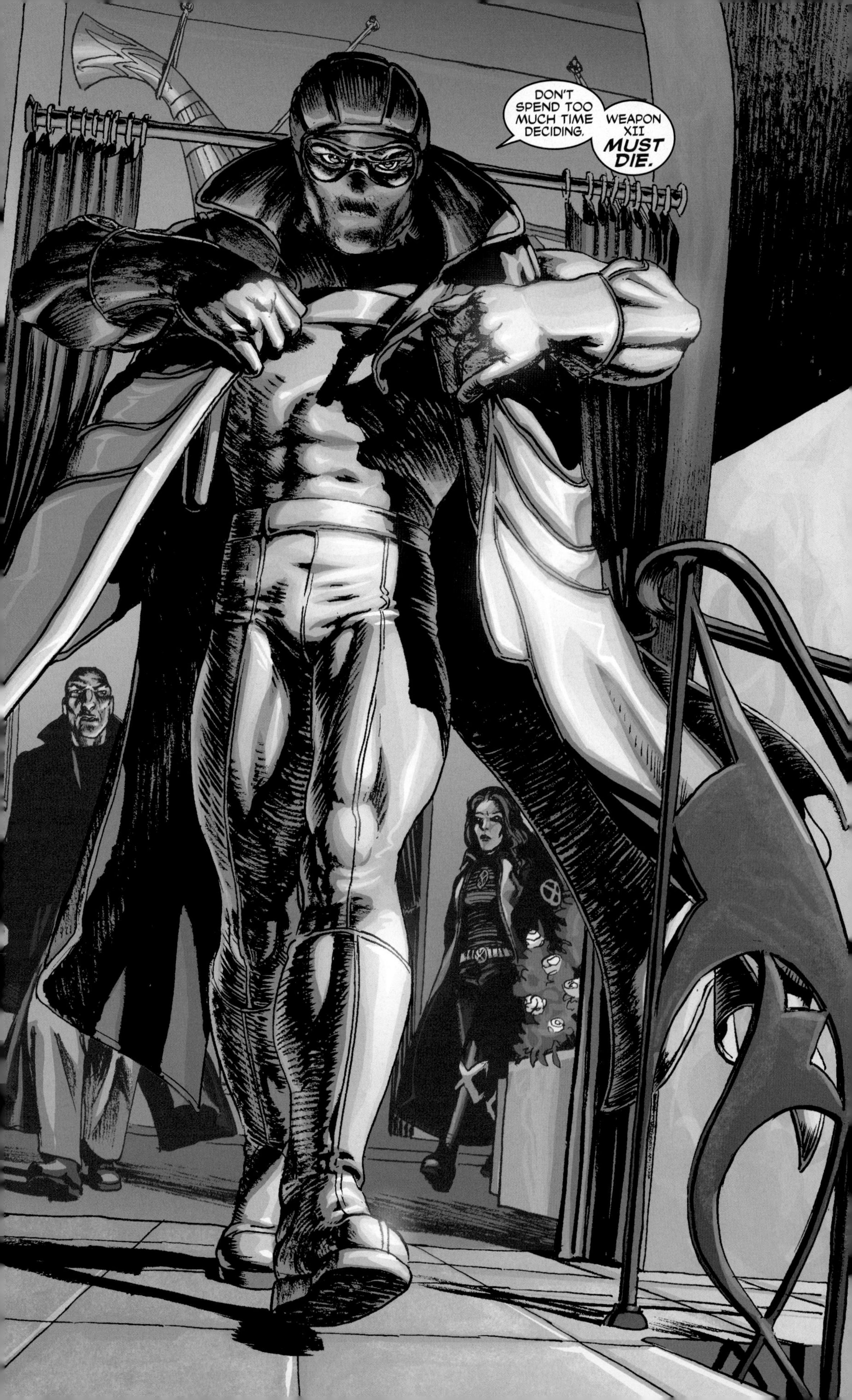
DON'T SPEND TOO MUCH TIME DECIDING.
WEAPON XII MUST DIE.

#130

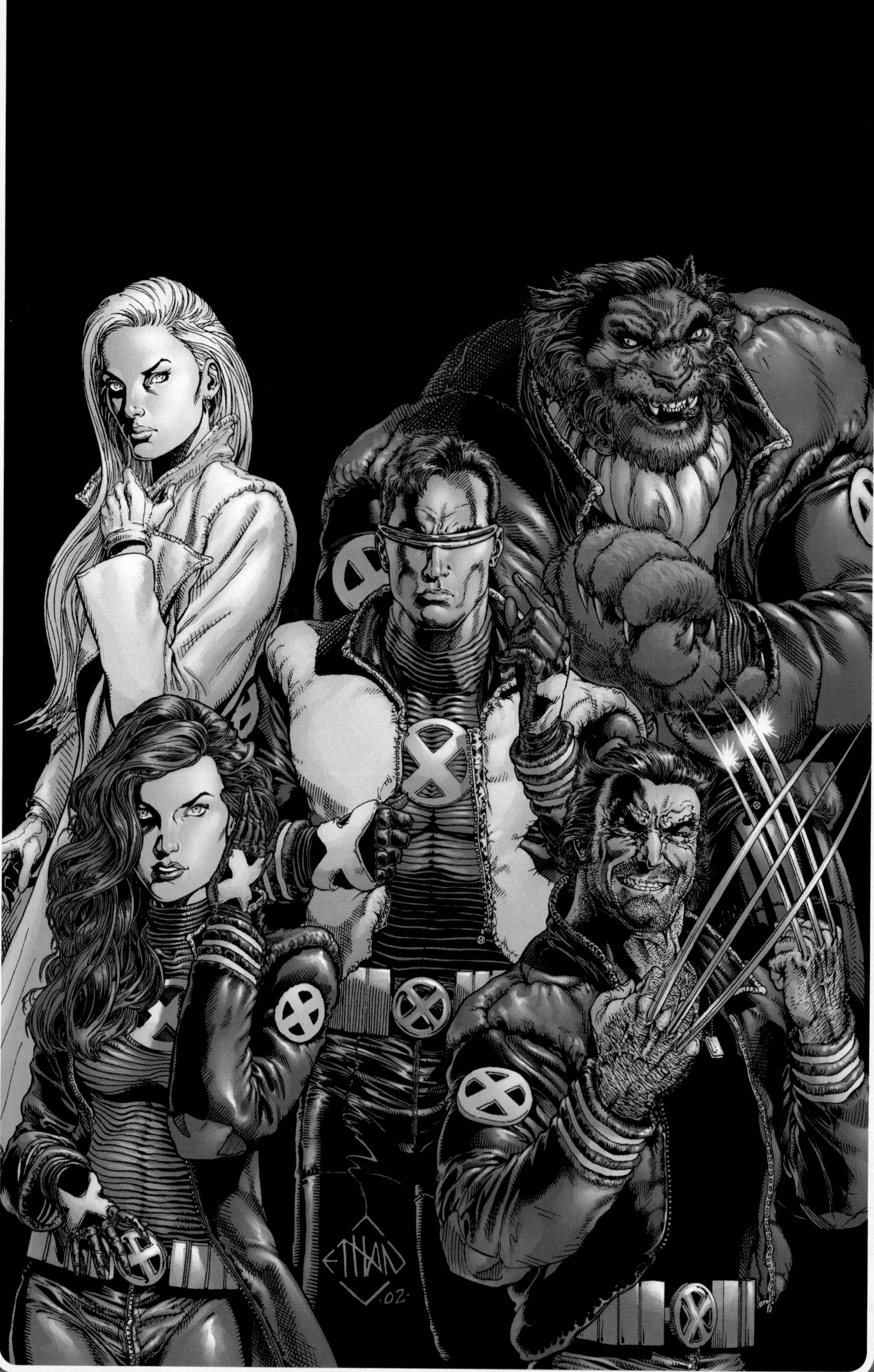

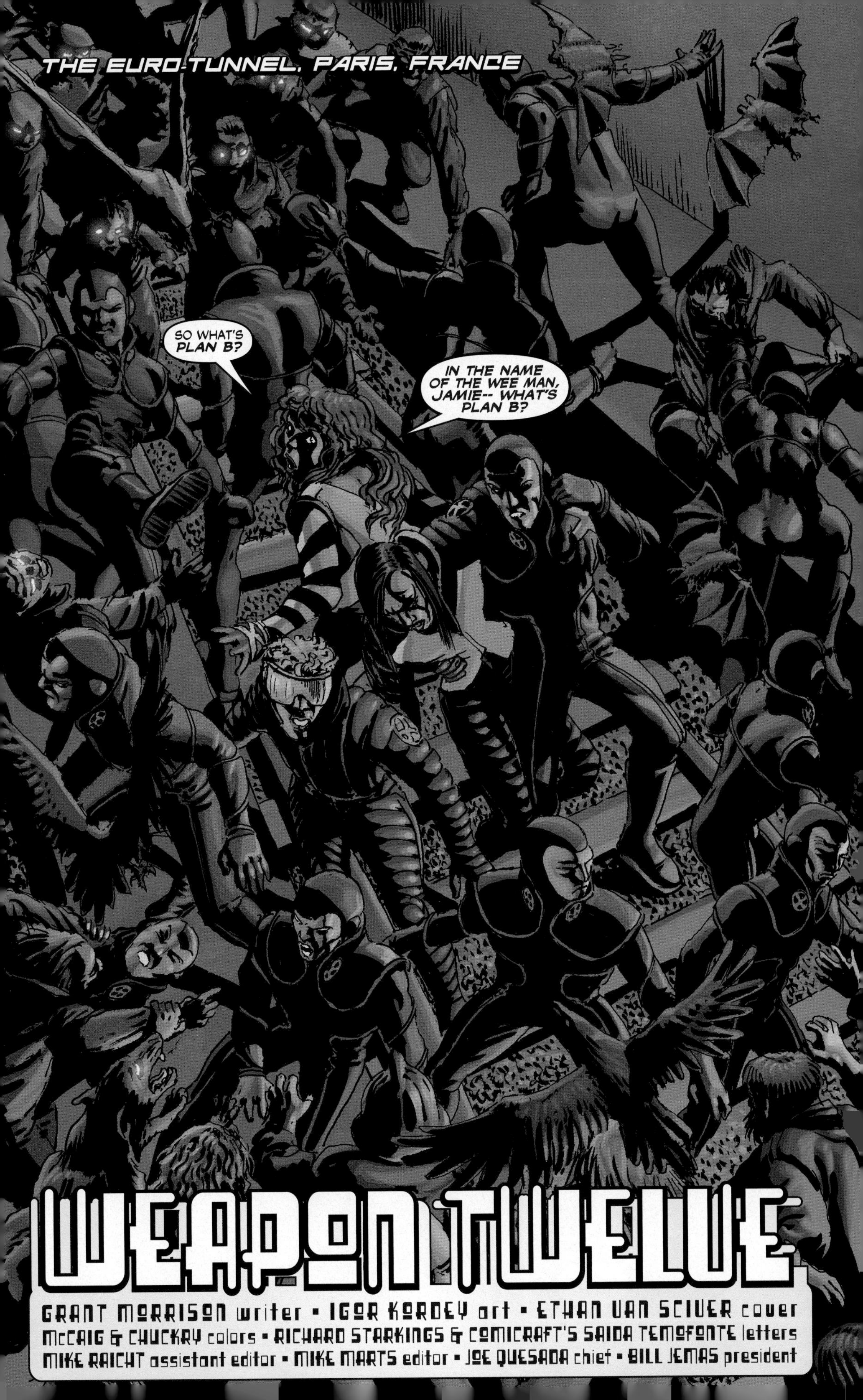
THE EURO-TUNNEL, PARIS, FRANCE
SO WHAT'S PLAN B?
IN THE NAME OF THE WEE MAN, JAMIE-- WHAT'S PLAN B?
WEAPON TWELVE
GRANT MORRISON writer • IGOR KORDEY art • ETHAN VAN SCIVER cover
McCAIG & CHUCKRY colors • RICHARD STARKINGS & COMICRAFT'S SAIDA TEMOFONTE letters
MIKE RAICHT assistant editor • MIKE MARTS editor • JOE QUESADA chief • BILL JEMAS president

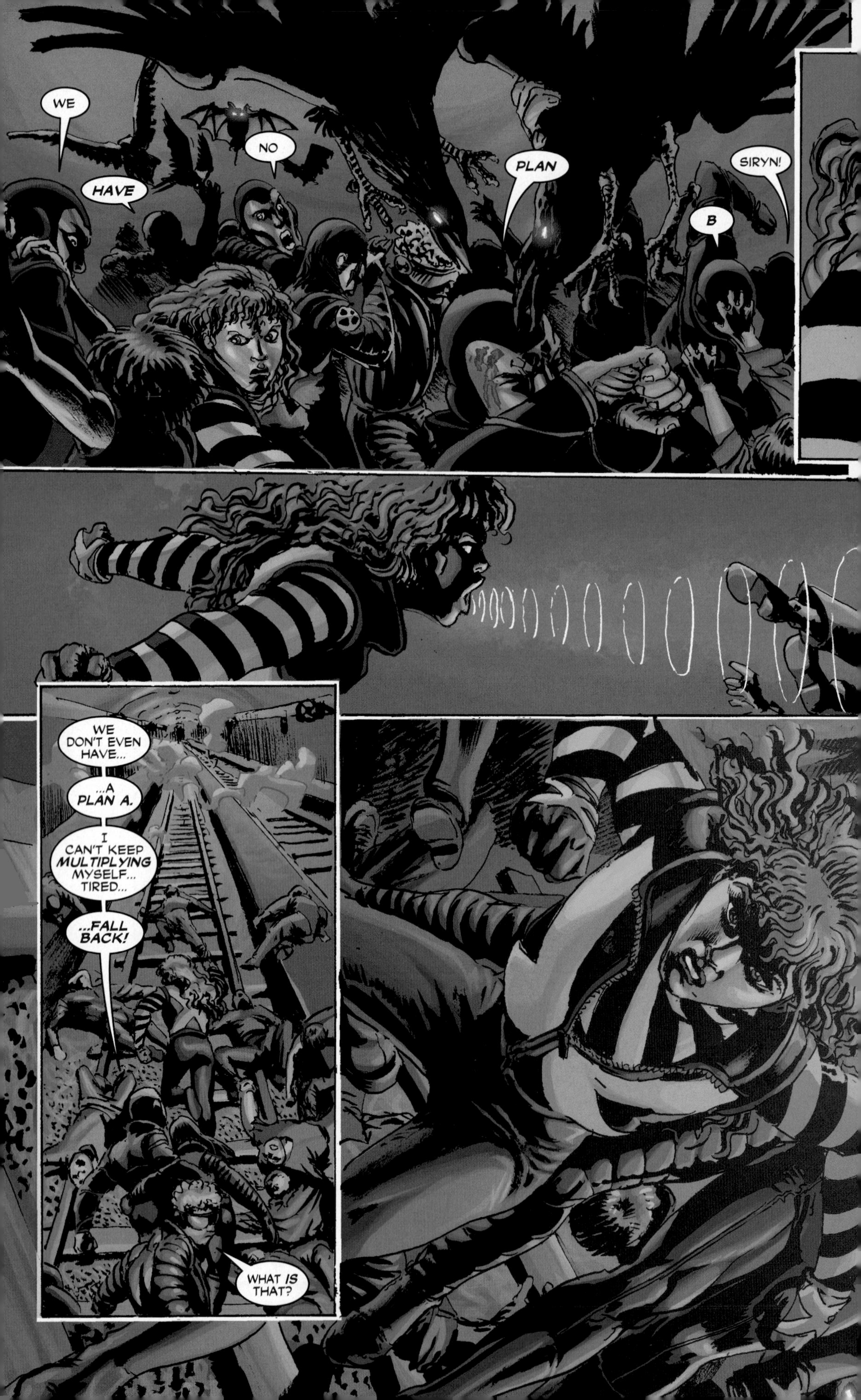
WE
HAVE
NO
PLAN
B
SIRYN!
WE DON'T EVEN HAVE...
...A PLAN A.
I CAN'T KEEP MULTIPLYING MYSELF... TIRED...
...FALL BACK!
WHAT IS THAT?

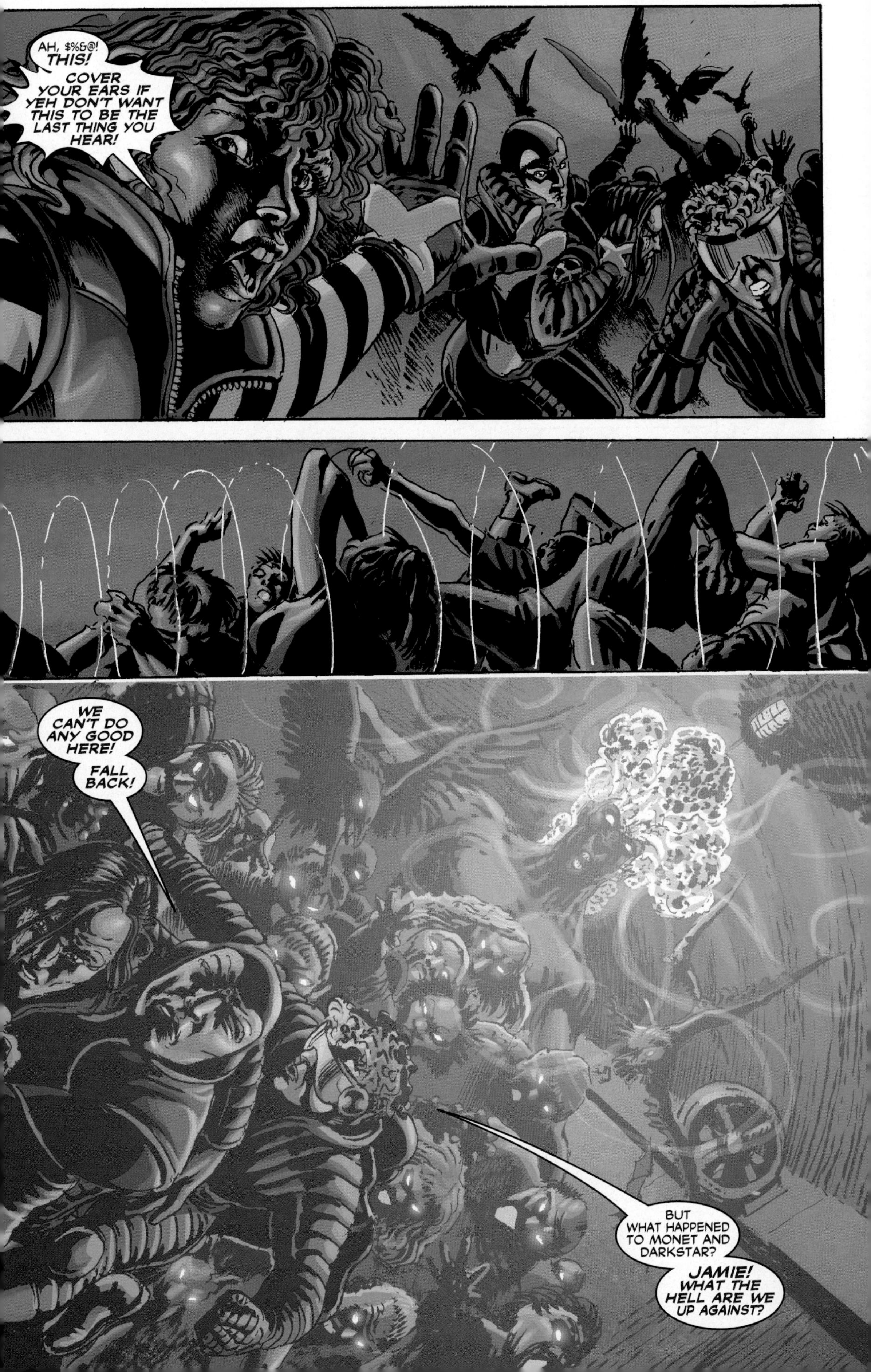
AH, $%&@! THIS!
COVER YOUR EARS IF YEH DON'T WANT THIS TO BE THE LAST THING YOU HEAR!
WE CAN'T DO ANY GOOD HERE!
FALL BACK!
BUT WHAT HAPPENED TO MONET AND DARKSTAR?
JAMIE! WHAT THE HELL ARE WE UP AGAINST?

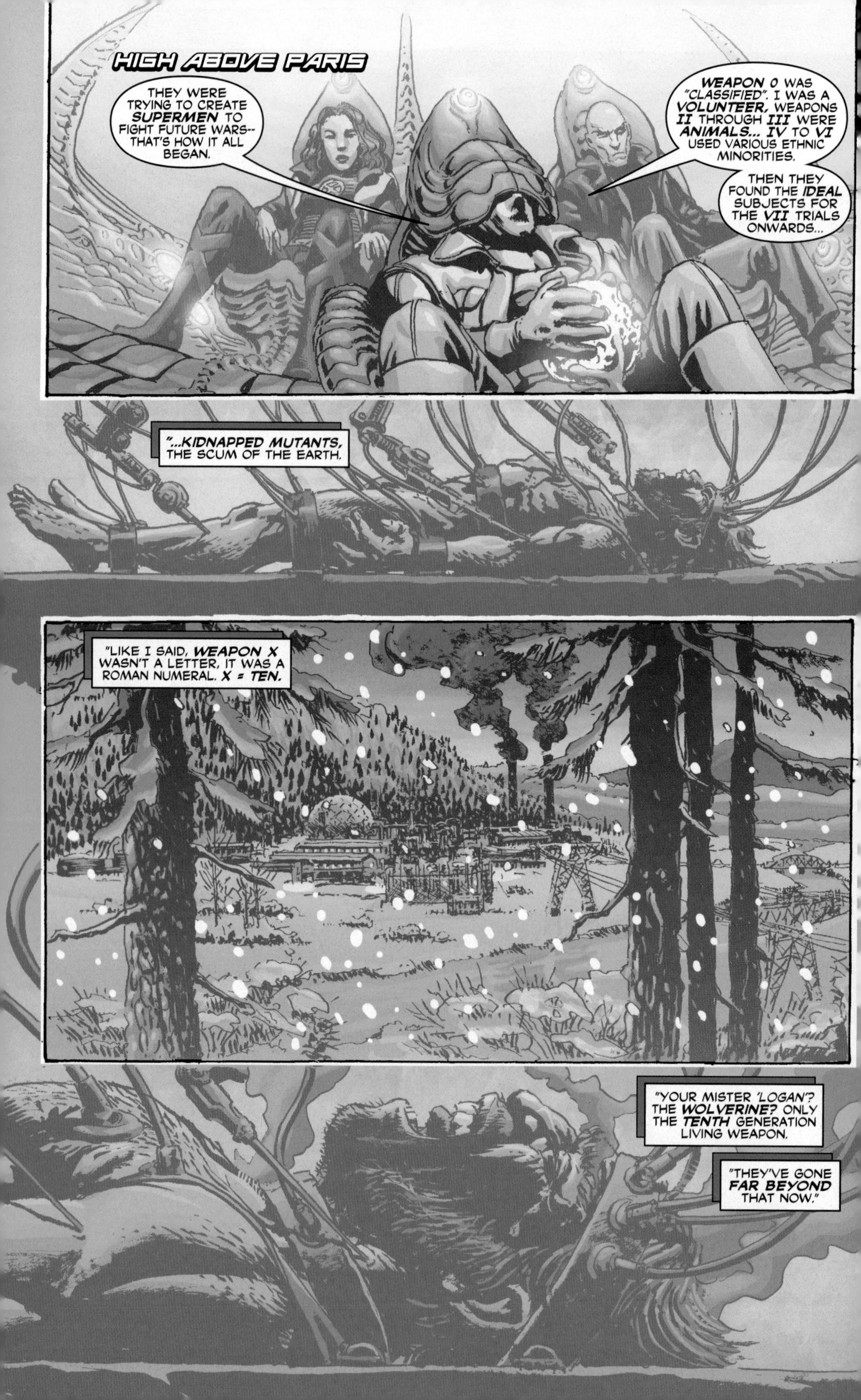
HIGH ABOVE PARIS
THEY WERE TRYING TO CREATE SUPERMEN TO FIGHT FUTURE WARS-- THAT'S HOW IT ALL BEGAN.
WEAPON 0 WAS "CLASSIFIED". I WAS A VOLUNTEER, WEAPONS II THROUGH III WERE ANIMALS... IV TO VI USED VARIOUS ETHNIC MINORITIES.
THEN THEY FOUND THE IDEAL SUBJECTS FOR THE VII TRIALS ONWARDS...
"...KIDNAPPED MUTANTS, THE SCUM OF THE EARTH.
"LIKE I SAID, WEAPON X WASN'T A LETTER, IT WAS A ROMAN NUMERAL. X = TEN.
"YOUR MISTER 'LOGAN'? THE WOLVERINE? ONLY THE TENTH GENERATION LIVING WEAPON.
"THEY'VE GONE FAR BEYOND THAT NOW."

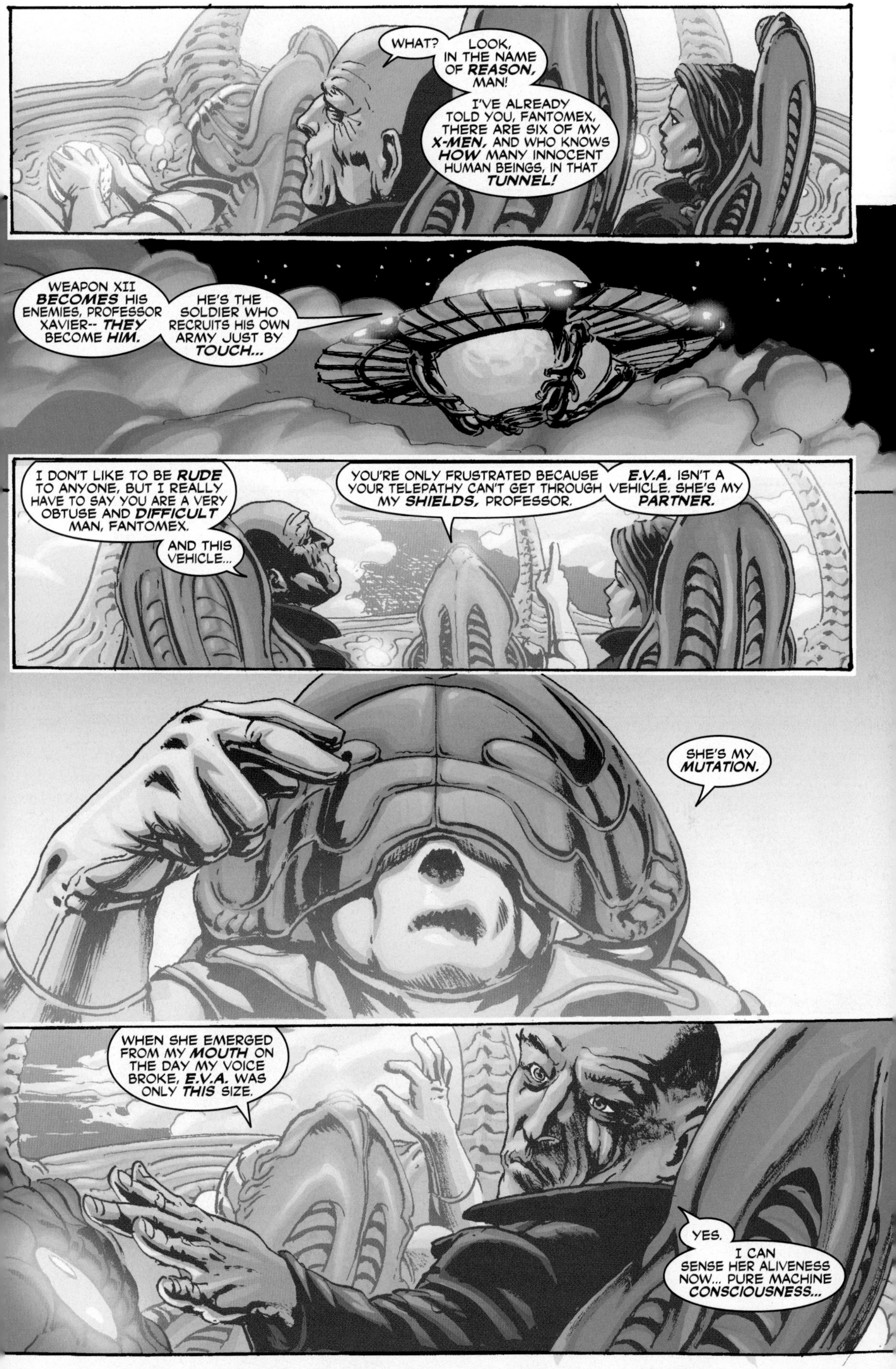
WHAT?
LOOK, IN THE NAME OF REASON, MAN!
I'VE ALREADY TOLD YOU, FANTOMEX, THERE ARE SIX OF MY X-MEN, AND WHO KNOWS HOW MANY INNOCENT HUMAN BEINGS, IN THAT TUNNEL!
WEAPON XII BECOMES HIS ENEMIES, PROFESSOR XAVIER-- THEY BECOME HIM.
HE'S THE SOLDIER WHO RECRUITS HIS OWN ARMY JUST BY TOUCH...
I DON'T LIKE TO BE RUDE TO ANYONE, BUT I REALLY HAVE TO SAY YOU ARE A VERY OBTUSE AND DIFFICULT MAN, FANTOMEX.
AND THIS VEHICLE...
YOU'RE ONLY FRUSTRATED BECAUSE YOUR TELEPATHY CAN'T GET THROUGH MY SHIELDS, PROFESSOR.
E.V.A. ISN'T A VEHICLE. SHE'S MY PARTNER.
SHE'S MY MUTATION.
WHEN SHE EMERGED FROM MY MOUTH ON THE DAY MY VOICE BROKE, E.V.A. WAS ONLY THIS SIZE.
YES.
I CAN SENSE HER ALIVENESS NOW... PURE MACHINE CONSCIOUSNESS...

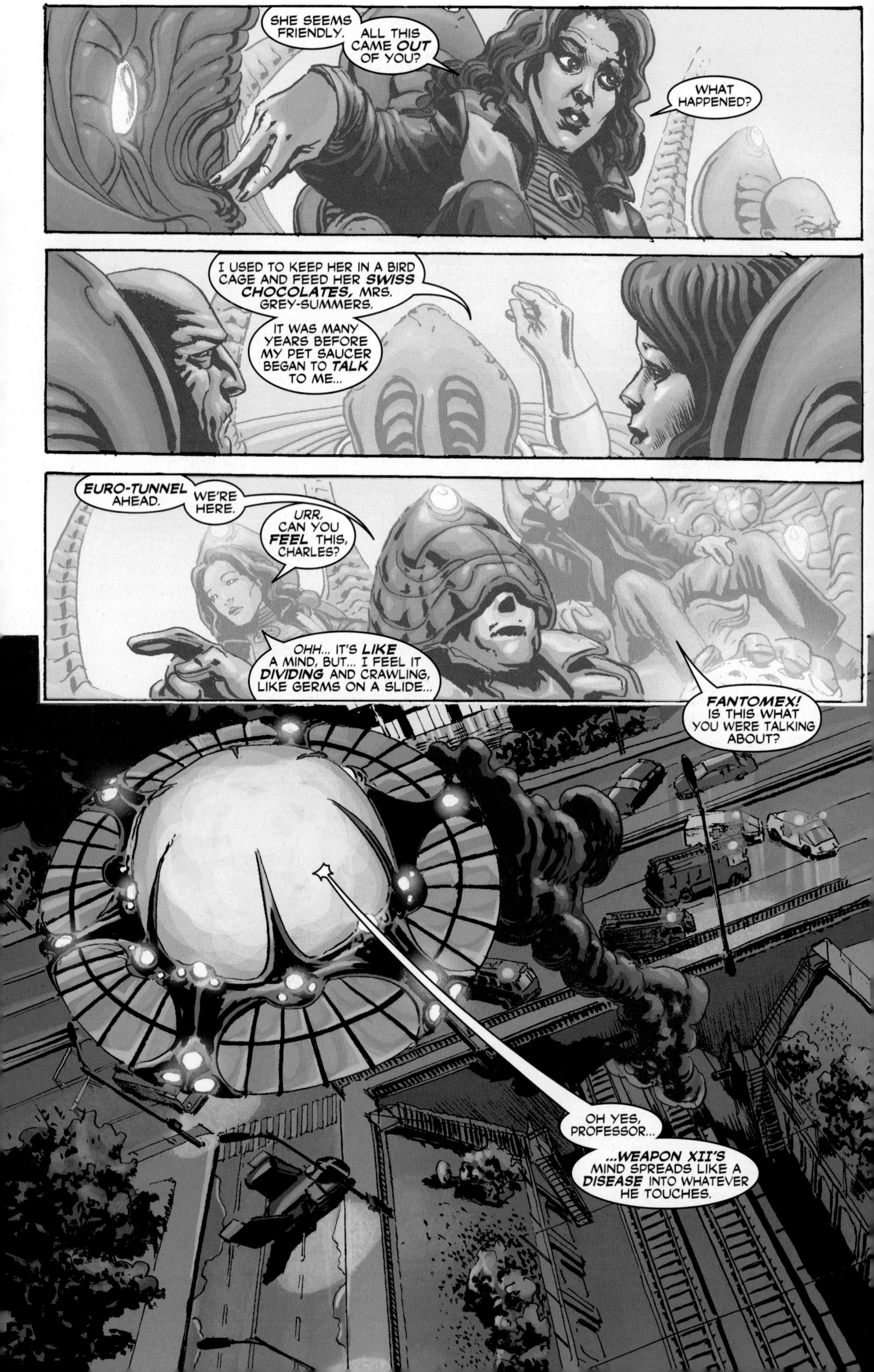
SHE SEEMS FRIENDLY.
ALL THIS CAME OUT OF YOU?
WHAT HAPPENED?
I USED TO KEEP HER IN A BIRD CAGE AND FEED HER SWISS CHOCOLATES, MRS. GREY-SUMMERS.
IT WAS MANY YEARS BEFORE MY PET SAUCER BEGAN TO TALK TO ME...
EURO-TUNNEL AHEAD.
WE'RE HERE.
URR, CAN YOU FEEL THIS, CHARLES?
OHH... IT'S LIKE A MIND, BUT... I FEEL IT DIVIDING AND CRAWLING, LIKE GERMS ON A SLIDE...
FANTOMEX! IS THIS WHAT YOU WERE TALKING ABOUT?
OH YES, PROFESSOR...
...WEAPON XII'S MIND SPREADS LIKE A DISEASE INTO WHATEVER HE TOUCHES.

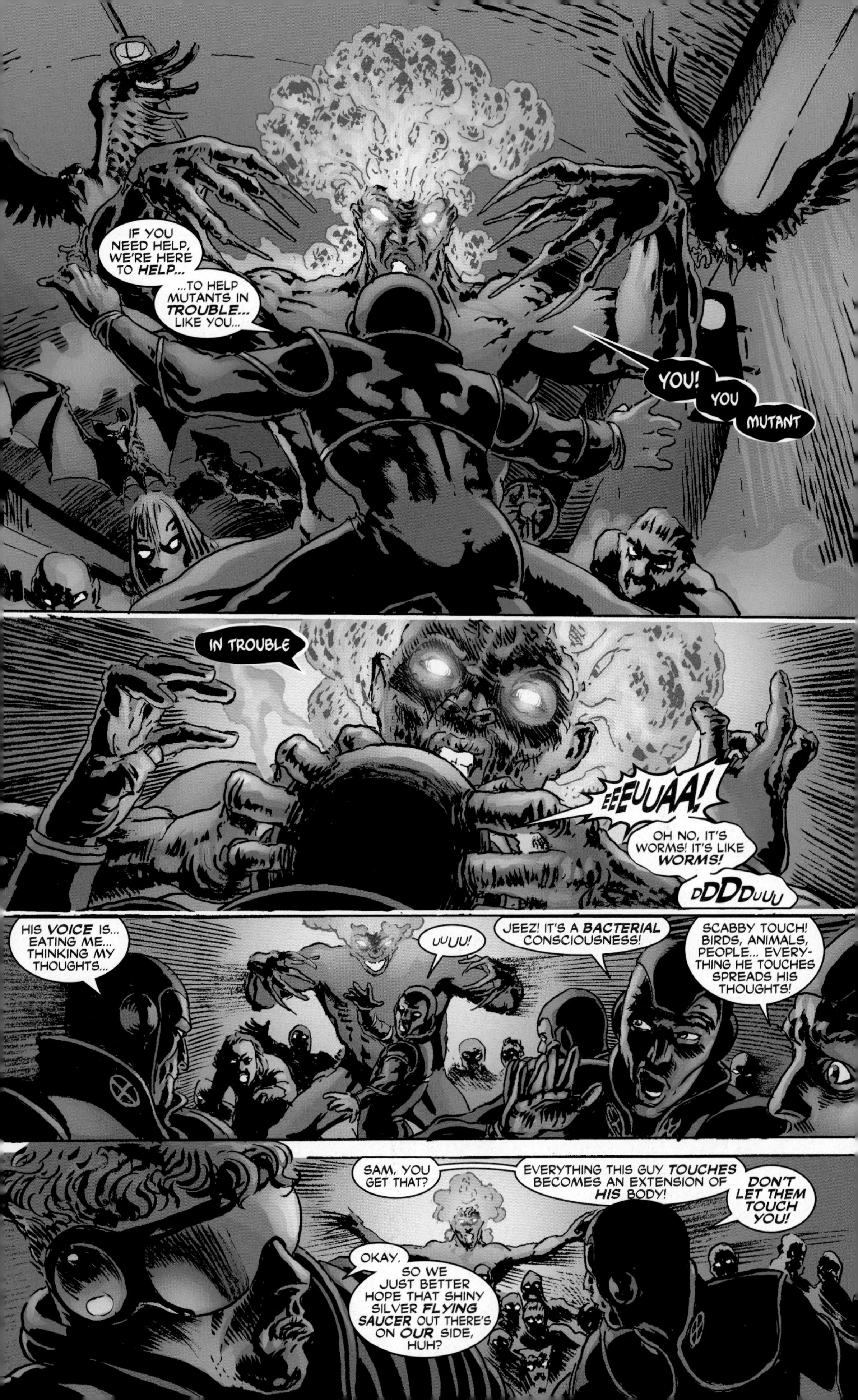

IF YOU NEED HELP, WE'RE HERE TO HELP...
...TO HELP MUTANTS IN TROUBLE... LIKE YOU...
YOU!
YOU
MUTANT
IN TROUBLE
EEEUUAA!
OH NO, IT'S WORMS! IT'S LIKE WORMS!
DDDDUUU
HIS VOICE IS... EATING ME... THINKING MY THOUGHTS...
UUUU!
JEEZ! IT'S A BACTERIAL CONSCIOUSNESS!
SCABBY TOUCH! BIRDS, ANIMALS, PEOPLE... EVERYTHING HE TOUCHES SPREADS HIS THOUGHTS!
SAM, YOU GET THAT?
EVERYTHING THIS GUY TOUCHES BECOMES AN EXTENSION OF HIS BODY!
DON'T LET THEM TOUCH YOU!
OKAY. SO WE JUST BETTER HOPE THAT SHINY SILVER FLYING SAUCER OUT THERE'S ON OUR SIDE, HUH?

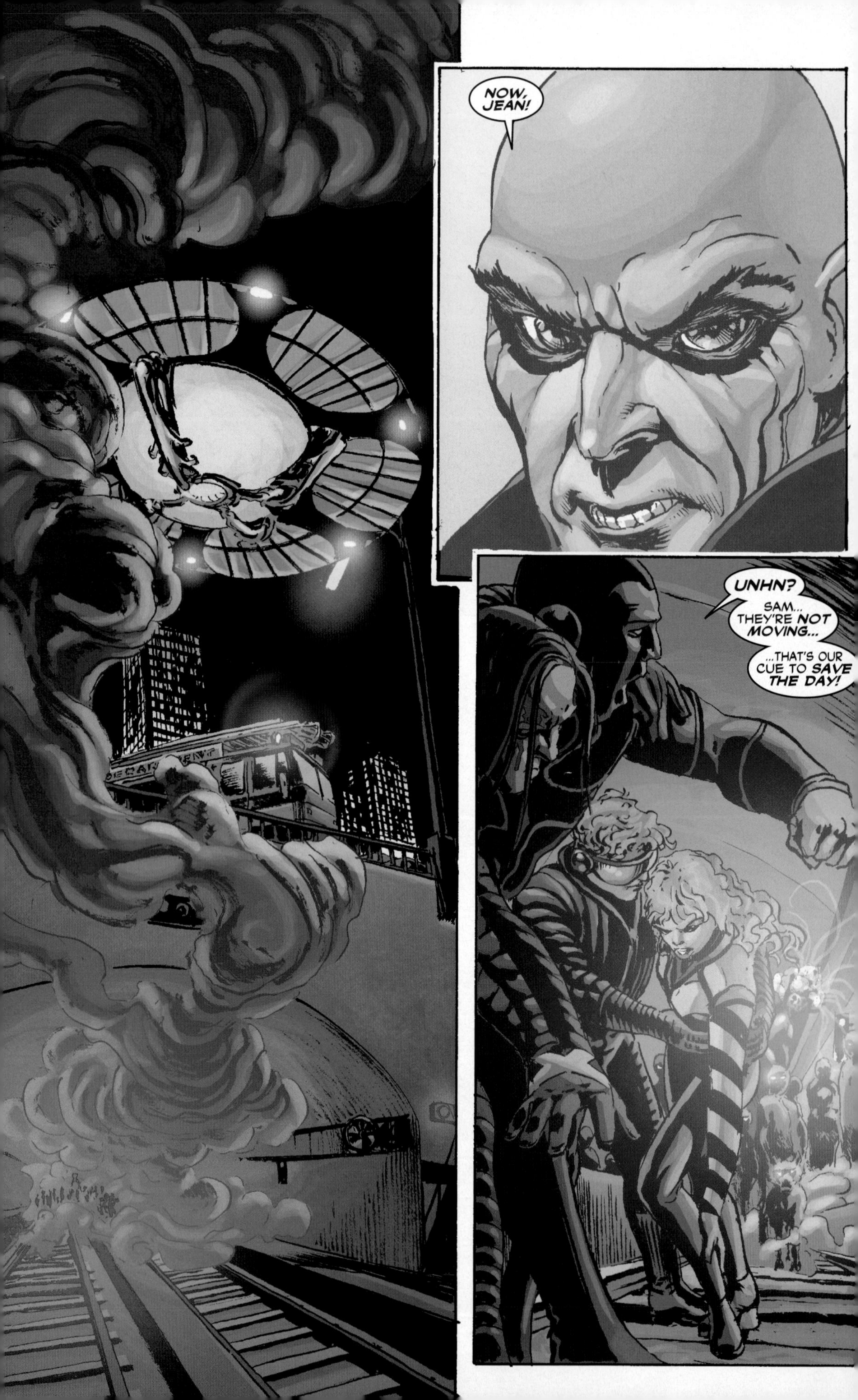
NOW, JEAN!
UNHN?
SAM... THEY'RE NOT MOVING...
...THAT'S OUR CUE TO SAVE THE DAY!

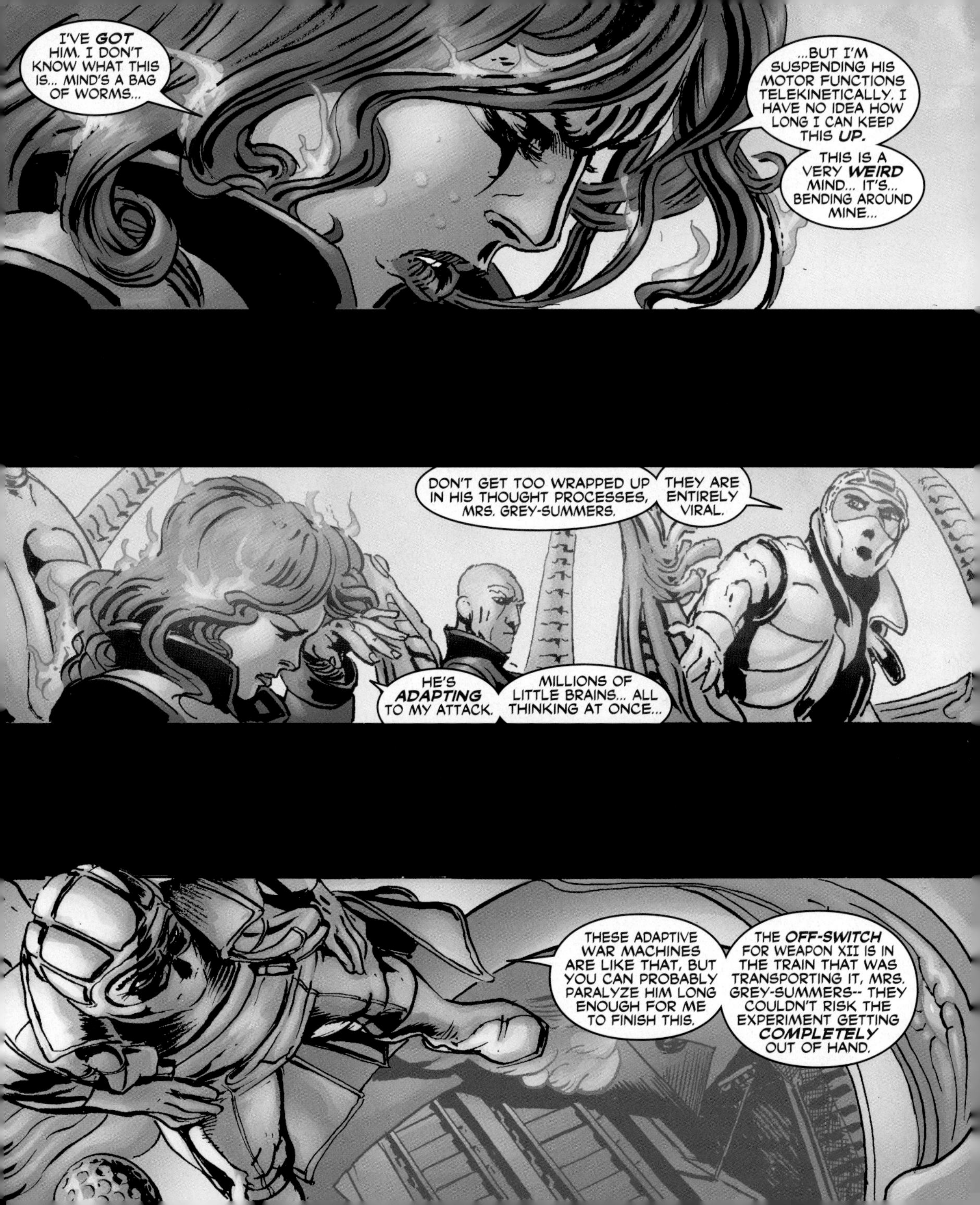
I'VE GOT HIM. I DON'T KNOW WHAT THIS IS... MIND'S A BAG OF WORMS...
...BUT I'M SUSPENDING HIS MOTOR FUNCTIONS TELEKINETICALLY. I HAVE NO IDEA HOW LONG I CAN KEEP THIS UP.
THIS IS A VERY WEIRD MIND... IT'S... BENDING AROUND MINE...
[redacted]
DON'T GET TOO WRAPPED UP IN HIS THOUGHT PROCESSES, MRS. GREY-SUMMERS.
THEY ARE ENTIRELY VIRAL.
HE'S ADAPTING TO MY ATTACK.
MILLIONS OF LITTLE BRAINS... ALL THINKING AT ONCE...
[redacted]
THESE ADAPTIVE WAR MACHINES ARE LIKE THAT, BUT YOU CAN PROBABLY PARALYZE HIM LONG ENOUGH FOR ME TO FINISH THIS.
THE OFF-SWITCH FOR WEAPON XII IS IN THE TRAIN THAT WAS TRANSPORTING IT, MRS. GREY-SUMMERS-- THEY COULDN'T RISK THE EXPERIMENT GETTING COMPLETELY OUT OF HAND.

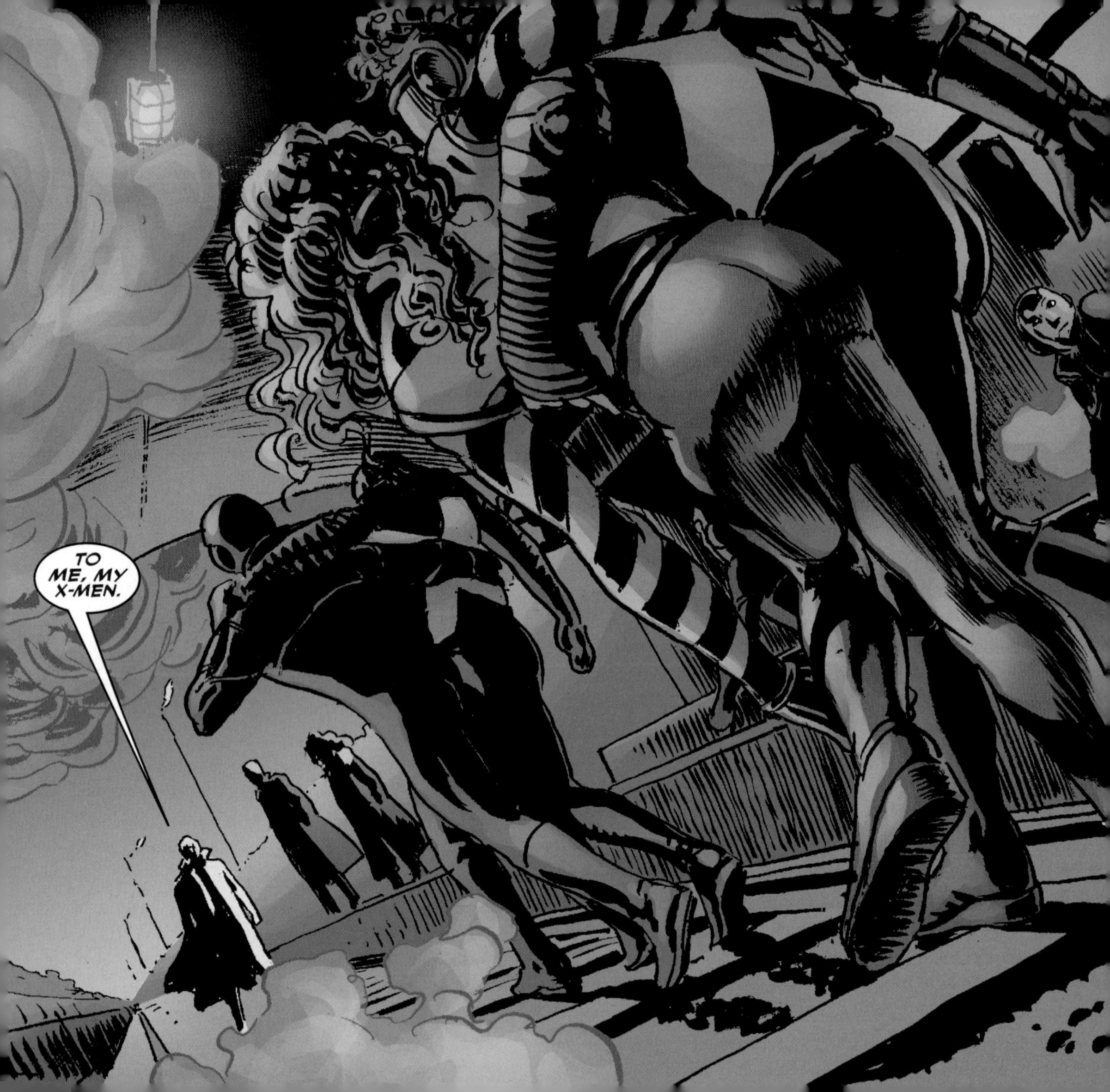
TO ME, MY X-MEN.

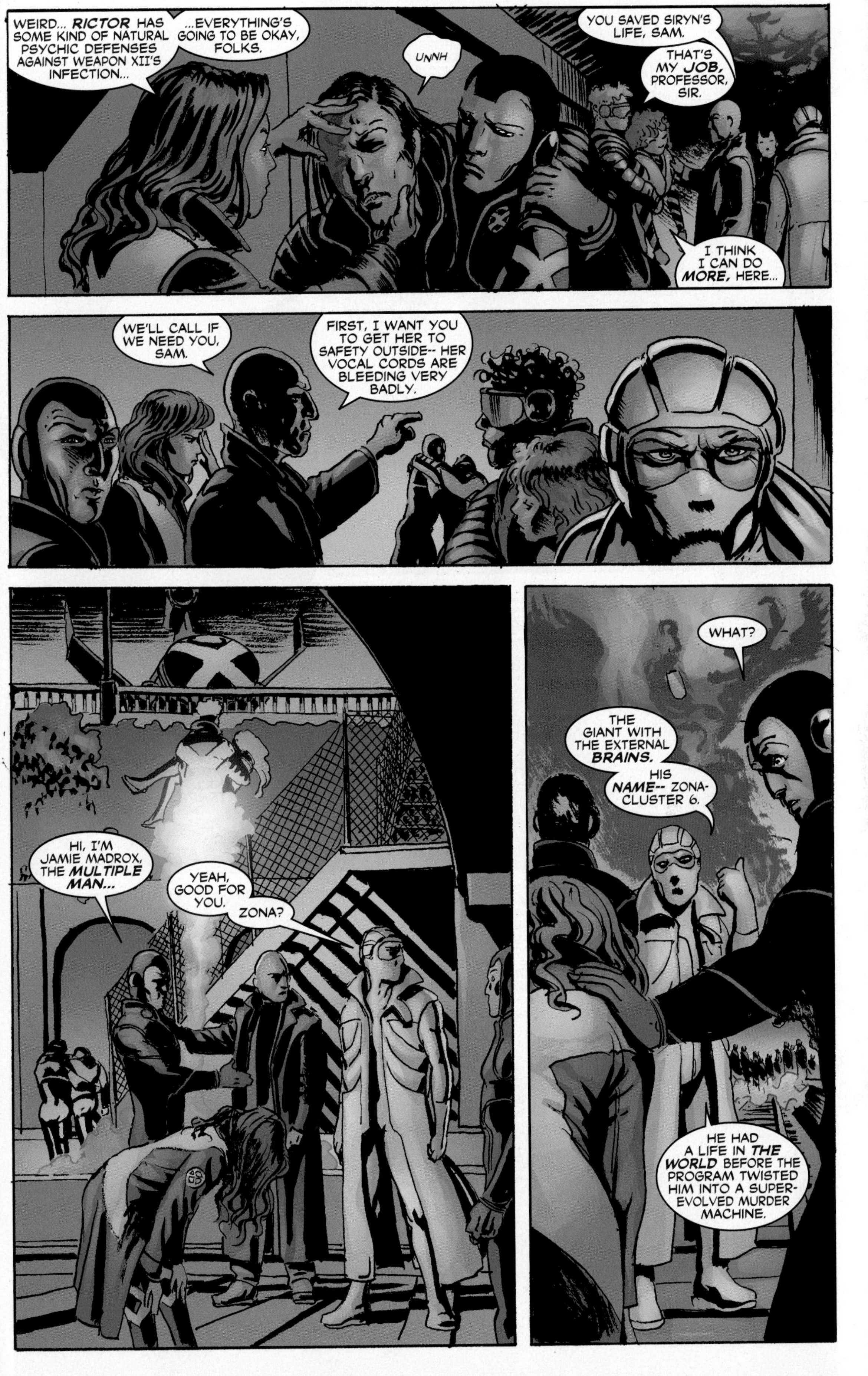

WEIRD... RICTOR HAS SOME KIND OF NATURAL PSYCHIC DEFENSES AGAINST WEAPON XII'S INFECTION...
...EVERYTHING'S GOING TO BE OKAY, FOLKS.
UNNH
YOU SAVED SIRYN'S LIFE, SAM.
THAT'S MY JOB, PROFESSOR, SIR.
I THINK I CAN DO MORE, HERE...
WE'LL CALL IF WE NEED YOU, SAM.
FIRST, I WANT YOU TO GET HER TO SAFETY OUTSIDE-- HER VOCAL CORDS ARE BLEEDING VERY BADLY.
HI, I'M JAMIE MADROX, THE MULTIPLE MAN...
YEAH, GOOD FOR YOU.
ZONA?
WHAT?
THE GIANT WITH THE EXTERNAL BRAINS.
HIS NAME-- ZONA-CLUSTER 6.
HE HAD A LIFE IN THE WORLD BEFORE THE PROGRAM TWISTED HIM INTO A SUPER-EVOLVED MURDER MACHINE.

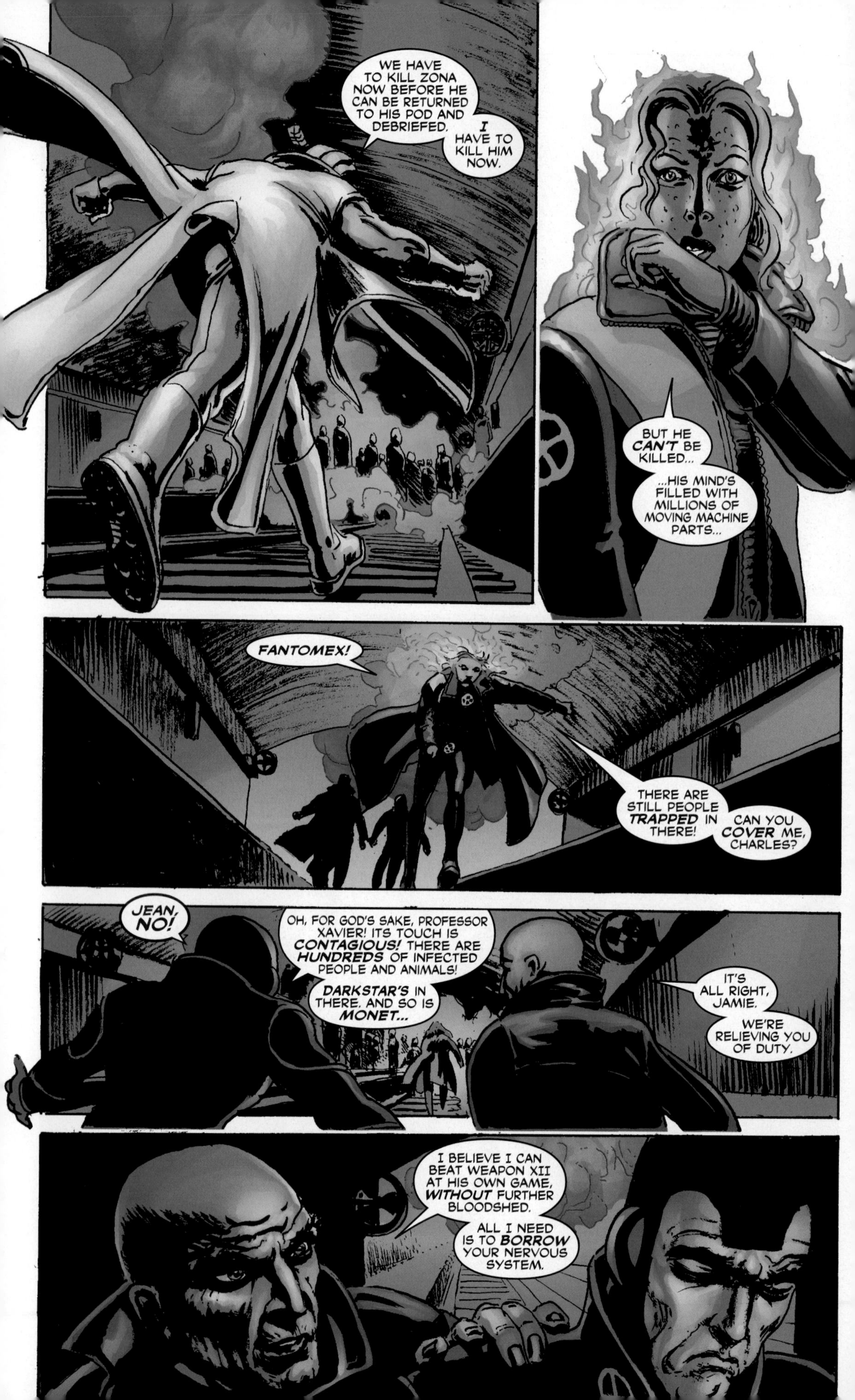
WE HAVE TO KILL ZONA NOW BEFORE HE CAN BE RETURNED TO HIS POD AND DEBRIEFED.
I HAVE TO KILL HIM NOW.
BUT HE CAN'T BE KILLED...
...HIS MIND'S FILLED WITH MILLIONS OF MOVING MACHINE PARTS...
FANTOMEX!
THERE ARE STILL PEOPLE TRAPPED IN THERE!
CAN YOU COVER ME, CHARLES?
JEAN, NO!
OH, FOR GOD'S SAKE, PROFESSOR XAVIER! ITS TOUCH IS CONTAGIOUS! THERE ARE HUNDREDS OF INFECTED PEOPLE AND ANIMALS!
DARKSTAR'S IN THERE. AND SO IS MONET...
IT'S ALL RIGHT, JAMIE.
WE'RE RELIEVING YOU OF DUTY.
I BELIEVE I CAN BEAT WEAPON XII AT HIS OWN GAME, WITHOUT FURTHER BLOODSHED.
ALL I NEED IS TO BORROW YOUR NERVOUS SYSTEM.

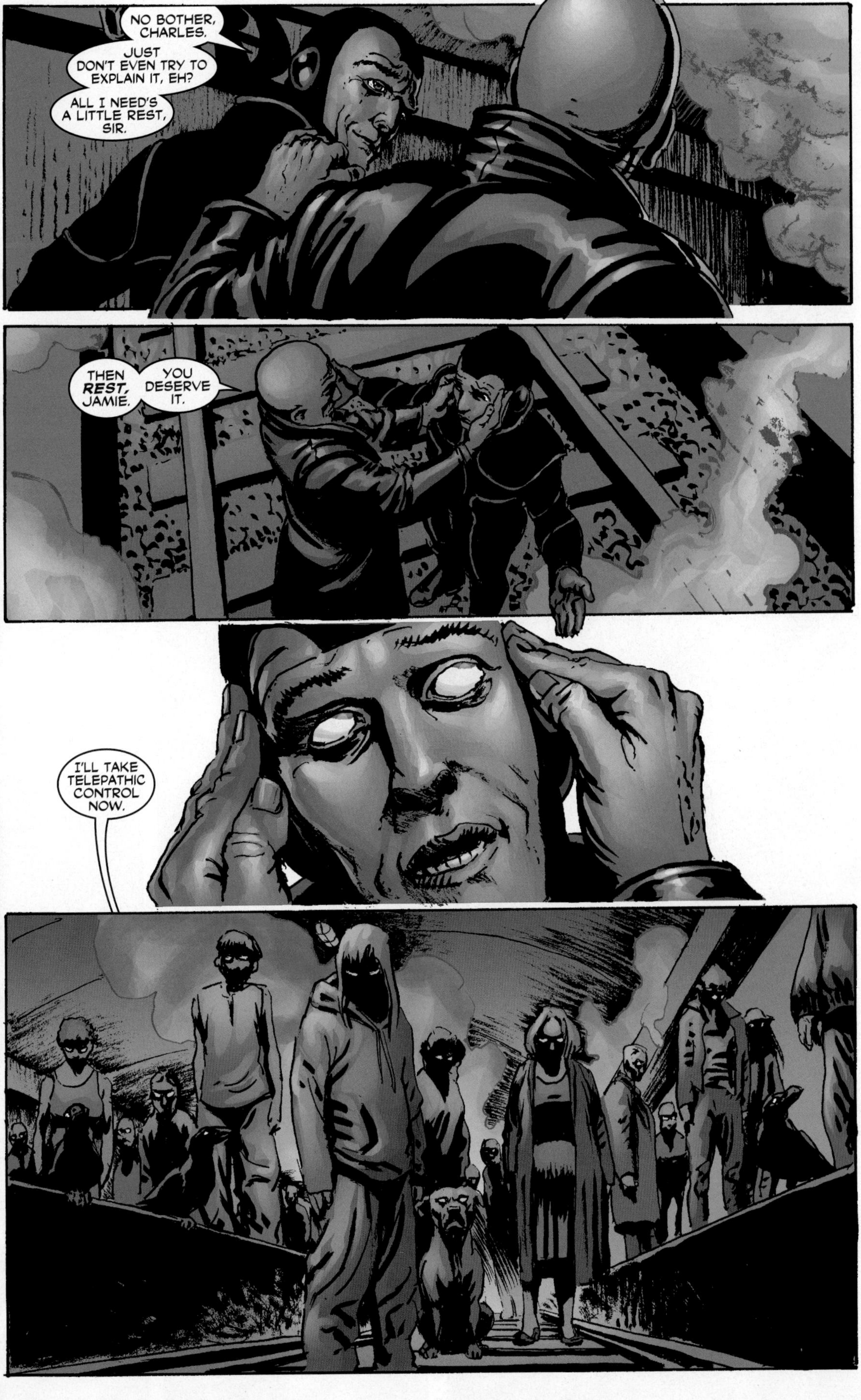
NO BOTHER, CHARLES.
JUST DON'T EVEN TRY TO EXPLAIN IT, EH?
ALL I NEED'S A LITTLE REST, SIR.
THEN REST, JAMIE.
YOU DESERVE IT.
I'LL TAKE TELEPATHIC CONTROL NOW.

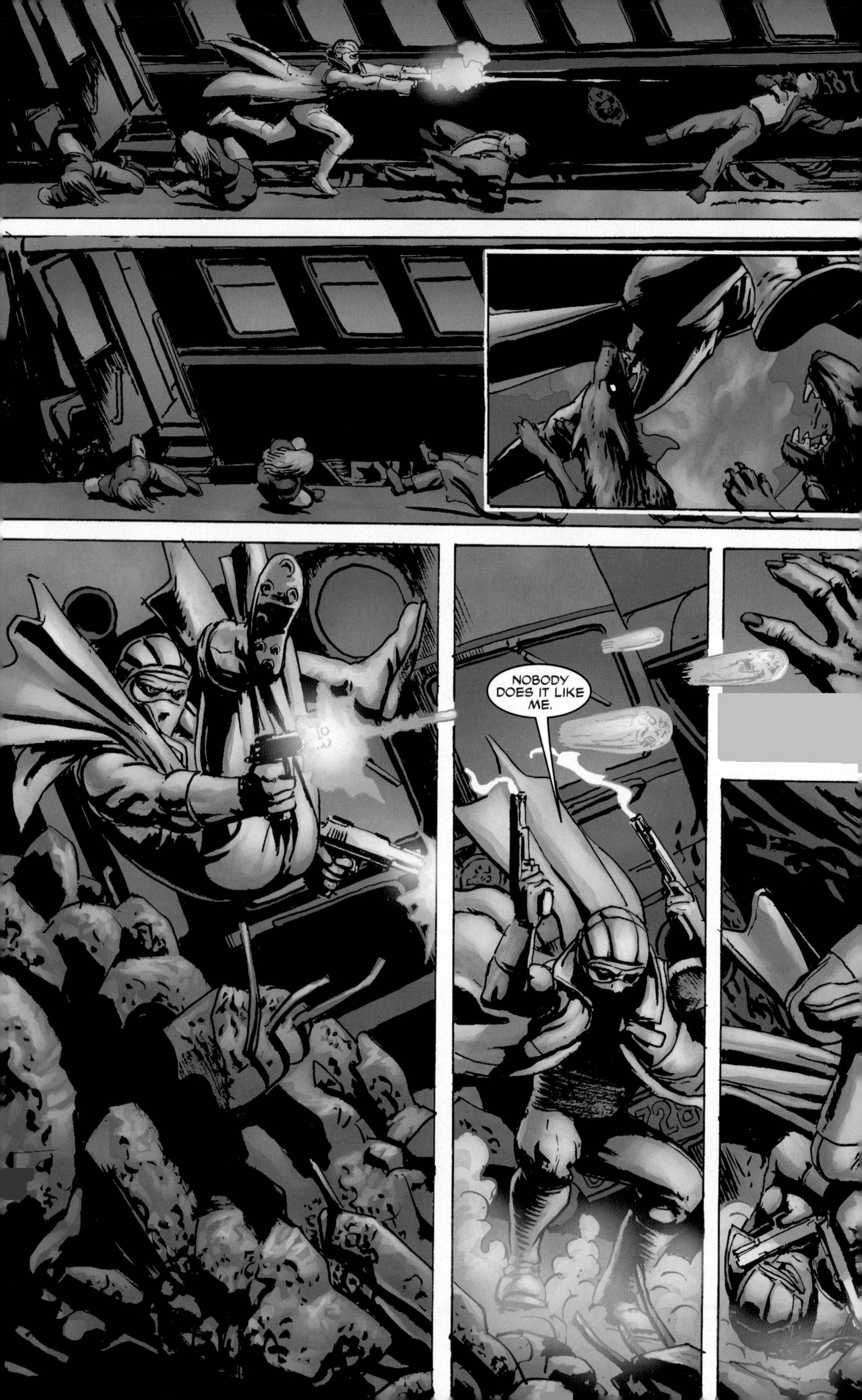
NOBODY DOES IT LIKE ME.

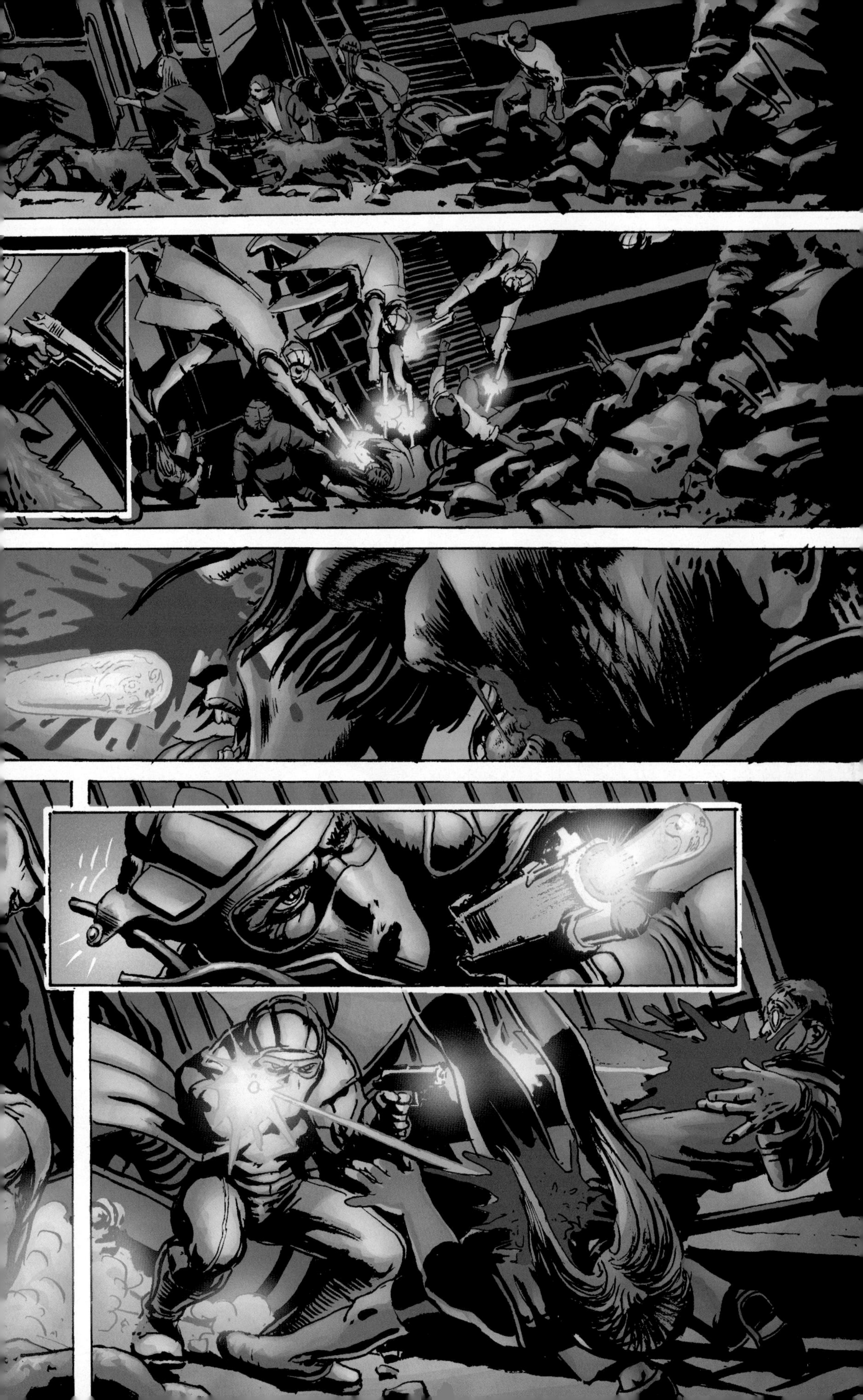

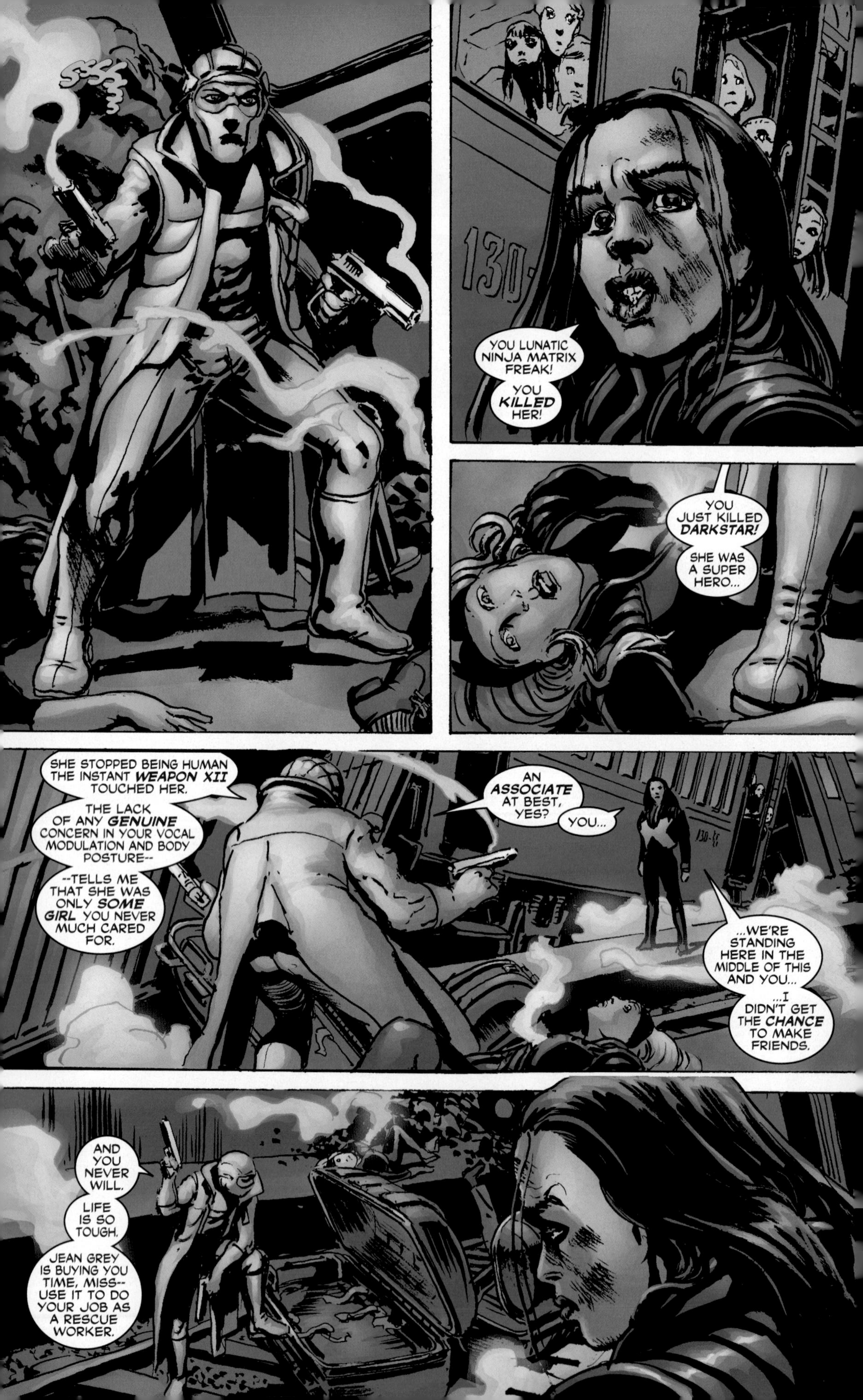
SSSSSS
YOU LUNATIC NINJA MATRIX FREAK!
YOU KILLED HER!
YOU JUST KILLED DARKSTAR!
SHE WAS A SUPER HERO...
SHE STOPPED BEING HUMAN THE INSTANT WEAPON XII TOUCHED HER.
THE LACK OF ANY GENUINE CONCERN IN YOUR VOCAL MODULATION AND BODY POSTURE--
--TELLS ME THAT SHE WAS ONLY SOME GIRL YOU NEVER MUCH CARED FOR.
AN ASSOCIATE AT BEST, YES?
YOU...
...WE'RE STANDING HERE IN THE MIDDLE OF THIS AND YOU...
...I DIDN'T GET THE CHANCE TO MAKE FRIENDS.
AND YOU NEVER WILL.
LIFE IS SO TOUGH.
JEAN GREY IS BUYING YOU TIME, MISS--USE IT TO DO YOUR JOB AS A RESCUE WORKER.

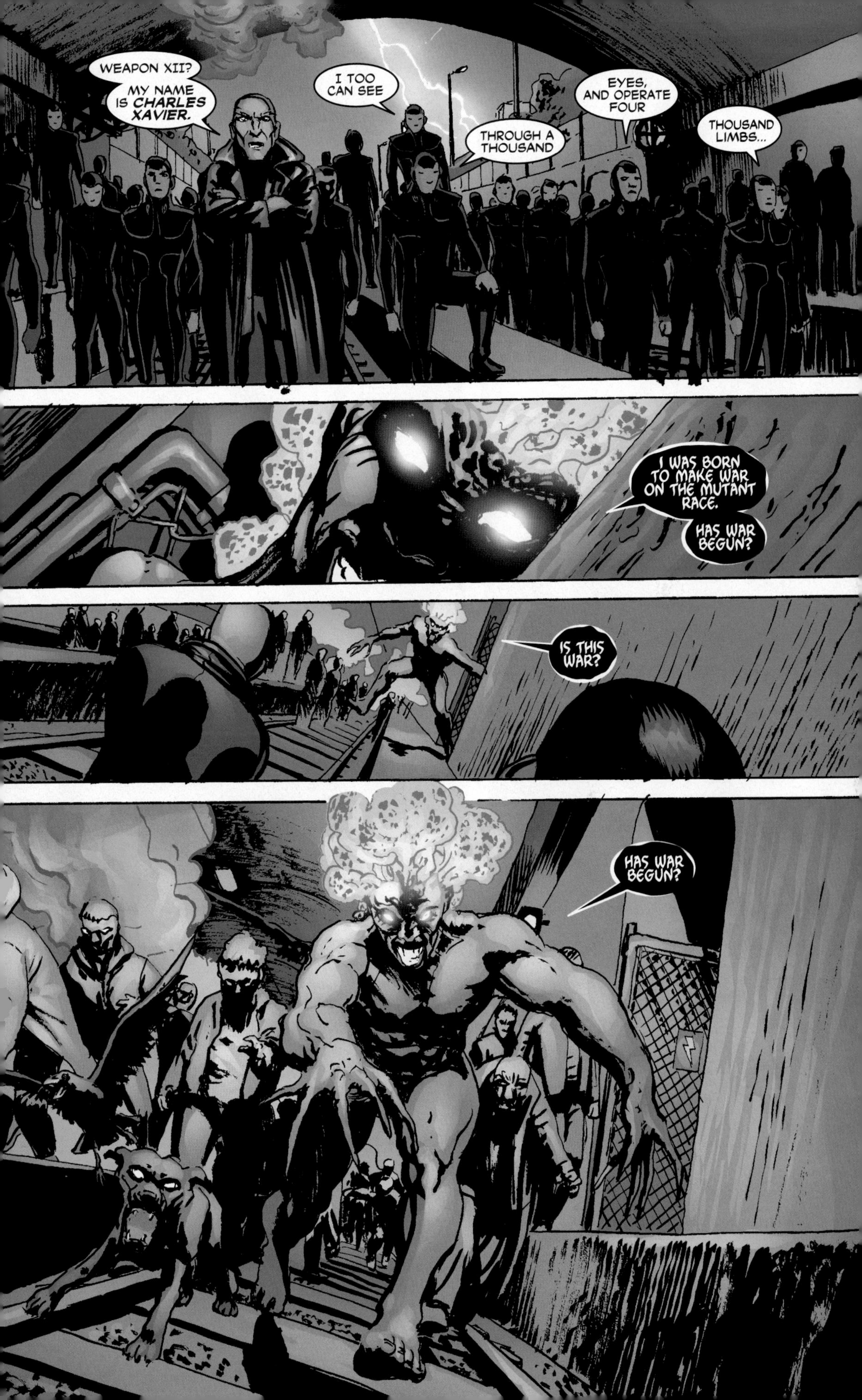
WEAPON XII?
MY NAME IS CHARLES XAVIER.
I TOO CAN SEE
THROUGH A THOUSAND
EYES, AND OPERATE FOUR
THOUSAND LIMBS...
I WAS BORN TO MAKE WAR ON THE MUTANT RACE.
HAS WAR BEGUN?
IS THIS WAR?
HAS WAR BEGUN?

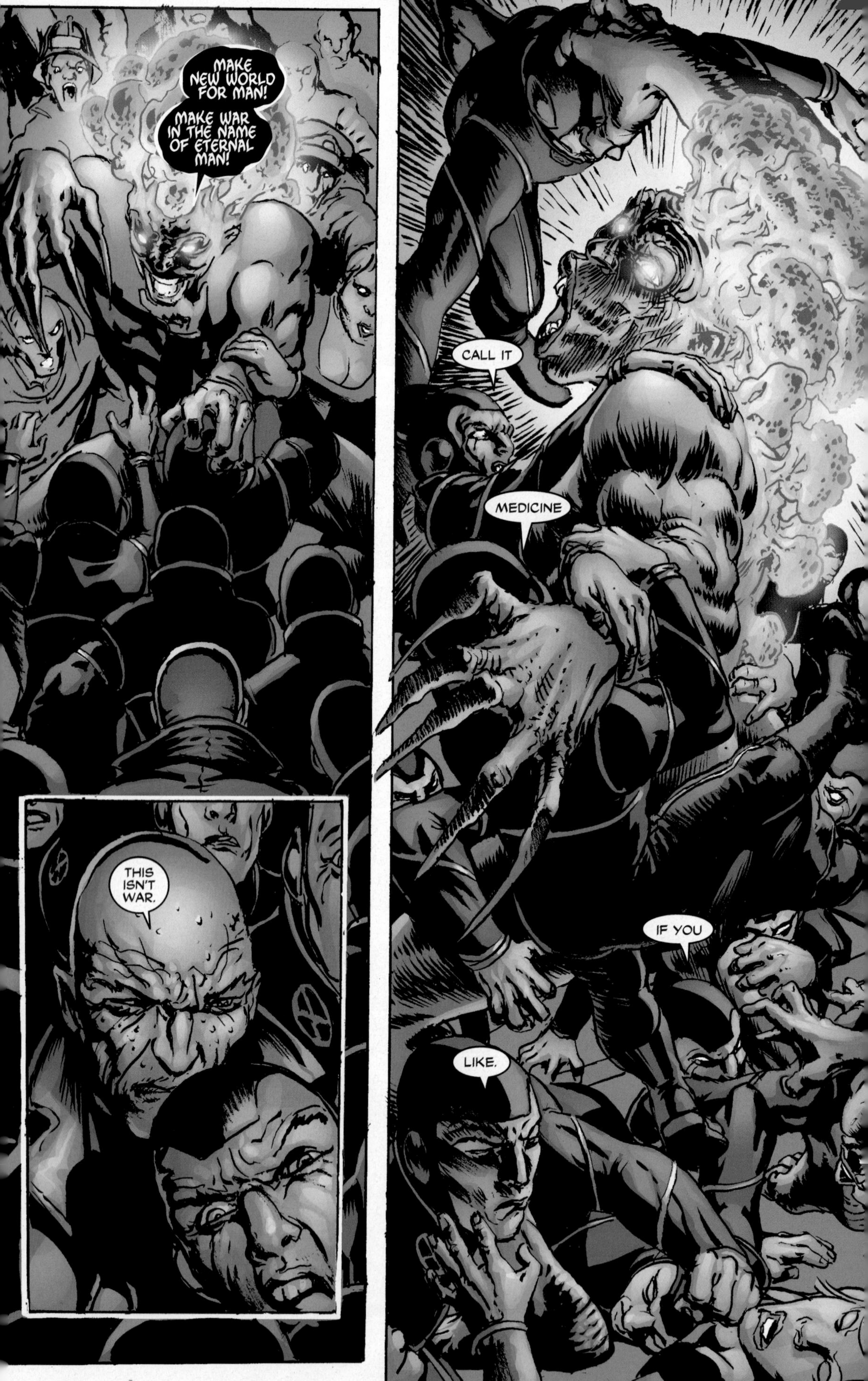
MAKE NEW WORLD FOR MAN!
MAKE WAR IN THE NAME OF ETERNAL MAN!
THIS ISN'T WAR.
CALL IT
MEDICINE
IF YOU
LIKE.

GET THE SURVIVORS *OUT*, MONET. THE WAY'S CLEAR.

JEAN? JEAN, THERE WERE NO PASSENGERS IN THE TRAIN.

EVERYTHING WENT NUTS AND... AND HE KILLED *DARKSTAR*.

BECAUSE IT WASN'T *HER* ANYMORE. TAKE IT EASY AND WALK SLOWLY BACK TOWARDS THE FLOODLIGHTS, MONET.

FANTOMEX?

HNN? AH!

AND THIS ONE OTHER...

FANTOMEX? I HATE TO BRING THIS UP, BUT IF THERE WAS ONLY *ONE* WEAPON XII...

...WHY ARE THERE *TWO* OF THESE CAGES?

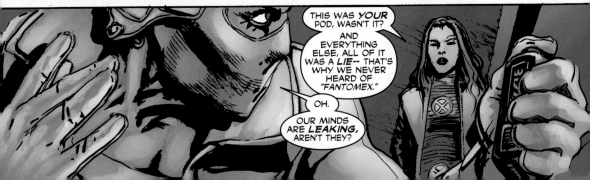

THIS WAS *YOUR* POD, WASN'T IT?

AND EVERYTHING ELSE, ALL OF IT WAS A *LIE*-- THAT'S WHY WE NEVER HEARD OF "FANTOMEX."

OH.

OUR MINDS ARE *LEAKING*, AREN'T THEY?

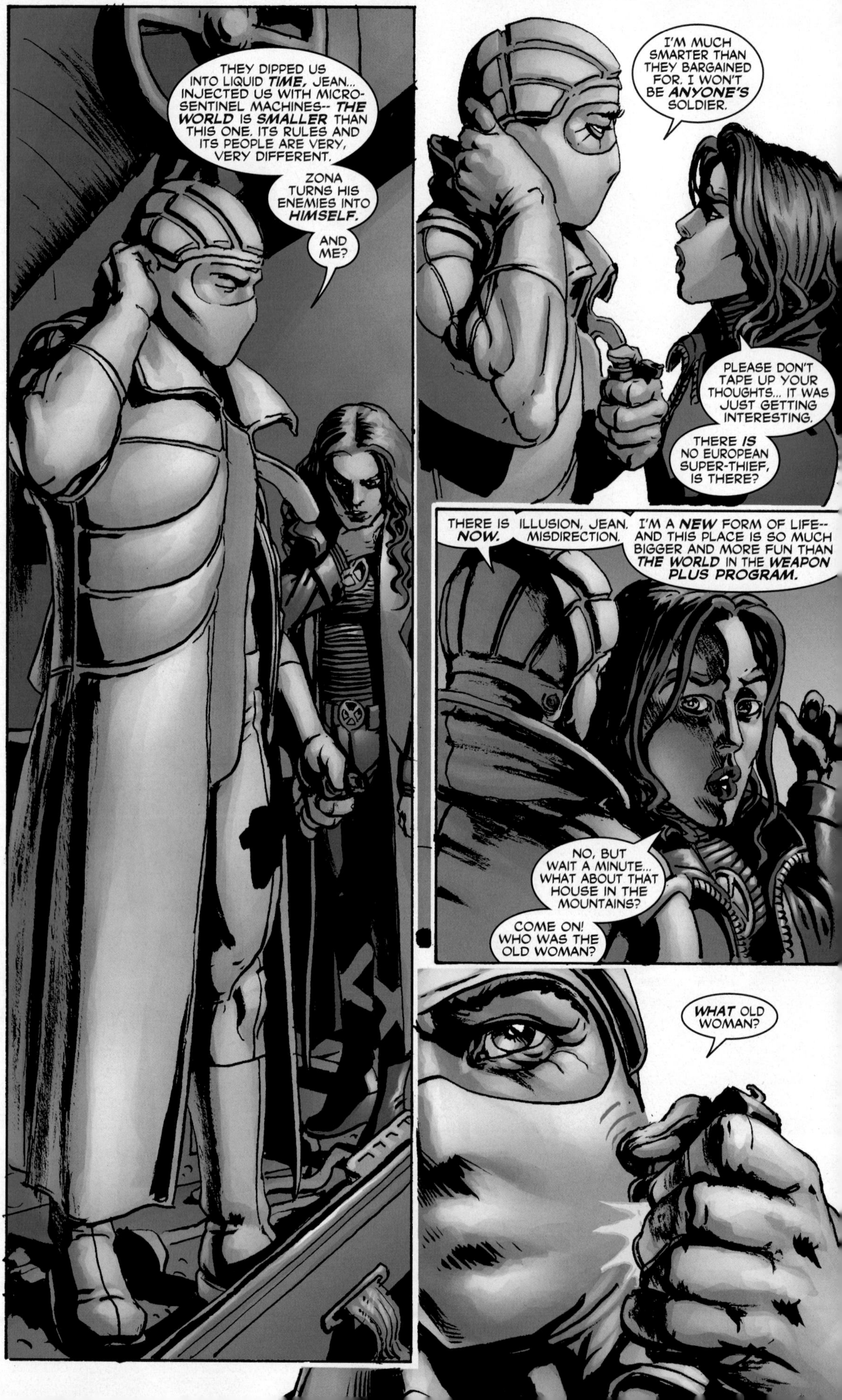
THEY DIPPED US INTO LIQUID TIME, JEAN... INJECTED US WITH MICRO-SENTINEL MACHINES-- THE WORLD IS SMALLER THAN THIS ONE. ITS RULES AND ITS PEOPLE ARE VERY, VERY DIFFERENT.
ZONA TURNS HIS ENEMIES INTO HIMSELF.
AND ME?
I'M MUCH SMARTER THAN THEY BARGAINED FOR. I WON'T BE ANYONE'S SOLDIER.
PLEASE DON'T TAPE UP YOUR THOUGHTS... IT WAS JUST GETTING INTERESTING.
THERE IS NO EUROPEAN SUPER-THIEF, IS THERE?
THERE IS NOW.
ILLUSION, JEAN. MISDIRECTION.
I'M A NEW FORM OF LIFE-- AND THIS PLACE IS SO MUCH BIGGER AND MORE FUN THAN THE WORLD IN THE WEAPON PLUS PROGRAM.
NO, BUT WAIT A MINUTE... WHAT ABOUT THAT HOUSE IN THE MOUNTAINS?
COME ON! WHO WAS THE OLD WOMAN?
WHAT OLD WOMAN?

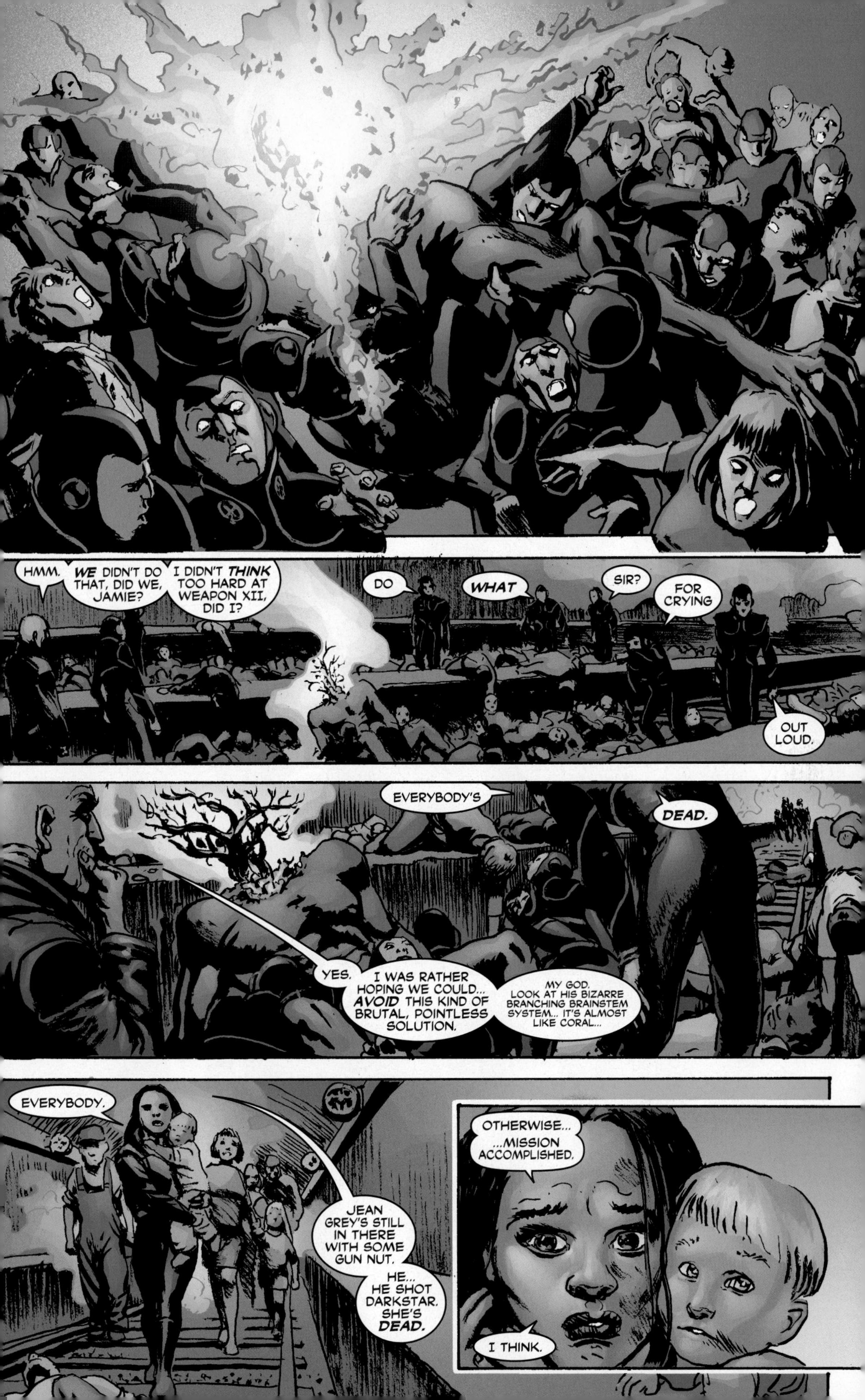
HMM.
WE DIDN'T DO THAT, DID WE, JAMIE?
I DIDN'T THINK TOO HARD AT WEAPON XII, DID I?
DO
WHAT
SIR?
FOR CRYING
OUT LOUD.
EVERYBODY'S
DEAD.
YES.
I WAS RATHER HOPING WE COULD... AVOID THIS KIND OF BRUTAL, POINTLESS SOLUTION.
MY GOD. LOOK AT HIS BIZARRE BRANCHING BRAINSTEM SYSTEM... IT'S ALMOST LIKE CORAL...
EVERYBODY.
JEAN GREY'S STILL IN THERE WITH SOME GUN NUT.
HE... HE SHOT DARKSTAR. SHE'S DEAD.
OTHERWISE... ...MISSION ACCOMPLISHED.
I THINK.

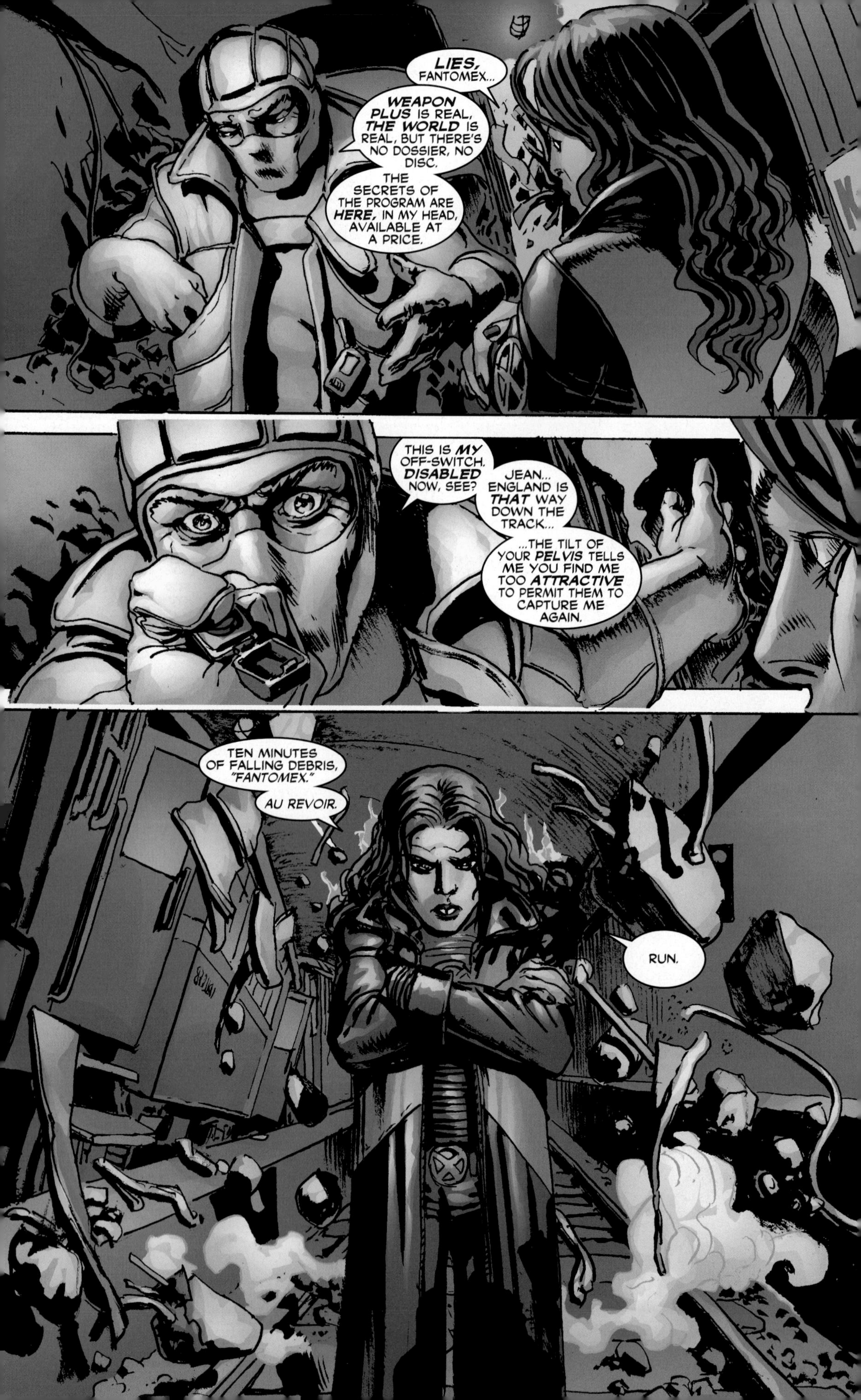
LIES, FANTOMEX...
WEAPON PLUS IS REAL, THE WORLD IS REAL, BUT THERE'S NO DOSSIER, NO DISC.
THE SECRETS OF THE PROGRAM ARE HERE, IN MY HEAD, AVAILABLE AT A PRICE.
THIS IS MY OFF-SWITCH. DISABLED NOW, SEE?
JEAN... ENGLAND IS THAT WAY DOWN THE TRACK...
...THE TILT OF YOUR PELVIS TELLS ME YOU FIND ME TOO ATTRACTIVE TO PERMIT THEM TO CAPTURE ME AGAIN.
TEN MINUTES OF FALLING DEBRIS, "FANTOMEX."
AU REVOIR.
RUN.

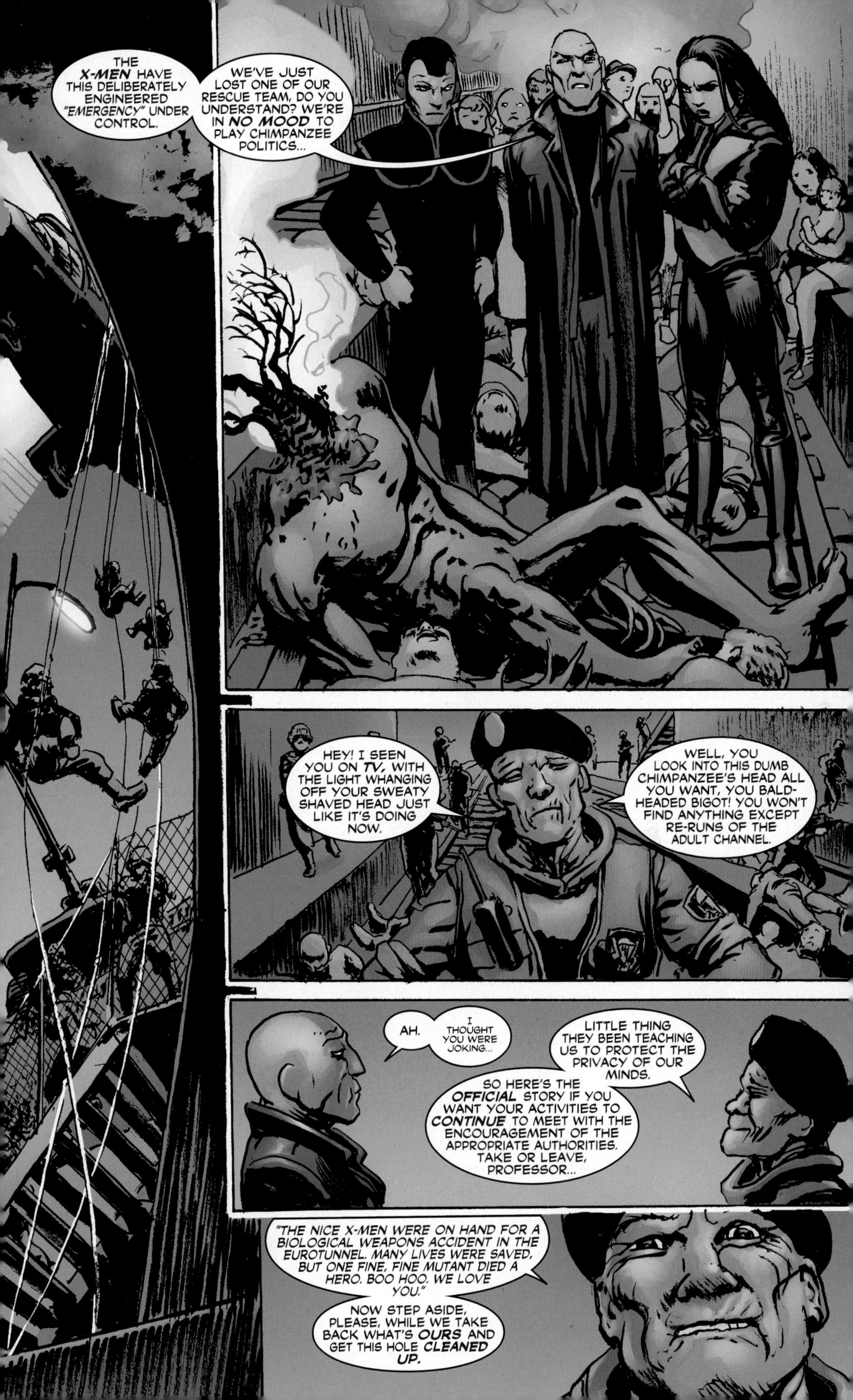
THE X-MEN HAVE THIS DELIBERATELY ENGINEERED "EMERGENCY" UNDER CONTROL.
WE'VE JUST LOST ONE OF OUR RESCUE TEAM, DO YOU UNDERSTAND? WE'RE IN NO MOOD TO PLAY CHIMPANZEE POLITICS...
HEY! I SEEN YOU ON TV, WITH THE LIGHT WHANGING OFF YOUR SWEATY SHAVED HEAD JUST LIKE IT'S DOING NOW.
WELL, YOU LOOK INTO THIS DUMB CHIMPANZEE'S HEAD ALL YOU WANT, YOU BALD-HEADED BIGOT! YOU WON'T FIND ANYTHING EXCEPT RE-RUNS OF THE ADULT CHANNEL.
AH.
I THOUGHT YOU WERE JOKING...
LITTLE THING THEY BEEN TEACHING US TO PROTECT THE PRIVACY OF OUR MINDS.
SO HERE'S THE OFFICIAL STORY IF YOU WANT YOUR ACTIVITIES TO CONTINUE TO MEET WITH THE ENCOURAGEMENT OF THE APPROPRIATE AUTHORITIES. TAKE OR LEAVE, PROFESSOR...
"THE NICE X-MEN WERE ON HAND FOR A BIOLOGICAL WEAPONS ACCIDENT IN THE EUROTUNNEL. MANY LIVES WERE SAVED, BUT ONE FINE, FINE MUTANT DIED A HERO. BOO HOO. WE LOVE YOU."
NOW STEP ASIDE, PLEASE, WHILE WE TAKE BACK WHAT'S OURS AND GET THIS HOLE CLEANED UP.

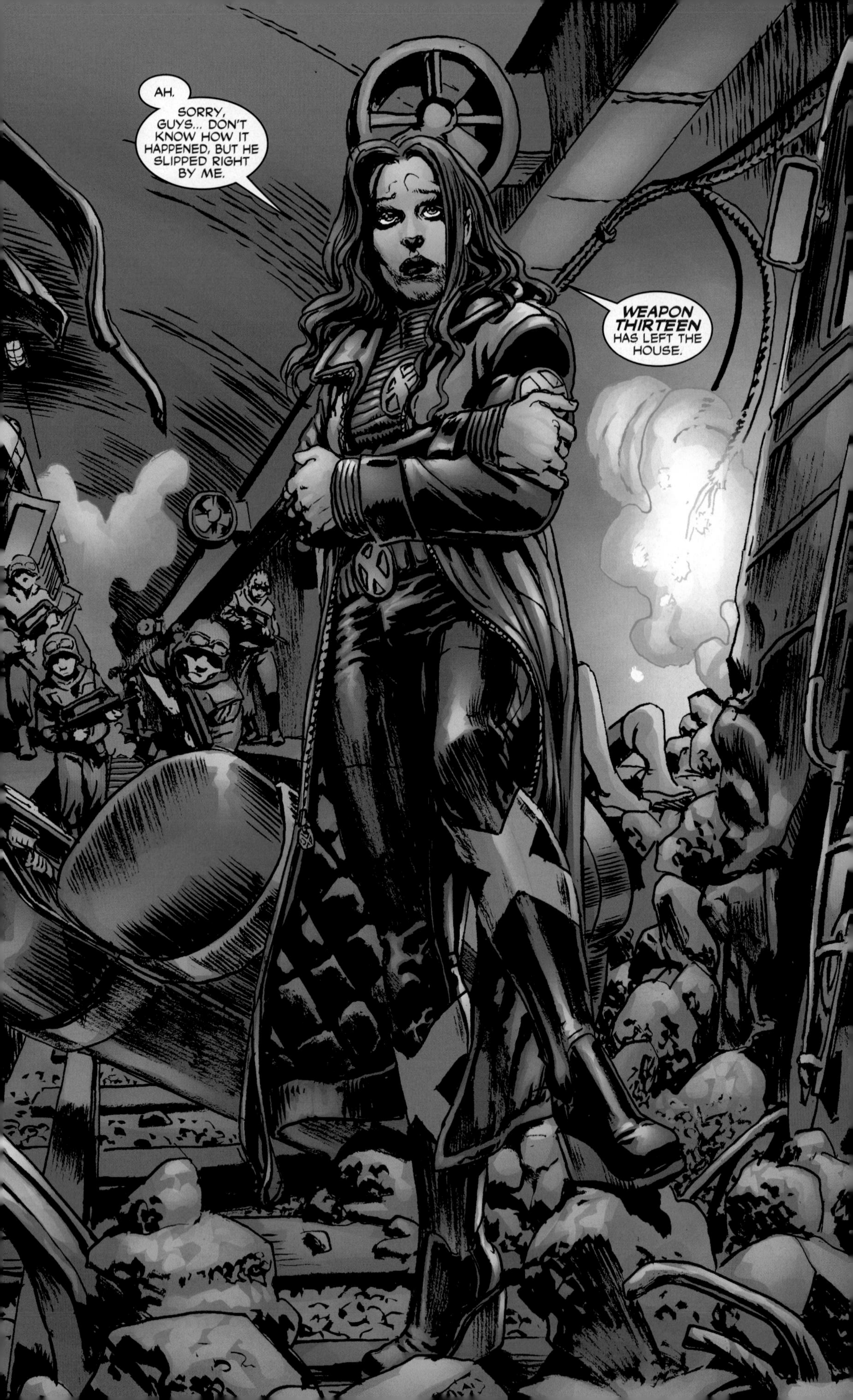
AH.
SORRY, GUYS... DON'T KNOW HOW IT HAPPENED, BUT HE SLIPPED RIGHT BY ME.
WEAPON THIRTEEN HAS LEFT THE HOUSE.

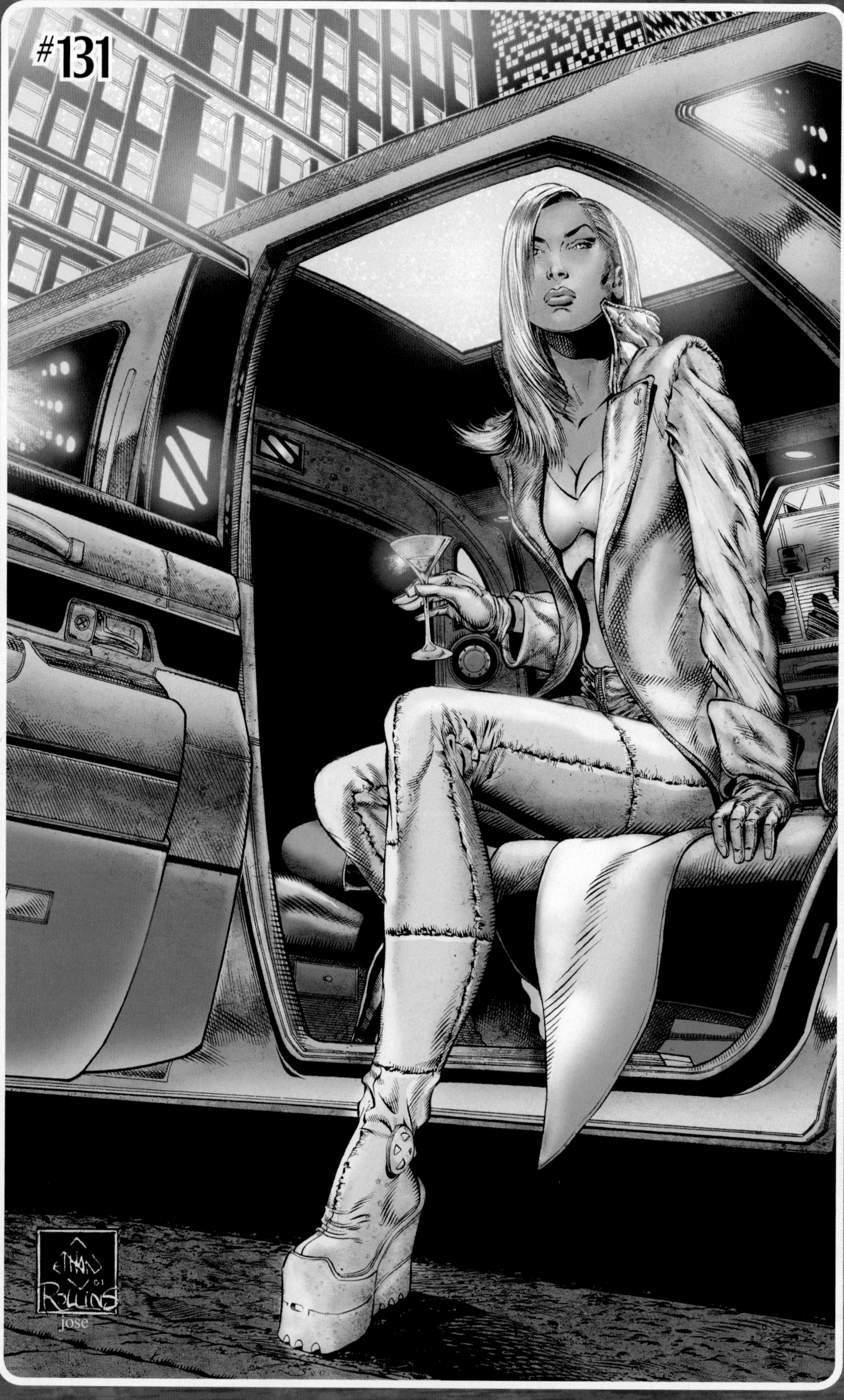
#131

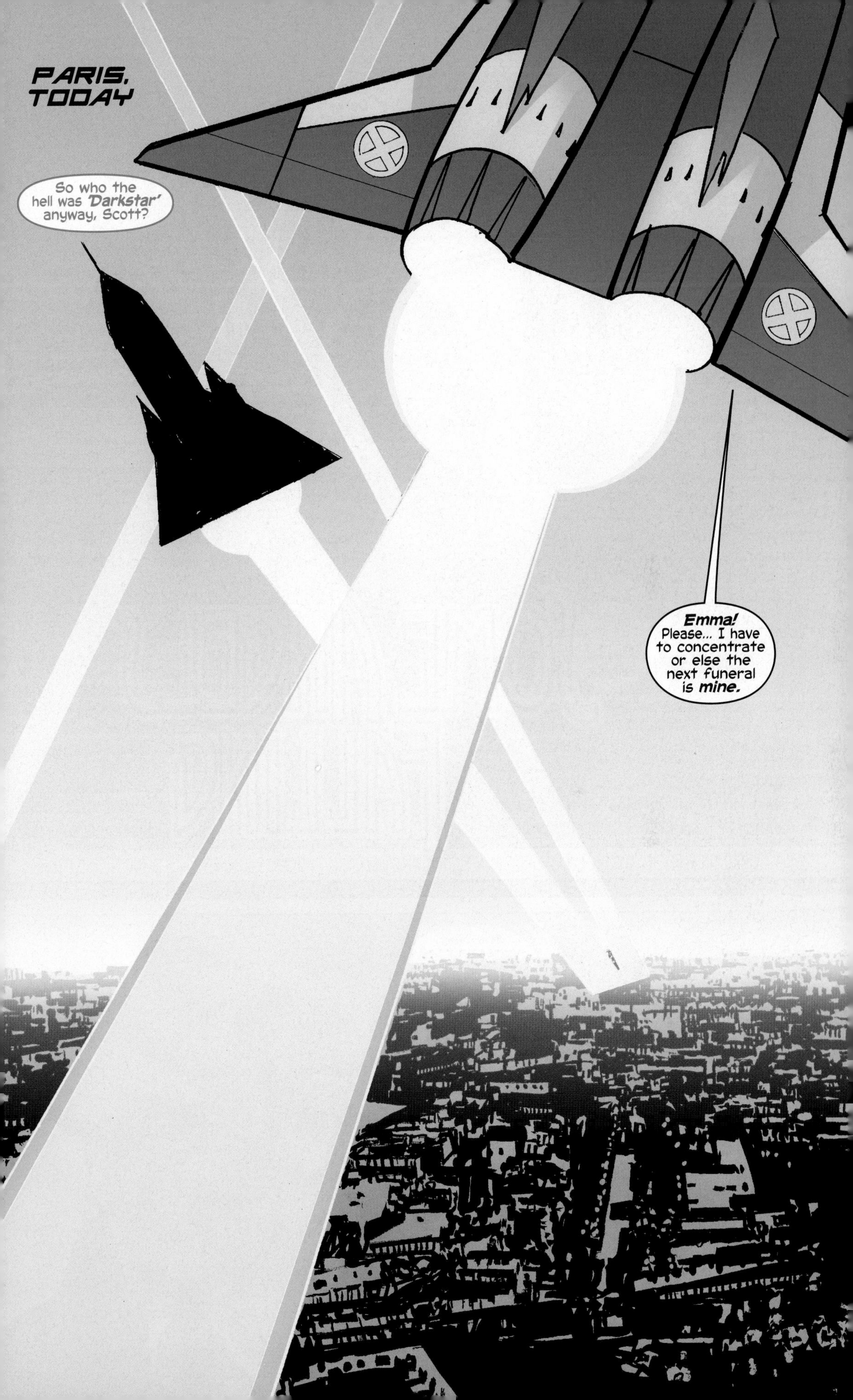
PARIS, TODAY
So who the hell was 'Darkstar' anyway, Scott?
Emma! Please... I have to concentrate or else the next funeral is mine.

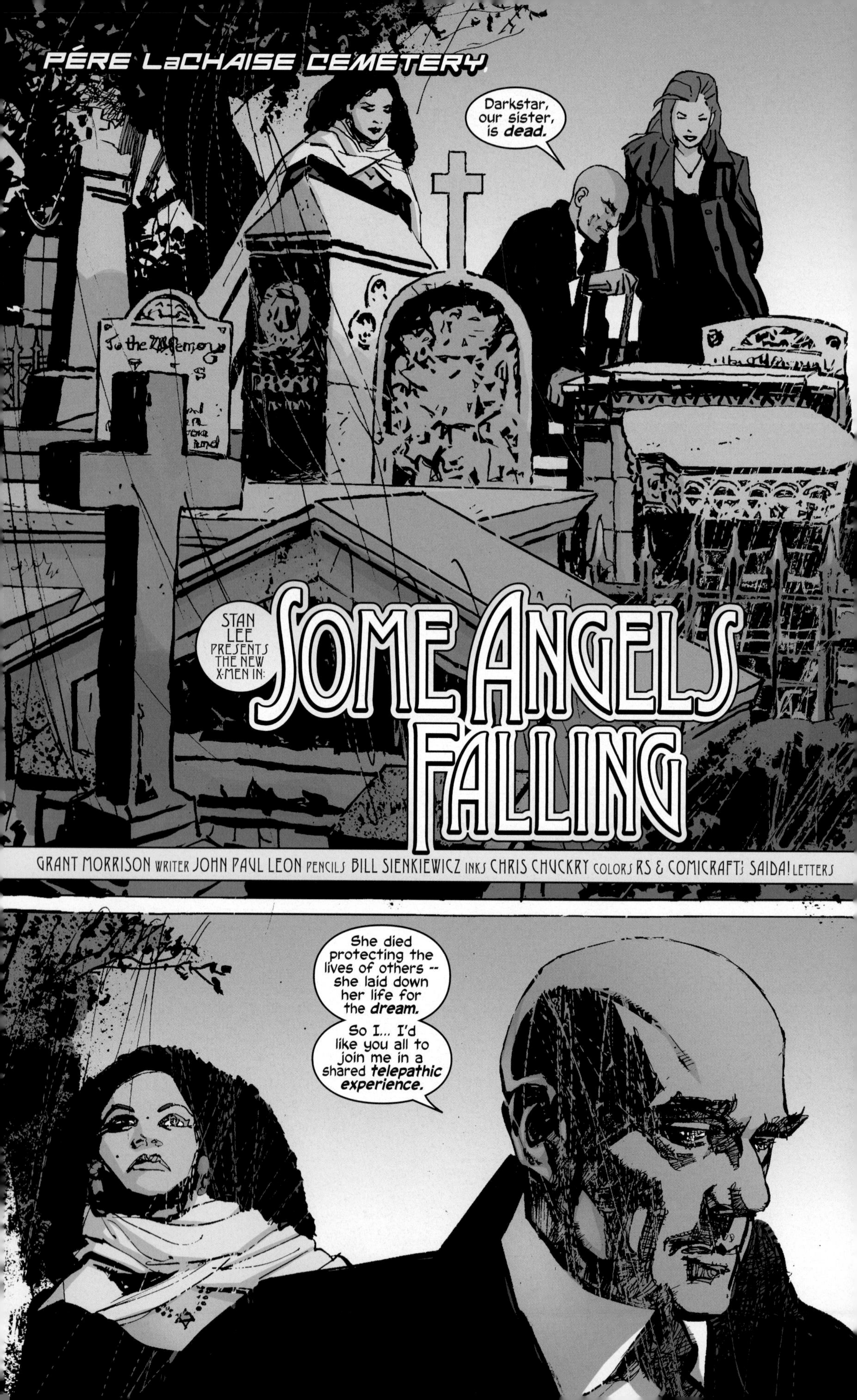
PÉRE LaCHAISE CEMETERY
Darkstar, our sister, is dead.
STAN LEE PRESENTS THE NEW X-MEN IN:
SOME ANGELS FALLING
GRANT MORRISON WRITER JOHN PAUL LEON PENCILS BILL SIENKIEWICZ INKS CHRIS CHUCKRY COLORS RS & COMICRAFT'S SAIDA! LETTERS
She died protecting the lives of others -- she laid down her life for the dream.
So I... I'd like you all to join me in a shared telepathic experience.

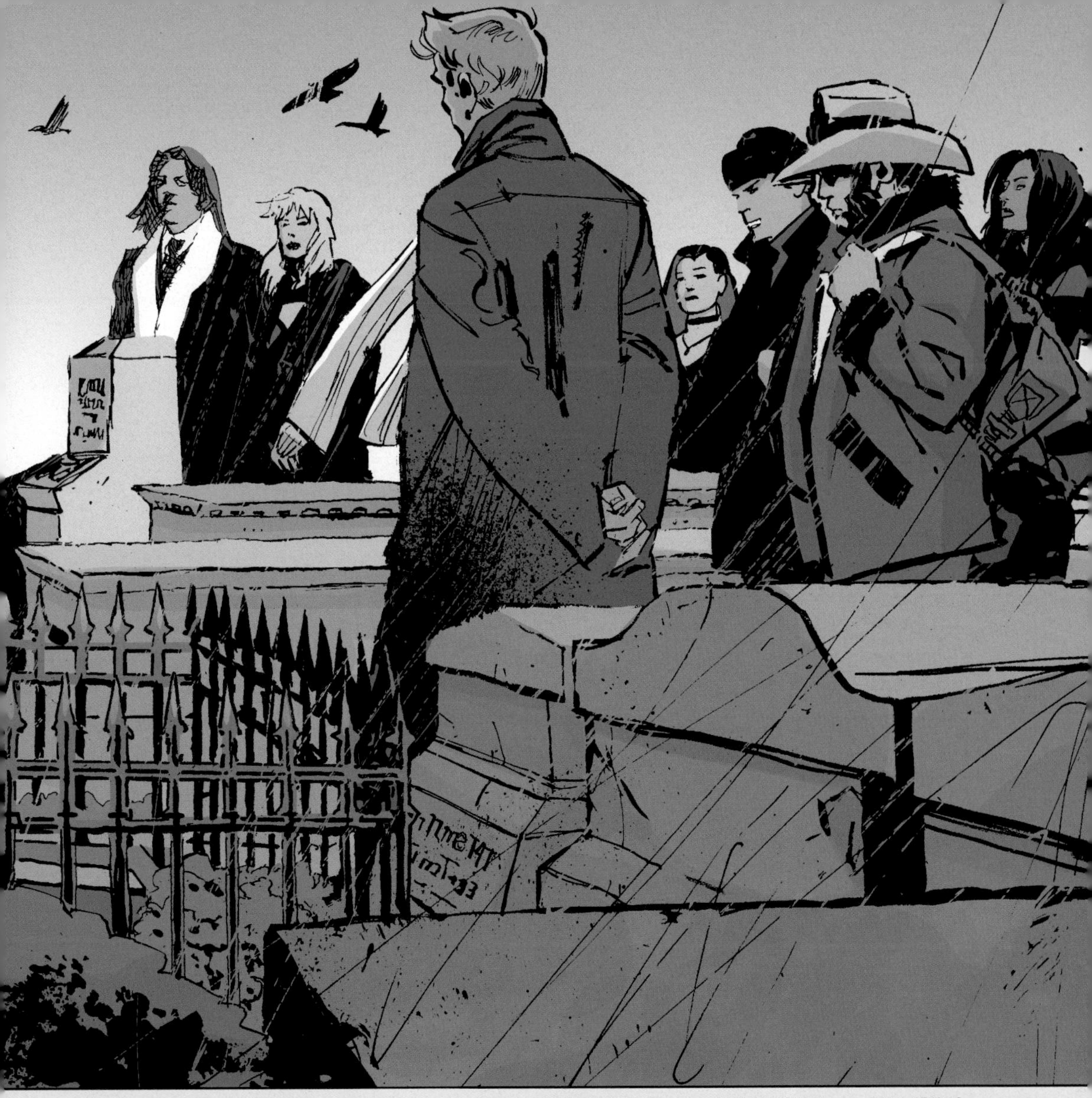

ETHAN VAN SCIVER COVER MIKE RAICHT & NOVA SUMA ASSISTANT EDITORS MIKE MARTS EDITOR JOE QUESADA CHIEF BILL JEMAS PRESIDENT

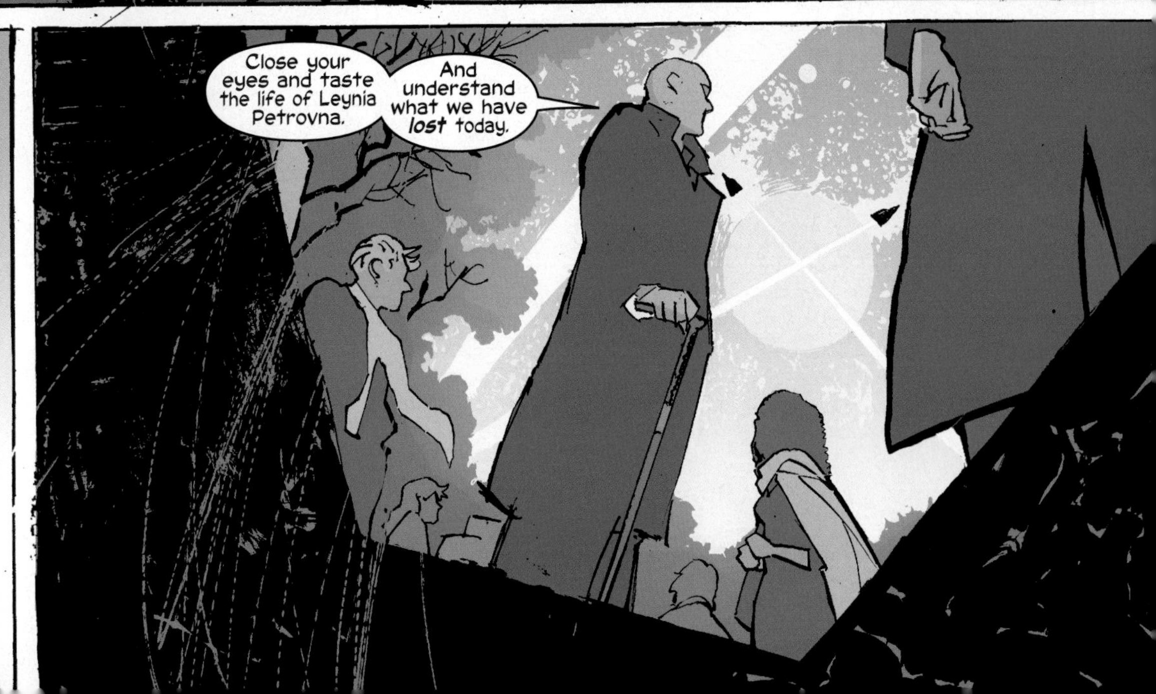
Close your eyes and taste the life of Leynia Petrovna.
And understand what we have *lost* today.

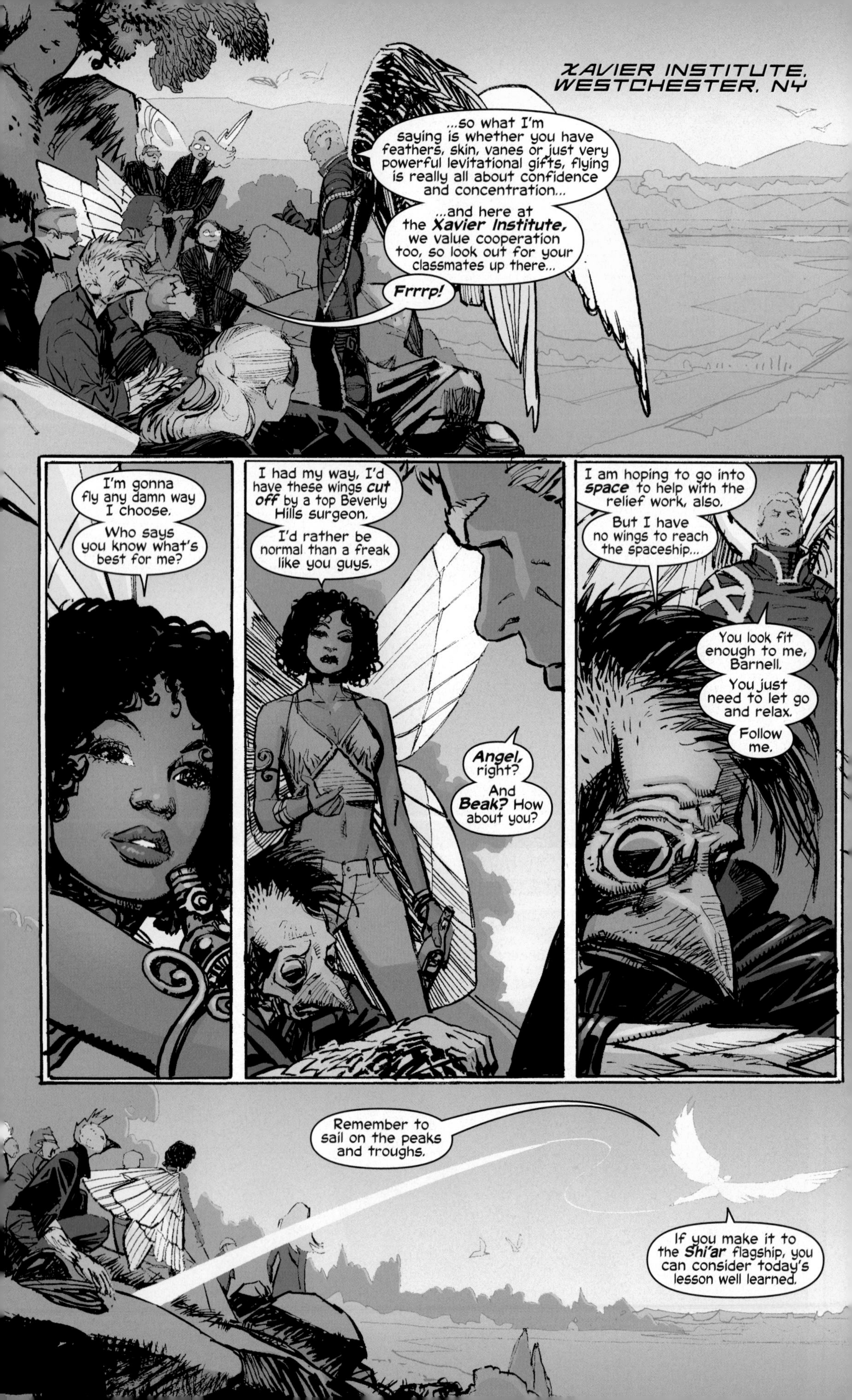

XAVIER INSTITUTE, WESTCHESTER, NY
...so what I'm saying is whether you have feathers, skin, vanes or just very powerful levitational gifts, flying is really all about confidence and concentration...
...and here at the Xavier Institute, we value cooperation too, so look out for your classmates up there...
Frrrp!
I'm gonna fly any damn way I choose.
Who says you know what's best for me?
I had my way, I'd have these wings cut off by a top Beverly Hills surgeon.
I'd rather be normal than a freak like you guys.
Angel, right?
And Beak? How about you?
I am hoping to go into space to help with the relief work, also.
But I have no wings to reach the spaceship...
You look fit enough to me, Barnell.
You just need to let go and relax.
Follow me.
Remember to sail on the peaks and troughs.
If you make it to the Shi'ar flagship, you can consider today's lesson well learned.

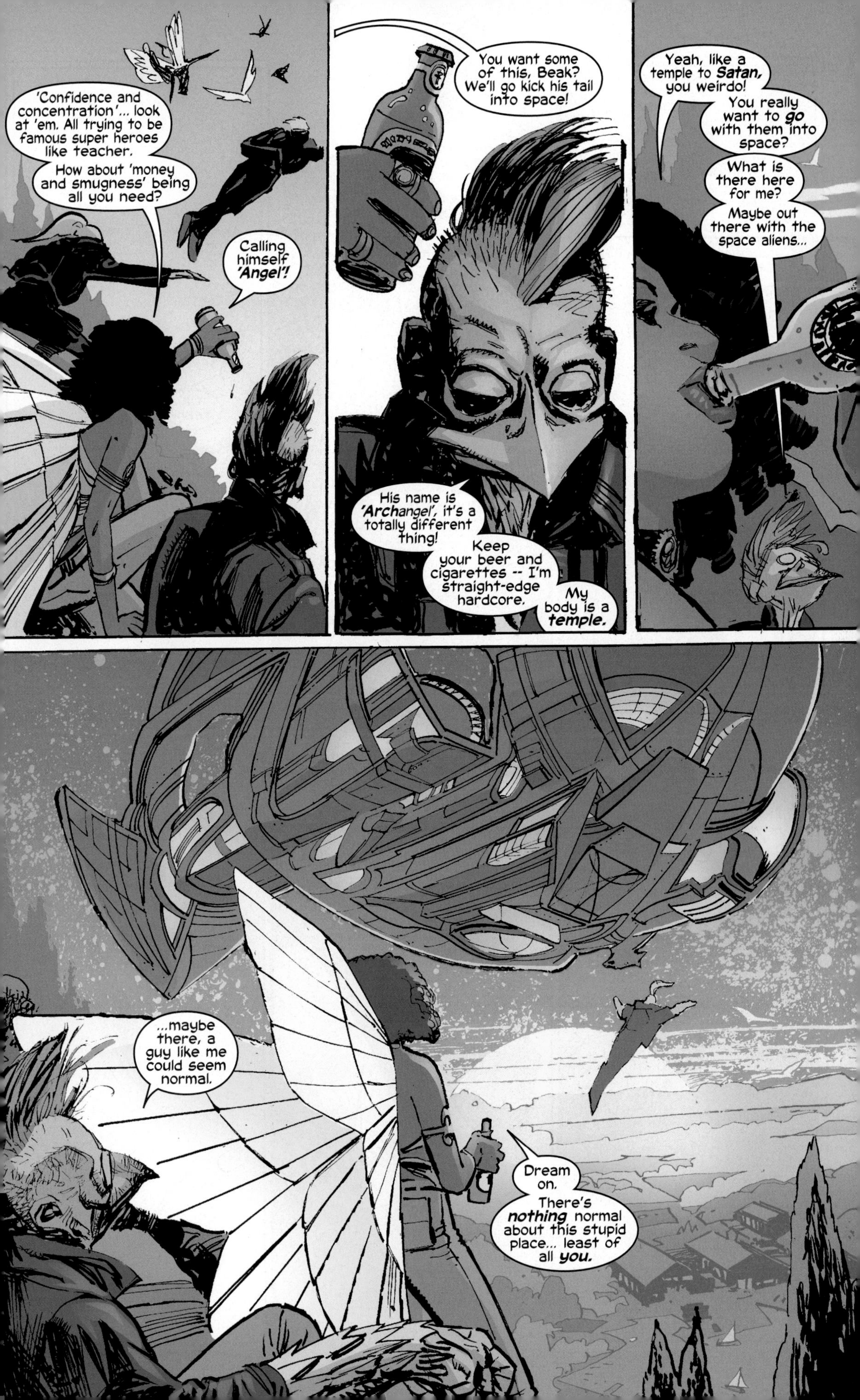
'Confidence and concentration'... look at 'em. All trying to be famous super heroes like teacher.
How about 'money and smugness' being all you need?
Calling himself 'Angel'!
You want some of this, Beak? We'll go kick his tail into space!
His name is 'Archangel', it's a totally different thing!
Keep your beer and cigarettes -- I'm straight-edge hardcore.
My body is a temple.
Yeah, like a temple to Satan, you weirdo!
You really want to go with them into space?
What is there here for me?
Maybe out there with the space aliens...
...maybe there, a guy like me could seem normal.
Dream on.
There's nothing normal about this stupid place... least of all you.

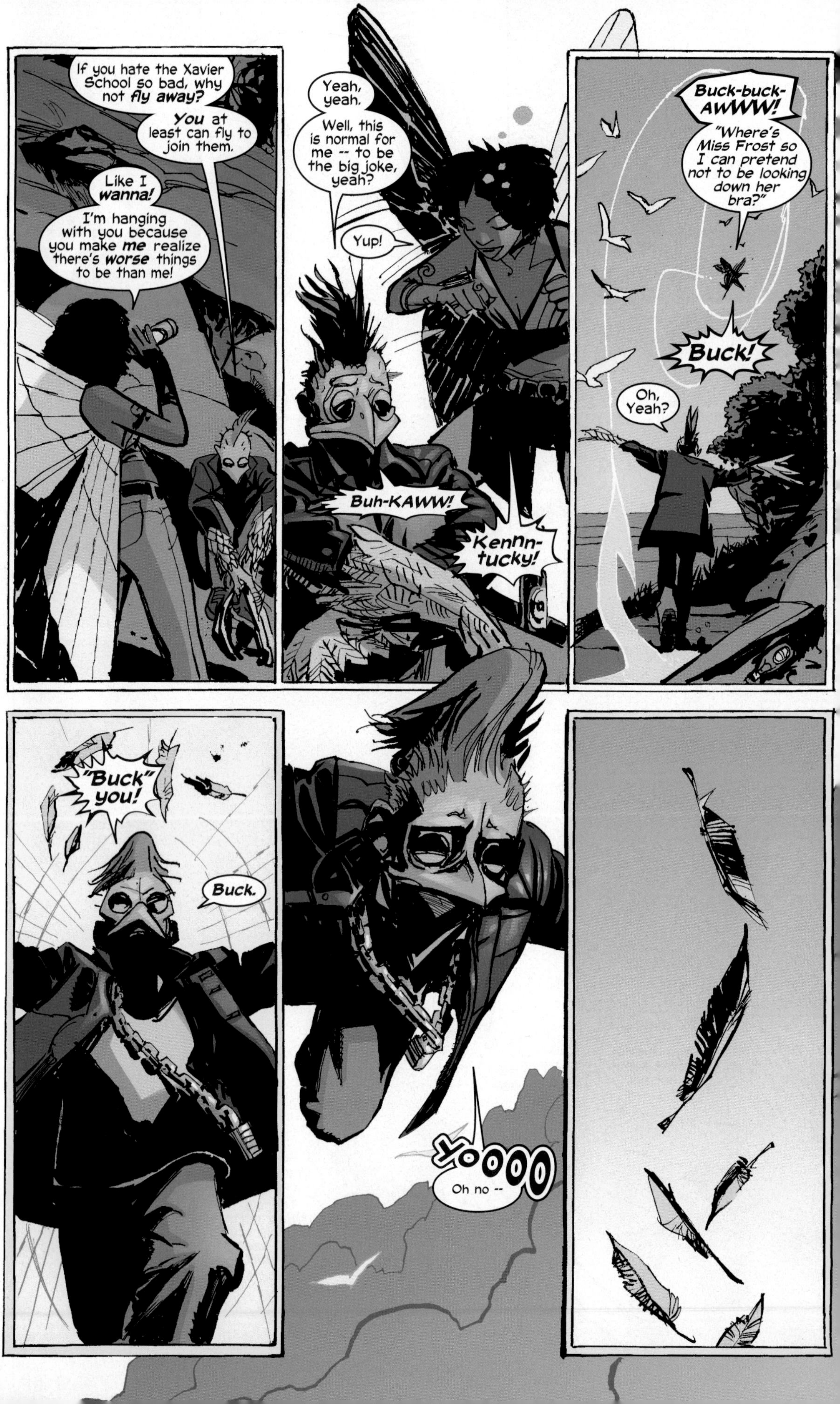
If you hate the Xavier School so bad, why not *fly away?*
You at least can fly to join them.
Like I *wanna!*
I'm hanging with you because you make *me* realize there's *worse* things to be than me!
Yeah, yeah.
Well, this is normal for me -- to be the big joke, yeah?
Yup!
Buh-KAWW!
Kennn-tucky!
Buck-buck-AWWW!
"Where's Miss Frost so I can pretend not to be looking down her bra?"
Buck!
Oh, Yeah?
"Buck" you!
Buck.
YOOOO
Oh no --

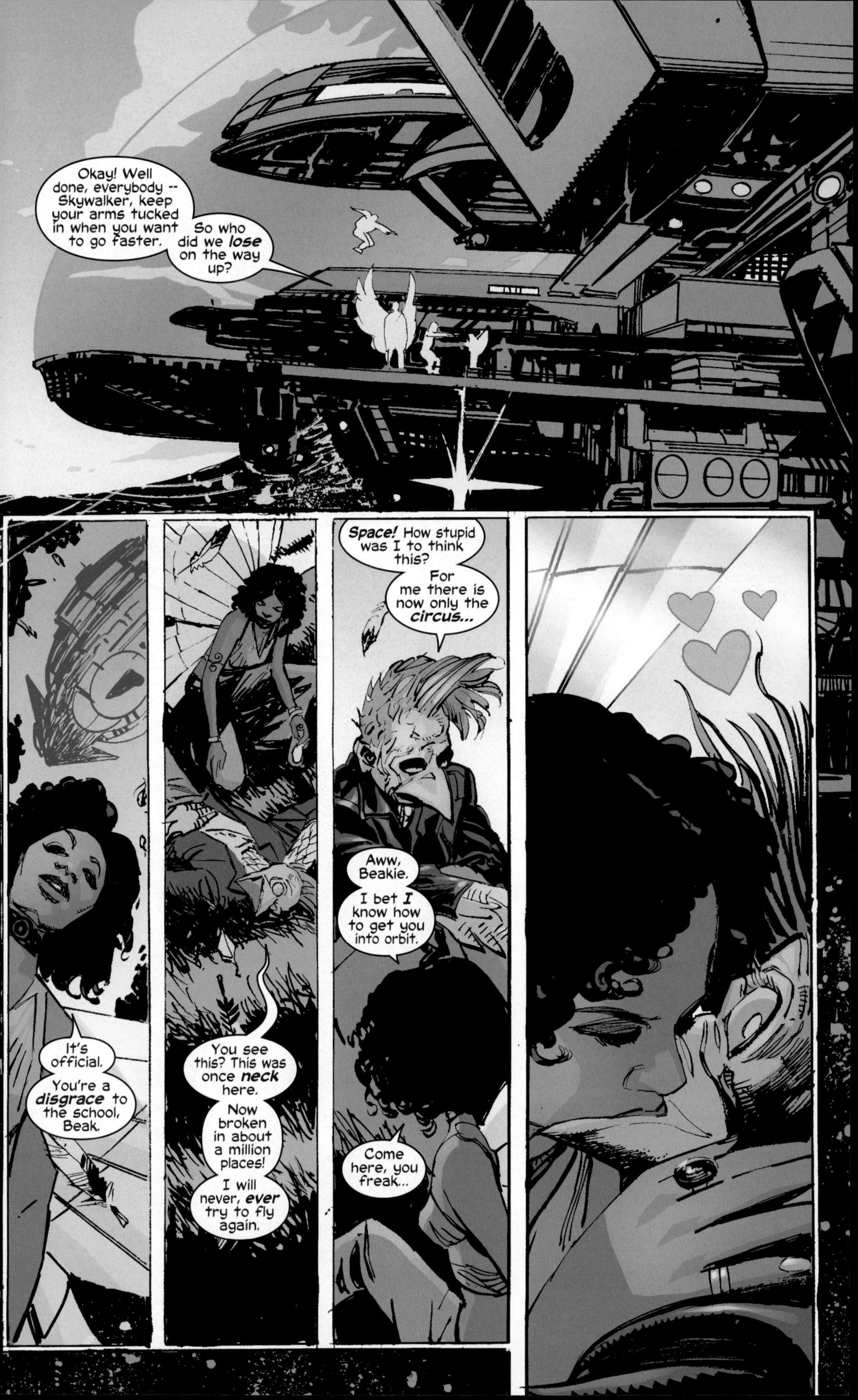

Okay! Well done, everybody -- Skywalker, keep your arms tucked in when you want to go faster.
So who did we *lose* on the way up?
It's official.
You're a *disgrace* to the school, Beak.
You see this? This was once *neck* here.
Now broken in about a million places!
I will never, *ever* try to fly again.
Space! How stupid was I to think this?
For me there is now only the *circus...*
Aww, Beakie.
I bet *I* know how to get you into orbit.
Come here, you freak...

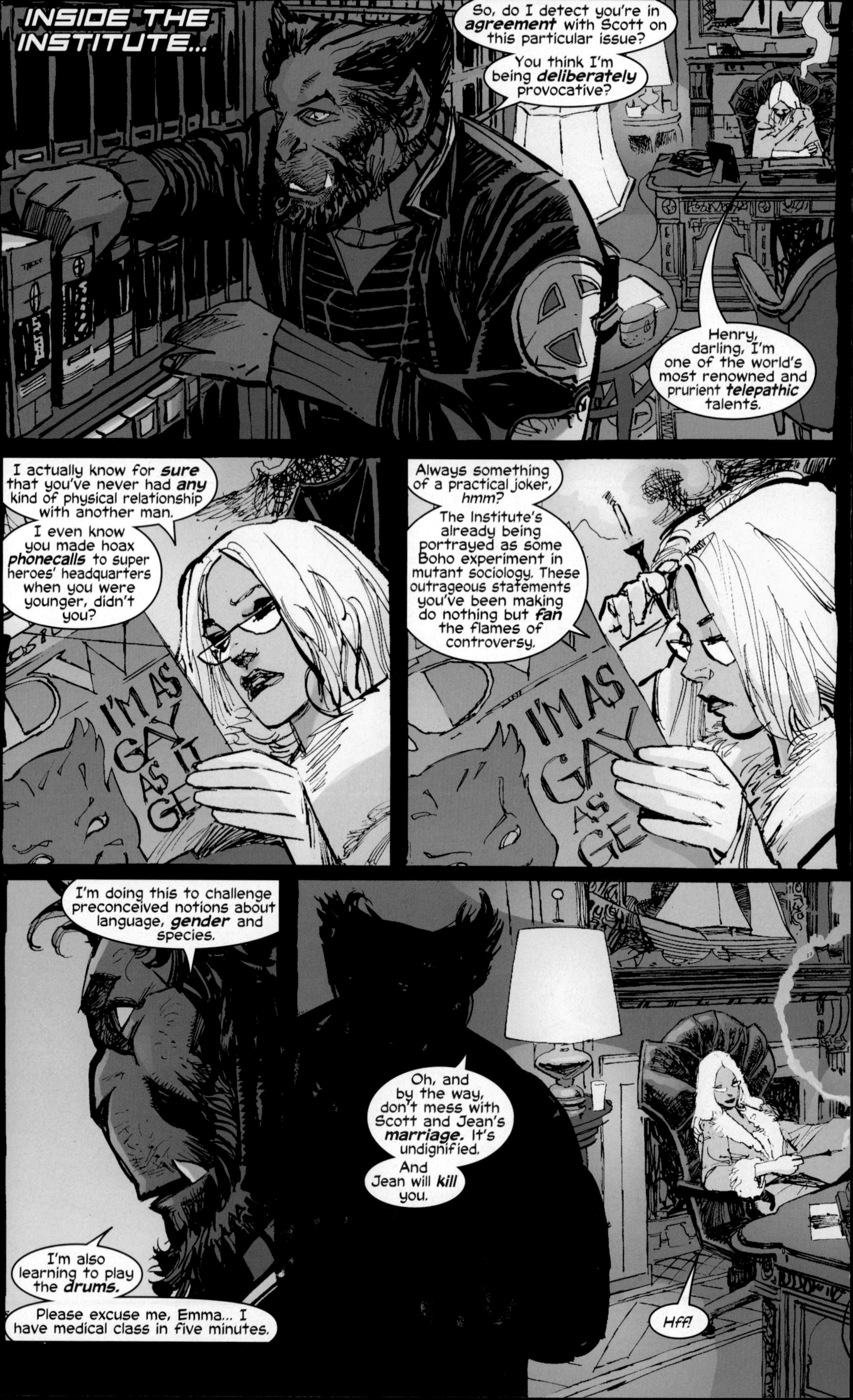
INSIDE THE INSTITUTE...
So, do I detect you're in agreement with Scott on this particular issue?
You think I'm being deliberately provocative?
Henry, darling, I'm one of the world's most renowned and prurient telepathic talents.
I actually know for sure that you've never had any kind of physical relationship with another man.
I even know you made hoax phonecalls to super heroes' headquarters when you were younger, didn't you?
Always something of a practical joker, hmm?
The Institute's already being portrayed as some Boho experiment in mutant sociology. These outrageous statements you've been making do nothing but fan the flames of controversy.
I'M AS GAY AS IT GE
I'm doing this to challenge preconceived notions about language, gender and species.
Oh, and by the way, don't mess with Scott and Jean's marriage. It's undignified.
And Jean will kill you.
I'm also learning to play the drums.
Please excuse me, Emma... I have medical class in five minutes.
Hff!

So how was *Madripoor*, Logan? *Kill* anyone?

Coupla bad guys.

First time you and Jeannie been together for weeks. You two should *talk* more.

I said, 'how was Madripoor?'

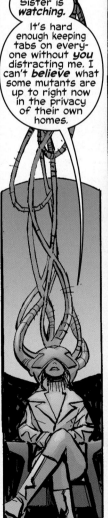

Boys! Big Sister is *watching*.

It's hard enough keeping tabs on everyone without *you* distracting me. I can't *believe* what some mutants are up to right now in the privacy of their own homes.

I was in the air most of the time... we didn't get a *chance* to talk.

All I'm saying...

Man's gotta mow his own lawn.

Rooowwr! Don't listen to him, Scott.

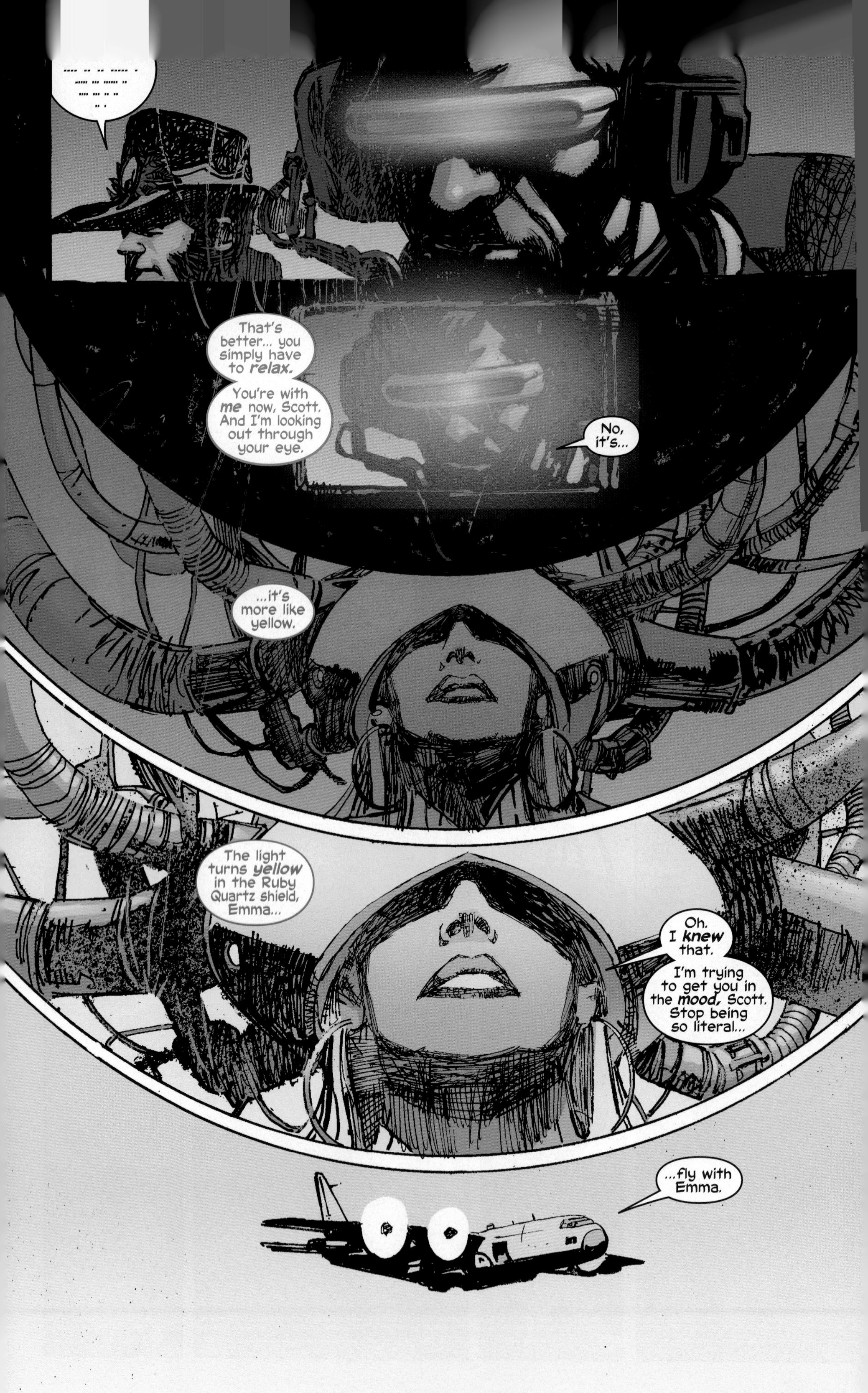
That's better... you simply have to *relax.*
You're with *me* now, Scott. And I'm looking out through your eye.
No, it's...
...it's more like yellow.
The light turns *yellow* in the Ruby Quartz shield, Emma...
Oh. I *knew* that.
I'm trying to get you in the *mood,* Scott. Stop being so literal...
...fly with Emma.

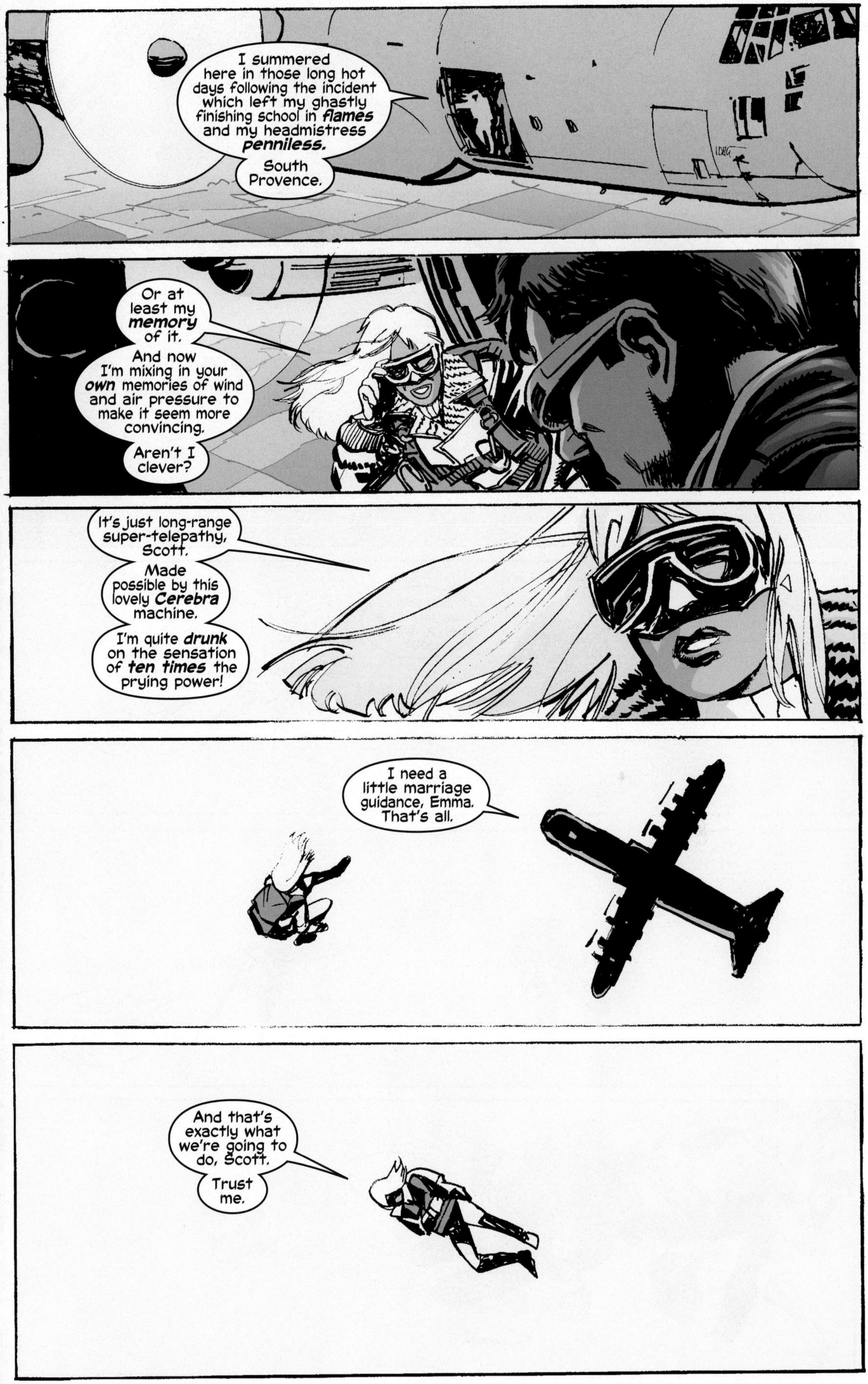

I summered here in those long hot days following the incident which left my ghastly finishing school in *flames* and my headmistress *penniless.*
South Provence.
Or at least my *memory* of it.
And now I'm mixing in your *own* memories of wind and air pressure to make it seem more convincing.
Aren't I clever?
It's just long-range super-telepathy, Scott.
Made possible by this lovely *Cerebra* machine.
I'm quite *drunk* on the sensation of *ten times* the prying power!
I need a little marriage guidance, Emma. That's all.
And that's exactly what we're going to do, Scott.
Trust me.

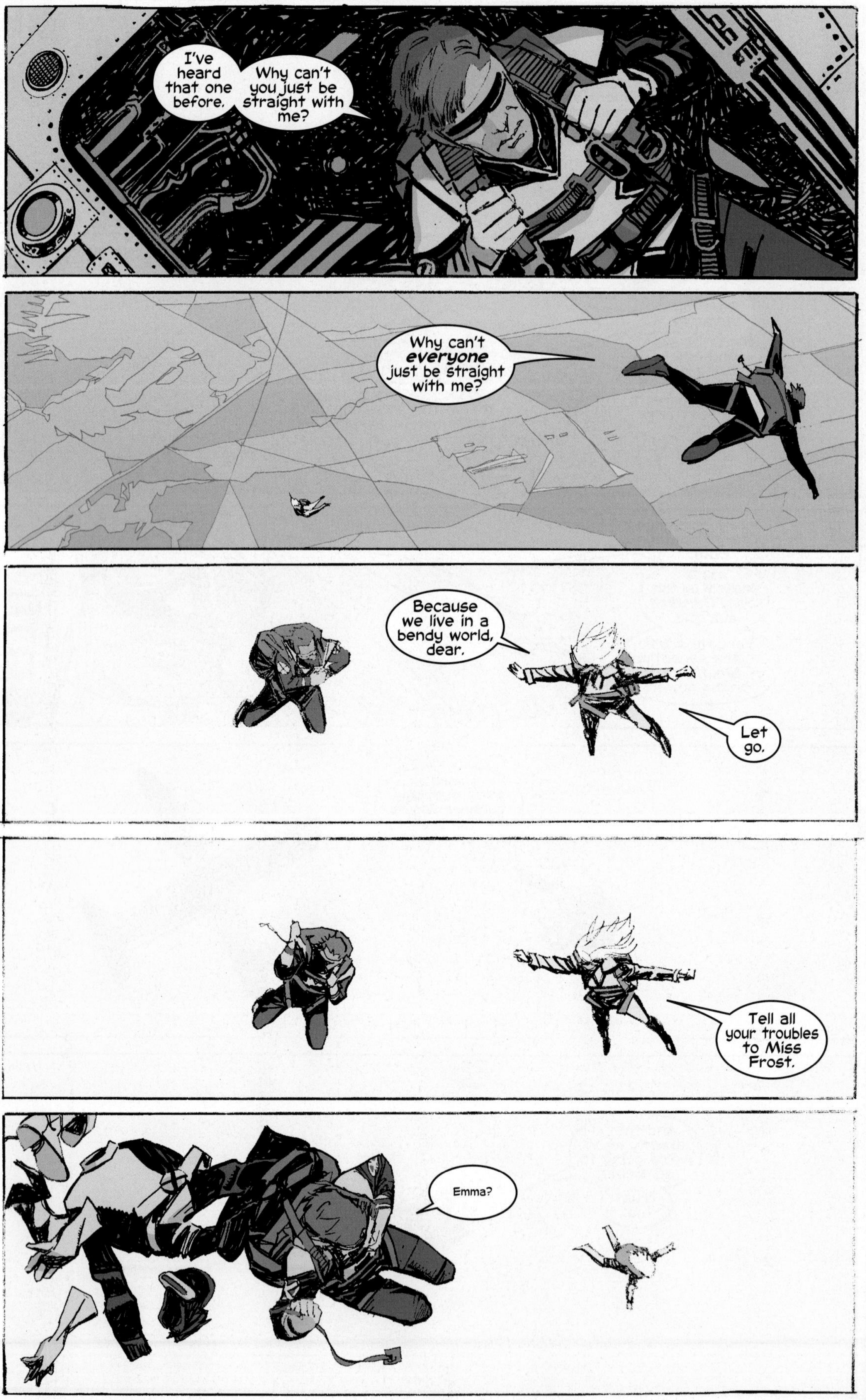
I've heard that one before.
Why can't you just be straight with me?
Why can't *everyone* just be straight with me?
Because we live in a bendy world, dear.
Let go.
Tell all your troubles to Miss Frost.
Emma?

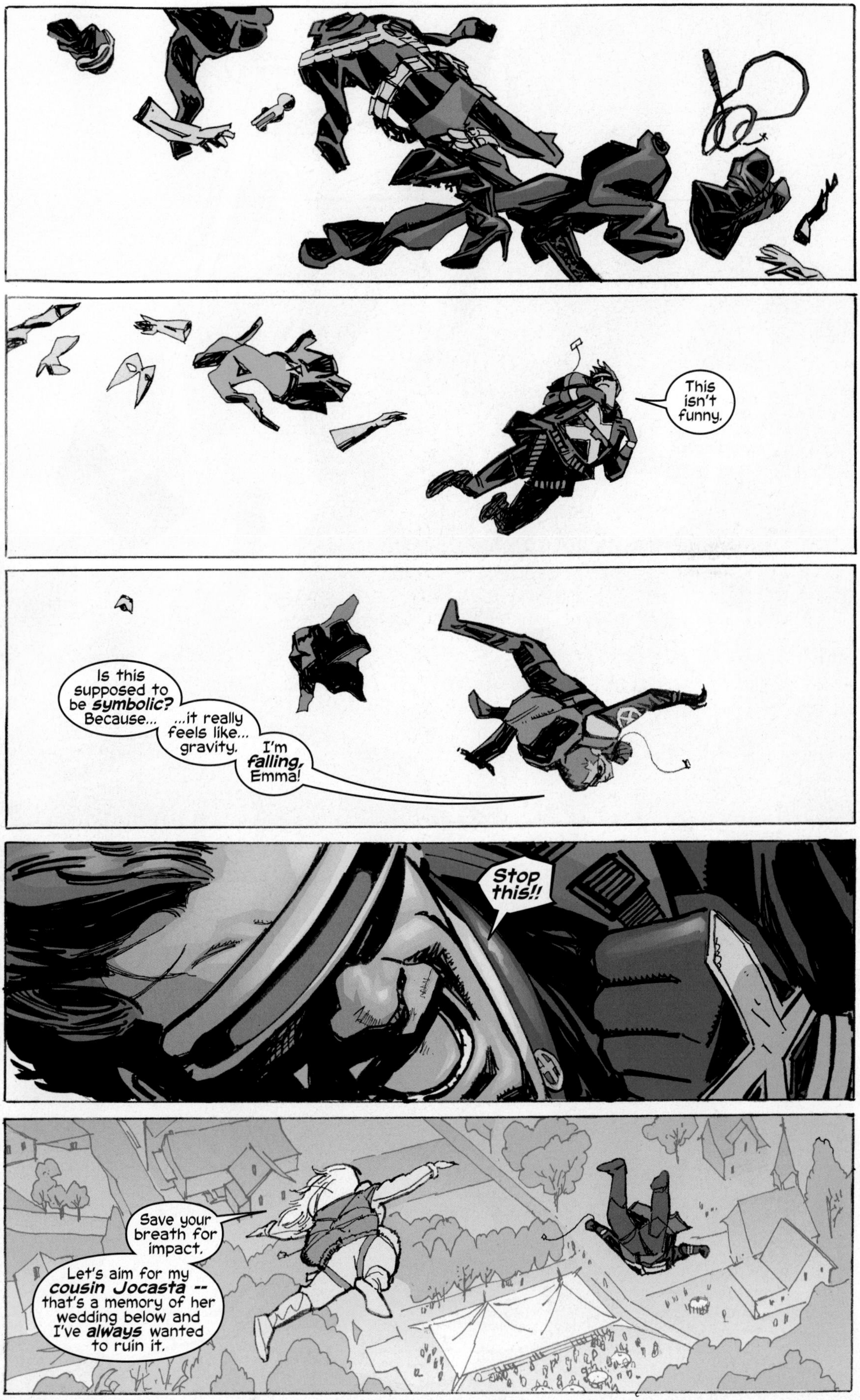

This isn't funny.
Is this supposed to be symbolic? Because...
...it really feels like... gravity.
I'm falling, Emma!
Stop this!!
Save your breath for impact.
Let's aim for my cousin Jocasta -- that's a memory of her wedding below and I've always wanted to ruin it.

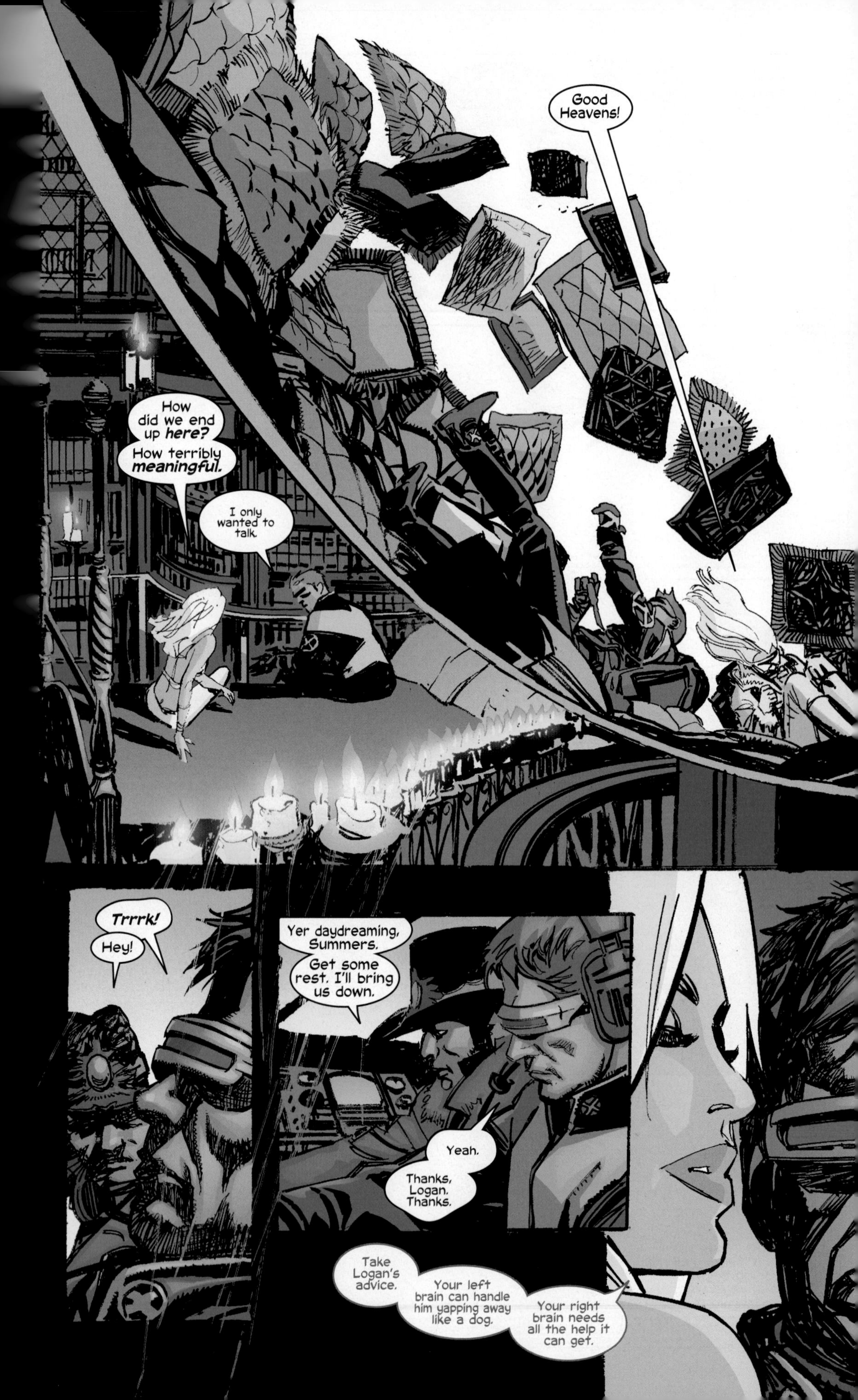
Good Heavens!
How did we end up *here?*
How terribly *meaningful.*
I only wanted to talk.
Trrrk!
Hey!
Yer daydreaming, Summers.
Get some rest. I'll bring us down.
Yeah.
Thanks, Logan. Thanks.
Take Logan's advice.
Your left brain can handle him yapping away like a dog.
Your right brain needs all the help it can get.

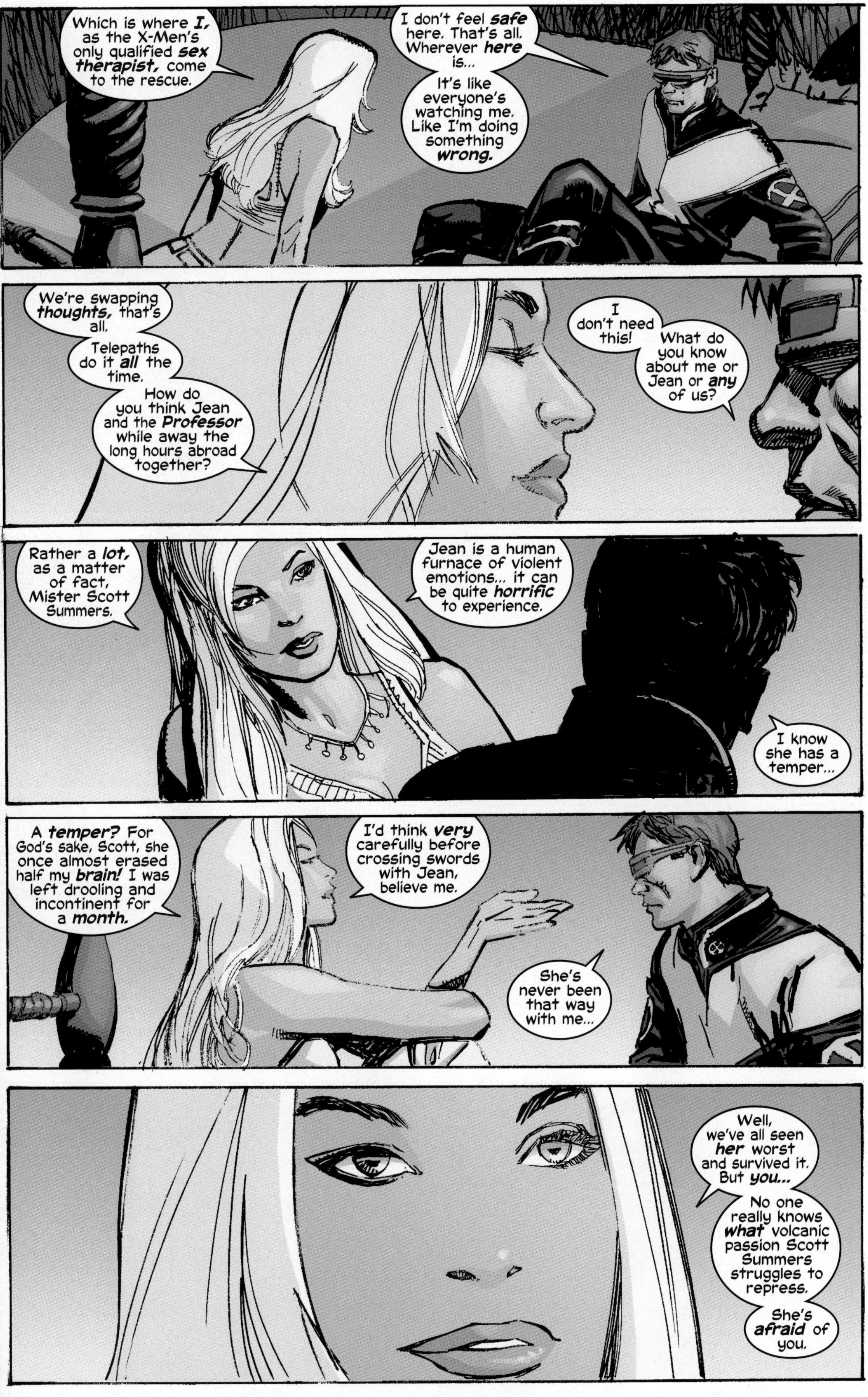
Which is where I, as the X-Men's only qualified sex therapist, come to the rescue.
I don't feel safe here. That's all. Wherever here is...
It's like everyone's watching me. Like I'm doing something wrong.
We're swapping thoughts, that's all.
Telepaths do it all the time.
How do you think Jean and the Professor while away the long hours abroad together?
I don't need this!
What do you know about me or Jean or any of us?
Rather a lot, as a matter of fact, Mister Scott Summers.
Jean is a human furnace of violent emotions... it can be quite horrific to experience.
I know she has a temper...
A temper? For God's sake, Scott, she once almost erased half my brain! I was left drooling and incontinent for a month.
I'd think very carefully before crossing swords with Jean, believe me.
She's never been that way with me...
Well, we've all seen her worst and survived it. But you...
No one really knows what volcanic passion Scott Summers struggles to repress.
She's afraid of you.

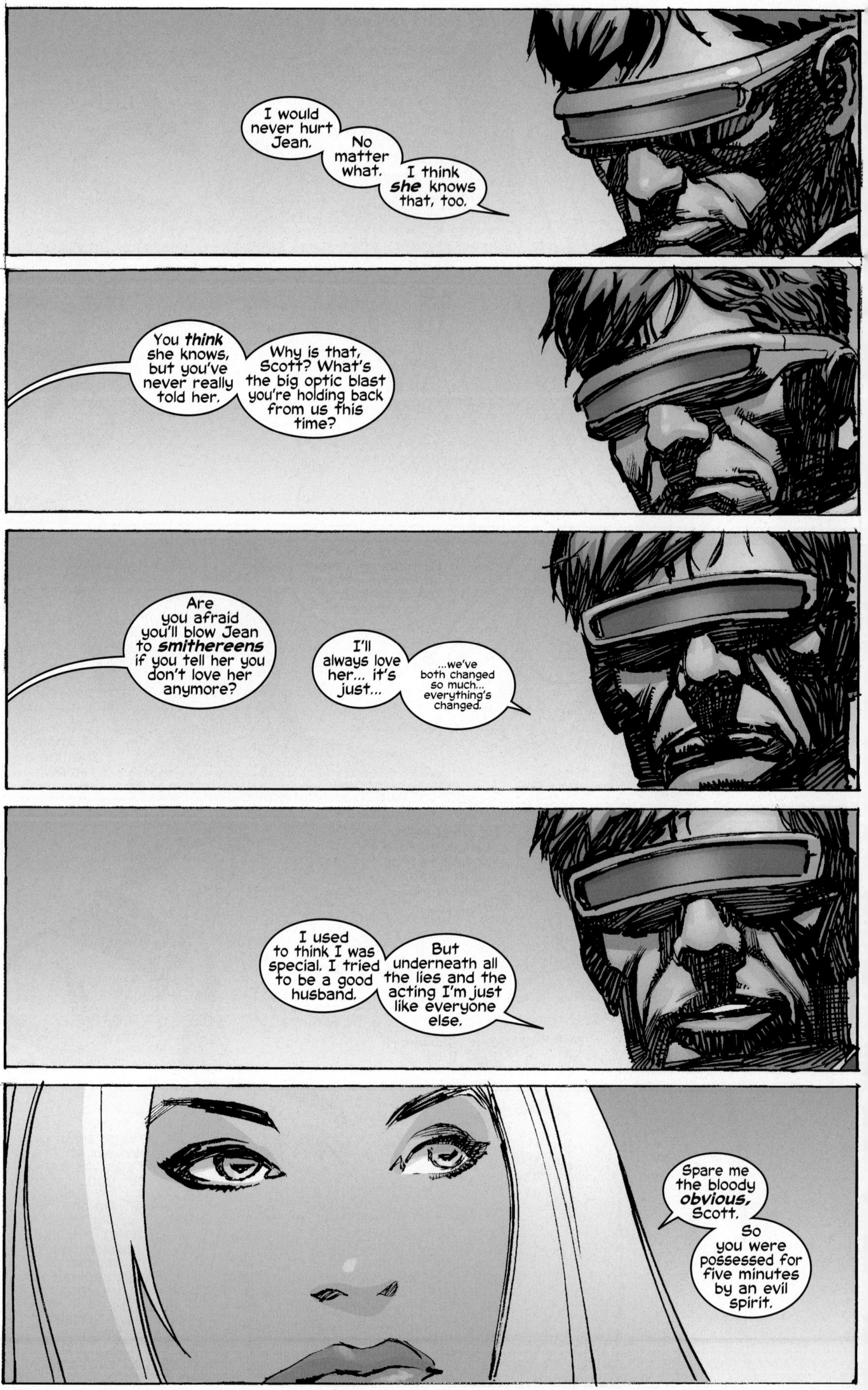

I would never hurt Jean.
No matter what.
I think *she* knows that, too.
You *think* she knows, but you've never really told her.
Why is that, Scott? What's the big optic blast you're holding back from us this time?
Are you afraid you'll blow Jean to *smithereens* if you tell her you don't love her anymore?
I'll always love her... it's just...
...we've both changed so much... everything's changed.
I used to think I was special. I tried to be a good husband.
But underneath all the lies and the acting I'm just like everyone else.
Spare me the bloody *obvious,* Scott.
So you were possessed for five minutes by an evil spirit.

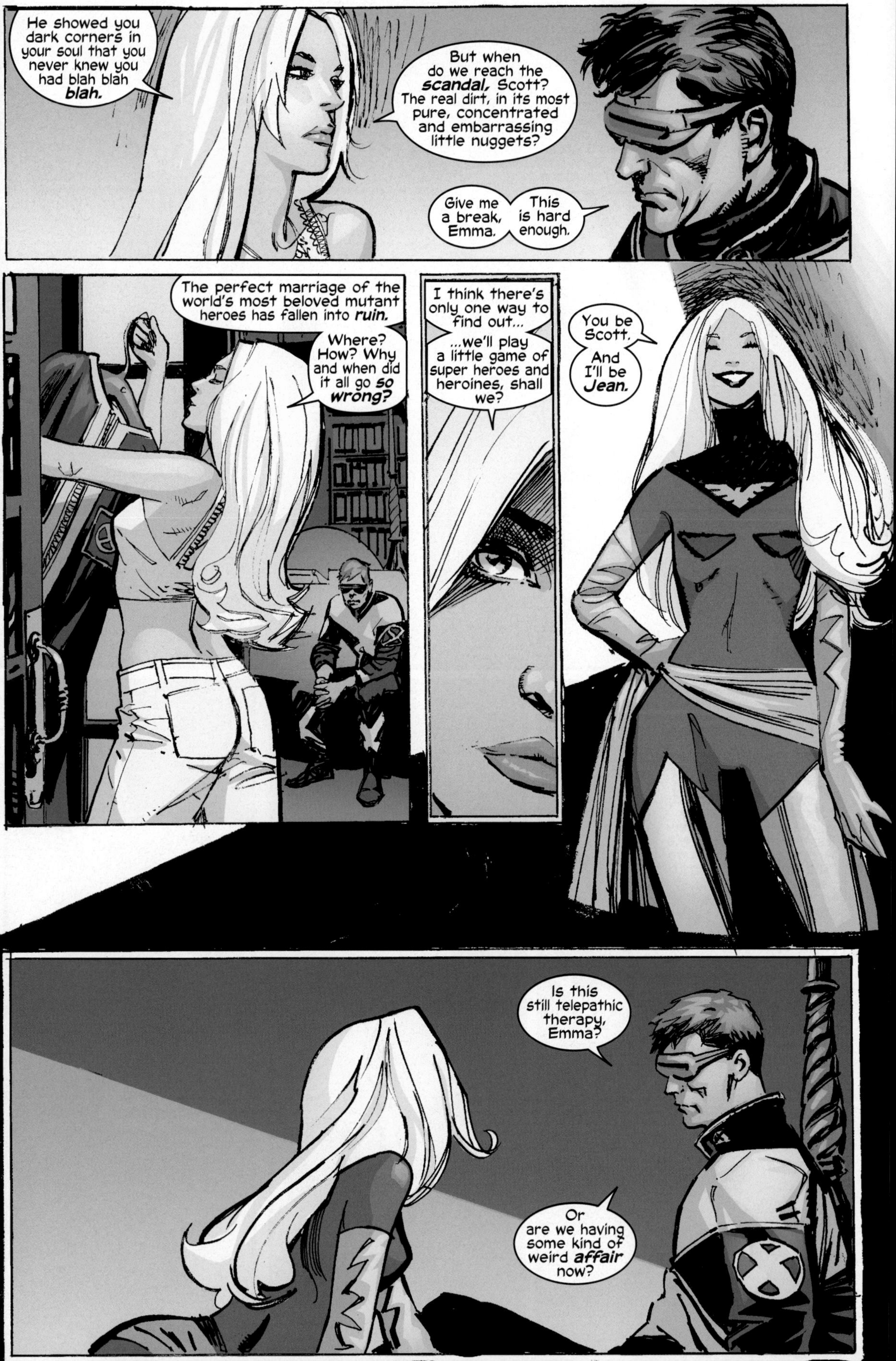
He showed you dark corners in your soul that you never knew you had blah blah **blah.**
But when do we reach the ***scandal,*** Scott? The real dirt, in its most pure, concentrated and embarrassing little nuggets?
Give me a break, Emma.
This is hard enough.
The perfect marriage of the world's most beloved mutant heroes has fallen into ***ruin.***
Where? How? Why and when did it all go ***so wrong?***
I think there's only one way to find out...
...we'll play a little game of super heroes and heroines, shall we?
You be Scott.
And I'll be ***Jean.***
Is this still telepathic therapy, Emma?
Or are we having some kind of weird ***affair*** now?

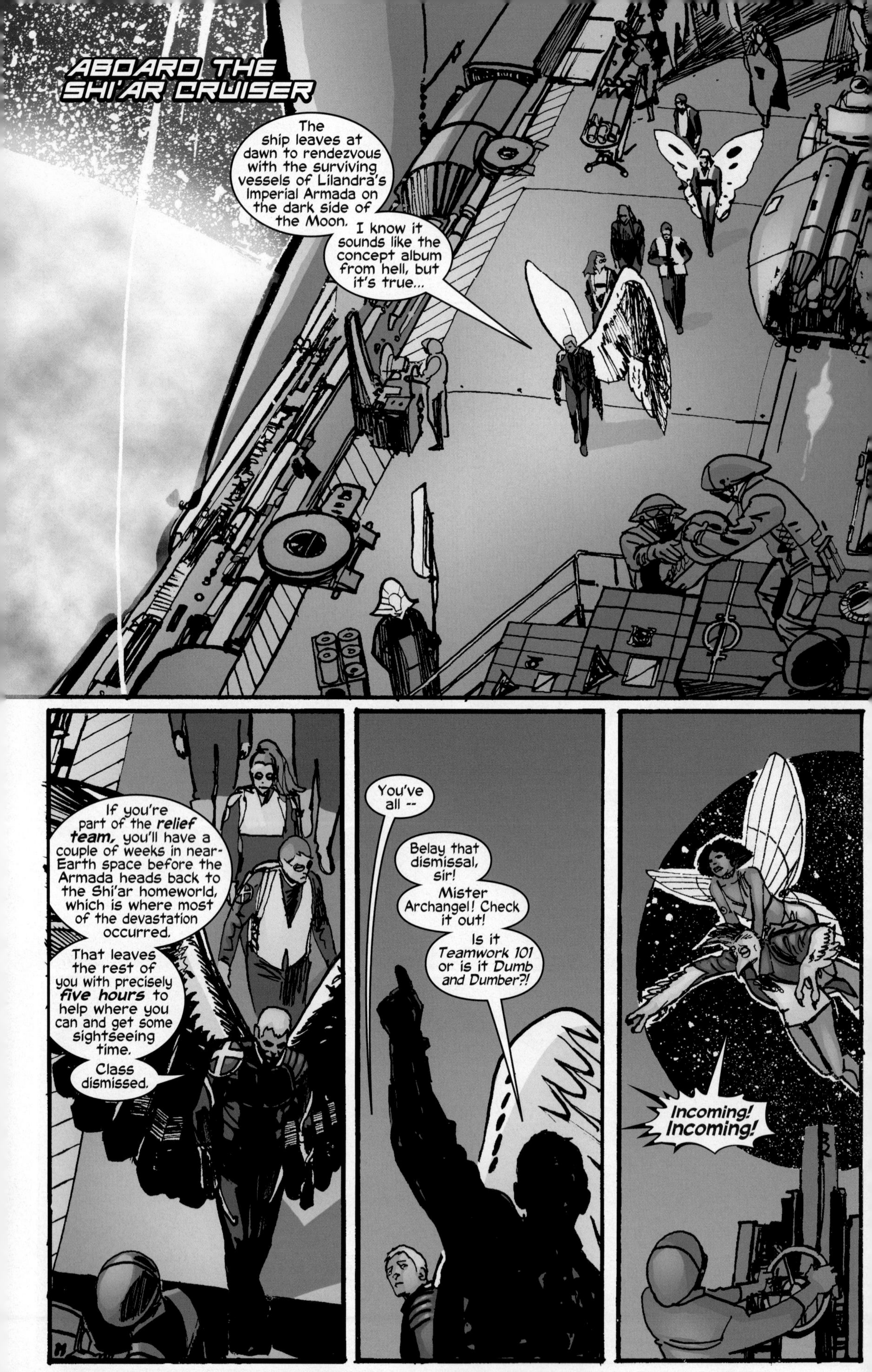
ABOARD THE SHI'AR CRUISER
The ship leaves at dawn to rendezvous with the surviving vessels of Lilandra's Imperial Armada on the dark side of the Moon.
I know it sounds like the concept album from hell, but it's true...
If you're part of the **relief team,** you'll have a couple of weeks in near-Earth space before the Armada heads back to the Shi'ar homeworld, which is where most of the devastation occurred.
That leaves the rest of you with precisely ***five hours*** to help where you can and get some sightseeing time.
Class dismissed.
You've all --
Belay that dismissal, sir!
Mister Archangel! Check it out!
Is it *Teamwork 101* or is it *Dumb and Dumber?!*
Incoming! Incoming!

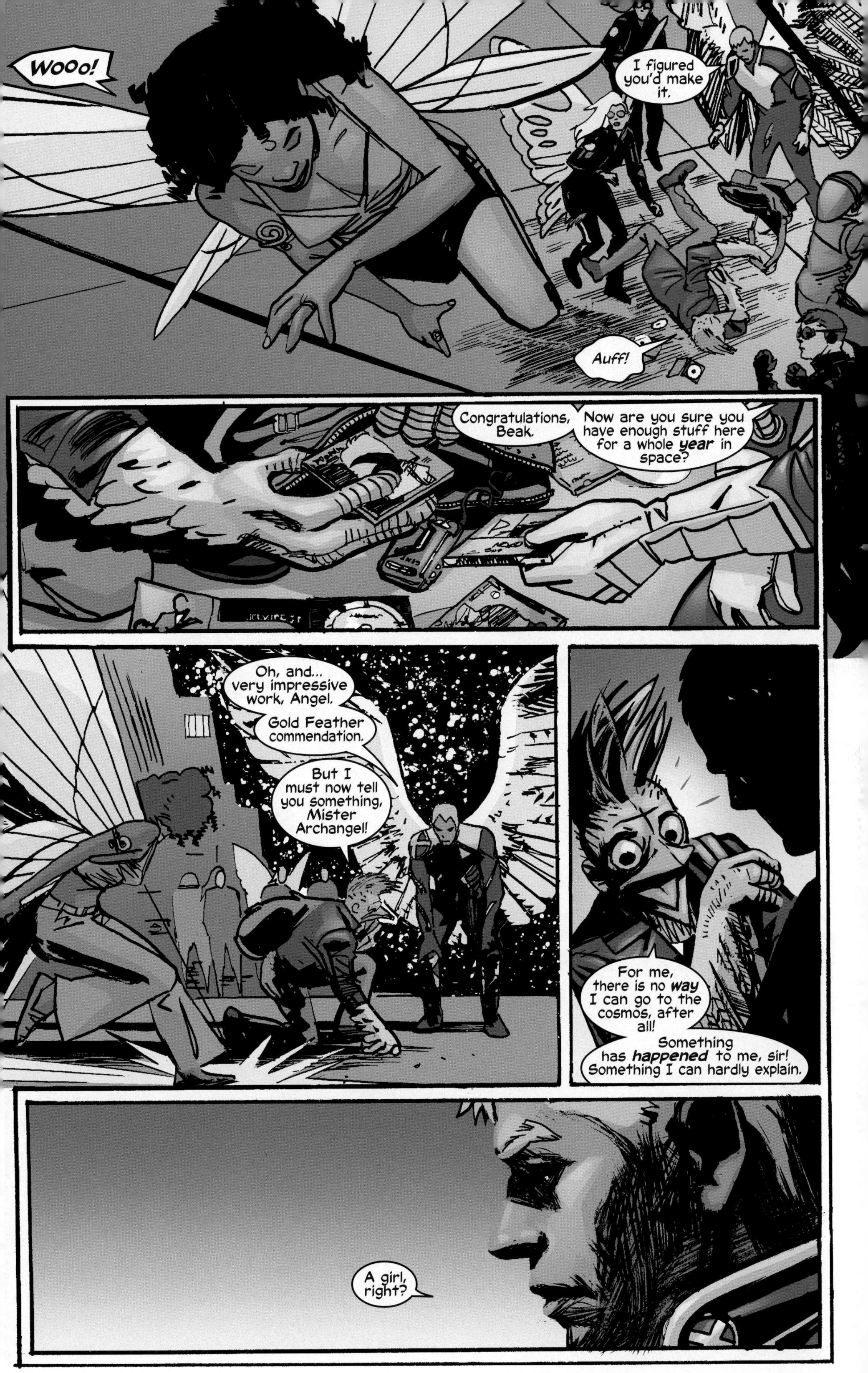
WOOO!
I figured you'd make it.
Auff!
Congratulations, Beak.
Now are you sure you have enough stuff here for a whole *year* in space?
Oh, and... very impressive work, Angel.
Gold Feather commendation.
But I must now tell you something, Mister Archangel!
For me, there is no *way* I can go to the cosmos, after all!
Something has *happened* to me, sir! Something I can hardly explain.
A girl, right?

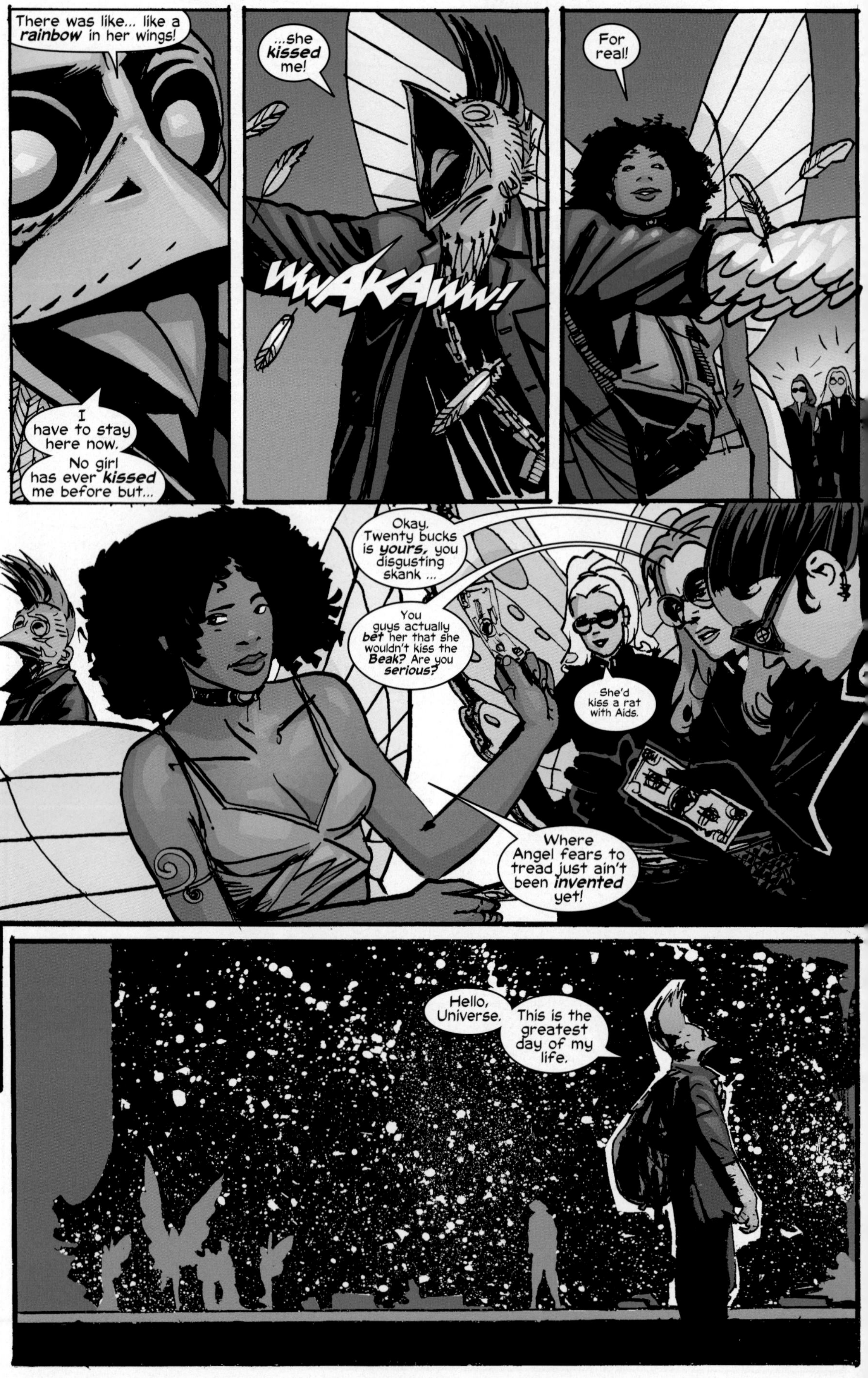
There was like... like a rainbow in her wings!
I have to stay here now.
No girl has ever kissed me before but...
...she kissed me!
WWAKAWW!
For real!
Okay. Twenty bucks is yours, you disgusting skank ...
You guys actually bet her that she wouldn't kiss the Beak? Are you serious?
She'd kiss a rat with Aids.
Where Angel fears to tread just ain't been invented yet!
Hello, Universe.
This is the greatest day of my life.

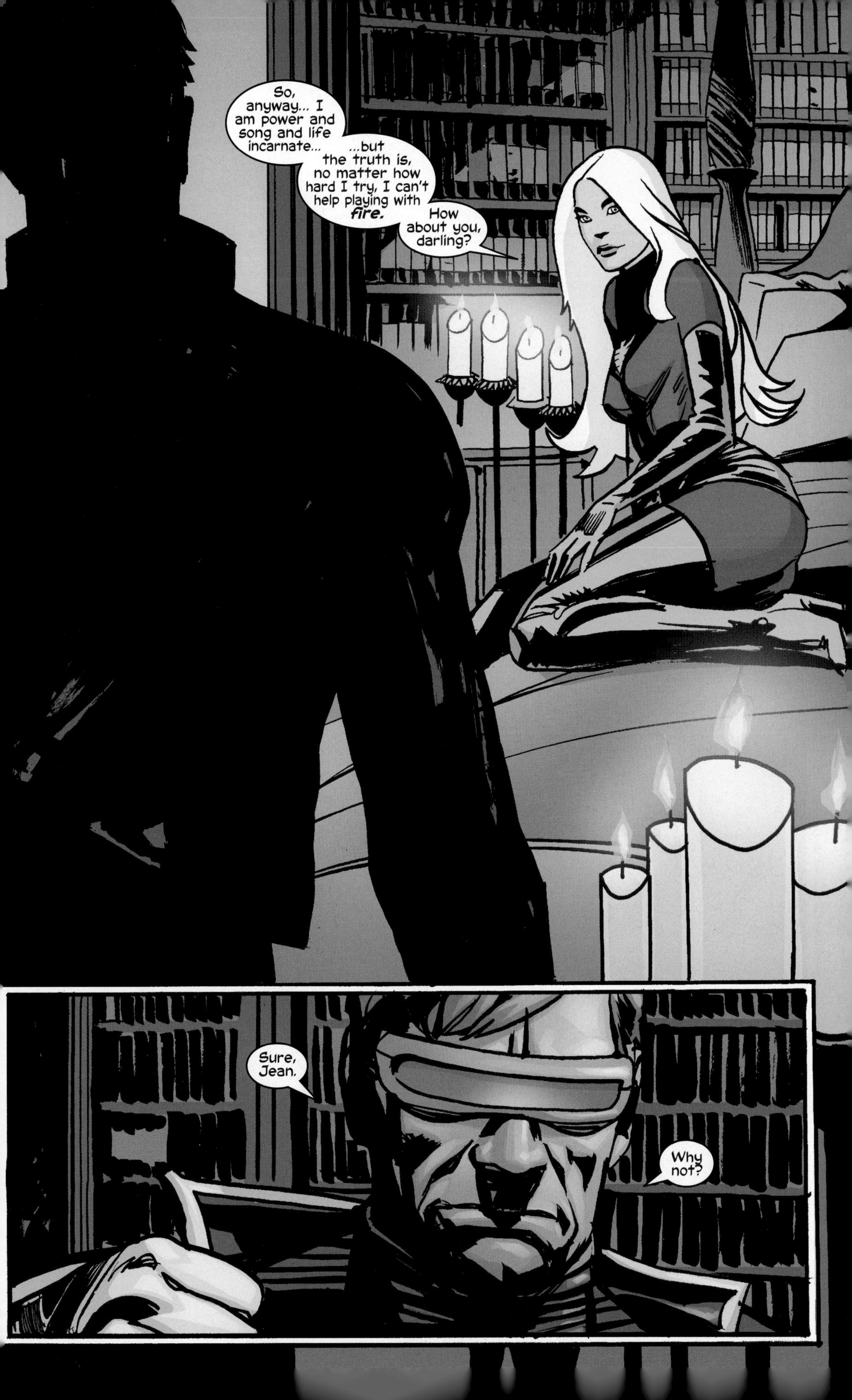
So, anyway... I am power and song and life incarnate...
...but the truth is, no matter how hard I try, I can't help playing with fire.
How about you, darling?
Sure, Jean.
Why not?

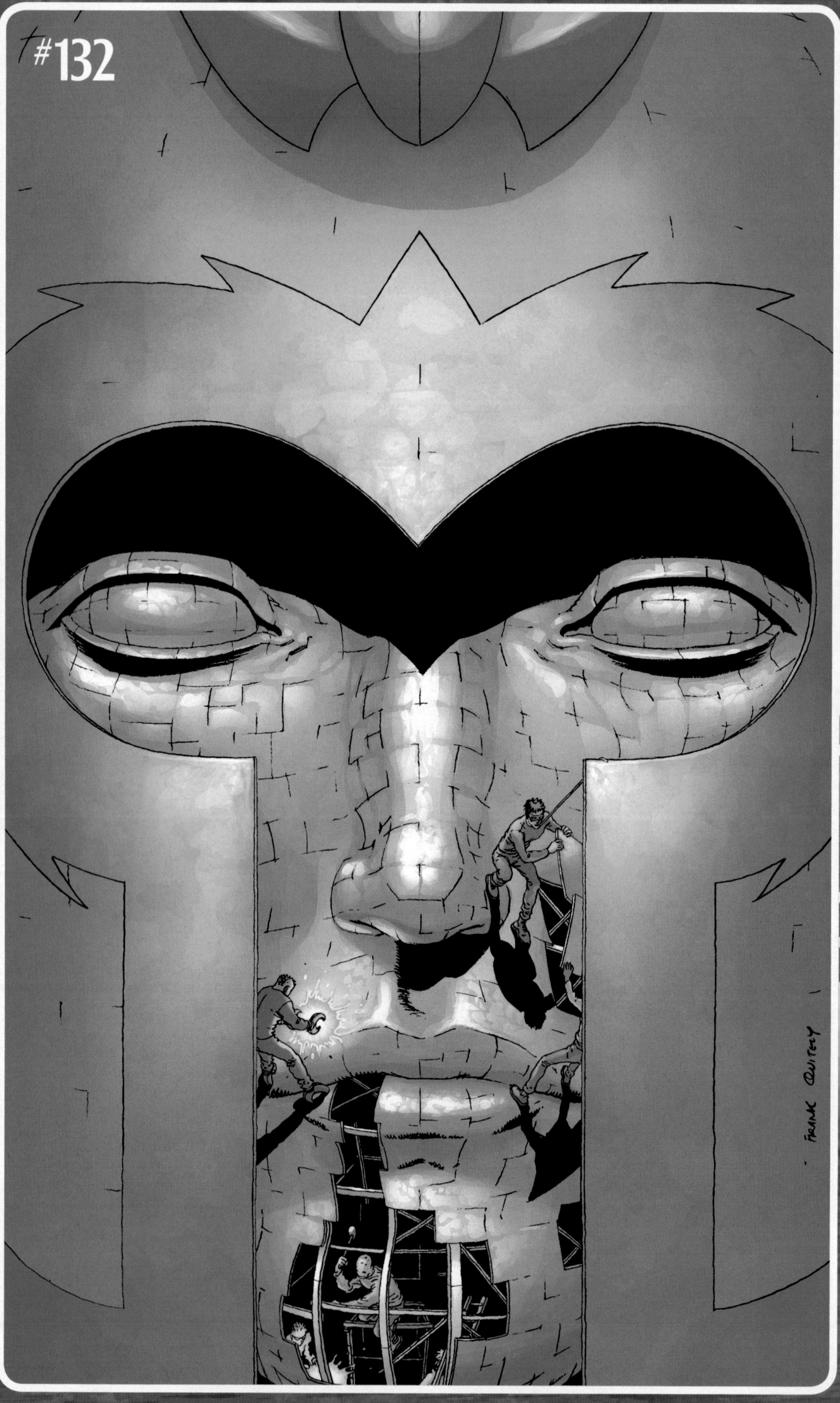
#132
FRANK QUITELY

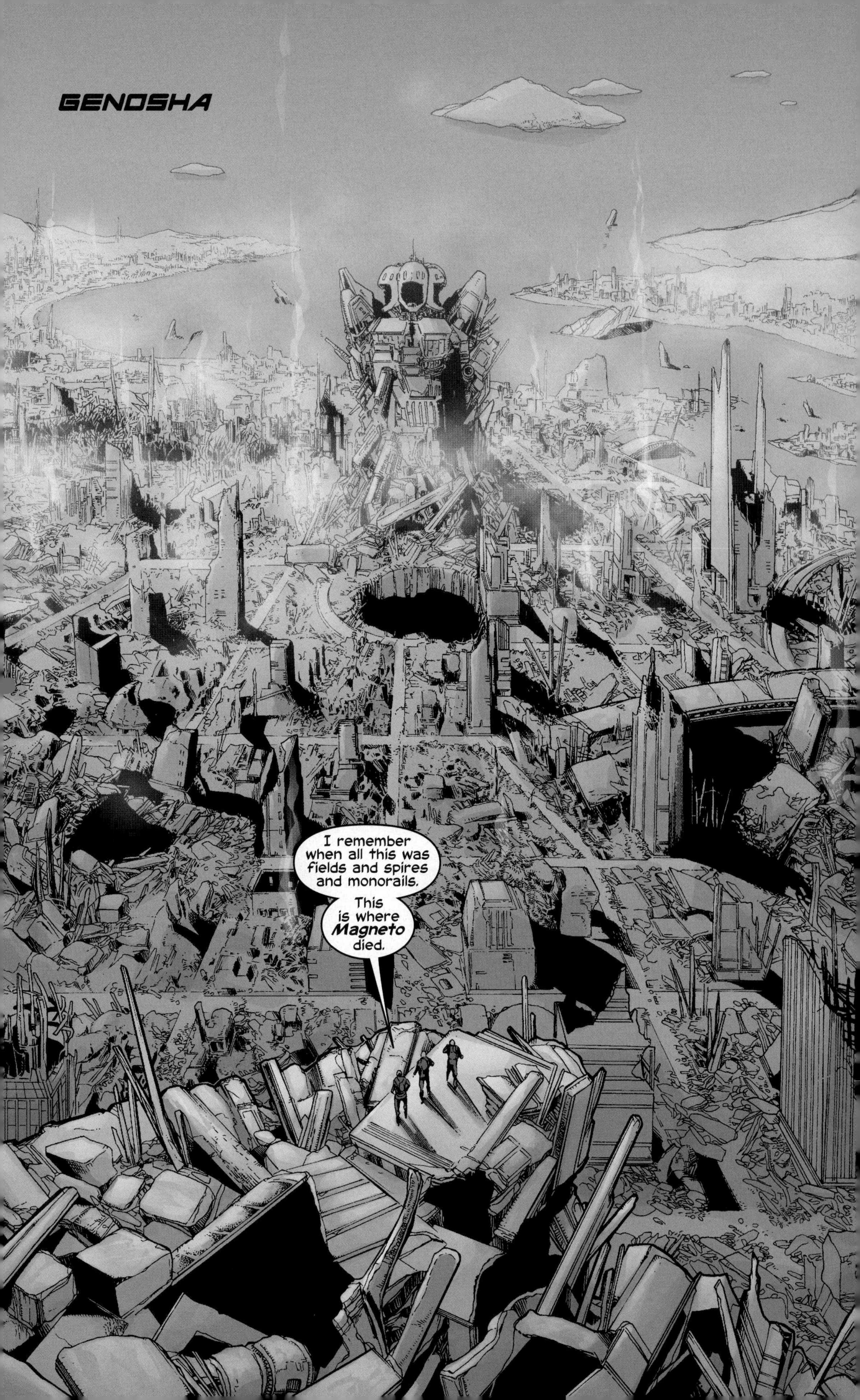
GENOSHA
I remember when all this was fields and spires and monorails.
This is where Magneto died.

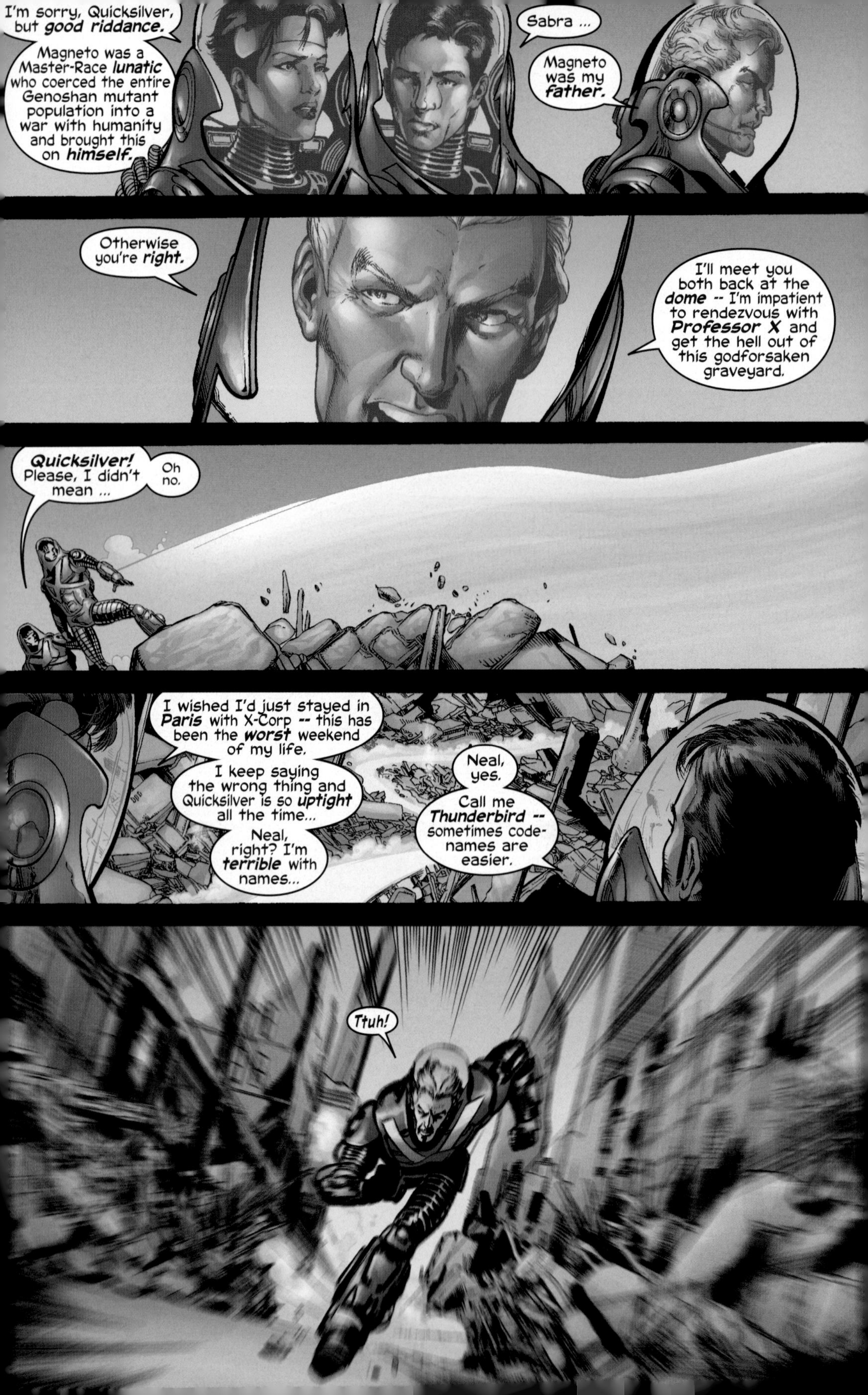
I'm sorry, Quicksilver, but good riddance.
Magneto was a Master-Race lunatic who coerced the entire Genoshan mutant population into a war with humanity and brought this on himself.
Sabra ...
Magneto was my father.
Otherwise you're right.
I'll meet you both back at the dome -- I'm impatient to rendezvous with Professor X and get the hell out of this godforsaken graveyard.
Quicksilver! Please, I didn't mean ...
Oh no.
I wished I'd just stayed in Paris with X-Corp -- this has been the worst weekend of my life.
I keep saying the wrong thing and Quicksilver is so uptight all the time...
Neal, right? I'm terrible with names...
Neal, yes.
Call me Thunderbird -- sometimes code-names are easier.
Ttuh!

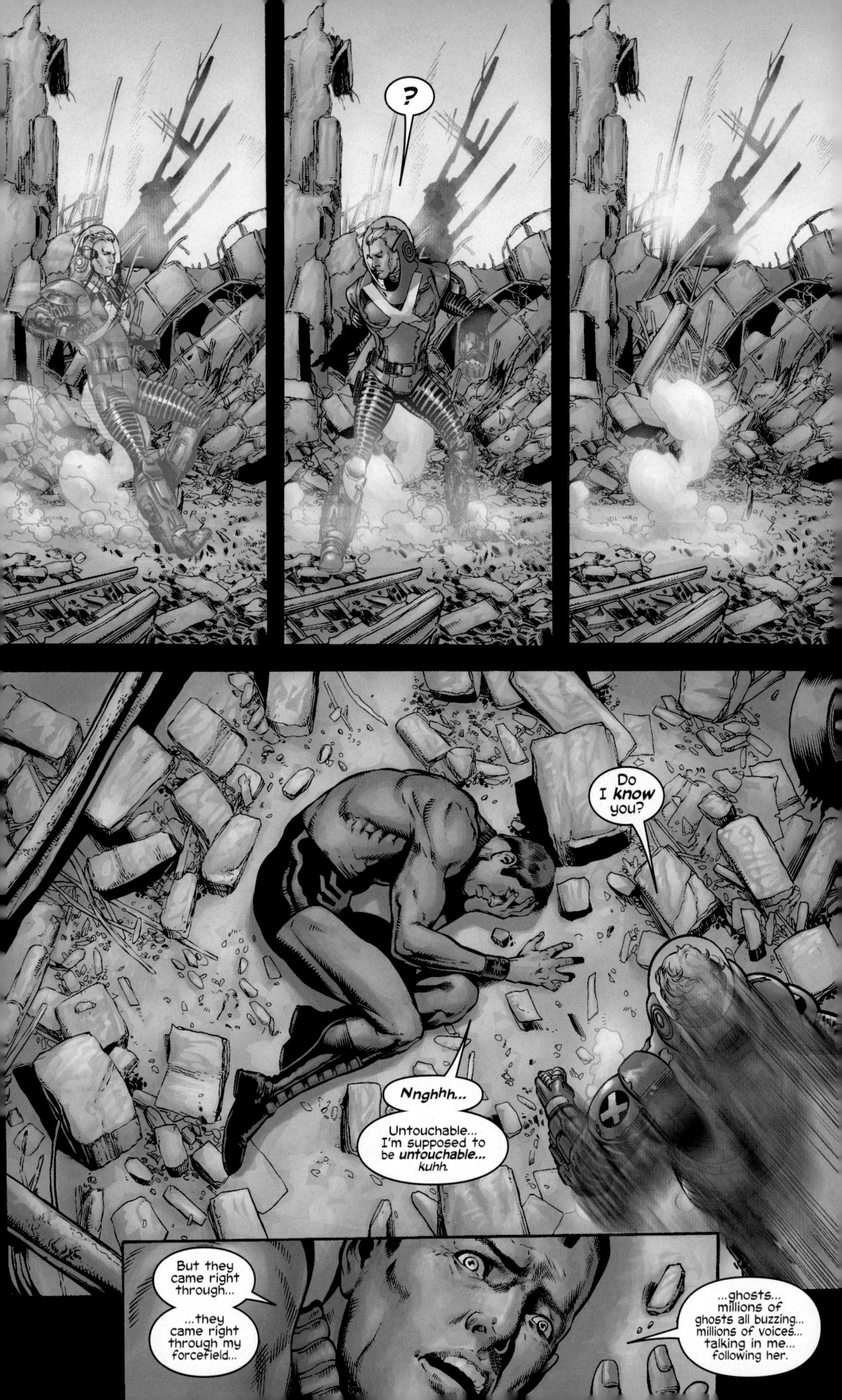
?
Do I know you?
Nnghhh...
Untouchable... I'm supposed to be untouchable... kuhh.
But they came right through...
...they came right through my forcefield...
...ghosts... millions of ghosts all buzzing... millions of voices... talking in me... following her.

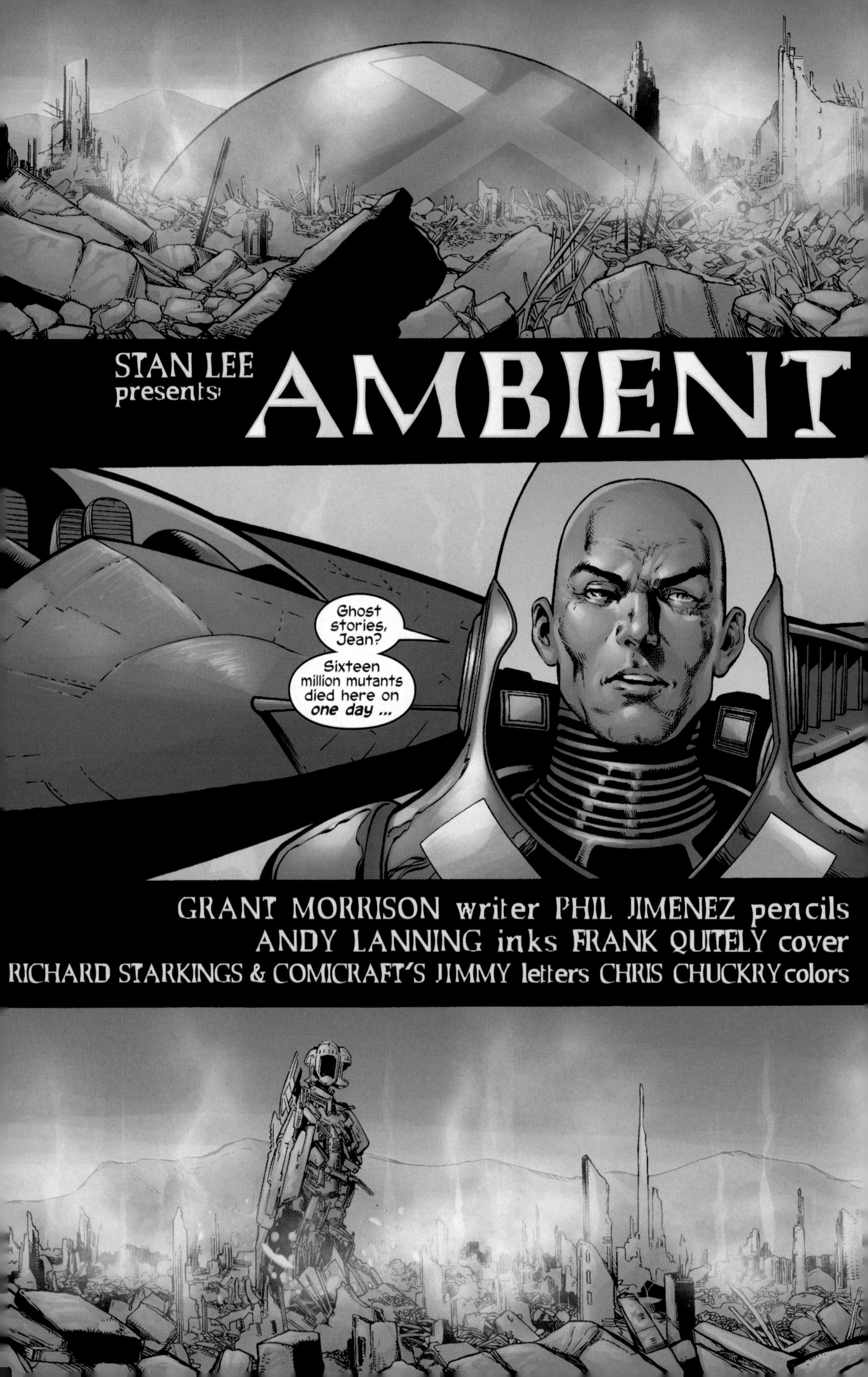
STAN LEE presents:
AMBIENT
Ghost stories, Jean?
Sixteen million mutants died here on *one day ...*
GRANT MORRISON writer PHIL JIMENEZ pencils
ANDY LANNING inks FRANK QUITELY cover
RICHARD STARKINGS & COMICRAFT'S JIMMY letters CHRIS CHUCKRY colors

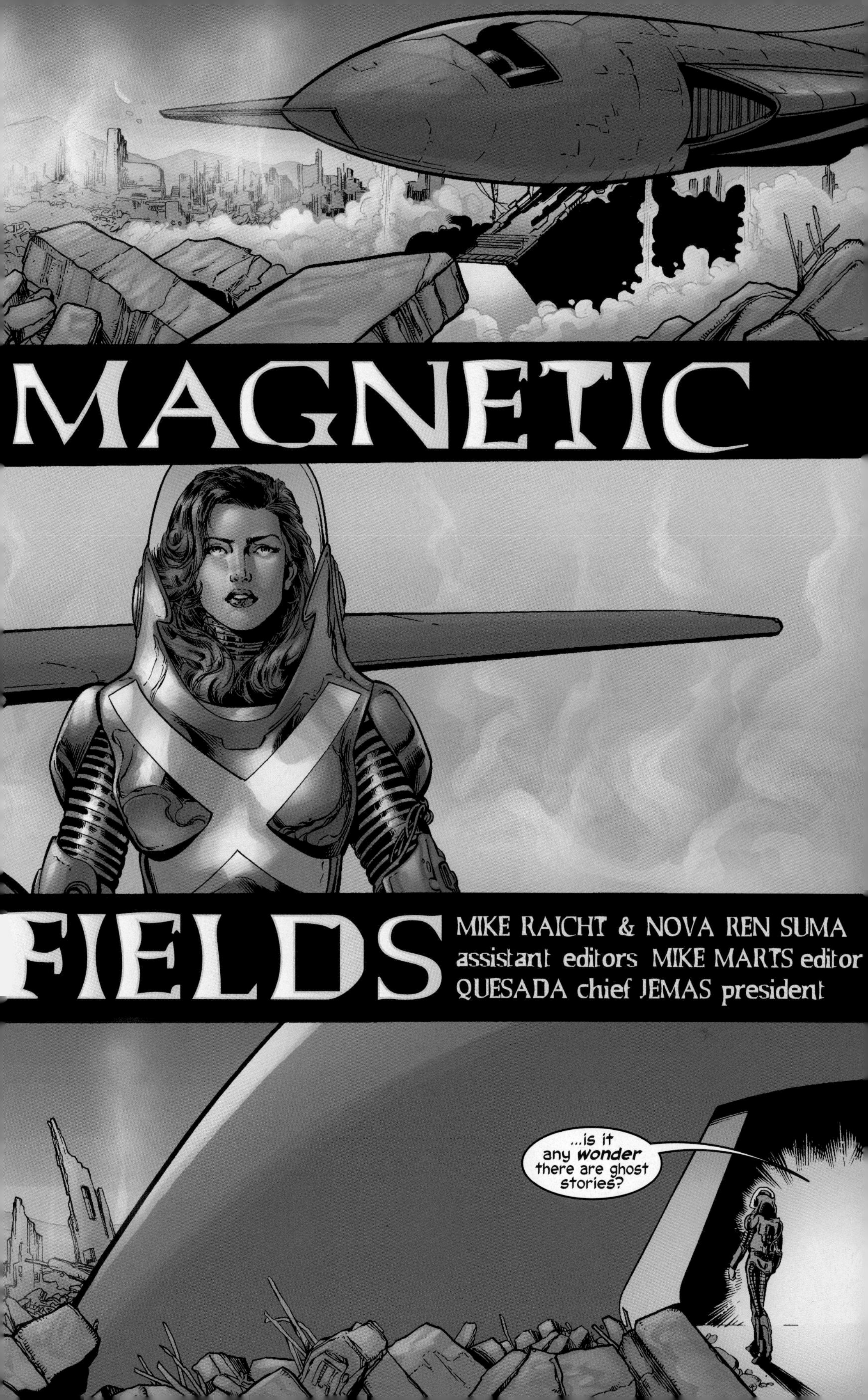
MAGNETIC
FIELDS
MIKE RAICHT & NOVA REN SUMA
assistant editors MIKE MARTS editor
QUESADA chief JEMAS president
...is it any wonder there are ghost stories?

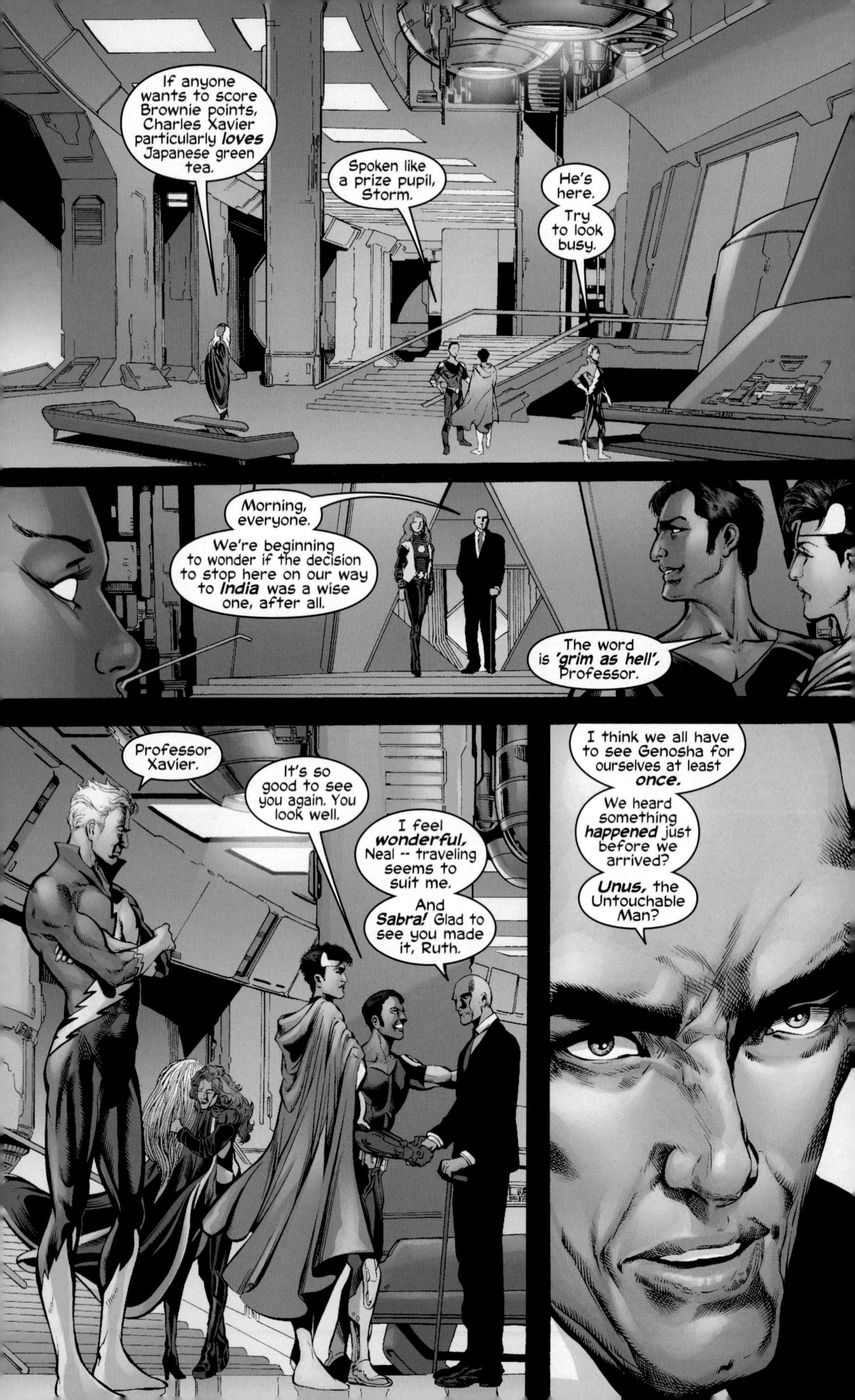
If anyone wants to score Brownie points, Charles Xavier particularly *loves* Japanese green tea.
Spoken like a prize pupil, Storm.
He's here.
Try to look busy.
Morning, everyone.
We're beginning to wonder if the decision to stop here on our way to *India* was a wise one, after all.
The word is *'grim as hell',* Professor.
Professor Xavier.
It's so good to see you again. You look well.
I feel *wonderful,* Neal -- traveling seems to suit me.
And *Sabra!* Glad to see you made it, Ruth.
I think we all have to see Genosha for ourselves at least *once.*
We heard something *happened* just before we arrived?
Unus, the Untouchable Man?

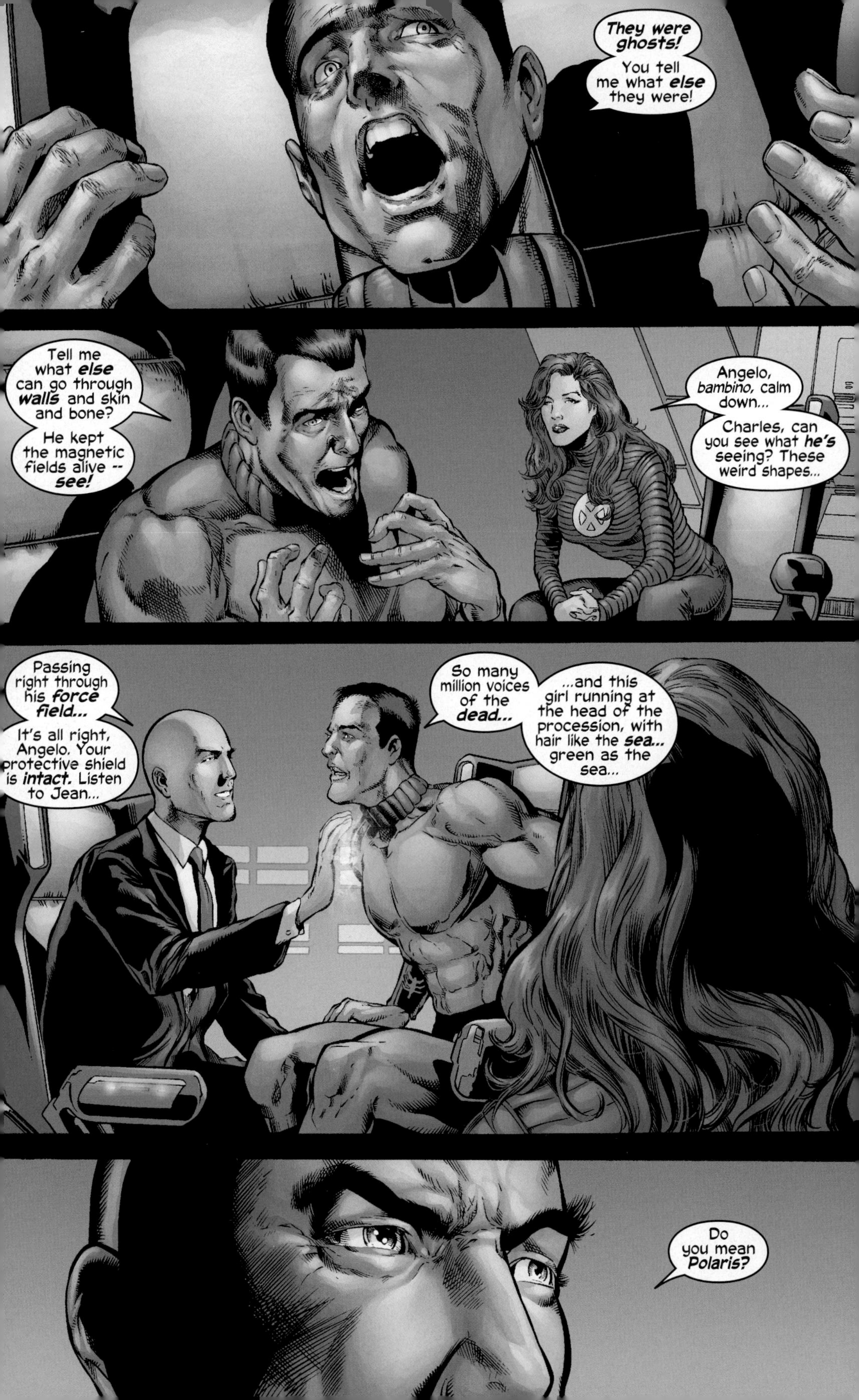
They were ghosts!
You tell me what else they were!
Tell me what else can go through walls and skin and bone?
He kept the magnetic fields alive -- see!
Angelo, bambino, calm down...
Charles, can you see what he's seeing? These weird shapes...
Passing right through his force field...
It's all right, Angelo. Your protective shield is intact. Listen to Jean...
So many million voices of the dead...
...and this girl running at the head of the procession, with hair like the sea... green as the sea...
Do you mean Polaris?

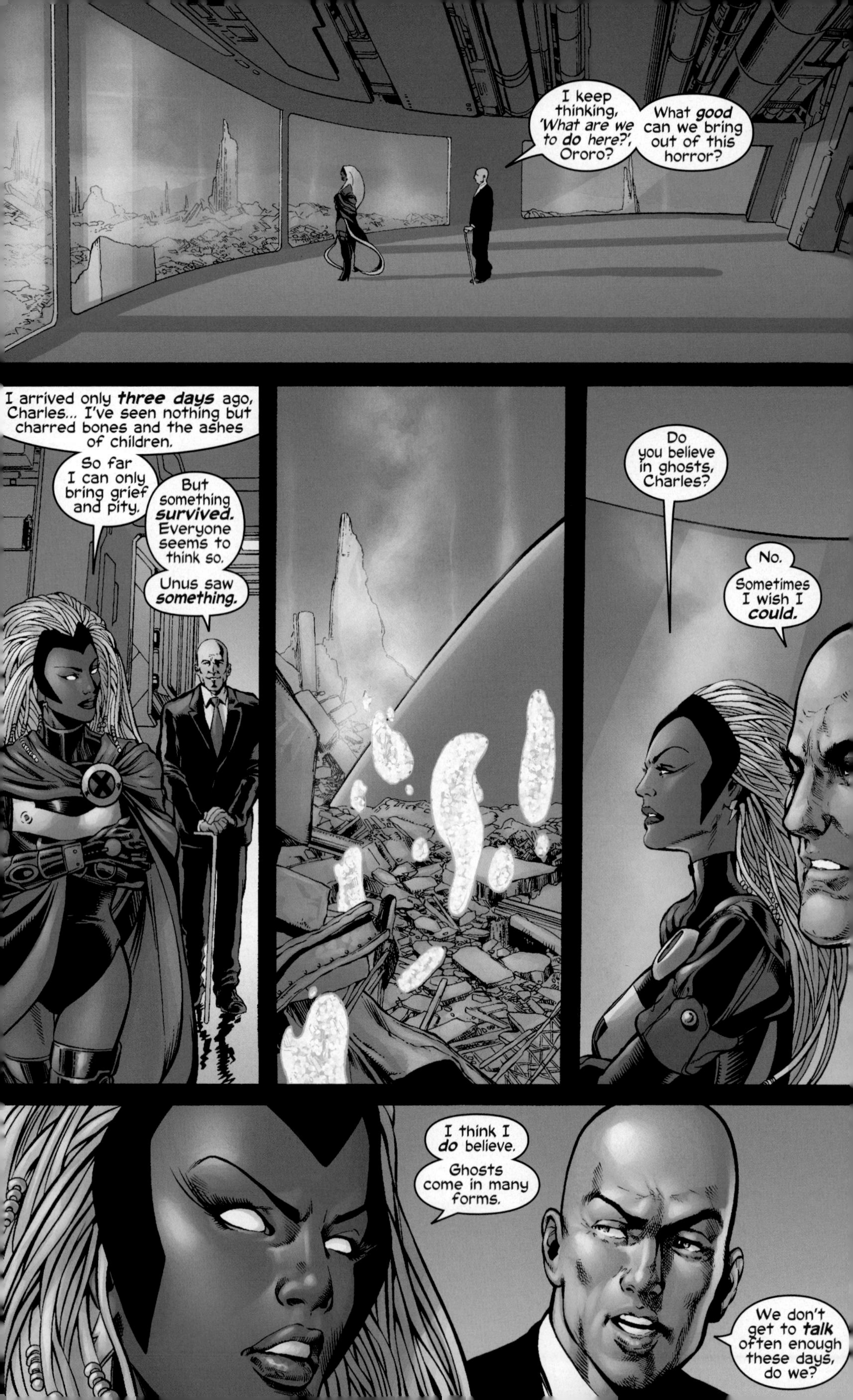
I keep thinking, 'What are we to do here?', Ororo?
What good can we bring out of this horror?
I arrived only three days ago, Charles... I've seen nothing but charred bones and the ashes of children.
So far I can only bring grief and pity.
But something survived. Everyone seems to think so.
Unus saw something.
Do you believe in ghosts, Charles?
No.
Sometimes I wish I could.
I think I do believe.
Ghosts come in many forms.
We don't get to talk often enough these days, do we?

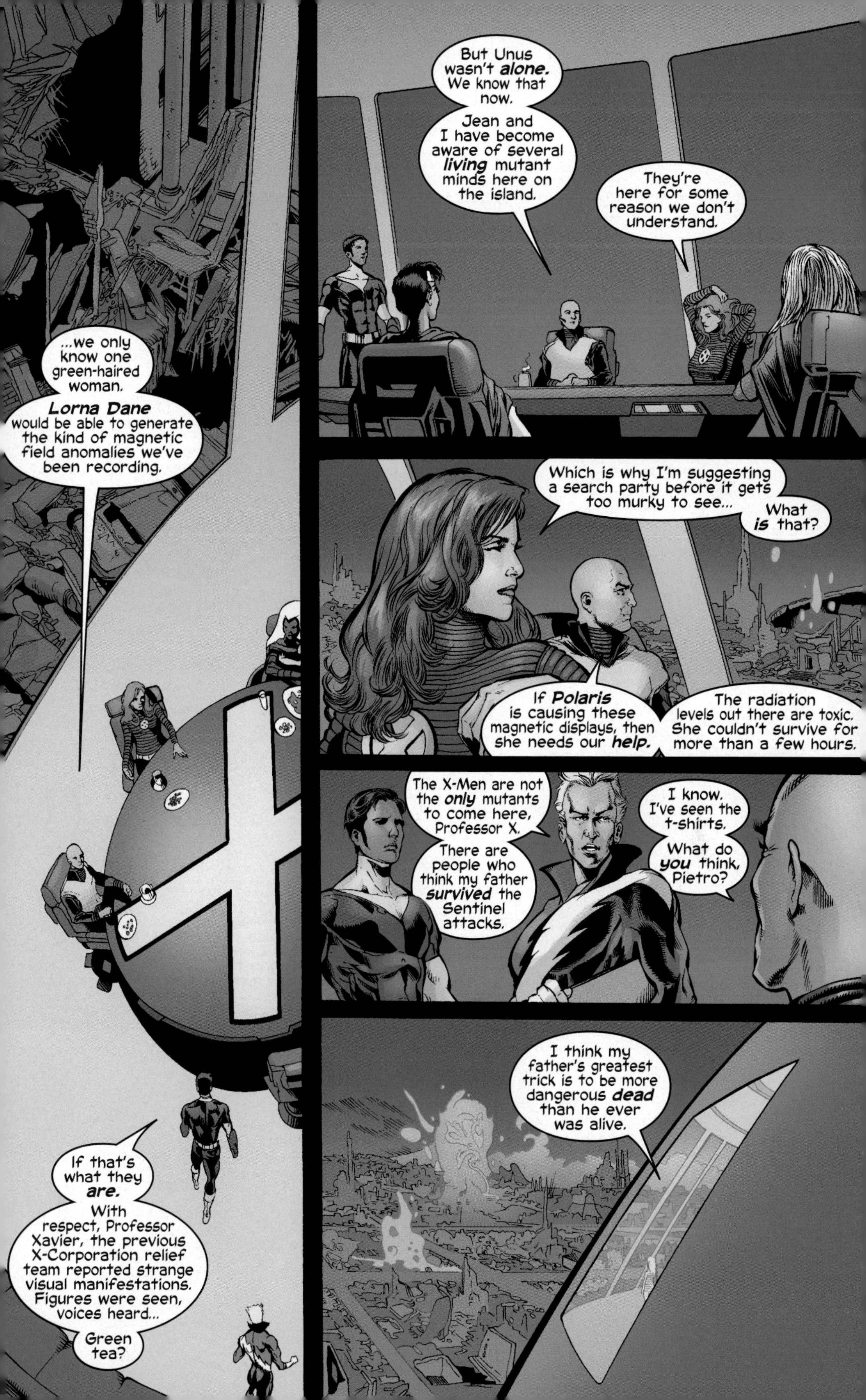
...we only know one green-haired woman.
Lorna Dane would be able to generate the kind of magnetic field anomalies we've been recording.
If that's what they are.
With respect, Professor Xavier, the previous X-Corporation relief team reported strange visual manifestations. Figures were seen, voices heard...
Green tea?
But Unus wasn't alone. We know that now.
Jean and I have become aware of several living mutant minds here on the island.
They're here for some reason we don't understand.
Which is why I'm suggesting a search party before it gets too murky to see...
What is that?
If Polaris is causing these magnetic displays, then she needs our help.
The radiation levels out there are toxic. She couldn't survive for more than a few hours.
The X-Men are not the only mutants to come here, Professor X.
There are people who think my father survived the Sentinel attacks.
I know. I've seen the t-shirts.
What do you think, Pietro?
I think my father's greatest trick is to be more dangerous dead than he ever was alive.

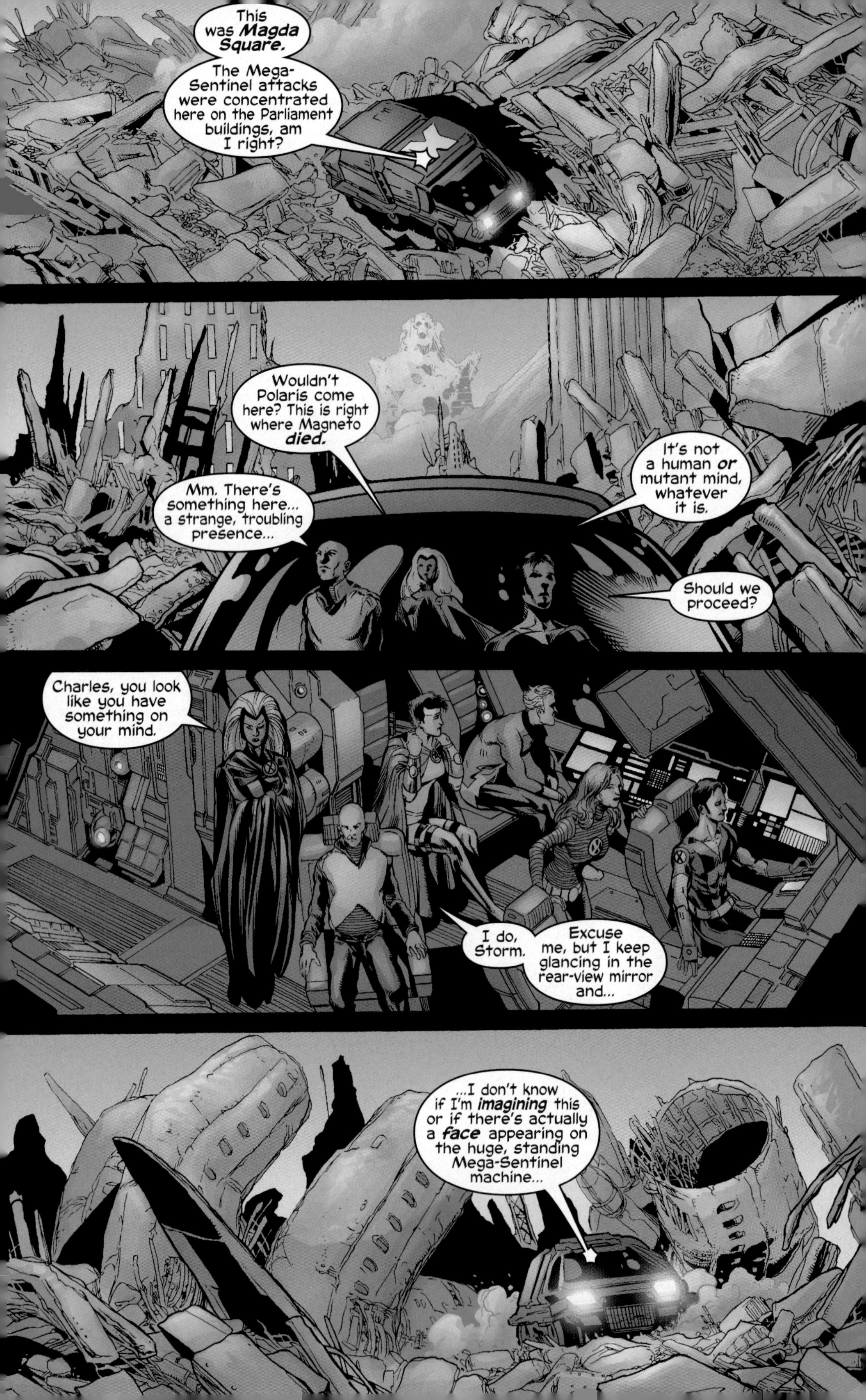
This was Magda Square.
The Mega-Sentinel attacks were concentrated here on the Parliament buildings, am I right?
Wouldn't Polaris come here? This is right where Magneto died.
Mm. There's something here... a strange, troubling presence...
It's not a human or mutant mind, whatever it is.
Should we proceed?
Charles, you look like you have something on your mind.
I do, Storm.
Excuse me, but I keep glancing in the rear-view mirror and...
...I don't know if I'm imagining this or if there's actually a face appearing on the huge, standing Mega-Sentinel machine...

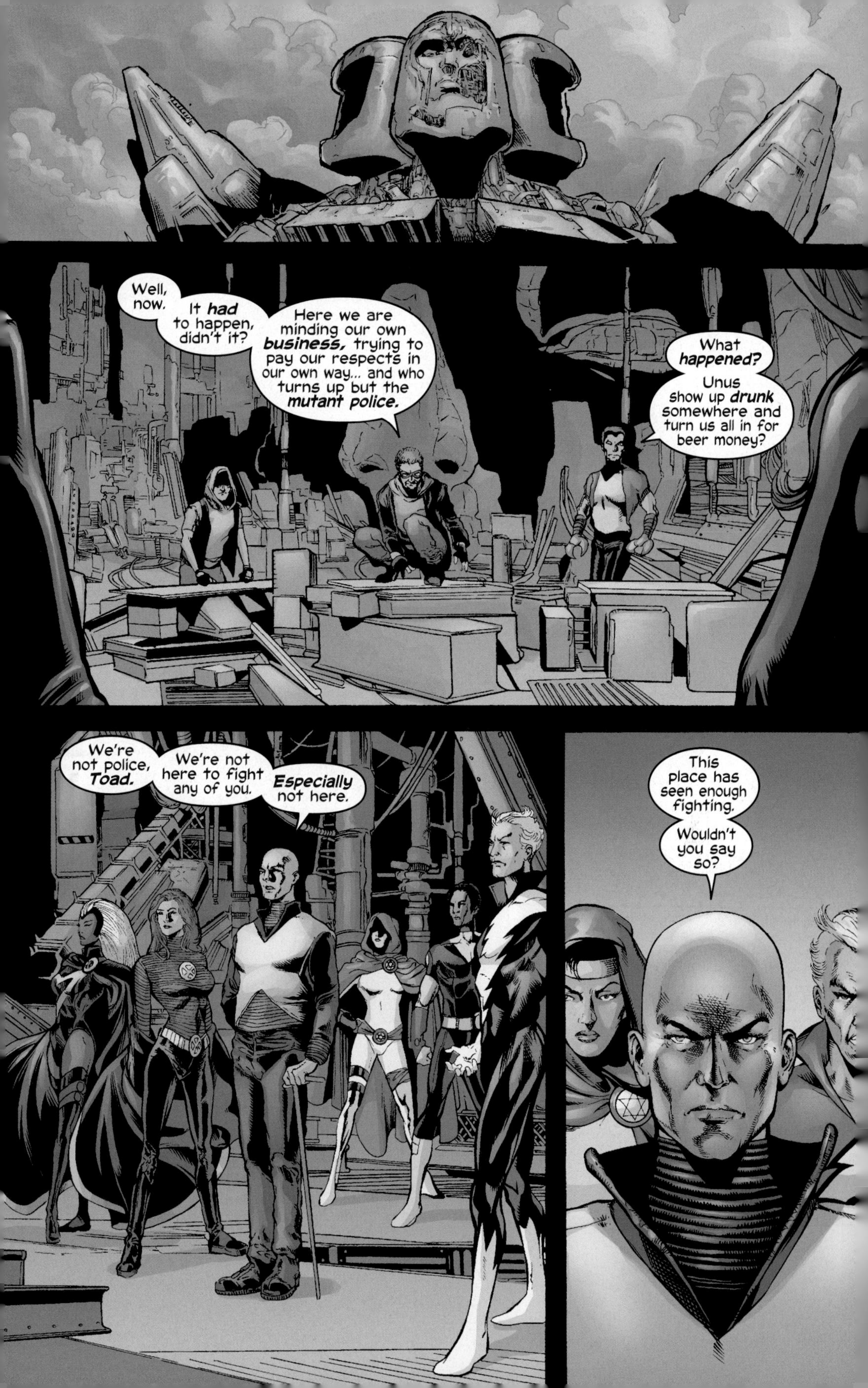
Well, now.
It had to happen, didn't it?
Here we are minding our own business, trying to pay our respects in our own way... and who turns up but the mutant police.
What happened?
Unus show up drunk somewhere and turn us all in for beer money?
We're not police, Toad.
We're not here to fight any of you.
Especially not here.
This place has seen enough fighting.
Wouldn't you say so?

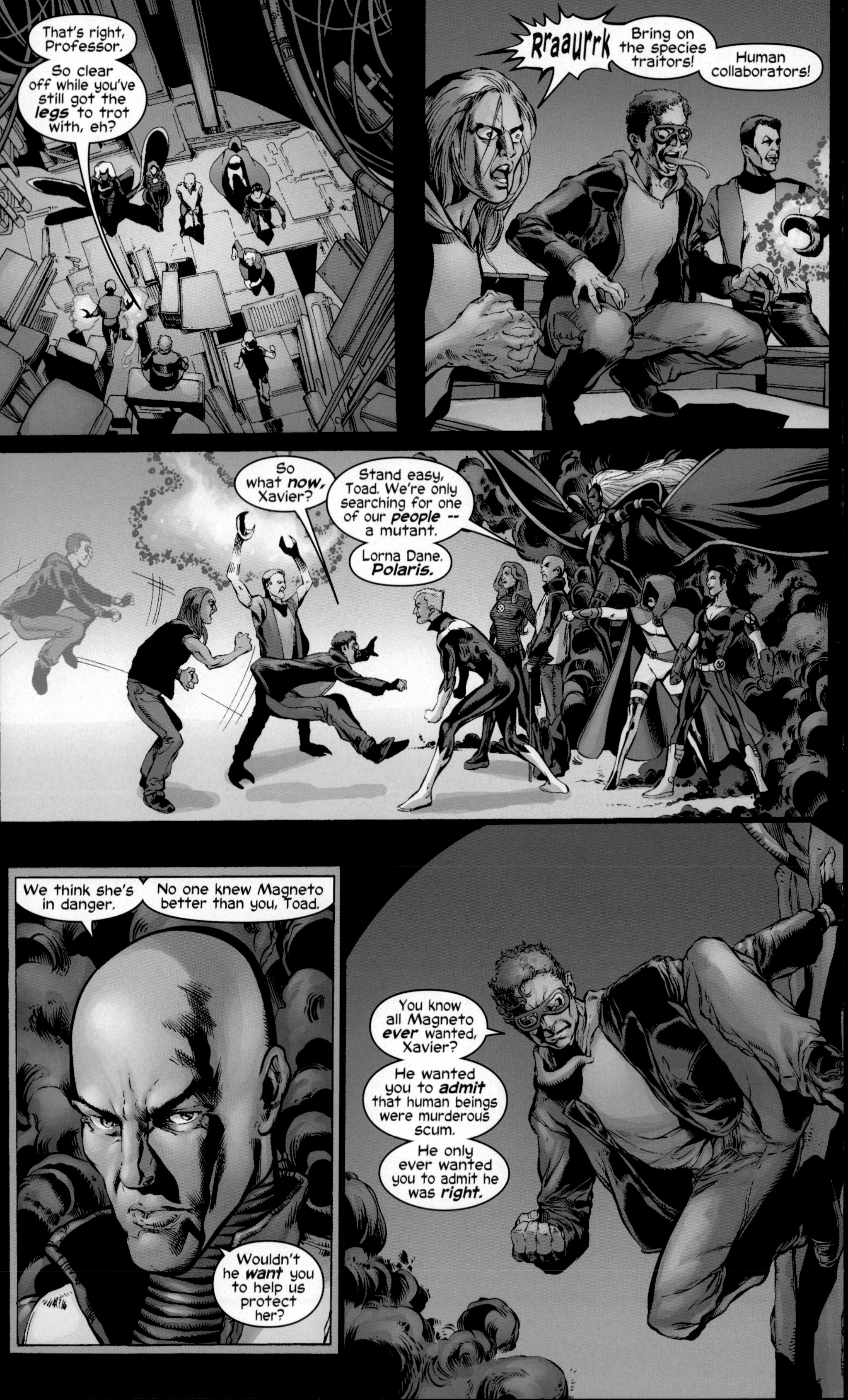
That's right, Professor.
So clear off while you've still got the legs to trot with, eh?
Rraaurrk
Bring on the species traitors!
Human collaborators!
So what now, Xavier?
Stand easy, Toad. We're only searching for one of our people -- a mutant.
Lorna Dane. Polaris.
We think she's in danger.
No one knew Magneto better than you, Toad.
Wouldn't he want you to help us protect her?
You know all Magneto ever wanted, Xavier?
He wanted you to admit that human beings were murderous scum.
He only ever wanted you to admit he was right.

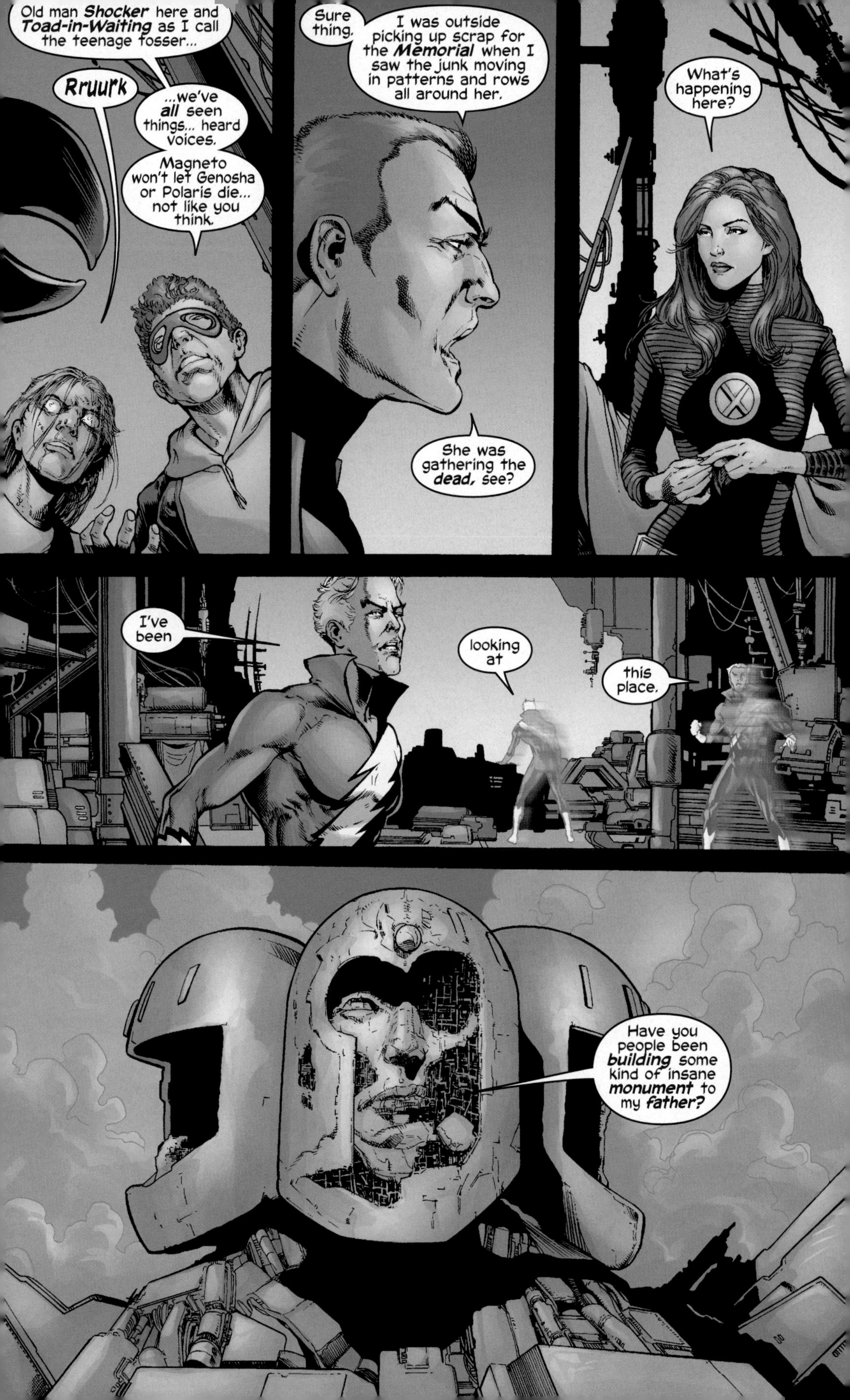
Old man **Shocker** here and **Toad-in-Waiting** as I call the teenage tosser...
Rruurk
...we've **all** seen things... heard voices.
Magneto won't let Genosha or Polaris die... not like you think.
Sure thing.
I was outside picking up scrap for the **Memorial** when I saw the junk moving in patterns and rows all around her.
She was gathering the **dead,** see?
What's happening here?
I've been
looking at
this place.
Have you people been **building** some kind of insane **monument** to my **father?**

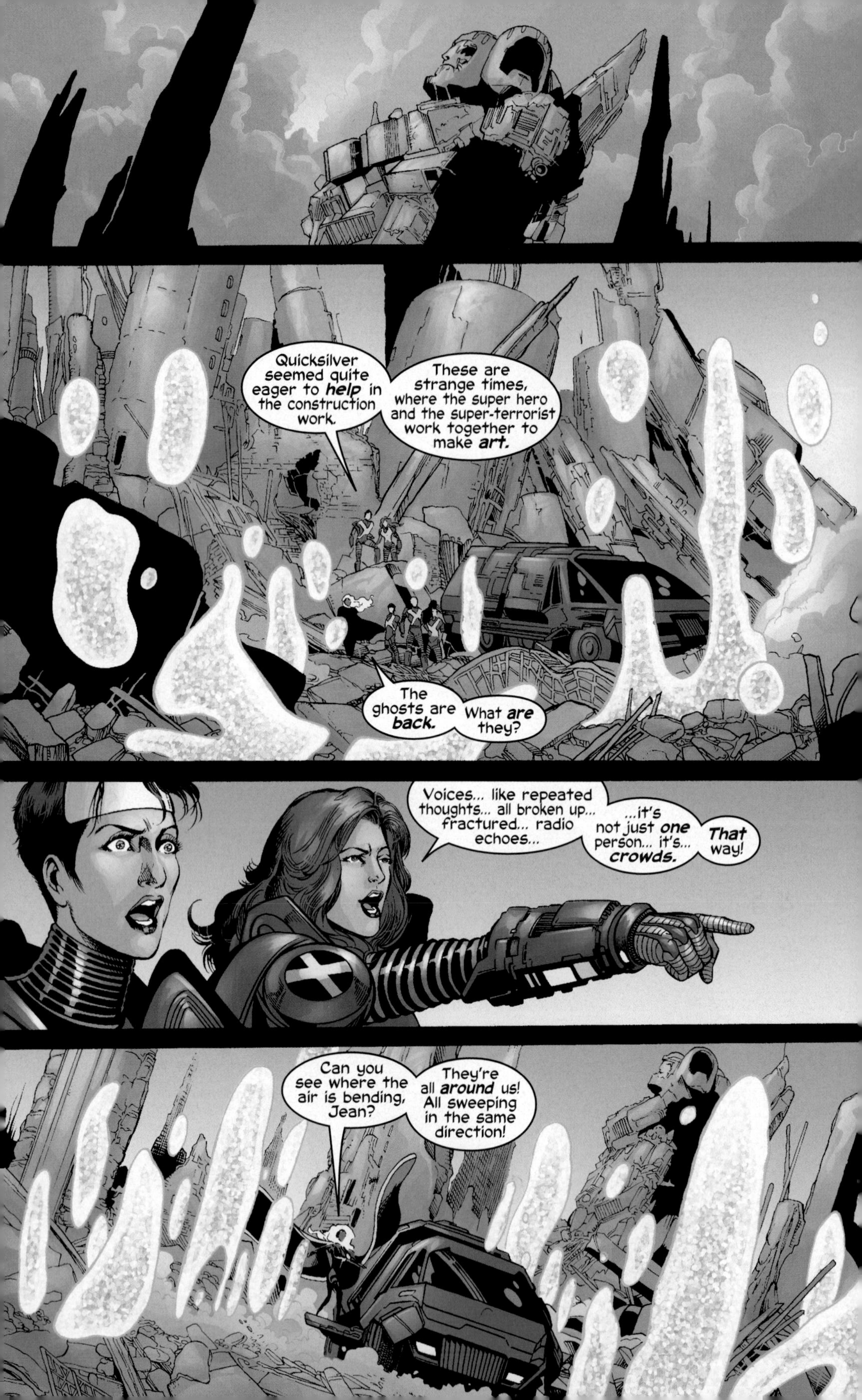
Quicksilver seemed quite eager to *help* in the construction work.
These are strange times, where the super hero and the super-terrorist work together to make *art.*
The ghosts are *back.*
What *are* they?
Voices... like repeated thoughts... all broken up... fractured... radio echoes...
...it's not just *one* person... it's... *crowds.*
That way!
Can you see where the air is bending, Jean?
They're all *around* us! All sweeping in the same direction!

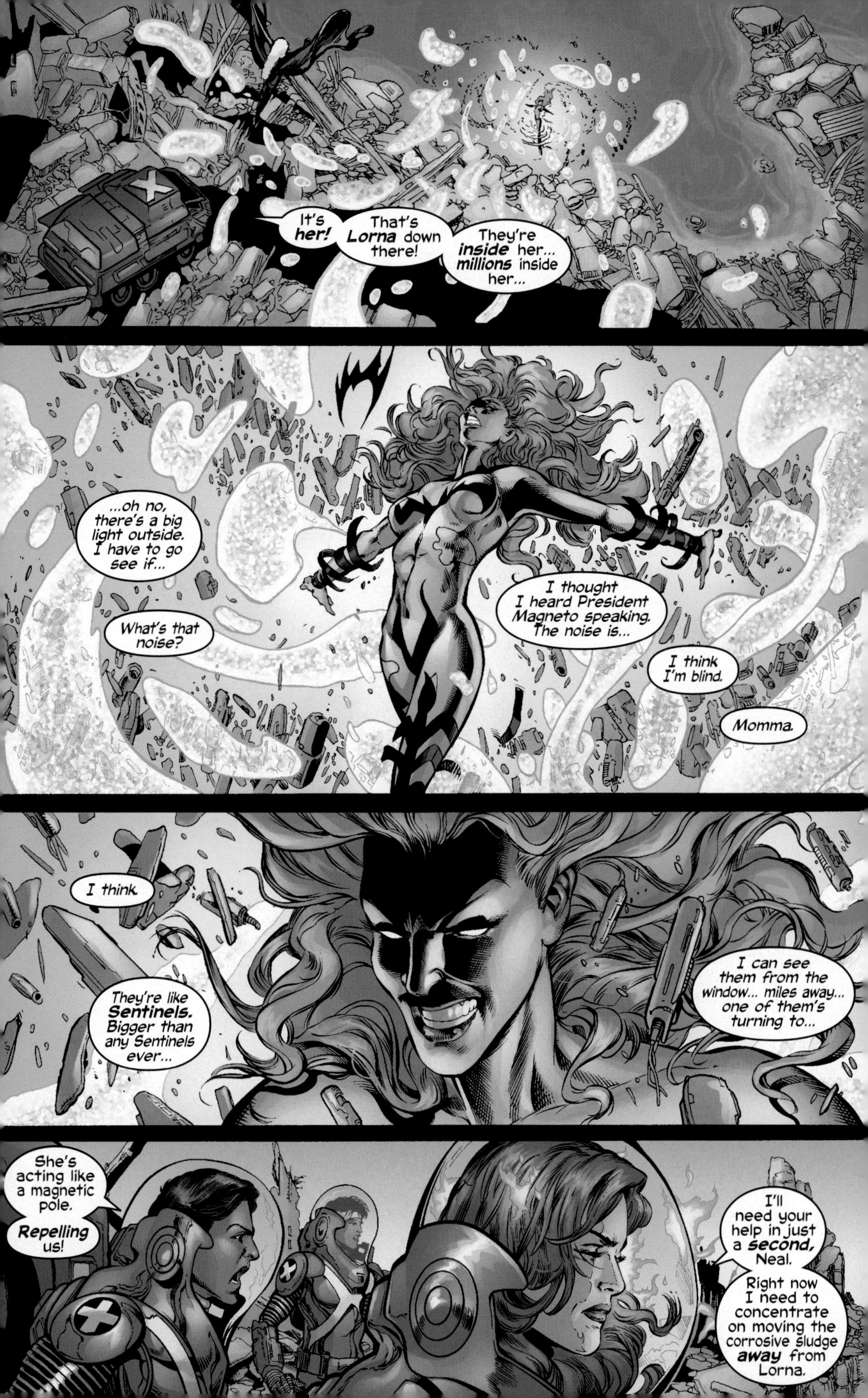

It's her!
That's Lorna down there!
They're inside her... millions inside her...
...oh no, there's a big light outside. I have to go see if...
What's that noise?
I thought I heard President Magneto speaking. The noise is...
I think I'm blind.
Momma.
I think.
They're like Sentinels. Bigger than any Sentinels ever...
I can see them from the window... miles away... one of them's turning to...
She's acting like a magnetic pole.
Repelling us!
I'll need your help in just a second, Neal.
Right now I need to concentrate on moving the corrosive sludge away from Lorna.

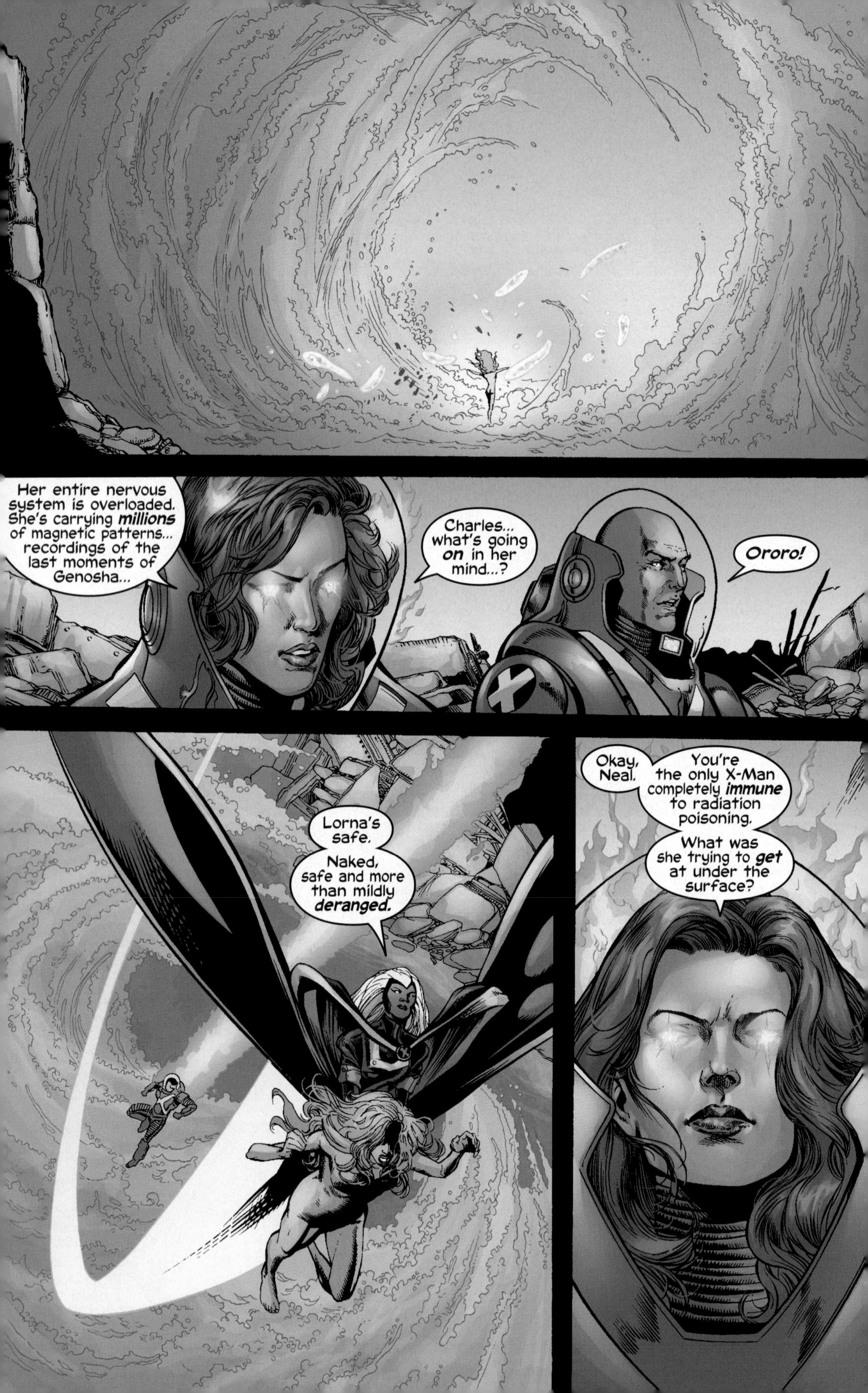
Her entire nervous system is overloaded. She's carrying *millions* of magnetic patterns... recordings of the last moments of Genosha...
Charles... what's going *on* in her mind...?
Ororo!
Lorna's safe.
Naked, safe and more than mildly *deranged.*
Okay, Neal.
You're the only X-Man completely *immune* to radiation poisoning.
What was she trying to *get* at under the surface?

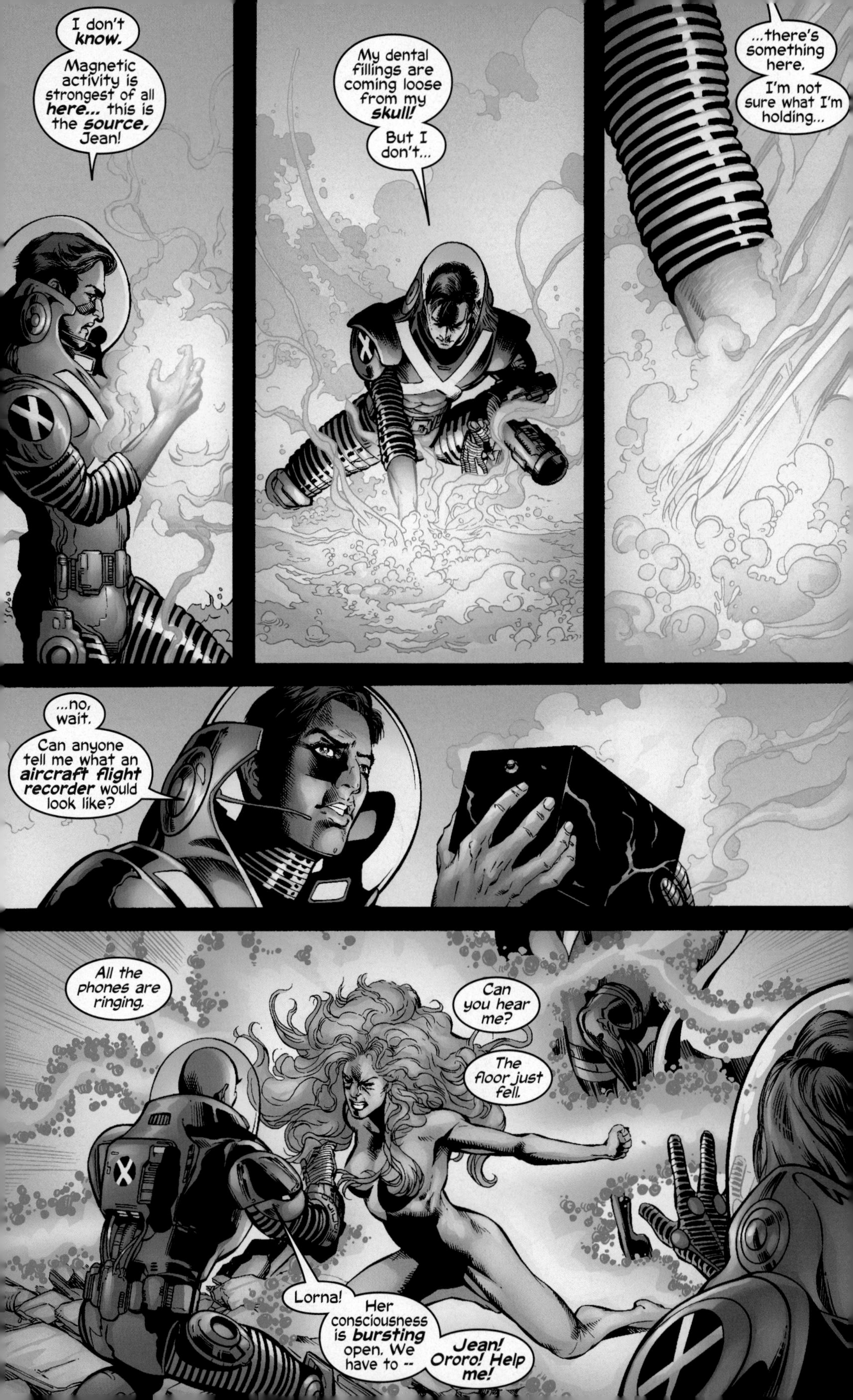
I don't **know.**
Magnetic activity is strongest of all **here...** this is the **source,** Jean!
My dental fillings are coming loose from my **skull!**
But I don't...
...there's something here.
I'm not sure what I'm holding...
...no, wait.
Can anyone tell me what an **aircraft flight recorder** would look like?
All the phones are ringing.
Can you hear me?
The floor just fell.
Lorna!
Her consciousness is **bursting** open. We have to --
Jean! Ororo! Help me!

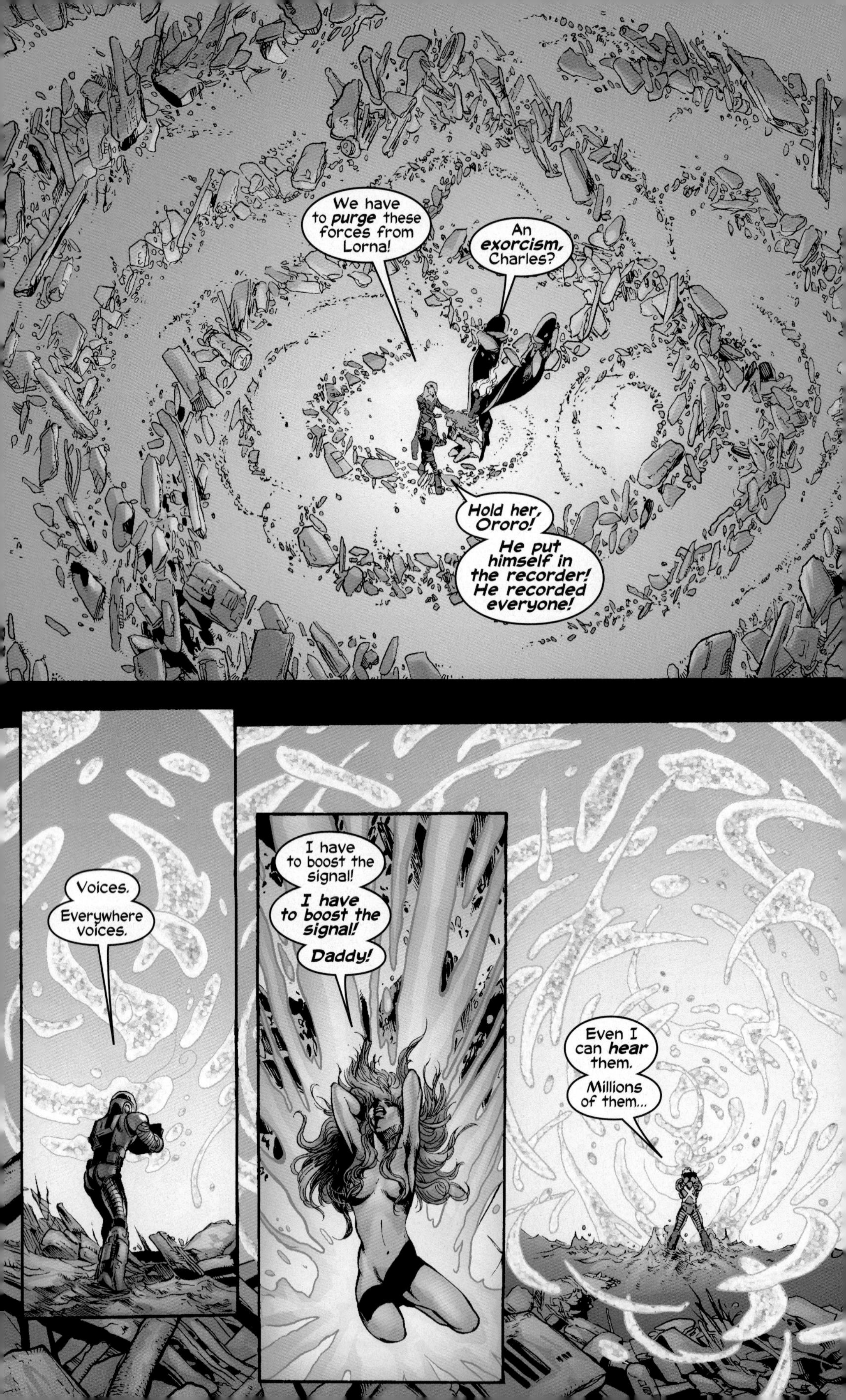
We have to purge these forces from Lorna!
An exorcism, Charles?
Hold her, Ororo!
He put himself in the recorder! He recorded everyone!
Voices.
Everywhere voices.
I have to boost the signal!
I have to boost the signal!
Daddy!
Even I can hear them.
Millions of them...

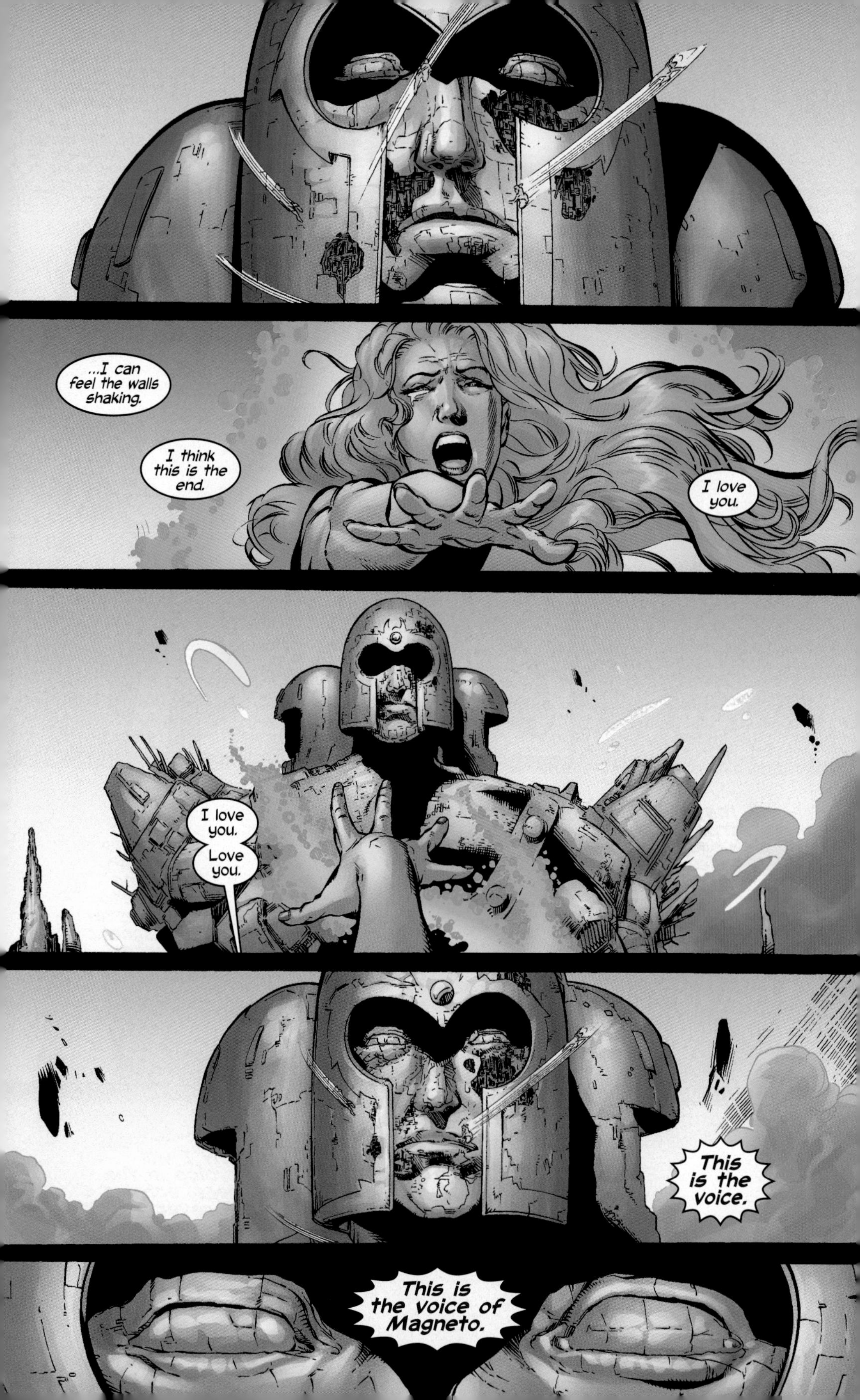
...I can feel the walls shaking.
I think this is the end.
I love you.
I love you.
Love you.
This is the voice.
This is the voice of Magneto.

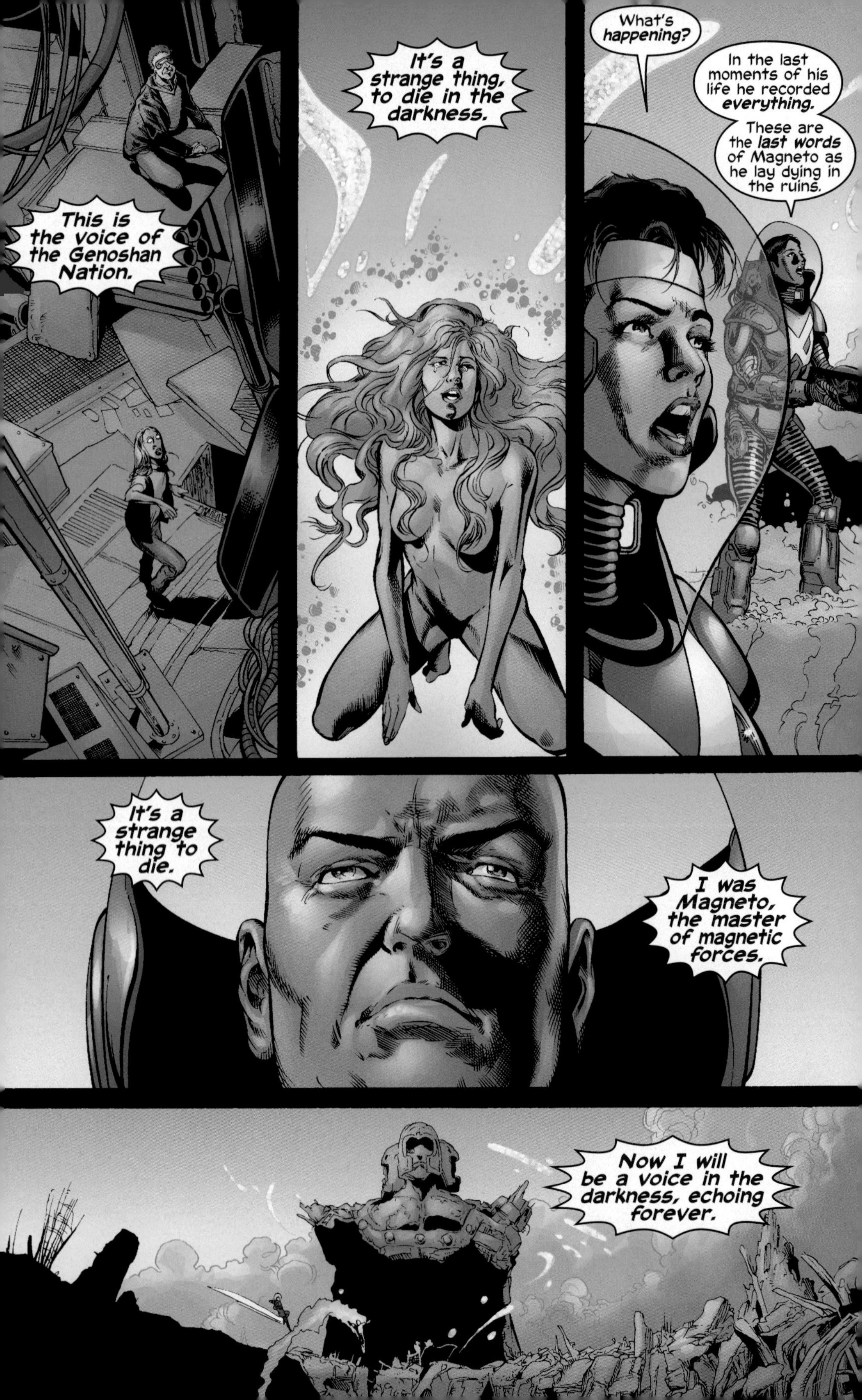
This is the voice of the Genoshan Nation.
It's a strange thing, to die in the darkness.
What's happening?
In the last moments of his life he recorded everything.
These are the last words of Magneto as he lay dying in the ruins.
It's a strange thing to die.
I was Magneto, the master of magnetic forces.
Now I will be a voice in the darkness, echoing forever.

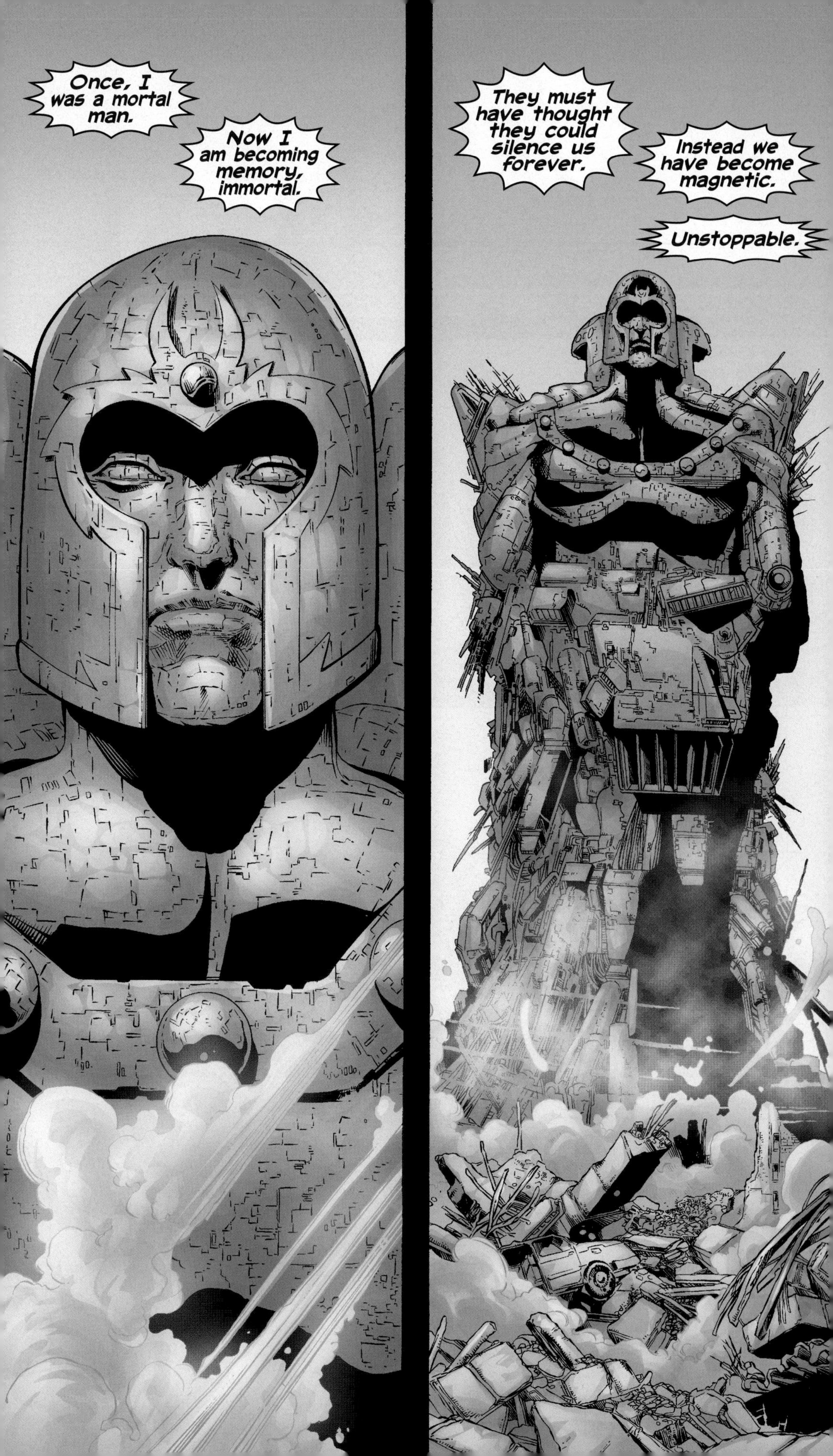
Once, I was a mortal man.
Now I am becoming memory, immortal.
They must have thought they could silence us forever.
Instead we have become magnetic.
Unstoppable.

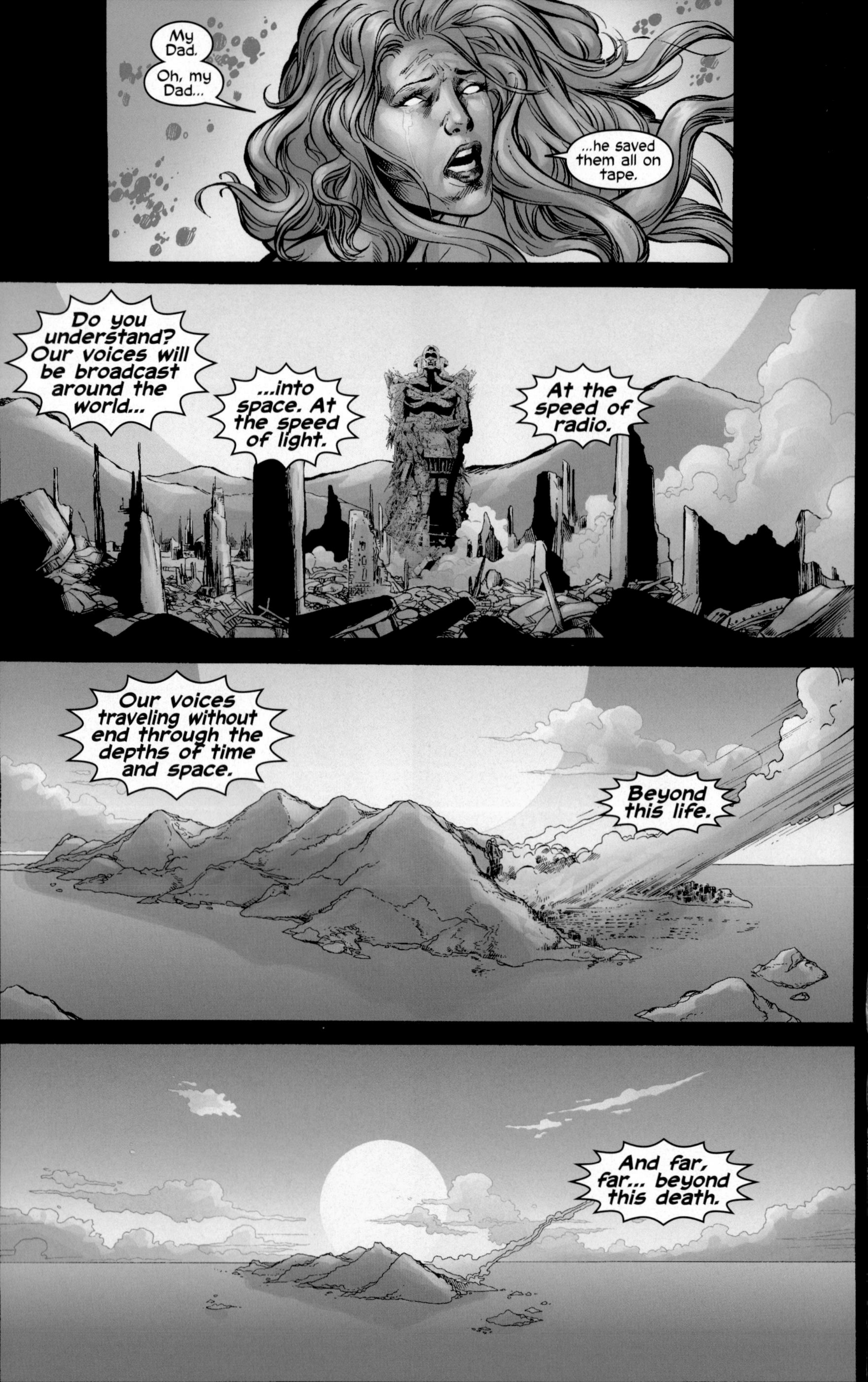
My Dad.
Oh, my Dad...
...he saved them all on tape.
Do you understand? Our voices will be broadcast around the world...
...into space. At the speed of light.
At the speed of radio.
Our voices traveling without end through the depths of time and space.
Beyond this life.
And far, far... beyond this death.

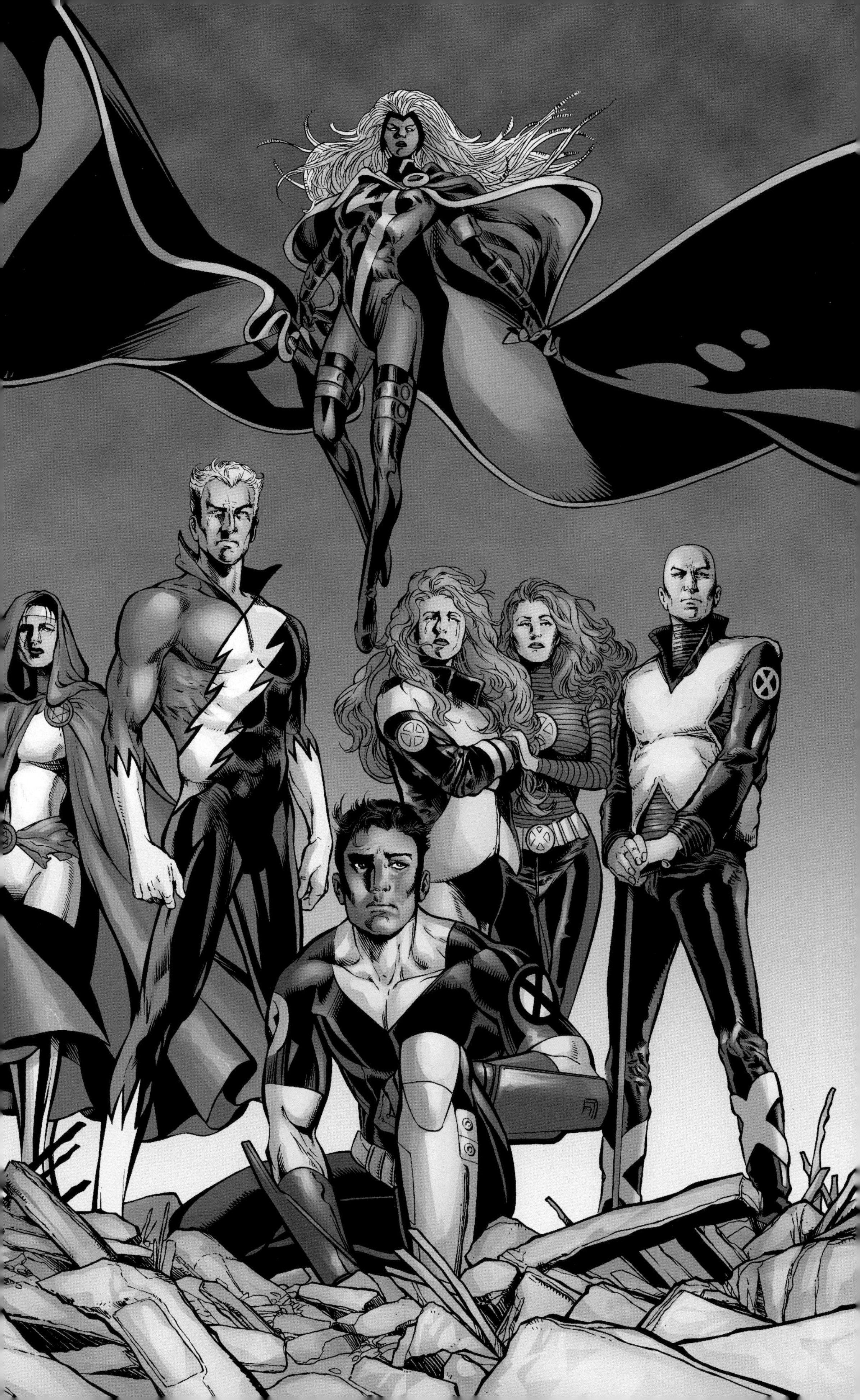

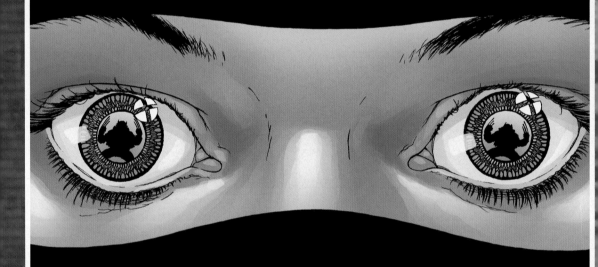

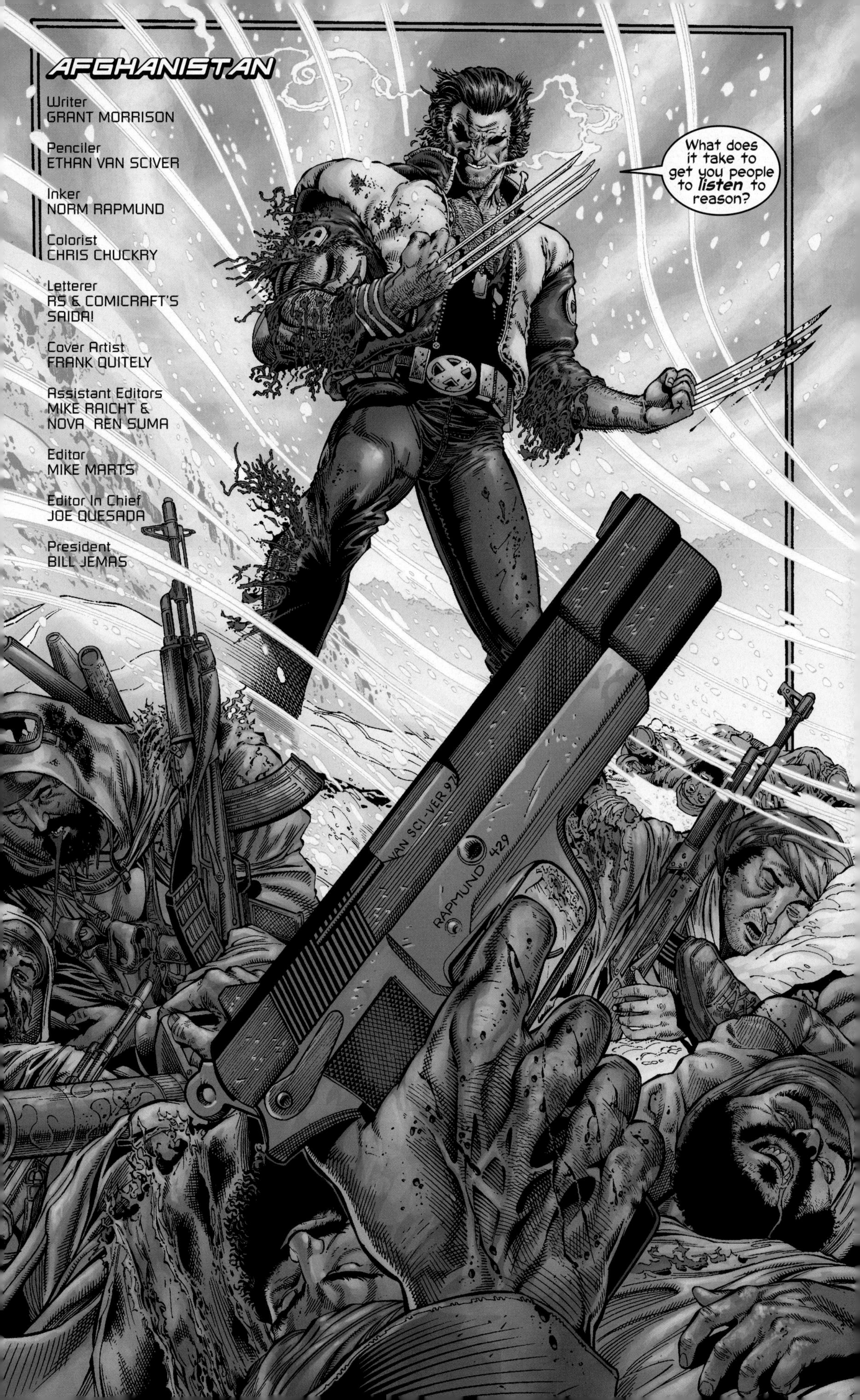
AFGHANISTAN
Writer
GRANT MORRISON
Penciler
ETHAN VAN SCIVER
Inker
NORM RAPMUND
Colorist
CHRIS CHUCKRY
Letterer
RS & COMICRAFT'S
SAIDA!
Cover Artist
FRANK QUITELY
Assistant Editors
MIKE RAICHT &
NOVA REN SUMA
Editor
MIKE MARTS
Editor In Chief
JOE QUESADA
President
BILL JEMAS
What does it take to get you people to *listen* to reason?
VAN SCI-VER 97
RAPMUND 429

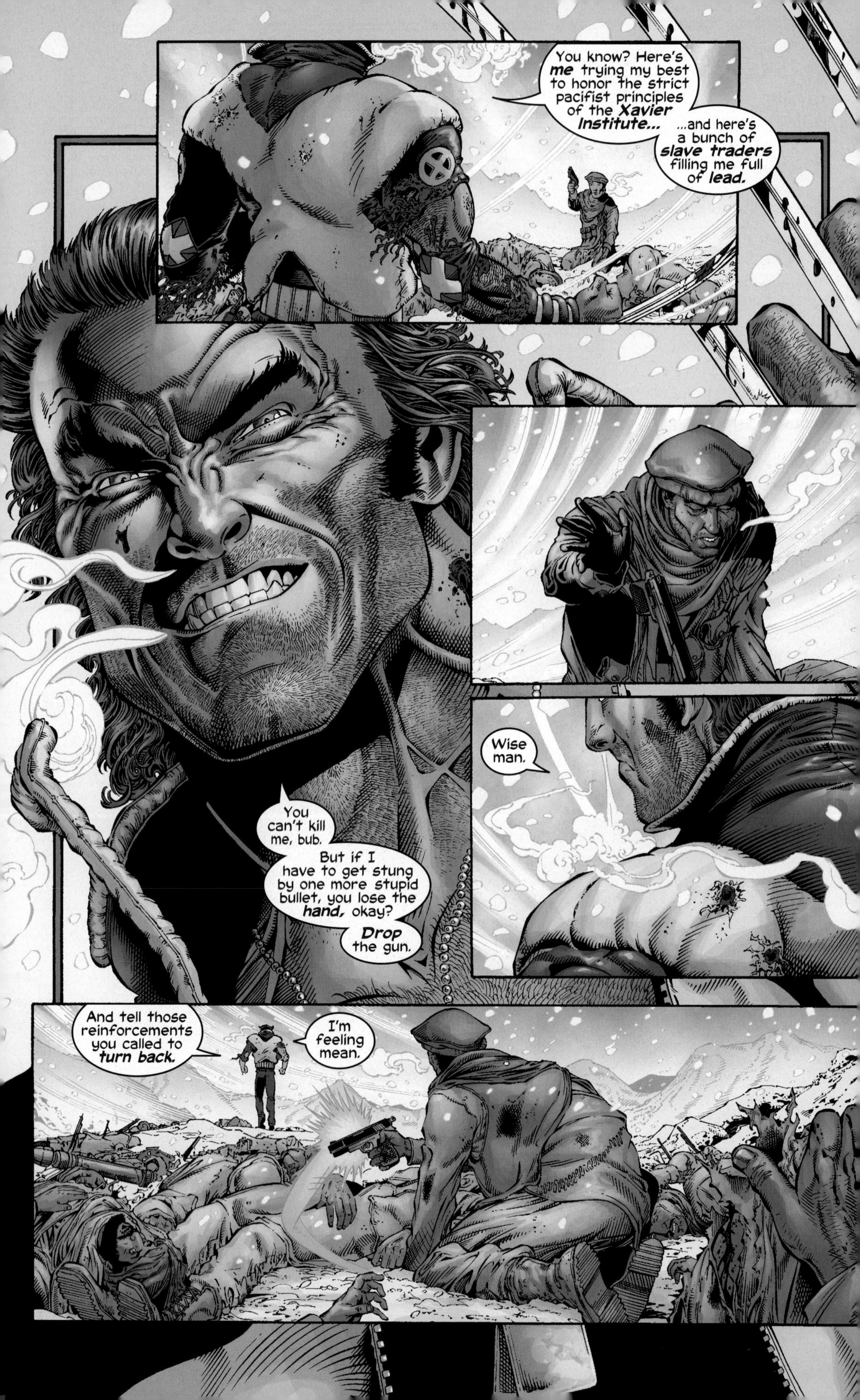
You know? Here's me trying my best to honor the strict pacifist principles of the Xavier Institute...
...and here's a bunch of slave traders filling me full of lead.
You can't kill me, bub.
But if I have to get stung by one more stupid bullet, you lose the hand, okay?
Drop the gun.
Wise man.
And tell those reinforcements you called to turn back.
I'm feeling mean.

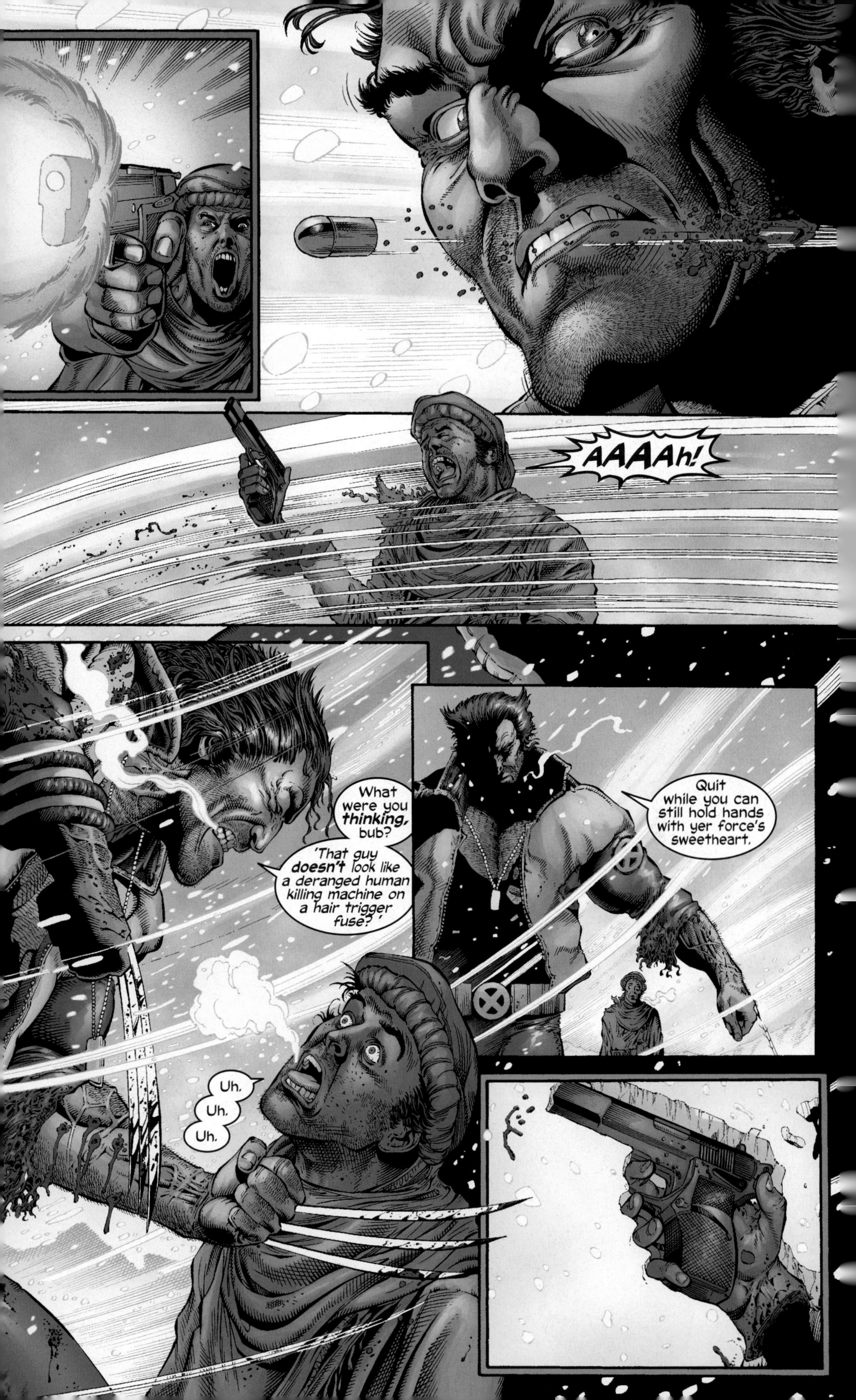
AAAAh!
What were you thinking, bub?
'That guy doesn't look like a deranged human killing machine on a hair trigger fuse?'
Quit while you can still hold hands with yer force's sweetheart.
Uh, Uh, Uh.

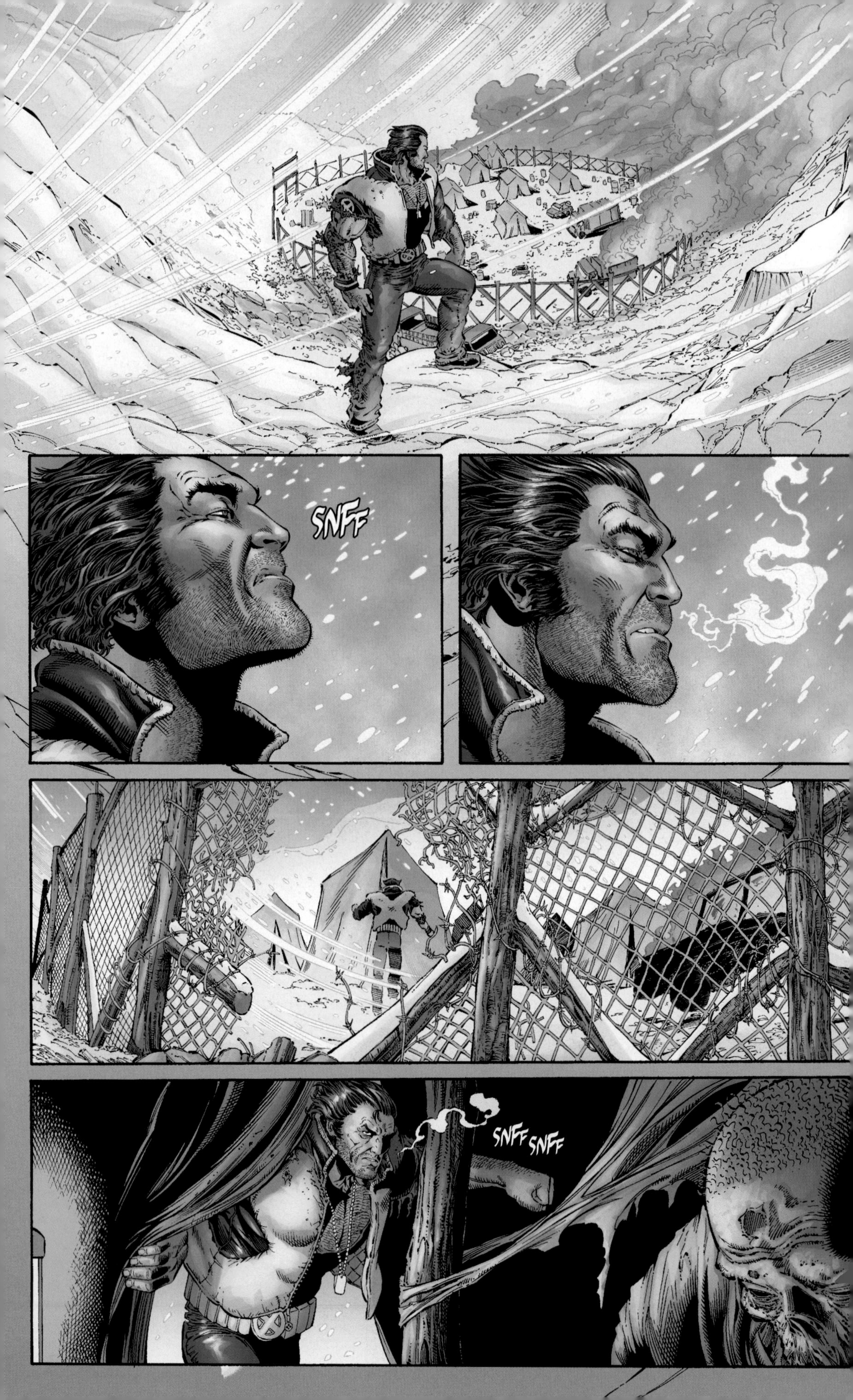
SNFF
SNFF SNFF

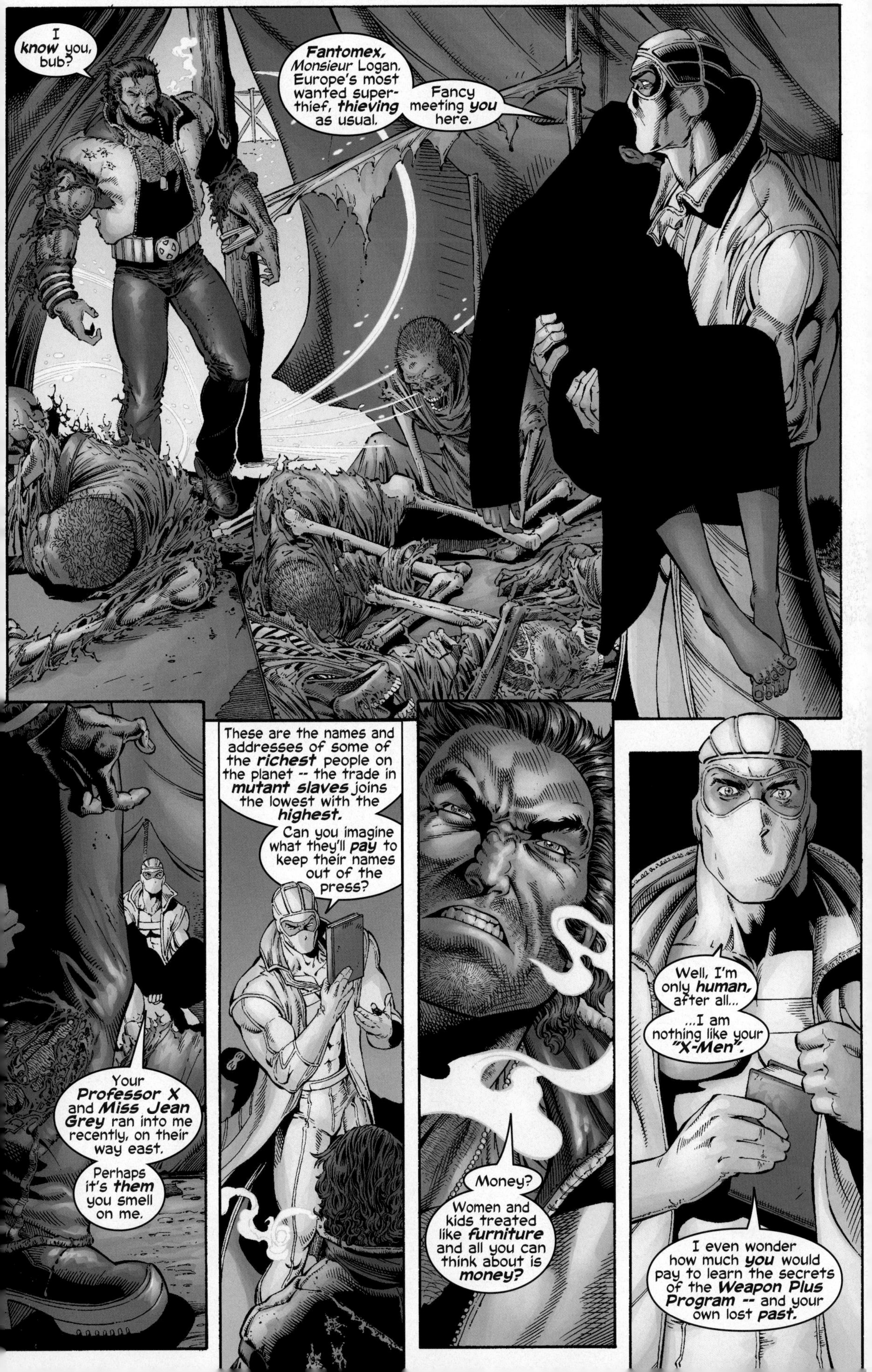
I know you, bub?
Fantomex, Monsieur Logan. Europe's most wanted super-thief, thieving as usual.
Fancy meeting you here.
Your Professor X and Miss Jean Grey ran into me recently, on their way east.
Perhaps it's them you smell on me.
These are the names and addresses of some of the richest people on the planet -- the trade in mutant slaves joins the lowest with the highest.
Can you imagine what they'll pay to keep their names out of the press?
Money?
Women and kids treated like furniture and all you can think about is money?
Well, I'm only human, after all...
...I am nothing like your "X-Men".
I even wonder how much you would pay to learn the secrets of the Weapon Plus Program -- and your own lost past.

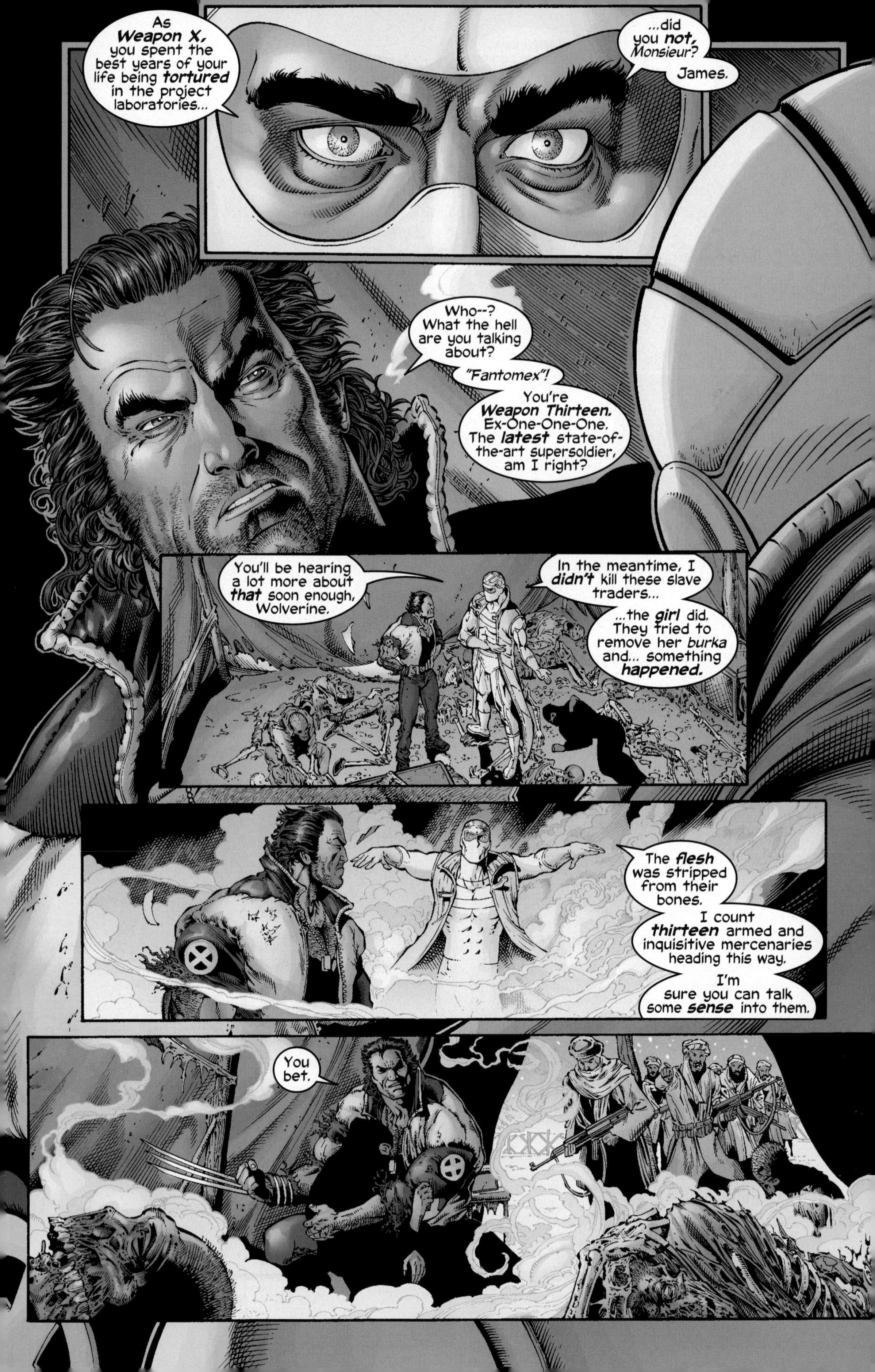
As Weapon X, you spent the best years of your life being tortured in the project laboratories...
...did you not, Monsieur?
James.
Who--? What the hell are you talking about?
"Fantomex"!
You're Weapon Thirteen. Ex-One-One-One. The latest state-of-the-art supersoldier, am I right?
You'll be hearing a lot more about that soon enough, Wolverine.
In the meantime, I didn't kill these slave traders...
...the girl did. They tried to remove her burka and... something happened.
The flesh was stripped from their bones.
I count thirteen armed and inquisitive mercenaries heading this way.
I'm sure you can talk some sense into them.
You bet.

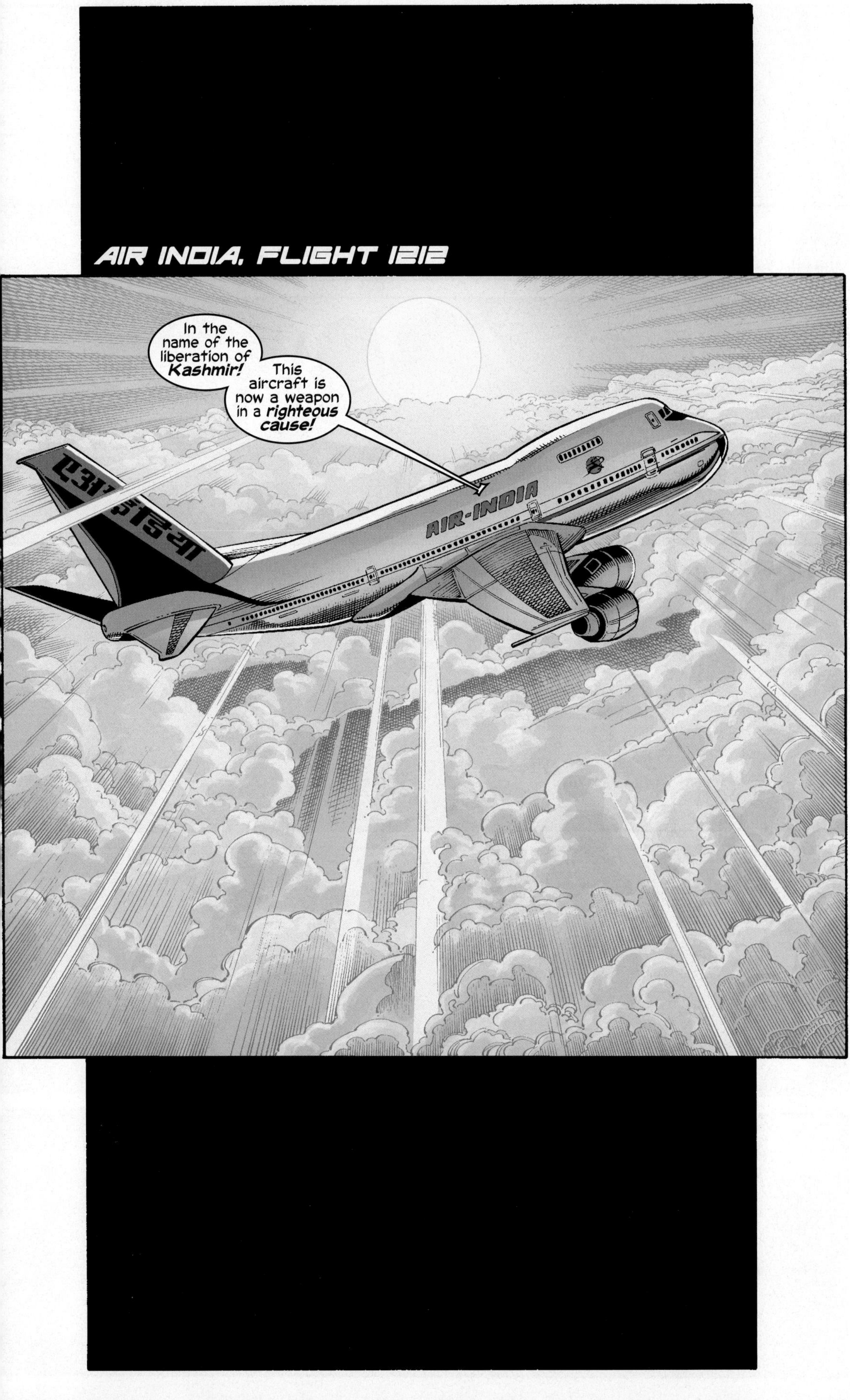
AIR INDIA, FLIGHT 1212
In the name of the liberation of *Kashmir!*
This aircraft is now a weapon in a *righteous cause!*
AIR-INDIA

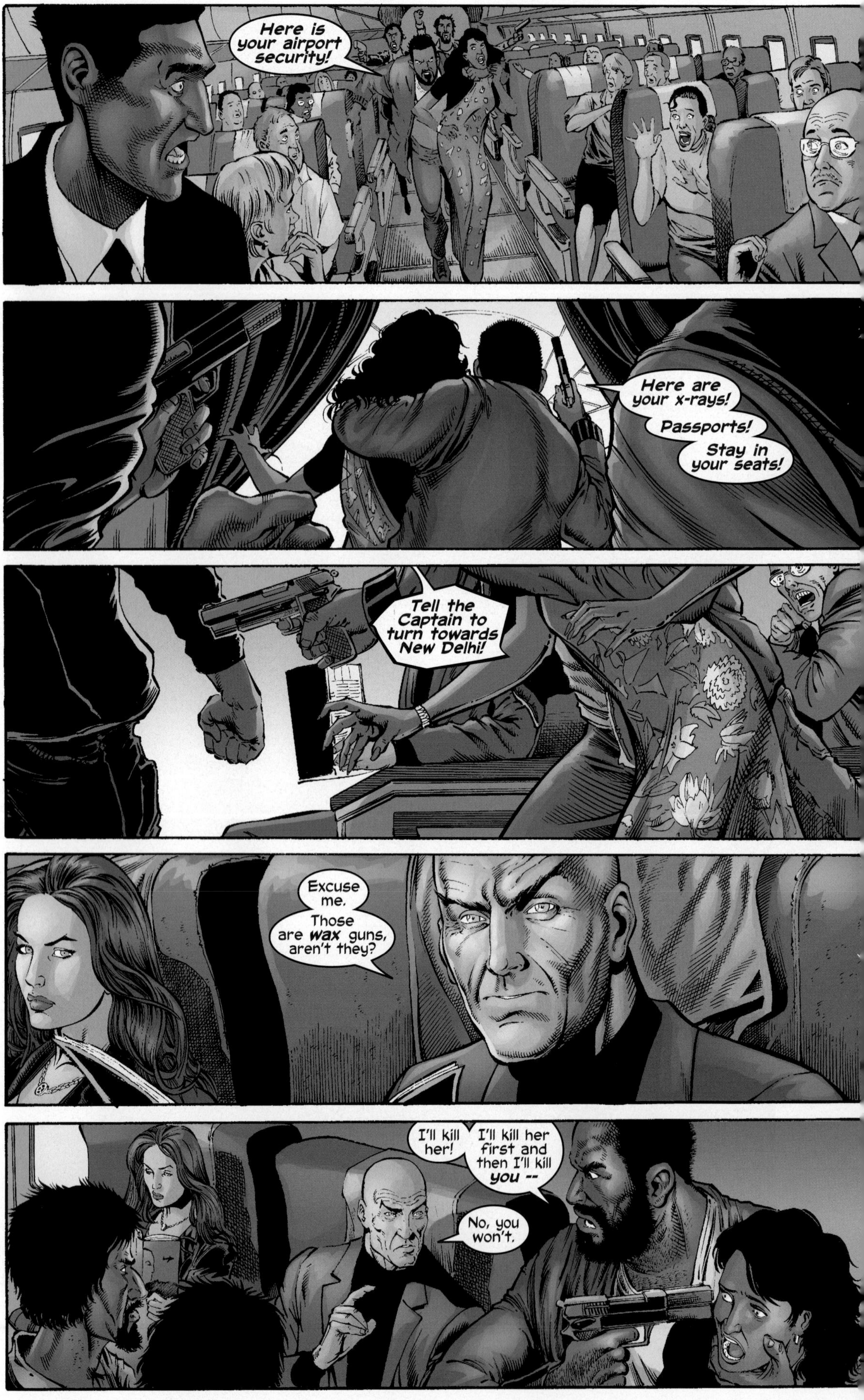
Here is your airport security!
Here are your x-rays!
Passports!
Stay in your seats!
Tell the Captain to turn towards New Delhi!
Excuse me.
Those are **wax** guns, aren't they?
I'll kill her!
I'll kill her first and then I'll kill **you --**
No, you won't.

SHUT UP!

I... you speak Pakistani... what should...

...what should we do instead?

Well, wouldn't it be much better for *everyone* if you all turned around and walked back to your seats? You could just stay there until we land at *Mumbai.*

And disarming the *bomb* in your bowel might be a very good idea, too, Mohammed.

Jean can probably do that for you -- she's *telekinetic.*

I'd just been reading about these so-called *"dirty bombs",* Jean...

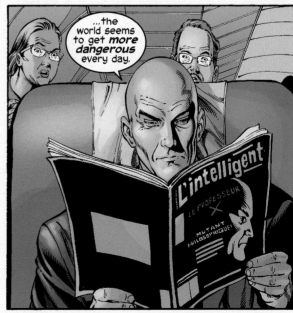

...the world seems to get *more dangerous* every day.

L'intelligent

LE PROFESSEUR X

MUTANT PHILOSOPHIQUE!

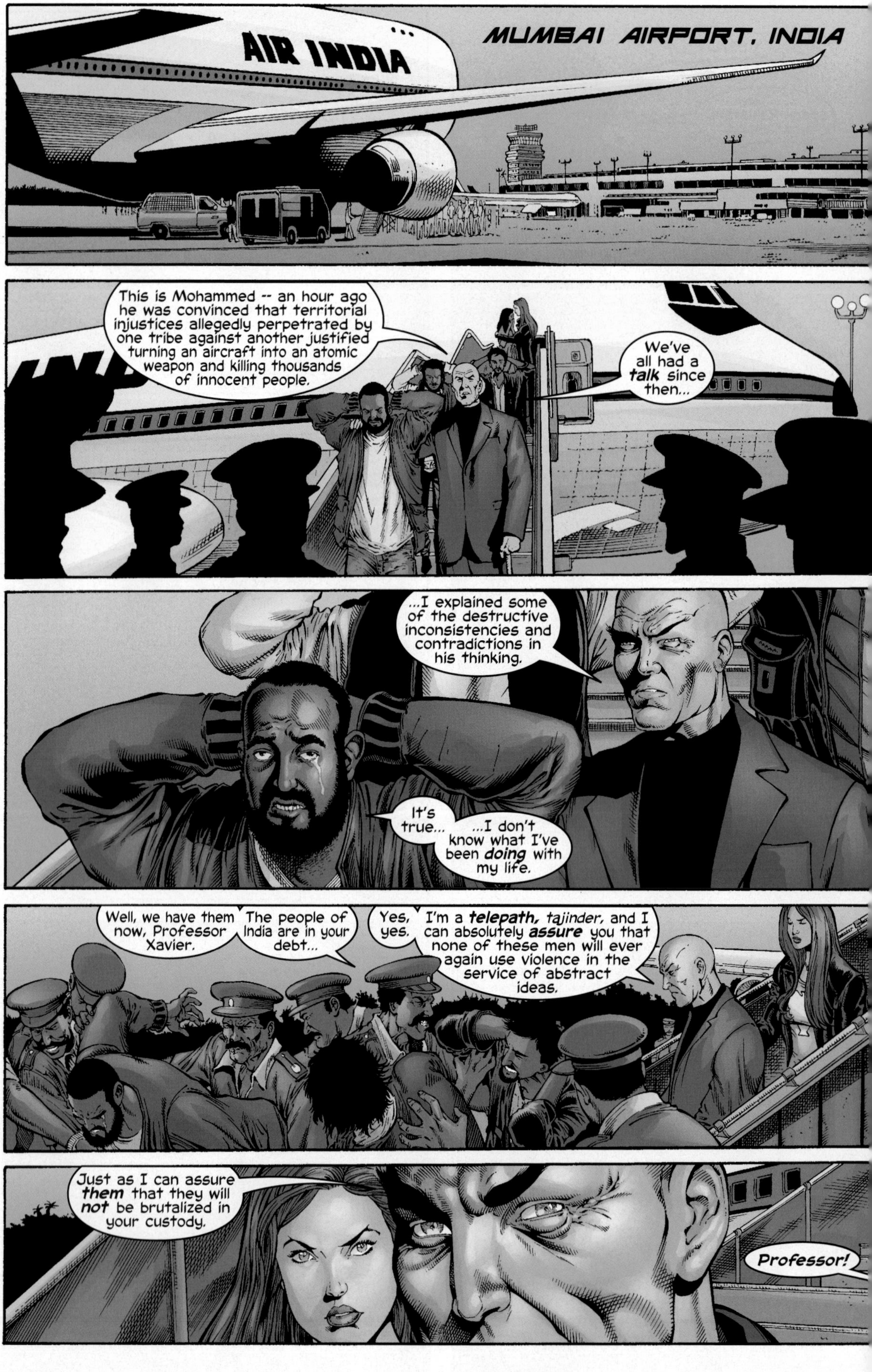
MUMBAI AIRPORT, INDIA
AIR INDIA
This is Mohammed -- an hour ago he was convinced that territorial injustices allegedly perpetrated by one tribe against another justified turning an aircraft into an atomic weapon and killing thousands of innocent people.
We've all had a talk since then...
...I explained some of the destructive inconsistencies and contradictions in his thinking.
It's true...
...I don't know what I've been doing with my life.
Well, we have them now, Professor Xavier.
The people of India are in your debt...
Yes, yes.
I'm a telepath, tajinder, and I can absolutely assure you that none of these men will ever again use violence in the service of abstract ideas.
Just as I can assure them that they will not be brutalized in your custody.
Professor!

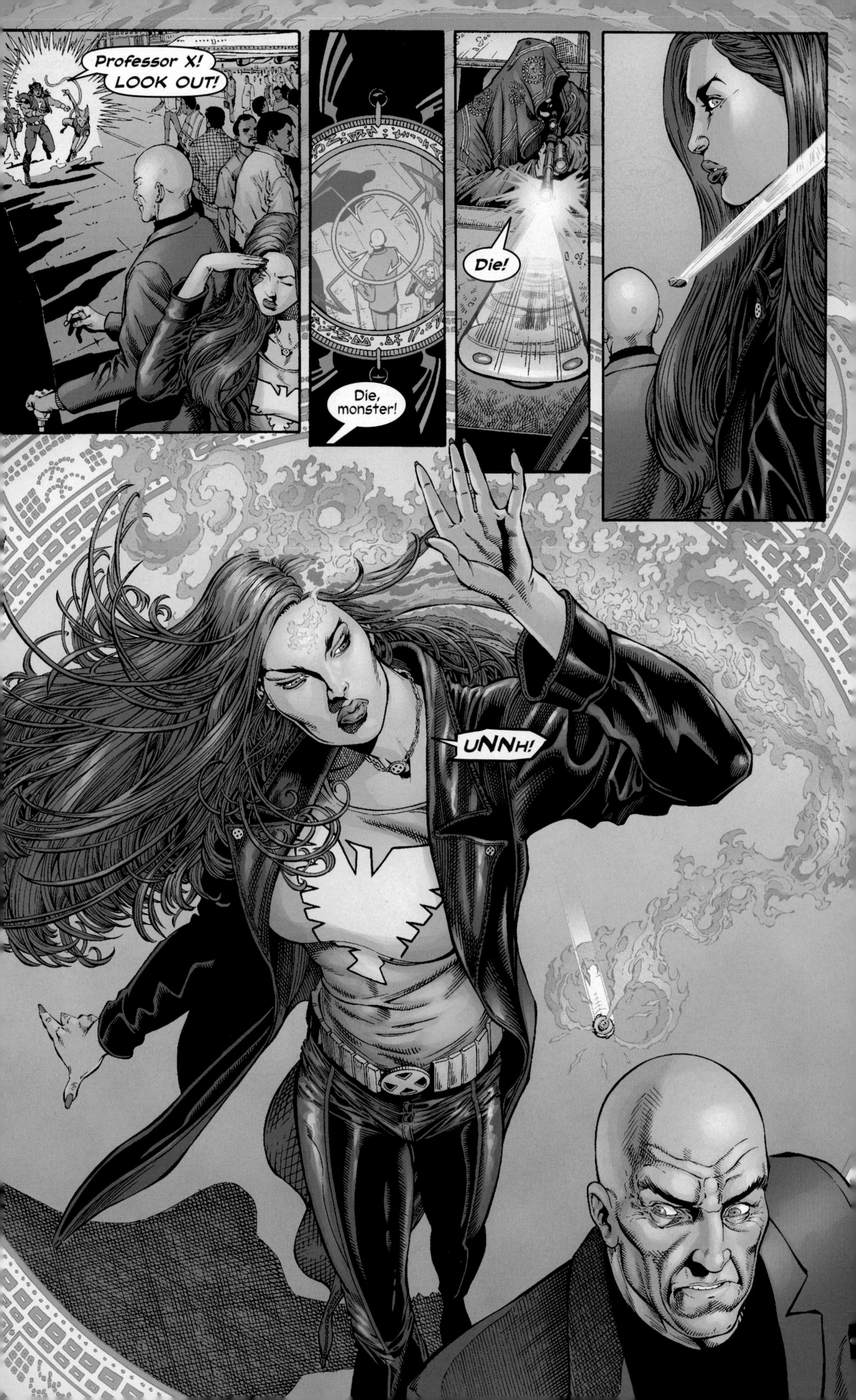
Professor X! LOOK OUT!
Die, monster!
Die!
UNNH!

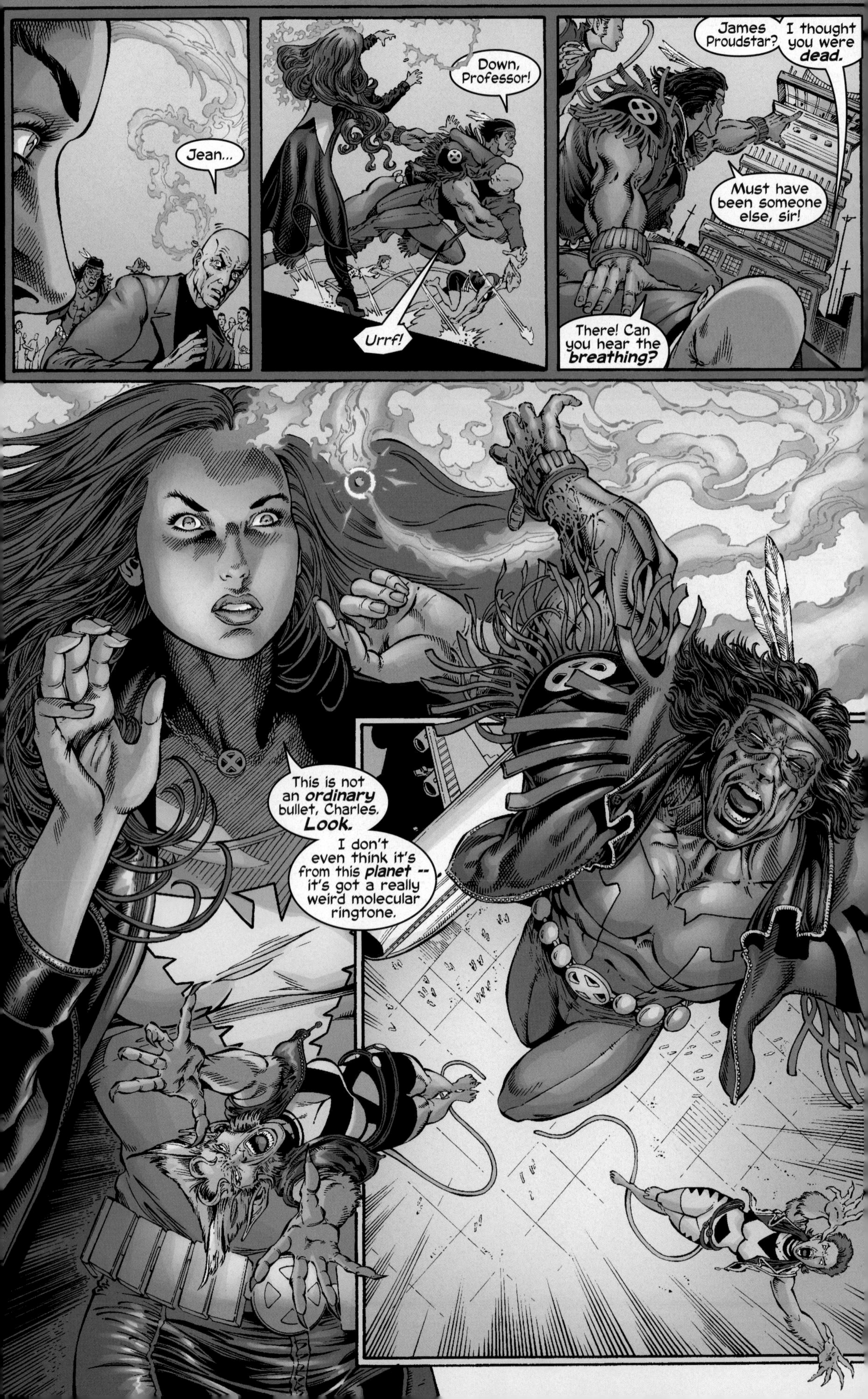
Jean...
Down, Professor!
Urrf!
James Proudstar?
I thought you were dead.
Must have been someone else, sir!
There! Can you hear the breathing?
This is not an ordinary bullet, Charles. Look.
I don't even think it's from this planet -- it's got a really weird molecular ringtone.

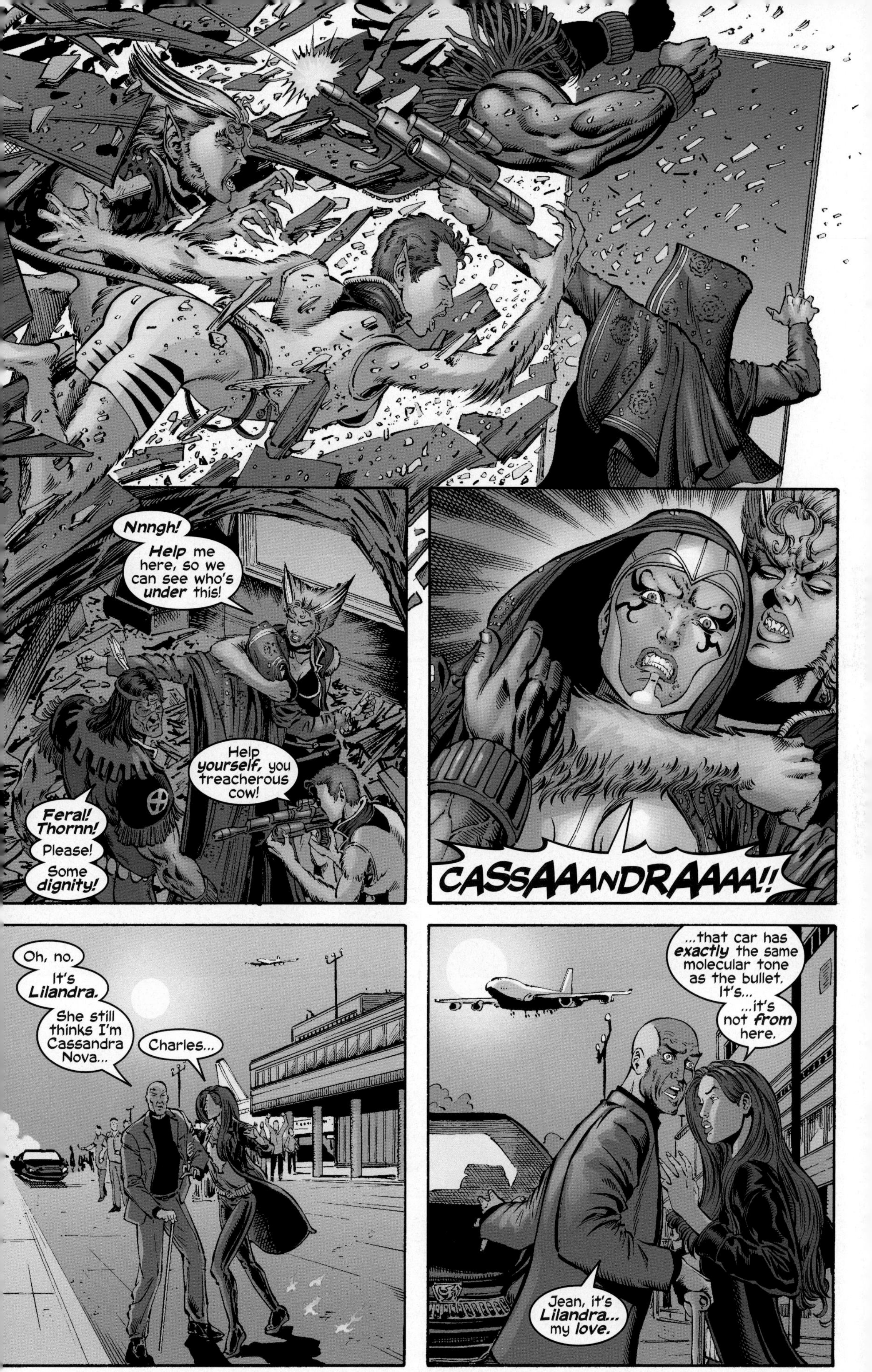
Nnngh!
Help me here, so we can see who's under this!
Help yourself, you treacherous cow!
Feral! Thornn!
Please!
Some dignity!
CASSAAANDRAAAA!!
Oh, no.
It's Lilandra.
She still thinks I'm Cassandra Nova...
Charles...
...that car has exactly the same molecular tone as the bullet. It's...
...it's not from here.
Jean, it's Lilandra... my love.

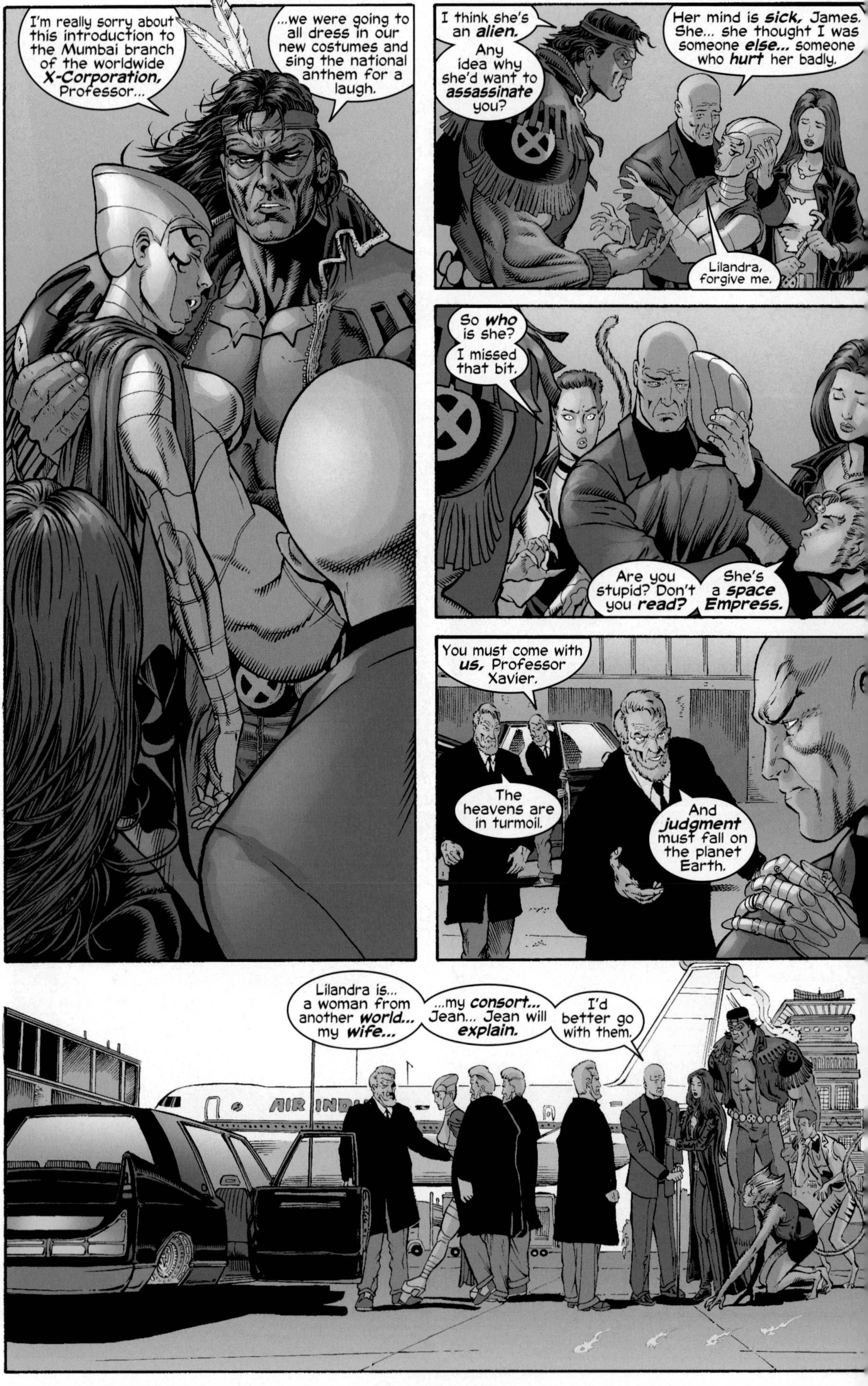

I'm really sorry about this introduction to the Mumbai branch of the worldwide X-Corporation, Professor...
...we were going to all dress in our new costumes and sing the national anthem for a laugh.
I think she's an alien.
Any idea why she'd want to assassinate you?
Her mind is sick, James. She... she thought I was someone else... someone who hurt her badly.
Lilandra, forgive me.
So who is she?
I missed that bit.
Are you stupid? Don't you read?
She's a space Empress.
You must come with us, Professor Xavier.
The heavens are in turmoil.
And judgment must fall on the planet Earth.
Lilandra is... a woman from another world... my wife...
...my consort... Jean... Jean will explain.
I'd better go with them.
AIR INDI

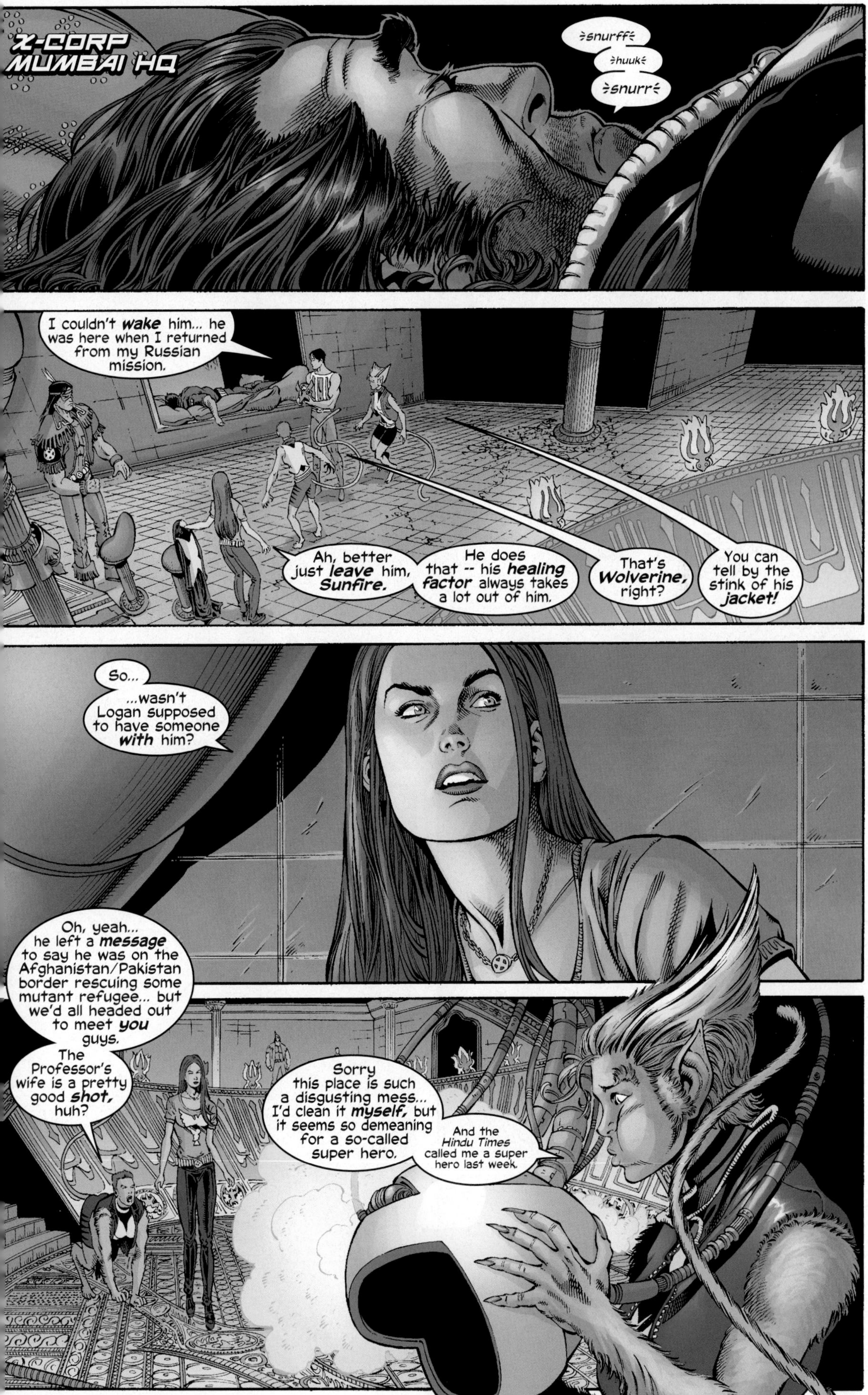
X-CORP MUMBAI HQ
≶snurff≶
≶huuk≶
≶snurr≶
I couldn't **wake** him... he was here when I returned from my Russian mission.
Ah, better just **leave** him, **Sunfire.**
He does that -- his **healing factor** always takes a lot out of him.
That's **Wolverine,** right?
You can tell by the stink of his **jacket!**
So...
...wasn't Logan supposed to have someone **with** him?
Oh, yeah... he left a **message** to say he was on the Afghanistan/Pakistan border rescuing some mutant refugee... but we'd all headed out to meet **you** guys.
The Professor's wife is a pretty good **shot,** huh?
Sorry this place is such a disgusting mess... I'd clean it **myself,** but it seems so demeaning for a so-called super hero.
And the *Hindu Times* called me a super hero last week.

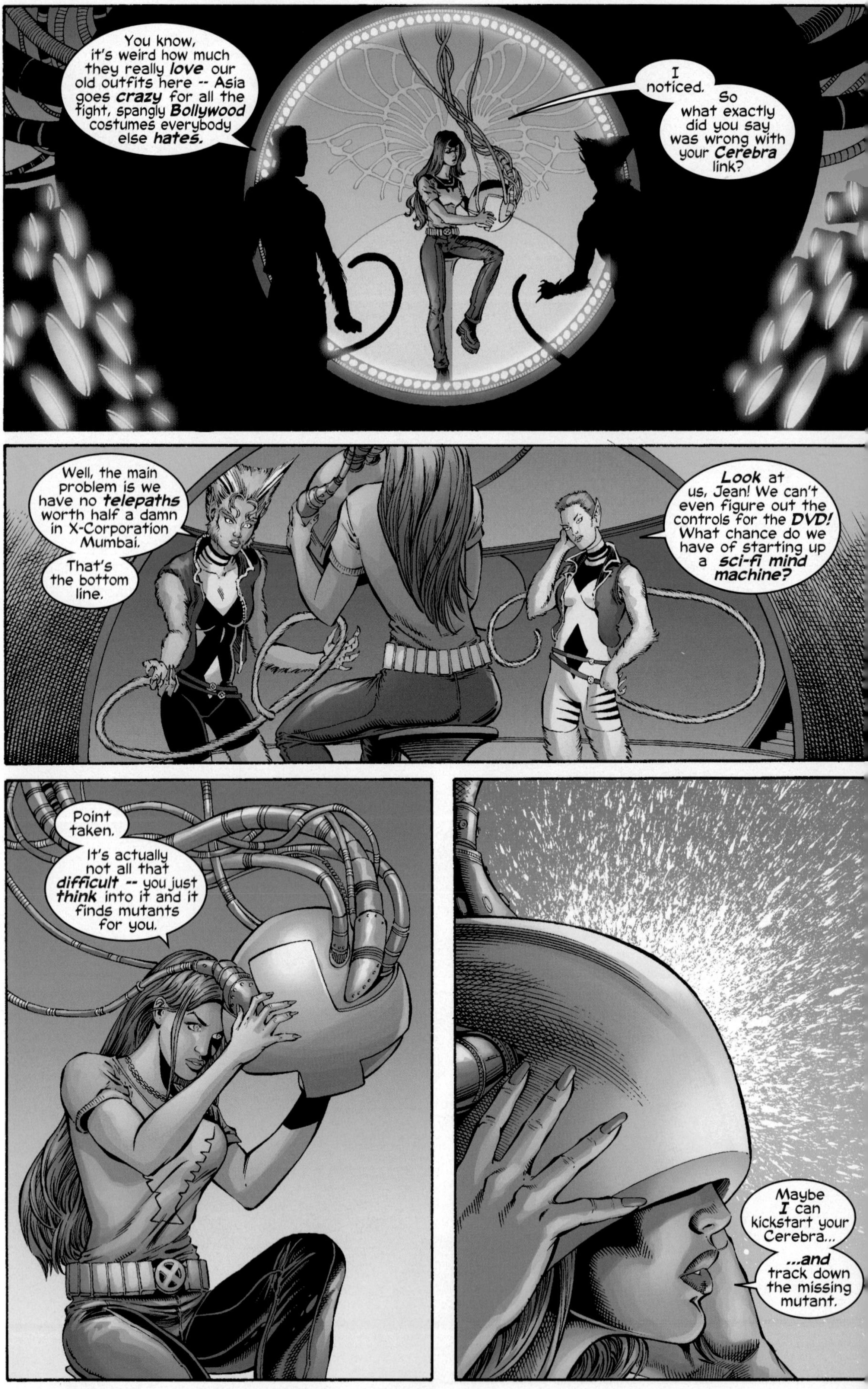

You know, it's weird how much they really love our old outfits here -- Asia goes crazy for all the tight, spangly Bollywood costumes everybody else hates.
I noticed.
So what exactly did you say was wrong with your Cerebra link?
Well, the main problem is we have no telepaths worth half a damn in X-Corporation Mumbai.
That's the bottom line.
Look at us, Jean! We can't even figure out the controls for the DVD! What chance do we have of starting up a sci-fi mind machine?
Point taken.
It's actually not all that difficult -- you just think into it and it finds mutants for you.
Maybe I can kickstart your Cerebra...
...and track down the missing mutant.

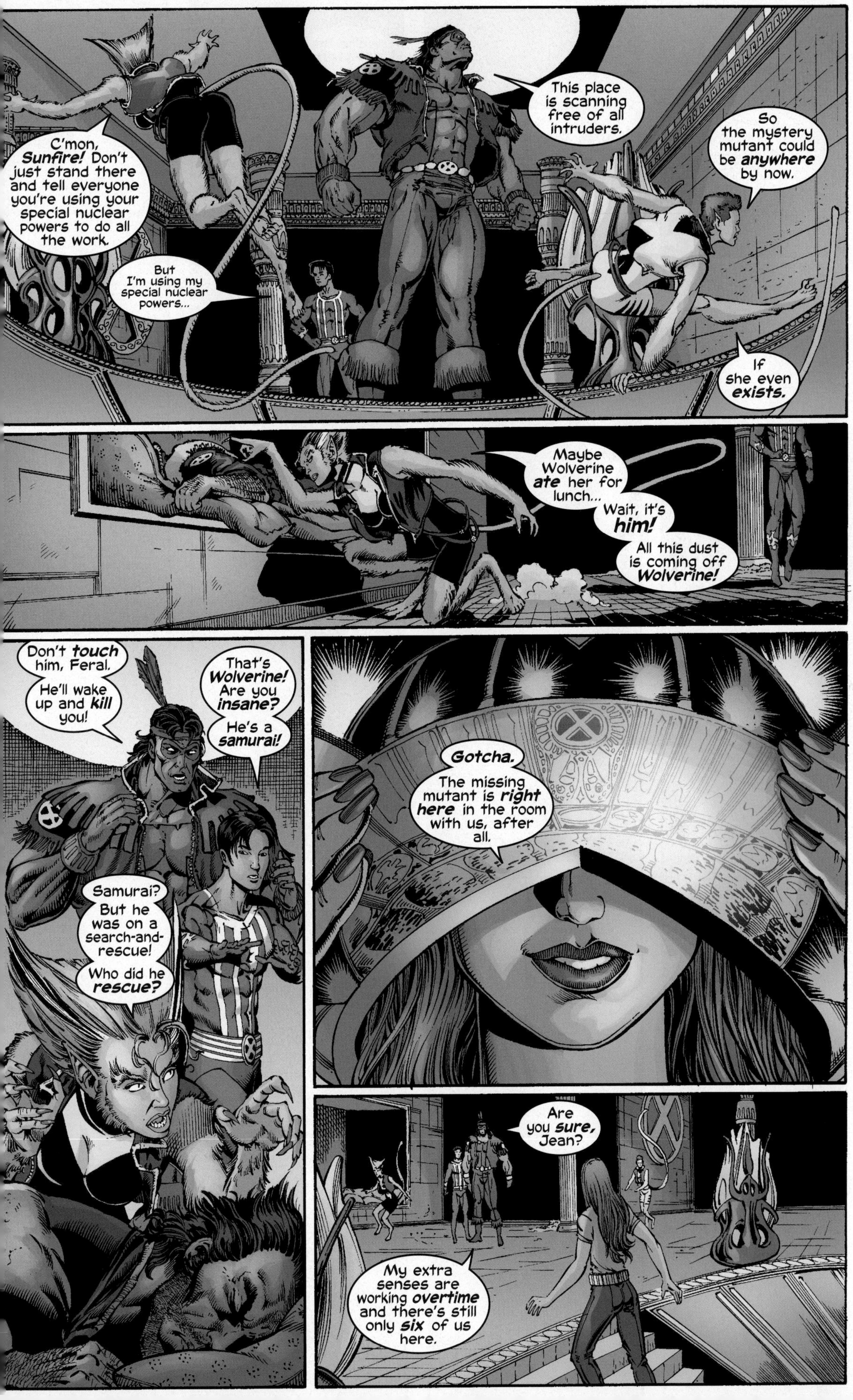

C'mon, Sunfire! Don't just stand there and tell everyone you're using your special nuclear powers to do all the work.
But I'm using my special nuclear powers...
This place is scanning free of all intruders.
So the mystery mutant could be anywhere by now.
If she even exists.
Maybe Wolverine ate her for lunch...
Wait, it's him!
All this dust is coming off Wolverine!
Don't touch him, Feral.
He'll wake up and kill you!
That's Wolverine! Are you insane?
He's a samurai!
Samurai? But he was on a search-and-rescue!
Who did he rescue?
Gotcha.
The missing mutant is right here in the room with us, after all.
Are you sure, Jean?
My extra senses are working overtime and there's still only six of us here.

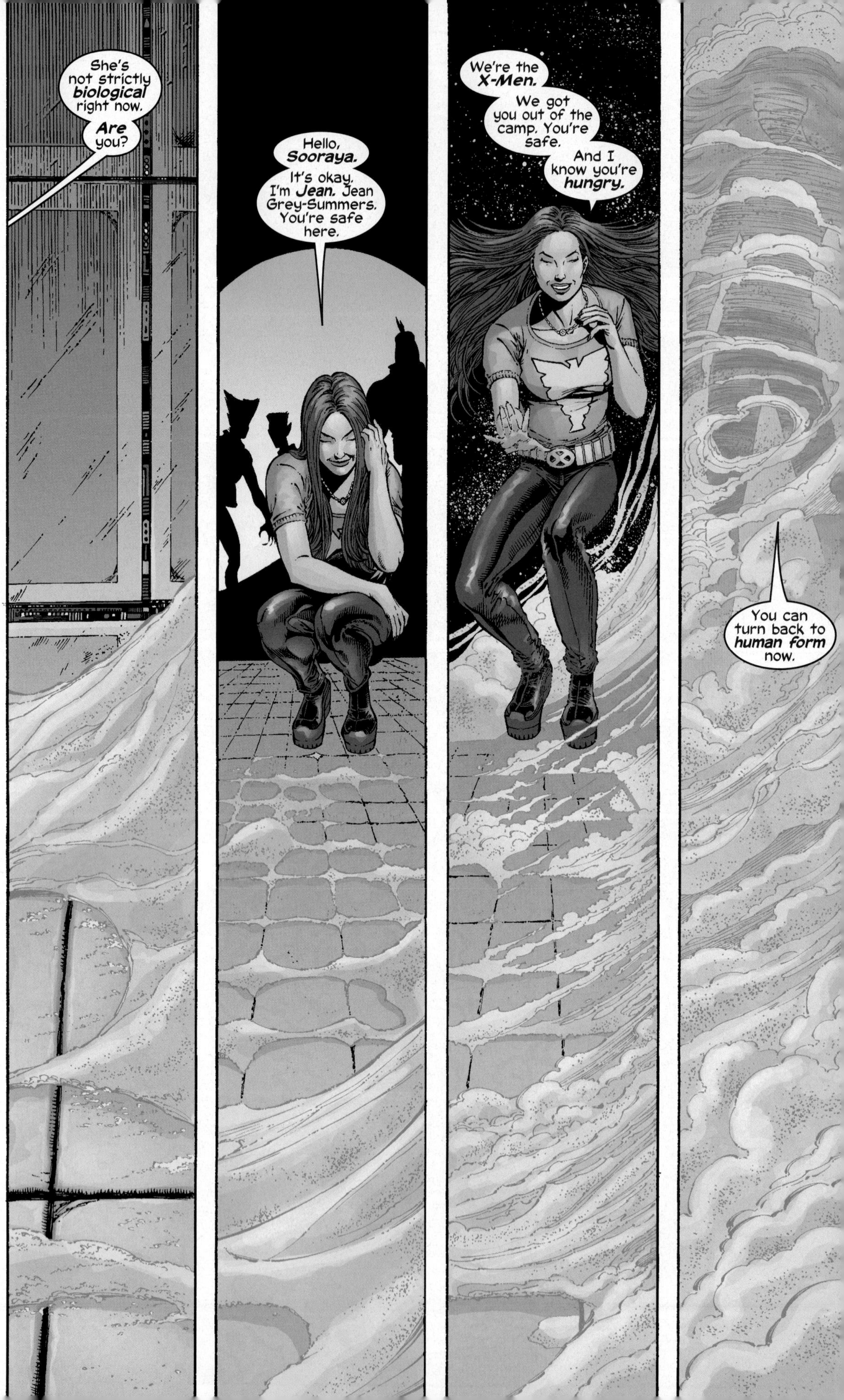
She's not strictly biological right now.
Are you?
Hello, Sooraya.
It's okay. I'm Jean. Jean Grey-Summers. You're safe here.
We're the X-Men.
We got you out of the camp. You're safe.
And I know you're hungry.
You can turn back to human form now.

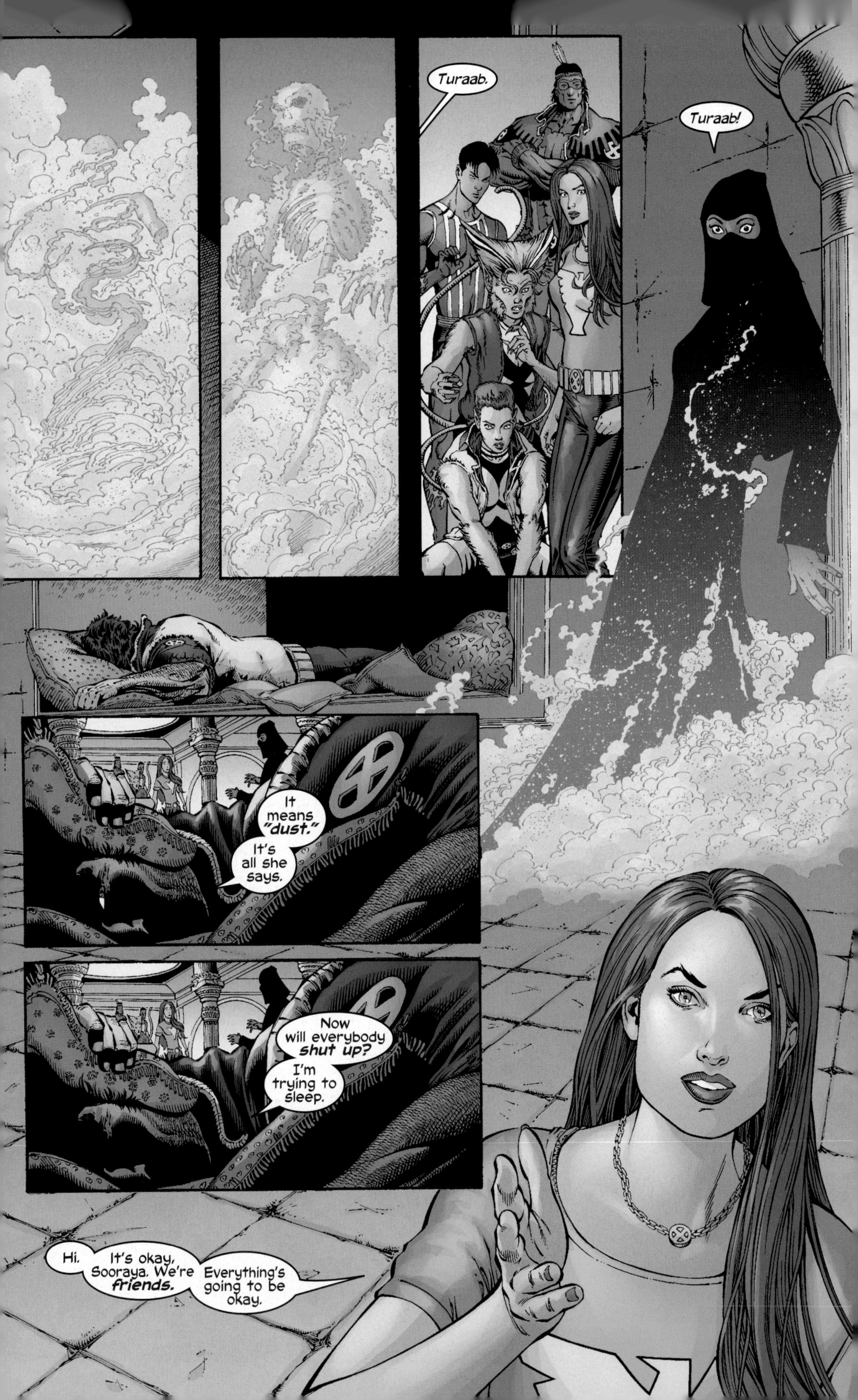
Turaab.
Turaab!
It means "dust."
It's all she says.
Now will everybody shut up?
I'm trying to sleep.
Hi.
It's okay, Sooraya. We're friends.
Everything's going to be okay.

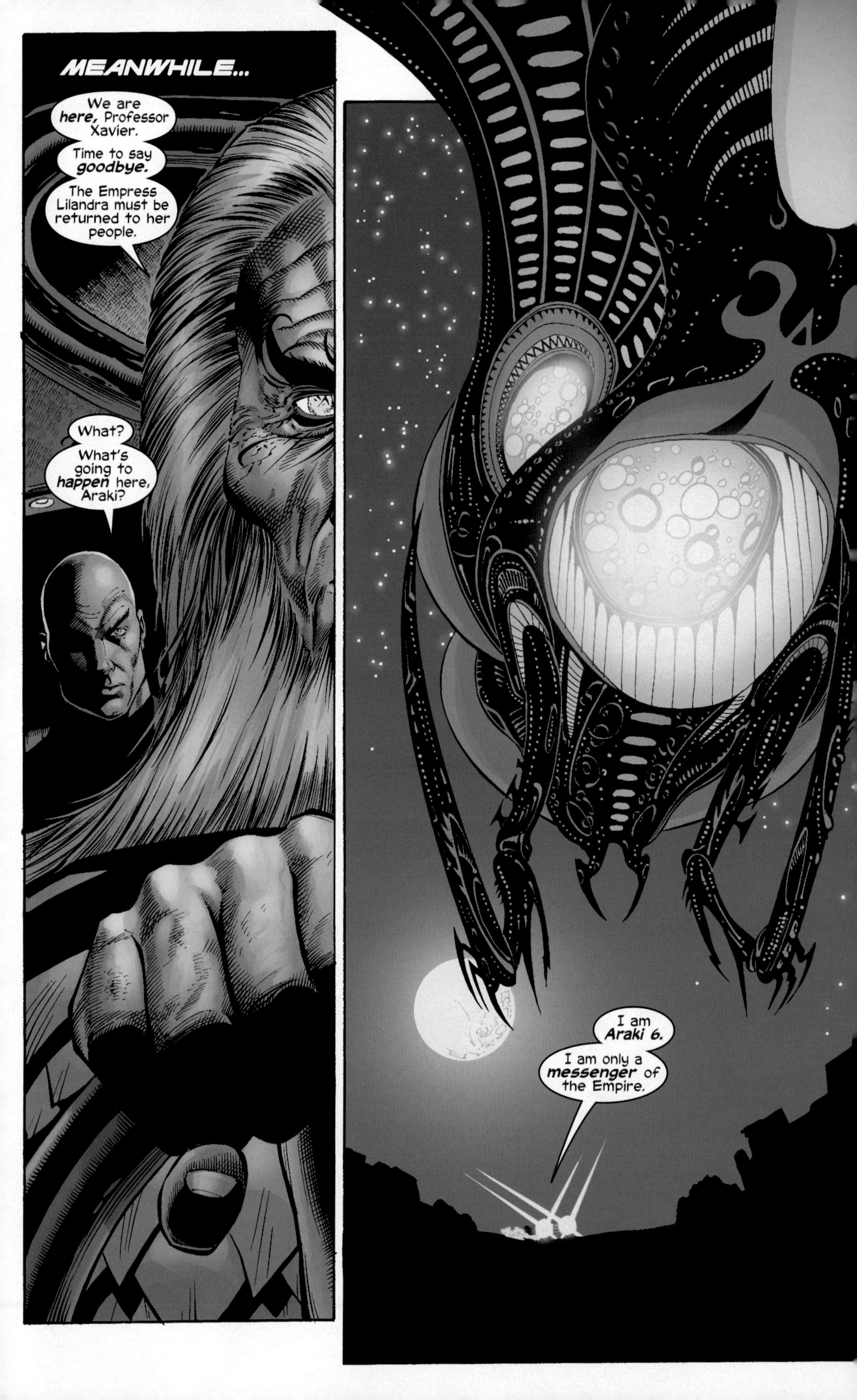
MEANWHILE...
We are here, Professor Xavier.
Time to say goodbye.
The Empress Lilandra must be returned to her people.
What?
What's going to happen here, Araki?
I am Araki 6.
I am only a messenger of the Empire.

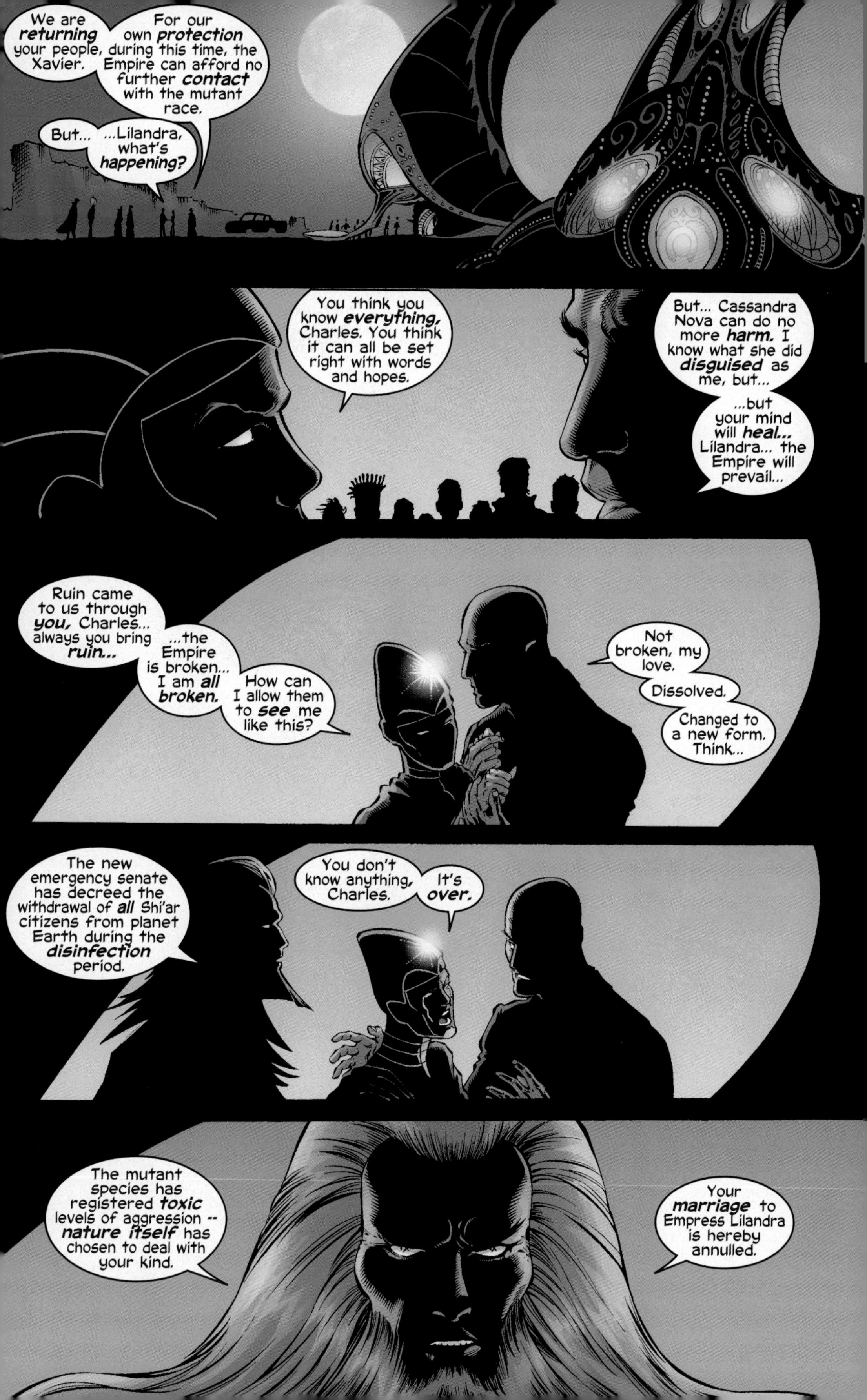
We are returning your people, Xavier.
For our own protection during this time, the Empire can afford no further contact with the mutant race.
But...
...Lilandra, what's happening?
You think you know everything, Charles. You think it can all be set right with words and hopes.
But... Cassandra Nova can do no more harm. I know what she did disguised as me, but...
...but your mind will heal... Lilandra... the Empire will prevail...
Ruin came to us through you, Charles... always you bring ruin...
...the Empire is broken... I am all broken.
How can I allow them to see me like this?
Not broken, my love.
Dissolved.
Changed to a new form. Think...
The new emergency senate has decreed the withdrawal of all Shi'ar citizens from planet Earth during the disinfection period.
You don't know anything, Charles.
It's over.
The mutant species has registered toxic levels of aggression -- nature itself has chosen to deal with your kind.
Your marriage to Empress Lilandra is hereby annulled.

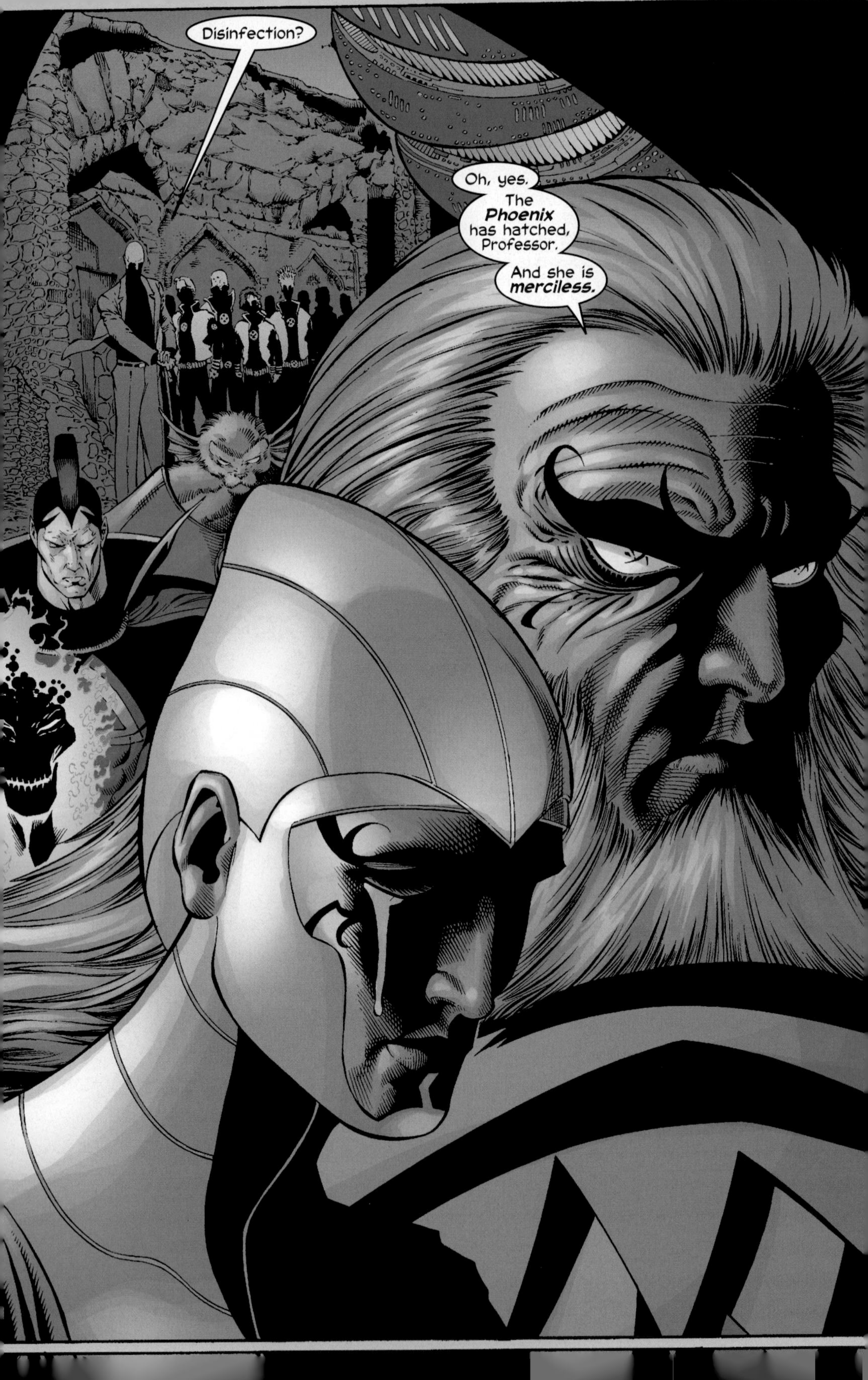
Disinfection?
Oh, yes.
The **Phoenix** has hatched, Professor.
And she is **merciless.**

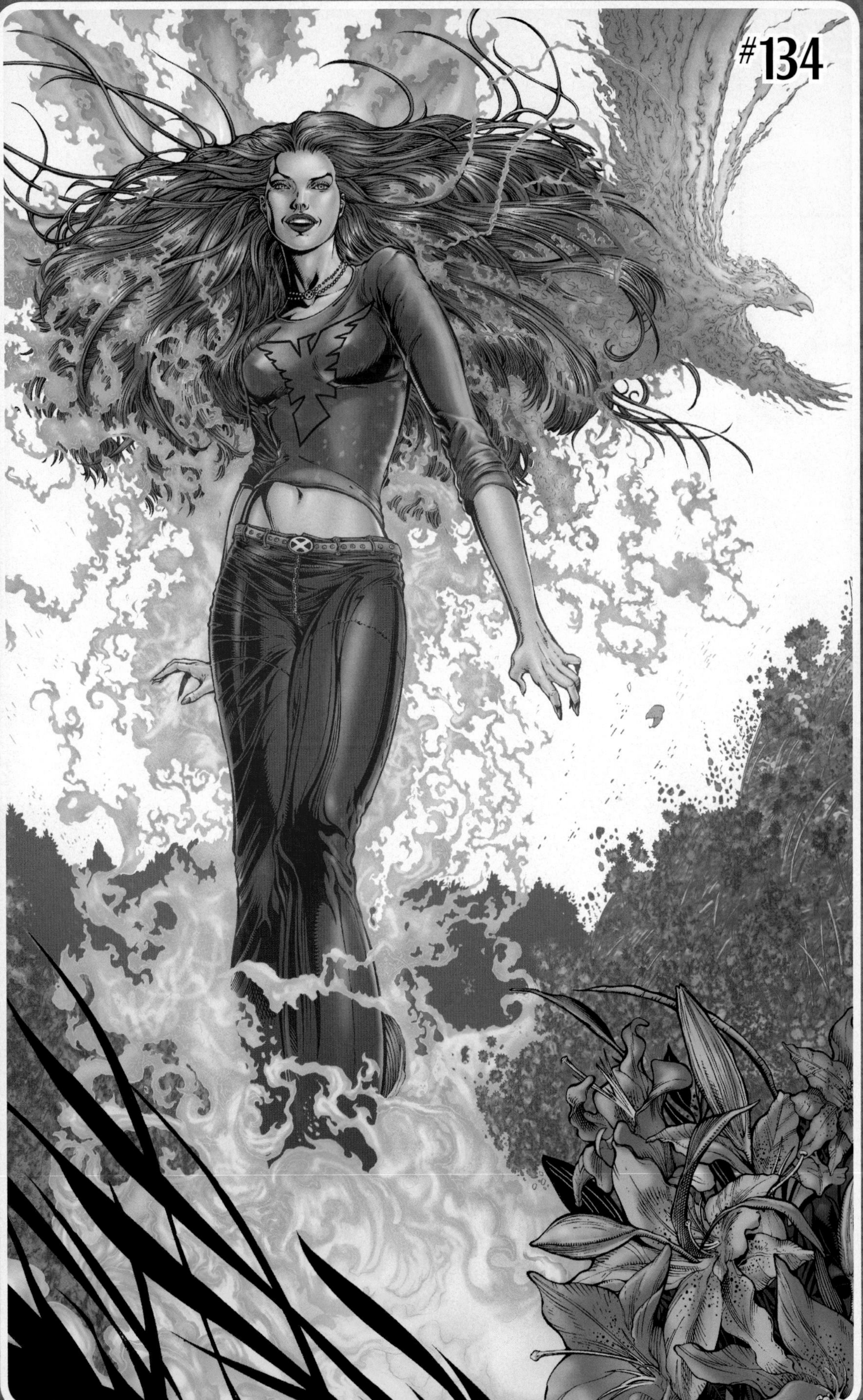
#134

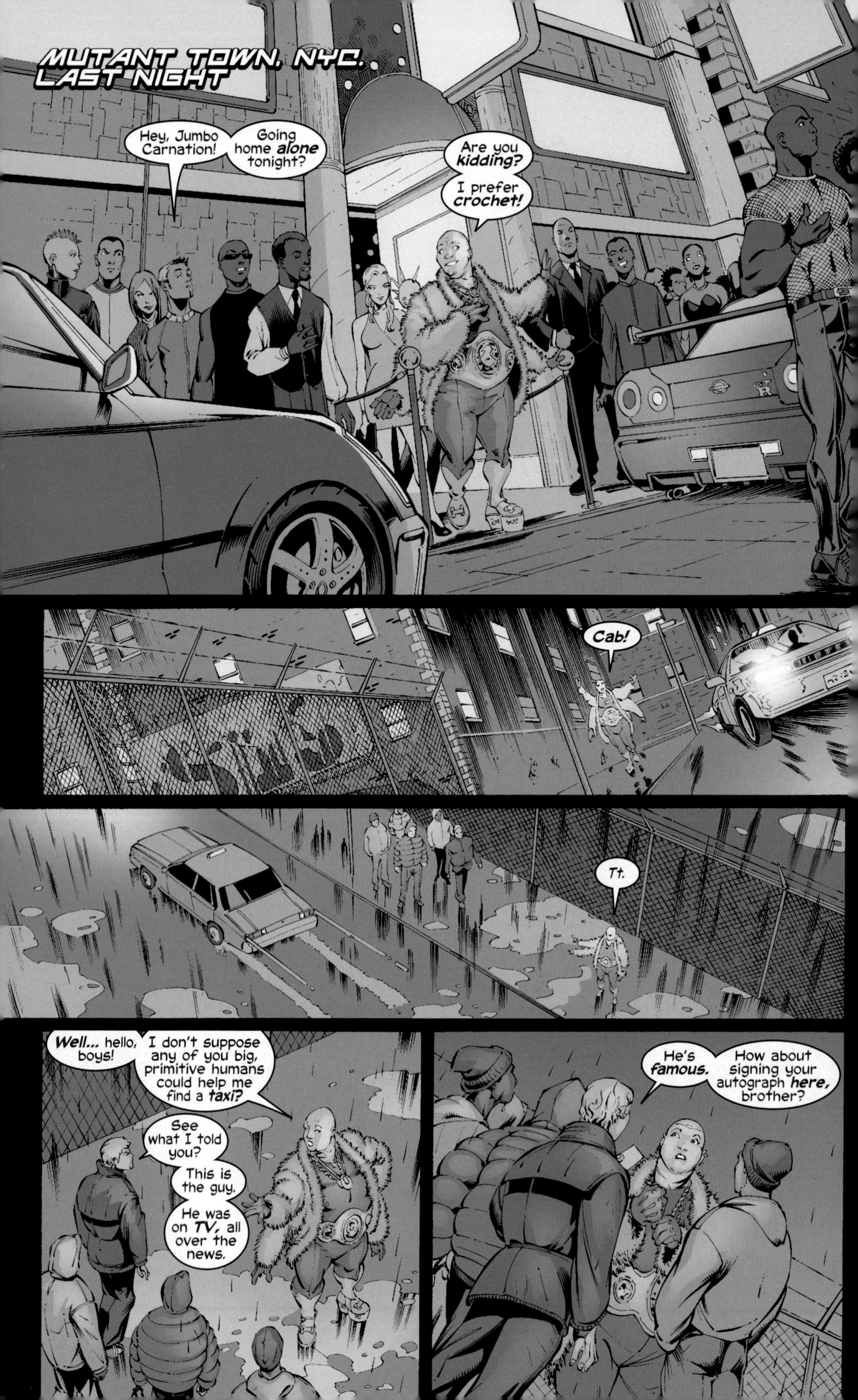
MUTANT TOWN, NYC. LAST NIGHT
Hey, Jumbo Carnation!
Going home alone tonight?
Are you kidding?
I prefer crochet!
Cab!
Tt.
Well... hello, boys!
I don't suppose any of you big, primitive humans could help me find a taxi?
See what I told you?
This is the guy.
He was on TV, all over the news.
He's famous.
How about signing your autograph here, brother?

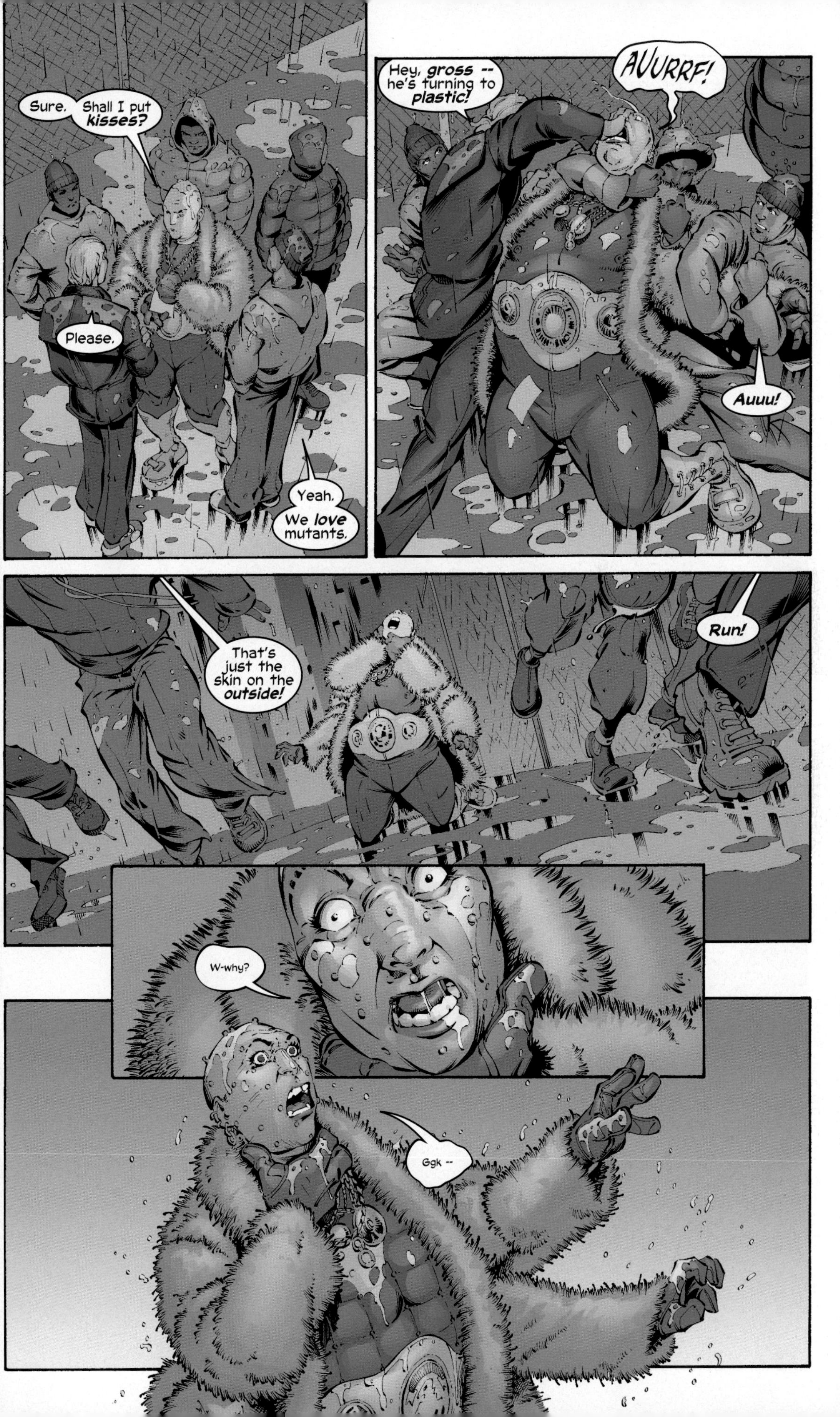
Sure.
Shall I put kisses?
Please.
Yeah.
We love mutants.
Hey, gross -- he's turning to plastic!
AUURRF!
Auuu!
That's just the skin on the outside!
Run!
W-why?
Ggk --

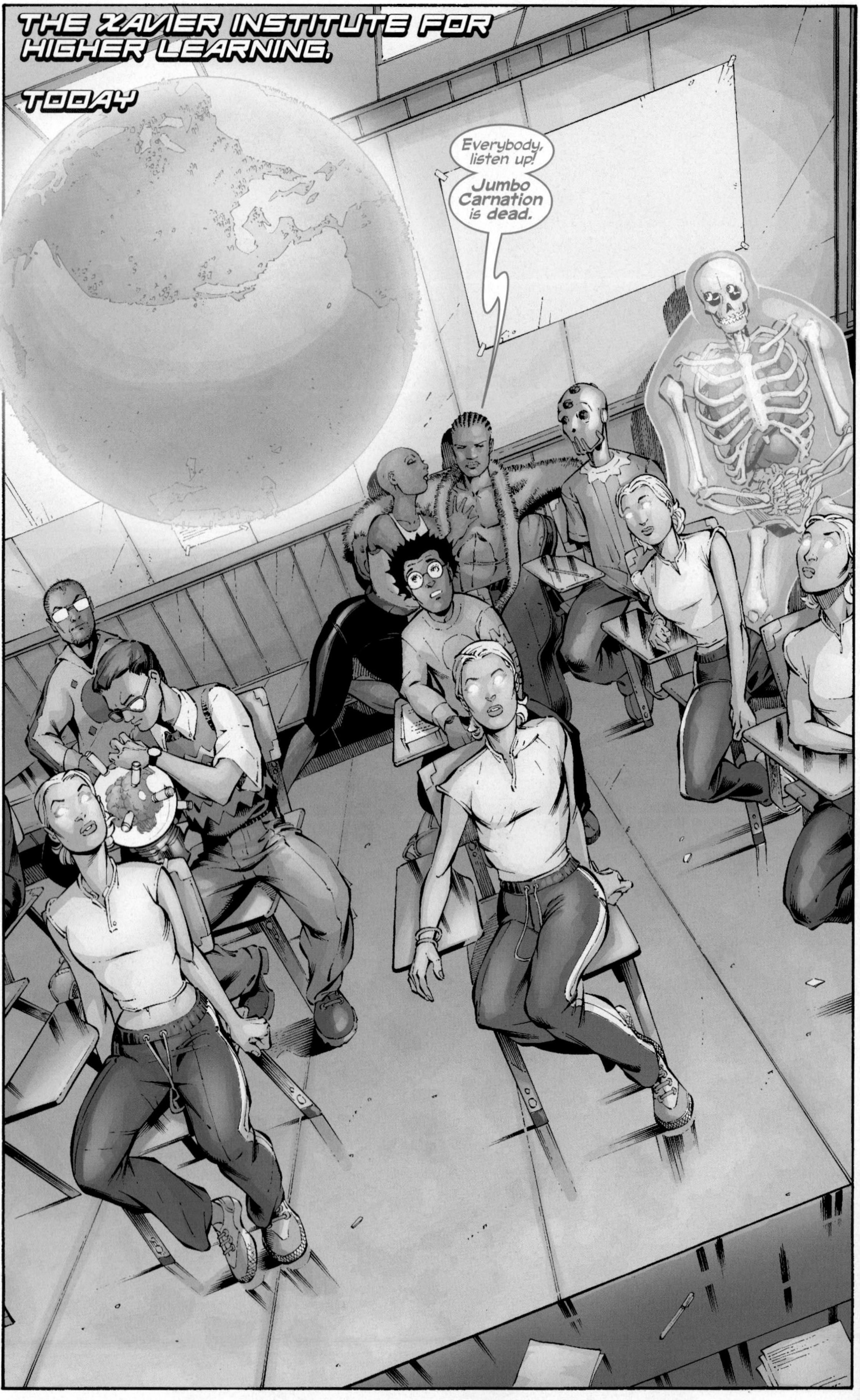
THE XAVIER INSTITUTE FOR HIGHER LEARNING.
TODAY
Everybody, listen up! Jumbo Carnation is dead.

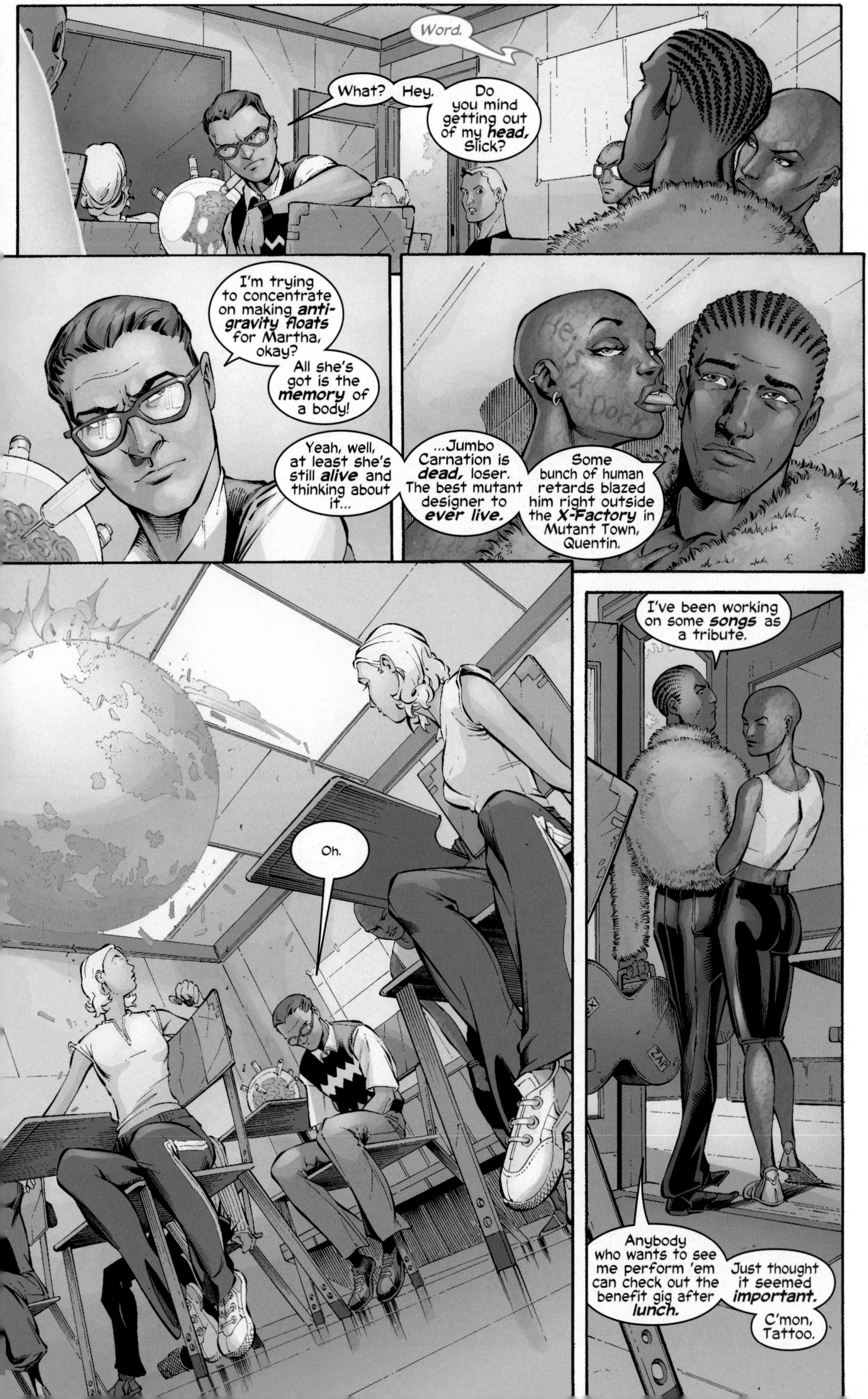
Word.
What?
Hey.
Do you mind getting out of my *head,* Slick?
I'm trying to concentrate on making *anti-gravity floats* for Martha, okay?
All she's got is the *memory* of a body!
Yeah, well, at least she's still *alive* and thinking about it...
...Jumbo Carnation is *dead,* loser. The best mutant designer to *ever live.*
Some bunch of human retards blazed him right outside the *X-Factory* in Mutant Town, Quentin.
Oh.
I've been working on some *songs* as a tribute.
ZAP
Anybody who wants to see me perform 'em can check out the benefit gig after *lunch.*
Just thought it seemed *important.*
C'mon, Tattoo.

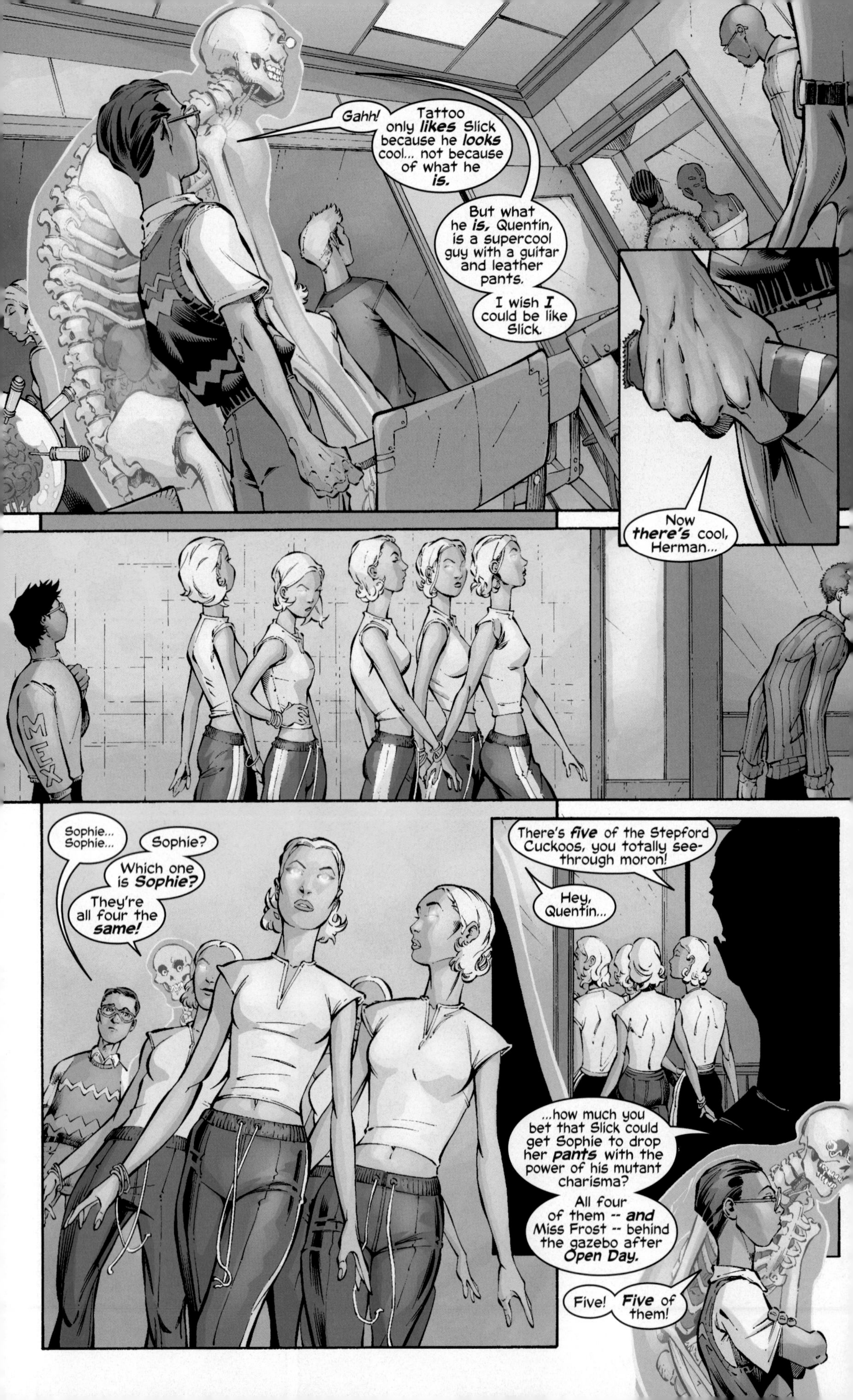
Gahh!
Tattoo only likes Slick because he looks cool... not because of what he is.
But what he is, Quentin, is a supercool guy with a guitar and leather pants.
I wish I could be like Slick.
Now there's cool, Herman...
MEX
Sophie... Sophie...
Sophie?
Which one is Sophie?
They're all four the same!
There's five of the Stepford Cuckoos, you totally see-through moron!
Hey, Quentin...
...how much you bet that Slick could get Sophie to drop her pants with the power of his mutant charisma?
All four of them -- and Miss Frost -- behind the gazebo after Open Day.
Five!
Five of them!

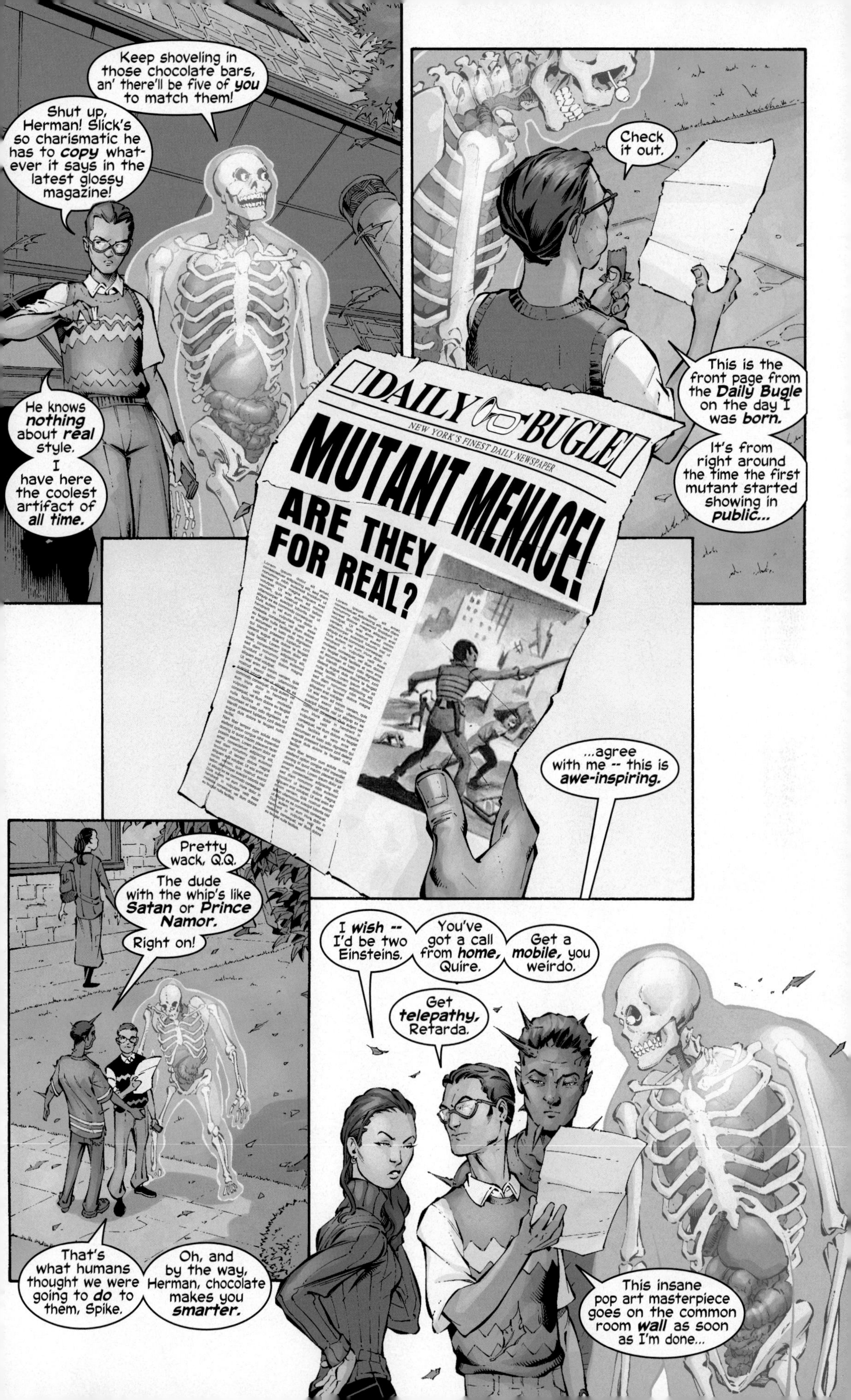

Keep shoveling in those chocolate bars, an' there'll be five of *you* to match them!
Shut up, Herman! Slick's so charismatic he has to *copy* whatever it says in the latest glossy magazine!
He knows *nothing* about *real* style.
I have here the coolest artifact of *all time.*
Check it out.
This is the front page from the *Daily Bugle* on the day I was *born.*
It's from right around the time the first mutant started showing in *public...*
DAILY BUGLE
NEW YORK'S FINEST DAILY NEWSPAPER
MUTANT MENACE!
ARE THEY FOR REAL?
...agree with me -- this is *awe-inspiring.*
Pretty wack, Q.Q.
The dude with the whip's like *Satan* or *Prince Namor.*
Right on!
That's what humans thought we were going to *do* to them, Spike.
Oh, and by the way, Herman, chocolate makes you *smarter.*
I *wish* -- I'd be two Einsteins.
You've got a call from *home,* Quire.
Get a *mobile,* you weirdo.
Get *telepathy,* Retarda.
This insane pop art masterpiece goes on the common room *wall* as soon as I'm done...

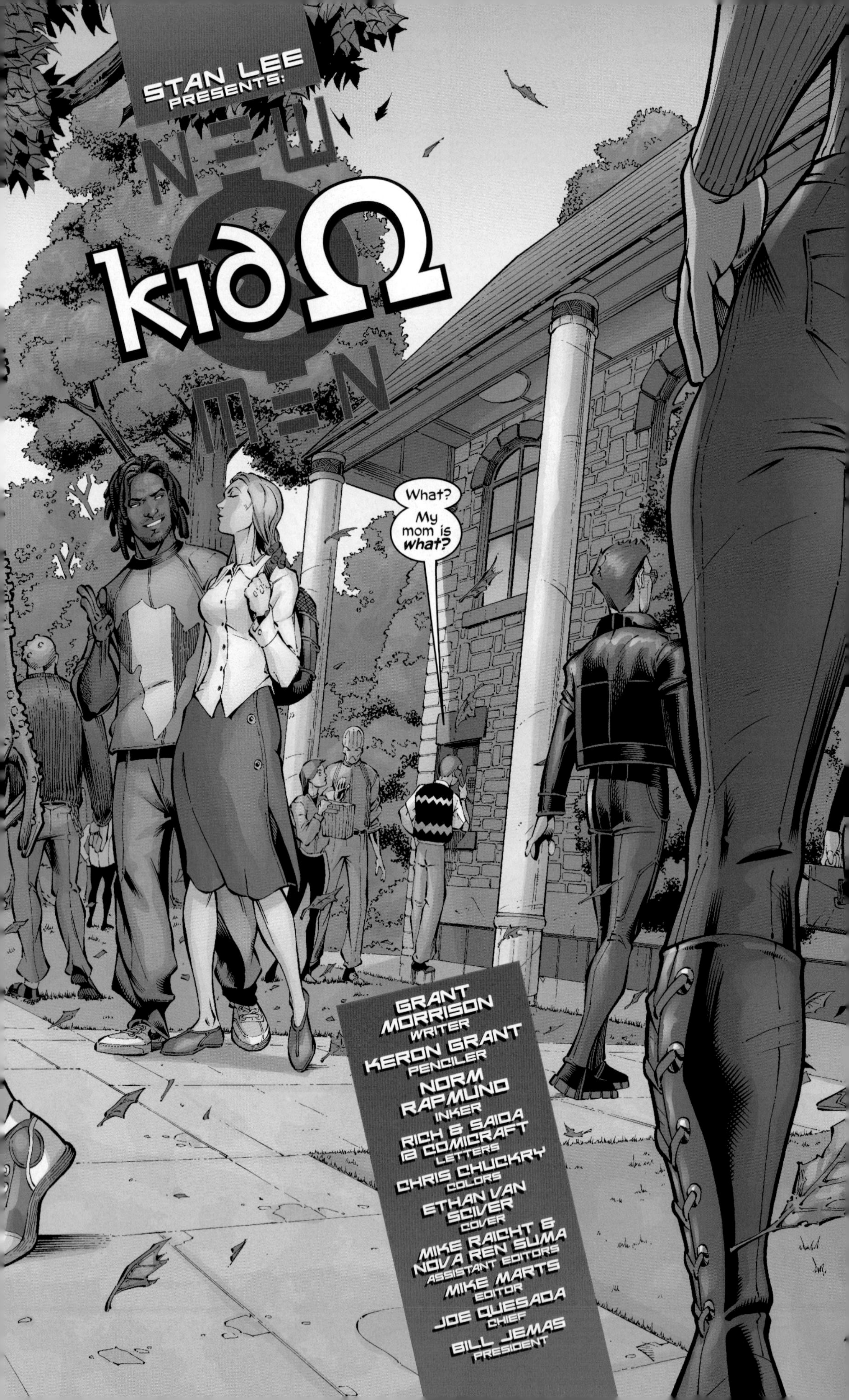
STAN LEE PRESENTS:
NEW X-MEN
KID Ω
What? My mom is what?
GRANT MORRISON WRITER
KERON GRANT PENCILER
NORM RAPMUND INKER
RICH & SAIDA
[2 COMICRAFT
LETTERS
CHRIS CHUCKRY COLORS
ETHAN VAN SCIVER COVER
MIKE RAICHT & NOVA REN SUMA ASSISTANT EDITORS
MIKE MARTS EDITOR
JOE QUESADA CHIEF
BILL JEMAS PRESIDENT

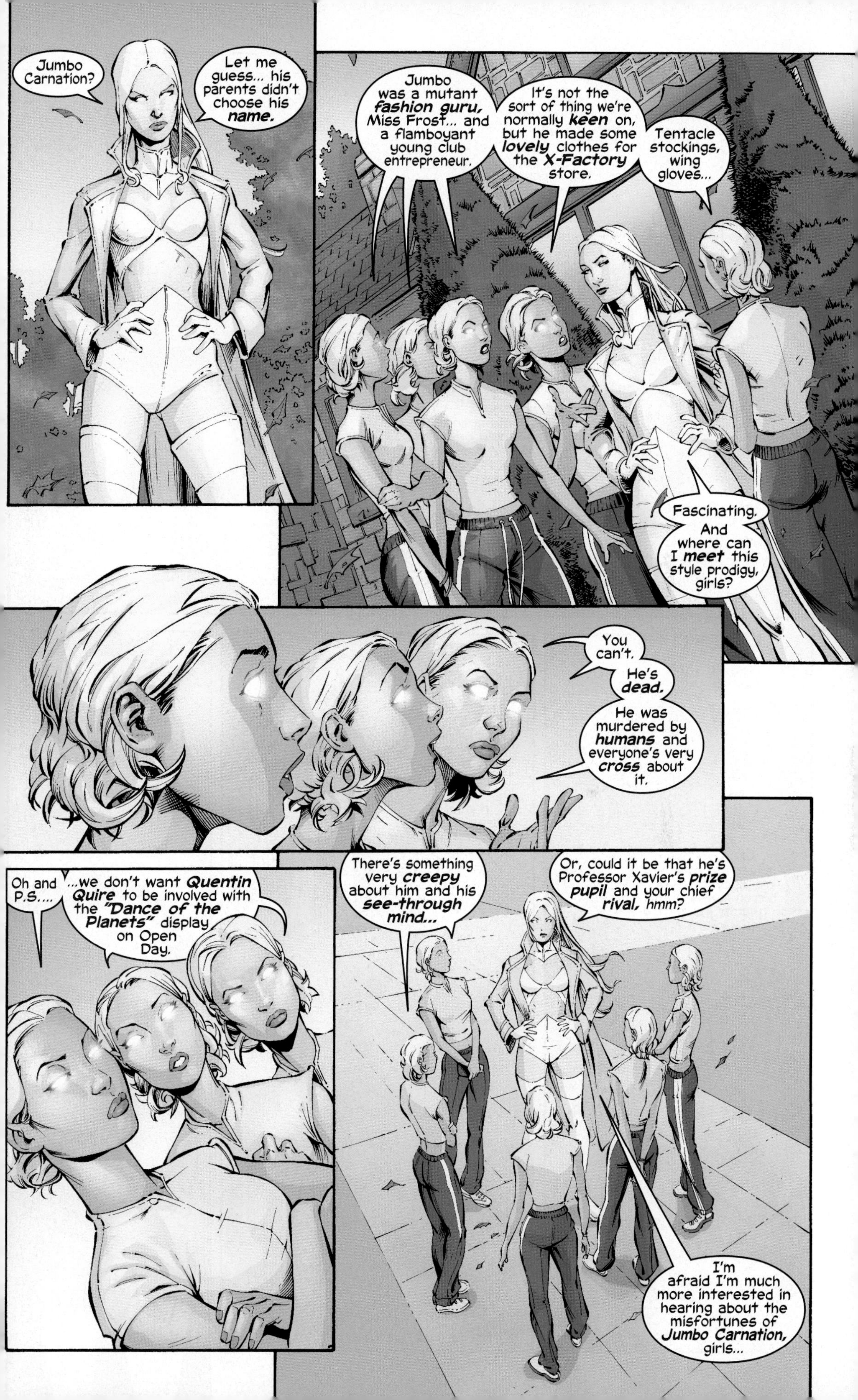

Jumbo Carnation?
Let me guess... his parents didn't choose his name.
Jumbo was a mutant fashion guru, Miss Frost... and a flamboyant young club entrepreneur.
It's not the sort of thing we're normally keen on, but he made some lovely clothes for the X-Factory store.
Tentacle stockings, wing gloves...
Fascinating. And where can I meet this style prodigy, girls?
You can't.
He's dead.
He was murdered by humans and everyone's very cross about it.
Oh and P.S....
...we don't want Quentin Quire to be involved with the "Dance of the Planets" display on Open Day.
There's something very creepy about him and his see-through mind...
Or, could it be that he's Professor Xavier's prize pupil and your chief rival, hmm?
I'm afraid I'm much more interested in hearing about the misfortunes of Jumbo Carnation, girls...

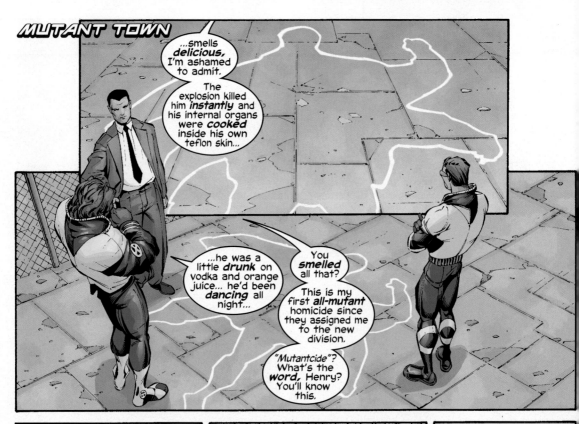

...smells *delicious,* I'm ashamed to admit.

The explosion killed him *instantly* and his internal organs were *cooked* inside his own teflon skin...

...he was a little *drunk* on vodka and orange juice... he'd been *dancing* all night...

You *smelled* all that?

This is my first *all-mutant* homicide since they assigned me to the new division.

"Mutantcide"? What's the *word,* Henry? You'll know this.

Homicide superior?

So, how *are* you, Henry?

Doctor McCoy here saved my *wife* and me during a super-terror meets woman-in-labor incident a few years ago, Cyclops.

I did?

Ah, *you* remember, Henry!

Oh, I'm sorry, Officer *Foster* -- all humans look *alike* to me.

It's all *save this* and *save that*...

Hahaha!

He cracks me up. He was like that all the way to the *hospital.* Driving a *tank,* would you believe it?

It's that *dry* humor.

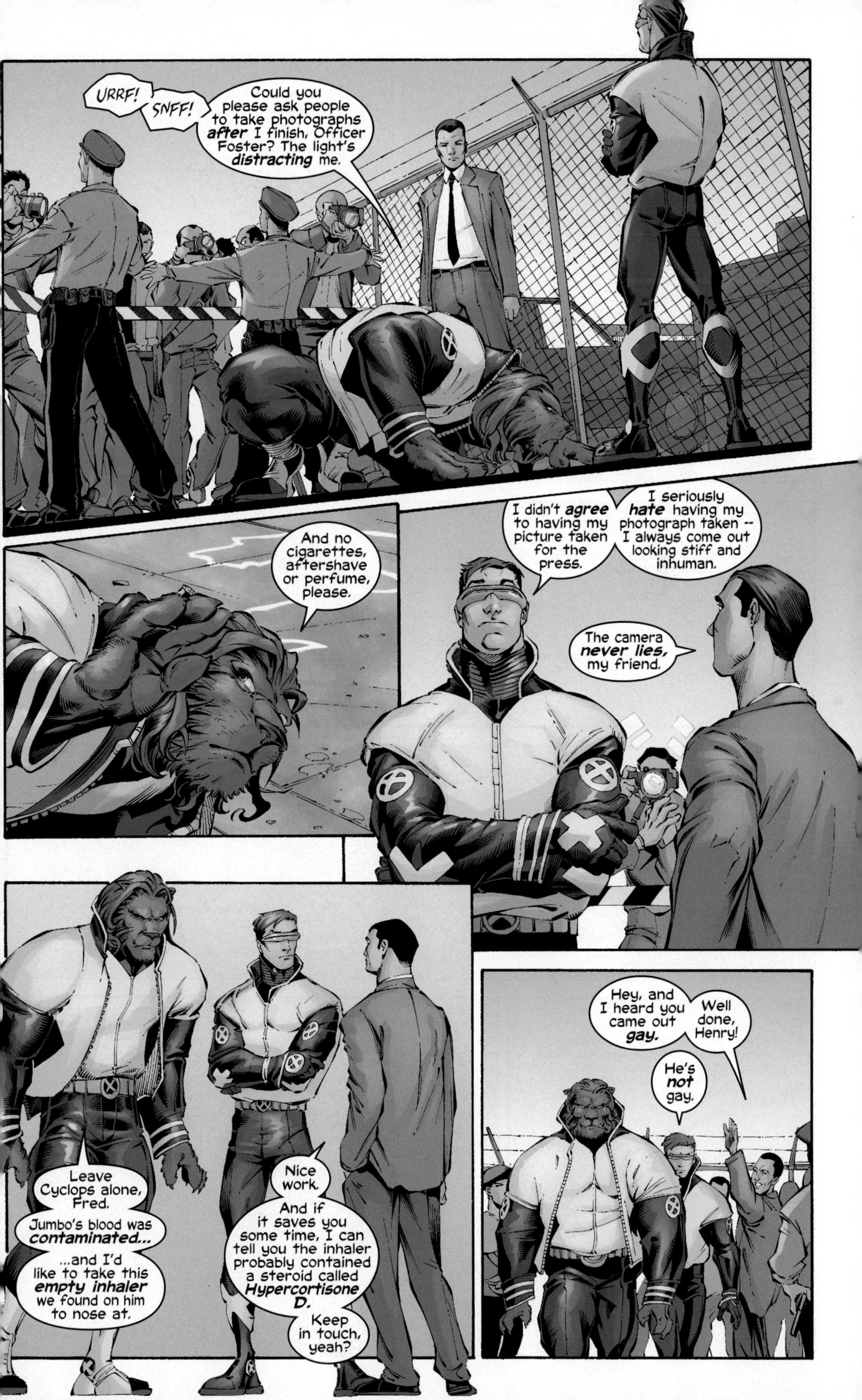
URRF!
SNFF!
Could you please ask people to take photographs **after** I finish, Officer Foster? The light's **distracting** me.
And no cigarettes, aftershave or perfume, please.
I didn't **agree** to having my picture taken for the press.
I seriously **hate** having my photograph taken -- I always come out looking stiff and inhuman.
The camera **never lies,** my friend.
Leave Cyclops alone, Fred.
Jumbo's blood was **contaminated...**
...and I'd like to take this **empty inhaler** we found on him to nose at.
Nice work.
And if it saves you some time, I can tell you the inhaler probably contained a steroid called **Hypercortisone D.**
Keep in touch, yeah?
Hey, and I heard you came out **gay.**
Well done, Henry!
He's **not** gay.

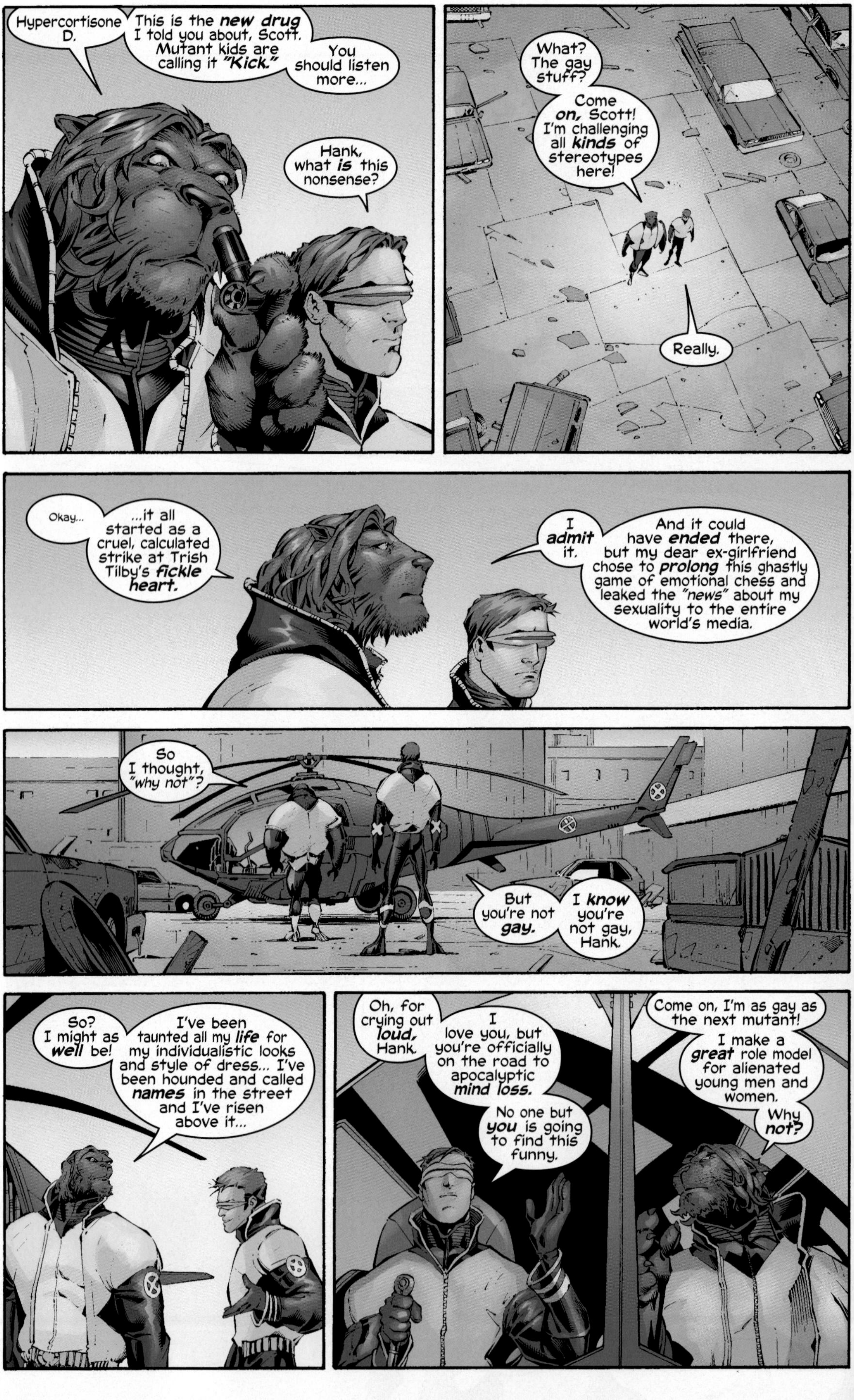
Hypercortisone D.
This is the new drug I told you about, Scott. Mutant kids are calling it "Kick."
You should listen more...
Hank, what is this nonsense?
What? The gay stuff?
Come on, Scott! I'm challenging all kinds of stereotypes here!
Really.
Okay...
...it all started as a cruel, calculated strike at Trish Tilby's fickle heart.
I admit it.
And it could have ended there, but my dear ex-girlfriend chose to prolong this ghastly game of emotional chess and leaked the "news" about my sexuality to the entire world's media.
So I thought, "why not"?
But you're not gay.
I know you're not gay, Hank.
So? I might as well be!
I've been taunted all my life for my individualistic looks and style of dress... I've been hounded and called names in the street and I've risen above it...
Oh, for crying out loud, Hank.
I love you, but you're officially on the road to apocalyptic mind loss.
No one but you is going to find this funny.
Come on, I'm as gay as the next mutant!
I make a great role model for alienated young men and women.
Why not?

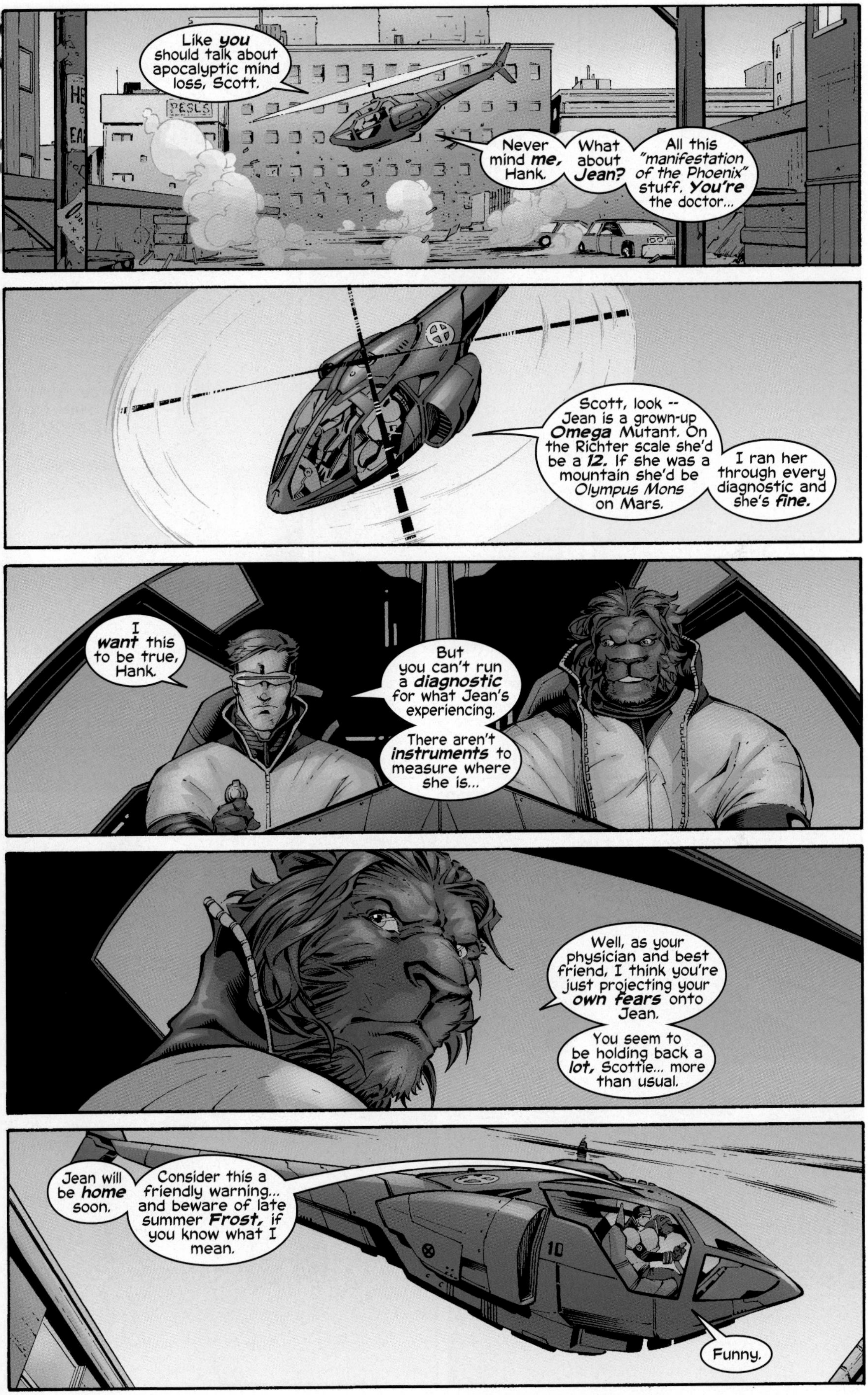
Like you should talk about apocalyptic mind loss, Scott.
Never mind me, Hank.
What about Jean?
All this "manifestation of the Phoenix" stuff. You're the doctor...
Scott, look -- Jean is a grown-up Omega Mutant. On the Richter scale she'd be a 12. If she was a mountain she'd be Olympus Mons on Mars.
I ran her through every diagnostic and she's fine.
I want this to be true, Hank.
But you can't run a diagnostic for what Jean's experiencing.
There aren't instruments to measure where she is...
Well, as your physician and best friend, I think you're just projecting your own fears onto Jean.
You seem to be holding back a lot, Scottie... more than usual.
Jean will be home soon.
Consider this a friendly warning... and beware of late summer Frost, if you know what I mean.
Funny.

You know, I caught a *whiff* of something back there that made me think about when we used to hang around the school *library,* remember?

While Warren and Bobby were out chasing girls?

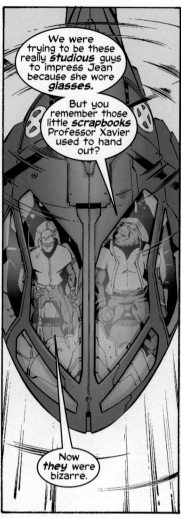

We were trying to be these really *studious* guys to impress Jean because she wore *glasses.*

But you remember those little *scrapbooks* Professor Xavier used to hand out?

Now *they* were bizarre.

And we had to learn to identify the *colors* for all the weird *costumes* the bad guys wore.

Whenever life seems strange, think about *that.*

Bobby used to have *nightmares* about that weird pendant...

Who *was* that guy?

El Tigre! My God, can't you still *see* those drawings with the beautiful water coloring?

The idea of Professor Xavier sitting up nights *hand painting* those things scarred my psyche more than any actual mutant terrorist ever could.

After Genosha, the old troublemakers don't seem to *bother,* do they?

Everyone's in *shock.*

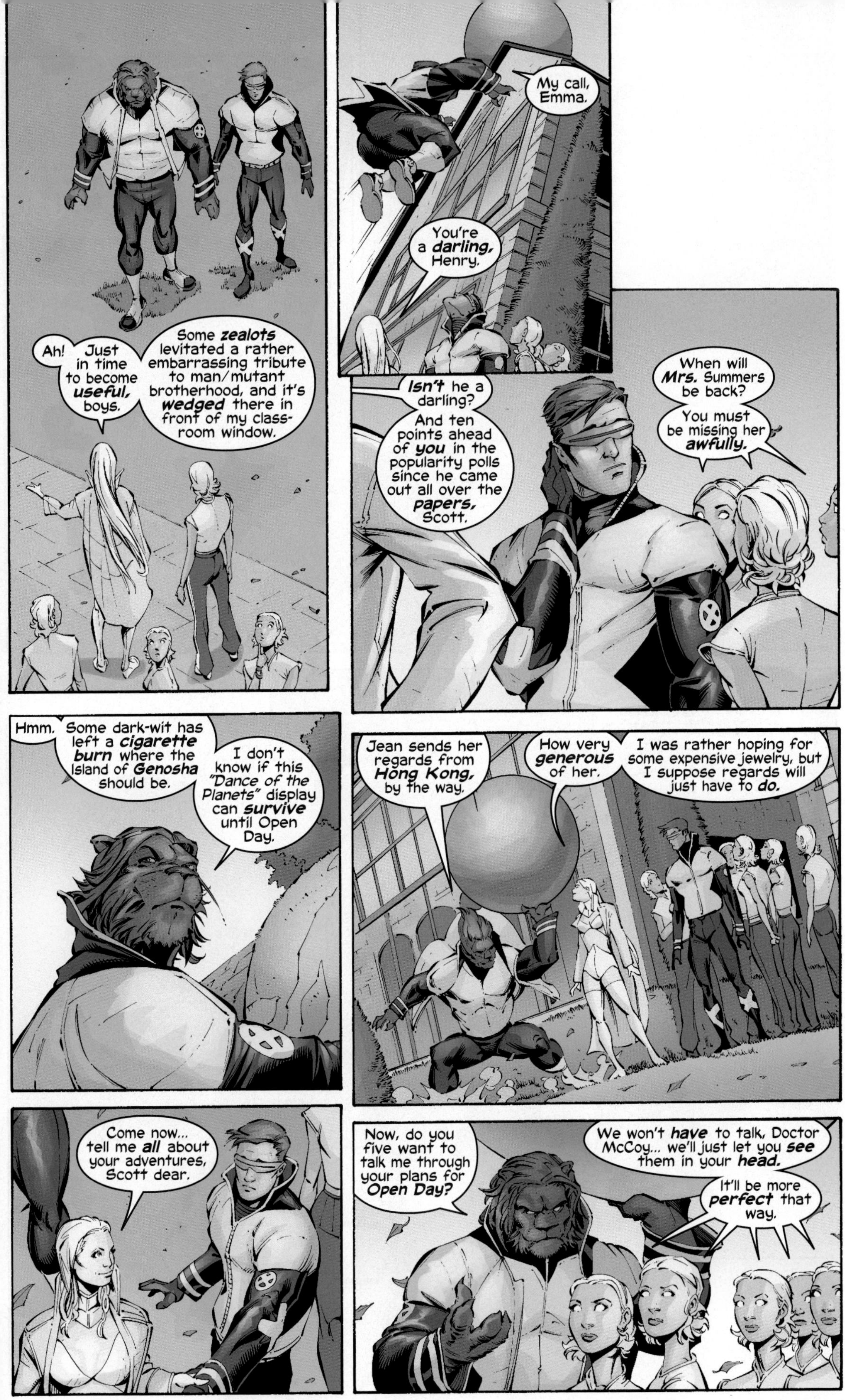

My call, Emma.
You're a darling, Henry.
Ah! Just in time to become useful, boys.
Some zealots levitated a rather embarrassing tribute to man/mutant brotherhood, and it's wedged there in front of my class-room window.
Isn't he a darling?
And ten points ahead of you in the popularity polls since he came out all over the papers, Scott.
When will Mrs. Summers be back?
You must be missing her awfully.
Hmm.
Some dark-wit has left a cigarette burn where the Island of Genosha should be.
I don't know if this "Dance of the Planets" display can survive until Open Day.
Jean sends her regards from Hong Kong, by the way.
How very generous of her.
I was rather hoping for some expensive jewelry, but I suppose regards will just have to do.
Come now... tell me all about your adventures, Scott dear.
Now, do you five want to talk me through your plans for Open Day?
We won't have to talk, Doctor McCoy... we'll just let you see them in your head.
It'll be more perfect that way.

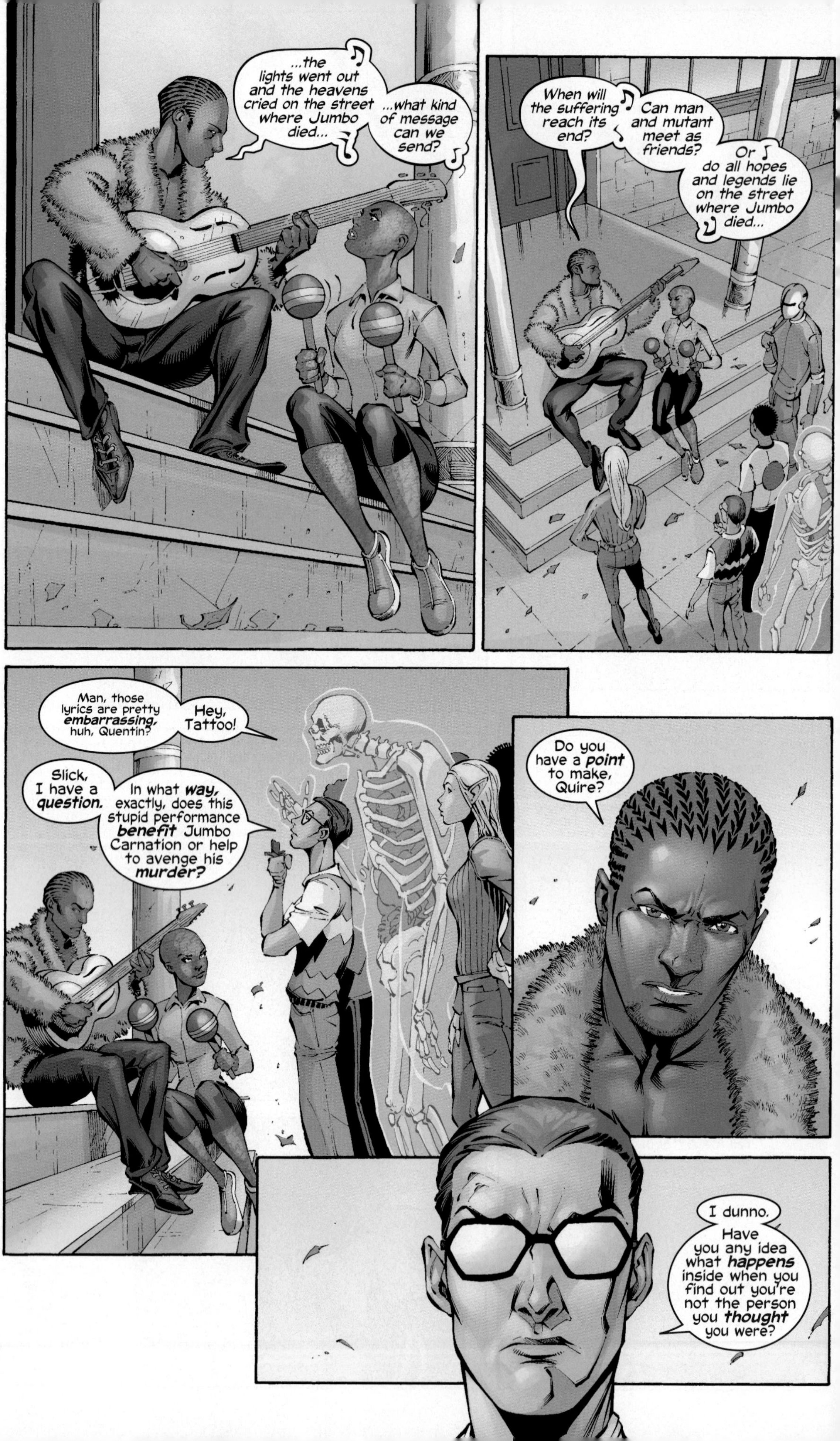

...the lights went out and the heavens cried on the street where Jumbo died...
...what kind of message can we send?
When will the suffering reach its end?
Can man and mutant meet as friends?
Or do all hopes and legends lie on the street where Jumbo died...
Man, those lyrics are pretty embarrassing, huh, Quentin?
Hey, Tattoo!
Slick, I have a question.
In what way, exactly, does this stupid performance benefit Jumbo Carnation or help to avenge his murder?
Do you have a point to make, Quire?
I dunno.
Have you any idea what happens inside when you find out you're not the person you thought you were?

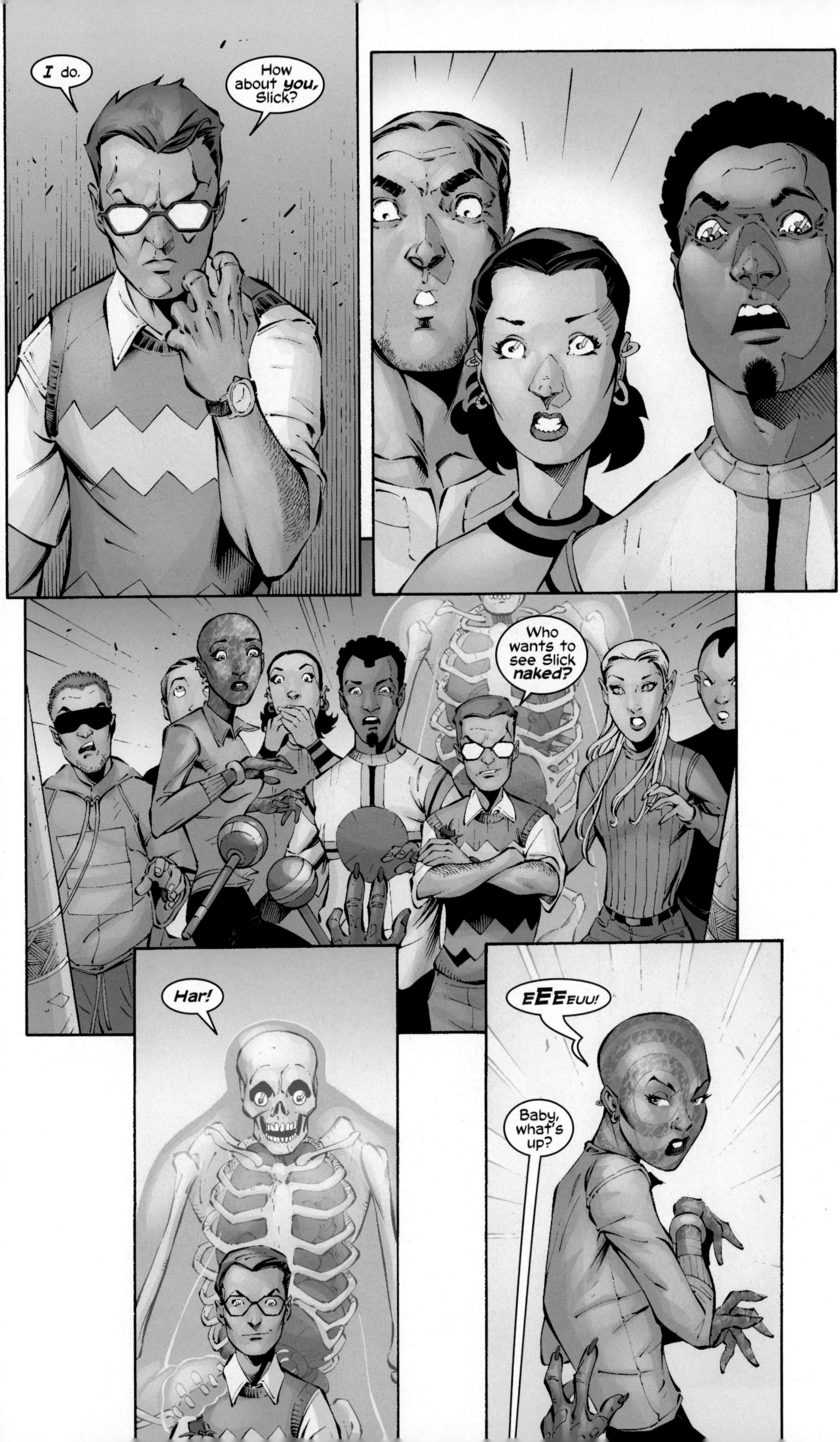
I do.
How about you, Slick?
Who wants to see Slick naked?
Har!
EEEEUU!
Baby, what's up?

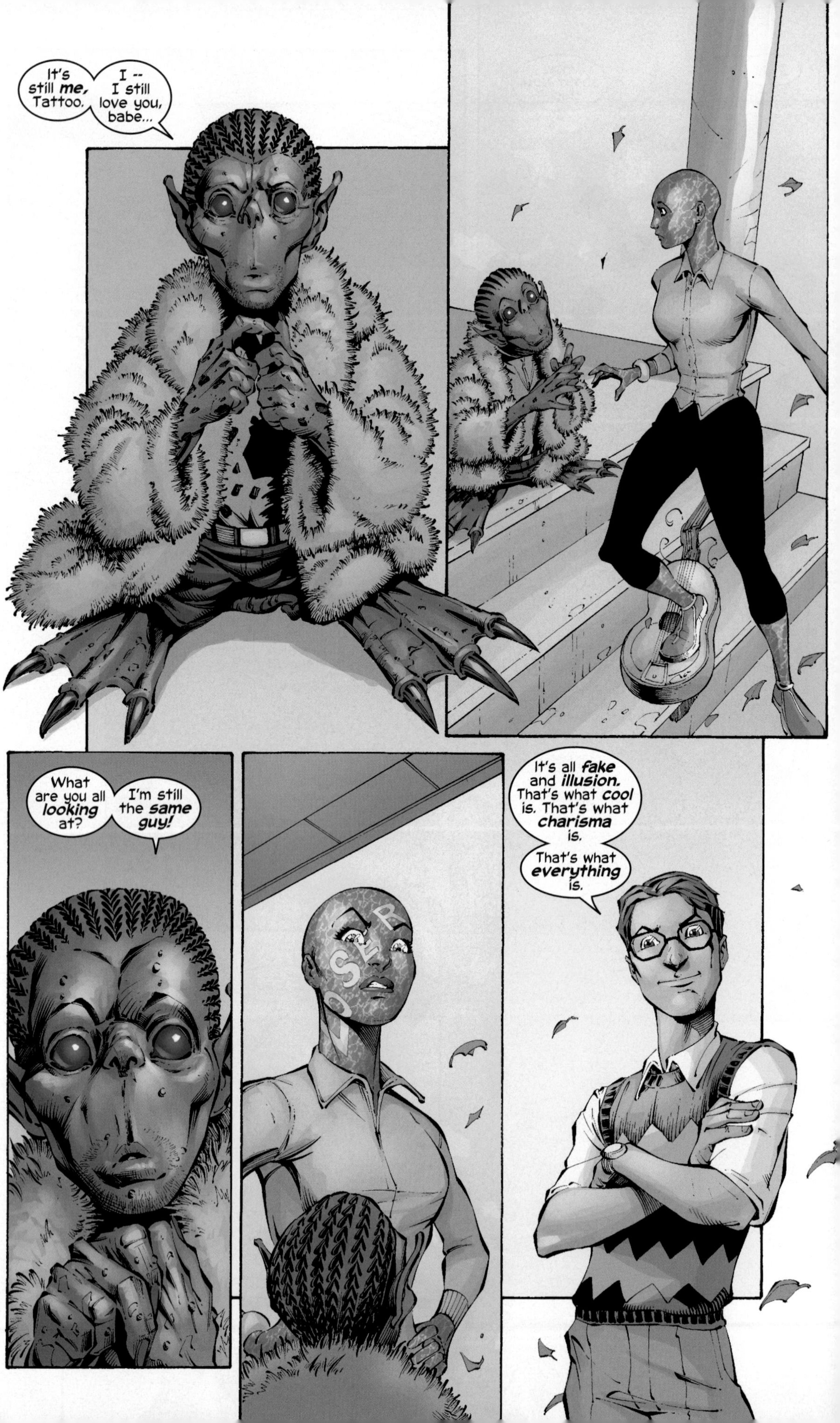
It's still **me,** Tattoo.
I -- I still love you, babe...
What are you all **looking** at?
I'm still the **same guy!**
It's all **fake** and **illusion.** That's what **cool** is. That's what **charisma** is.
That's what **everything** is.

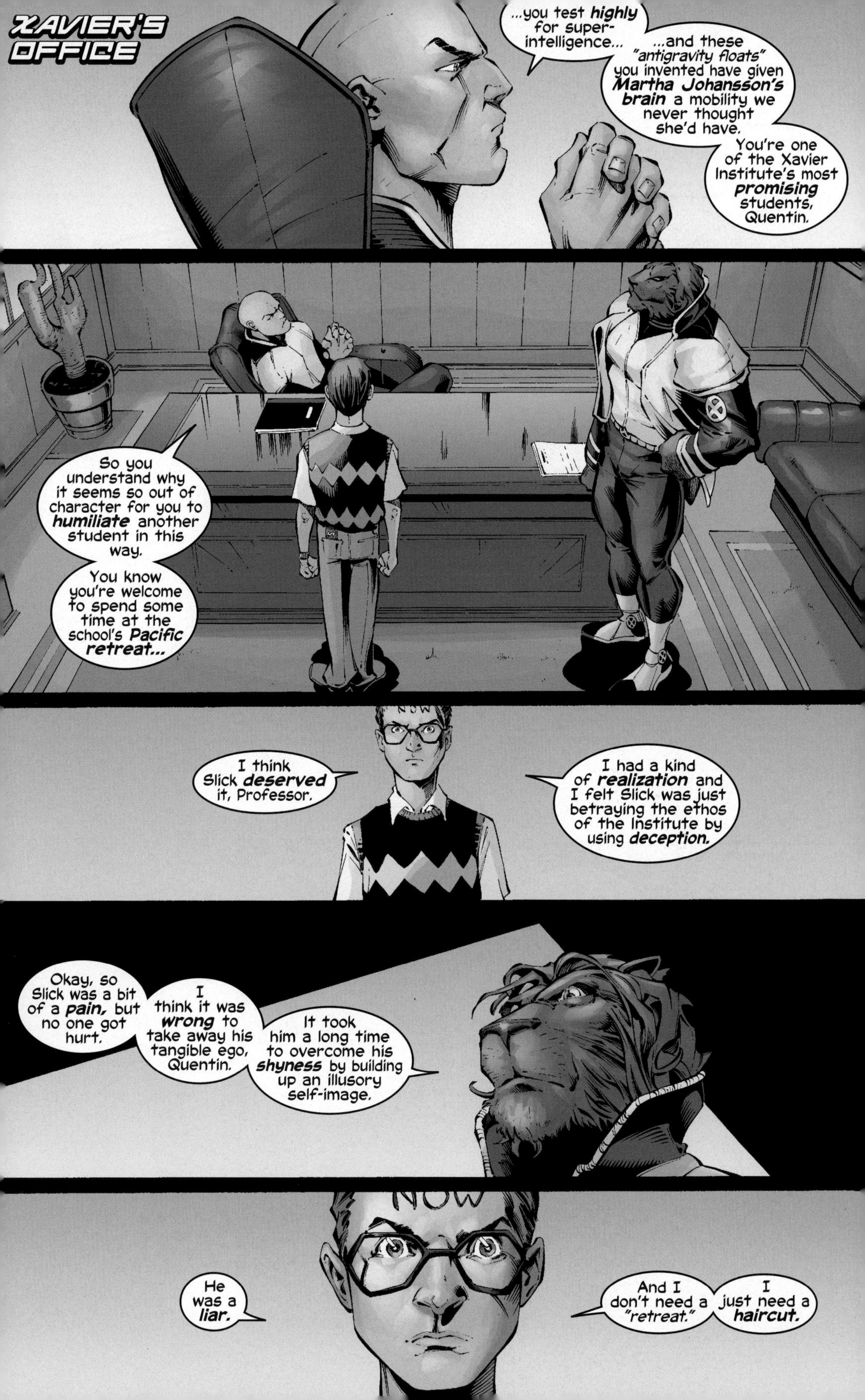
XAVIER'S OFFICE
...you test **highly** for super-intelligence...
...and these *"antigravity floats"* you invented have given **Martha Johansson's brain** a mobility we never thought she'd have.
You're one of the Xavier Institute's most **promising** students, Quentin.
So you understand why it seems so out of character for you to **humiliate** another student in this way.
You know you're welcome to spend some time at the school's **Pacific retreat...**
I think Slick **deserved** it, Professor.
I had a kind of **realization** and I felt Slick was just betraying the ethos of the Institute by using **deception.**
Okay, so Slick was a bit of a **pain,** but no one got hurt.
I think it was **wrong** to take away his tangible ego, Quentin.
It took him a long time to overcome his **shyness** by building up an illusory self-image.
He was a **liar.**
And I don't need a "retreat."
I just need a **haircut.**

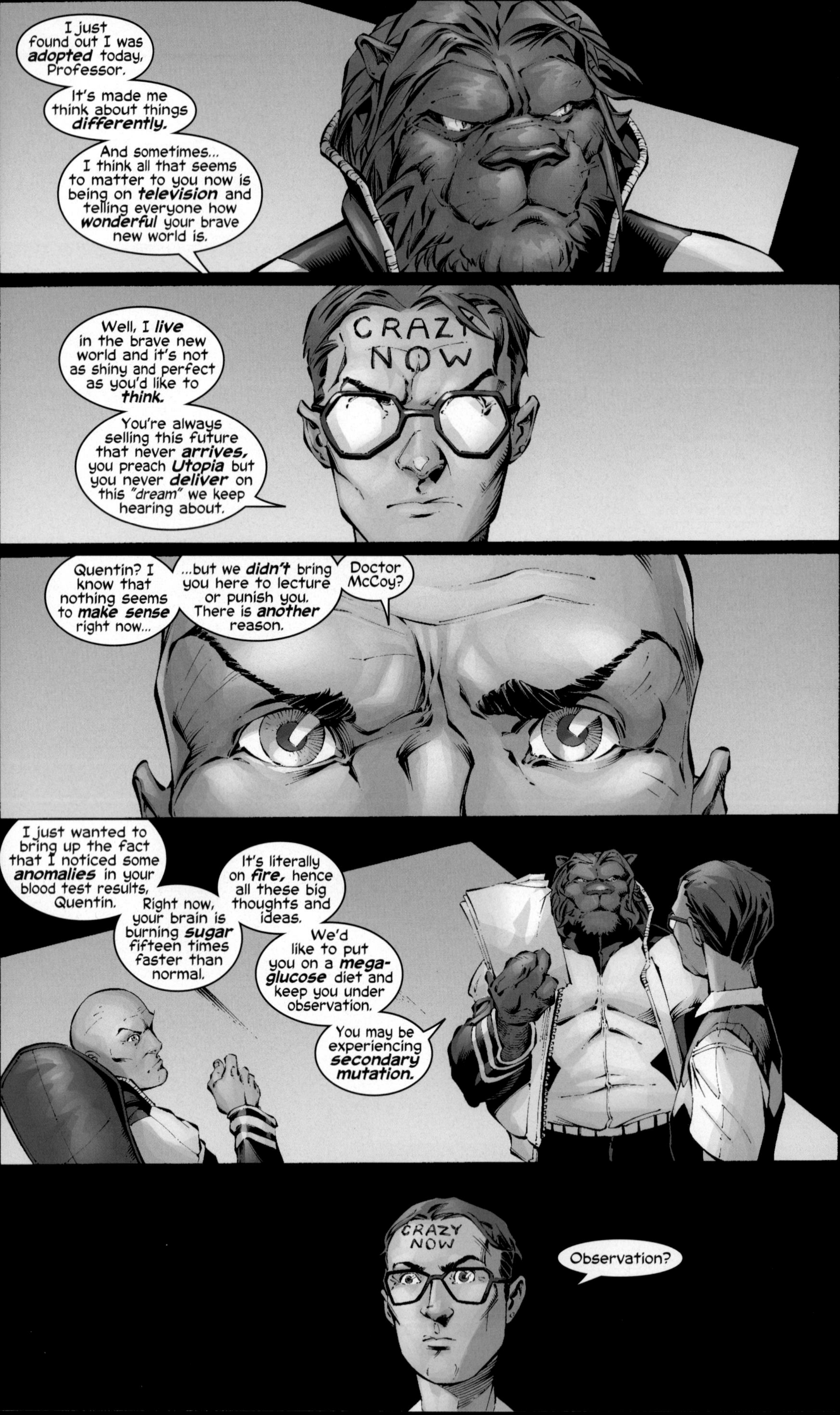

I just found out I was adopted today, Professor.
It's made me think about things differently.
And sometimes... I think all that seems to matter to you now is being on television and telling everyone how wonderful your brave new world is.
CRAZY NOW
Well, I live in the brave new world and it's not as shiny and perfect as you'd like to think.
You're always selling this future that never arrives, you preach Utopia but you never deliver on this "dream" we keep hearing about.
Quentin? I know that nothing seems to make sense right now...
...but we didn't bring you here to lecture or punish you. There is another reason.
Doctor McCoy?
I just wanted to bring up the fact that I noticed some anomalies in your blood test results, Quentin.
Right now, your brain is burning sugar fifteen times faster than normal.
It's literally on fire, hence all these big thoughts and ideas.
We'd like to put you on a mega-glucose diet and keep you under observation.
You may be experiencing secondary mutation.
CRAZY NOW
Observation?

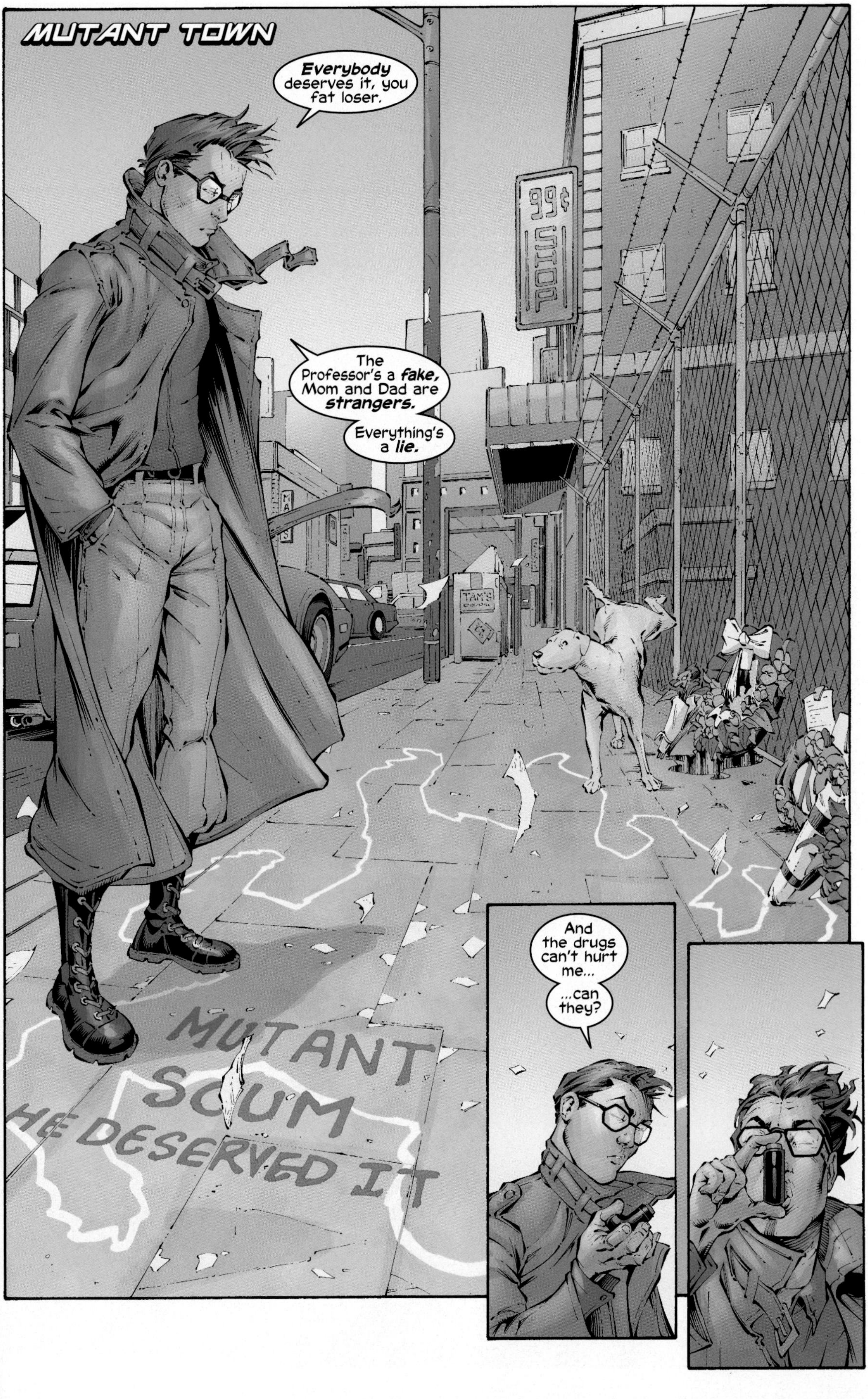
MUTANT TOWN
Everybody deserves it, you fat loser.
The Professor's a fake, Mom and Dad are strangers.
Everything's a lie.
99¢ SHOP
TAM'S
MUTANT SCUM HE DESERVED IT
And the drugs can't hurt me...
...can they?

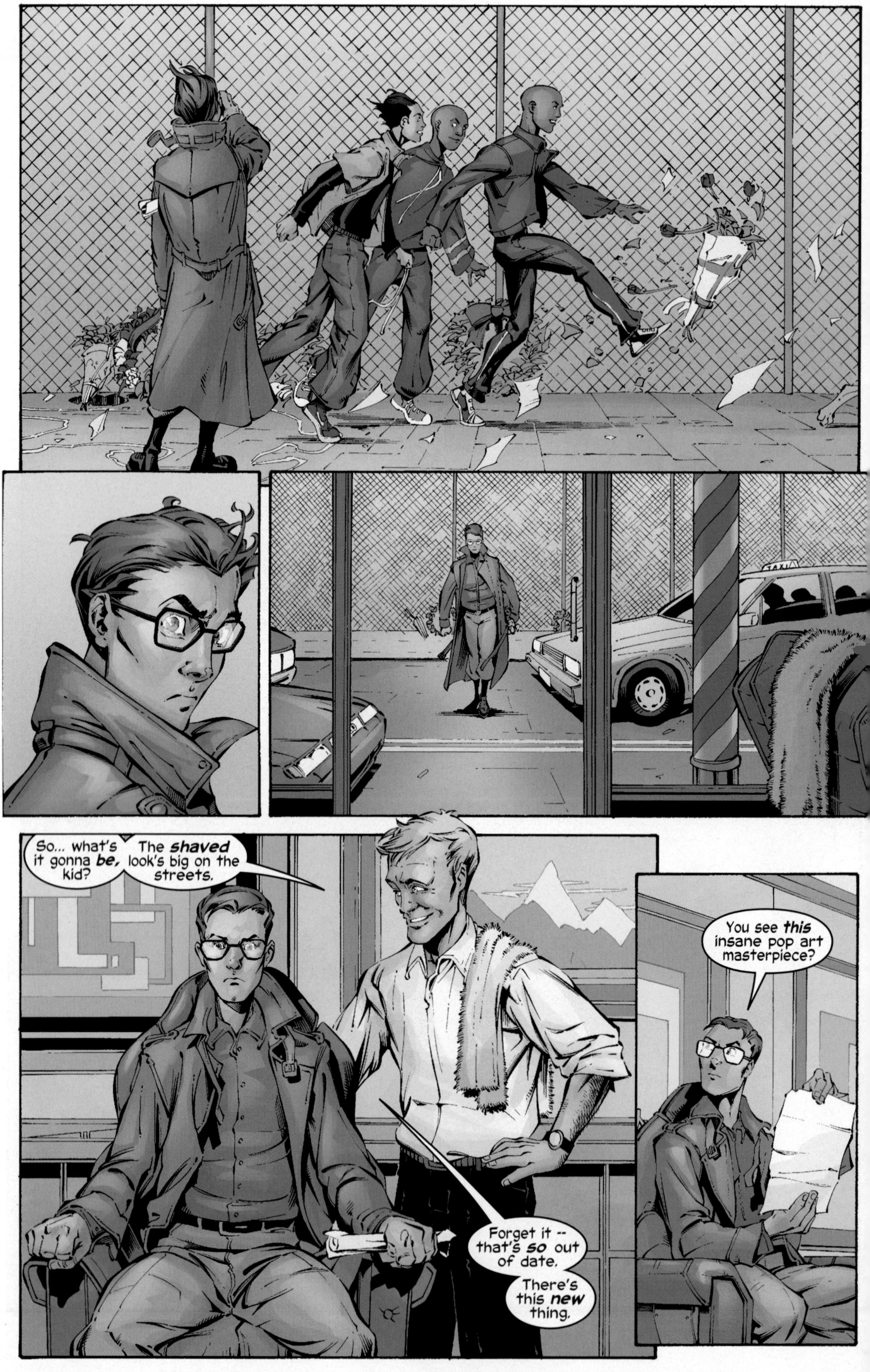
So... what's it gonna be, kid?
The shaved look's big on the streets.
Forget it -- that's so out of date.
There's this new thing.
You see this insane pop art masterpiece?

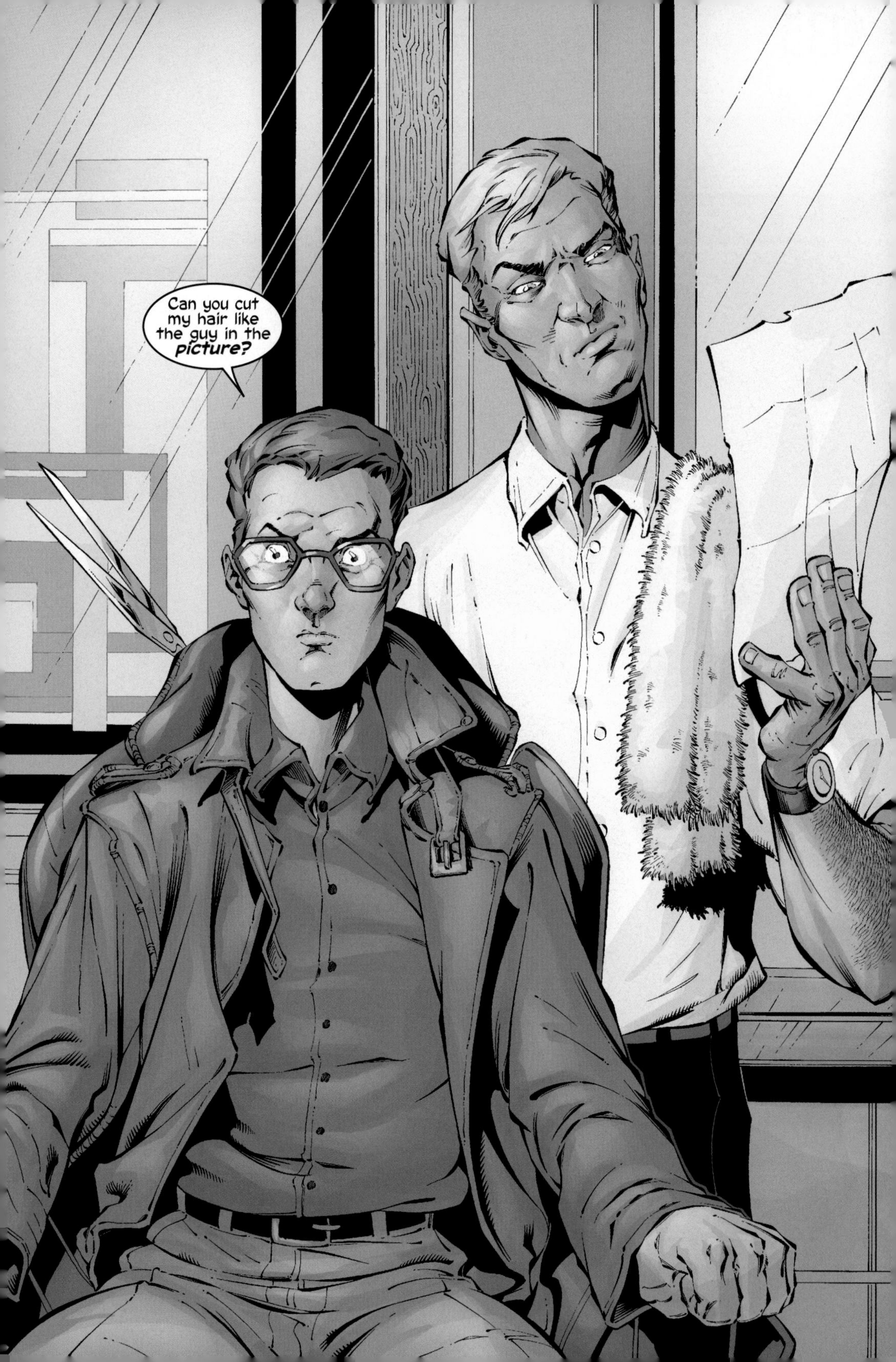
Can you cut my hair like the guy in the *picture?*

#135

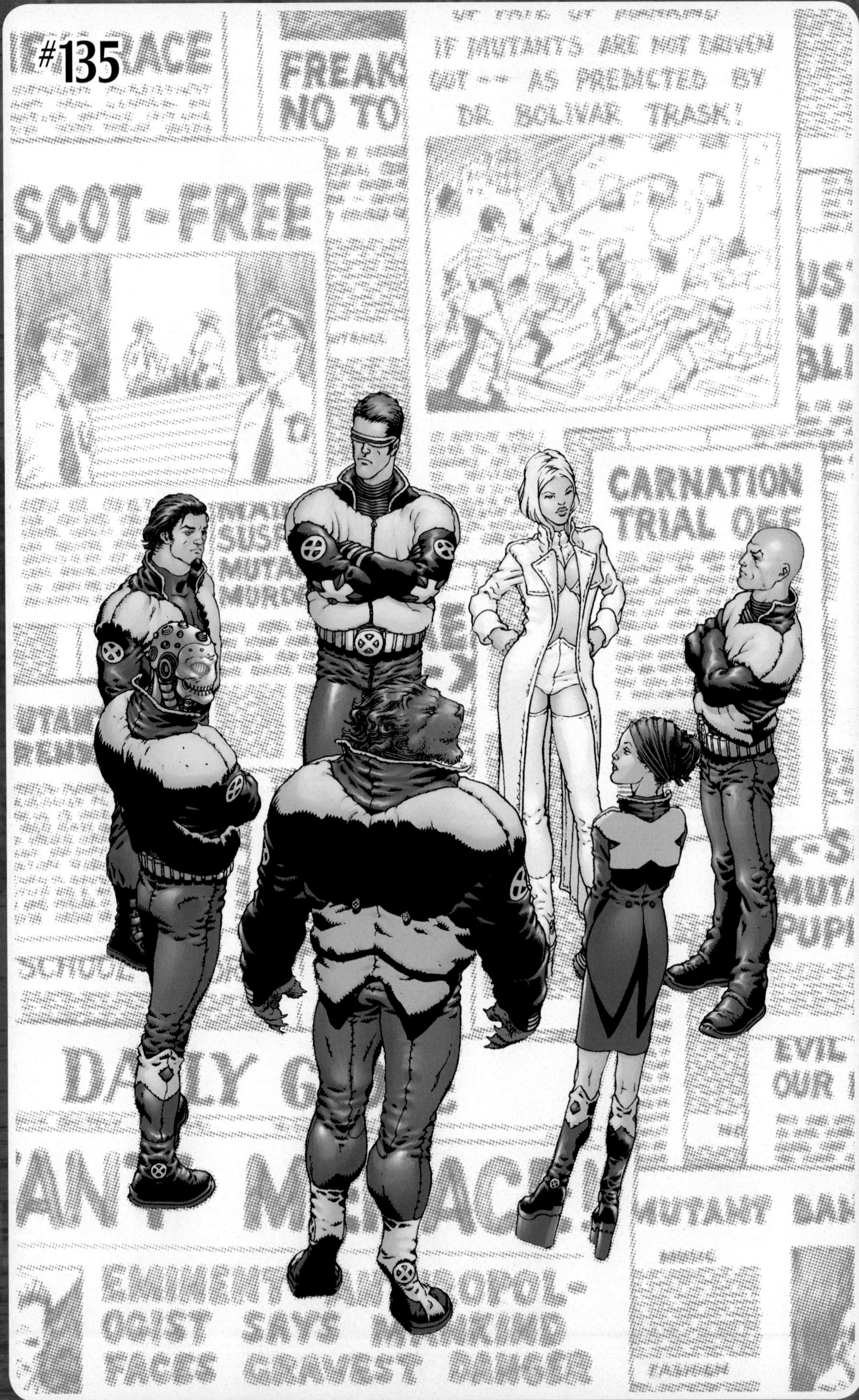
IF MUTANTS ARE NOT DRIVEN
OUT -- AS PREDICTED BY
DR. BOLIVAR TRASK!
SCOT-FREE
CARNATION
TRIAL OFF
SCHOOL
MUTANT
FACES GRAVEST DANGER

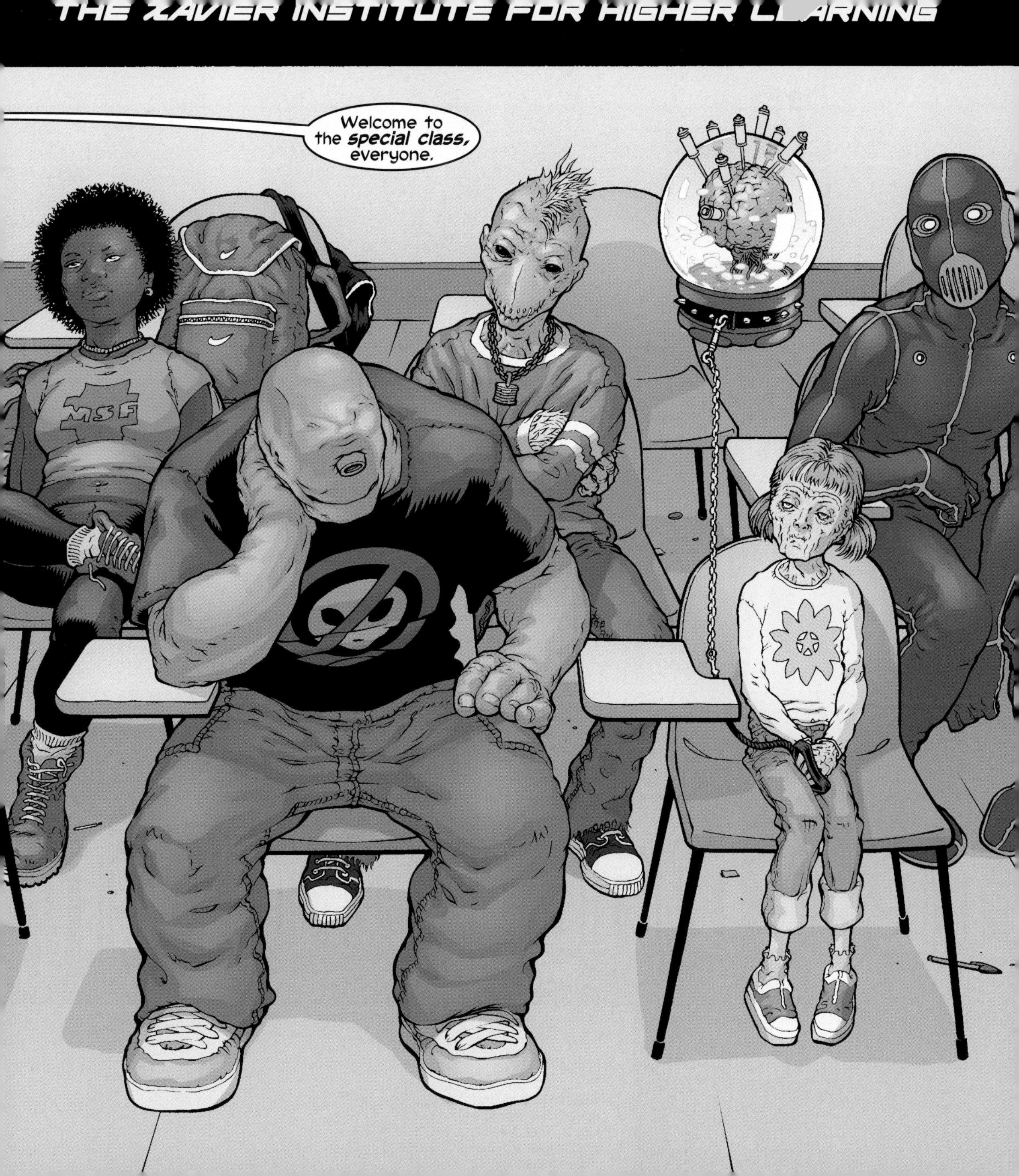
THE XAVIER INSTITUTE FOR HIGHER LEARNING
Welcome to the *special class,* everyone.
MSF

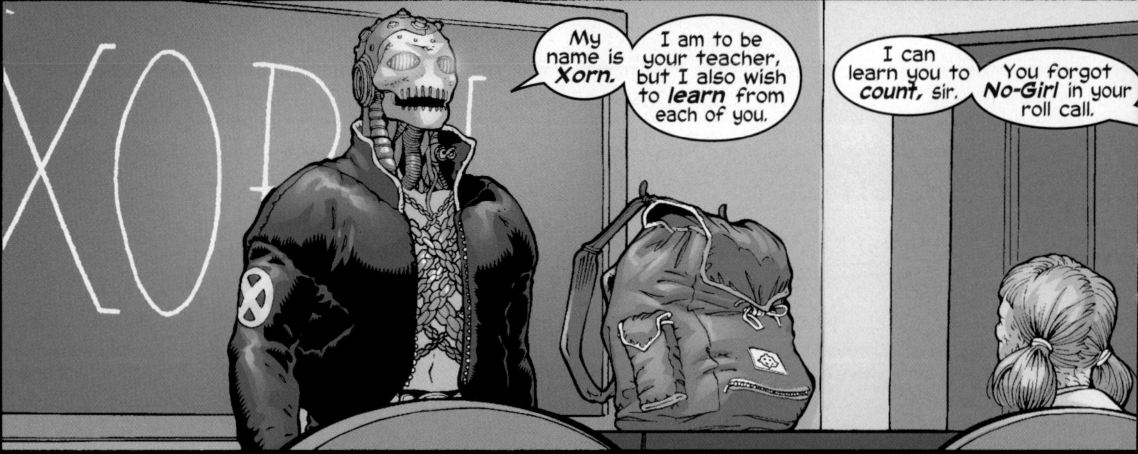
My name is *Xorn.*
I am to be your teacher, but I also wish to *learn* from each of you.
I can learn you to *count,* sir.
You forgot *No-Girl* in your roll call.

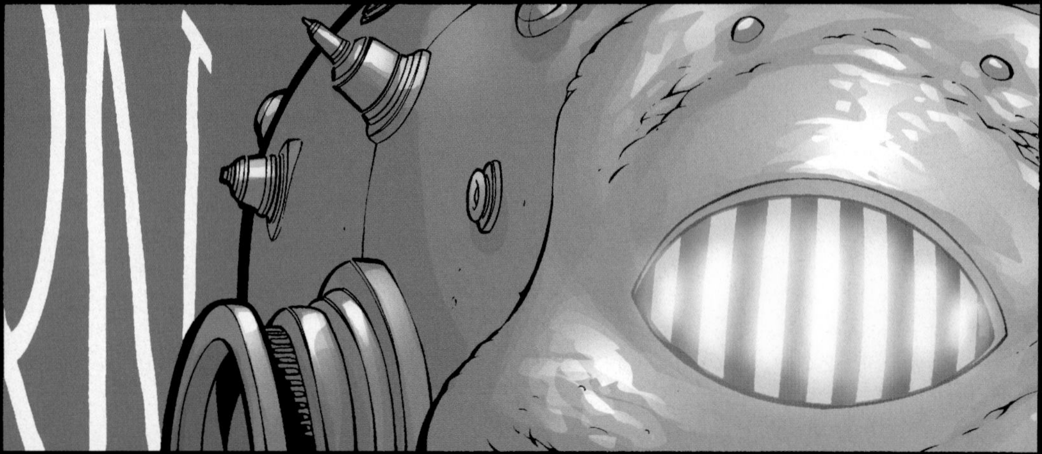

teaching children

richard starkings & comicraft's saida
letters
nova ren suma & mike raicht
assistant editors
mike marts
editor
joe quesada
chief
bill jemas
president

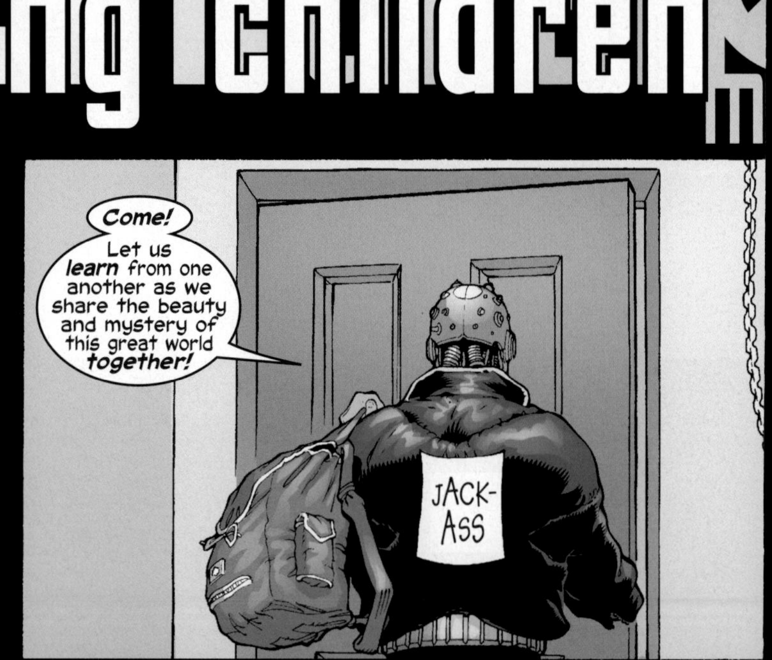
Come! Let us *learn* from one another as we share the beauty and mystery of this great world *together!*
JACK-ASS

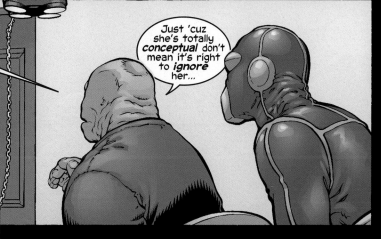

Just 'cuz she's totally *conceptual* don't mean it's right to *ignore* her...

grant morrison
writer

frank quitely
pencils

tim townsend
inks

chris chuckry
colors

Then let me see once more... *Angel, Basilisk, Beak, Martha, Ernst, Dummy.*

Still no *No-Girl.*

Perhaps she has gone ahead and waits for us outside...

about fractals frac

You bet, Mister Xorn!

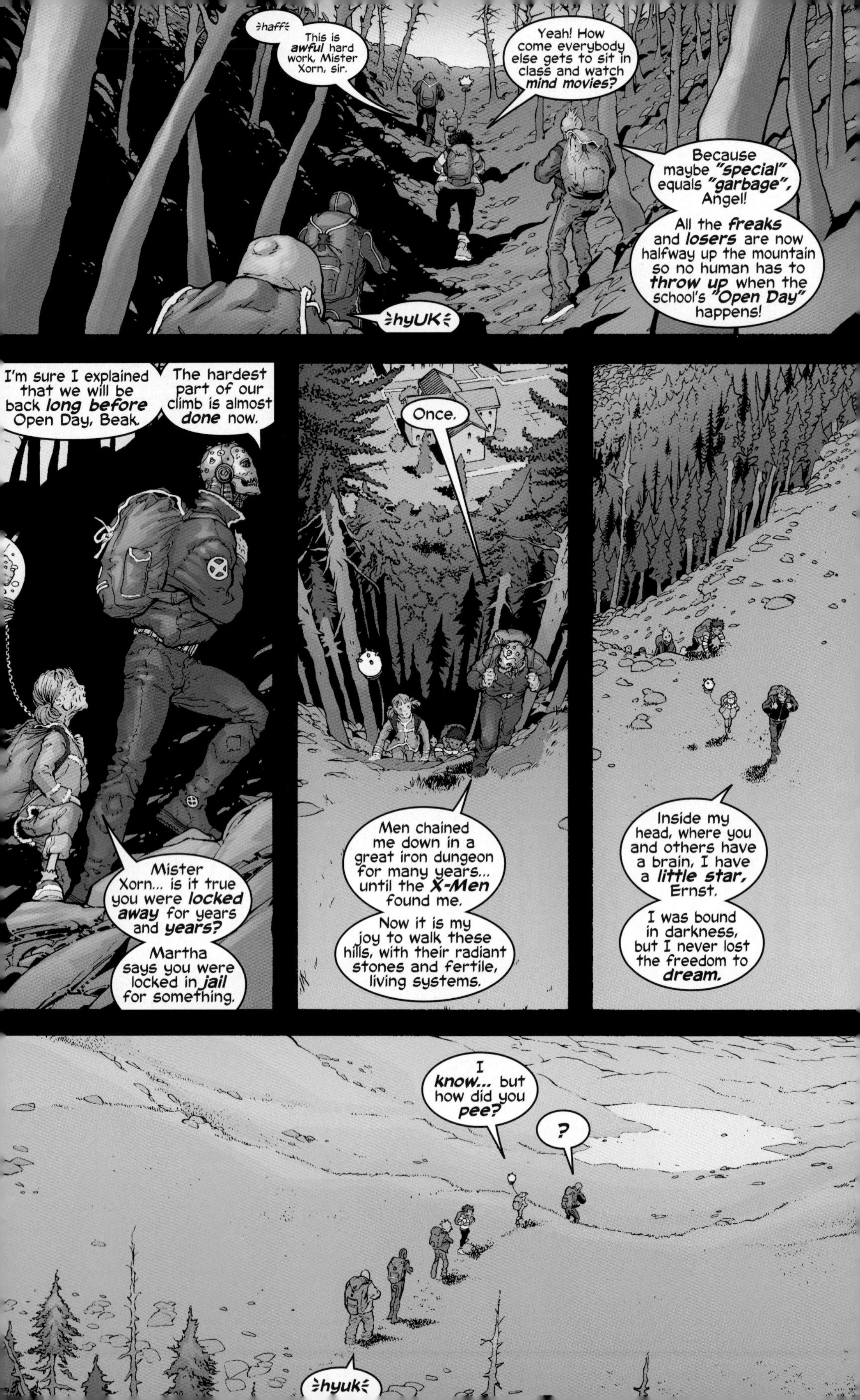

≷haff≶
This is awful hard work, Mister Xorn, sir.
Yeah! How come everybody else gets to sit in class and watch mind movies?
Because maybe "special" equals "garbage", Angel!
All the freaks and losers are now halfway up the mountain so no human has to throw up when the school's "Open Day" happens!
≷hyUK≶
I'm sure I explained that we will be back long before Open Day, Beak.
The hardest part of our climb is almost done now.
Mister Xorn... is it true you were locked away for years and years?
Martha says you were locked in jail for something.
Once.
Men chained me down in a great iron dungeon for many years... until the X-Men found me.
Now it is my joy to walk these hills, with their radiant stones and fertile, living systems.
Inside my head, where you and others have a brain, I have a little star, Ernst.
I was bound in darkness, but I never lost the freedom to dream.
I know... but how did you pee?
?
≷hyuk≶

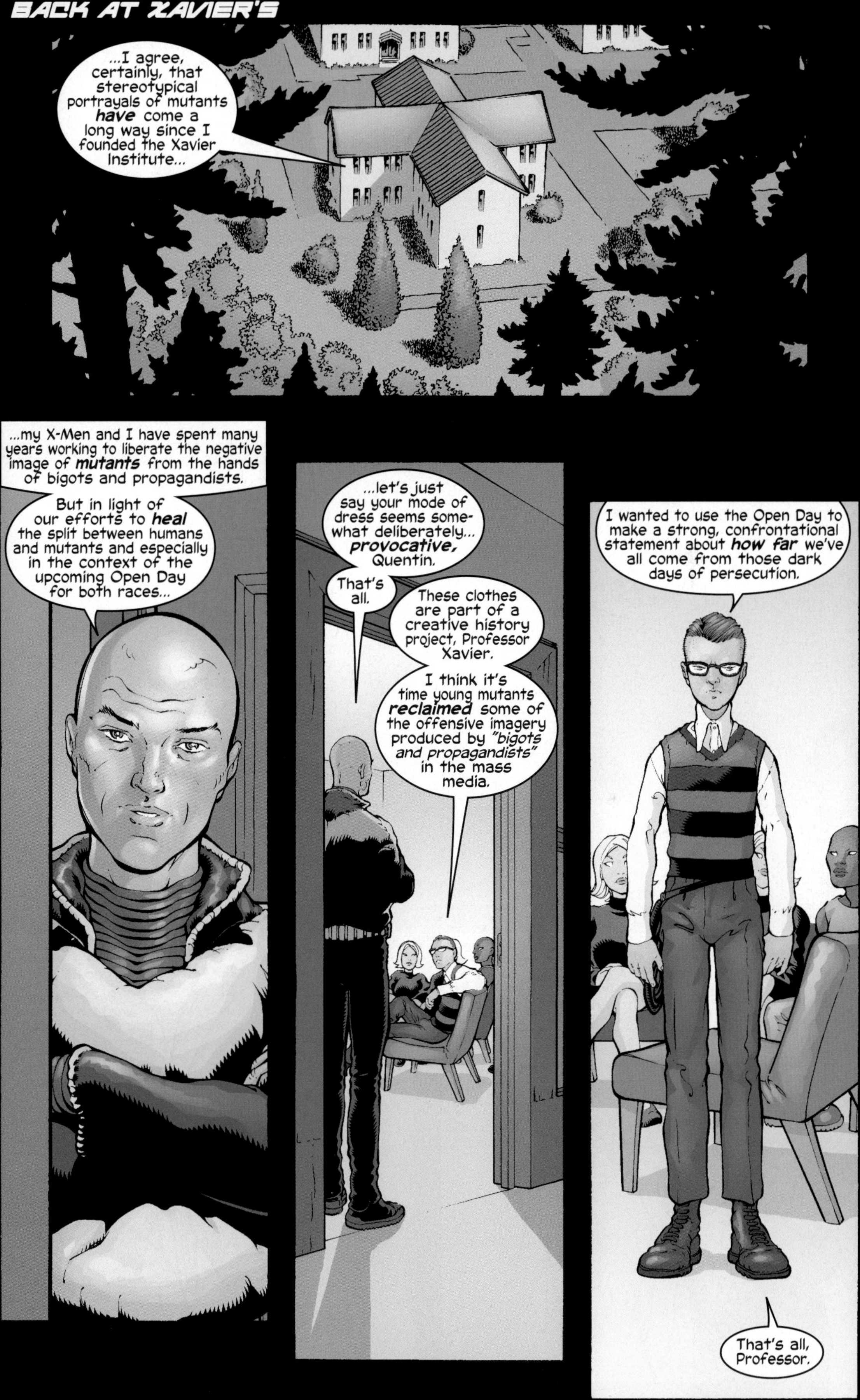
BACK AT XAVIER'S
...I agree, certainly, that stereotypical portrayals of mutants **have** come a long way since I founded the Xavier Institute...
...my X-Men and I have spent many years working to liberate the negative image of **mutants** from the hands of bigots and propagandists.
But in light of our efforts to **heal** the split between humans and mutants and especially in the context of the upcoming Open Day for both races...
...let's just say your mode of dress seems somewhat deliberately... ***provocative,*** Quentin.
That's all.
These clothes are part of a creative history project, Professor Xavier.
I think it's time young mutants ***reclaimed*** some of the offensive imagery produced by *"bigots and propagandists"* in the mass media.
I wanted to use the Open Day to make a strong, confrontational statement about ***how far*** we've all come from those dark days of persecution.
That's all, Professor.

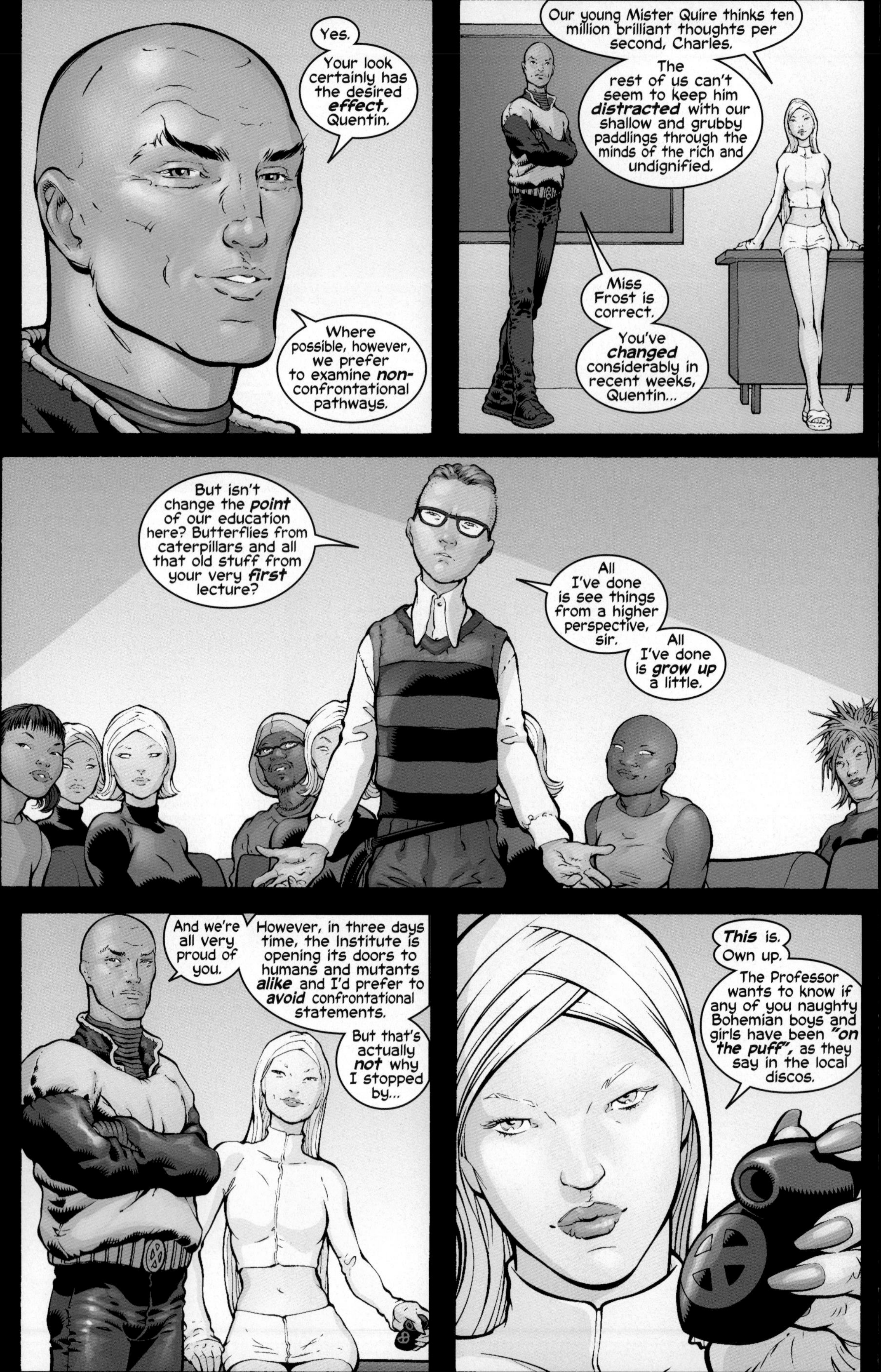

Yes.
Your look certainly has the desired *effect,* Quentin.
Where possible, however, we prefer to examine *non*-confrontational pathways.
Our young Mister Quire thinks ten million brilliant thoughts per second, Charles.
The rest of us can't seem to keep him *distracted* with our shallow and grubby paddlings through the minds of the rich and undignified.
Miss Frost is correct.
You've *changed* considerably in recent weeks, Quentin...
But isn't change the *point* of our education here? Butterflies from caterpillars and all that old stuff from your very *first* lecture?
All I've done is see things from a higher perspective, sir.
All I've done is *grow up* a little.
And we're all very proud of you.
However, in three days time, the Institute is opening its doors to humans and mutants *alike* and I'd prefer to *avoid* confrontational statements.
But that's actually *not* why I stopped by...
This is.
Own up.
The Professor wants to know if any of you naughty Bohemian boys and girls have been *"on the puff"*, as they say in the local discos.

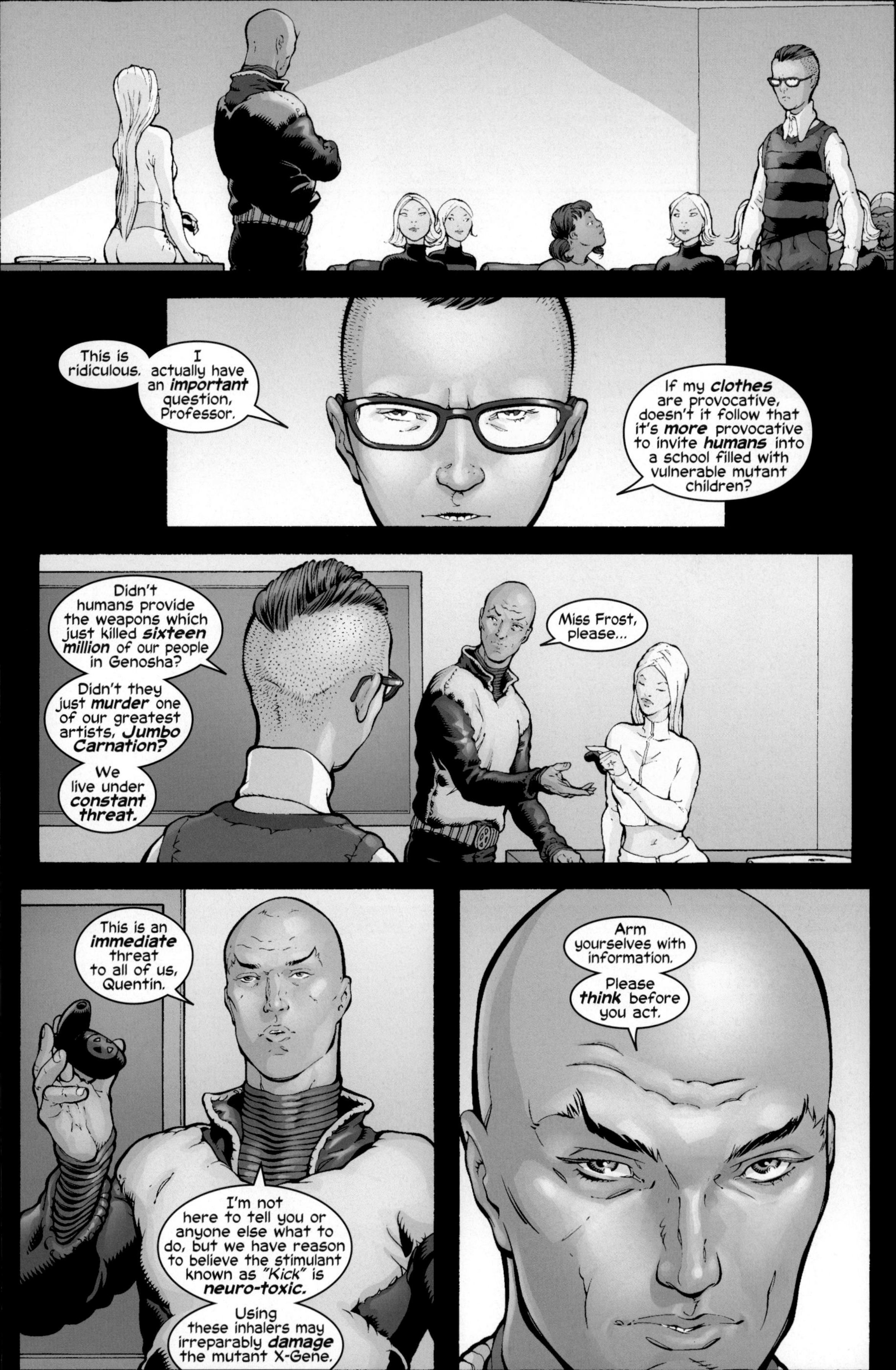
This is ridiculous.
I actually have an important question, Professor.
If my clothes are provocative, doesn't it follow that it's more provocative to invite humans into a school filled with vulnerable mutant children?
Didn't humans provide the weapons which just killed sixteen million of our people in Genosha?
Didn't they just murder one of our greatest artists, Jumbo Carnation?
We live under constant threat.
Miss Frost, please...
This is an immediate threat to all of us, Quentin.
I'm not here to tell you or anyone else what to do, but we have reason to believe the stimulant known as "Kick" is neuro-toxic.
Using these inhalers may irreparably damage the mutant X-Gene.
Arm yourselves with information.
Please think before you act.

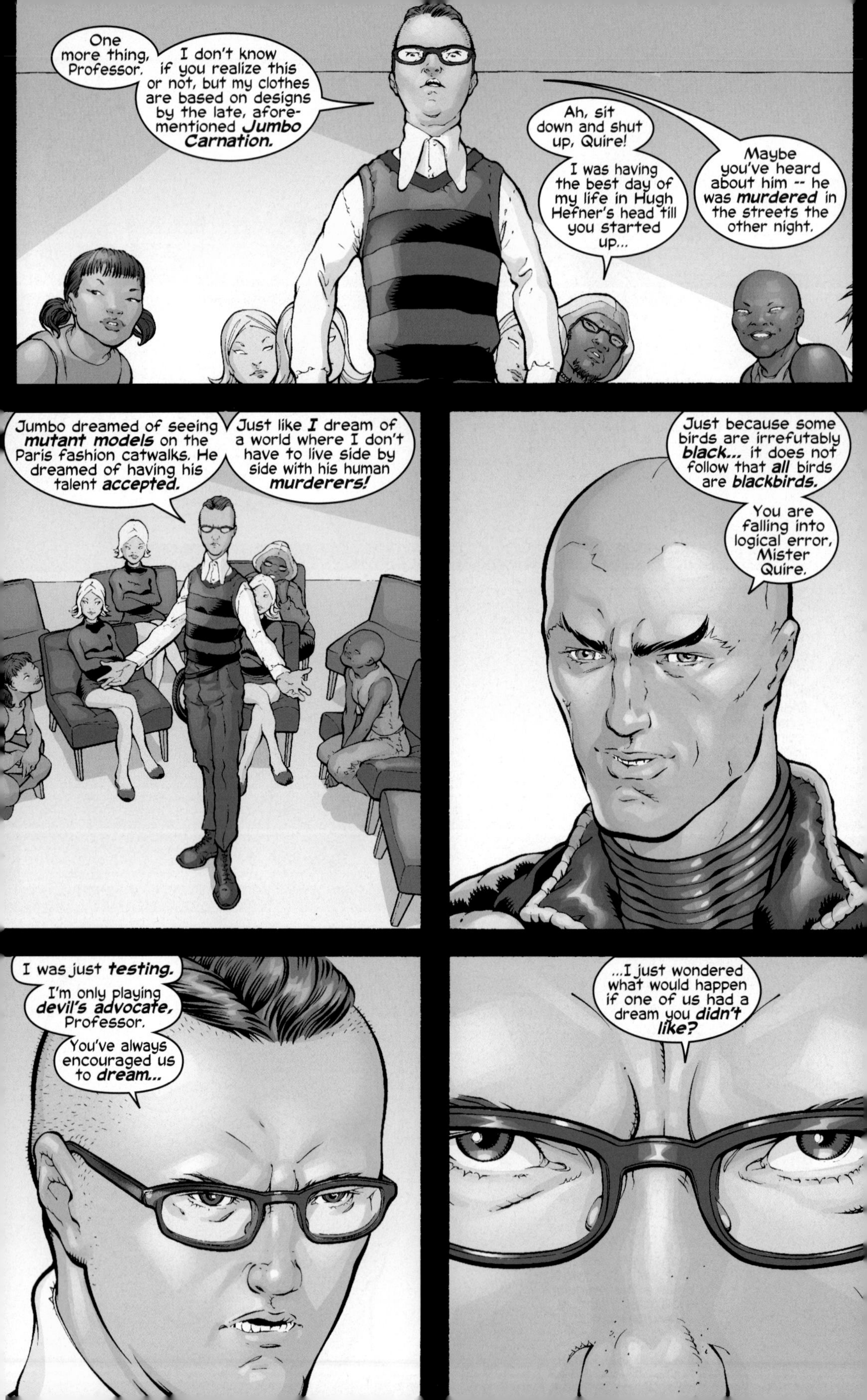
One more thing, Professor.
I don't know if you realize this or not, but my clothes are based on designs by the late, aforementioned *Jumbo Carnation.*
Ah, sit down and shut up, Quire!
I was having the best day of my life in Hugh Hefner's head till you started up...
Maybe you've heard about him -- he was *murdered* in the streets the other night.
Jumbo dreamed of seeing *mutant models* on the Paris fashion catwalks. He dreamed of having his talent *accepted.*
Just like *I* dream of a world where I don't have to live side by side with his human *murderers!*
Just because some birds are irrefutably *black...* it does not follow that *all* birds are *blackbirds.*
You are falling into logical error, Mister Quire.
I was just *testing.*
I'm only playing *devil's advocate,* Professor.
You've always encouraged us to *dream...*
...I just wondered what would happen if one of us had a dream you *didn't like?*

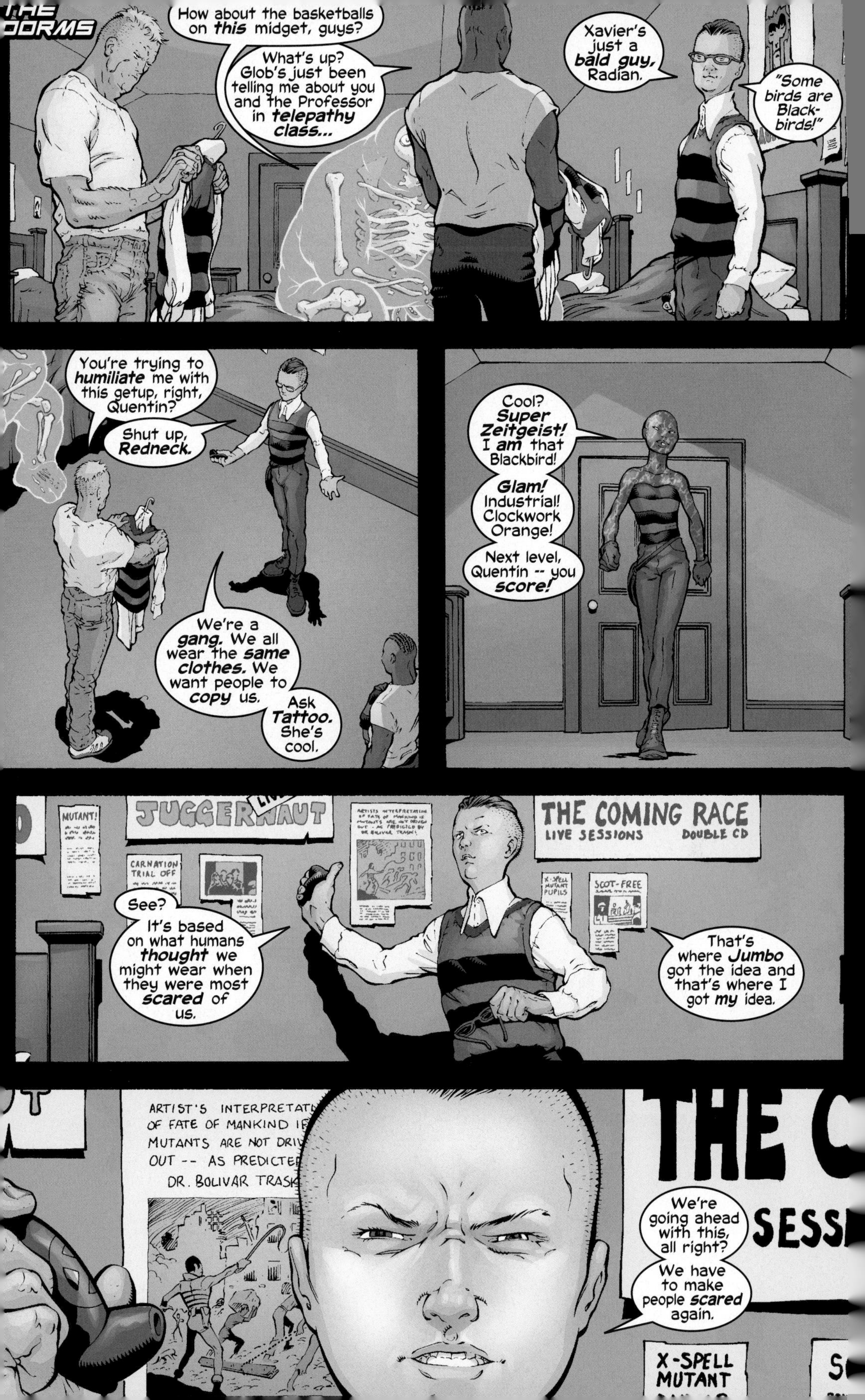
THE DORMS
How about the basketballs on this midget, guys?
What's up? Glob's just been telling me about you and the Professor in telepathy class...
Xavier's just a bald guy, Radian.
"Some birds are Blackbirds!"
You're trying to humiliate me with this getup, right, Quentin?
Shut up, Redneck.
We're a gang. We all wear the same clothes. We want people to copy us.
Ask Tattoo. She's cool.
Cool? Super Zeitgeist! I am that Blackbird!
Glam! Industrial! Clockwork Orange!
Next level, Quentin -- you score!
MUTANT!
JUGGERNAUT
CARNATION TRIAL OFF
THE COMING RACE
LIVE SESSIONS DOUBLE CD
X-SPELL MUTANT PUPILS
SCOT-FREE
See?
It's based on what humans thought we might wear when they were most scared of us.
That's where Jumbo got the idea and that's where I got my idea.
ARTIST'S INTERPRETAT
OF FATE OF MANKIND IF
MUTANTS ARE NOT DRIV
OUT -- AS PREDICTE
DR. BOLIVAR TRASK
THE C
SESS
We're going ahead with this, all right?
We have to make people scared again.
X-SPELL MUTANT

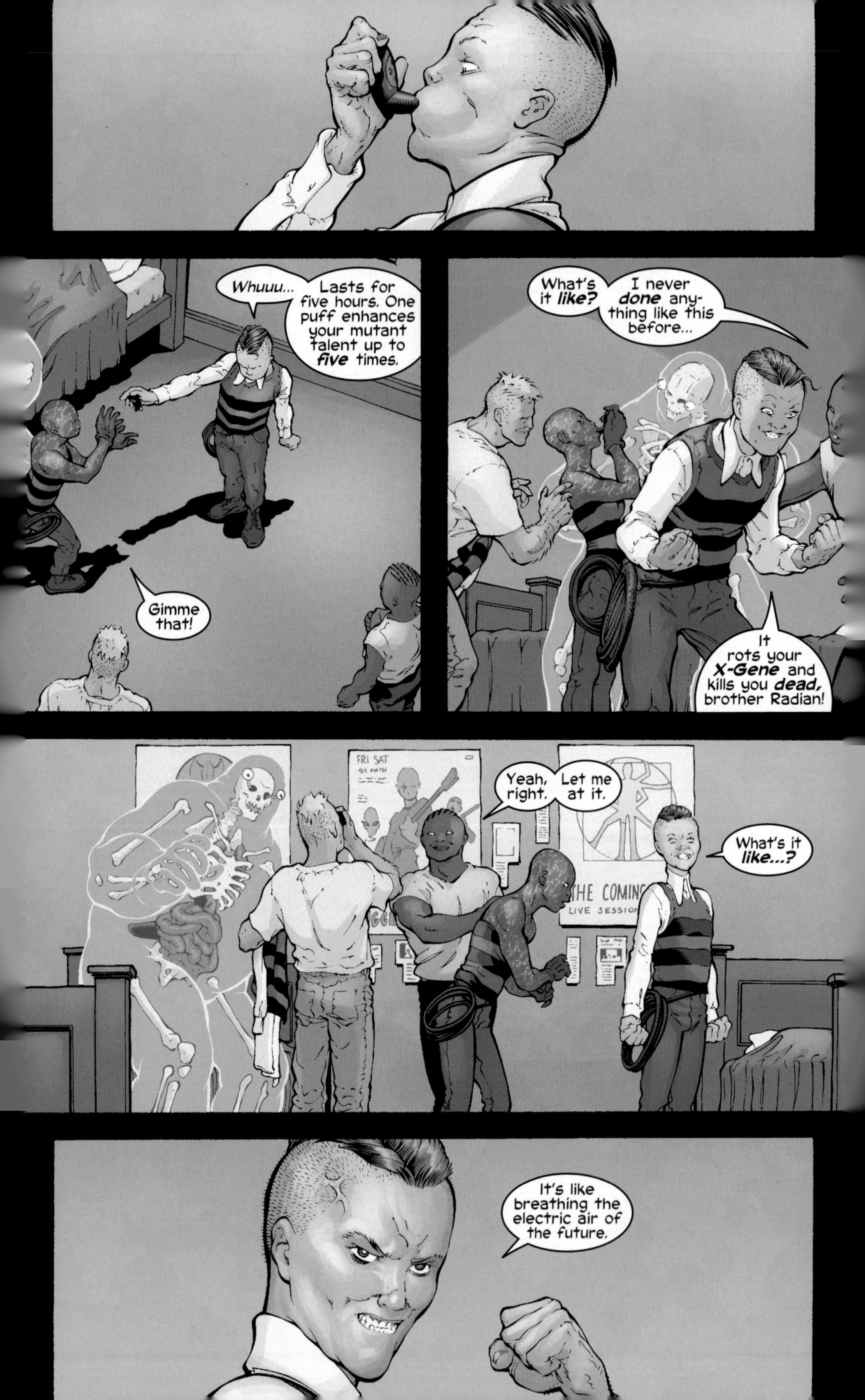

Whuuu...
Lasts for five hours. One puff enhances your mutant talent up to *five* times.
Gimme that!
What's it *like?*
I never *done* anything like this before...
It rots your *X-Gene* and kills you *dead,* brother Radian!
FRI SAT
Yeah, right.
Let me at it.
THE COMING
LIVE SESSION
What's it *like...?*
It's like breathing the electric air of the future.

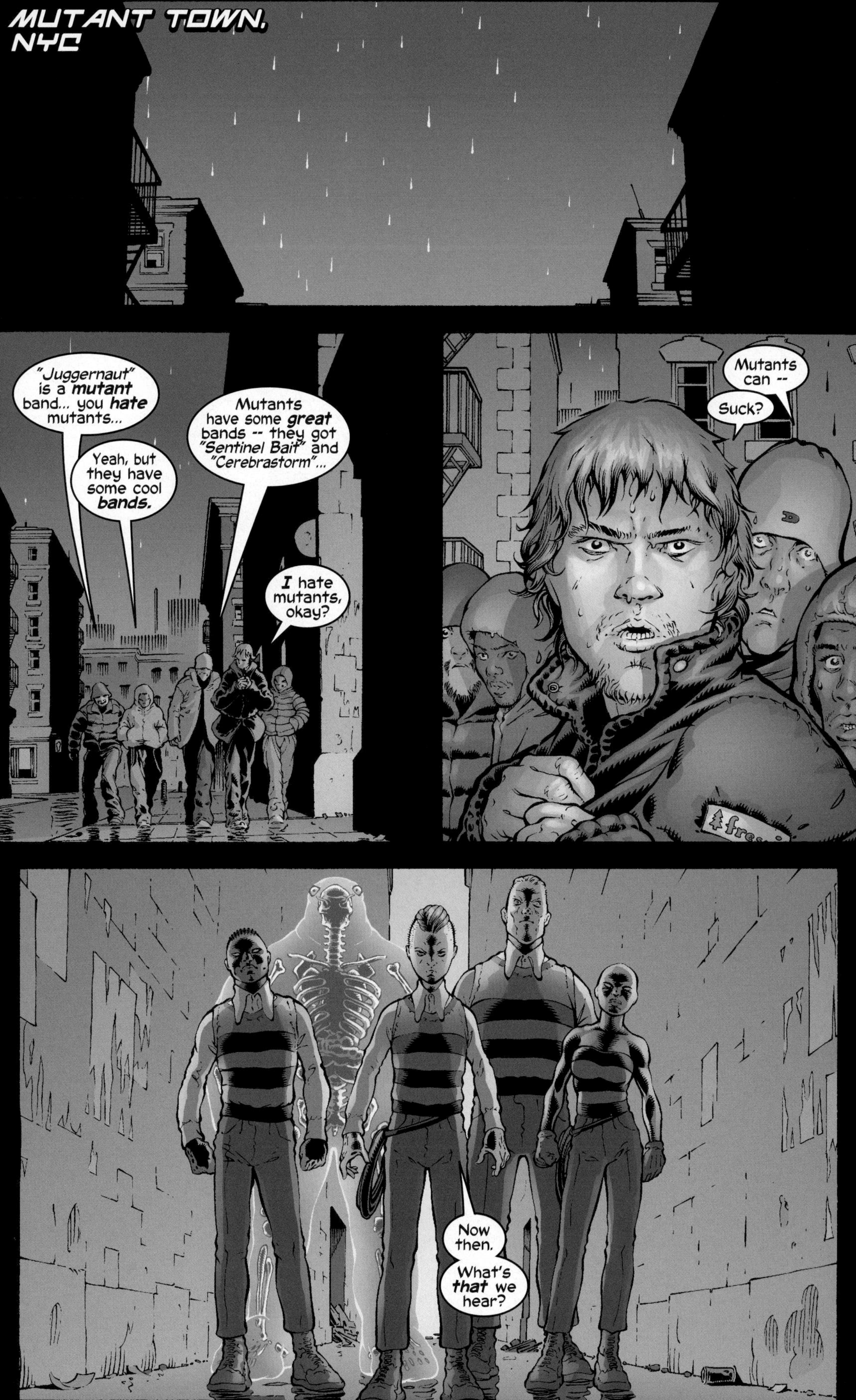
MUTANT TOWN, NYC
"Juggernaut" is a mutant band... you hate mutants...
Yeah, but they have some cool bands.
Mutants have some great bands -- they got "Sentinel Bait" and "Cerebrastorm"...
I hate mutants, okay?
Mutants can --
Suck?
Now then.
What's that we hear?

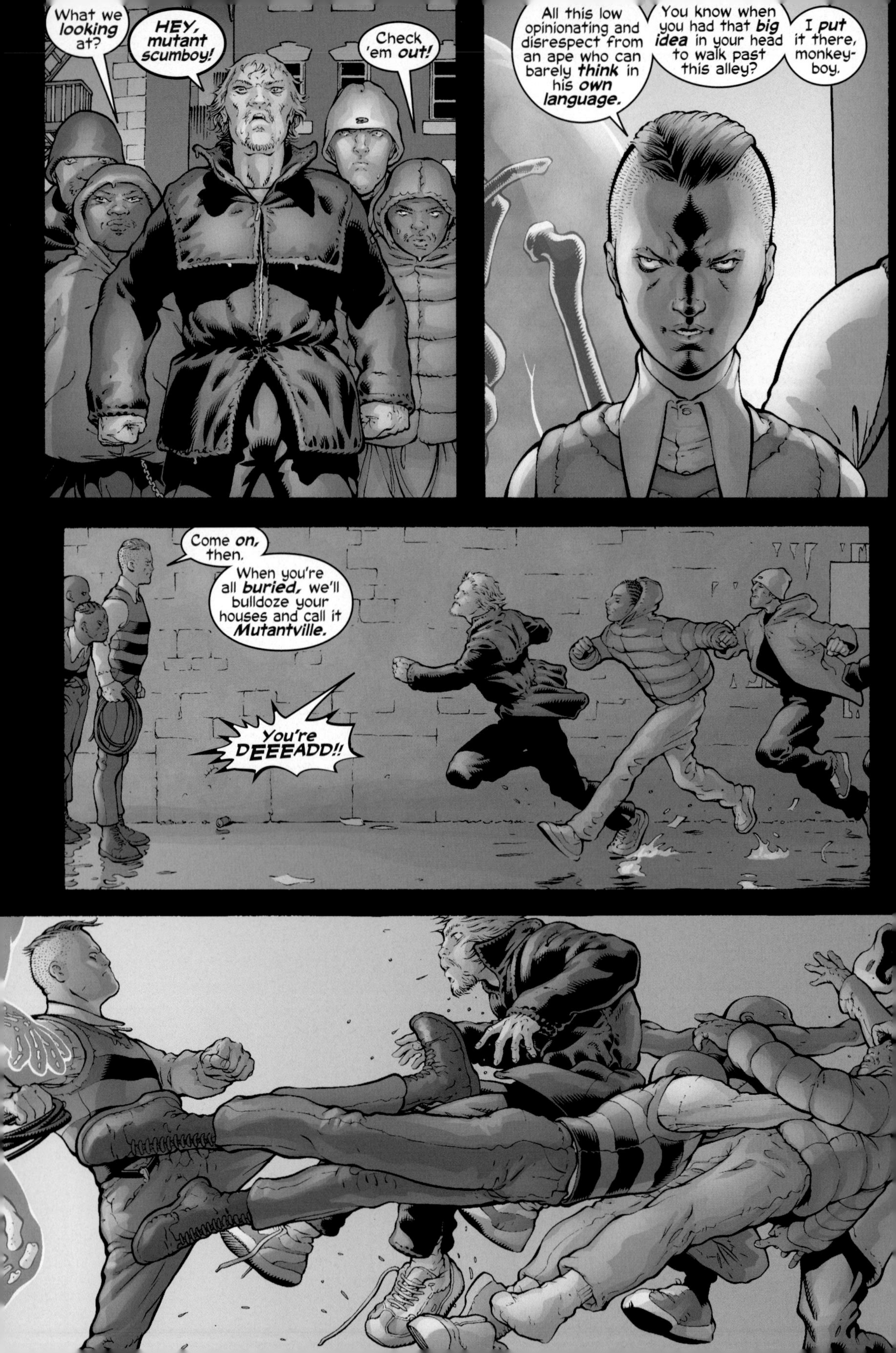
What we looking at?
HEY, mutant scumboy!
Check 'em out!
All this low opinionating and disrespect from an ape who can barely think in his own language.
You know when you had that big idea in your head to walk past this alley?
I put it there, monkey-boy.
Come on, then.
When you're all buried, we'll bulldoze your houses and call it Mutantville.
You're DEEEADD!!

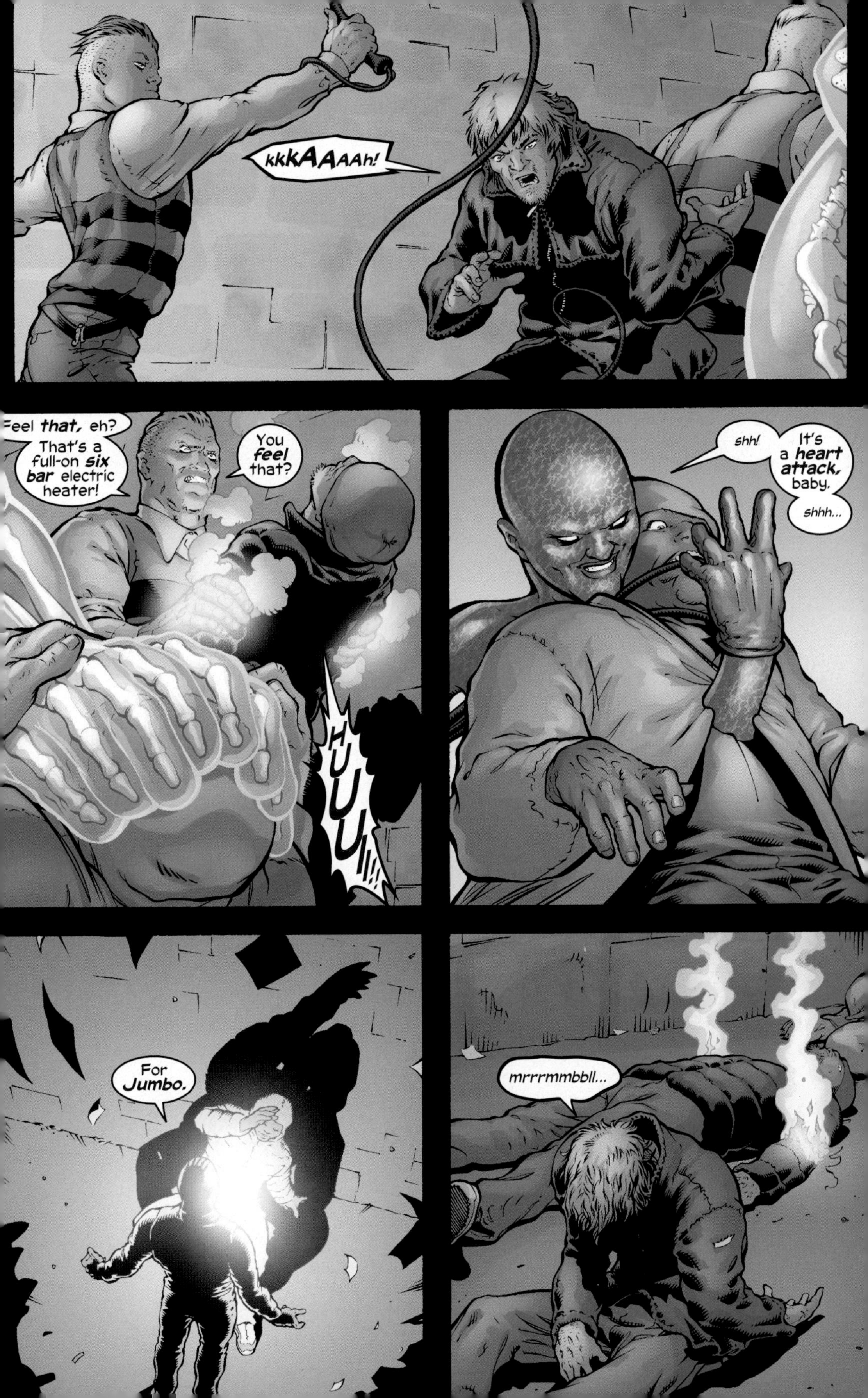
kkKAAAAh!
Feel that, eh? That's a full-on six bar electric heater!
You feel that?
HUUU!!!!
shh!
It's a heart attack, baby.
shhh...
For Jumbo.
mrrrmmbbll...

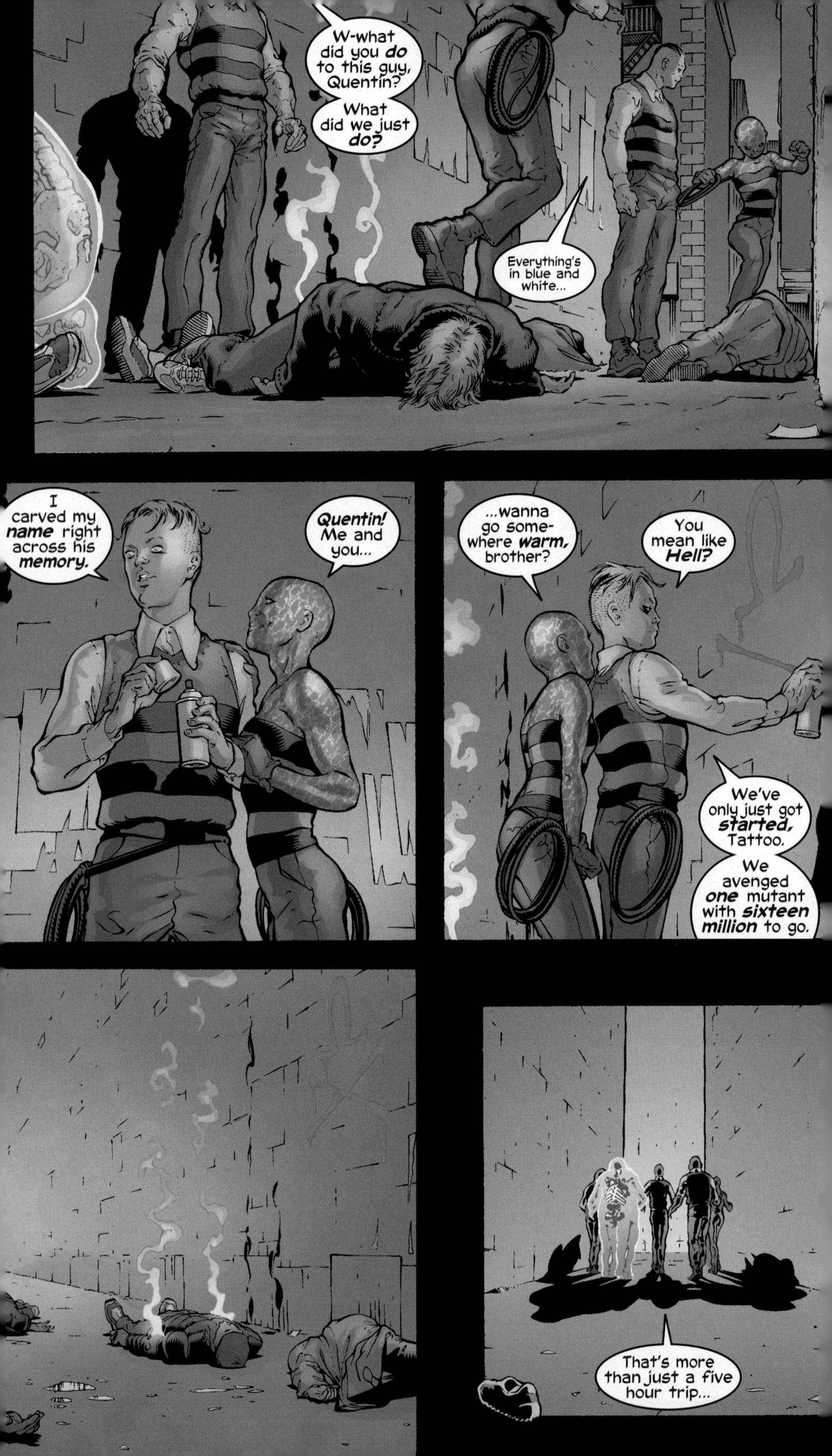
W-what did you do to this guy, Quentin?
What did we just do?
Everything's in blue and white...
I carved my name right across his memory.
Quentin! Me and you...
...wanna go some-where warm, brother?
You mean like Hell?
We've only just got started, Tattoo.
We avenged one mutant with sixteen million to go.
That's more than just a five hour trip...

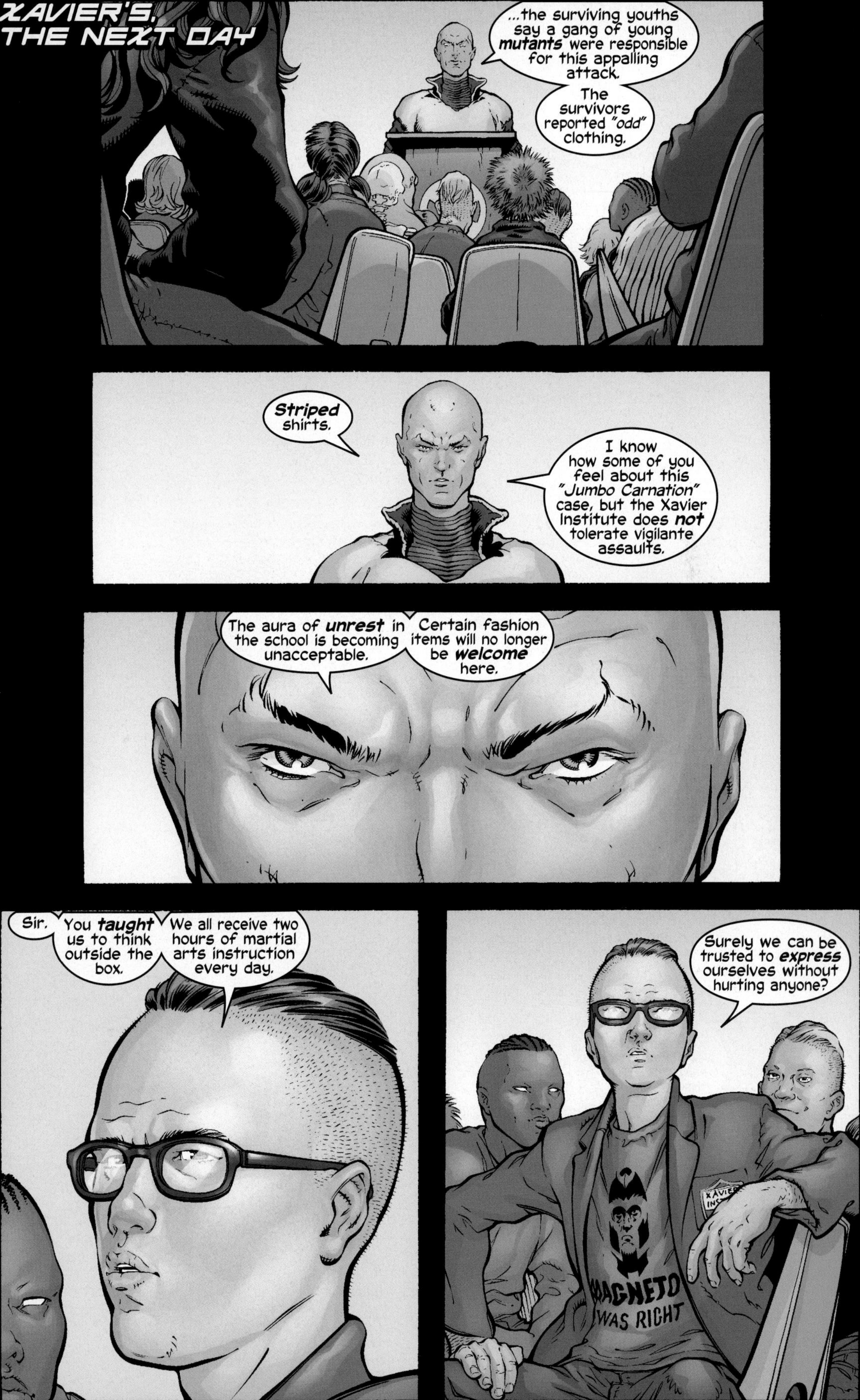
XAVIER'S, THE NEXT DAY
...the surviving youths say a gang of young mutants were responsible for this appalling attack.
The survivors reported "odd" clothing.
Striped shirts.
I know how some of you feel about this "Jumbo Carnation" case, but the Xavier Institute does not tolerate vigilante assaults.
The aura of unrest in the school is becoming unacceptable.
Certain fashion items will no longer be welcome here.
Sir.
You taught us to think outside the box.
We all receive two hours of martial arts instruction every day.
Surely we can be trusted to express ourselves without hurting anyone?
MAGNETO WAS RIGHT

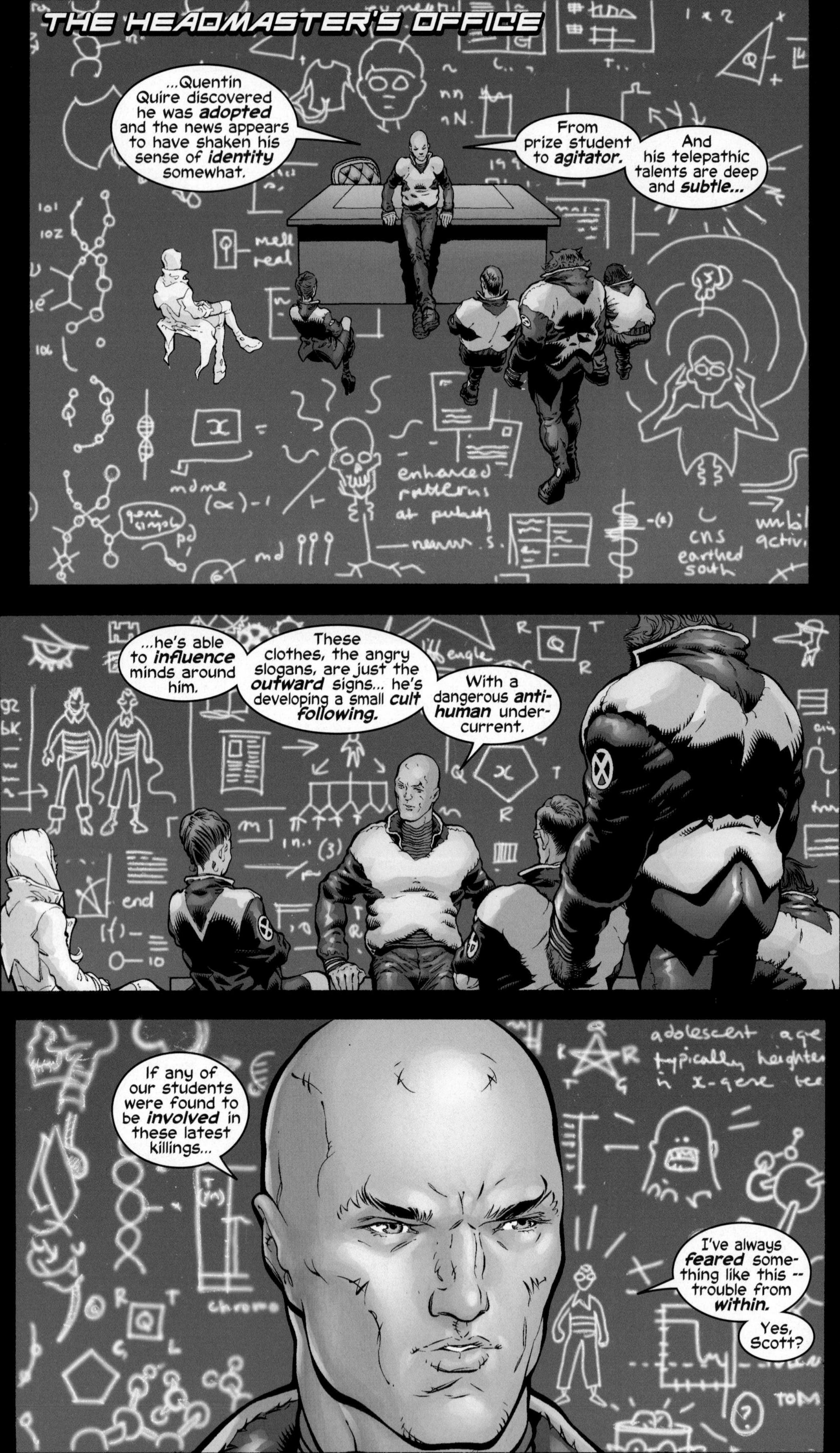
THE HEADMASTER'S OFFICE
...Quentin Quire discovered he was *adopted* and the news appears to have shaken his sense of *identity* somewhat.
From prize student to *agitator.*
And his telepathic talents are deep and *subtle...*
...he's able to *influence* minds around him.
These clothes, the angry slogans, are just the *outward* signs... he's developing a small *cult following.*
With a dangerous *anti-human* under-current.
If any of our students were found to be *involved* in these latest killings...
I've always *feared* some-thing like this -- trouble from *within.*
Yes, Scott?

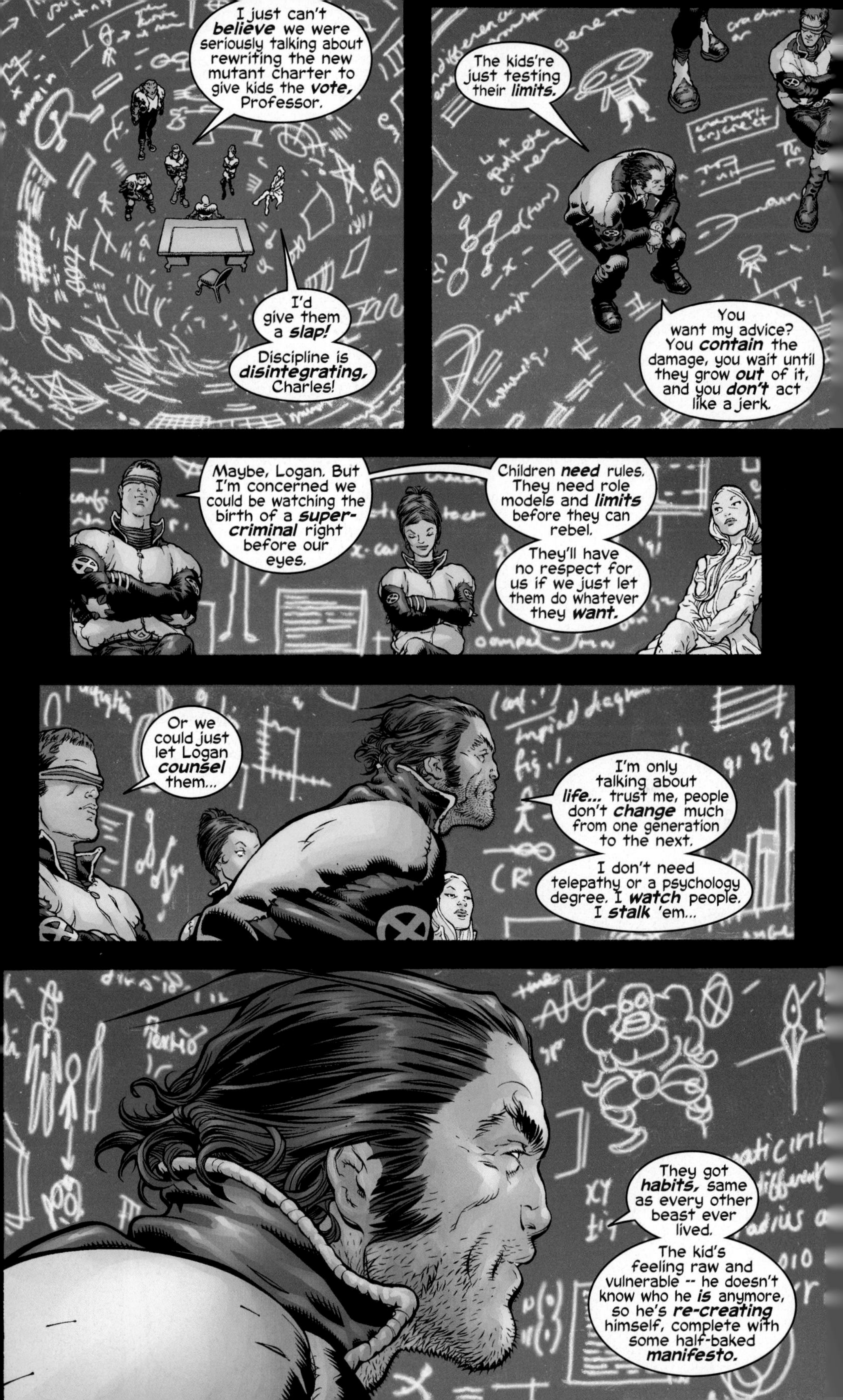
I just can't believe we were seriously talking about rewriting the new mutant charter to give kids the vote, Professor.
I'd give them a slap!
Discipline is disintegrating, Charles!
The kids're just testing their limits.
You want my advice? You contain the damage, you wait until they grow out of it, and you don't act like a jerk.
Maybe, Logan. But I'm concerned we could be watching the birth of a super-criminal right before our eyes.
Children need rules. They need role models and limits before they can rebel.
They'll have no respect for us if we just let them do whatever they want.
Or we could just let Logan counsel them...
I'm only talking about life... trust me, people don't change much from one generation to the next.
I don't need telepathy or a psychology degree. I watch people. I stalk 'em...
They got habits, same as every other beast ever lived.
The kid's feeling raw and vulnerable -- he doesn't know who he is anymore, so he's re-creating himself, complete with some half-baked manifesto.

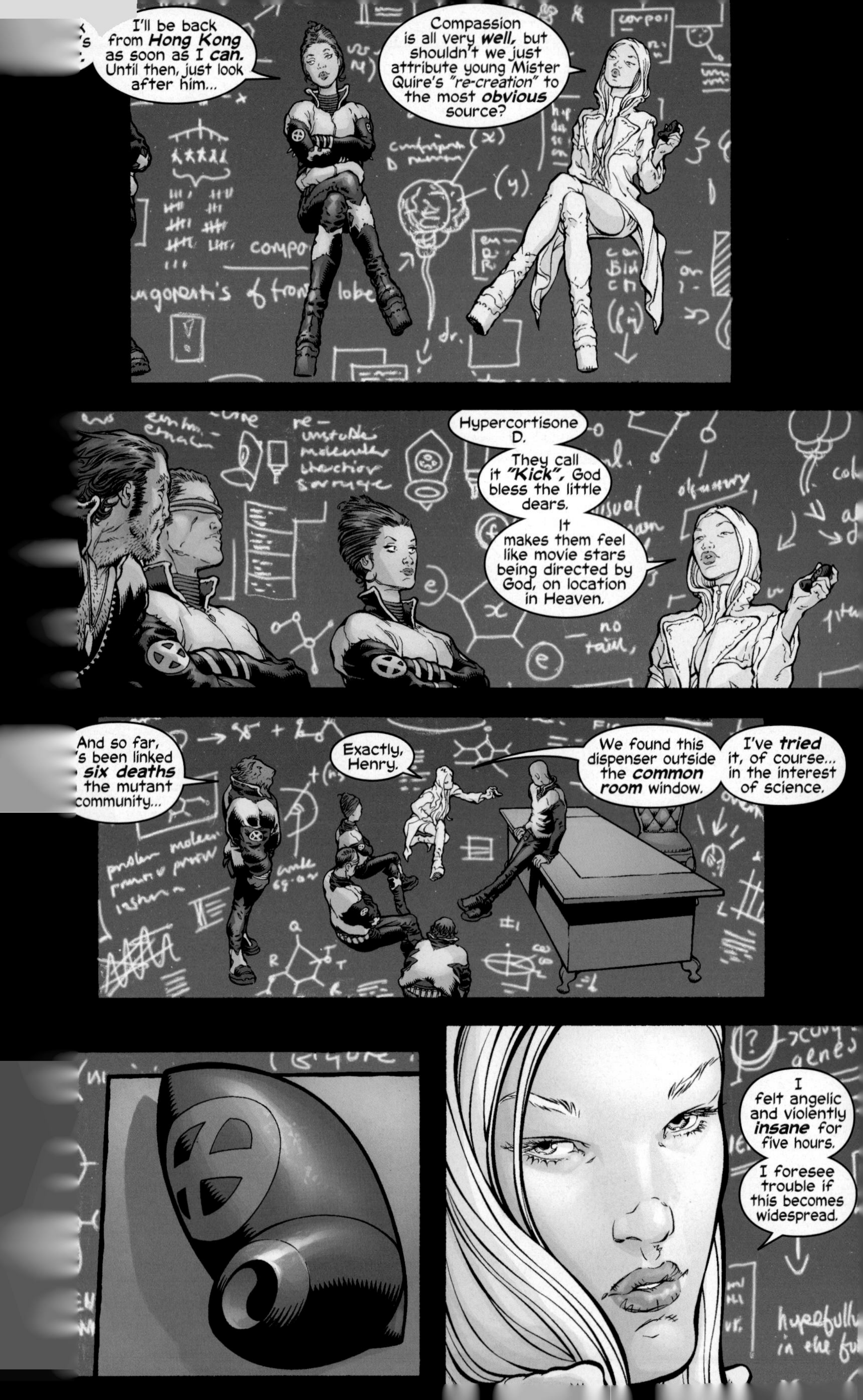
I'll be back from Hong Kong as soon as I can. Until then, just look after him...
Compassion is all very well, but shouldn't we just attribute young Mister Quire's "re-creation" to the most obvious source?
Hypercortisone D.
They call it "Kick", God bless the little dears.
It makes them feel like movie stars being directed by God, on location in Heaven.
And so far, 's been linked six deaths the mutant community...
Exactly, Henry.
We found this dispenser outside the common room window.
I've tried it, of course... in the interest of science.
I felt angelic and violently insane for five hours.
I foresee trouble if this becomes widespread.

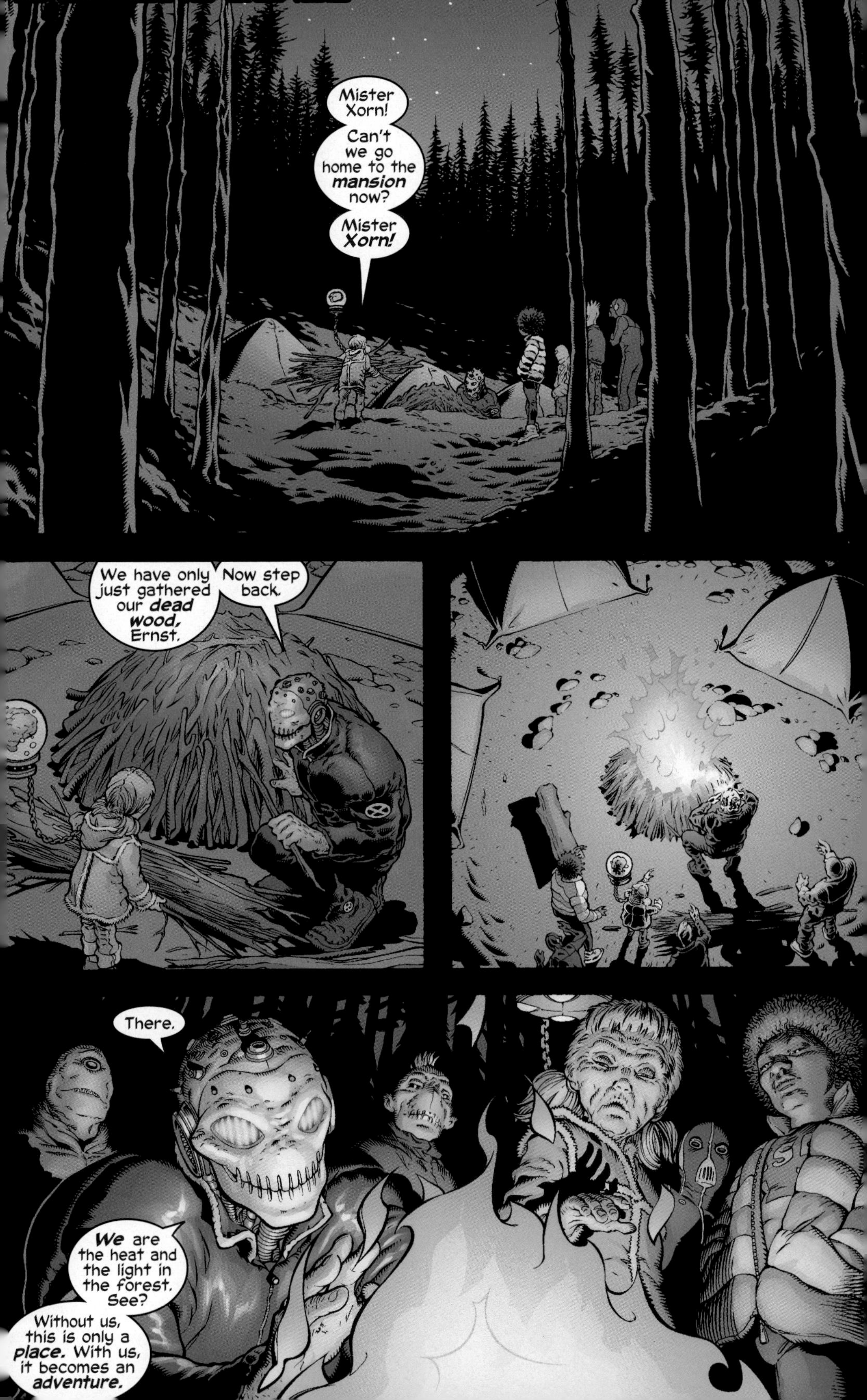
Mister Xorn!
Can't we go home to the *mansion* now?
Mister *Xorn!*
We have only just gathered our *dead wood,* Ernst.
Now step back.
There.
We are the heat and the light in the forest. See?
Without us, this is only a *place.* With us, it becomes an *adventure.*

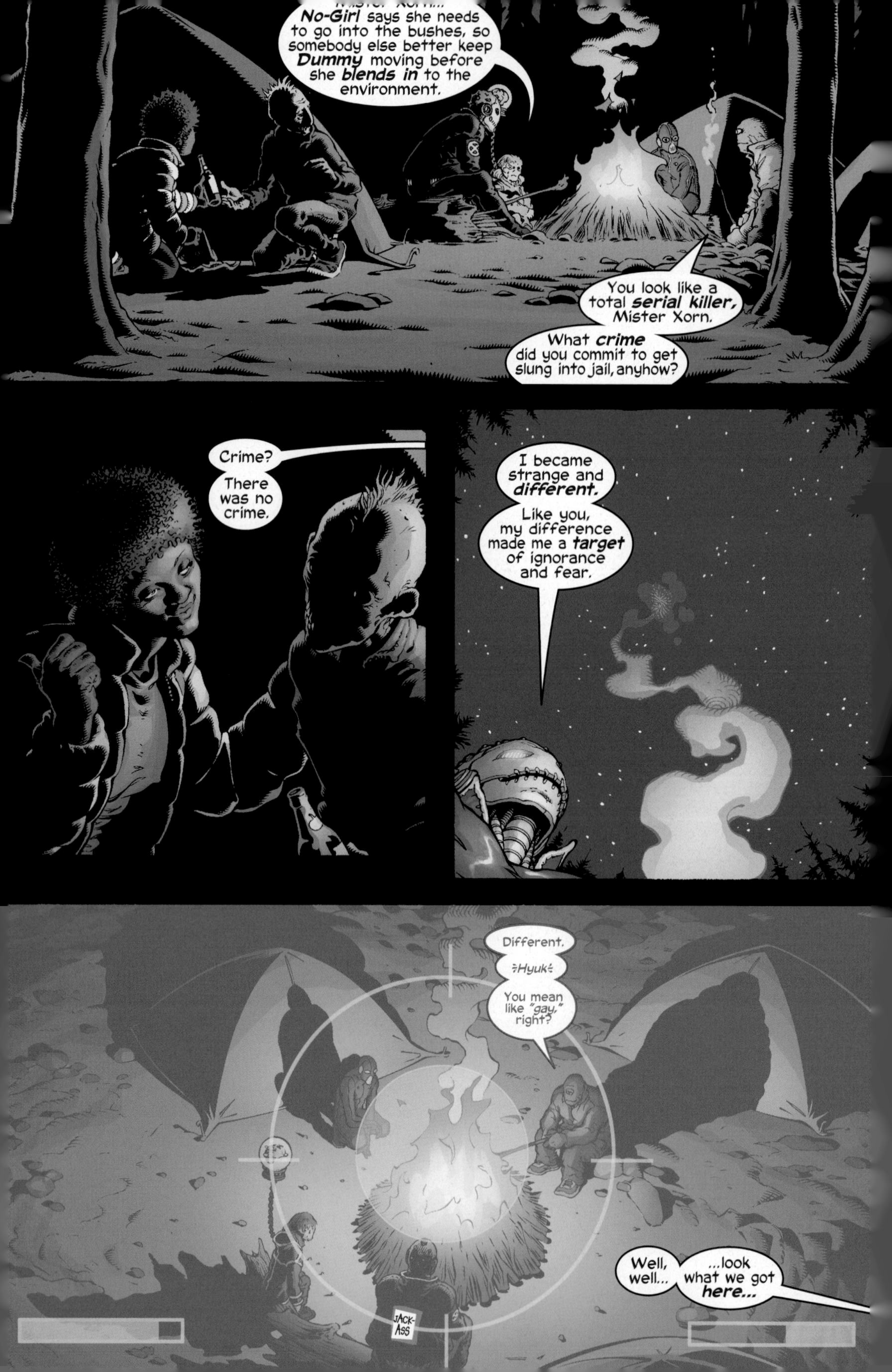
No-Girl says she needs to go into the bushes, so somebody else better keep Dummy moving before she blends in to the environment.
You look like a total serial killer, Mister Xorn.
What crime did you commit to get slung into jail, anyhow?
Crime?
There was no crime.
I became strange and different.
Like you, my difference made me a target of ignorance and fear.
Different.
Hyuk
You mean like "gay," right?
Well, well...
...look what we got here...
JACK-ASS

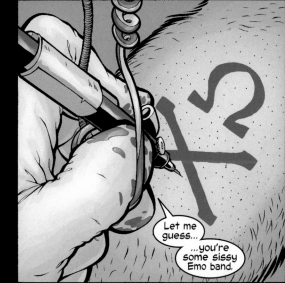

Let me guess...

...you're some sissy Emo band.

You're suburban Neo-Nazis.

Frat boys on dope!

I *told* you this is what we'd look like!

What did I *say?!* We're gonna look like a bunch of *frat boys!*

I'll tell him what we are.

Everybody's heard of the *X-Men*, right?

Well, we're the *next generation.* Like on *TV.*

The *improved* version.

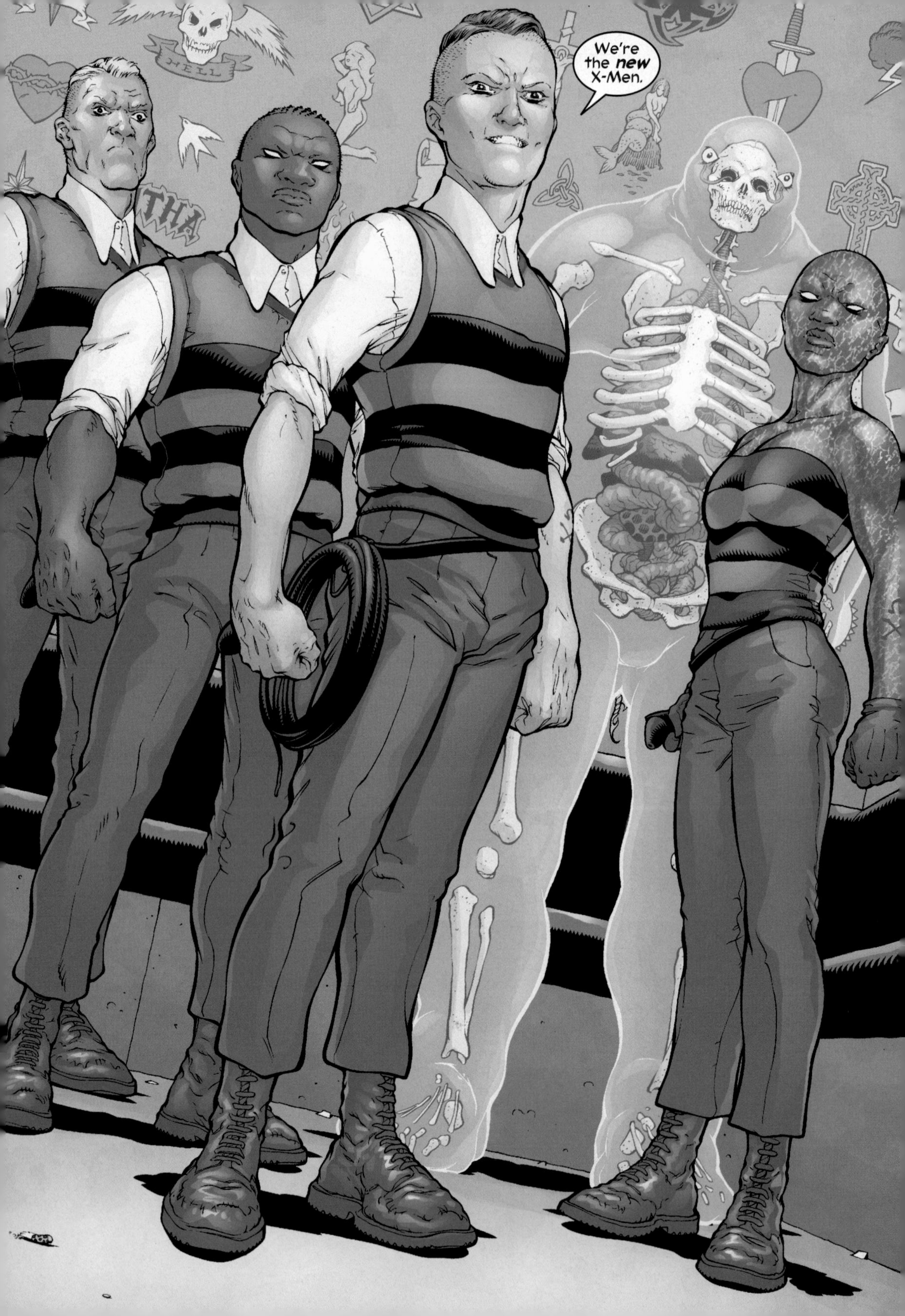
We're the new X-Men.

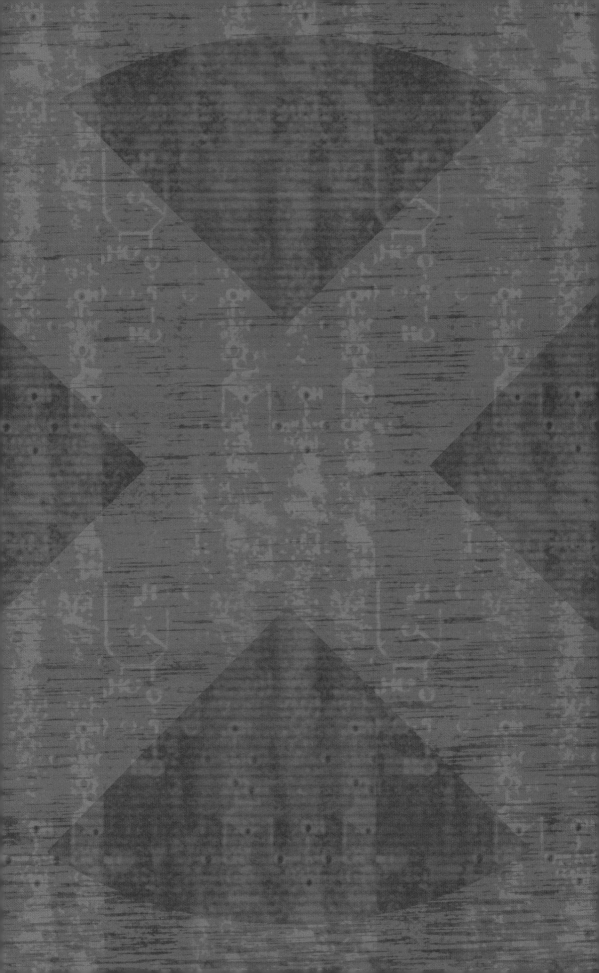

#136

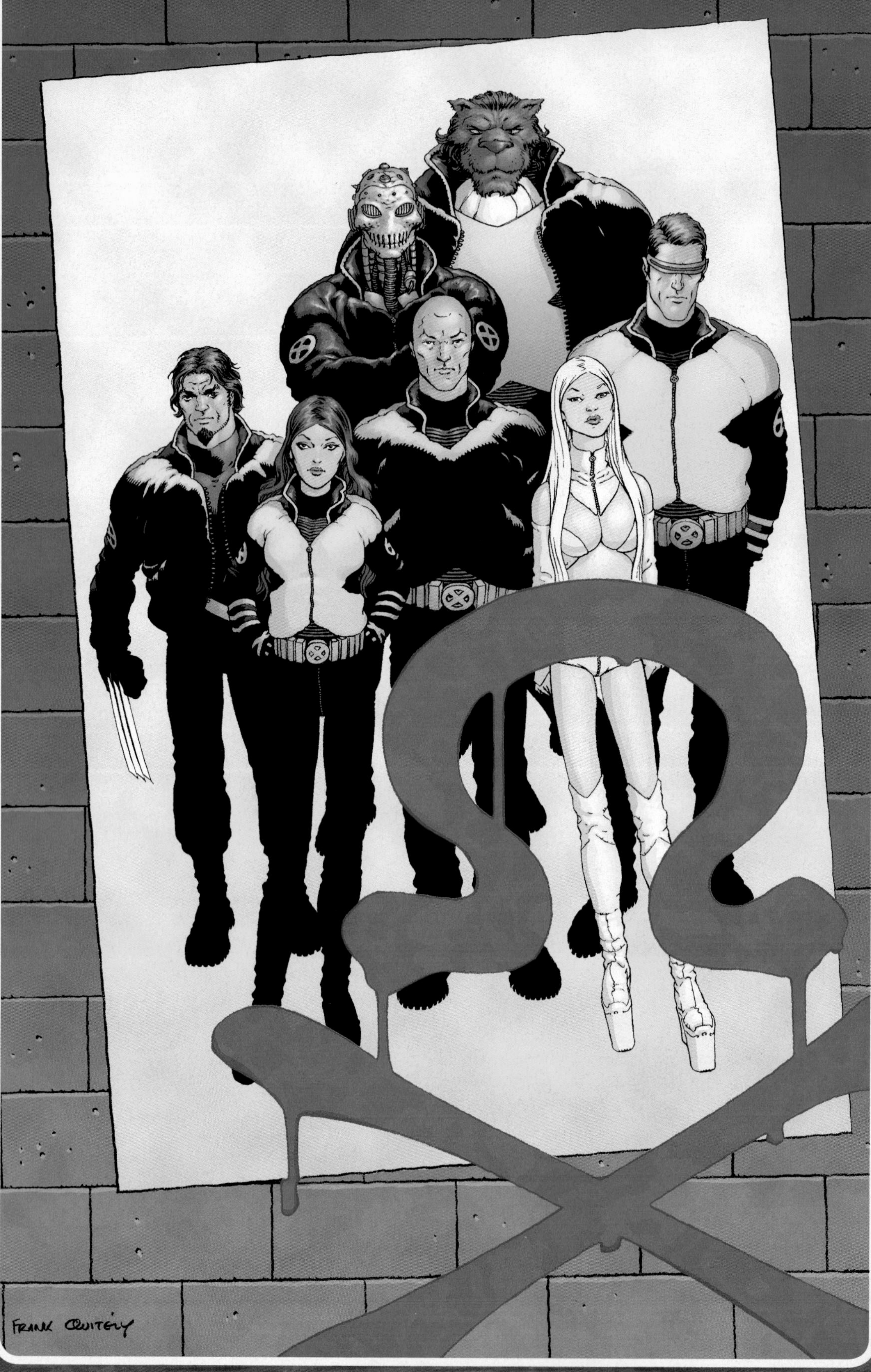
FRANK QUITELY

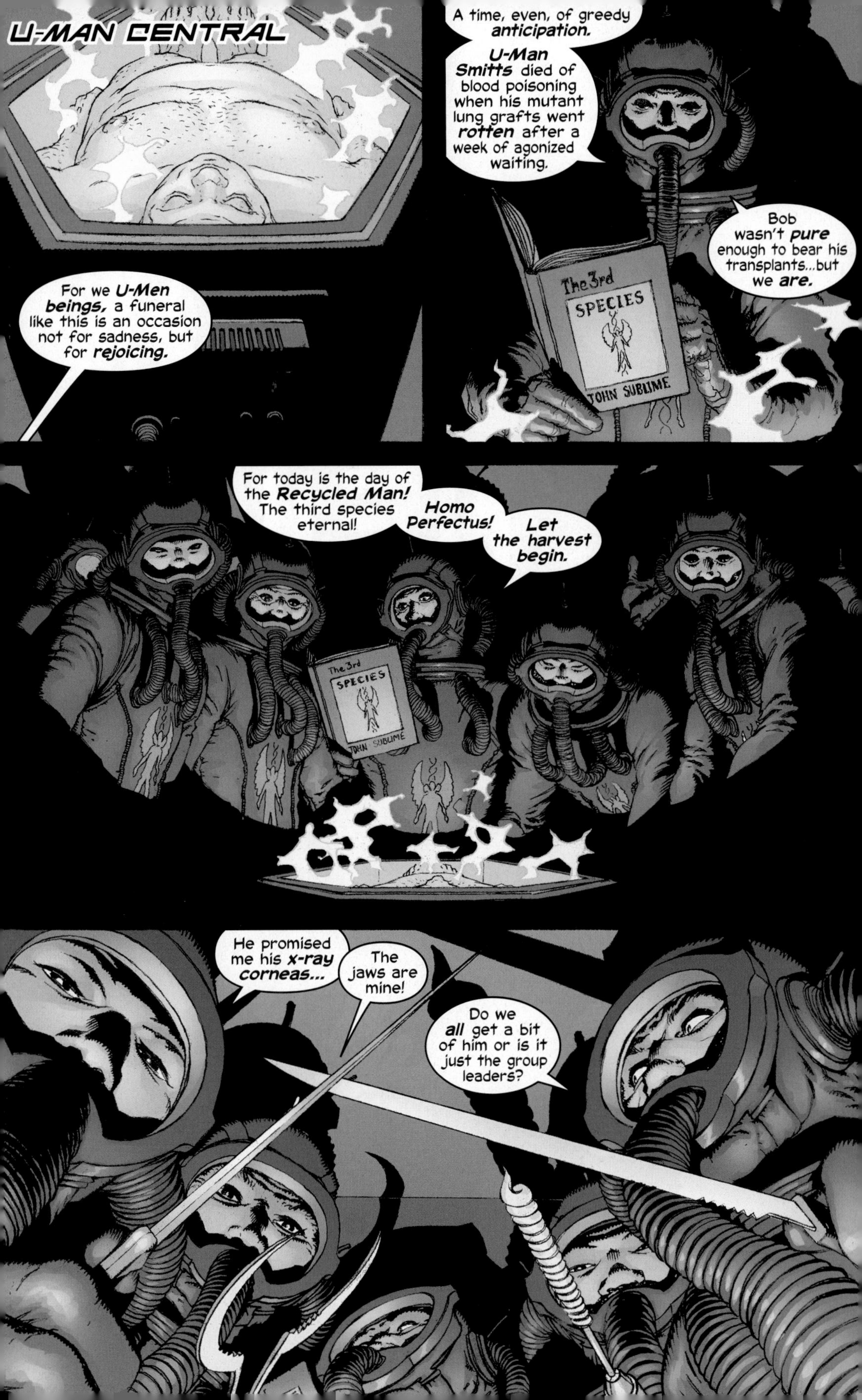

U-MAN CENTRAL
For we U-Men beings, a funeral like this is an occasion not for sadness, but for rejoicing.
A time, even, of greedy anticipation.
U-Man Smitts died of blood poisoning when his mutant lung grafts went rotten after a week of agonized waiting.
Bob wasn't pure enough to bear his transplants...but we are.
The 3rd SPECIES JOHN SUBLIME
For today is the day of the Recycled Man! The third species eternal!
Homo Perfectus!
Let the harvest begin.
The 3rd SPECIES JOHN SUBLIME
He promised me his x-ray corneas...
The jaws are mine!
Do we all get a bit of him or is it just the group leaders?

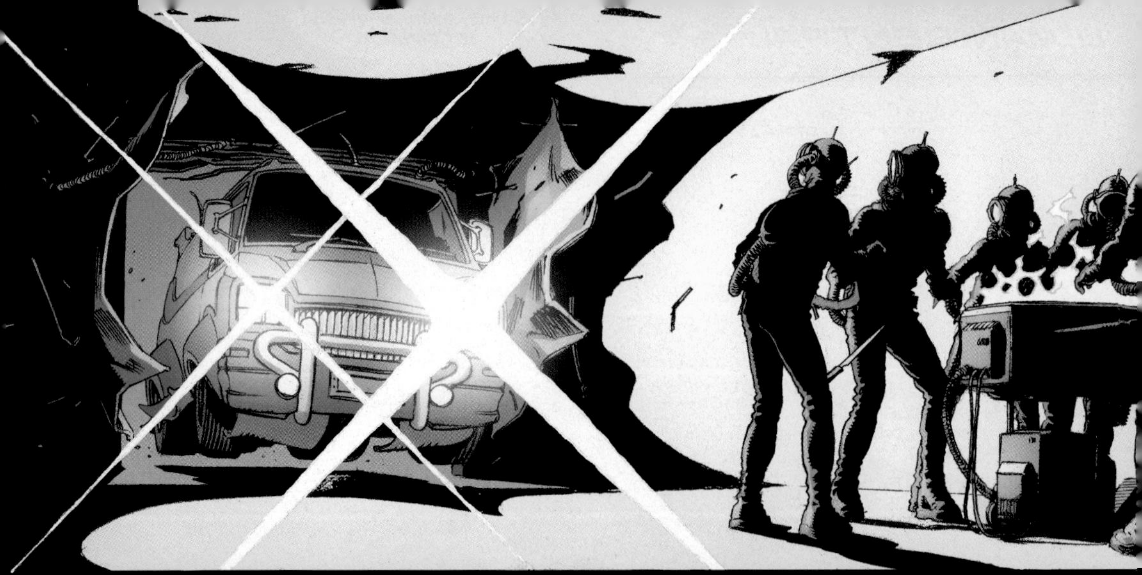

GRANT MORRISON
WRITER

FRANK QUITELY
WITH AVALON STUDIOS
ART

CHRIS CHUCKRY
COLORS

RICHARD STARKINGS & COMICRAFT'S WES!
LETTERS

MIKE RAICHT & NOVA REN SUMA
ASSISTANT EDITORS

MIKE MARTS
EDITOR

JOE QUESADA
EDITOR IN CHIEF

BILL JEMAS
PRESIDENT

NEW X-MEN

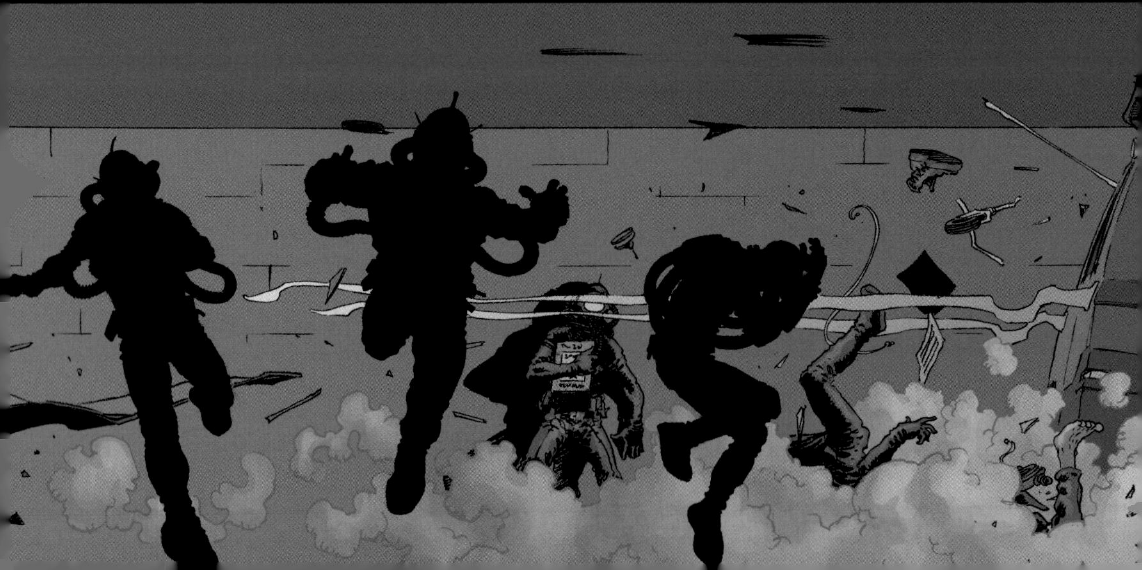

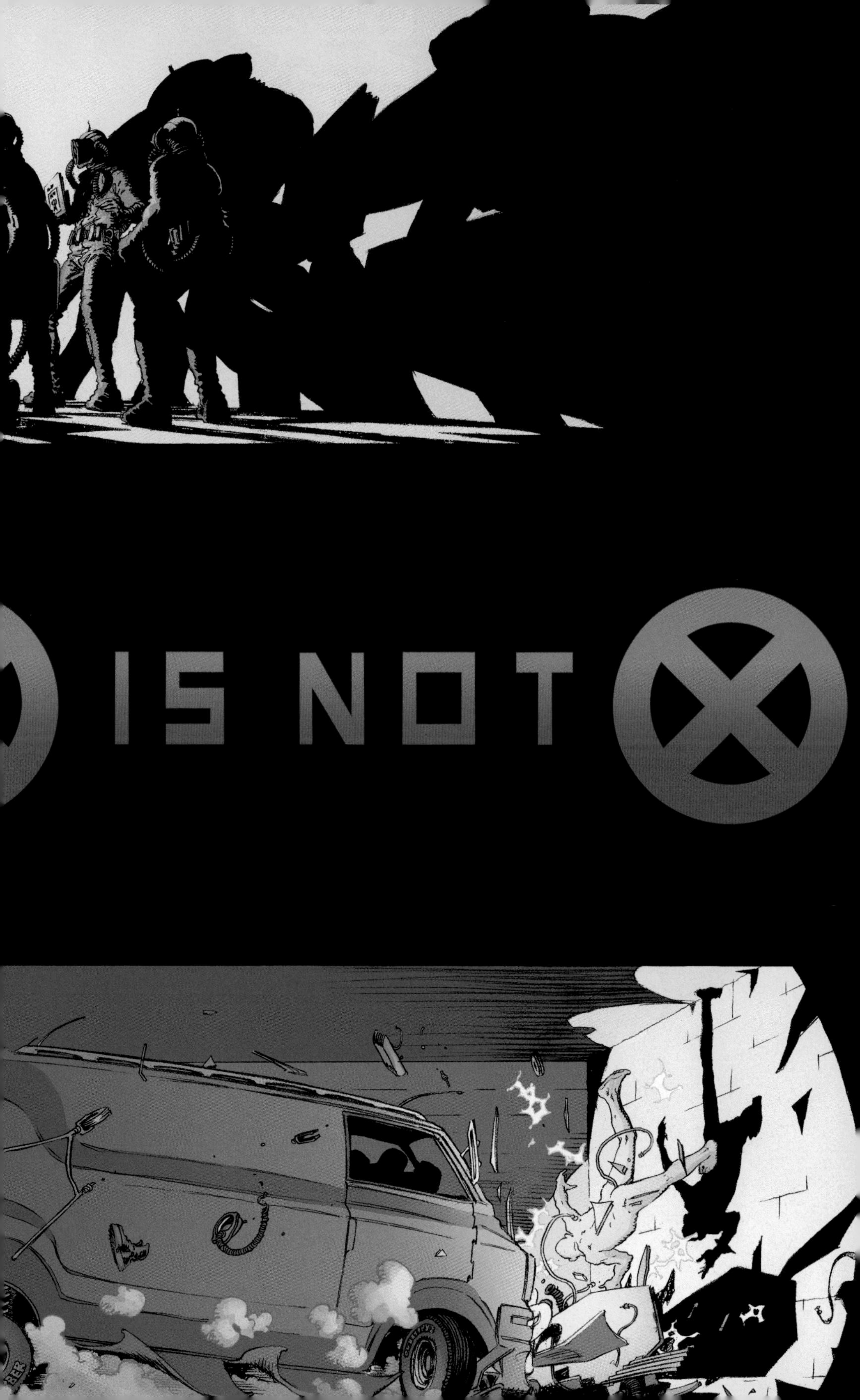
IS NOT

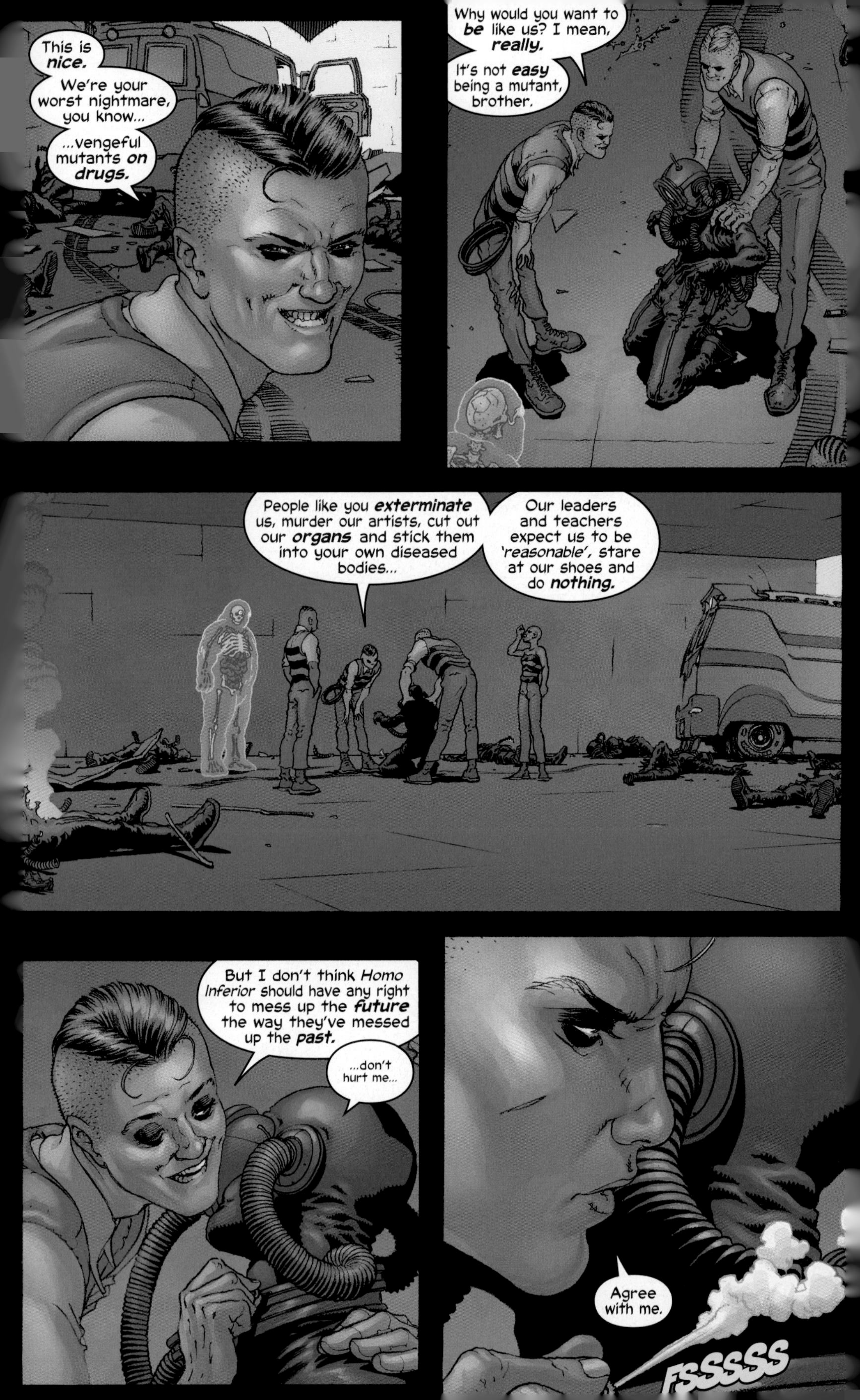
This is nice.
We're your worst nightmare, you know...
...vengeful mutants on drugs.
Why would you want to be like us? I mean, really.
It's not easy being a mutant, brother.
People like you exterminate us, murder our artists, cut out our organs and stick them into your own diseased bodies...
Our leaders and teachers expect us to be 'reasonable', stare at our shoes and do nothing.
But I don't think Homo Inferior should have any right to mess up the future the way they've messed up the past.
...don't hurt me...
Agree with me.
FSSSSS

I can't touch the ground... I have to breathe pure air...

...it's my religion...please...I can't touch the fallen world until it's made perfect...

Get some *Kick* into your lungs, *Redneck*, my man!

Gimme five-bar electric death!

I spent the last of my savings on this suit...please don't ruin it...

You're not a *religion.* You're a cannibal freak who met some like-minded losers in a seedy chatroom and decided to create a *Do-It-Yourself* species...using *pieces* of *our* people.

Citizen Redneck? Citizen Herman?

New X Justice.

Hey, Quentin...

...you want we should tell this guy what Herman's *made* from...

...before it's *too late* for him to hear?

You mean *Bio-Paraffin?* Living wax?

EEEAAUU

The world hasn't *fallen*, you ignorant ape...

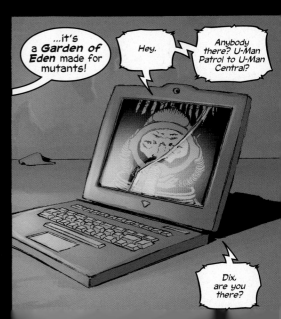

...it's a *Garden of Eden* made for mutants!

Hey.

Anybody there? U-Man Patrol to U-Man Central?

Dix, are you there?

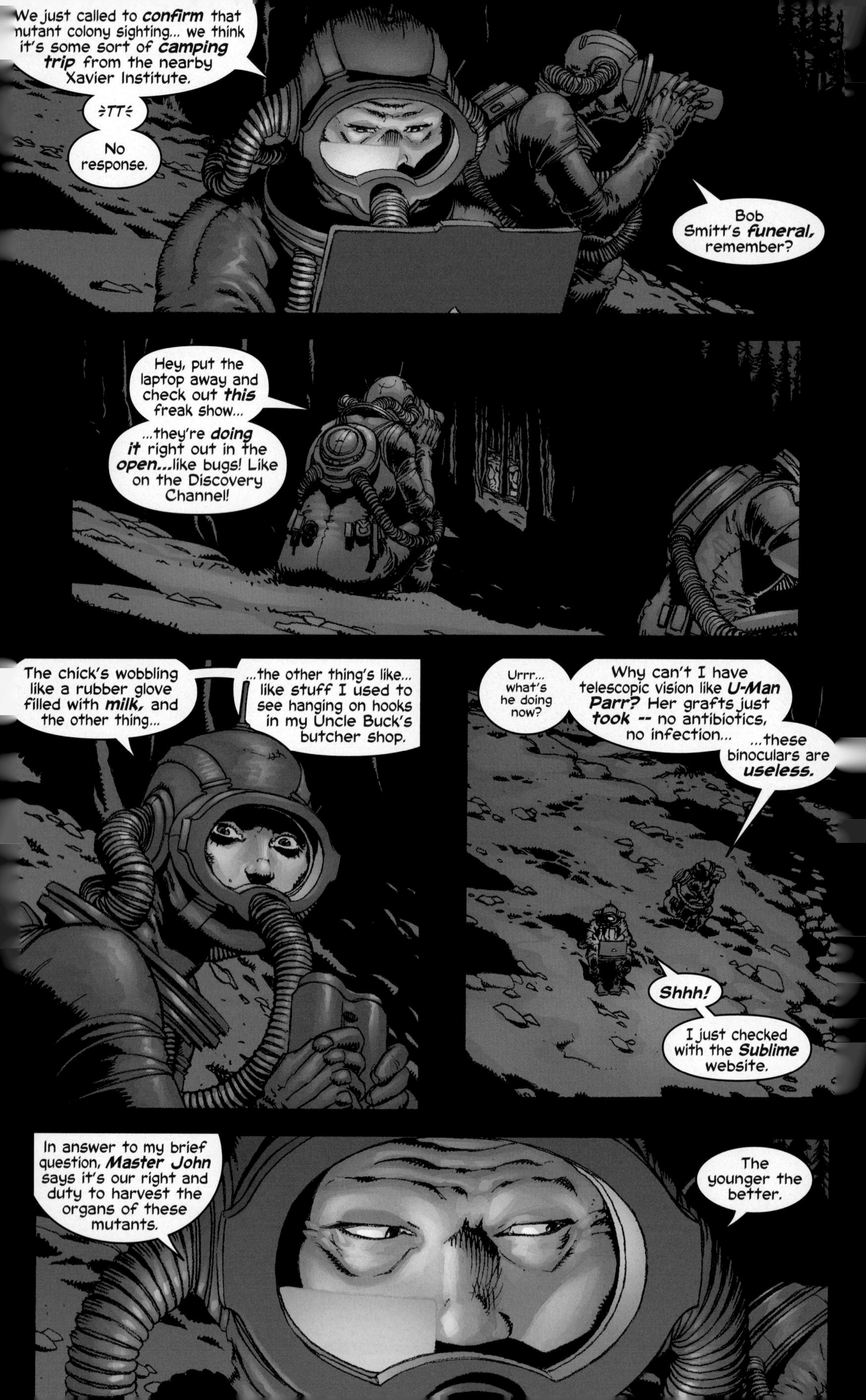
We just called to confirm that mutant colony sighting... we think it's some sort of camping trip from the nearby Xavier Institute.
≠TT≠
No response.
Bob Smitt's funeral, remember?
Hey, put the laptop away and check out this freak show...
...they're doing it right out in the open...like bugs! Like on the Discovery Channel!
The chick's wobbling like a rubber glove filled with milk, and the other thing...
...the other thing's like... like stuff I used to see hanging on hooks in my Uncle Buck's butcher shop.
Urrr... what's he doing now?
Why can't I have telescopic vision like U-Man Parr? Her grafts just took -- no antibiotics, no infection...
...these binoculars are useless.
Shhh!
I just checked with the Sublime website.
In answer to my brief question, Master John says it's our right and duty to harvest the organs of these mutants.
The younger the better.

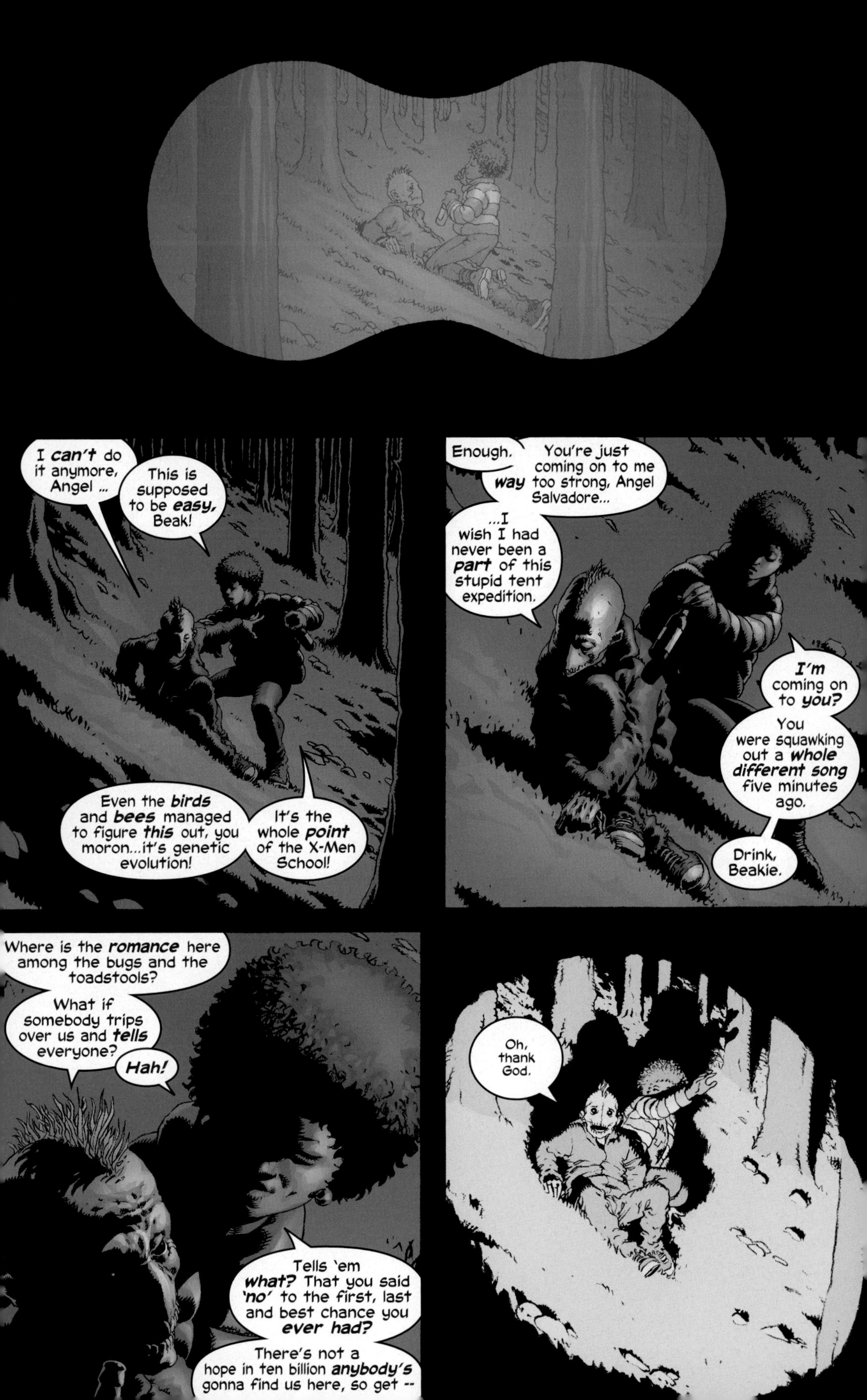

I can't do it anymore, Angel ...
This is supposed to be easy, Beak!
Even the birds and bees managed to figure this out, you moron...it's genetic evolution!
It's the whole point of the X-Men School!
Enough.
You're just coming on to me way too strong, Angel Salvadore...
...I wish I had never been a part of this stupid tent expedition.
I'm coming on to you?
You were squawking out a whole different song five minutes ago.
Drink, Beakie.
Where is the romance here among the bugs and the toadstools?
What if somebody trips over us and tells everyone?
Hah!
Tells 'em what? That you said 'no' to the first, last and best chance you ever had?
There's not a hope in ten billion anybody's gonna find us here, so get --
Oh, thank God.

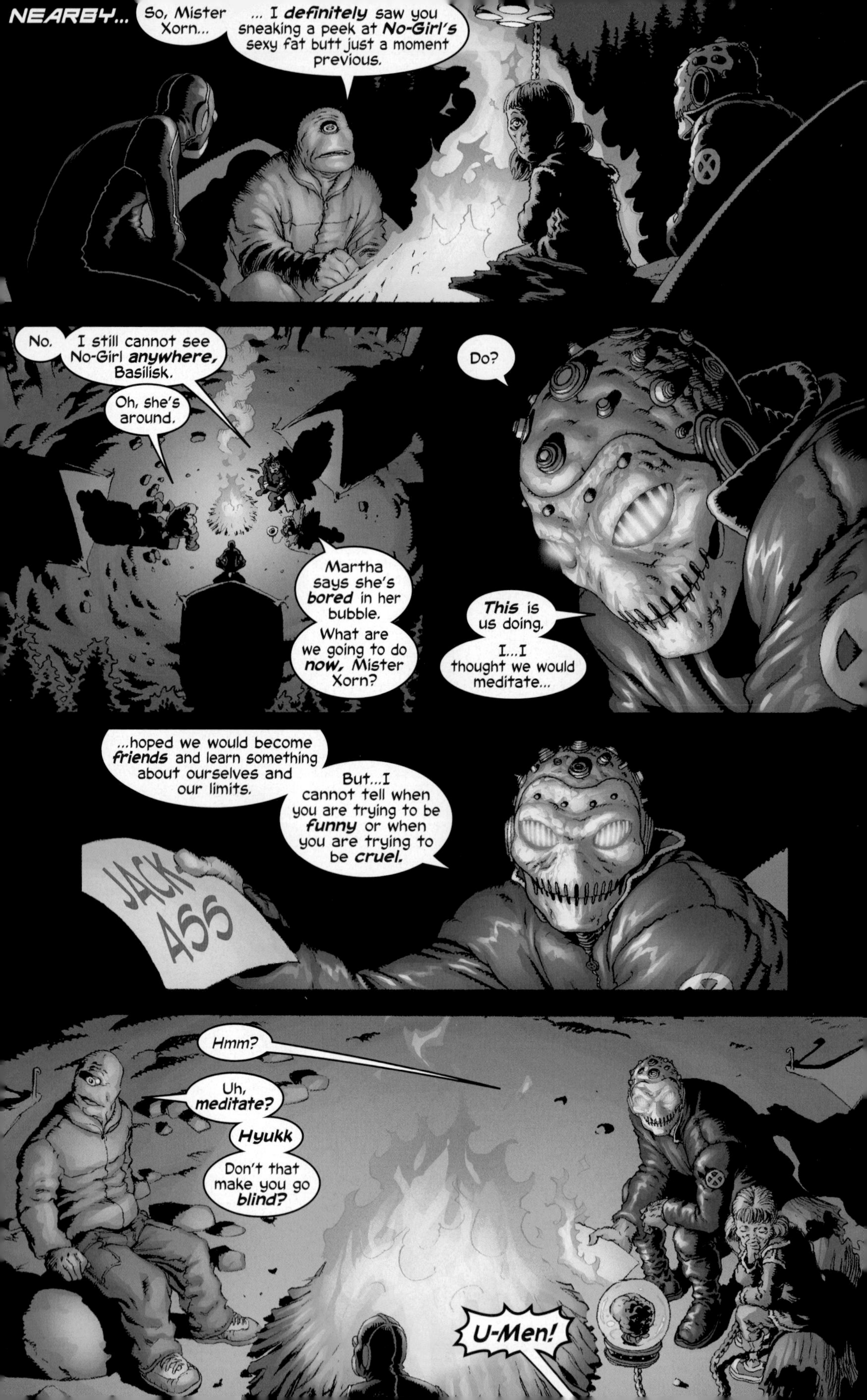
NEARBY...
So, Mister Xorn...
... I definitely saw you sneaking a peek at No-Girl's sexy fat butt just a moment previous.
No.
I still cannot see No-Girl anywhere, Basilisk.
Oh, she's around.
Martha says she's bored in her bubble.
What are we going to do now, Mister Xorn?
Do?
This is us doing.
I...I thought we would meditate...
...hoped we would become friends and learn something about ourselves and our limits.
But...I cannot tell when you are trying to be funny or when you are trying to be cruel.
JACK-ASS
Hmm?
Uh, meditate?
Hyukk
Don't that make you go blind?
U-Men!

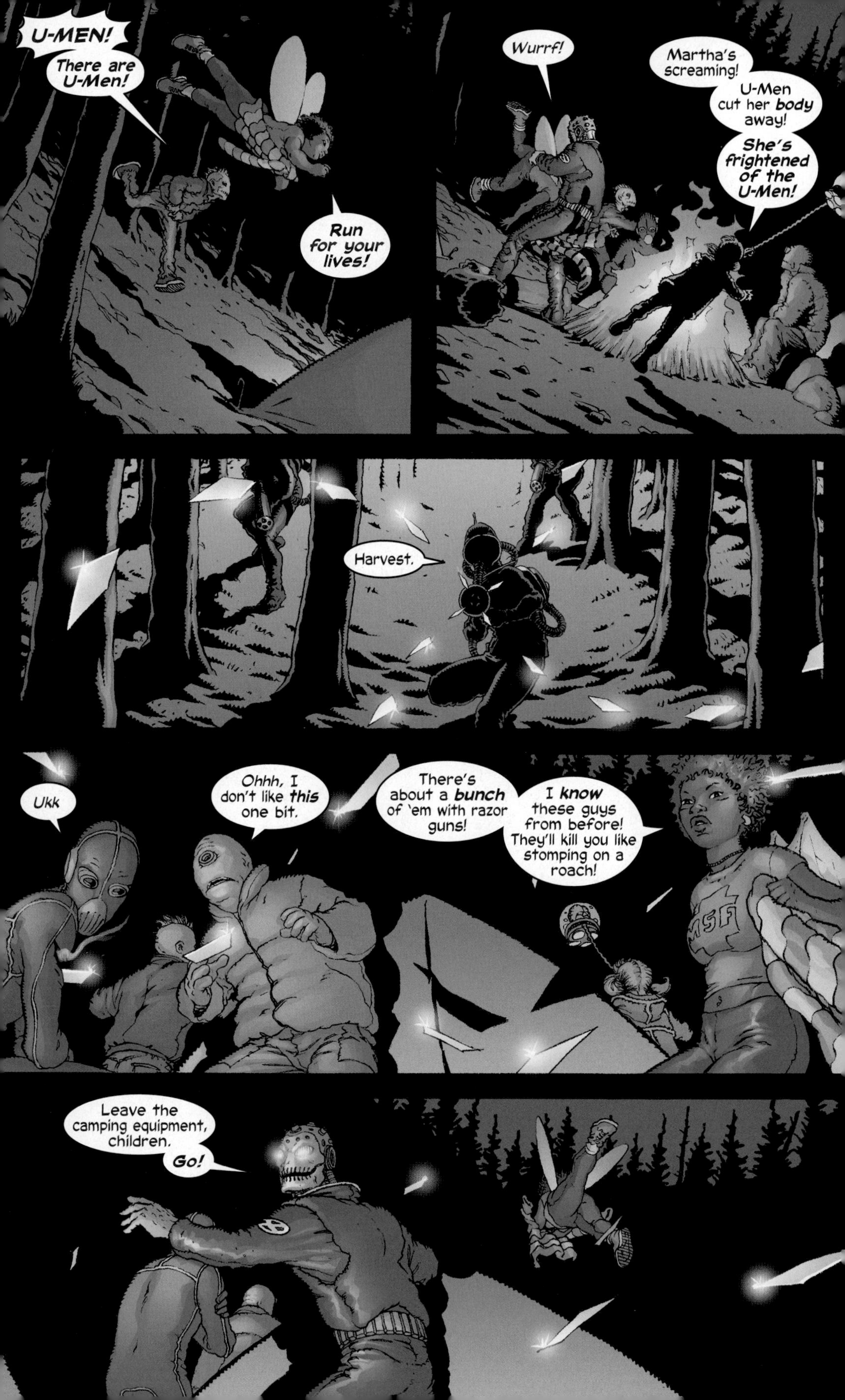
U-MEN!
There are U-Men!
Run for your lives!
Wurrf!
Martha's screaming!
U-Men cut her body away!
She's frightened of the U-Men!
Harvest.
Ukk
Ohhh, I don't like this one bit.
There's about a bunch of 'em with razor guns!
I know these guys from before! They'll kill you like stomping on a roach!
Leave the camping equipment, children.
Go!

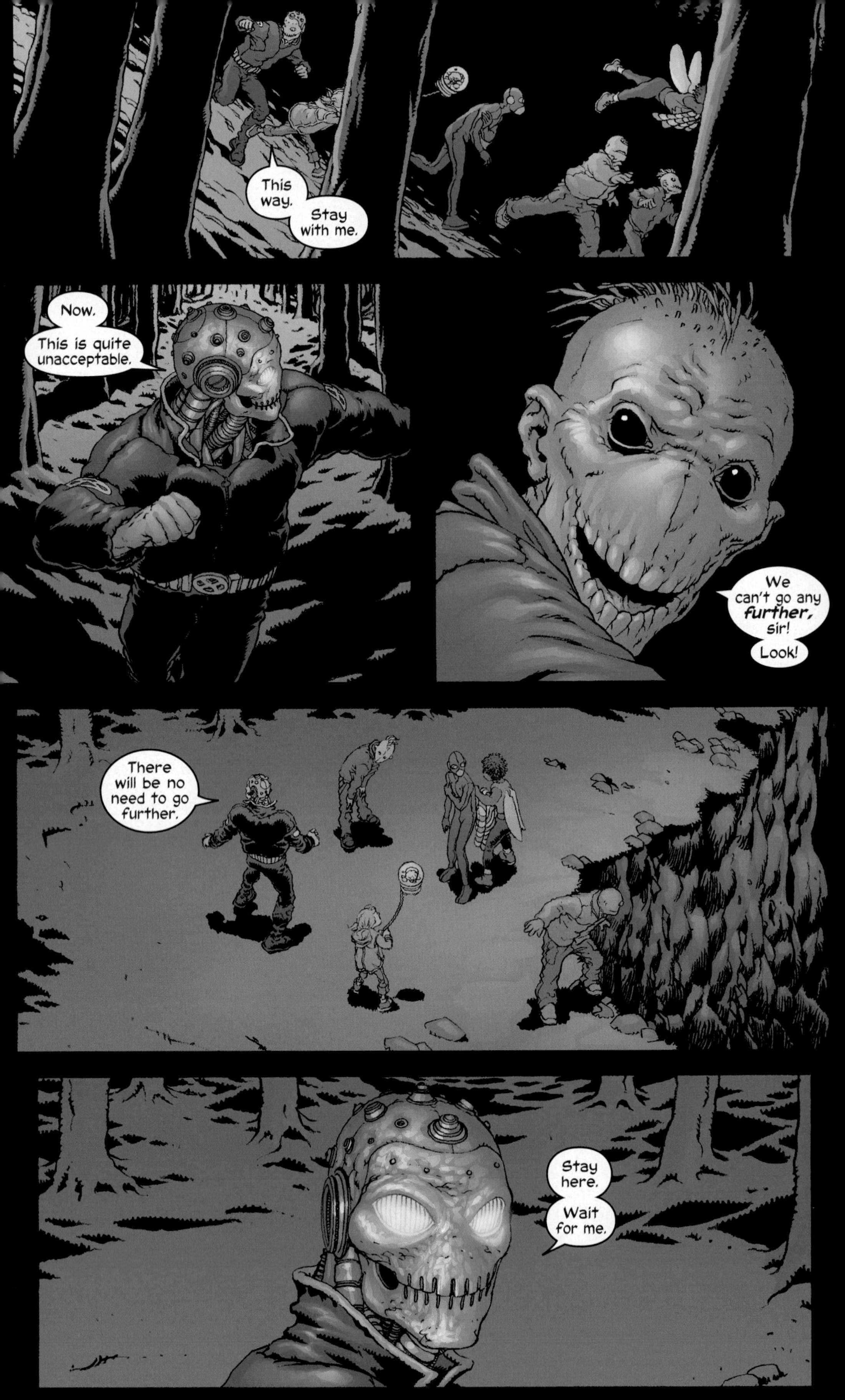
This way.
Stay with me.
Now.
This is quite unacceptable.
We can't go any **further,** sir!
Look!
There will be no need to go further.
Stay here.
Wait for me.

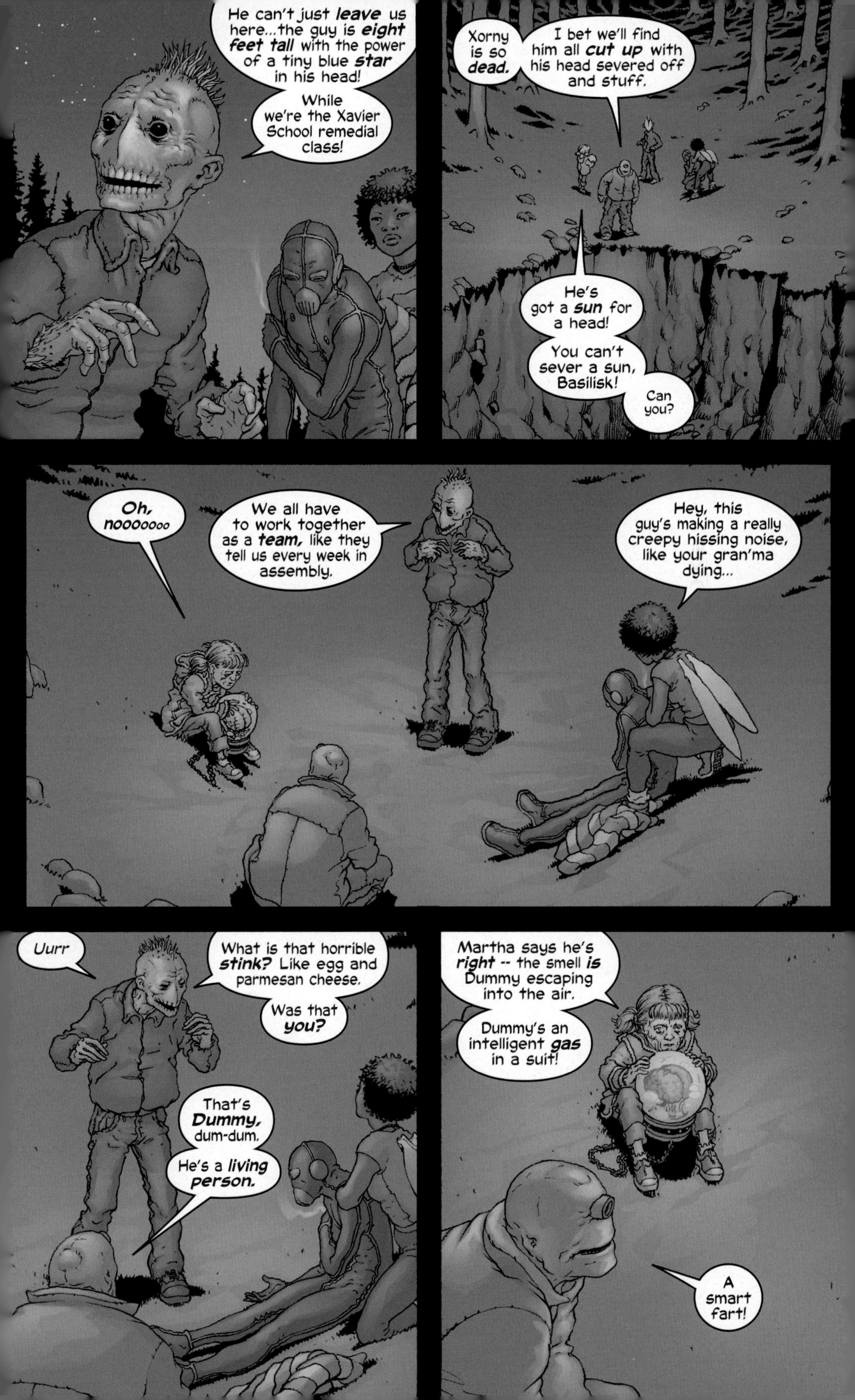
He can't just leave us here...the guy is eight feet tall with the power of a tiny blue star in his head!
While we're the Xavier School remedial class!
Xorny is so dead.
I bet we'll find him all cut up with his head severed off and stuff.
He's got a sun for a head!
You can't sever a sun, Basilisk!
Can you?
Oh, nooooooo
We all have to work together as a team, like they tell us every week in assembly.
Hey, this guy's making a really creepy hissing noise, like your gran'ma dying...
Uurr
What is that horrible stink? Like egg and parmesan cheese.
Was that you?
That's Dummy, dum-dum.
He's a living person.
Martha says he's right -- the smell is Dummy escaping into the air.
Dummy's an intelligent gas in a suit!
A smart fart!

So when did common sense stand on its head and make *you* the leader anyhow, Beakum?

You are the ones who *make* me the leader by standing there doing @&@$!

You guys make *me* look like the *X-Men!*

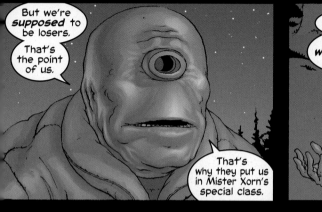

But we're *supposed* to be losers. That's the point of us.

That's why they put us in Mister Xorn's special class.

No way! No *way* are we losers!

Do *I* look like a loser to you?

You'll *never* be X-Man material, Beak! And Angel's only here 'cause she likes the taste of finger-lickin' frozen chicken!

Hyukk

Okay, leader... ...fifteen minutes ago, you were begging me to tell you what went where -- now *you're* the big man with the plan?

Why is everybody now *picking* on me? We are in a death and life situation!

You are the one who can *fly*, Angel, so fly for *help!!*

What kind?

Psychiatric?

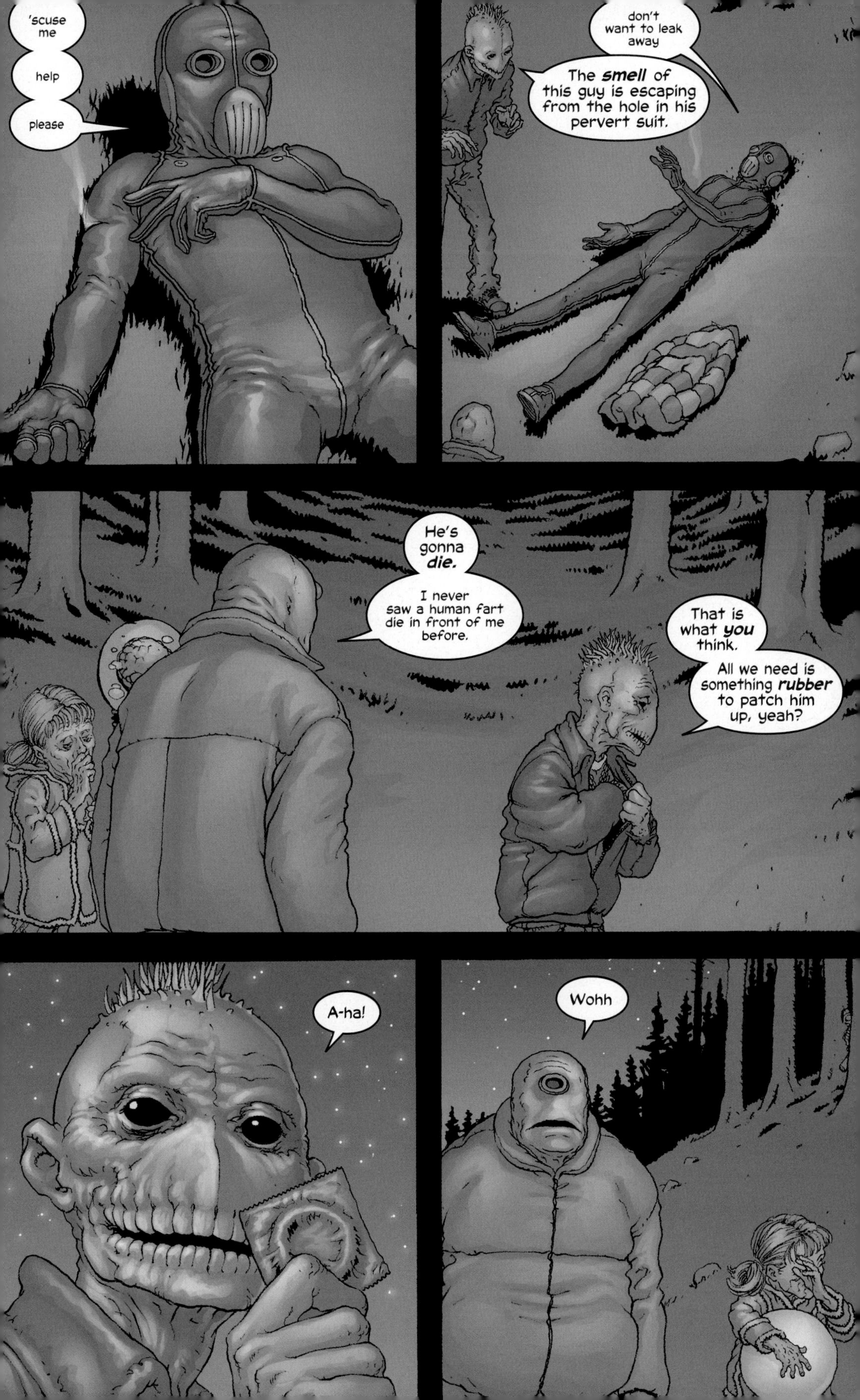
'scuse me
help
please
don't want to leak away
The **smell** of this guy is escaping from the hole in his pervert suit.
He's gonna **die.**
I never saw a human fart die in front of me before.
That is what **you** think.
All we need is something **rubber** to patch him up, yeah?
A-ha!
Wohh

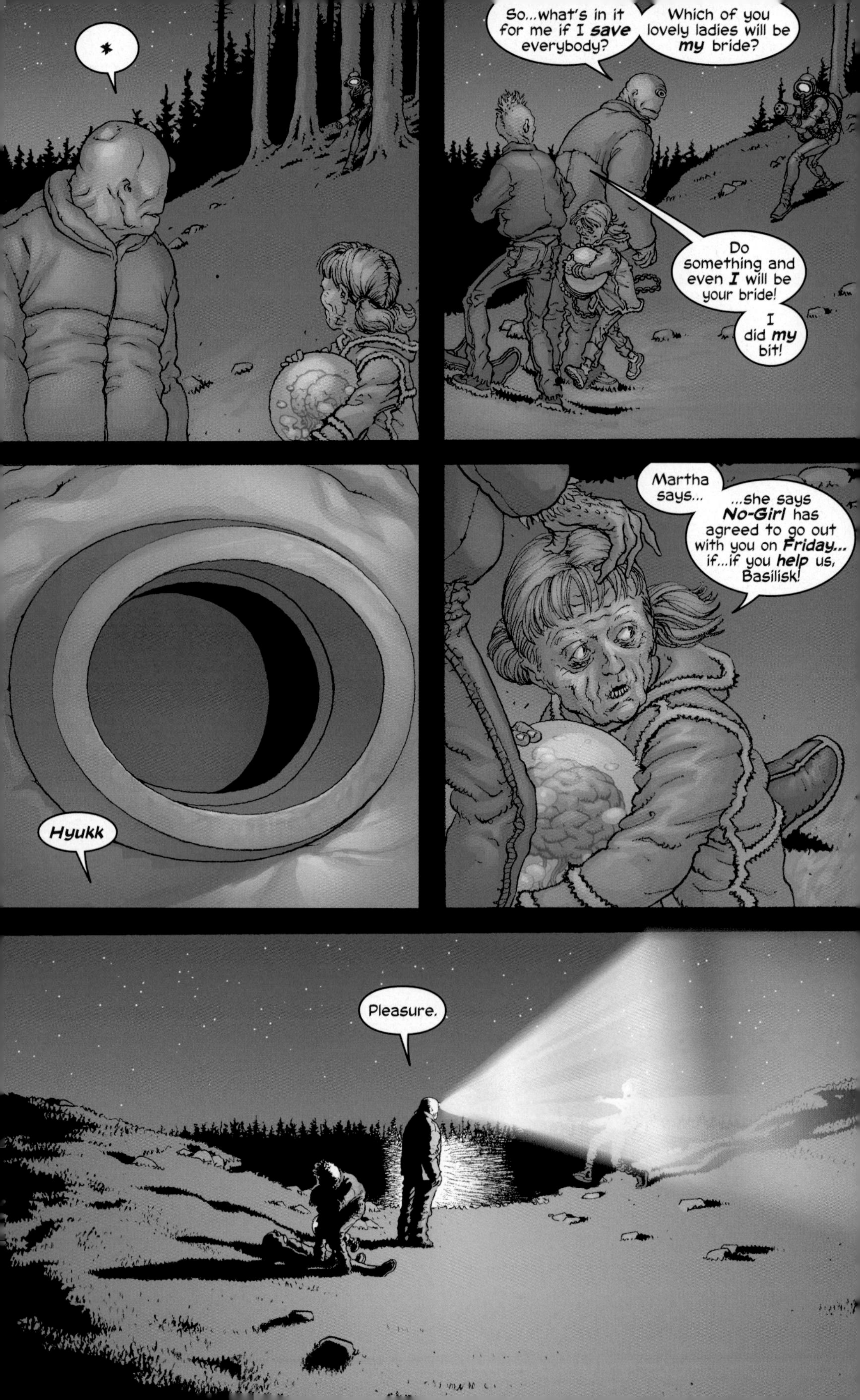
*
So...what's in it for me if I ***save*** everybody?
Which of you lovely ladies will be ***my*** bride?
Do something and even ***I*** will be your bride!
I did ***my*** bit!
Hyukk
Martha says...
...she says ***No-Girl*** has agreed to go out with you on ***Friday...*** if...if you ***help*** us, Basilisk!
Pleasure.

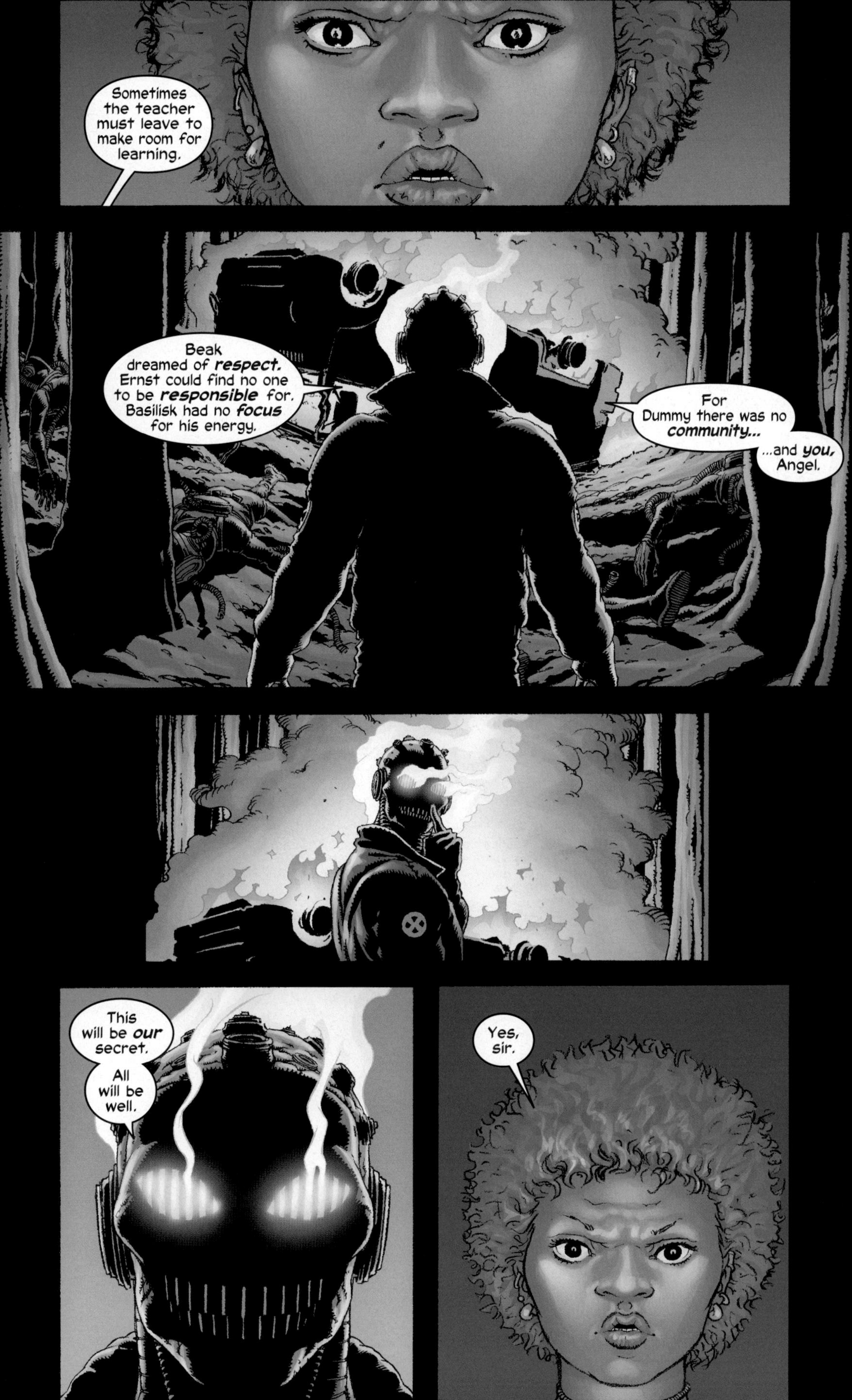
Sometimes the teacher must leave to make room for learning.
Beak dreamed of **respect.** Ernst could find no one to be **responsible** for. Basilisk had no **focus** for his energy.
For Dummy there was no **community...**
...and **you,** Angel.
This will be **our** secret.
All will be well.
Yes, sir.

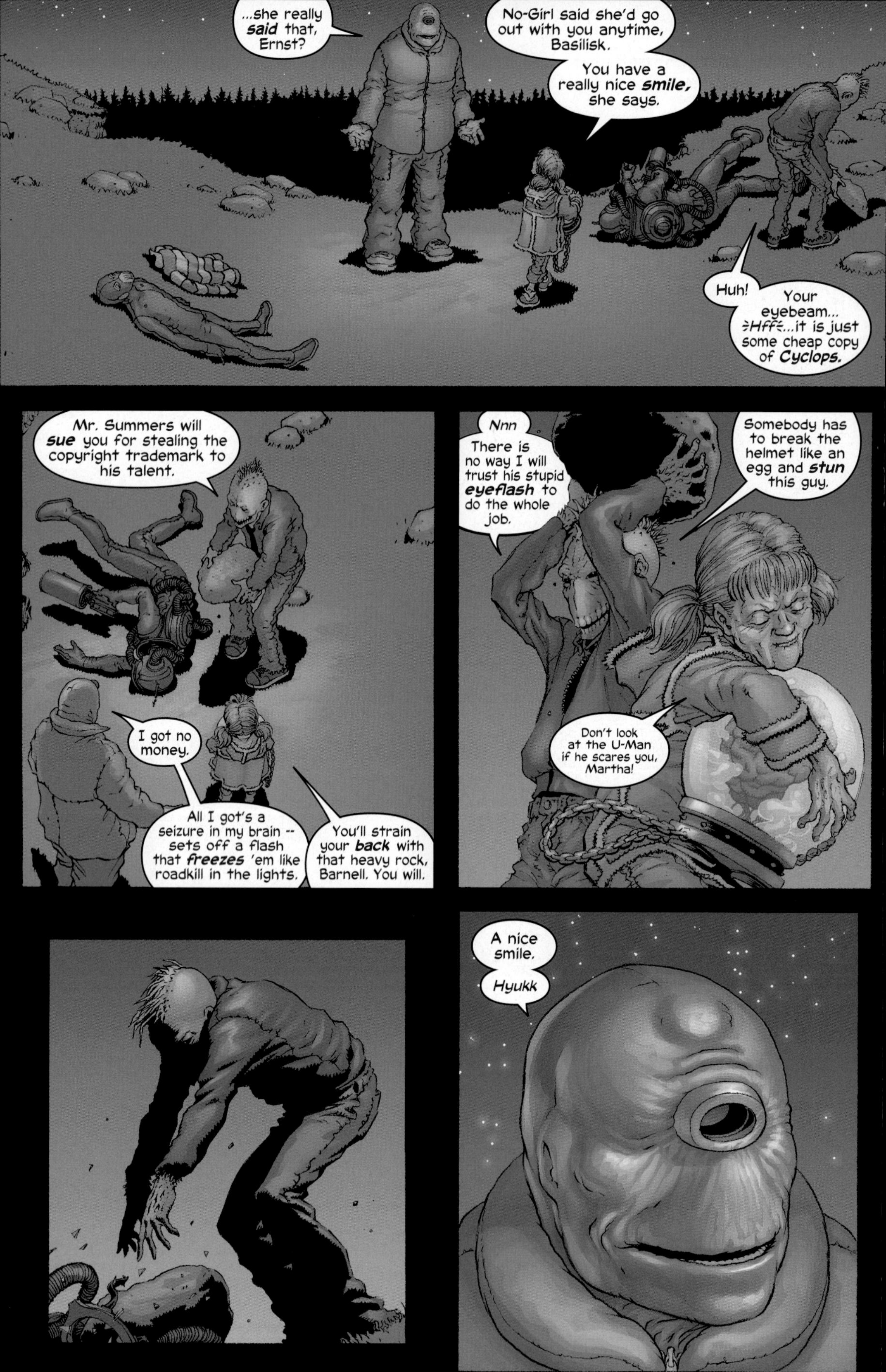
...she really said that, Ernst?
No-Girl said she'd go out with you anytime, Basilisk.
You have a really nice smile, she says.
Huh!
Your eyebeam... Hff...it is just some cheap copy of Cyclops.
Mr. Summers will sue you for stealing the copyright trademark to his talent.
I got no money.
All I got's a seizure in my brain -- sets off a flash that freezes 'em like roadkill in the lights.
You'll strain your back with that heavy rock, Barnell. You will.
Nnn
There is no way I will trust his stupid eyeflash to do the whole job.
Somebody has to break the helmet like an egg and stun this guy.
Don't look at the U-Man if he scares you, Martha!
A nice smile.
Hyukk

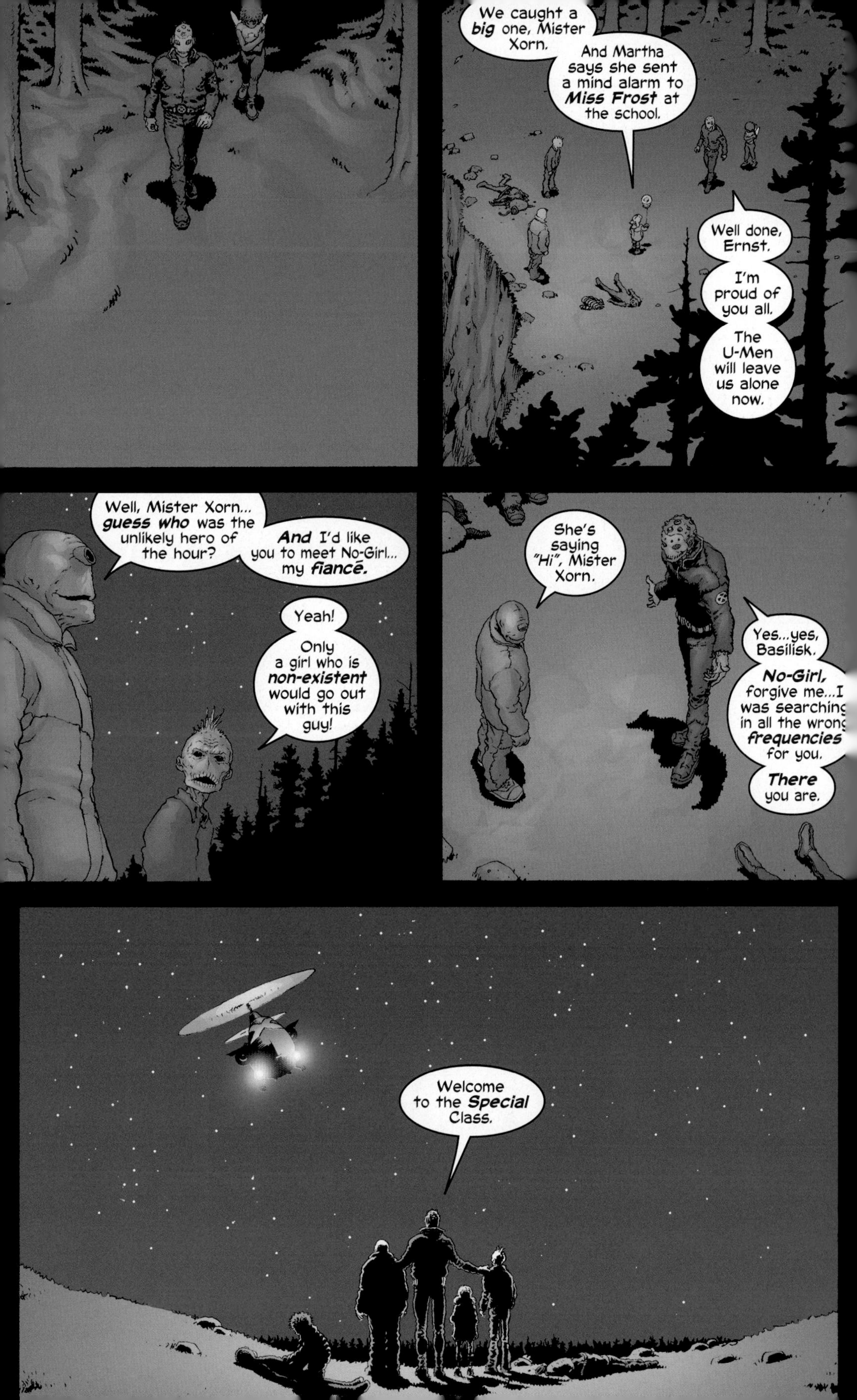
We caught a *big* one, Mister Xorn.
And Martha says she sent a mind alarm to *Miss Frost* at the school.
Well done, Ernst.
I'm proud of you all.
The U-Men will leave us alone now.
Well, Mister Xorn... *guess who* was the unlikely hero of the hour?
And I'd like you to meet No-Girl... my *fiancé.*
Yeah!
Only a girl who is *non-existent* would go out with this guy!
She's saying "Hi", Mister Xorn.
Yes...yes, Basilisk.
No-Girl, forgive me...I was searching in all the wrong *frequencies* for you.
There you are.
Welcome to the *Special* Class.

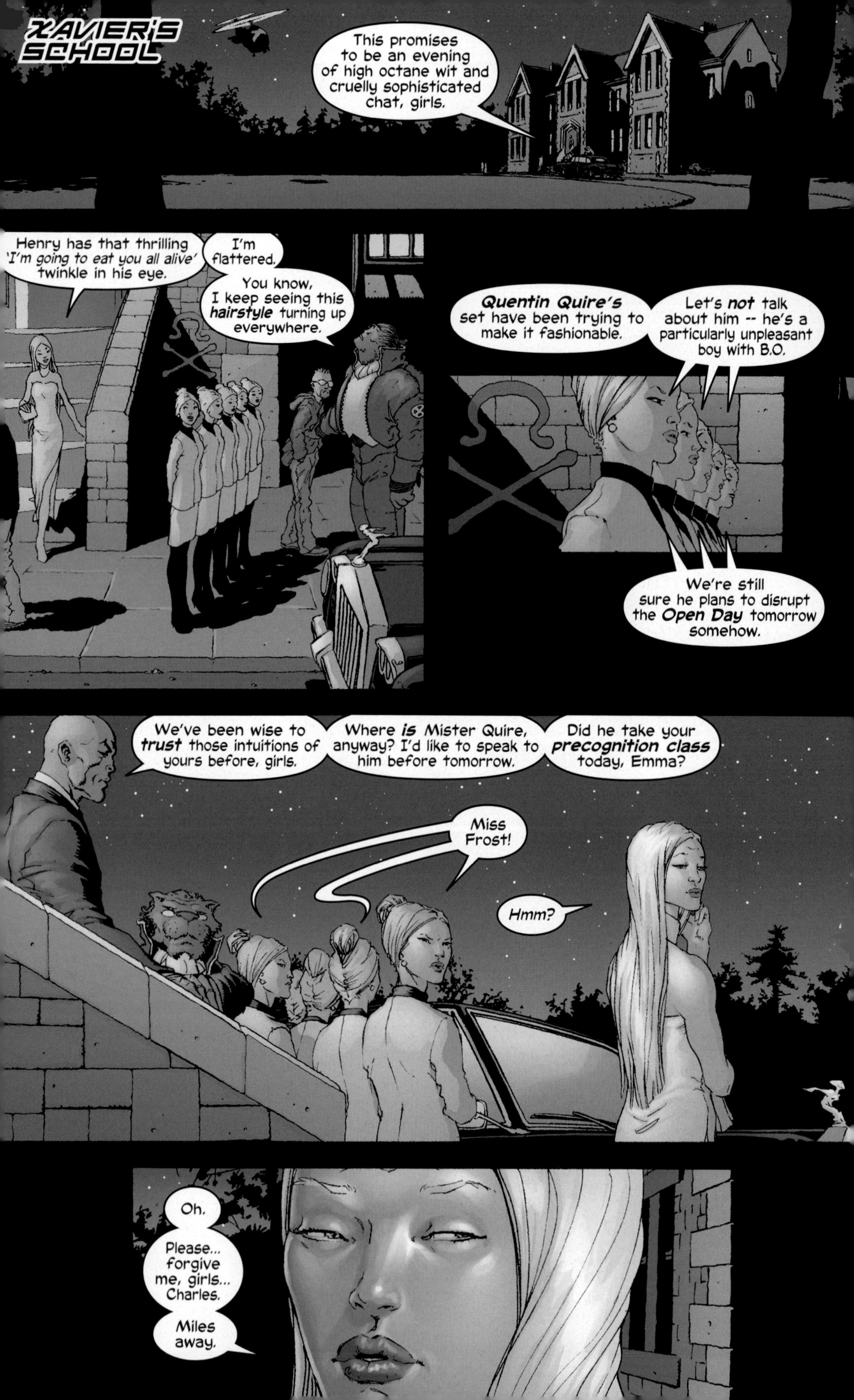
XAVIER'S SCHOOL
This promises to be an evening of high octane wit and cruelly sophisticated chat, girls.
Henry has that thrilling 'I'm going to eat you all alive' twinkle in his eye.
I'm flattered.
You know, I keep seeing this hairstyle turning up everywhere.
Quentin Quire's set have been trying to make it fashionable.
Let's not talk about him -- he's a particularly unpleasant boy with B.O.
We're still sure he plans to disrupt the Open Day tomorrow somehow.
We've been wise to trust those intuitions of yours before, girls.
Where is Mister Quire, anyway? I'd like to speak to him before tomorrow.
Did he take your precognition class today, Emma?
Miss Frost!
Hmm?
Oh.
Please... forgive me, girls... Charles.
Miles away.

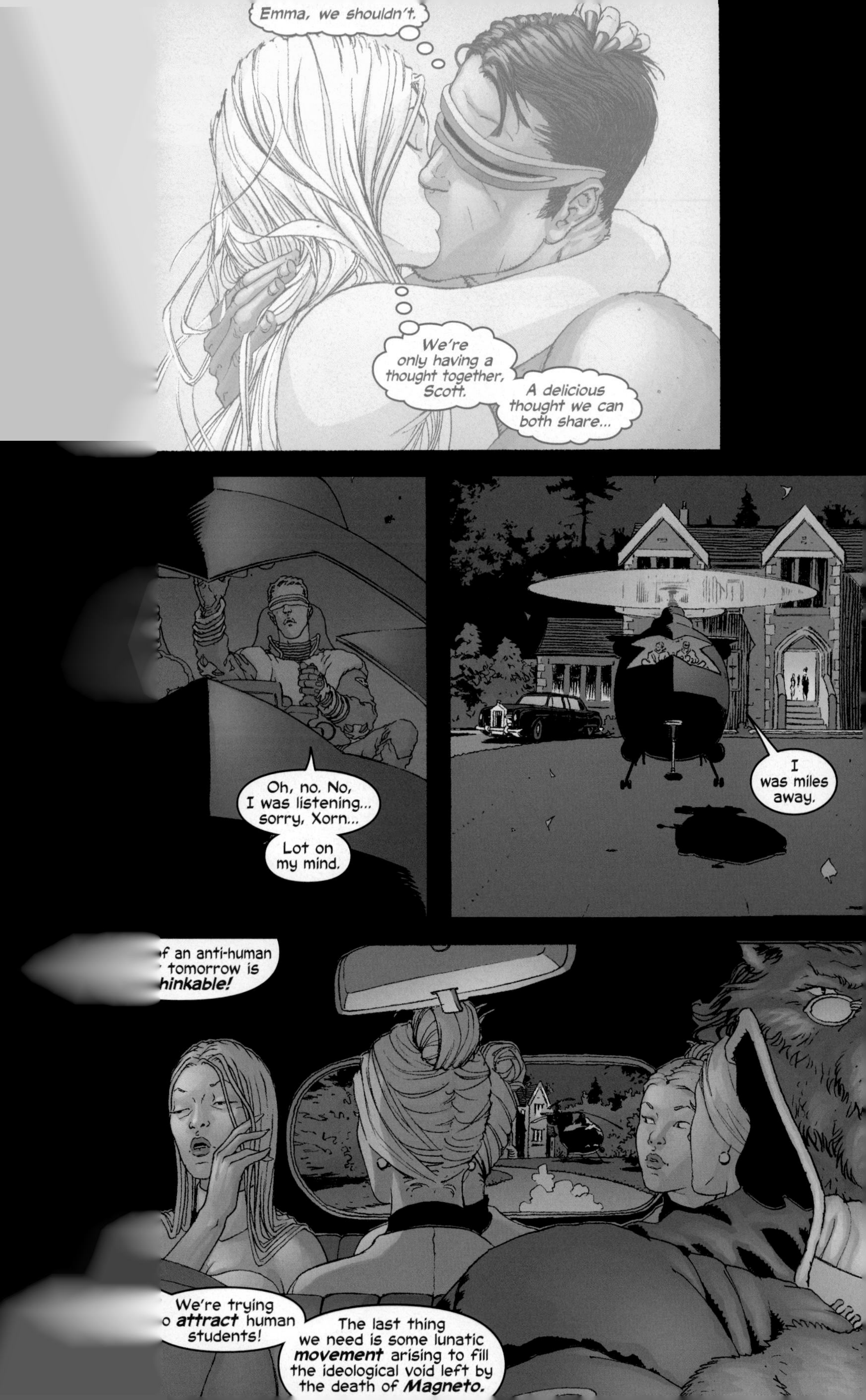
Emma, we shouldn't.
We're only having a thought together, Scott.
A delicious thought we can both share...
Oh, no. No, I was listening... sorry, Xorn...
Lot on my mind.
I was miles away.
f an anti-human
tomorrow is
hinkable!
We're trying
o attract human students!
The last thing we need is some lunatic movement arising to fill the ideological void left by the death of Magneto.

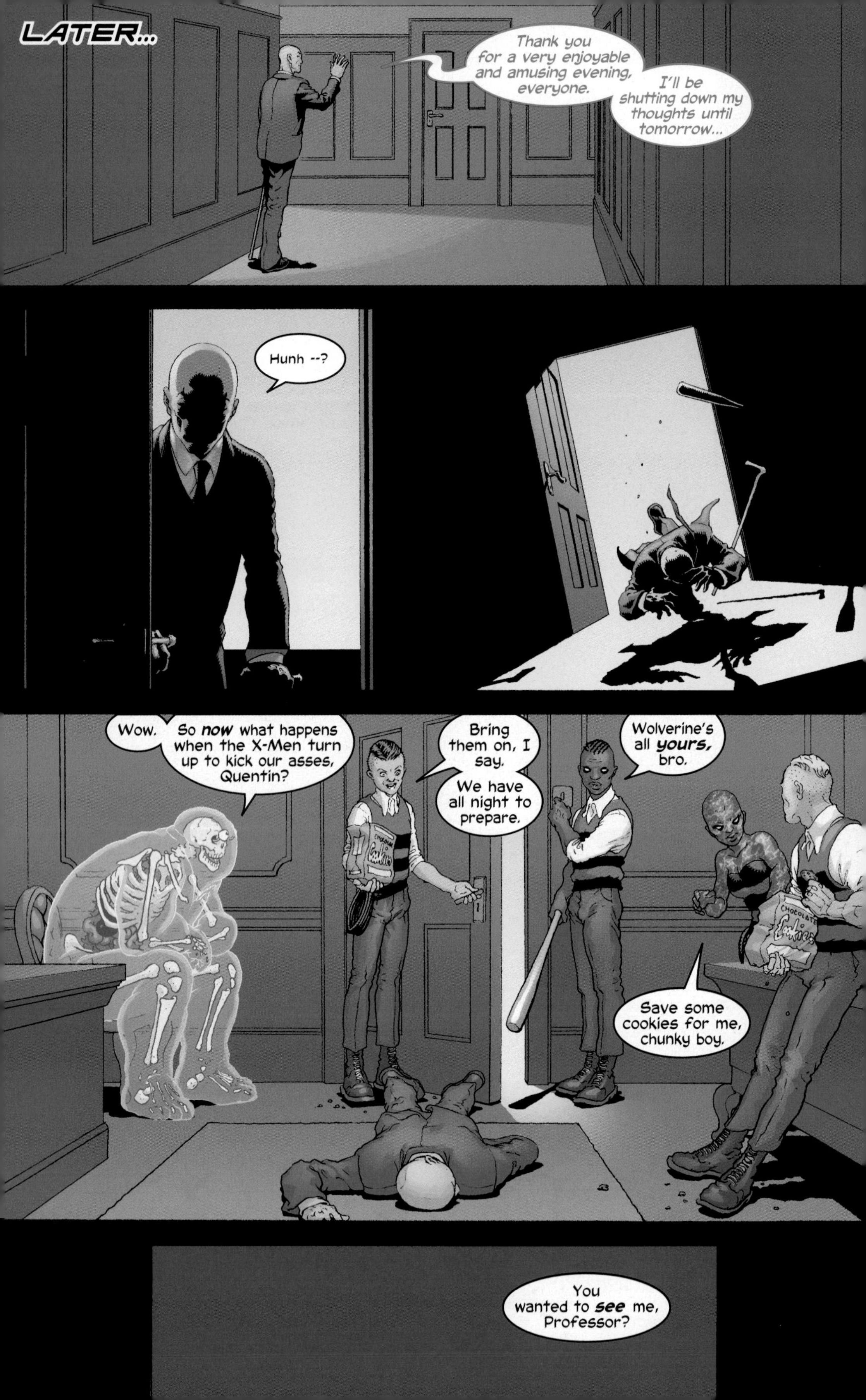
LATER...
Thank you for a very enjoyable and amusing evening, everyone.
I'll be shutting down my thoughts until tomorrow...
Hunh --?
Wow.
So now what happens when the X-Men turn up to kick our asses, Quentin?
Bring them on, I say.
We have all night to prepare.
Wolverine's all yours, bro.
Save some cookies for me, chunky boy.
You wanted to see me, Professor?

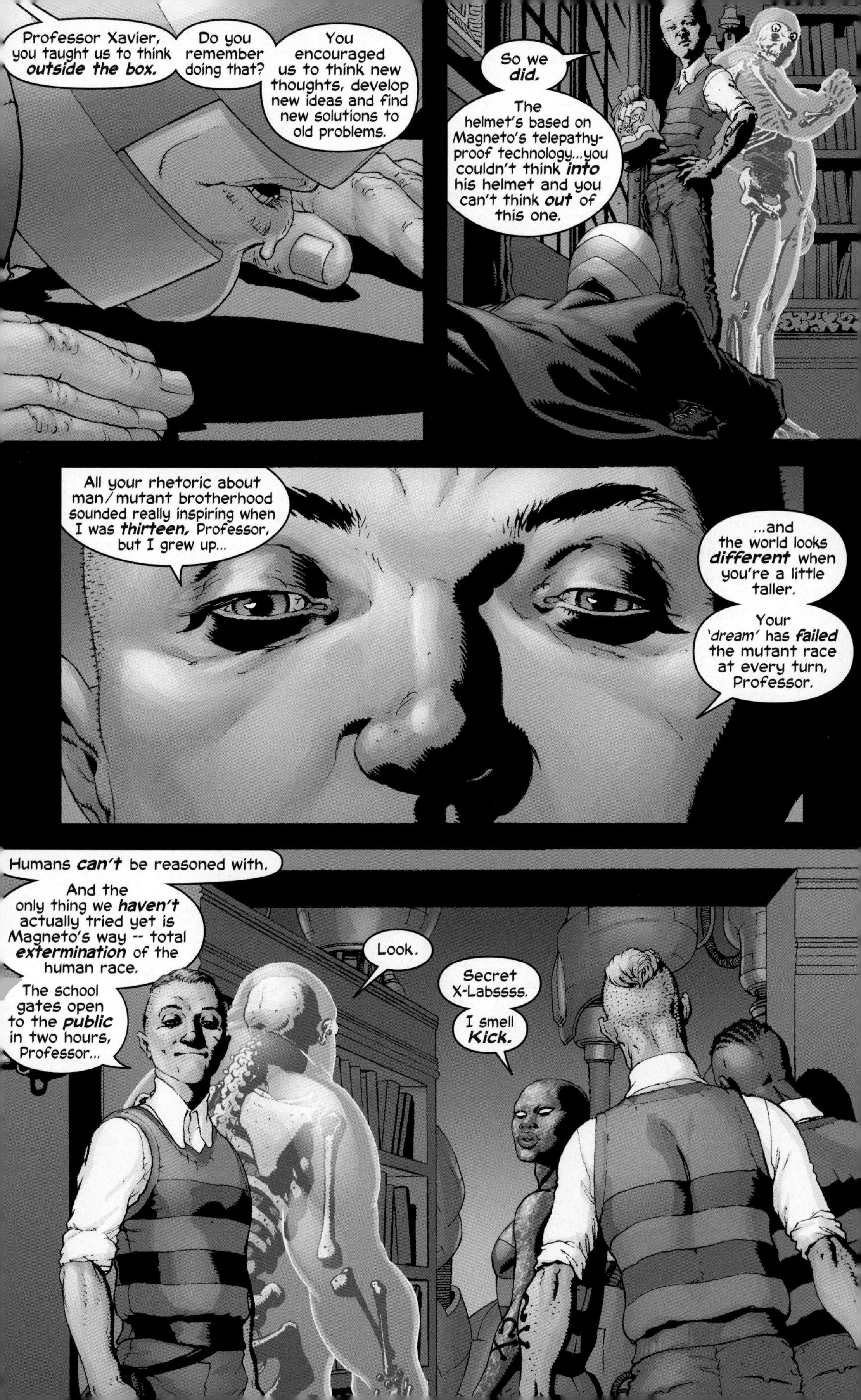

Professor Xavier, you taught us to think *outside the box.*
Do you remember doing that?
You encouraged us to think new thoughts, develop new ideas and find new solutions to old problems.
So we *did.*
The helmet's based on Magneto's telepathy-proof technology...you couldn't think *into* his helmet and you can't think *out* of this one.
All your rhetoric about man/mutant brotherhood sounded really inspiring when I was *thirteen,* Professor, but I grew up...
...and the world looks *different* when you're a little taller.
Your *'dream'* has *failed* the mutant race at every turn, Professor.
Humans *can't* be reasoned with.
And the only thing we *haven't* actually tried yet is Magneto's way -- total *extermination* of the human race.
The school gates open to the *public* in two hours, Professor...
Look.
Secret X-Labssss.
I smell *Kick.*

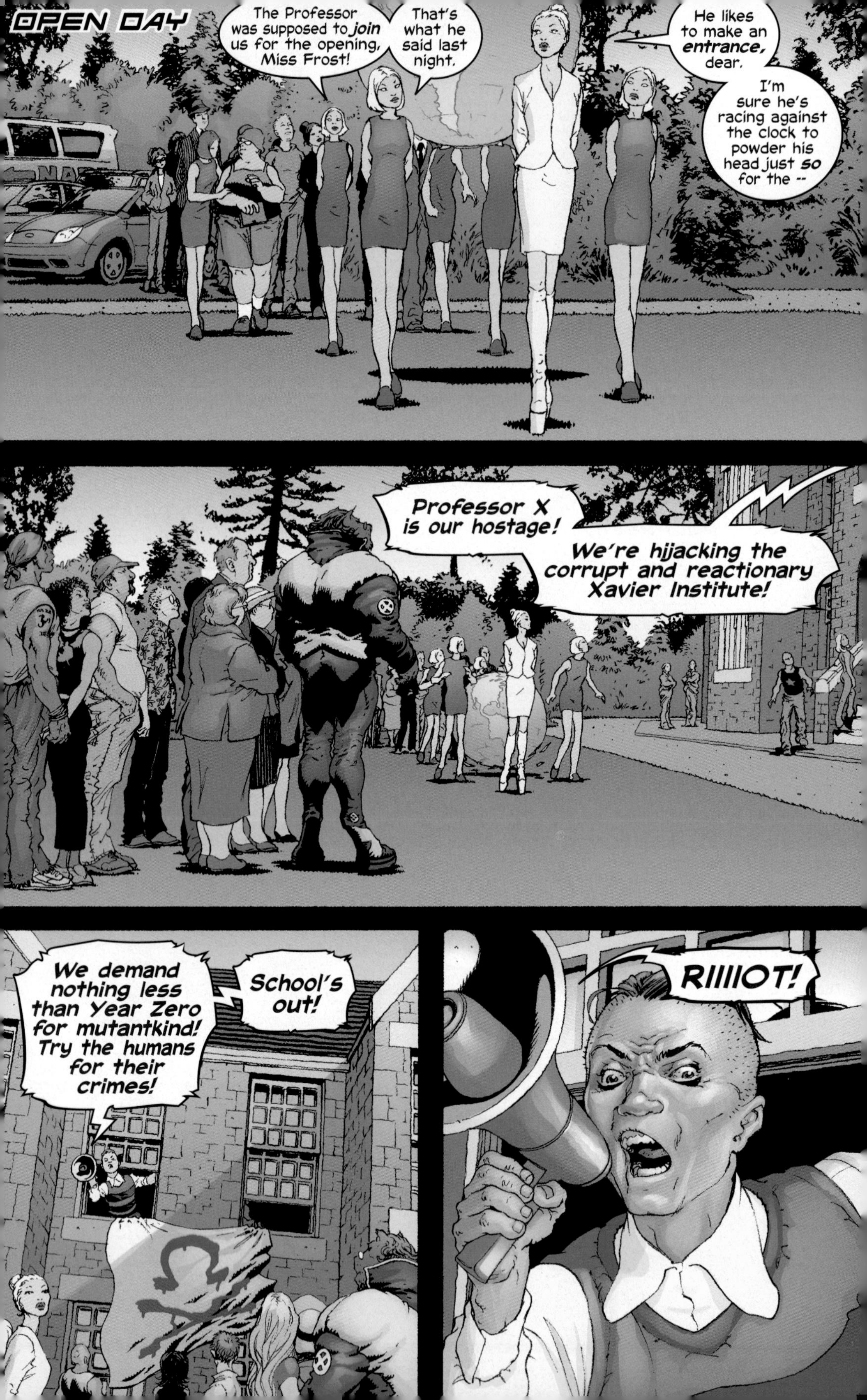
OPEN DAY
The Professor was supposed to join us for the opening, Miss Frost!
That's what he said last night.
He likes to make an entrance, dear.
I'm sure he's racing against the clock to powder his head just so for the --
Professor X is our hostage!
We're hijacking the corrupt and reactionary Xavier Institute!
We demand nothing less than Year Zero for mutantkind! Try the humans for their crimes!
School's out!
RIIIIOT!

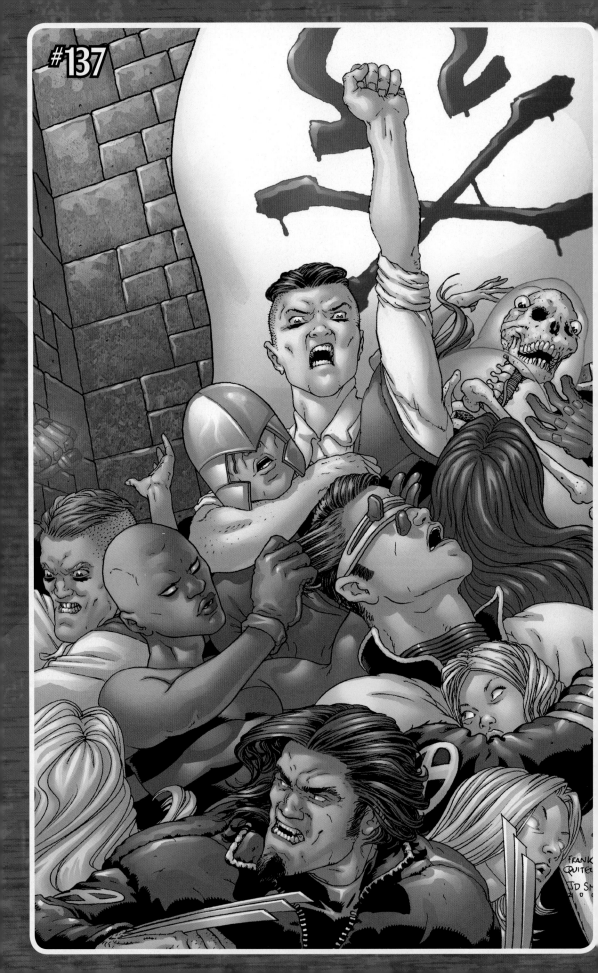

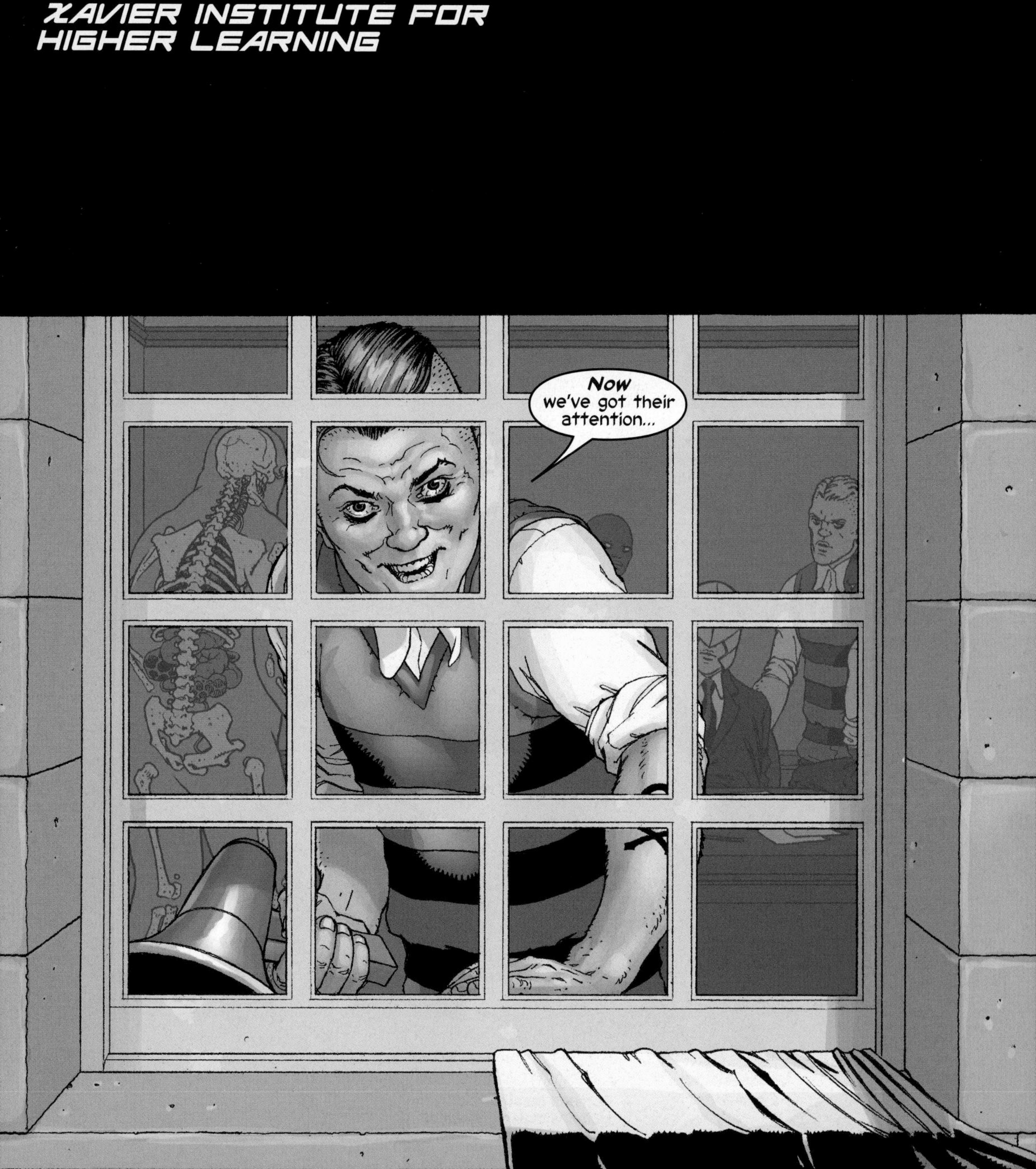
XAVIER INSTITUTE FOR HIGHER LEARNING
Now we've got their attention...

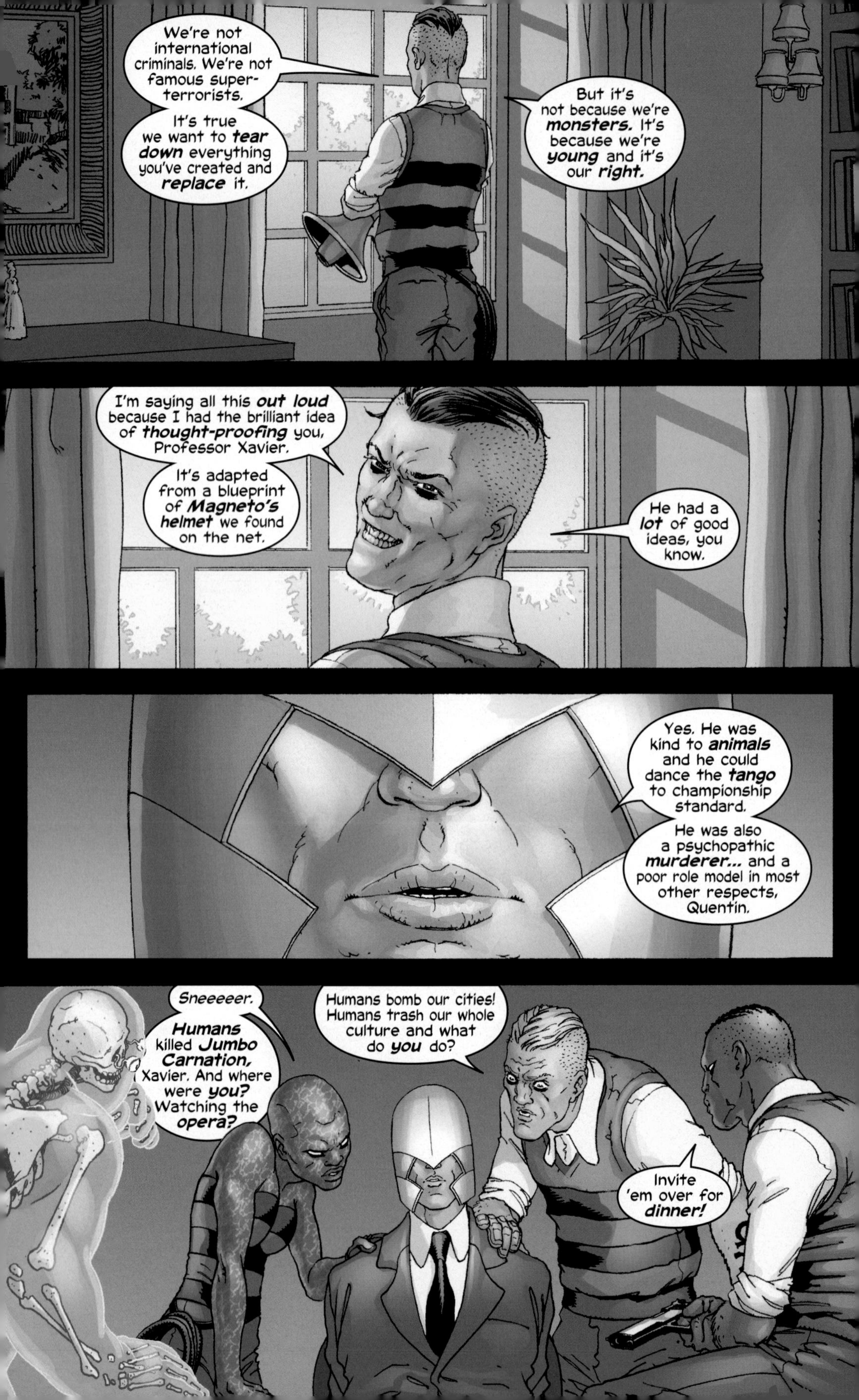

We're not international criminals. We're not famous super-terrorists.
It's true we want to tear down everything you've created and replace it.
But it's not because we're monsters. It's because we're young and it's our right.
I'm saying all this out loud because I had the brilliant idea of thought-proofing you, Professor Xavier.
It's adapted from a blueprint of Magneto's helmet we found on the net.
He had a lot of good ideas, you know.
Yes. He was kind to animals and he could dance the tango to championship standard.
He was also a psychopathic murderer... and a poor role model in most other respects, Quentin.
Sneeeeer.
Humans killed Jumbo Carnation, Xavier. And where were you? Watching the opera?
Humans bomb our cities! Humans trash our whole culture and what do you do?
Invite 'em over for dinner!

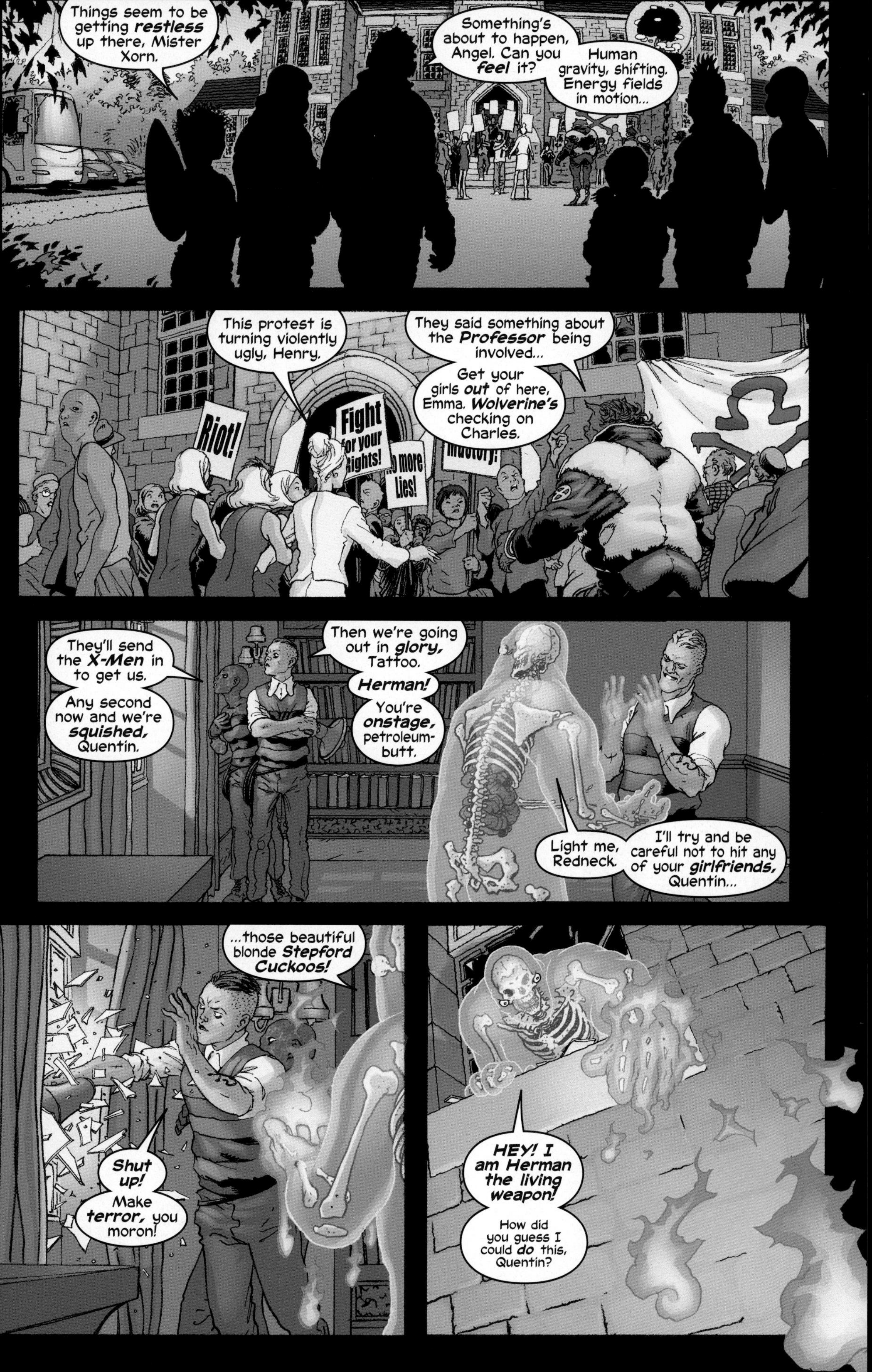

137

Things seem to be getting ***restless*** up there, Mister Xorn.
Something's about to happen, Angel. Can you ***feel*** it?
Human gravity, shifting. Energy fields in motion...
This protest is turning violently ugly, Henry.
They said something about the ***Professor*** being involved...
Get your girls ***out*** of here, Emma. ***Wolverine's*** checking on Charles.
Riot!
Fight for your Rights!
They'll send the ***X-Men*** in to get us.
Any second now and we're ***squished,*** Quentin.
Then we're going out in ***glory,*** Tattoo.
Herman!
You're ***onstage,*** petroleum-butt.
Light me, Redneck.
I'll try and be careful not to hit any of your ***girlfriends,*** Quentin...
...those beautiful blonde ***Stepford Cuckoos!***
Shut up!
Make ***terror,*** you moron!
HEY! I am Herman the living weapon!
How did you guess I could ***do*** this, Quentin?

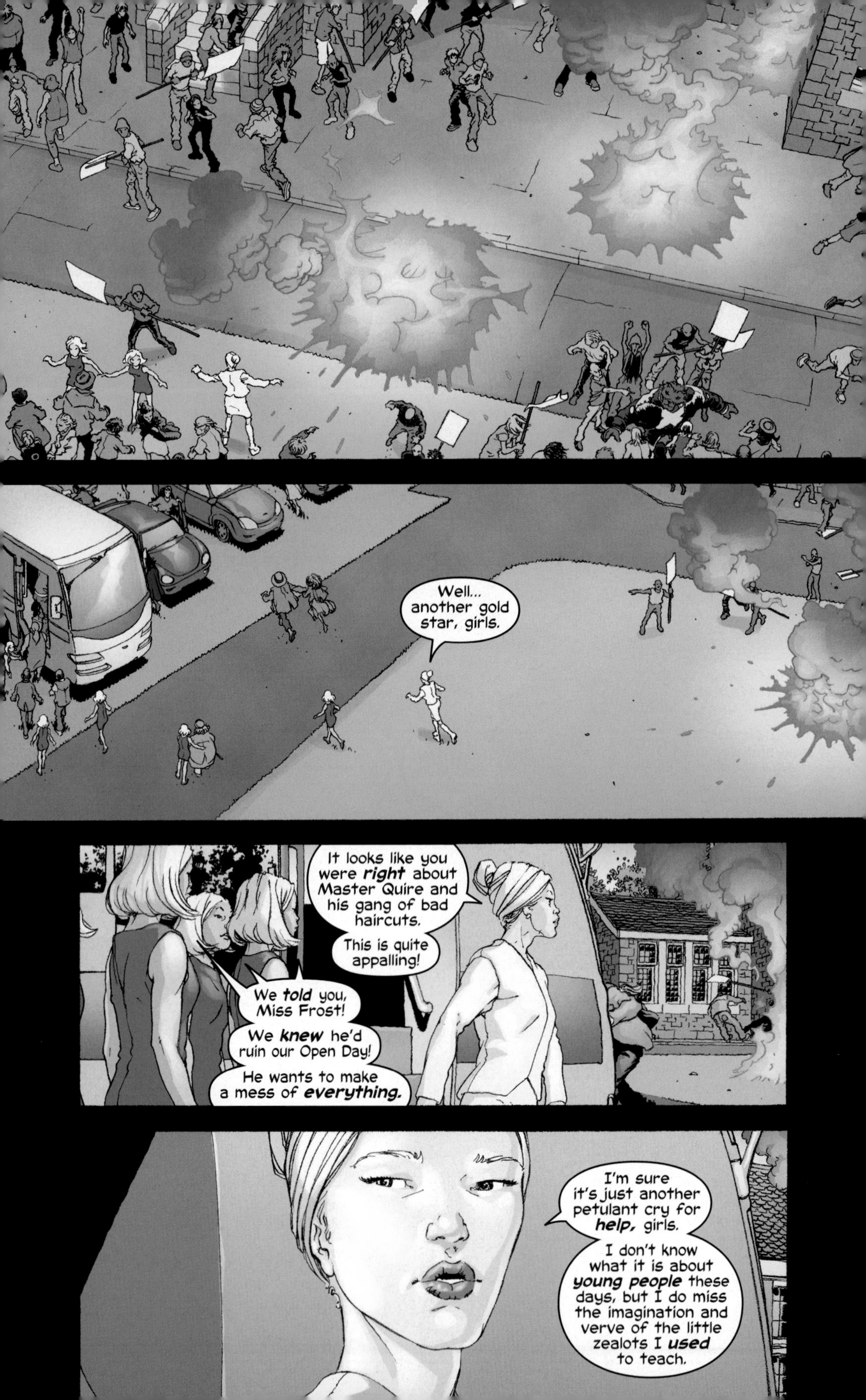
Well... another gold star, girls.
It looks like you were right about Master Quire and his gang of bad haircuts.
This is quite appalling!
We told you, Miss Frost!
We knew he'd ruin our Open Day!
He wants to make a mess of everything.
I'm sure it's just another petulant cry for help, girls.
I don't know what it is about young people these days, but I do miss the imagination and verve of the little zealots I used to teach.

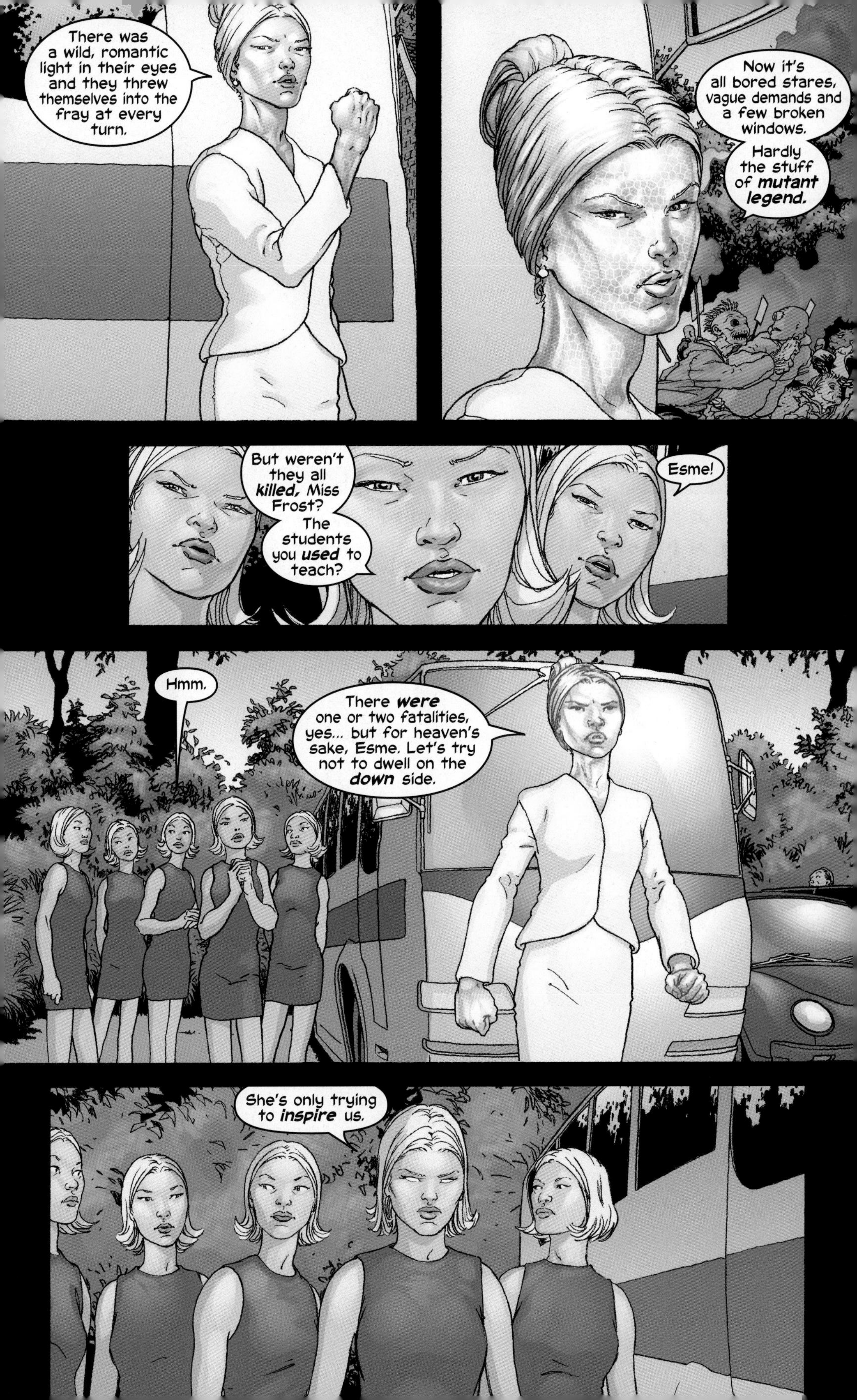
There was a wild, romantic light in their eyes and they threw themselves into the fray at every turn.
Now it's all bored stares, vague demands and a few broken windows.
Hardly the stuff of **mutant legend.**
But weren't they all ***killed,*** Miss Frost?
The students you ***used*** to teach?
Esme!
Hmm.
There ***were*** one or two fatalities, yes... but for heaven's sake, Esme. Let's try not to dwell on the ***down*** side.
She's only trying to ***inspire*** us.

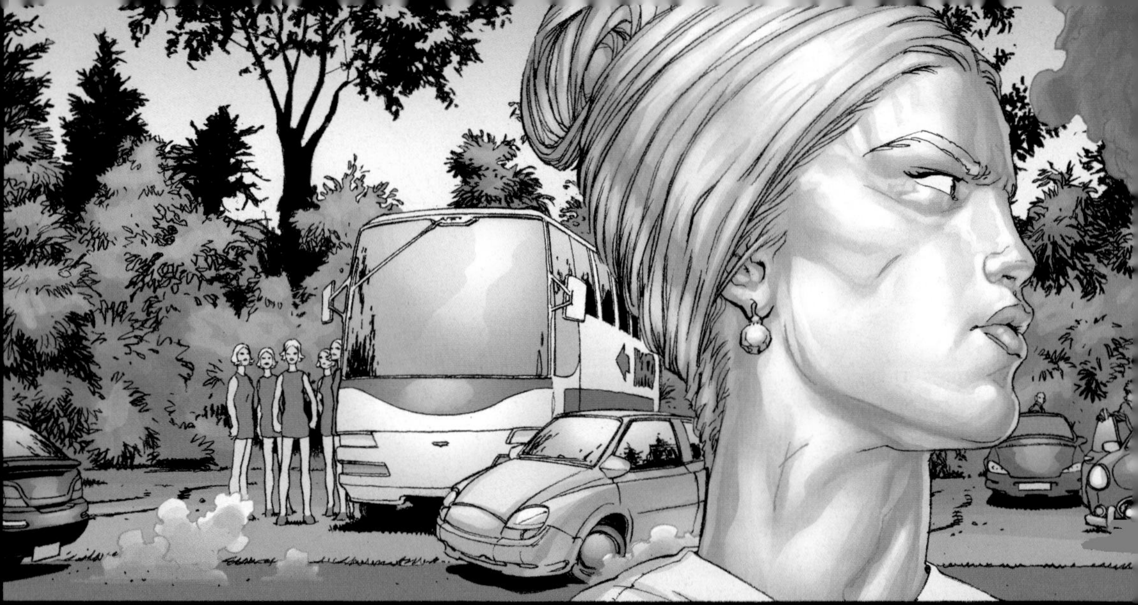

GRANT MORRISON WRITER
FRANK QUITELY ART
WITH AVALON STUDIOS

RIOT AT

CHRIS CHUCKRY COLORS
RICHARD STARKINGS LETTERS
WITH COMICRAFT'S JIMMY!
MIKE RAICHT AND NOVA REN SUMA
ASSISTANT EDITORS

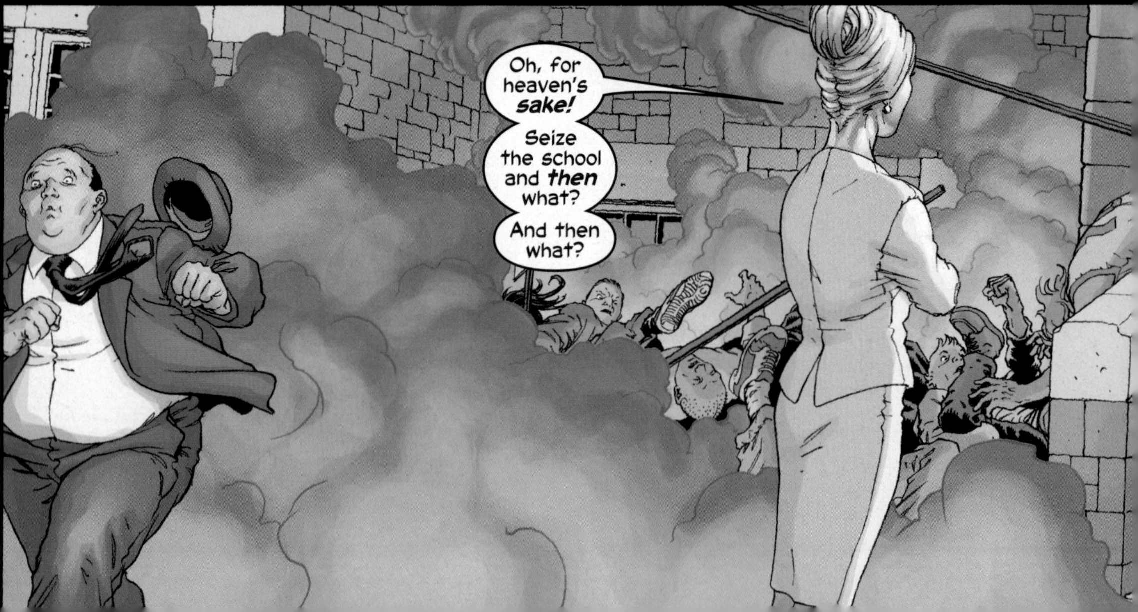
Oh, for heaven's *sake!*
Seize the school and *then* what?
And then what?

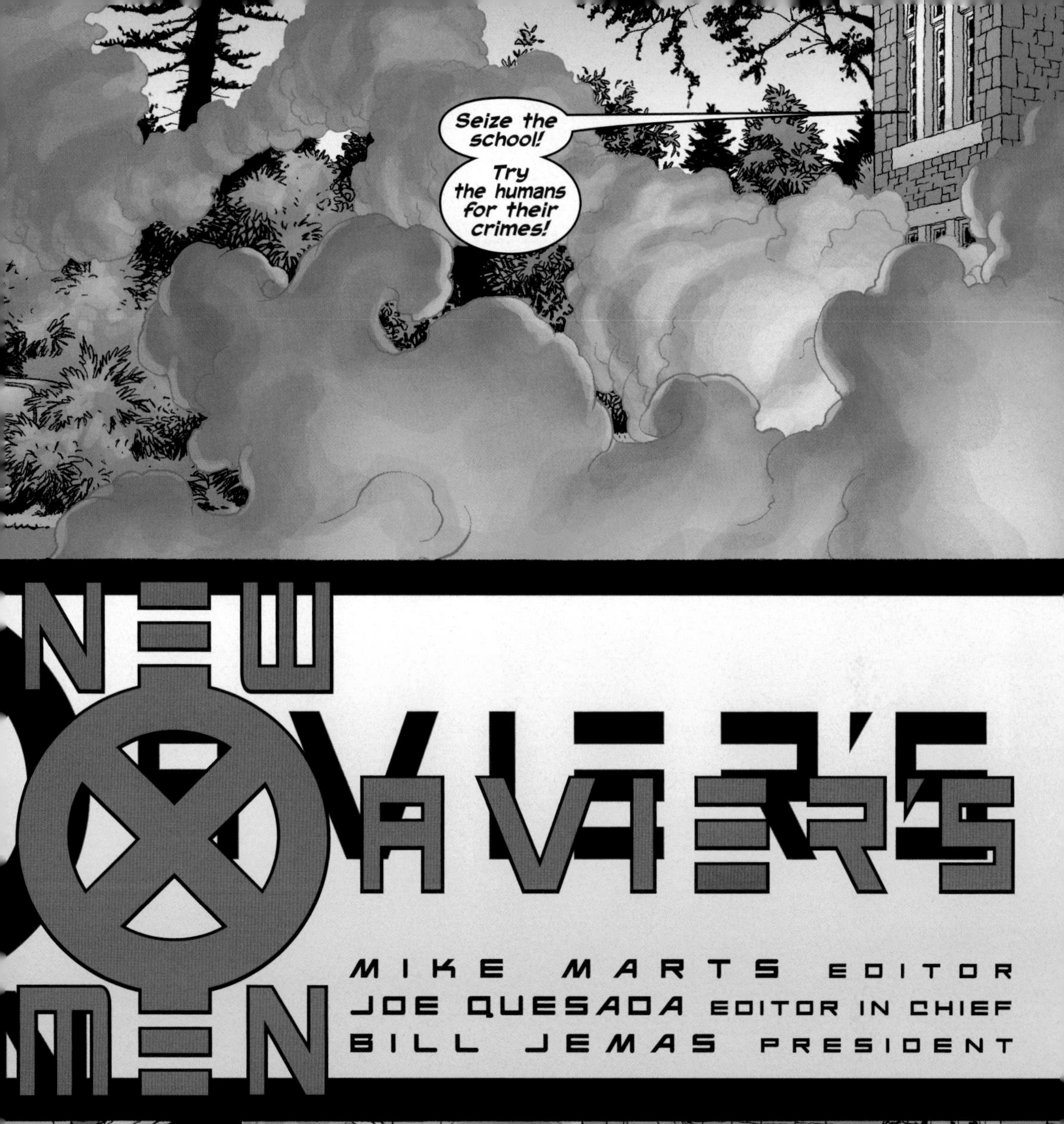
Seize the school!
Try the humans for their crimes!

NEW X-MEN
XAVIER'S

MIKE MARTS EDITOR
JOE QUESADA EDITOR IN CHIEF
BILL JEMAS PRESIDENT

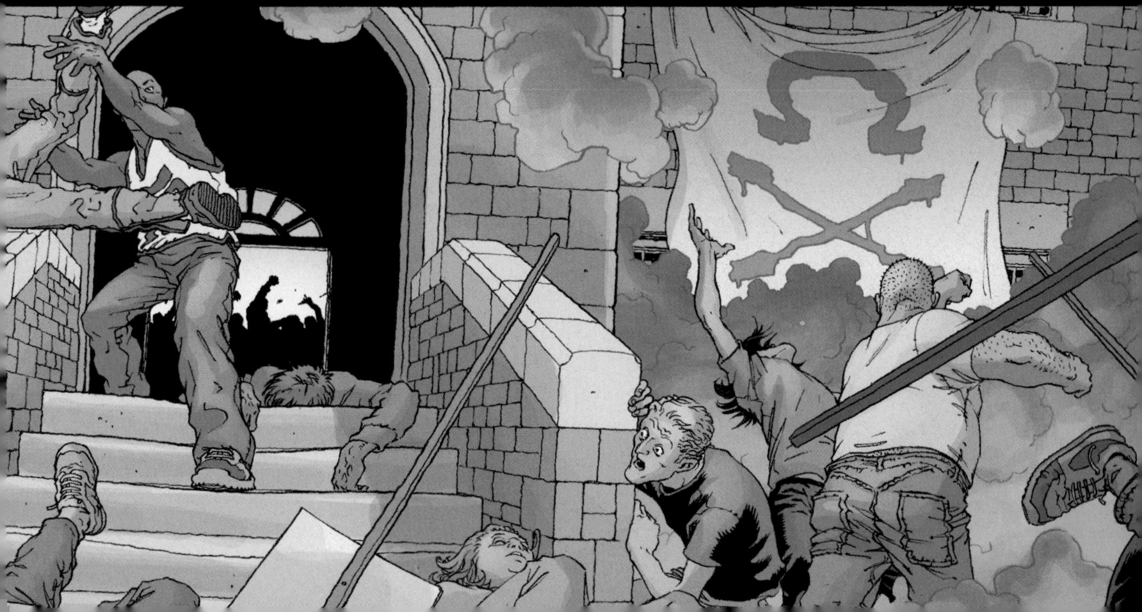

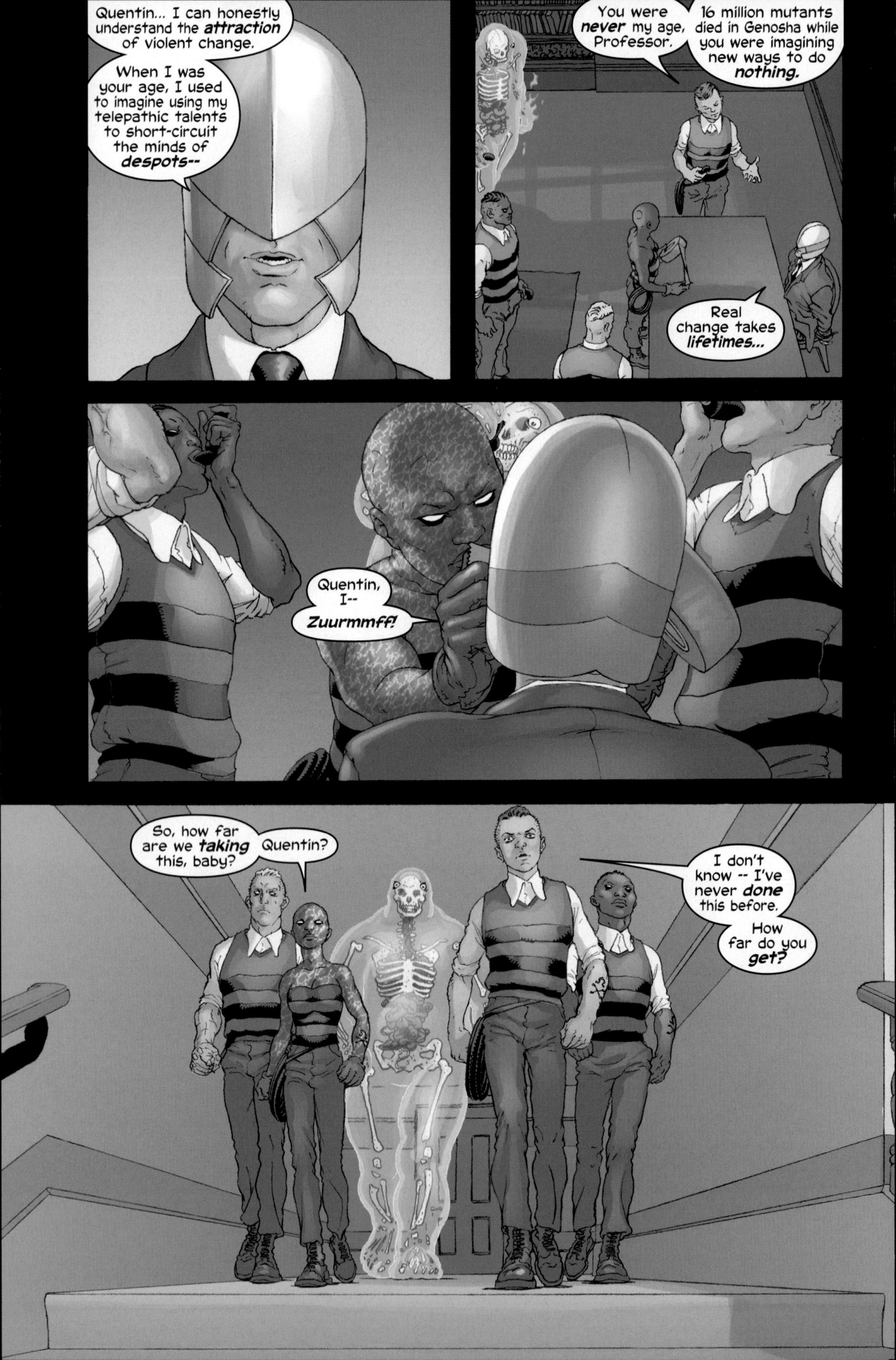

Quentin... I can honestly understand the attraction of violent change.
When I was your age, I used to imagine using my telepathic talents to short-circuit the minds of despots--
You were never my age, Professor.
16 million mutants died in Genosha while you were imagining new ways to do nothing.
Real change takes lifetimes...
Quentin, I--
Zuurmmff!
So, how far are we taking this, baby?
Quentin?
I don't know -- I've never done this before.
How far do you get?

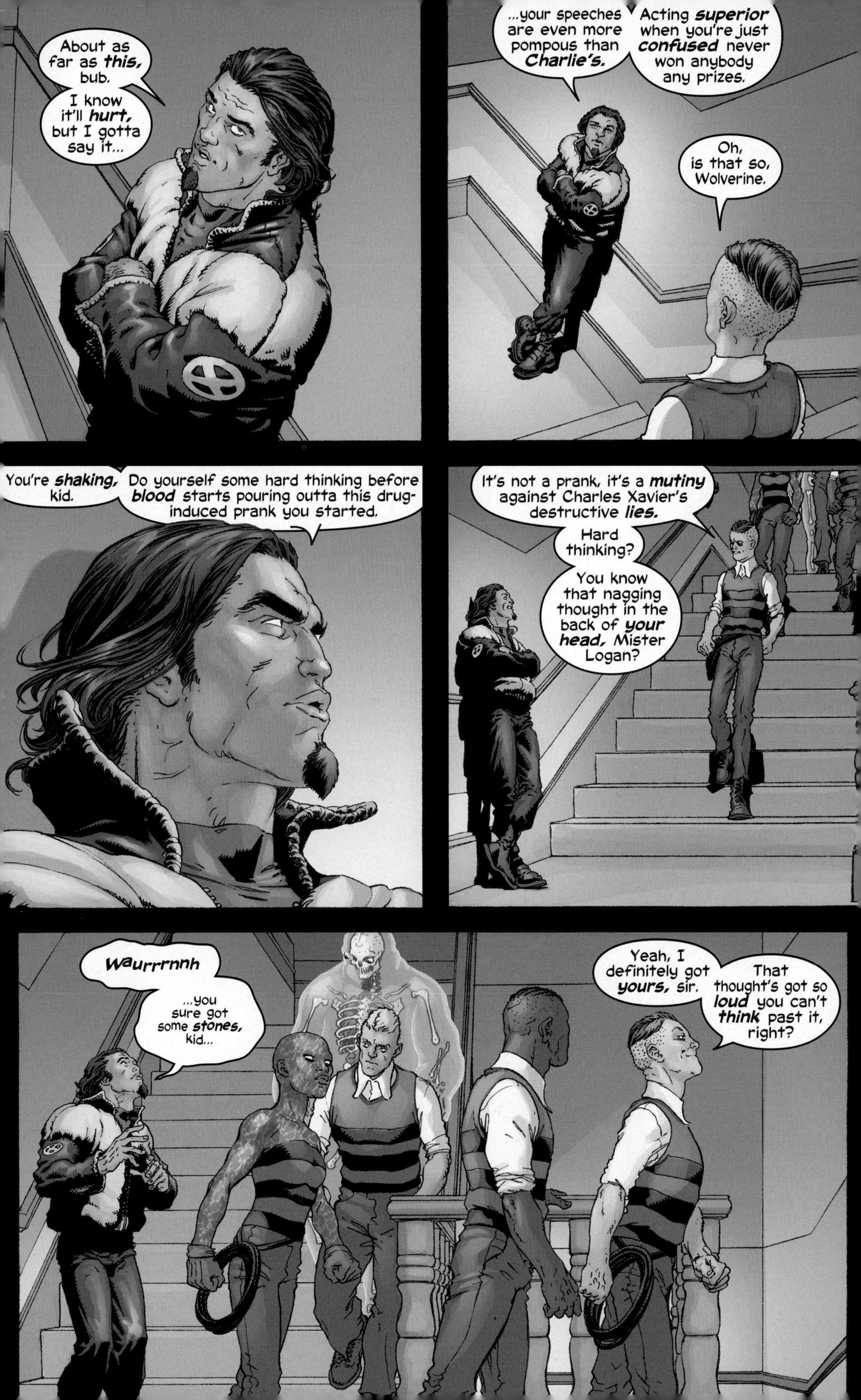
About as far as this, bub.
I know it'll hurt, but I gotta say it...
...your speeches are even more pompous than Charlie's.
Acting superior when you're just confused never won anybody any prizes.
Oh, is that so, Wolverine.
You're shaking, kid.
Do yourself some hard thinking before blood starts pouring outta this drug-induced prank you started.
It's not a prank, it's a mutiny against Charles Xavier's destructive lies.
Hard thinking?
You know that nagging thought in the back of your head, Mister Logan?
Waurrrnnh
...you sure got some stones, kid...
Yeah, I definitely got yours, sir.
That thought's got so loud you can't think past it, right?

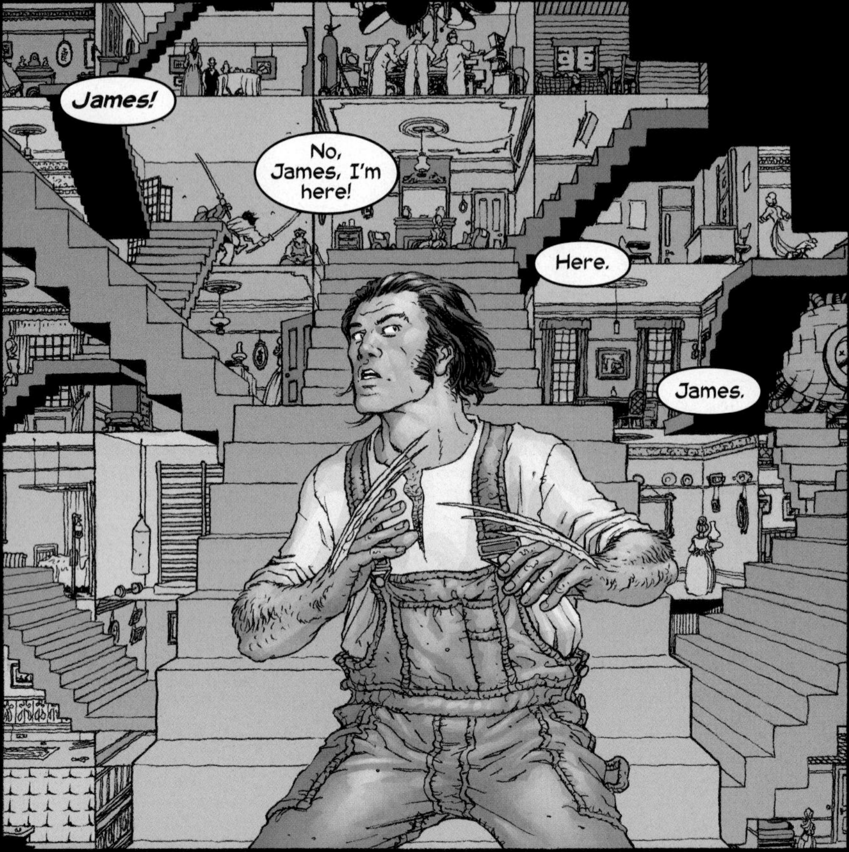
James!
No, James, I'm here!
Here.
James.

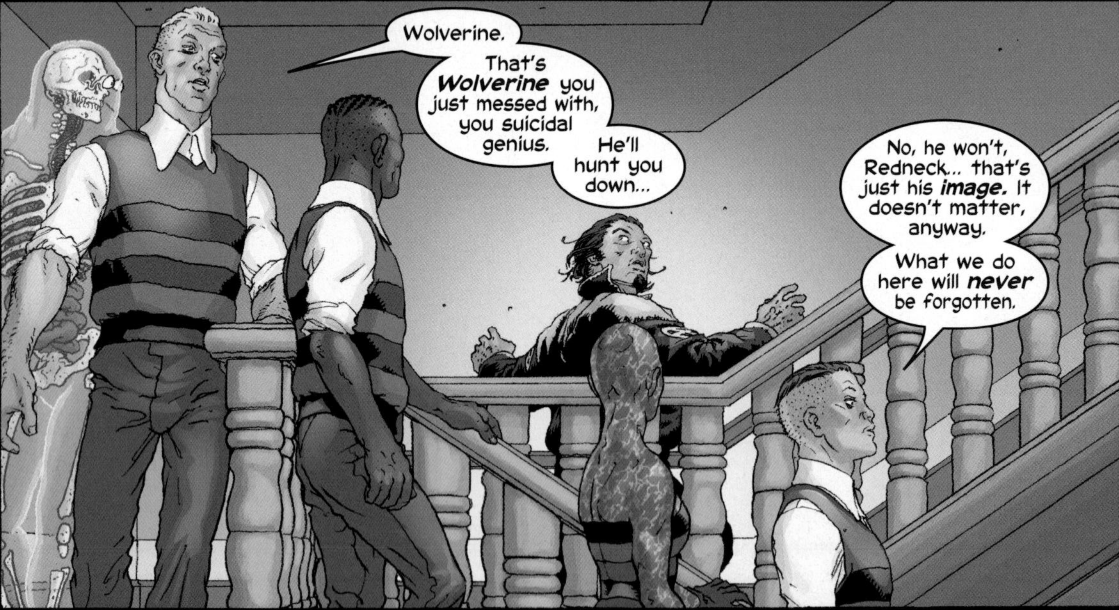
Wolverine.
That's *Wolverine* you just messed with, you suicidal genius.
He'll hunt you down...
No, he won't, Redneck... that's just his *image.* It doesn't matter, anyway.
What we do here will *never* be forgotten.

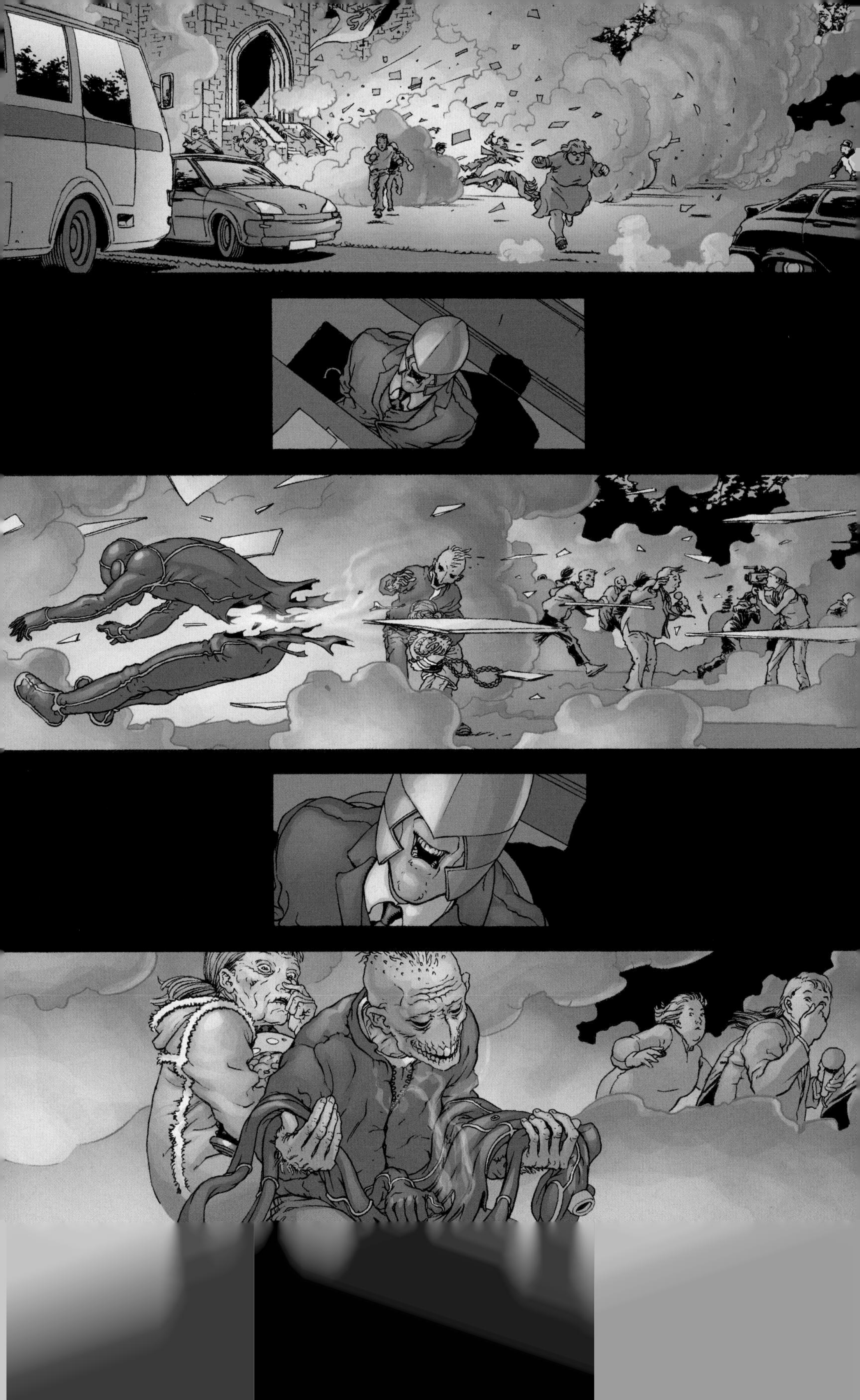

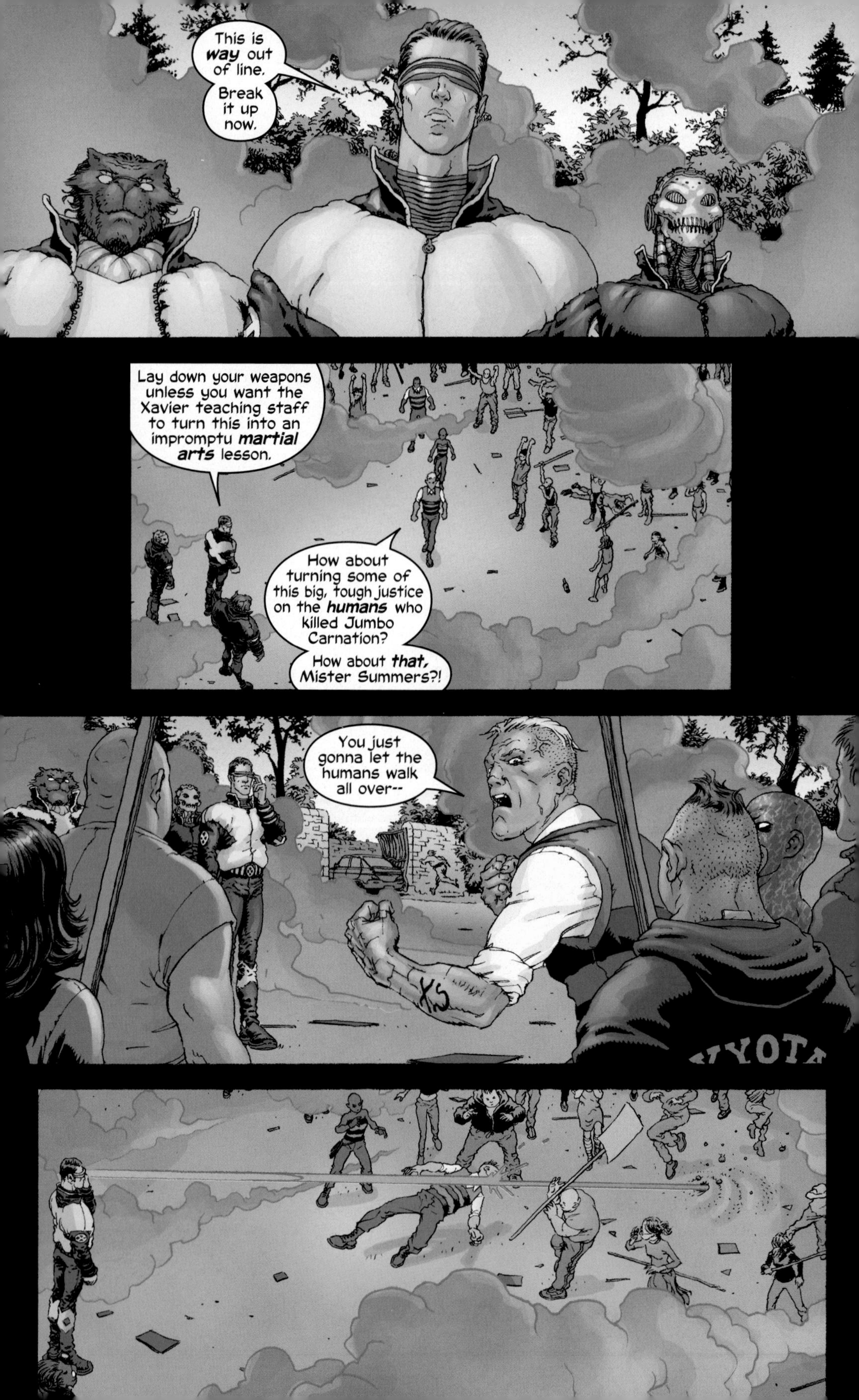
This is *way* out of line.
Break it up now.
Lay down your weapons unless you want the Xavier teaching staff to turn this into an impromptu *martial arts* lesson.
How about turning some of this big, tough justice on the *humans* who killed Jumbo Carnation?
How about *that,* Mister Summers?!
You just gonna let the humans walk all over--
XS
YOTA

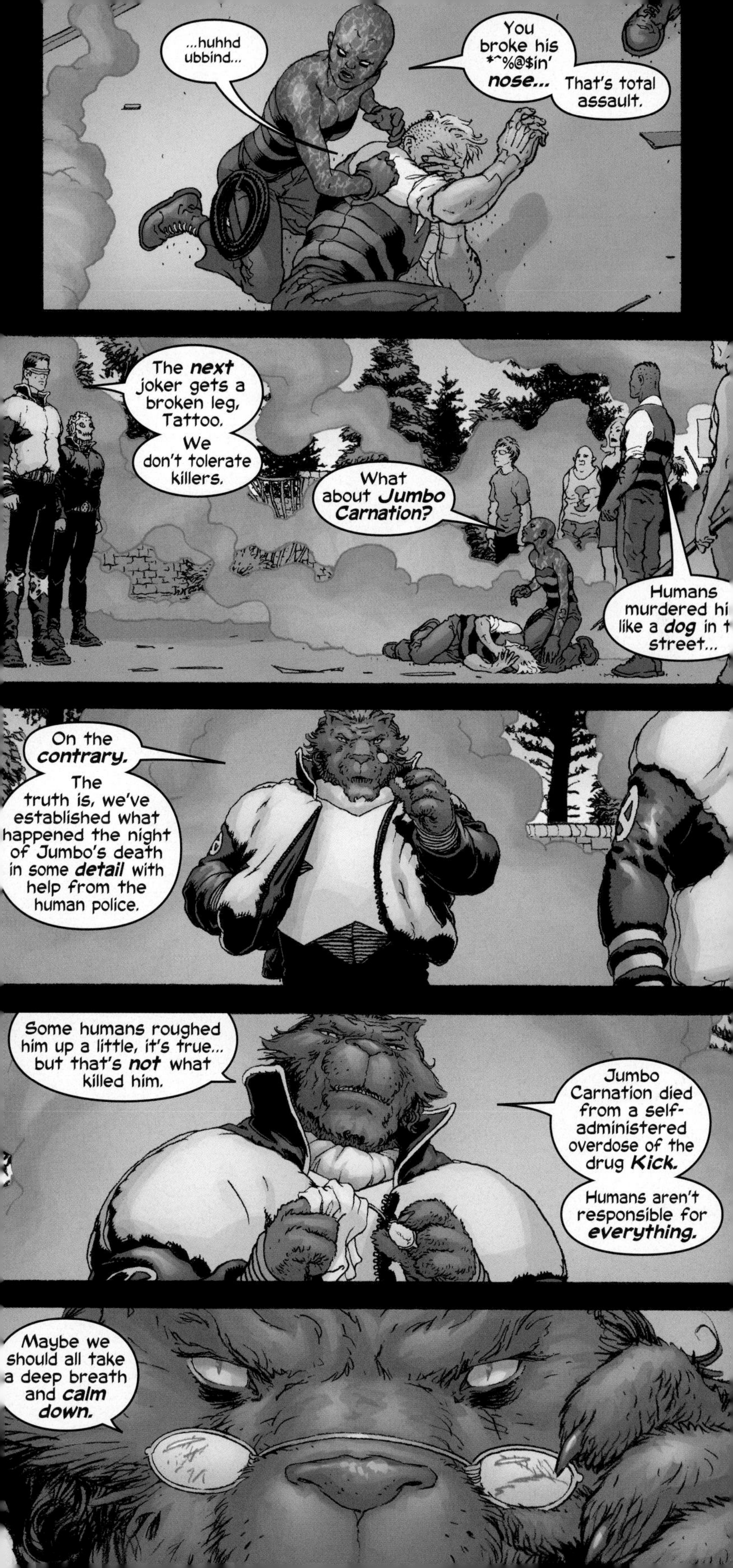
...huhhd ubbind...
You broke his *^%@$in' nose... That's total assault.
The next joker gets a broken leg, Tattoo.
We don't tolerate killers.
What about Jumbo Carnation?
Humans murdered hi like a dog in t street...
On the contrary.
The truth is, we've established what happened the night of Jumbo's death in some detail with help from the human police.
Some humans roughed him up a little, it's true... but that's not what killed him.
Jumbo Carnation died from a self-administered overdose of the drug Kick.
Humans aren't responsible for everything.
Maybe we should all take a deep breath and calm down.

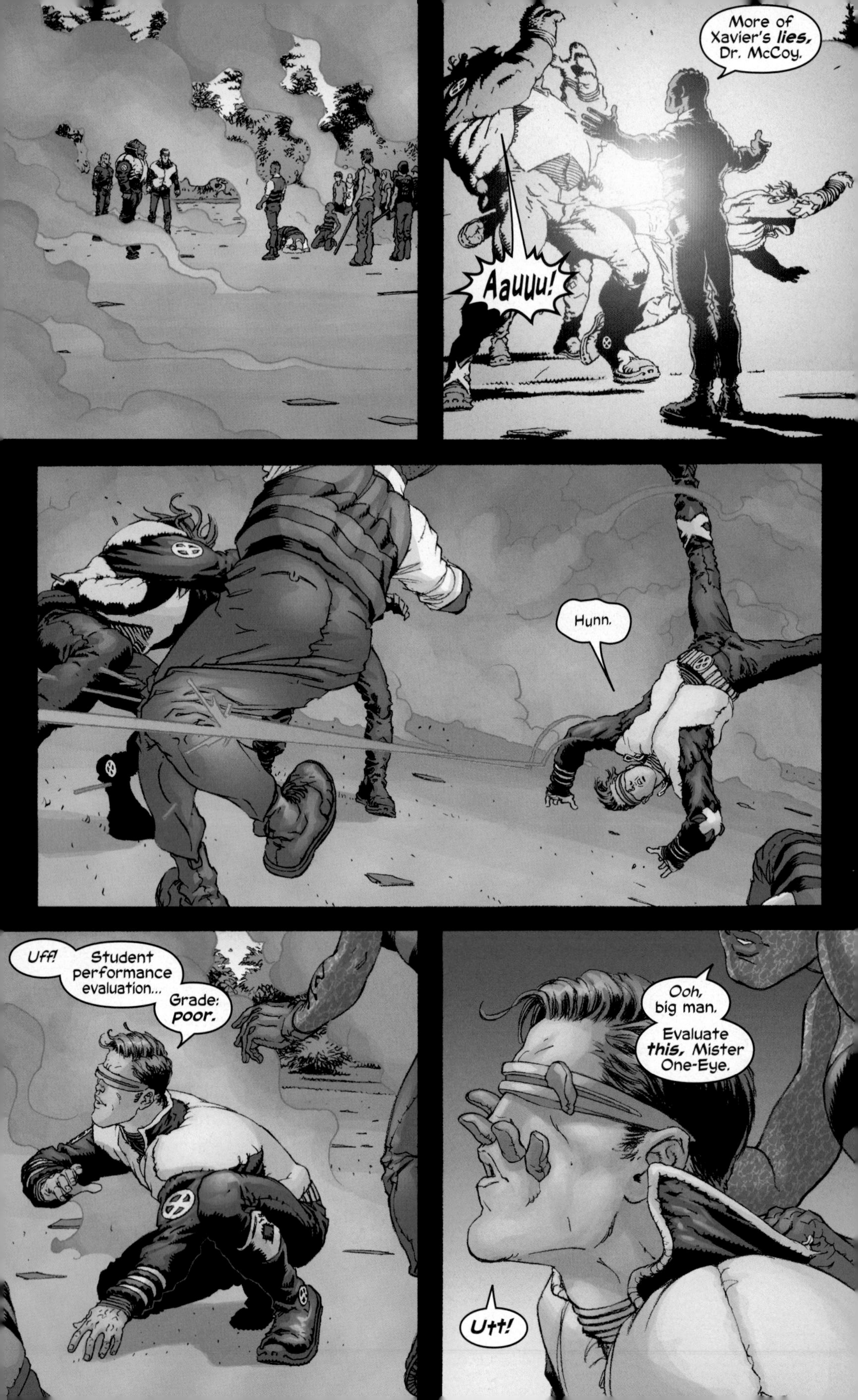
More of Xavier's ***lies,*** Dr. McCoy.
Aauuu!
Hunn.
Uff!
Student performance evaluation...
Grade: ***poor.***
Ooh, big man.
Evaluate ***this,*** Mister One-Eye.
Utt!

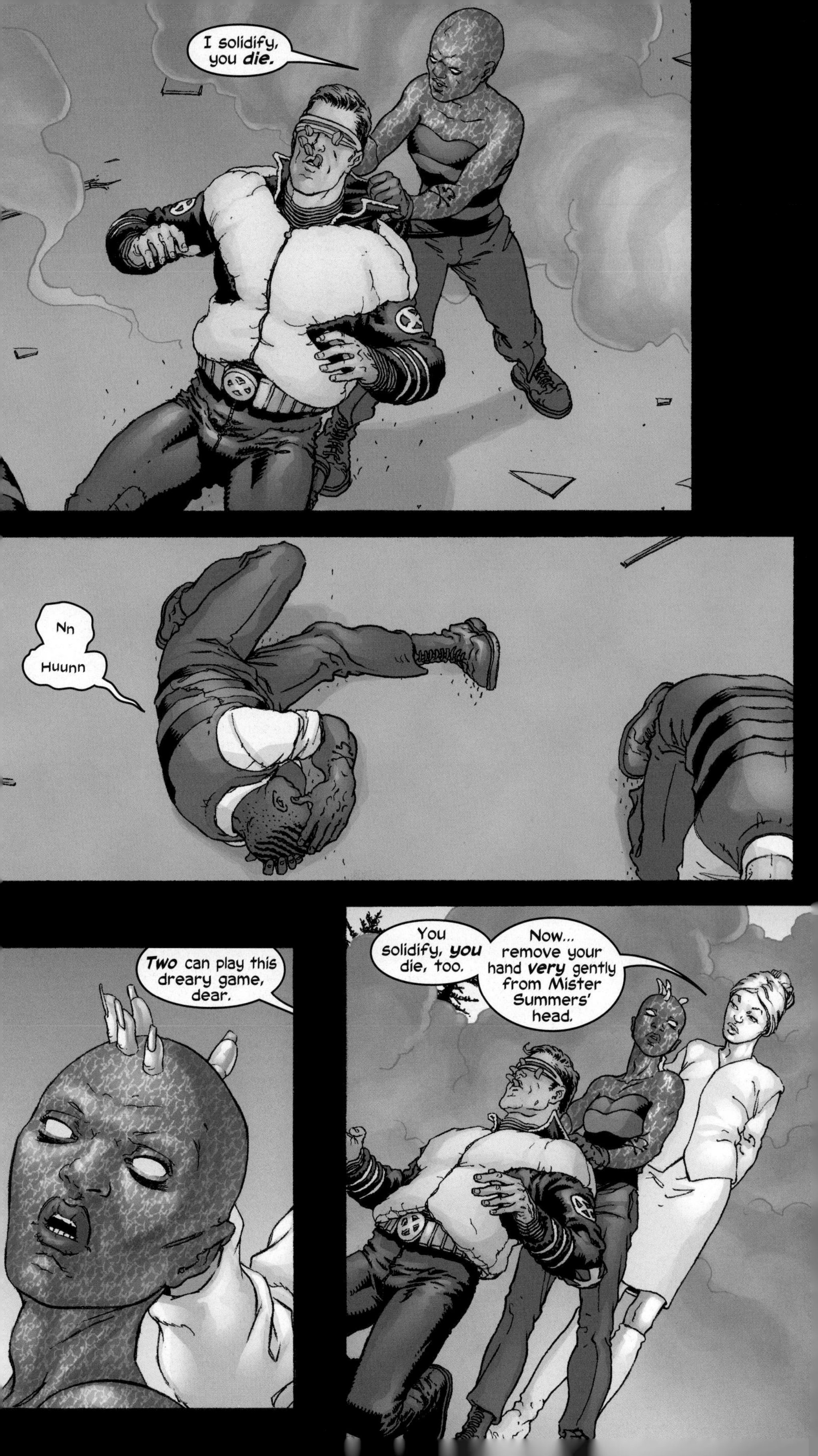
I solidify, you *die.*
Nn
Huunn
Two can play this dreary game, dear.
You solidify, *you* die, too.
Now... remove your hand *very* gently from Mister Summers' head.

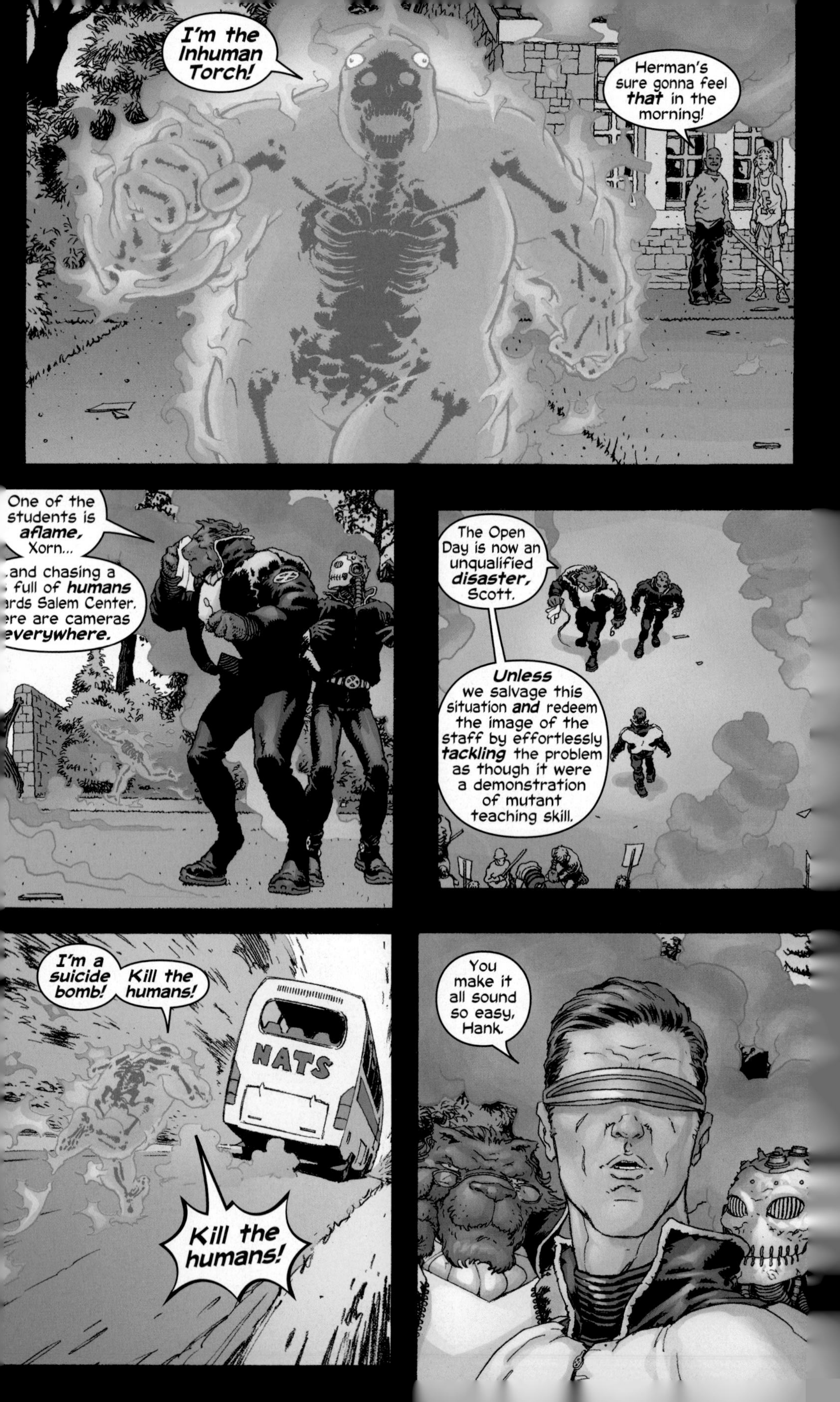

I'm the Inhuman Torch!
Herman's sure gonna feel **that** in the morning!
One of the students is ***aflame,*** Xorn...
.and chasing a
; full of ***humans***
ards Salem Center.
ere are cameras
everywhere.
The Open Day is now an unqualified ***disaster,*** Scott.
Unless we salvage this situation ***and*** redeem the image of the staff by effortlessly ***tackling*** the problem as though it were a demonstration of mutant teaching skill.
I'm a suicide bomb!
Kill the humans!
NATS
Kill the humans!
You make it all sound so easy, Hank.

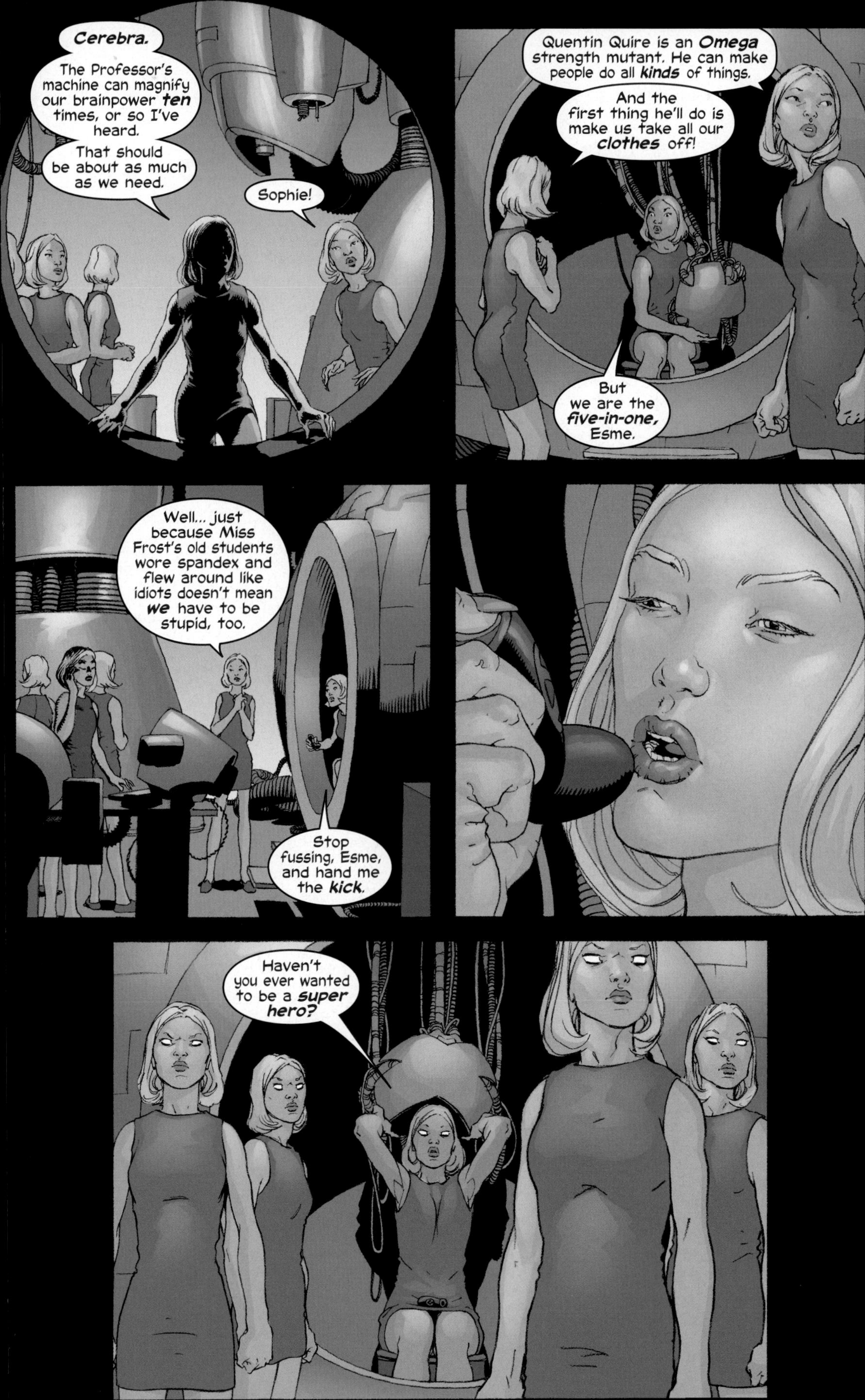
Cerebra.
The Professor's machine can magnify our brainpower ten times, or so I've heard.
That should be about as much as we need.
Sophie!
Quentin Quire is an Omega strength mutant. He can make people do all kinds of things.
And the first thing he'll do is make us take all our clothes off!
But we are the five-in-one, Esme.
Well... just because Miss Frost's old students wore spandex and flew around like idiots doesn't mean we have to be stupid, too.
Stop fussing, Esme, and hand me the kick.
Haven't you ever wanted to be a super hero?

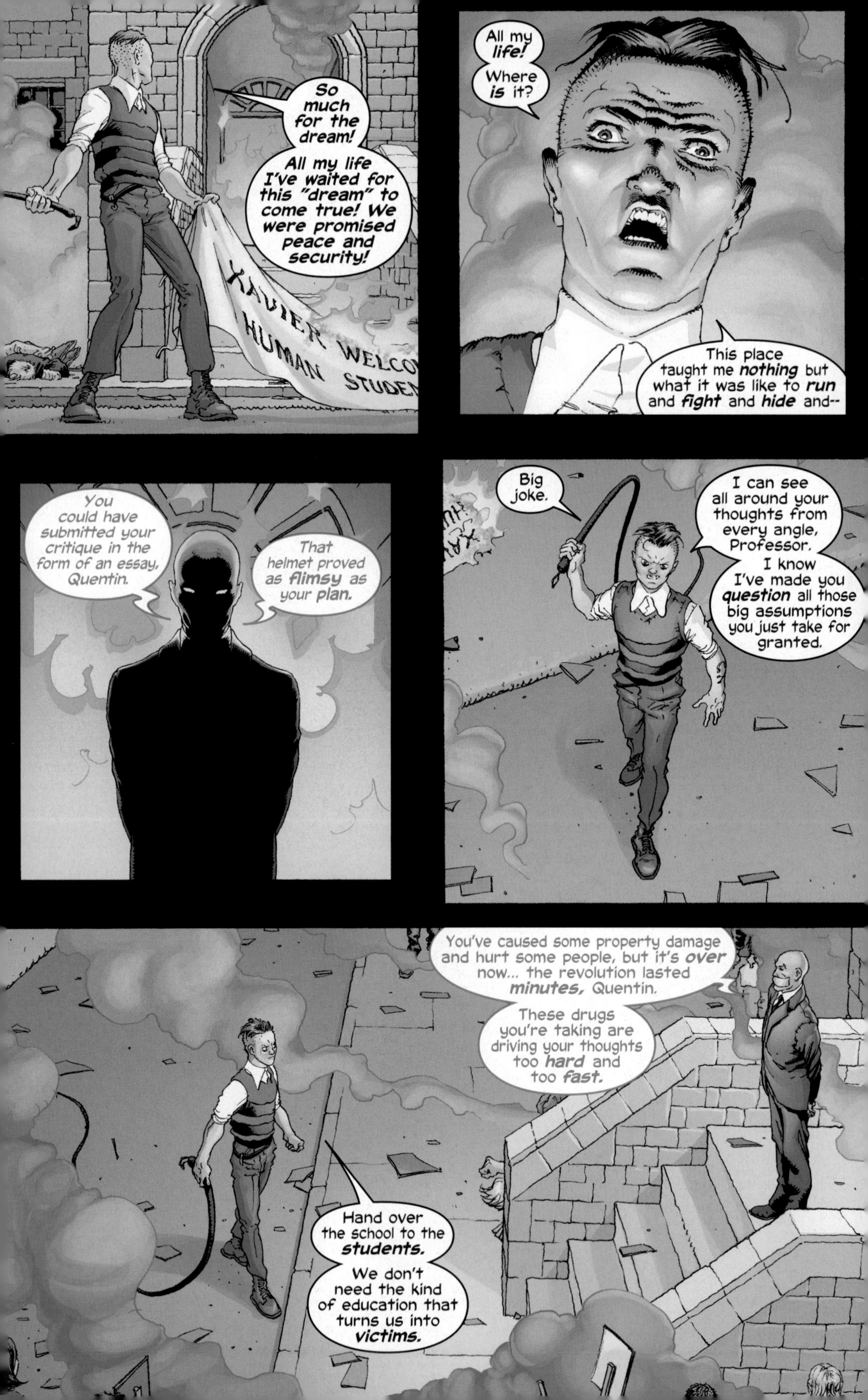

So much for the dream!
All my life I've waited for this "dream" to come true! We were promised peace and security!
XAVIER WELCO HUMAN STUDEN
All my life!
Where is it?
This place taught me nothing but what it was like to run and fight and hide and--
You could have submitted your critique in the form of an essay, Quentin.
That helmet proved as flimsy as your plan.
Big joke.
I can see all around your thoughts from every angle, Professor.
I know I've made you question all those big assumptions you just take for granted.
You've caused some property damage and hurt some people, but it's over now... the revolution lasted minutes, Quentin.
These drugs you're taking are driving your thoughts too hard and too fast.
Hand over the school to the students.
We don't need the kind of education that turns us into victims.

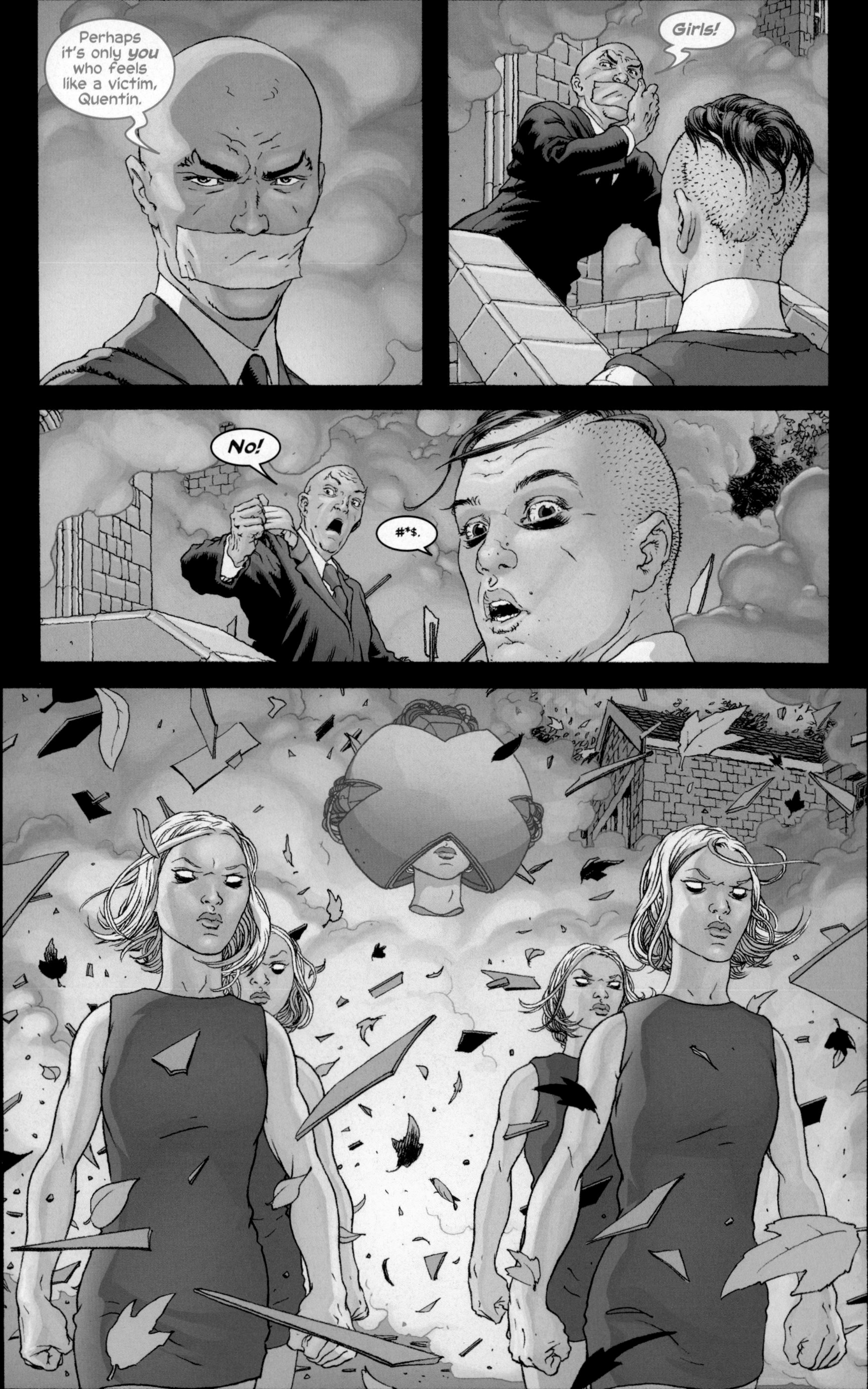
Perhaps it's only you who feels like a victim, Quentin.
Girls!
No!
#*$.

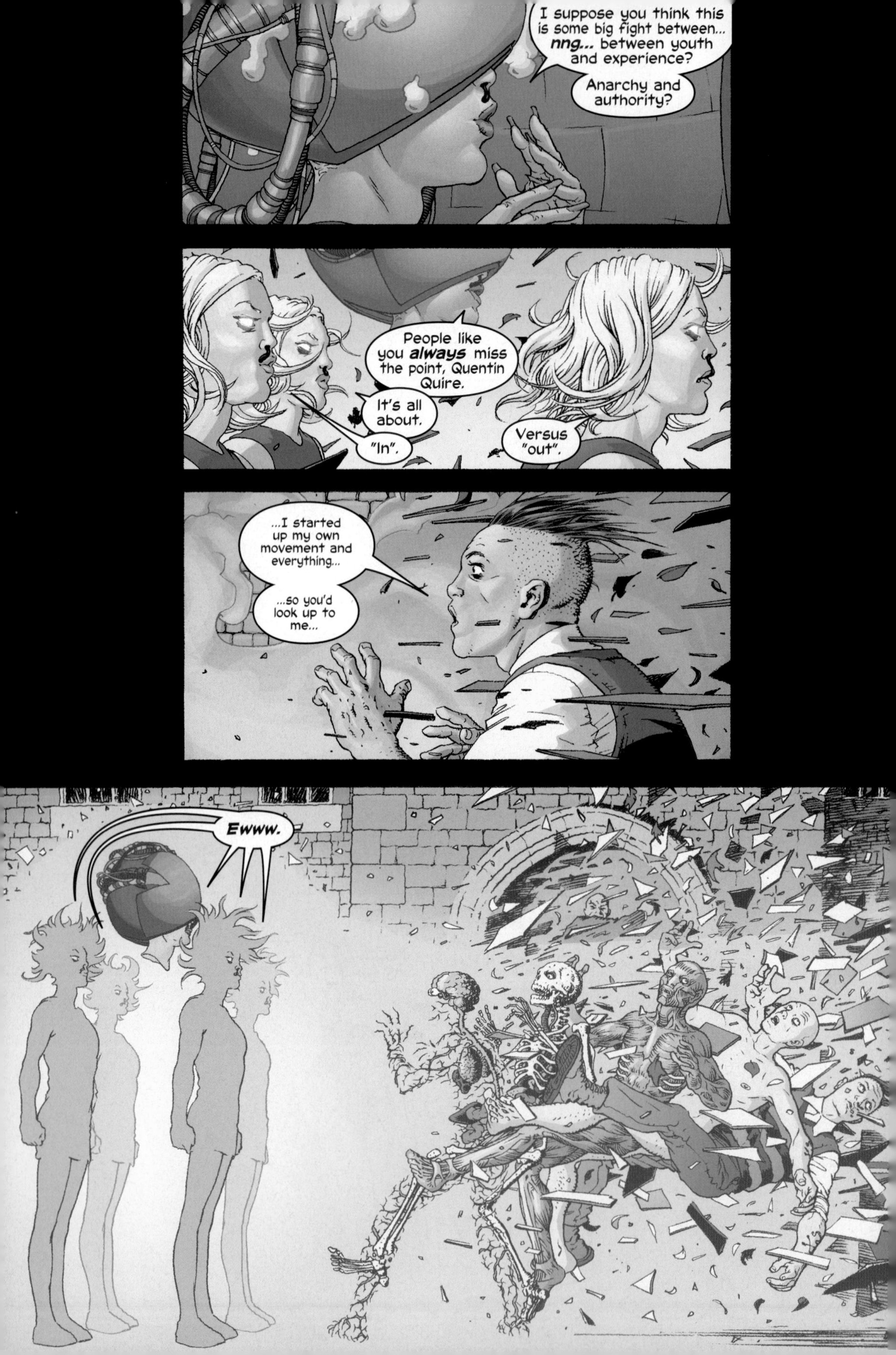
I suppose you think this is some big fight between... nng... between youth and experience?
Anarchy and authority?
People like you always miss the point, Quentin Quire.
It's all about.
"In".
Versus "out".
...I started up my own movement and everything...
...so you'd look up to me...
Ewww.

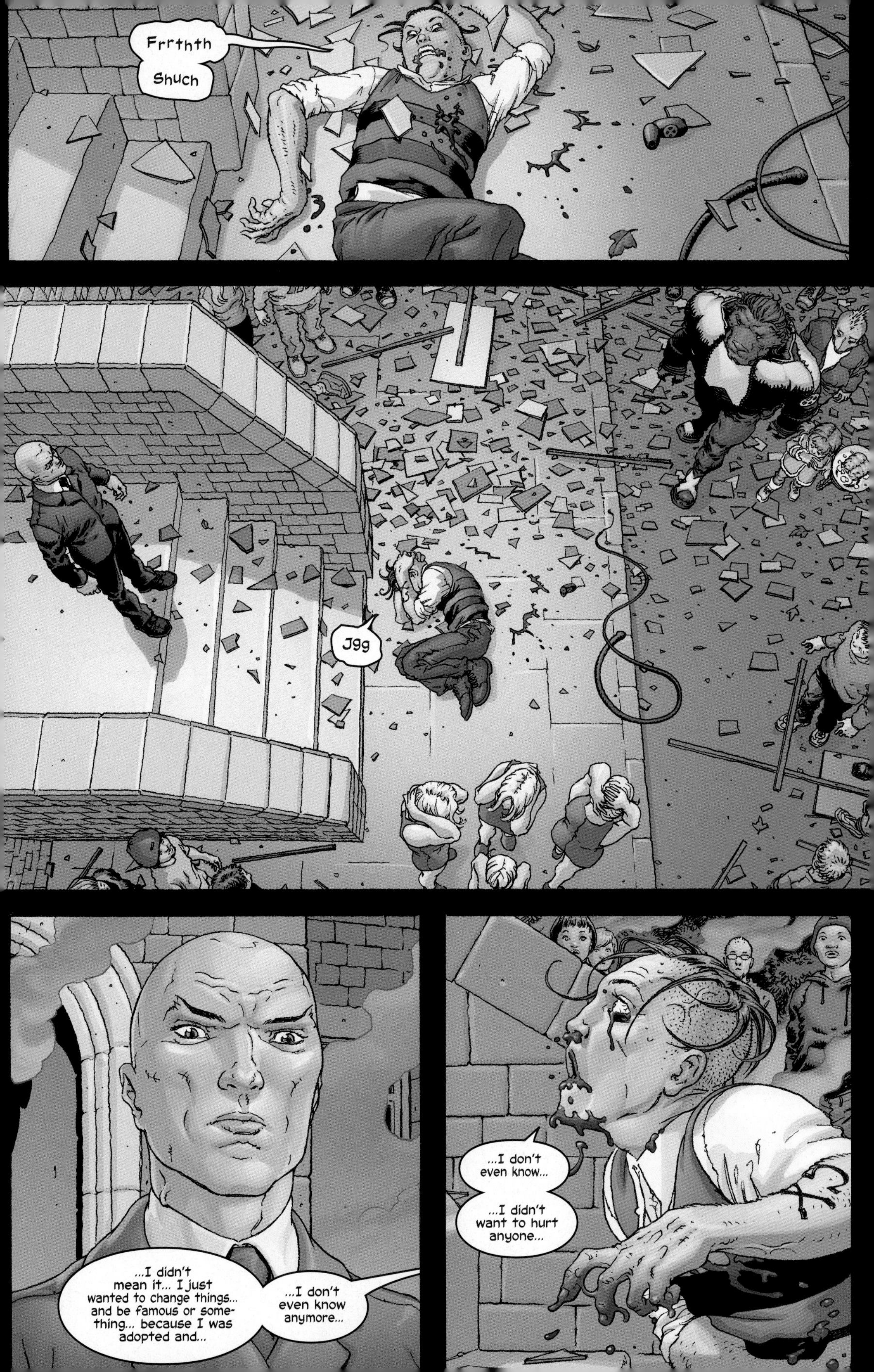
Frrthth
Shuch
Jgg
...I didn't mean it... I just wanted to change things... and be famous or something... because I was adopted and...
...I don't even know anymore...
...I don't even know...
...I didn't want to hurt anyone...

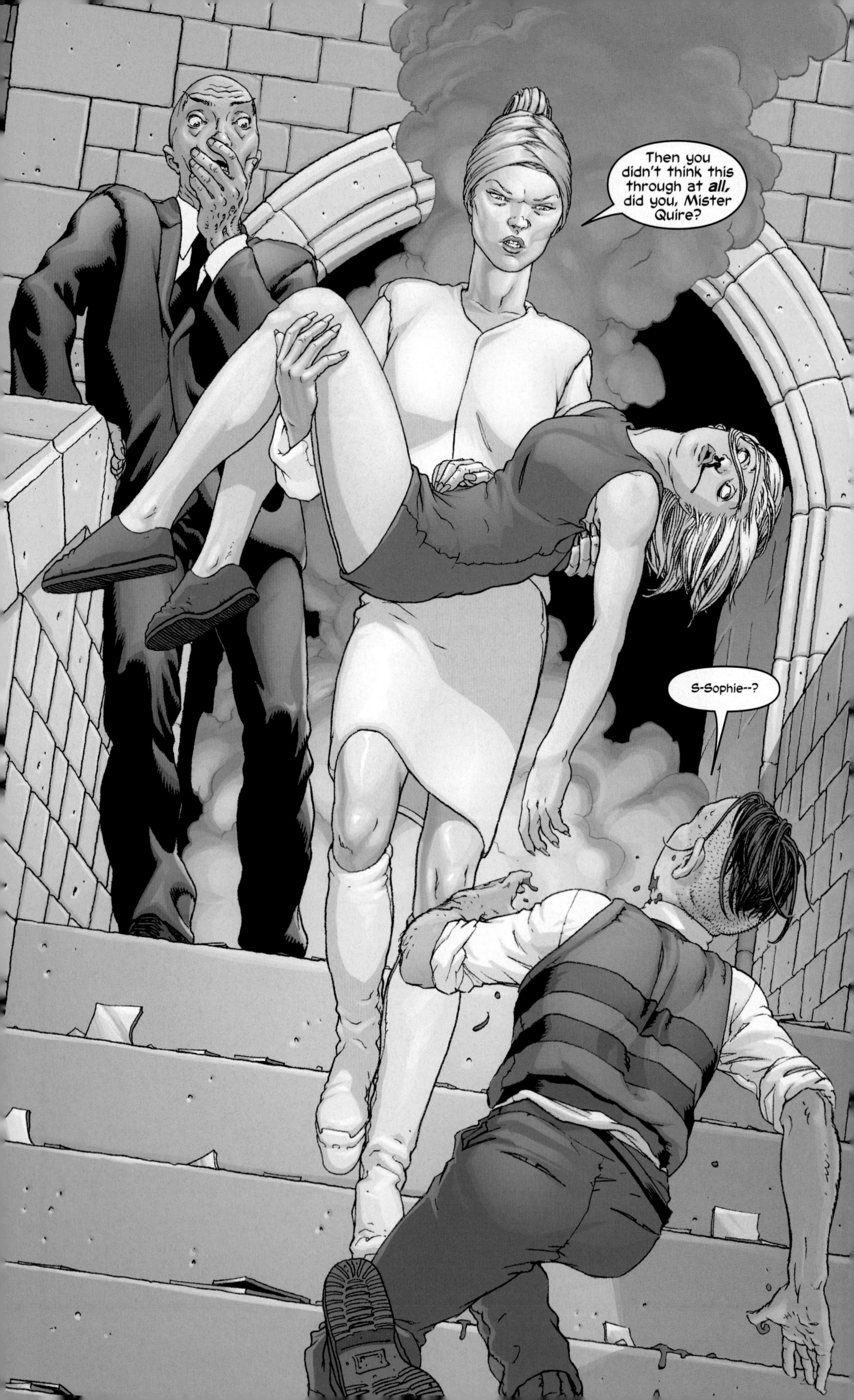
Then you didn't think this through at *all,* did you, Mister Quire?
S-Sophie--?

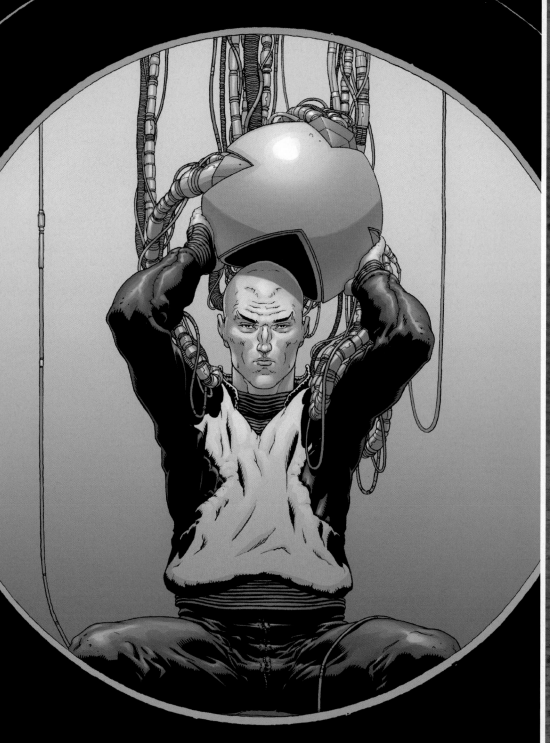

138

FRANK QUITELY

The Prime of Miss Emma Frost

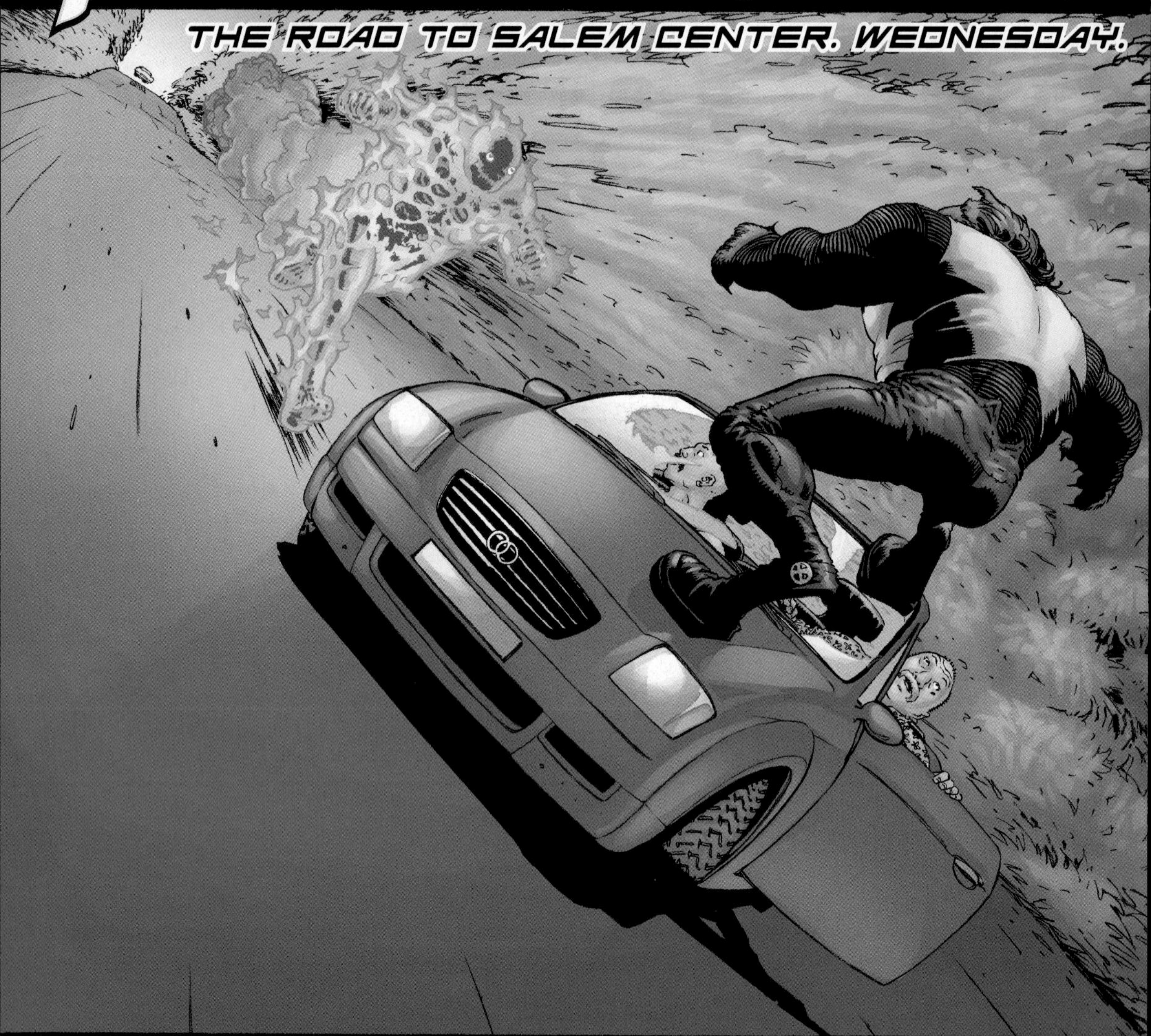
THE ROAD TO SALEM CENTER. WEDNESDAY.

GRANT MORRISON WRITER | FRANK QUITELY WITH AVALON STUDIOS ART | CHRIS CHUCKRY COLORS

RICHARD STARKINGS WITH COMICRAFT'S ALBERT DESCHESNE LETTERS
NOVA REN SUMA ASSISTANT EDITOR MIKE RAICHT ASSOCIATE EDITOR MIKE MARTS EDITOR
JOE QUESADA EDITOR IN CHIEF BILL JEMAS PRESIDENT

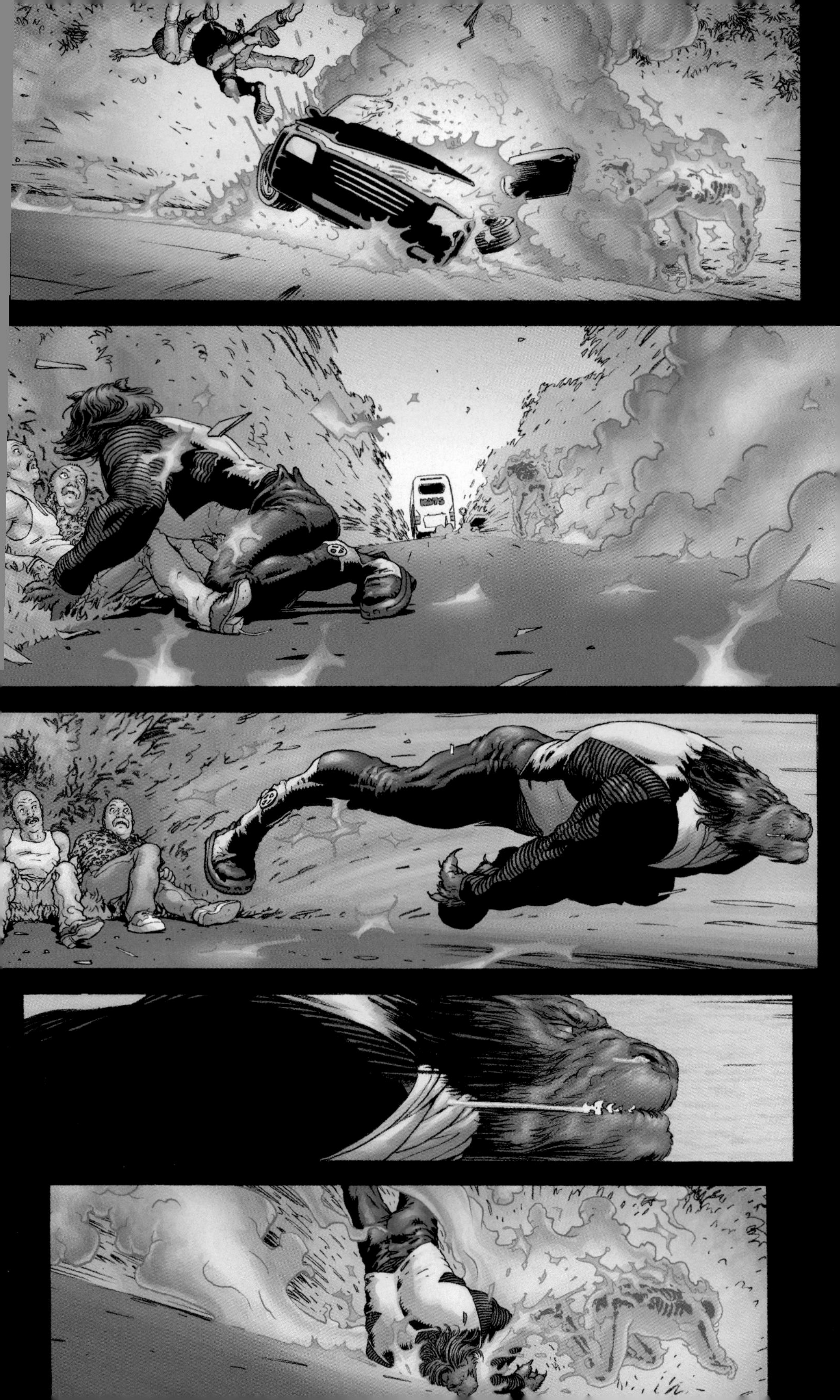

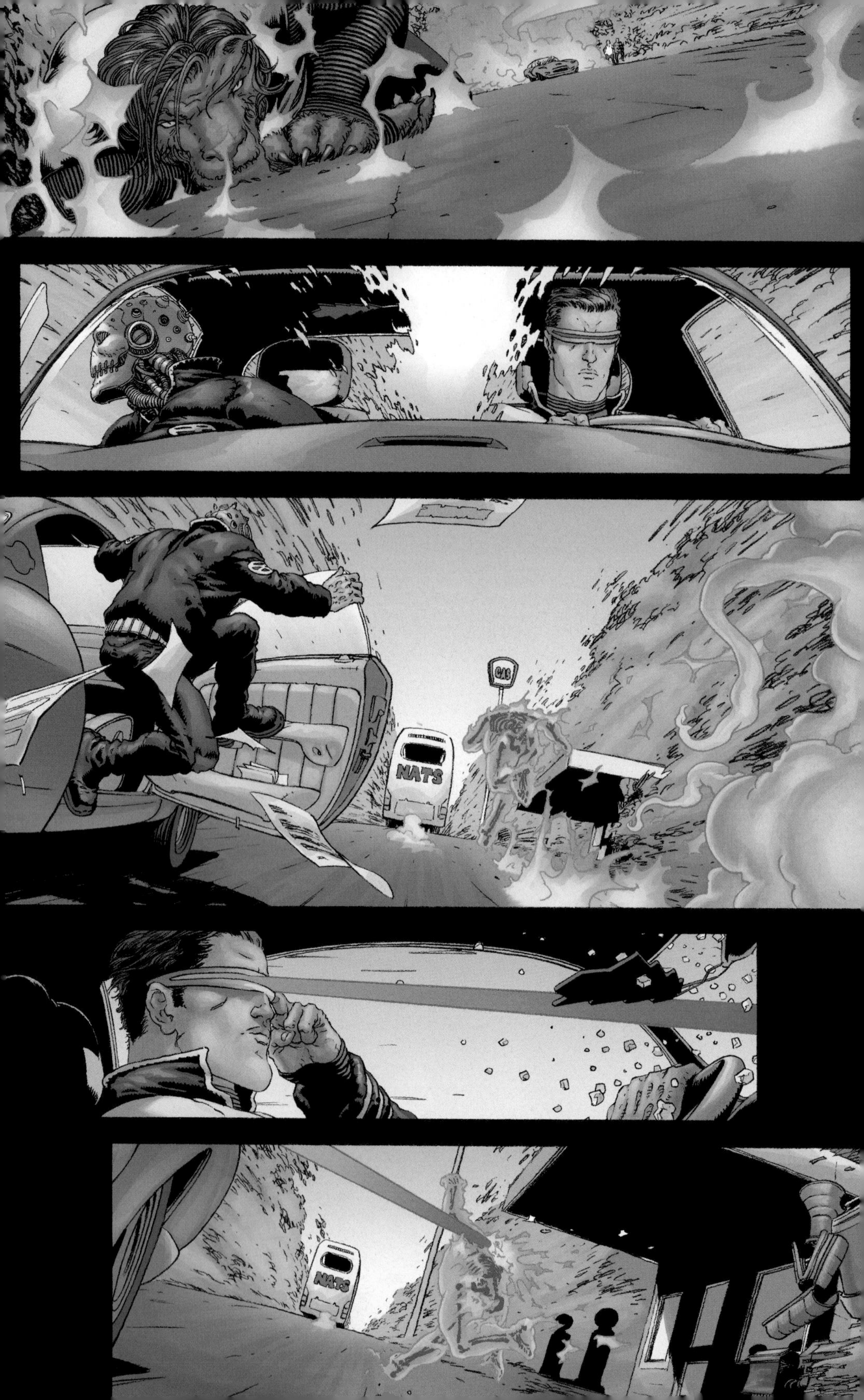
GAS
NATS

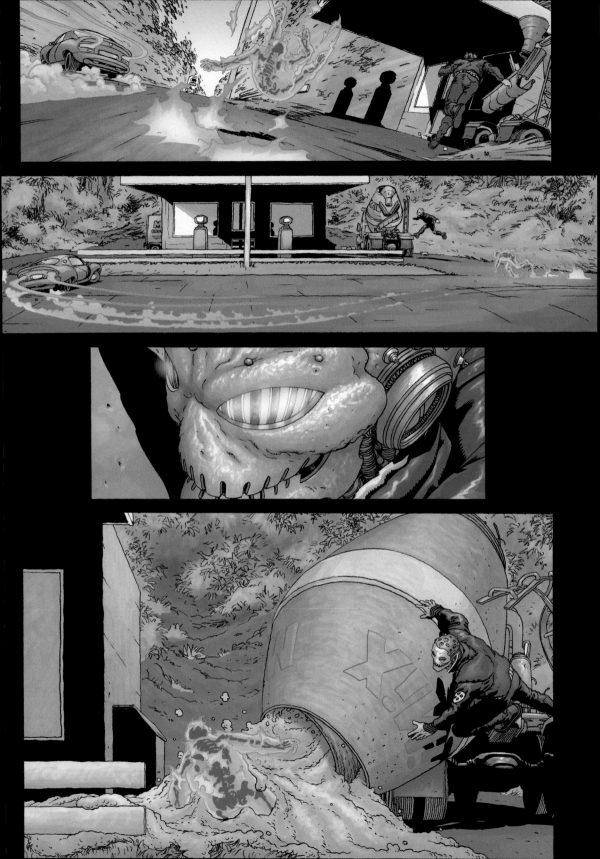

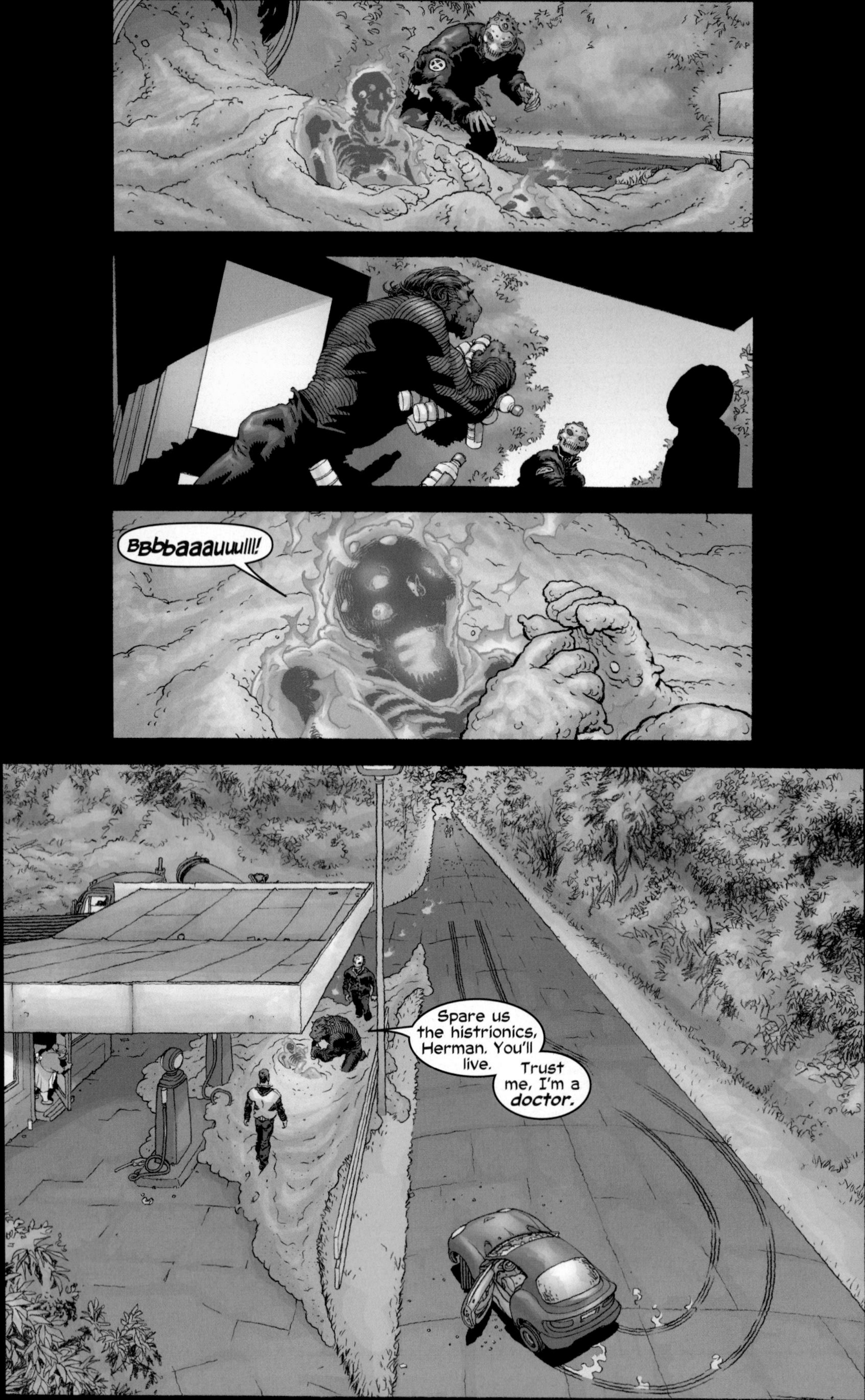
BBbbaaauuulll!
Spare us the histrionics, Herman. You'll live.
Trust me, I'm a *doctor.*

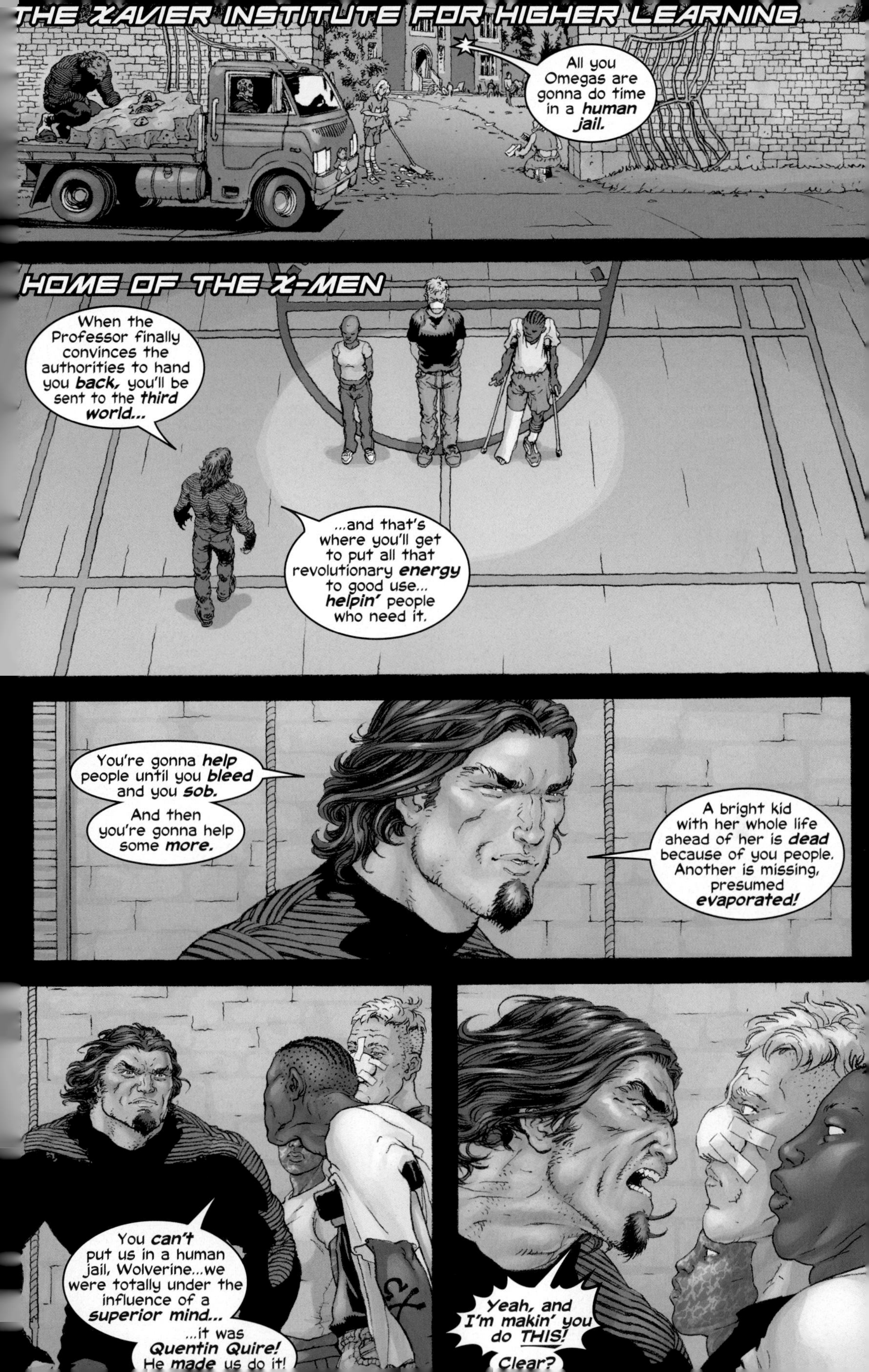
THE XAVIER INSTITUTE FOR HIGHER LEARNING
All you Omegas are gonna do time in a human jail.
HOME OF THE X-MEN
When the Professor finally convinces the authorities to hand you back, you'll be sent to the third world...
...and that's where you'll get to put all that revolutionary energy to good use... helpin' people who need it.
You're gonna help people until you bleed and you sob.
And then you're gonna help some more.
A bright kid with her whole life ahead of her is dead because of you people. Another is missing, presumed evaporated!
You can't put us in a human jail, Wolverine...we were totally under the influence of a superior mind...
...it was Quentin Quire! He made us do it!
Yeah, and I'm makin' you do THIS!
Clear?

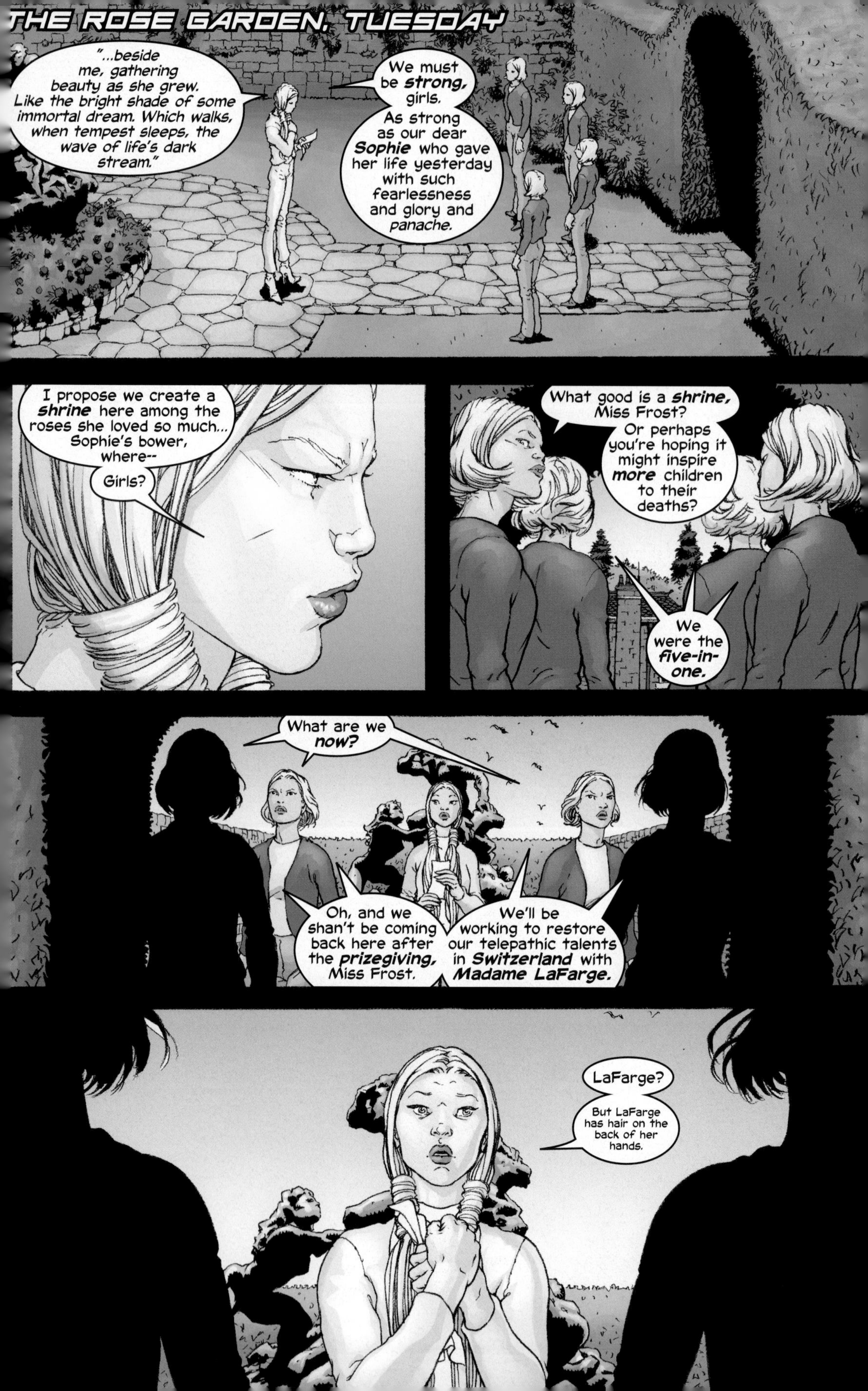
THE ROSE GARDEN, TUESDAY
"...beside me, gathering beauty as she grew. Like the bright shade of some immortal dream. Which walks, when tempest sleeps, the wave of life's dark stream."
We must be strong, girls.
As strong as our dear Sophie who gave her life yesterday with such fearlessness and glory and panache.
I propose we create a shrine here among the roses she loved so much... Sophie's bower, where--
Girls?
What good is a shrine, Miss Frost?
Or perhaps you're hoping it might inspire more children to their deaths?
We were the five-in-one.
What are we now?
Oh, and we shan't be coming back here after the prizegiving, Miss Frost.
We'll be working to restore our telepathic talents in Switzerland with Madame LaFarge.
LaFarge?
But LaFarge has hair on the back of her hands.

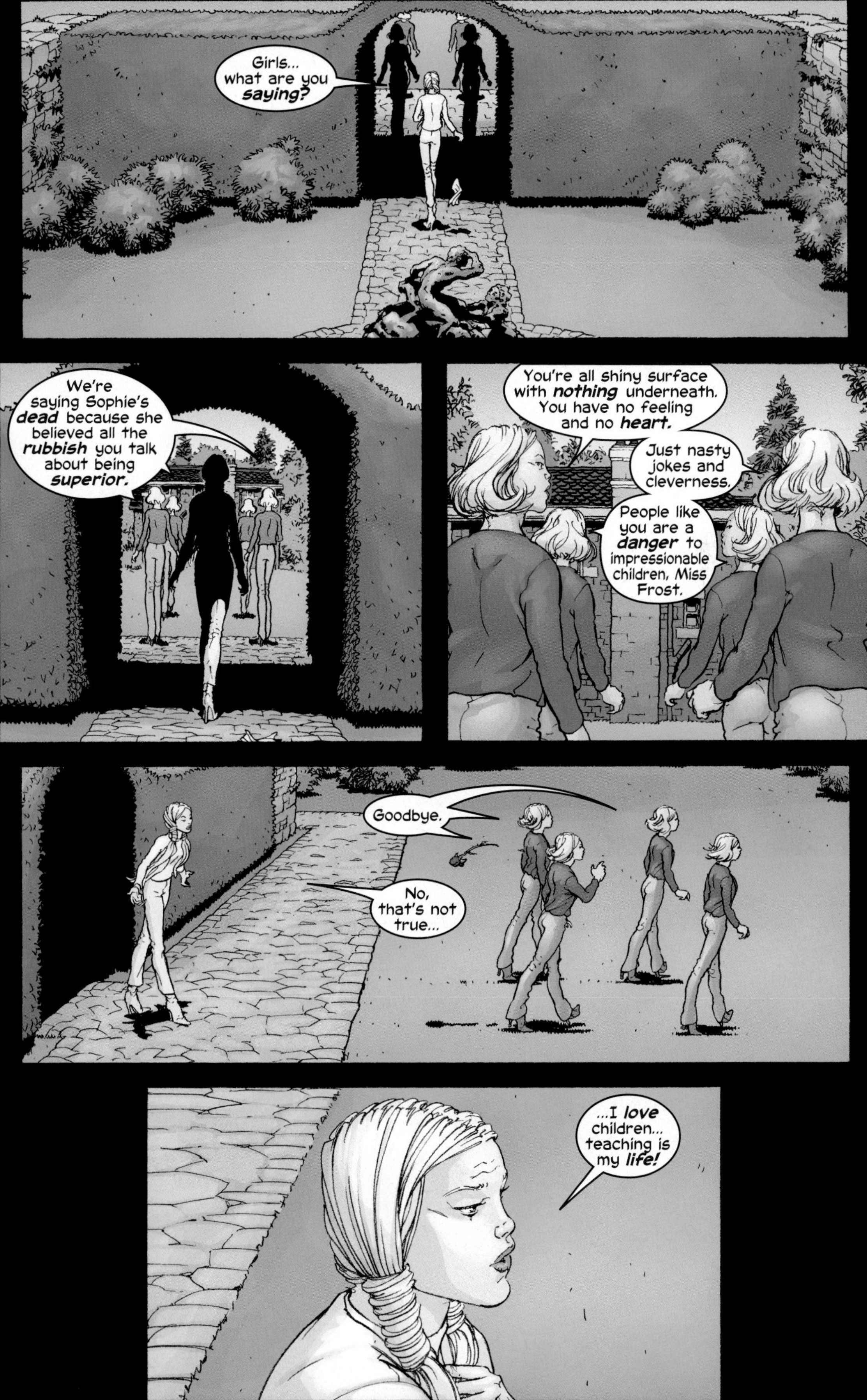
Girls... what are you *saying?*
We're saying Sophie's *dead* because she believed all the *rubbish* you talk about being *superior.*
You're all shiny surface with *nothing* underneath. You have no feeling and no *heart.*
Just nasty jokes and cleverness.
People like you are a *danger* to impressionable children, Miss Frost.
Goodbye.
No, that's not true...
...I *love* children... teaching is my *life!*

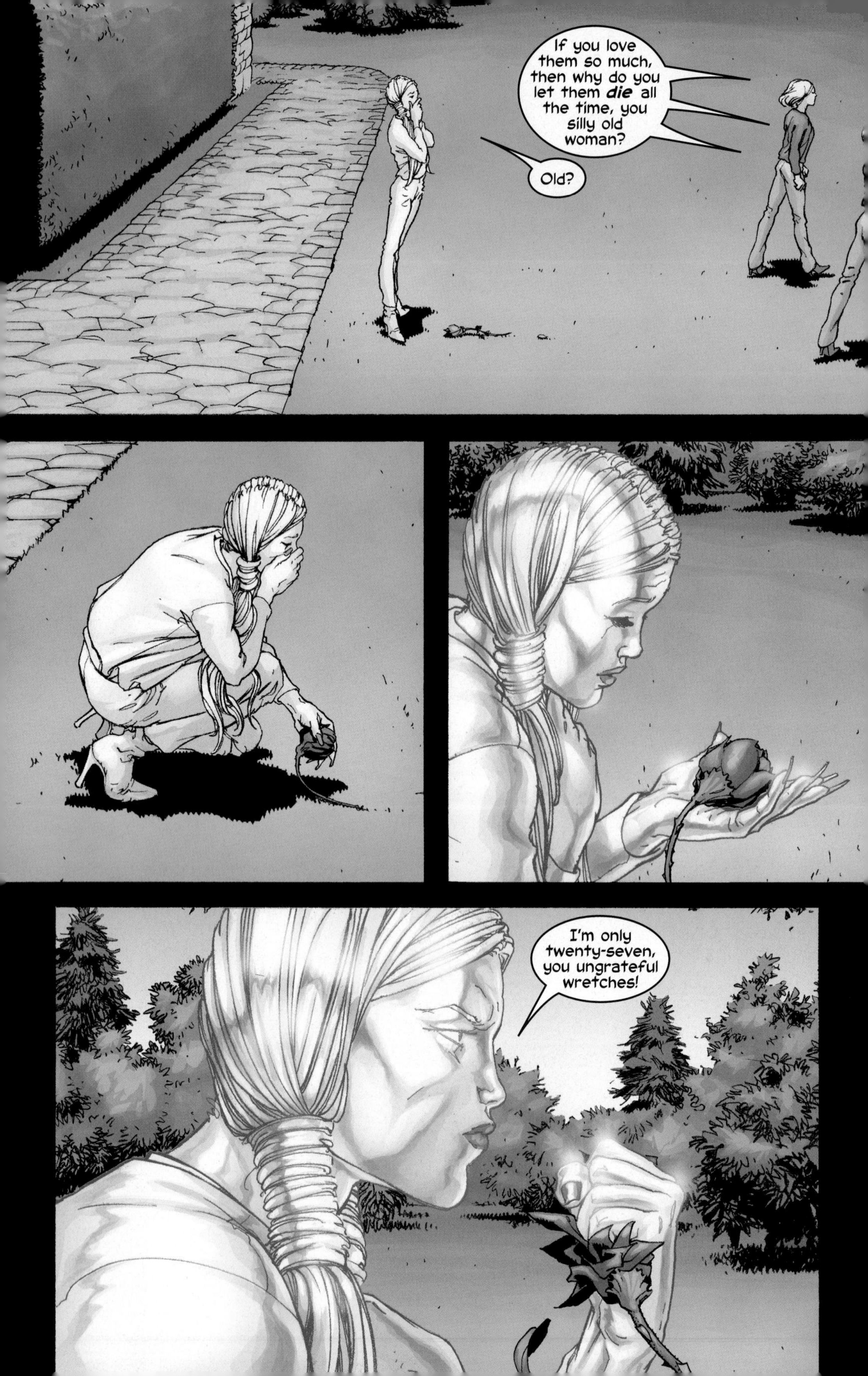
If you love them so much, then why do you let them *die* all the time, you silly old woman?
Old?
I'm only twenty-seven, you ungrateful wretches!

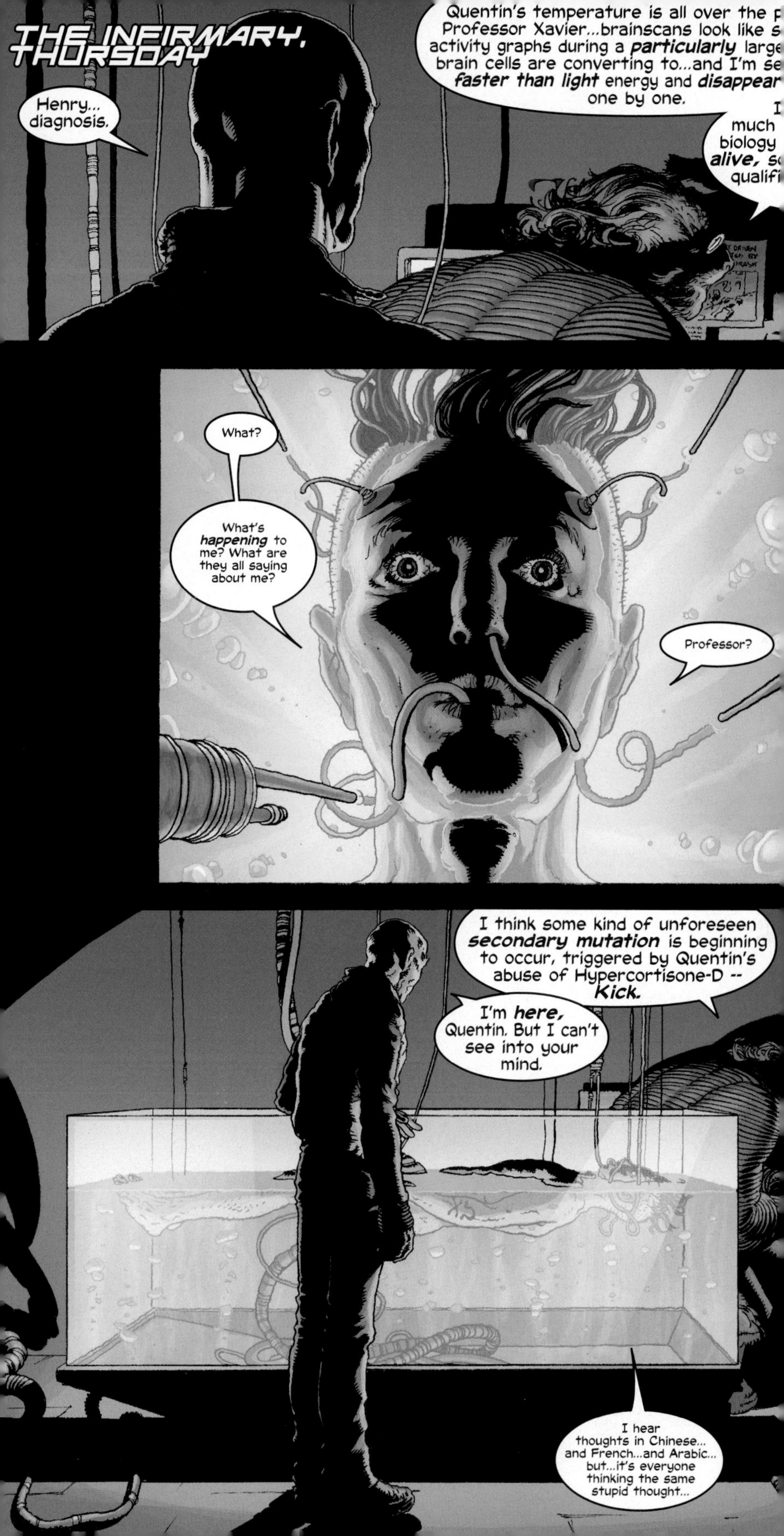
THE INFIRMARY, THURSDAY
Henry... diagnosis.
Quentin's temperature is all over the
Professor Xavier...brainscans look like
activity graphs during a particularly
brain cells are converting to...and I'm
faster than light energy and
one by one.
much
biology
alive,
What?
What's happening to me? What are they all saying about me?
Professor?
I think some kind of unforeseen secondary mutation is beginning to occur, triggered by Quentin's abuse of Hypercortisone-D -- Kick.
I'm here, Quentin. But I can't see into your mind.
I hear thoughts in Chinese... and French...and Arabic... but...it's everyone thinking the same stupid thought...

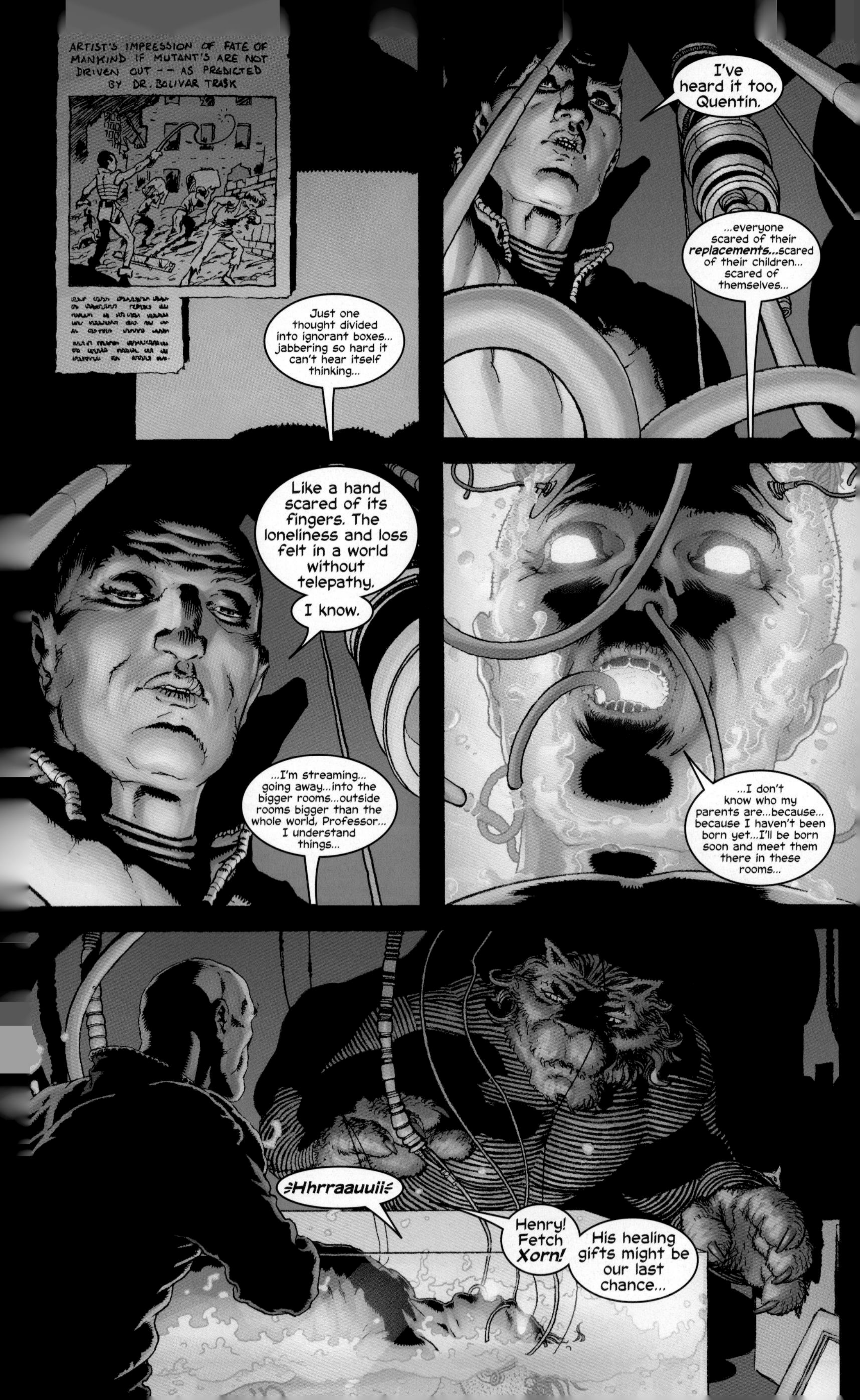

ARTIST'S IMPRESSION OF FATE OF MANKIND IF MUTANT'S ARE NOT DRIVEN OUT -- AS PREDICTED BY DR. BOLIVAR TRASK
Just one thought divided into ignorant boxes... jabbering so hard it can't hear itself thinking...
I've heard it too, Quentin.
...everyone scared of their replacements...scared of their children... scared of themselves...
Like a hand scared of its fingers. The loneliness and loss felt in a world without telepathy.
I know.
...I'm streaming... going away...into the bigger rooms...outside rooms bigger than the whole world, Professor... I understand things...
...I don't know who my parents are...because... because I haven't been born yet...I'll be born soon and meet them there in these rooms...
Hhrraauuii
Henry! Fetch Xorn!
His healing gifts might be our last chance...

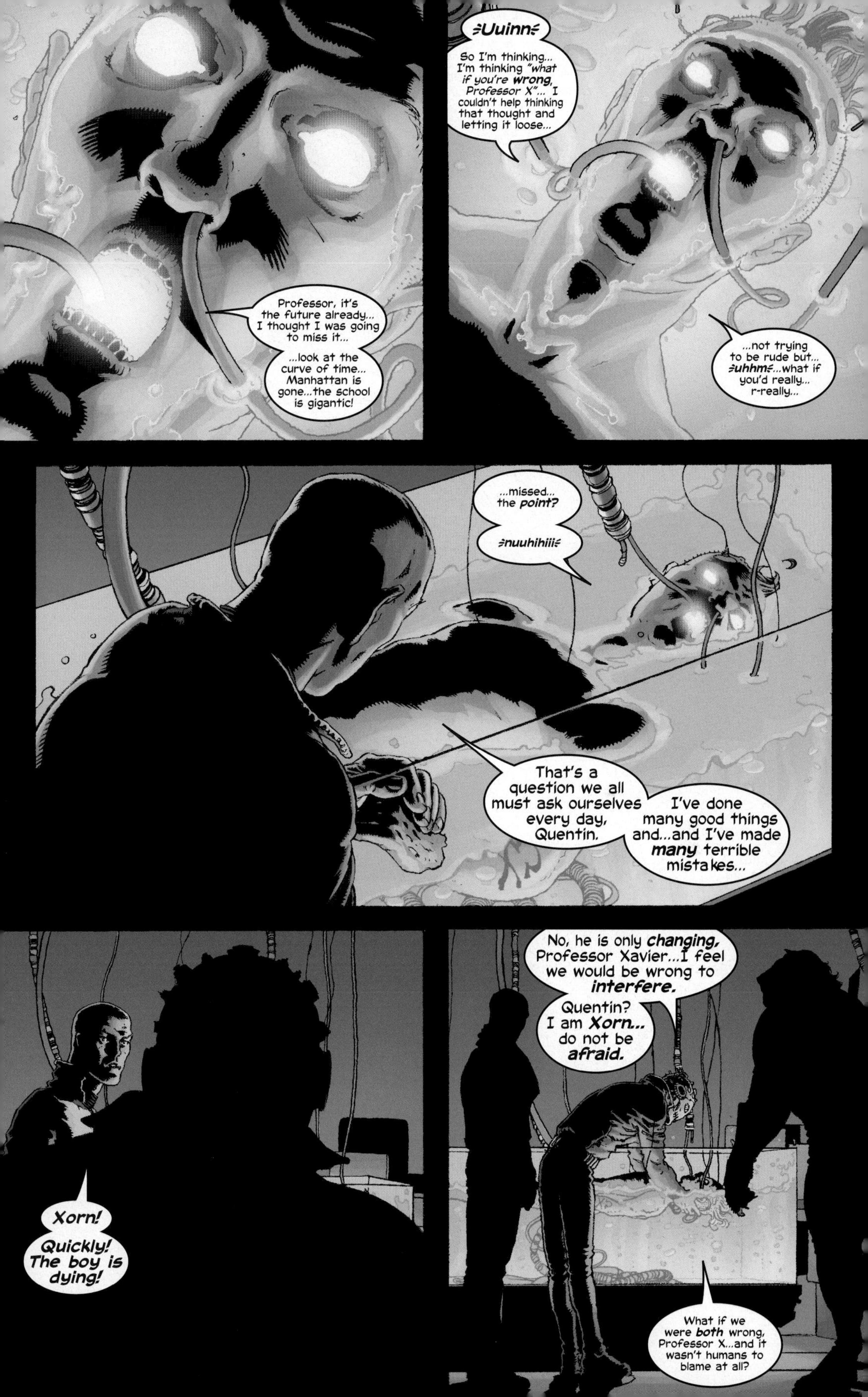

Professor, it's the future already... I thought I was going to miss it...
...look at the curve of time... Manhattan is gone...the school is gigantic!
Uuinn
So I'm thinking... I'm thinking "what if you're wrong, Professor X"... I couldn't help thinking that thought and letting it loose...
...not trying to be rude but... uhhm...what if you'd really... r-really...
...missed... the point?
nuuhihiii
That's a question we all must ask ourselves every day, Quentin.
I've done many good things and...and I've made many terrible mistakes...
Xorn! Quickly! The boy is dying!
No, he is only changing, Professor Xavier...I feel we would be wrong to interfere.
Quentin? I am Xorn... do not be afraid.
What if we were both wrong, Professor X...and it wasn't humans to blame at all?

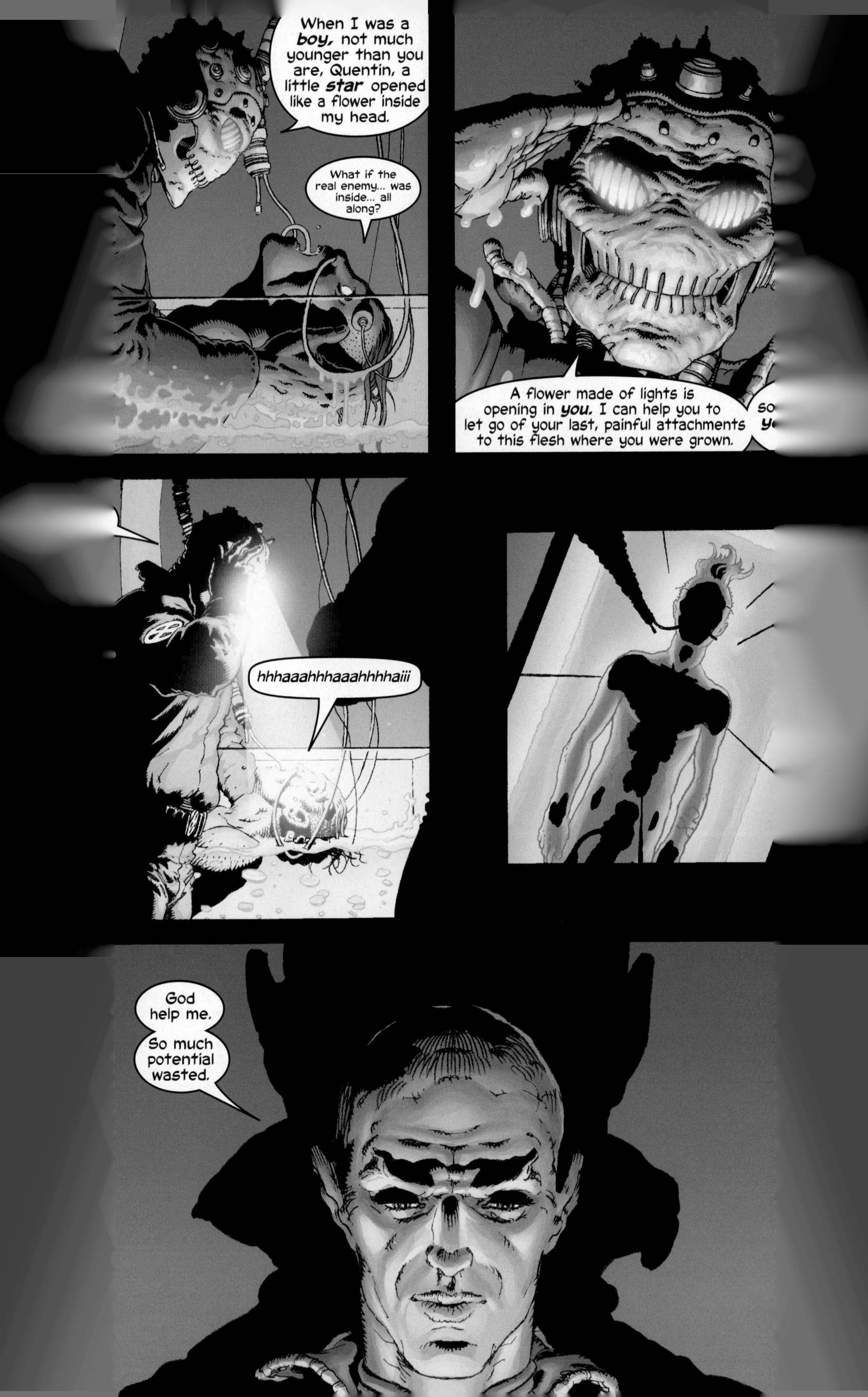

When I was a boy, not much younger than you are, Quentin, a little star opened like a flower inside my head.
What if the real enemy... was inside... all along?
A flower made of lights is opening in you. I can help you to let go of your last, painful attachments to this flesh where you were grown.
hhhaaahhhaaahhhhaiii
God help me.
So much potential wasted.

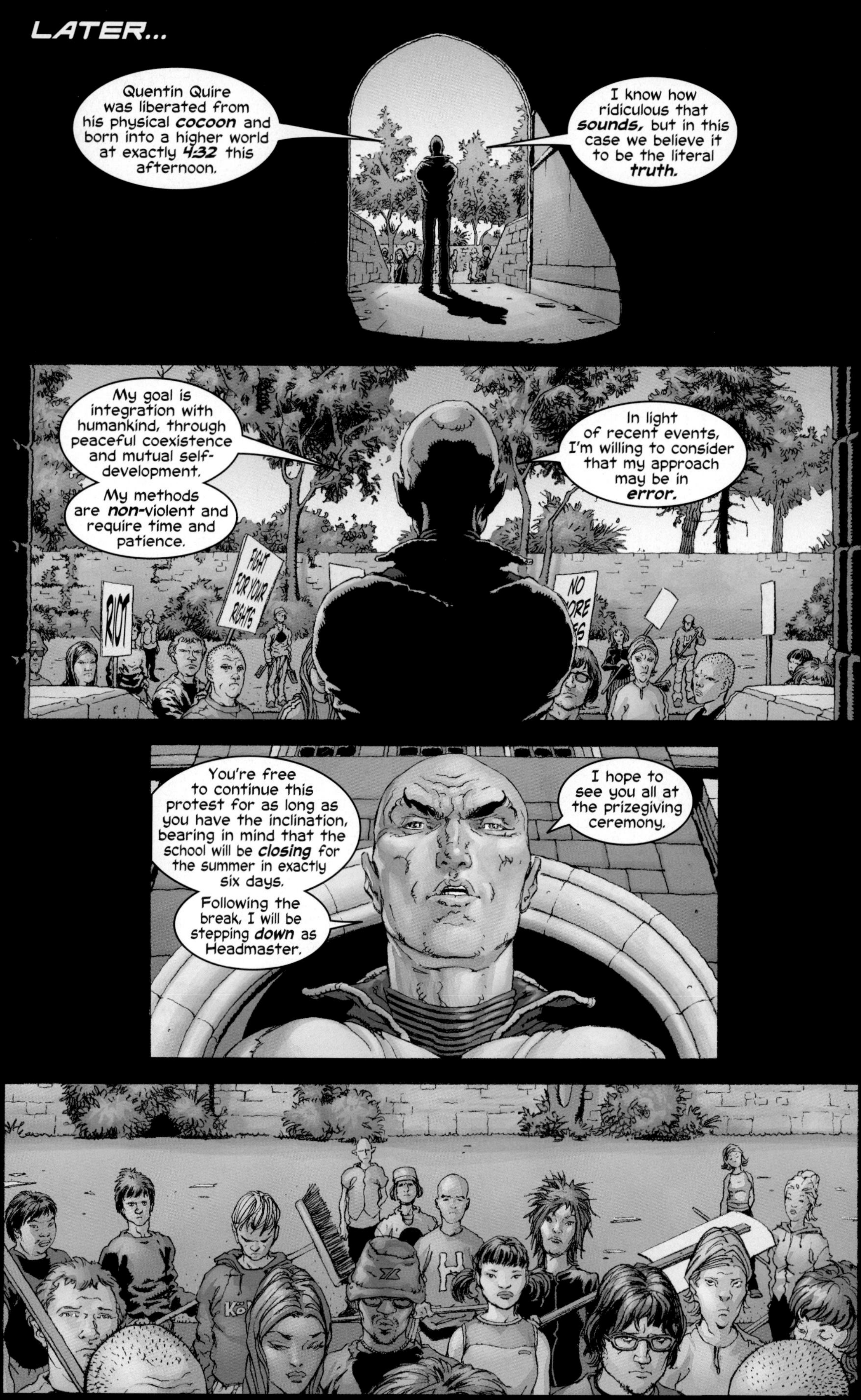
LATER...
Quentin Quire was liberated from his physical *cocoon* and born into a higher world at exactly *4:32* this afternoon.
I know how ridiculous that *sounds,* but in this case we believe it to be the literal *truth.*
My goal is integration with humankind, through peaceful coexistence and mutual self-development.
My methods are *non-*violent and require time and patience.
In light of recent events, I'm willing to consider that my approach may be in *error.*
RIOT
FIGHT FOR YOUR RIGHTS
You're free to continue this protest for as long as you have the inclination, bearing in mind that the school will be *closing* for the summer in exactly six days.
Following the break, I will be stepping *down* as Headmaster.
I hope to see you all at the prizegiving ceremony.

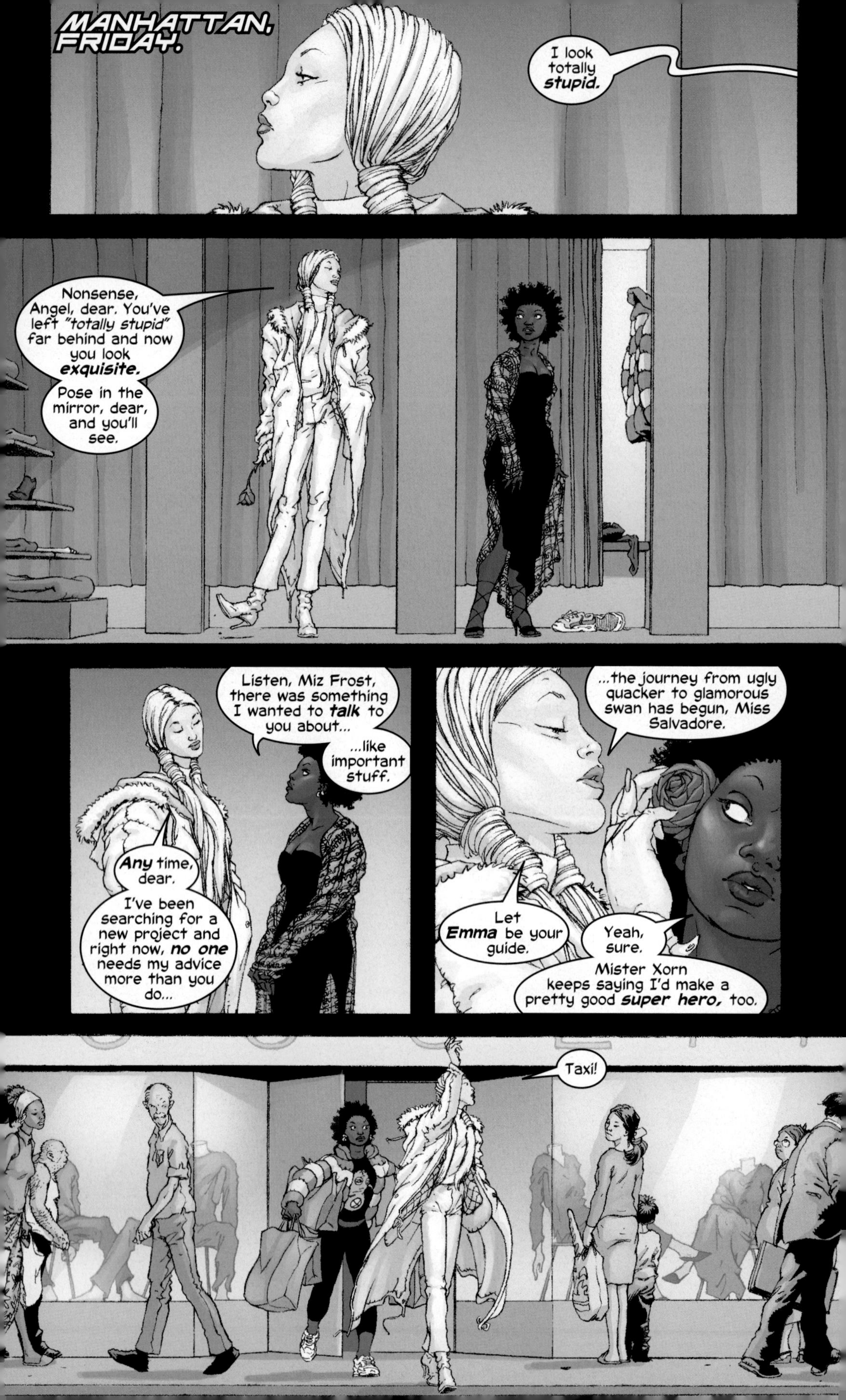

MANHATTAN, FRIDAY.
I look totally stupid.
Nonsense, Angel, dear. You've left "totally stupid" far behind and now you look exquisite.
Pose in the mirror, dear, and you'll see.
Listen, Miz Frost, there was something I wanted to talk to you about...
...like important stuff.
Any time, dear.
I've been searching for a new project and right now, no one needs my advice more than you do...
...the journey from ugly quacker to glamorous swan has begun, Miss Salvadore.
Let Emma be your guide.
Yeah, sure.
Mister Xorn keeps saying I'd make a pretty good super hero, too.
Taxi!

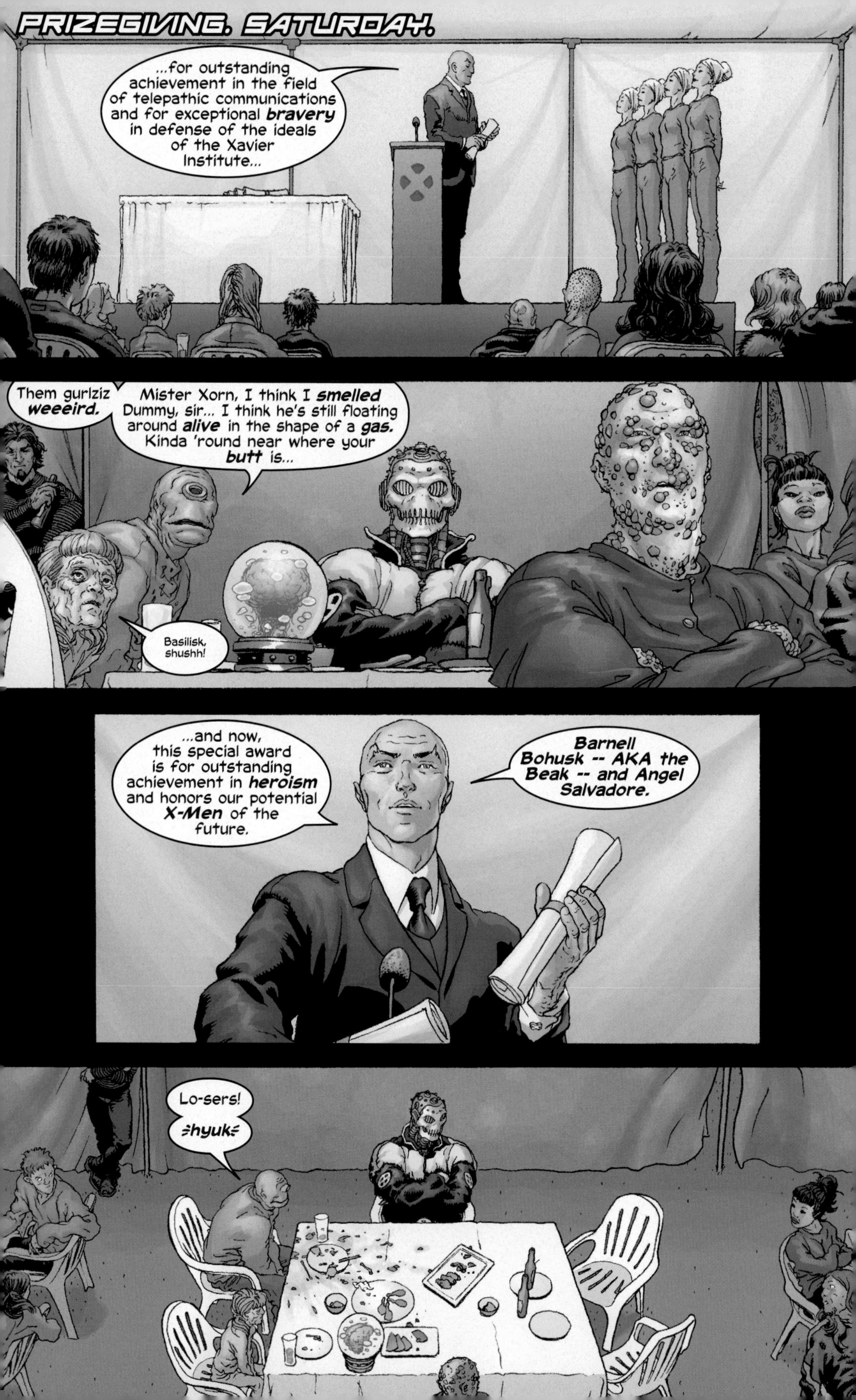
PRIZEGIVING. SATURDAY.
...for outstanding achievement in the field of telepathic communications and for exceptional bravery in defense of the ideals of the Xavier Institute...
Them gurlziz weeeird.
Mister Xorn, I think I smelled Dummy, sir... I think he's still floating around alive in the shape of a gas. Kinda 'round near where your butt is...
Basilisk, shushh!
...and now, this special award is for outstanding achievement in heroism and honors our potential X-Men of the future.
Barnell Bohusk -- AKA the Beak -- and Angel Salvadore.
Lo-sers!
hyuk

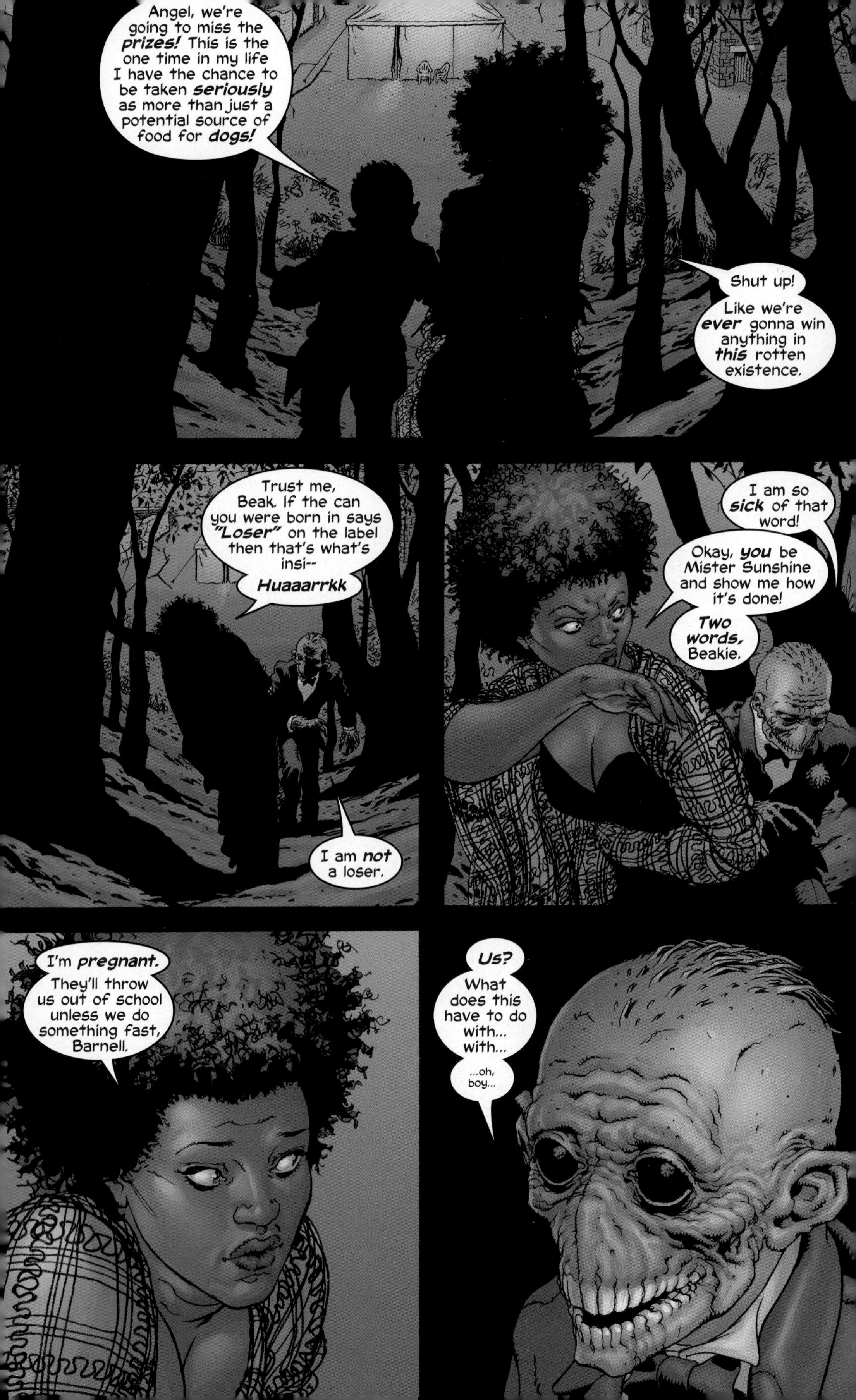
Angel, we're going to miss the ***prizes!*** This is the one time in my life I have the chance to be taken ***seriously*** as more than just a potential source of food for ***dogs!***
Shut up!
Like we're ***ever*** gonna win anything in ***this*** rotten existence.
Trust me, Beak. If the can you were born in says ***"Loser"*** on the label then that's what's insi--
Huaaarrkk
I am ***not*** a loser.
I am so ***sick*** of that word!
Okay, ***you*** be Mister Sunshine and show me how it's done!
Two words, Beakie.
I'm ***pregnant.***
They'll throw us out of school unless we do something fast, Barnell.
Us?
What does this have to do with... with...
...oh, boy...

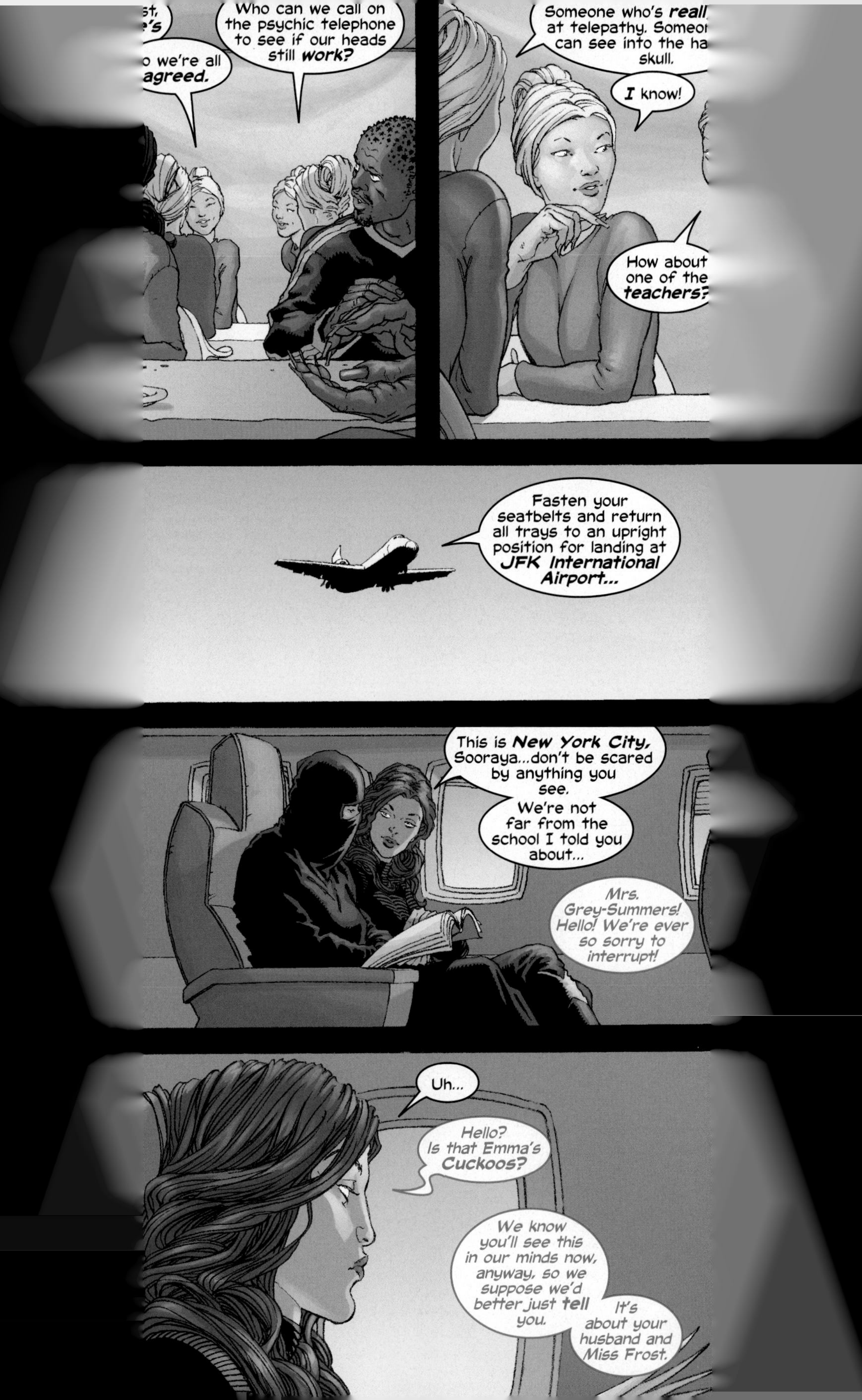

o we're all agreed.
Who can we call on the psychic telephone to see if our heads still work?
Someone who's reall at telepathy. Someo can see into the ha skull.
I know!
How about one of the teachers?
Fasten your seatbelts and return all trays to an upright position for landing at JFK International Airport...
This is New York City, Sooraya...don't be scared by anything you see.
We're not far from the school I told you about...
Mrs. Grey-Summers! Hello! We're ever so sorry to interrupt!
Uh...
Hello? Is that Emma's Cuckoos?
We know you'll see this in our minds now, anyway, so we suppose we'd better just tell you.
It's about your husband and Miss Frost.

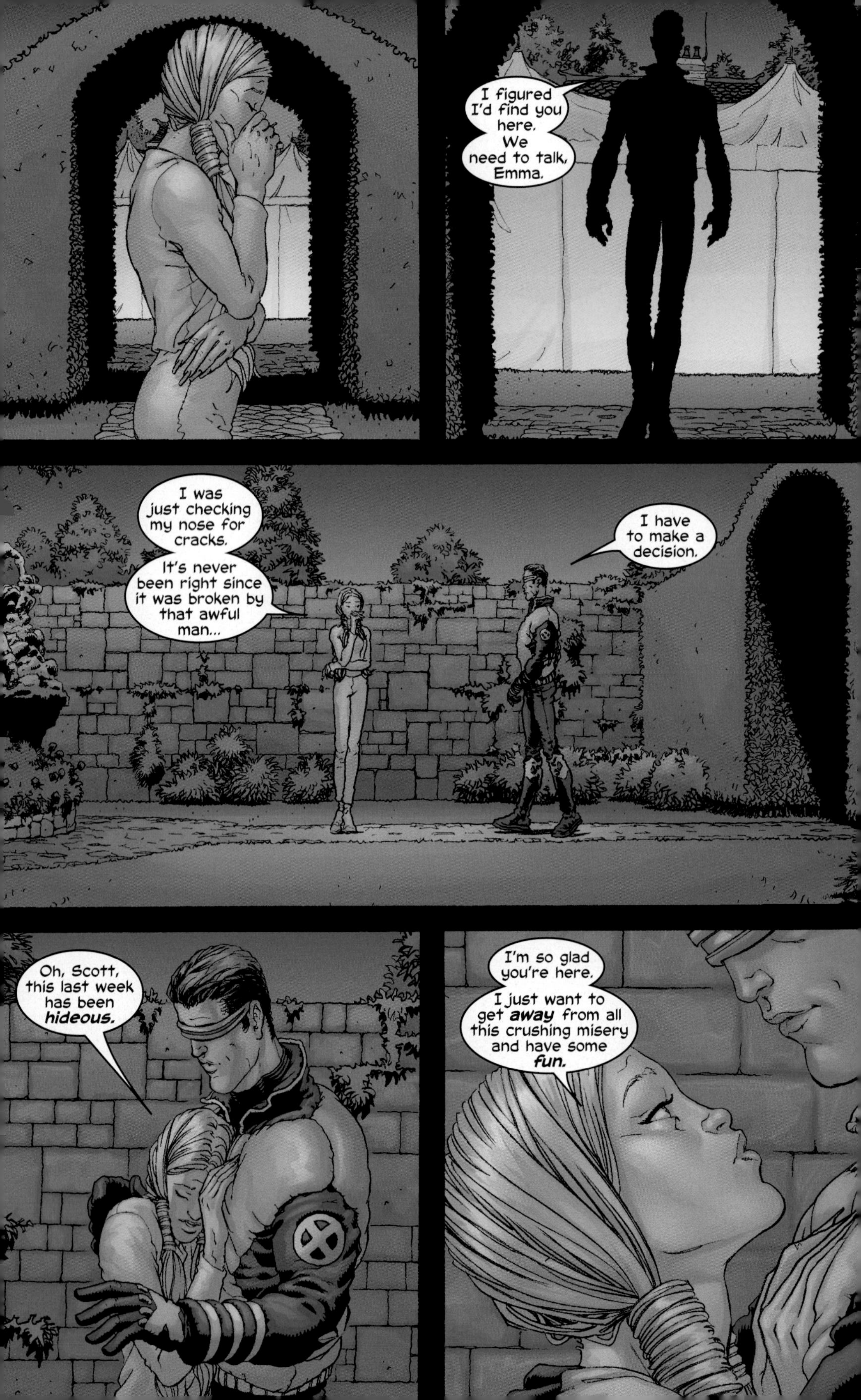
I figured I'd find you here.
We need to talk, Emma.
I was just checking my nose for cracks.
It's never been right since it was broken by that awful man...
I have to make a decision.
Oh, Scott, this last week has been ***hideous.***
I'm so glad you're here.
I just want to get ***away*** from all this crushing misery and have some ***fun.***

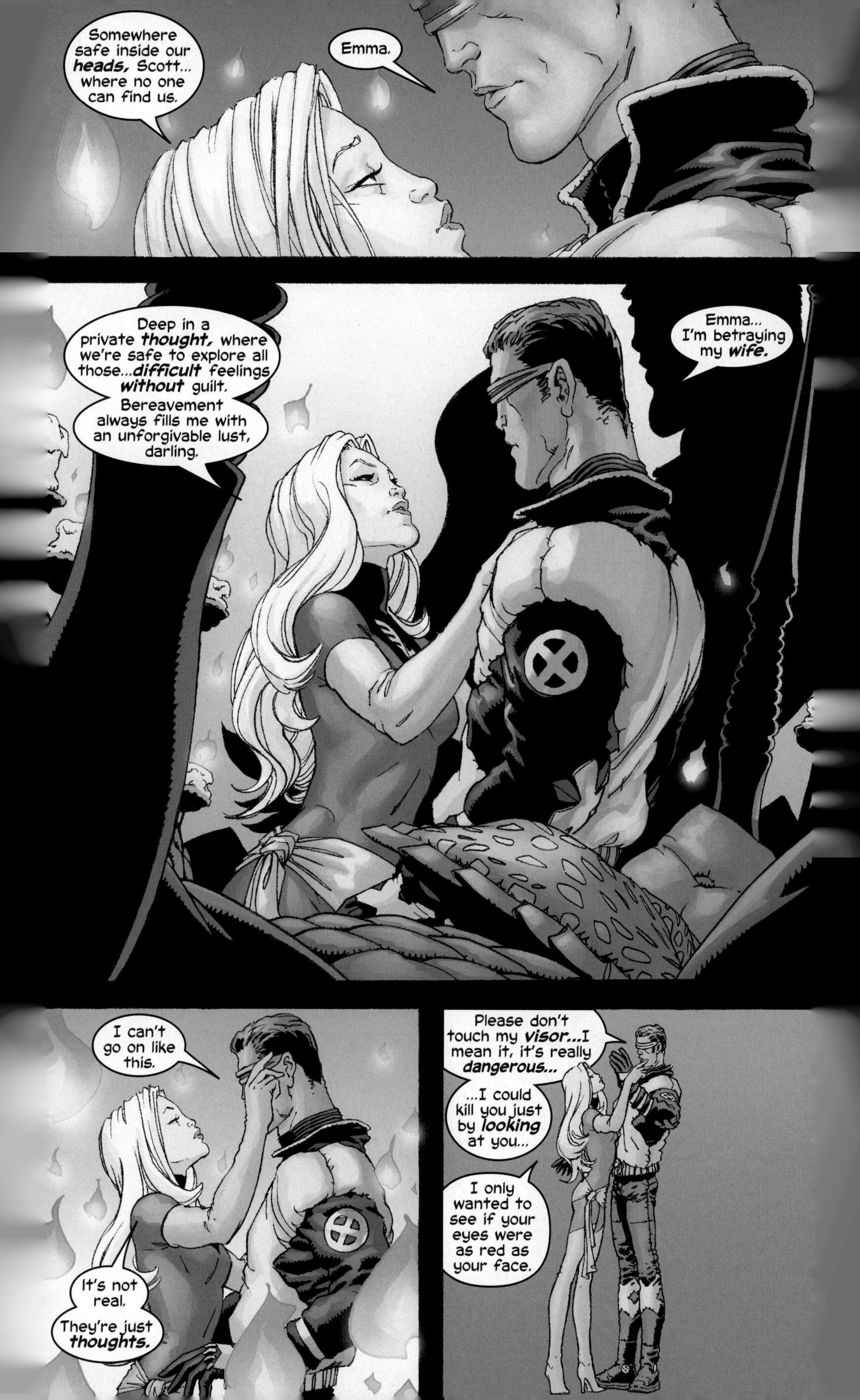
Somewhere safe inside our heads, Scott... where no one can find us.
Emma.
Deep in a private thought, where we're safe to explore all those...difficult feelings without guilt.
Bereavement always fills me with an unforgivable lust, darling.
Emma... I'm betraying my wife.
I can't go on like this.
It's not real.
They're just thoughts.
Please don't touch my visor...I mean it, it's really dangerous...
...I could kill you just by looking at you...
I only wanted to see if your eyes were as red as your face.

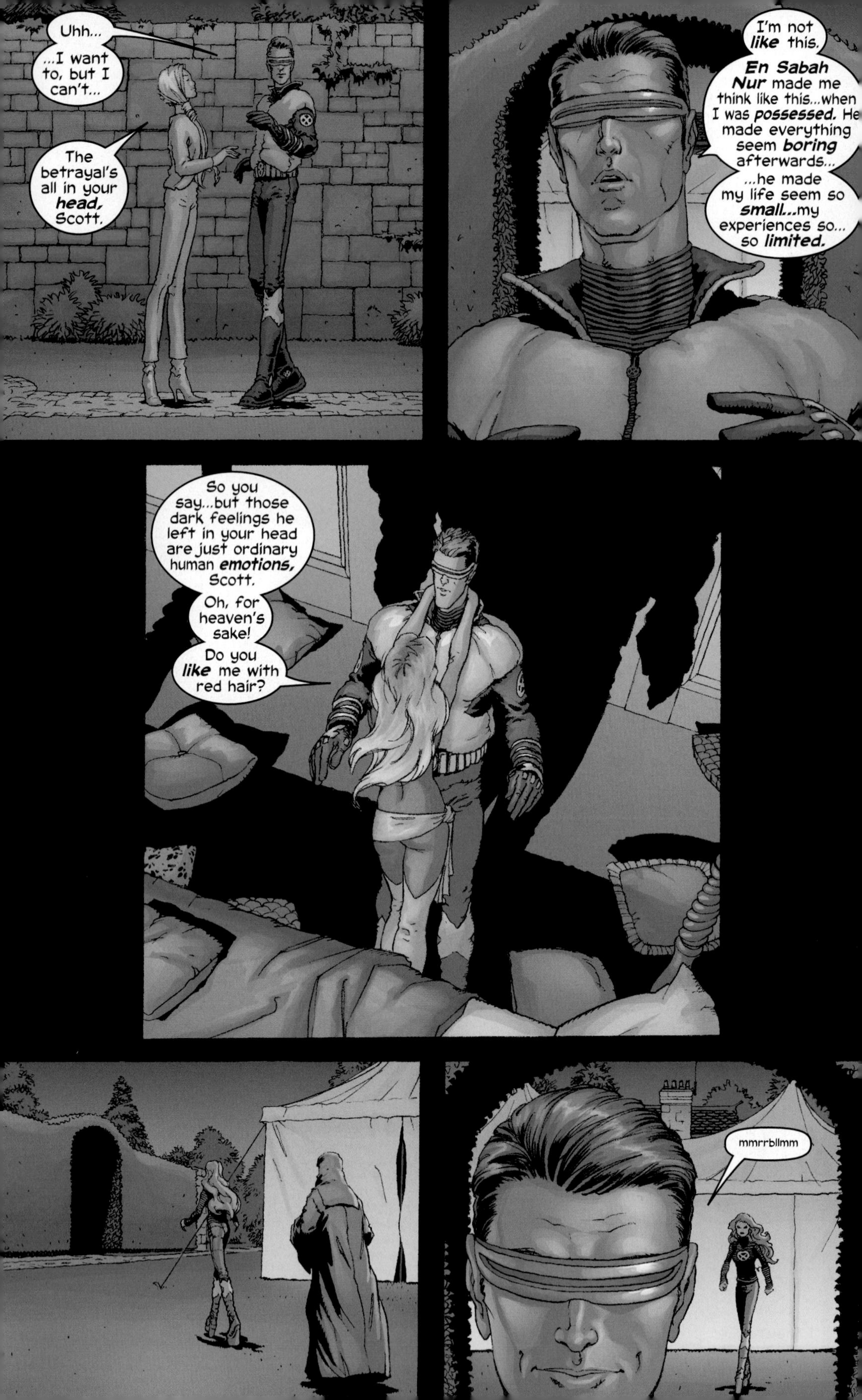

Uhh...
...I want to, but I can't...
The betrayal's all in your head, Scott.
I'm not like this.
En Sabah Nur made me think like this...when I was possessed. He made everything seem boring afterwards...
...he made my life seem so small...my experiences so... so limited.
So you say...but those dark feelings he left in your head are just ordinary human emotions, Scott.
Oh, for heaven's sake!
Do you like me with red hair?
mmrrbllmm

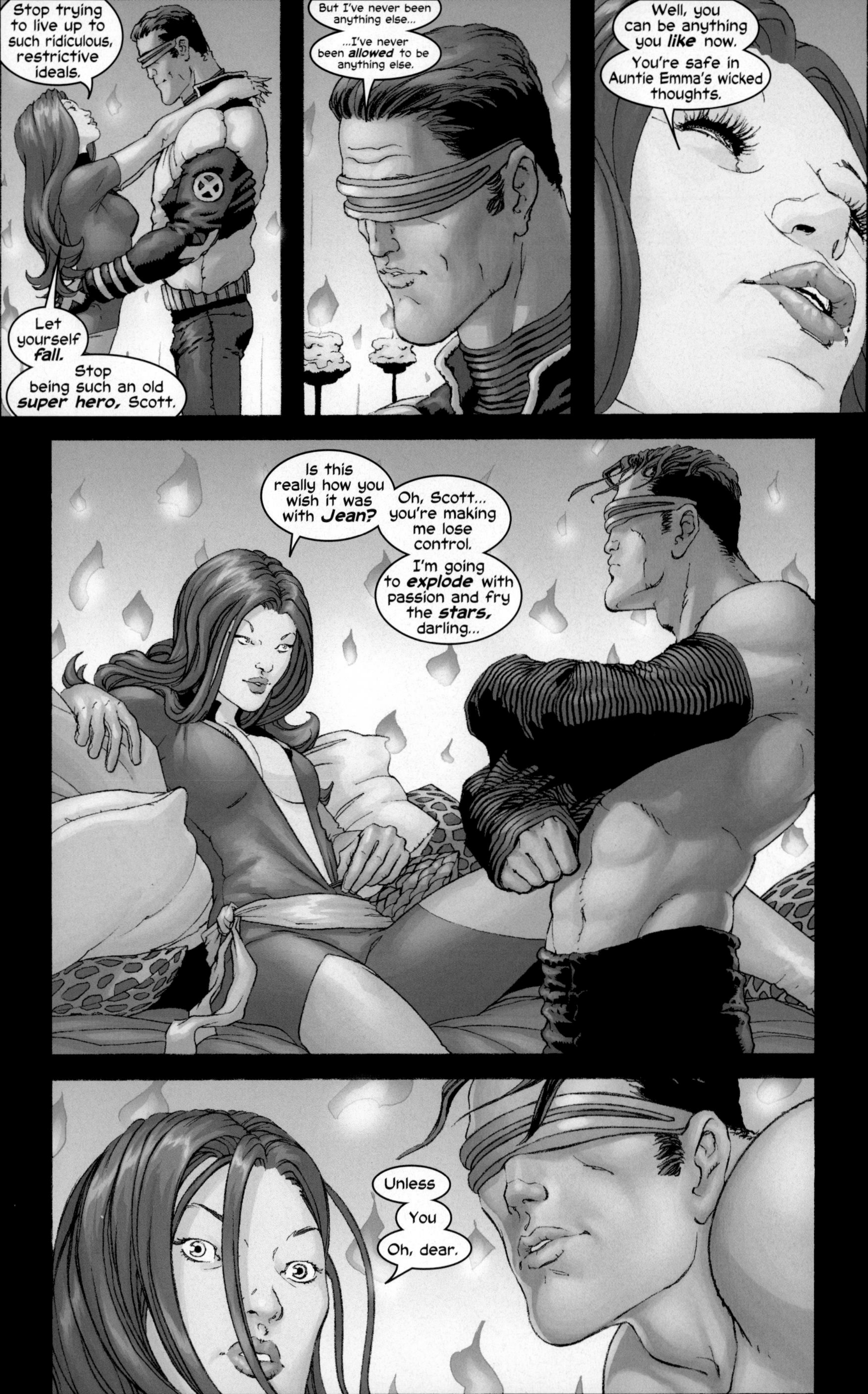
Stop trying to live up to such ridiculous, restrictive ideals.
Let yourself fall.
Stop being such an old super hero, Scott.
But I've never been anything else...
...I've never been allowed to be anything else.
Well, you can be anything you like now.
You're safe in Auntie Emma's wicked thoughts.
Is this really how you wish it was with Jean?
Oh, Scott... you're making me lose control.
I'm going to explode with passion and fry the stars, darling...
Unless
You
Oh, dear.

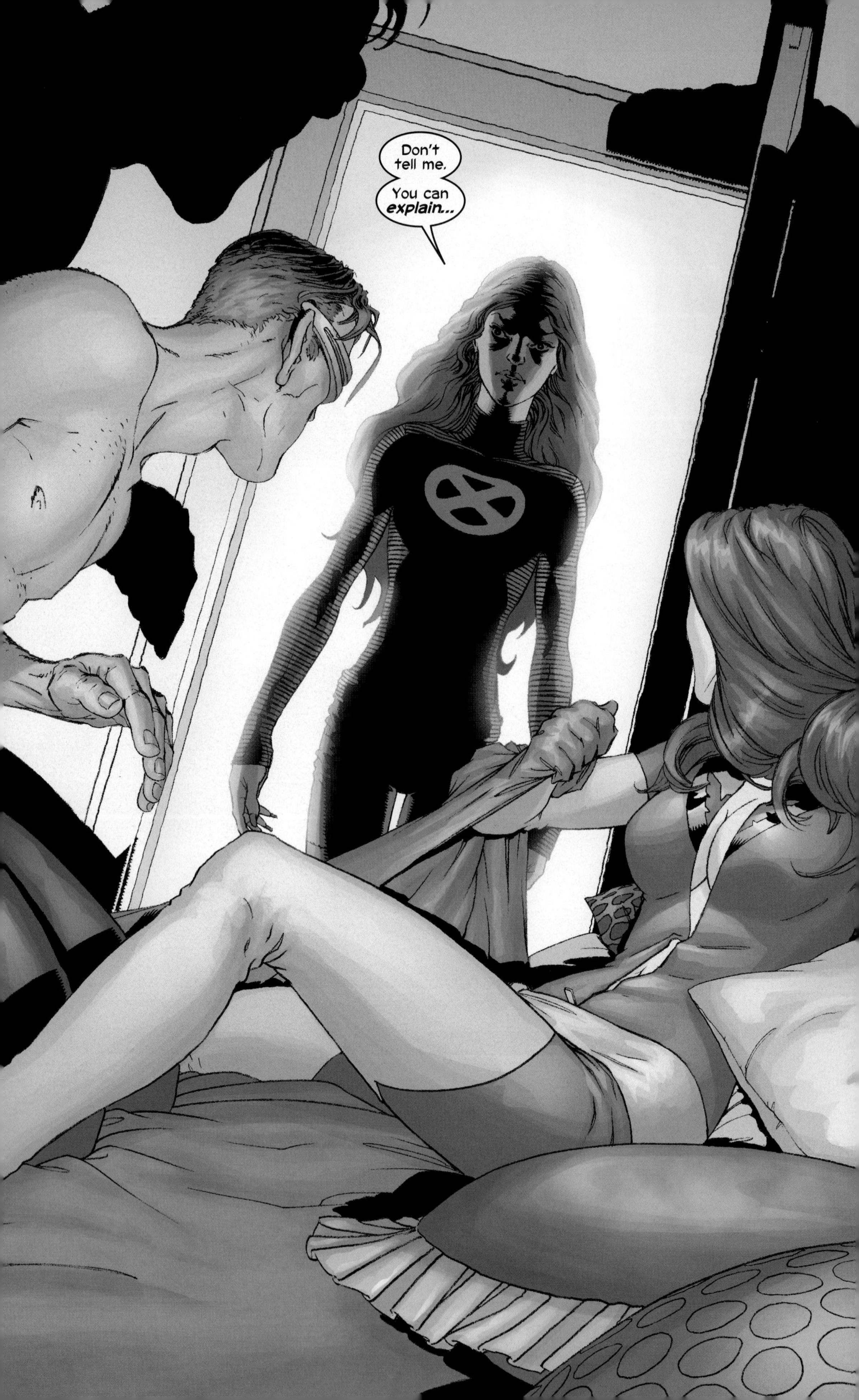
Don't tell me.
You can *explain...*

#139

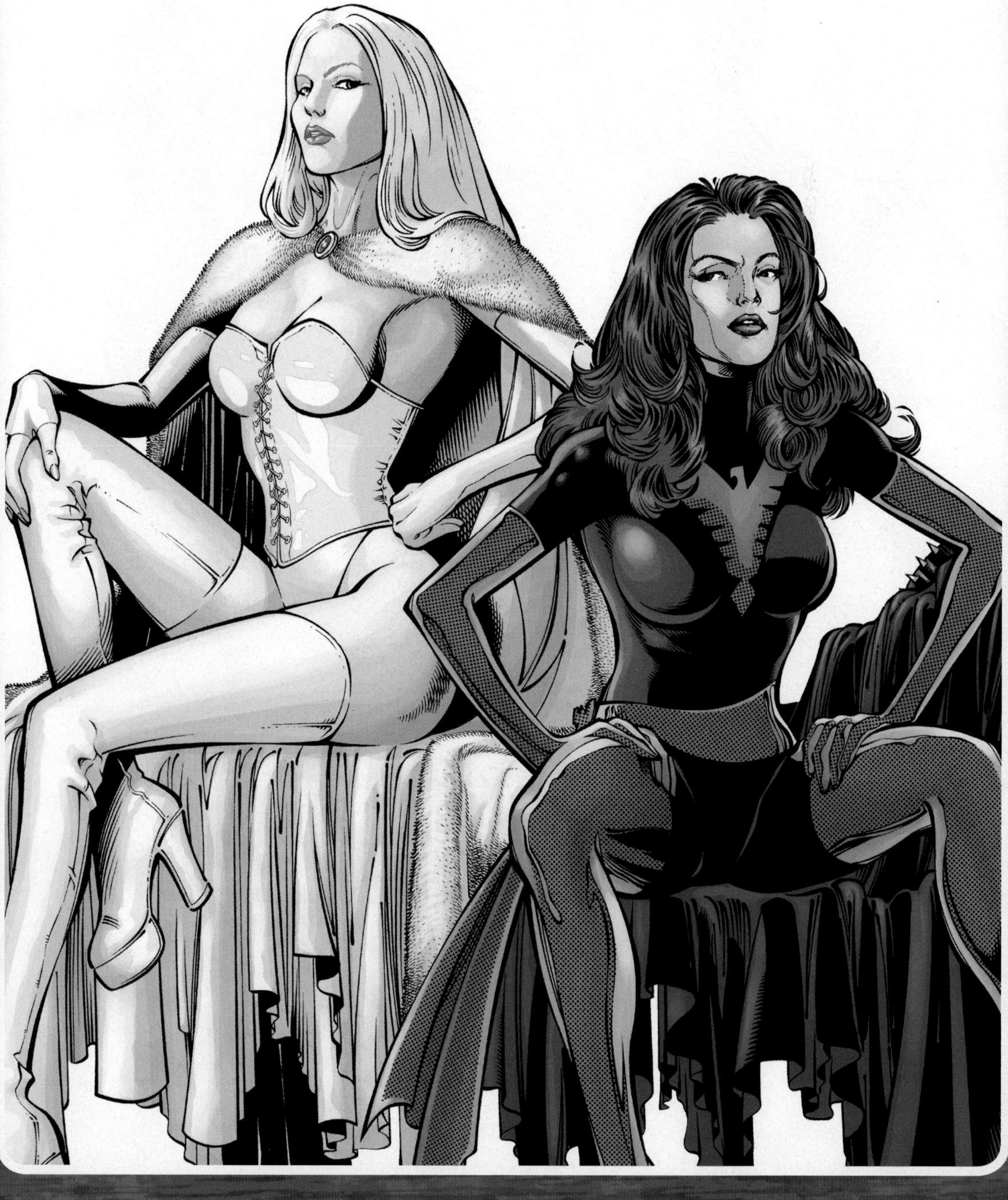

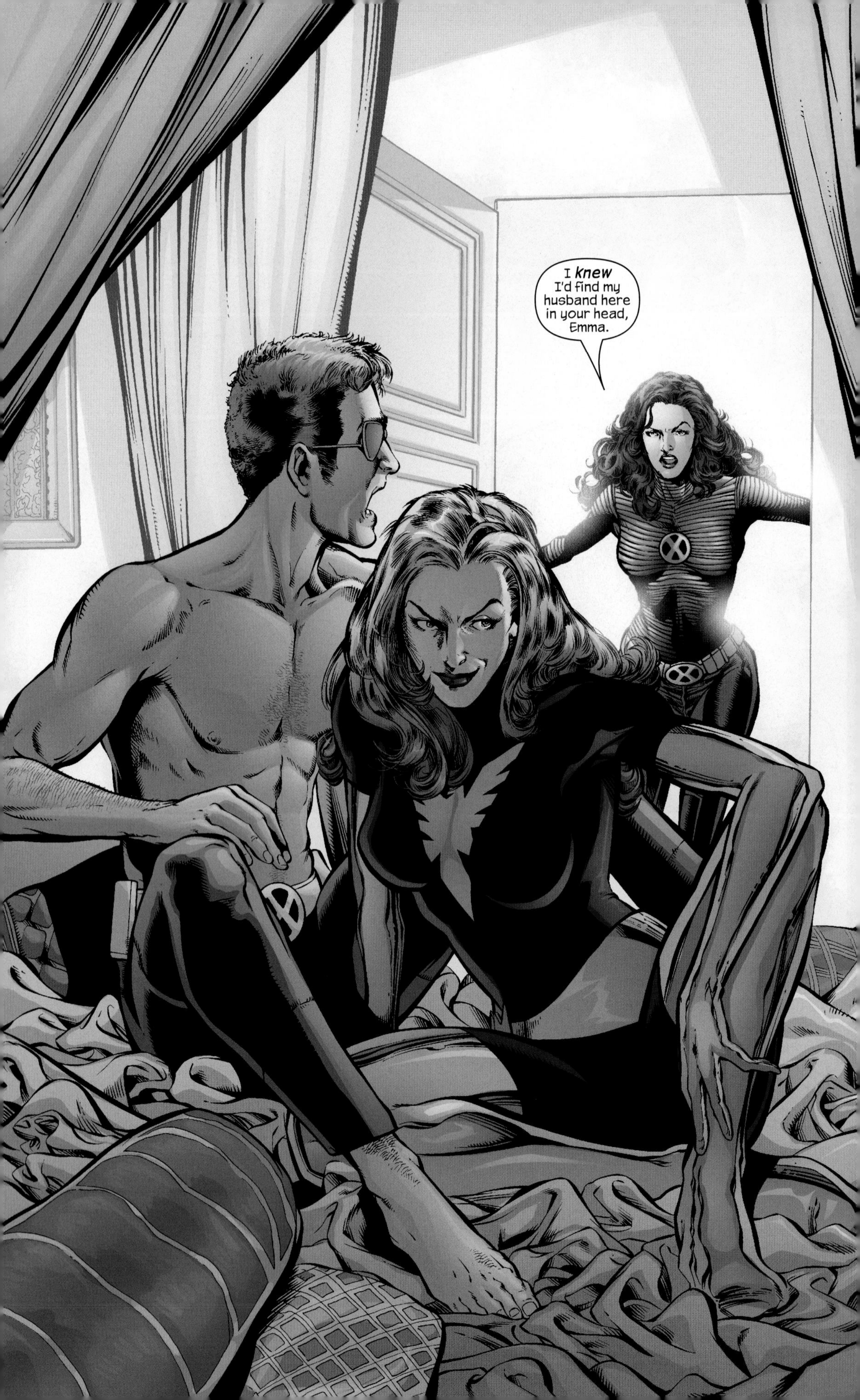
I knew I'd find my husband here in your head, Emma.

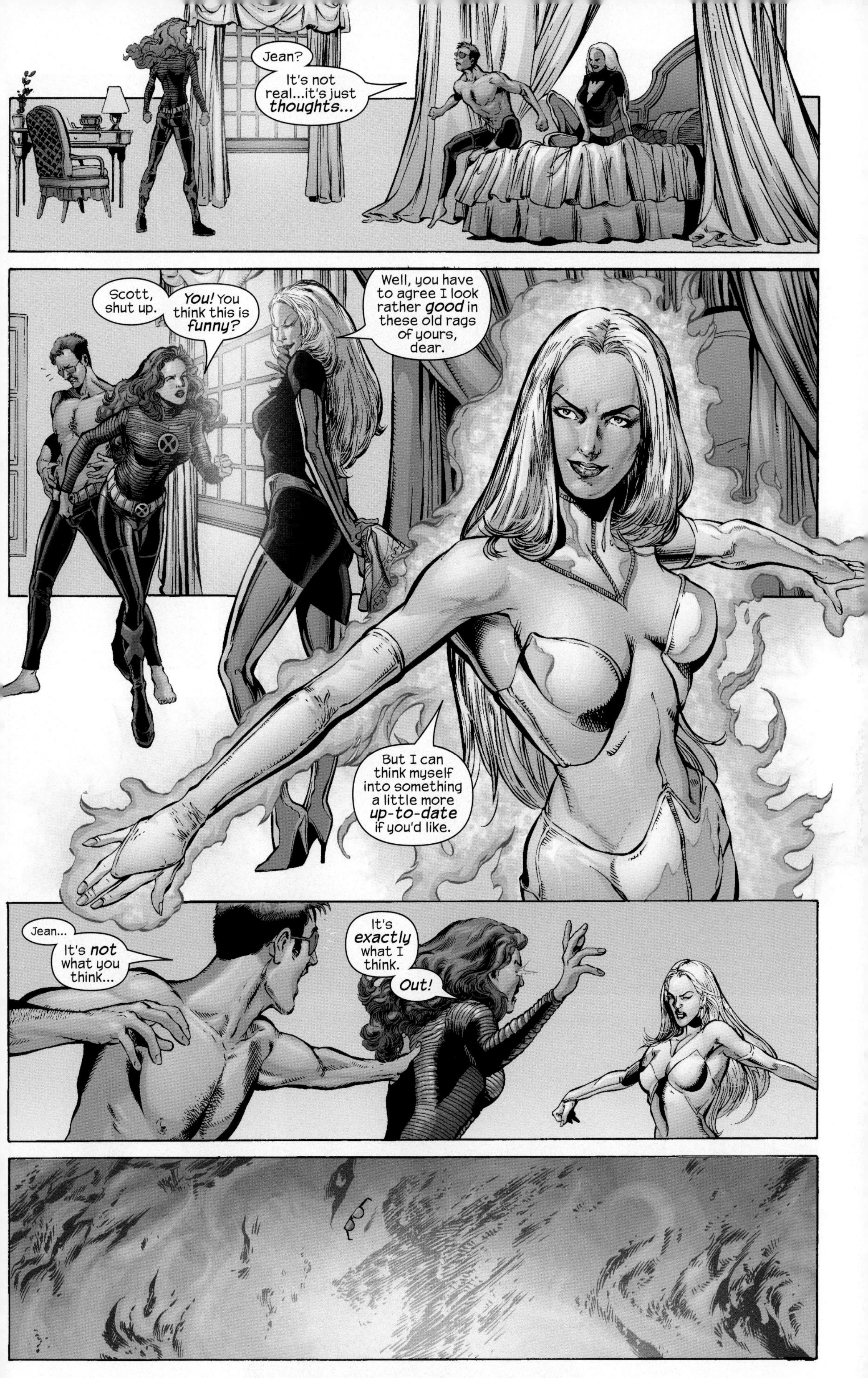
Jean?
It's not real...it's just *thoughts...*
Scott, shut up.
You! You think this is *funny?*
Well, you have to agree I look rather *good* in these old rags of yours, dear.
But I can think myself into something a little more *up-to-date* if you'd like.
Jean...
It's *not* what you think...
It's *exactly* what I think.
Out!

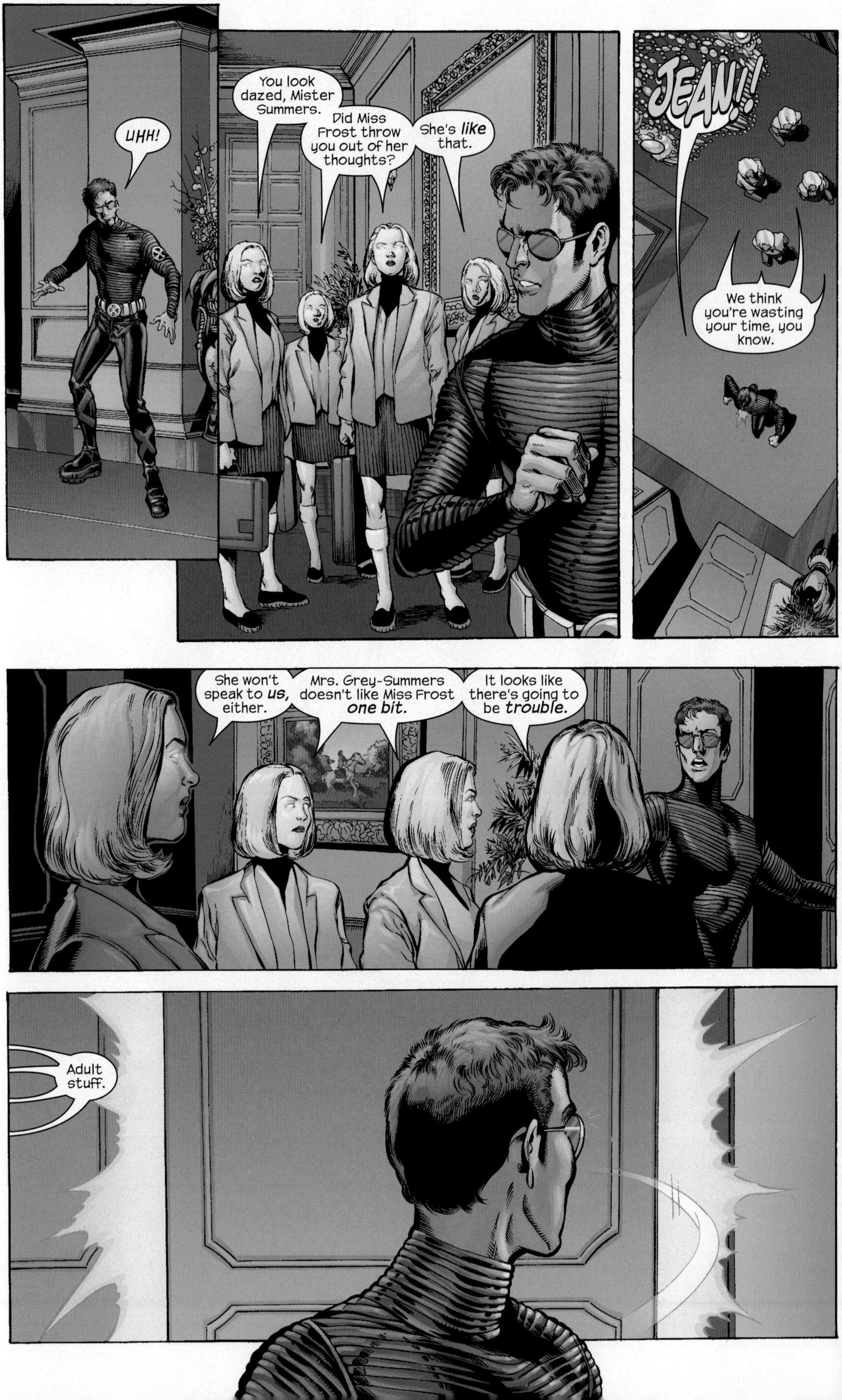
UHH!
You look dazed, Mister Summers.
Did Miss Frost throw you out of her thoughts?
She's *like* that.
JEAN!!
We think you're wasting your time, you know.
She won't speak to *us*, either.
Mrs. Grey-Summers doesn't like Miss Frost *one bit.*
It looks like there's going to be *trouble.*
Adult stuff.

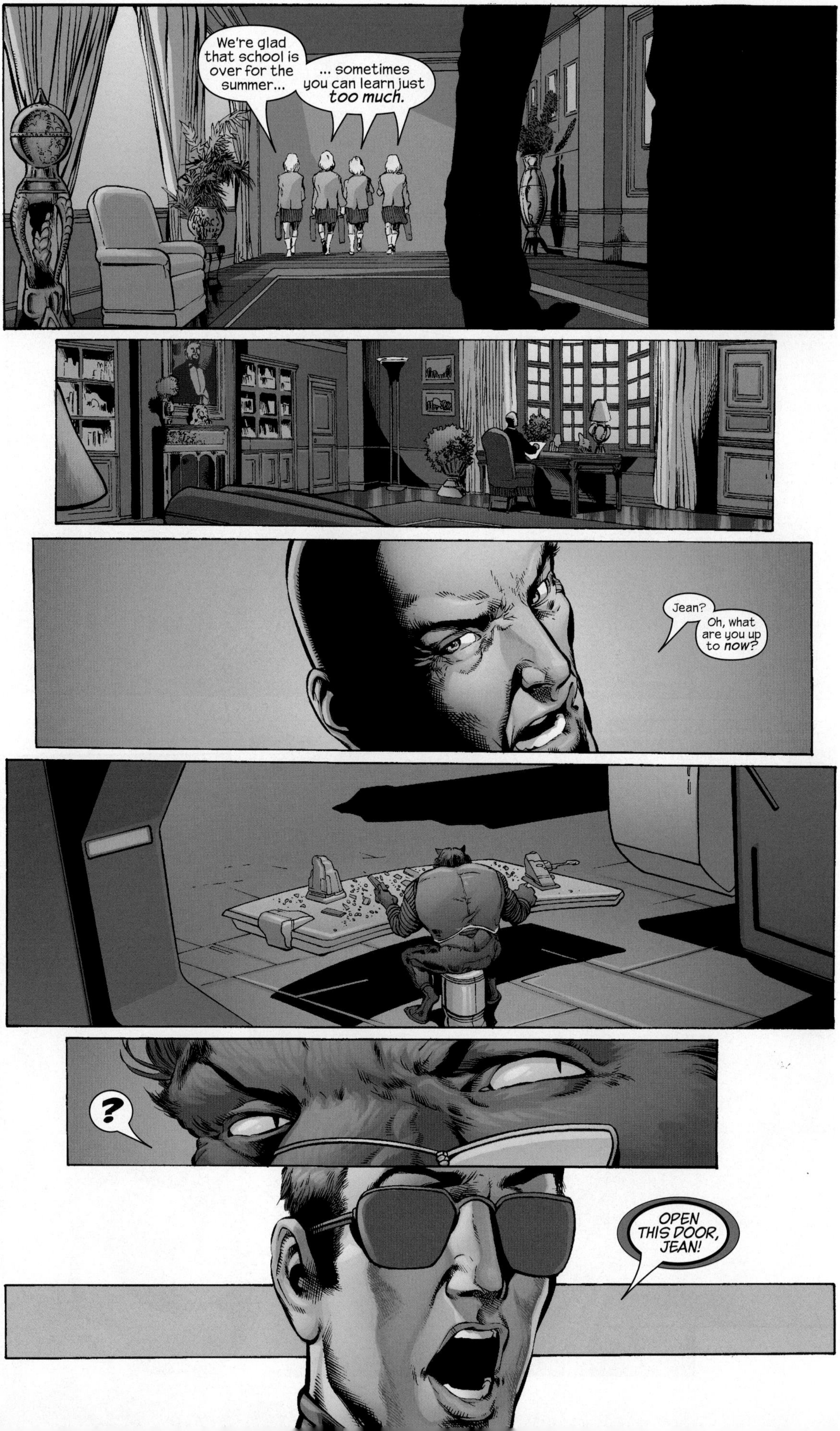

We're glad that school is over for the summer...
... sometimes you can learn just *too much.*
Jean? Oh, what are you up to *now?*
?
OPEN THIS DOOR, JEAN!

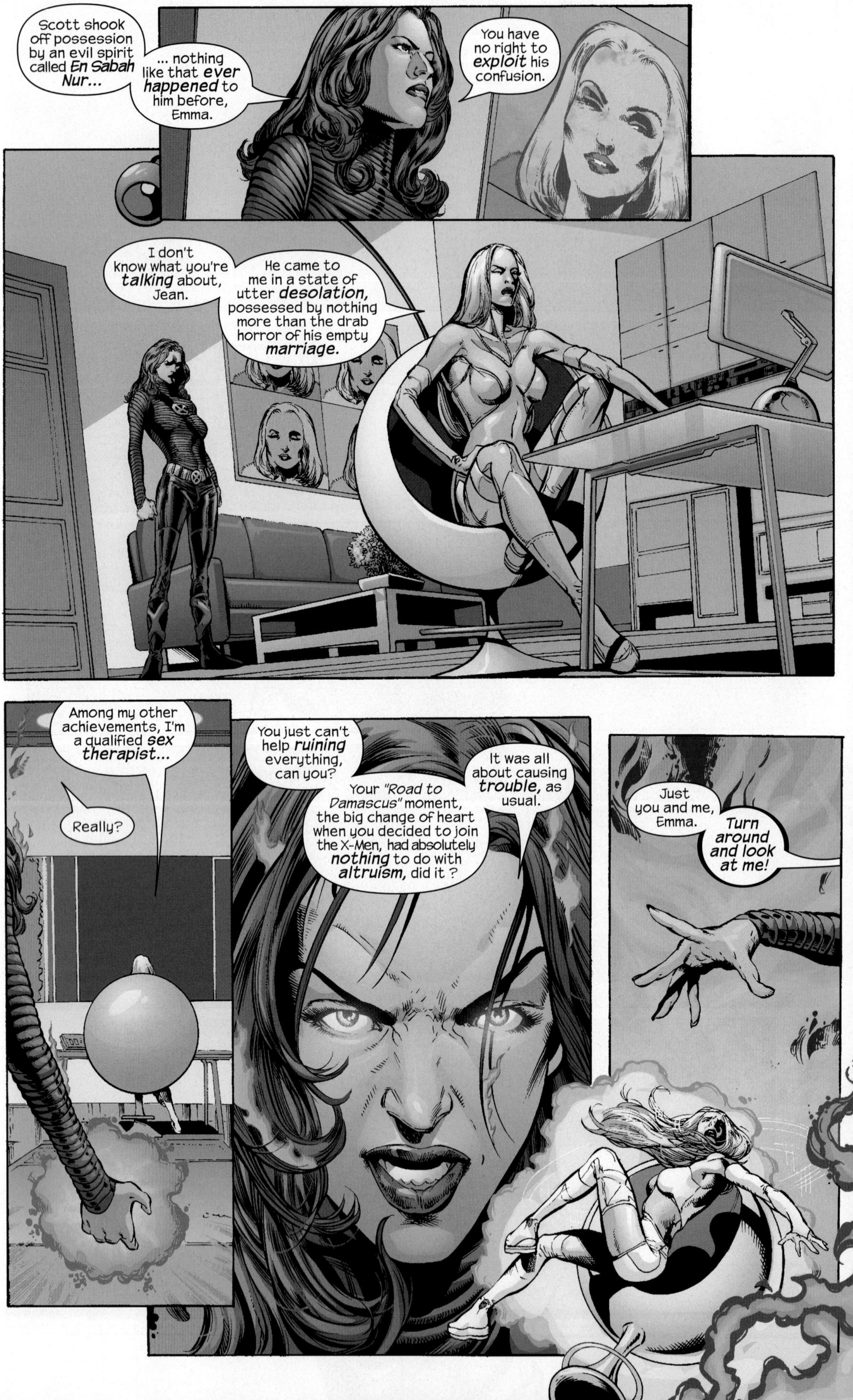
Scott shook off possession by an evil spirit called *En Sabah Nur*...
... nothing like that **ever happened** to him before, Emma.
You have no right to ***exploit*** his confusion.
I don't know what you're ***talking*** about, Jean.
He came to me in a state of utter ***desolation,*** possessed by nothing more than the drab horror of his empty ***marriage.***
Among my other achievements, I'm a qualified ***sex therapist...***
Really?
You just can't help ***ruining*** everything, can you?
Your *"Road to Damascus"* moment, the big change of heart when you decided to join the X-Men, had absolutely ***nothing*** to do with ***altruism,*** did it ?
It was all about causing ***trouble,*** as usual.
Just you and me, Emma.
Turn around and look at me!

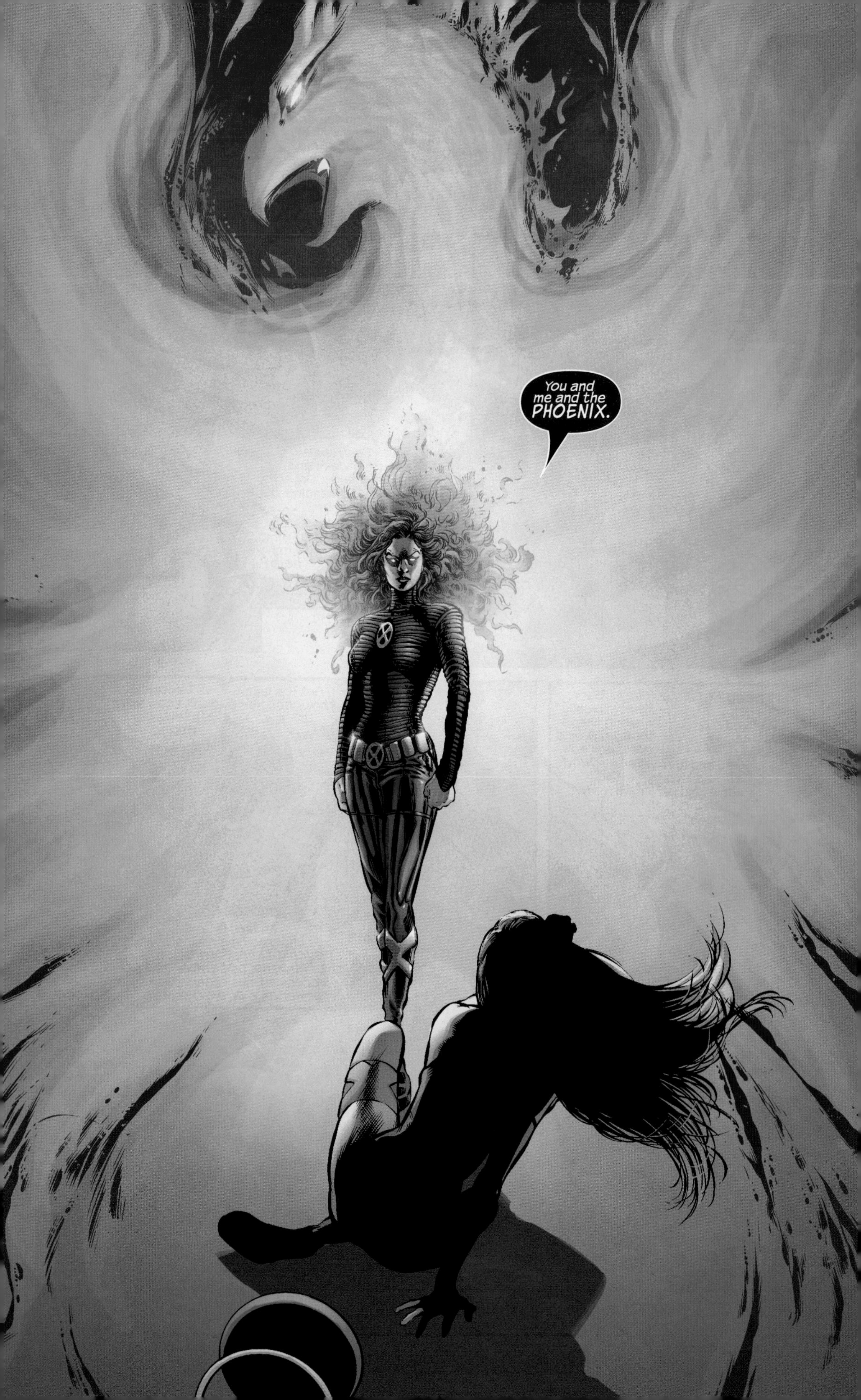
You and me and the PHOENIX.

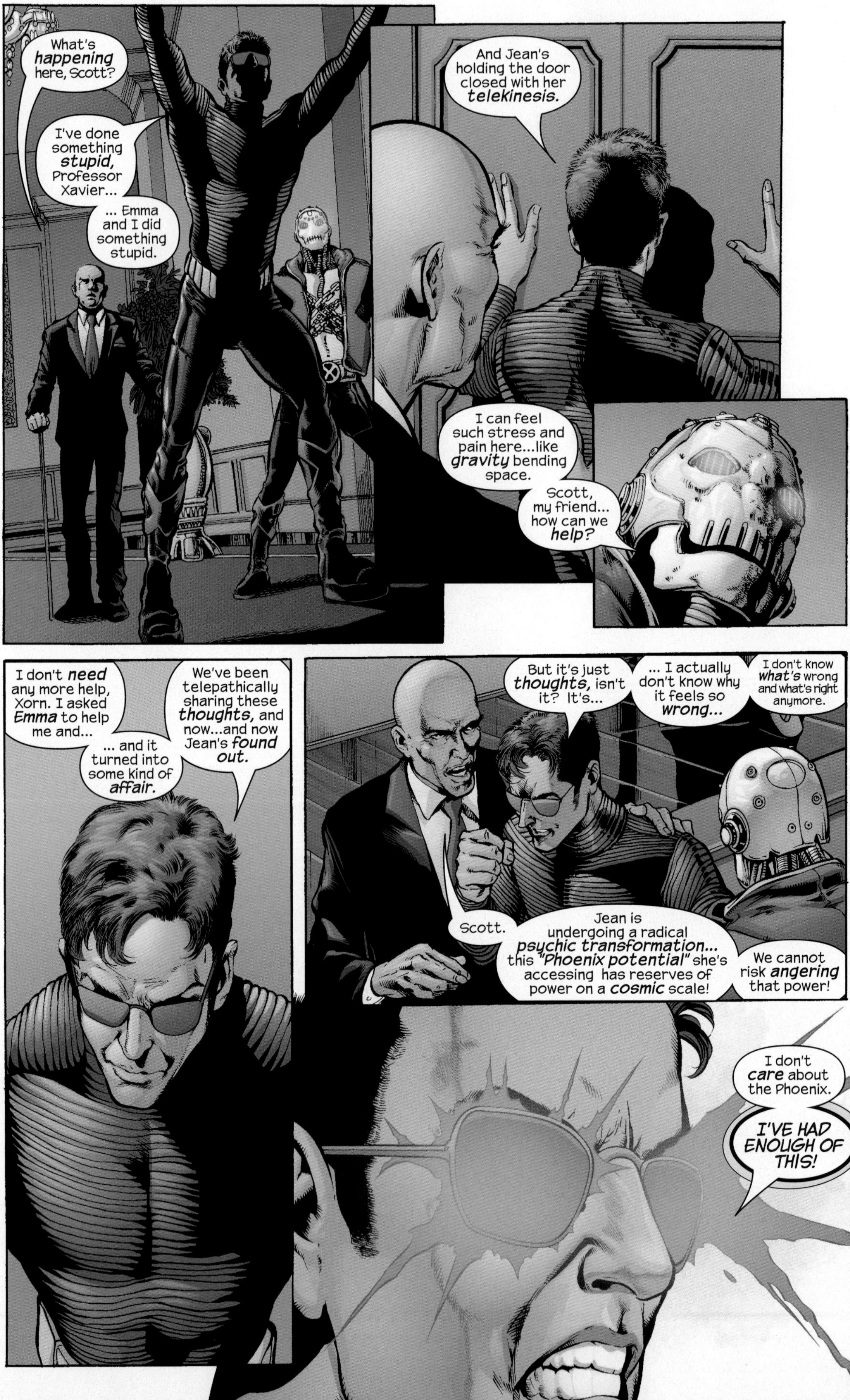
What's happening here, Scott?
I've done something stupid, Professor Xavier...
... Emma and I did something stupid.
And Jean's holding the door closed with her telekinesis.
I can feel such stress and pain here...like gravity bending space.
Scott, my friend... how can we help?
I don't need any more help, Xorn. I asked Emma to help me and...
... and it turned into some kind of affair.
We've been telepathically sharing these thoughts, and now...and now Jean's found out.
But it's just thoughts, isn't it? It's...
... I actually don't know why it feels so wrong...
I don't know what's wrong and what's right anymore.
Scott.
Jean is undergoing a radical psychic transformation... this "Phoenix potential" she's accessing has reserves of power on a cosmic scale!
We cannot risk angering that power!
I don't care about the Phoenix.
I'VE HAD ENOUGH OF THIS!

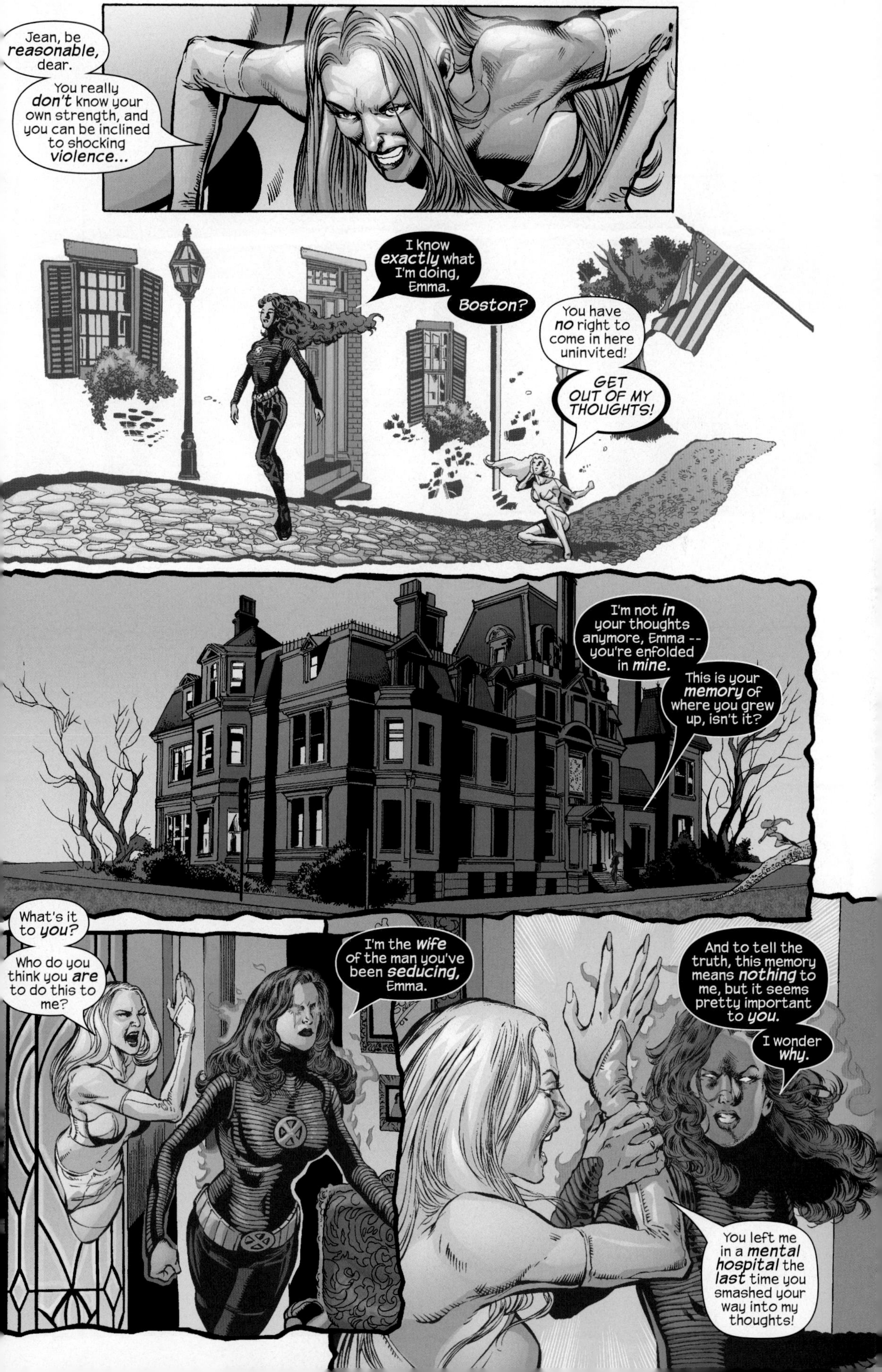
Jean, be reasonable, dear.
You really don't know your own strength, and you can be inclined to shocking violence...
I know exactly what I'm doing, Emma.
Boston?
You have no right to come in here uninvited!
GET OUT OF MY THOUGHTS!
I'm not in your thoughts anymore, Emma -- you're enfolded in mine.
This is your memory of where you grew up, isn't it?
What's it to you?
Who do you think you are to do this to me?
I'm the wife of the man you've been seducing, Emma.
And to tell the truth, this memory means nothing to me, but it seems pretty important to you.
I wonder why.
You left me in a mental hospital the last time you smashed your way into my thoughts!

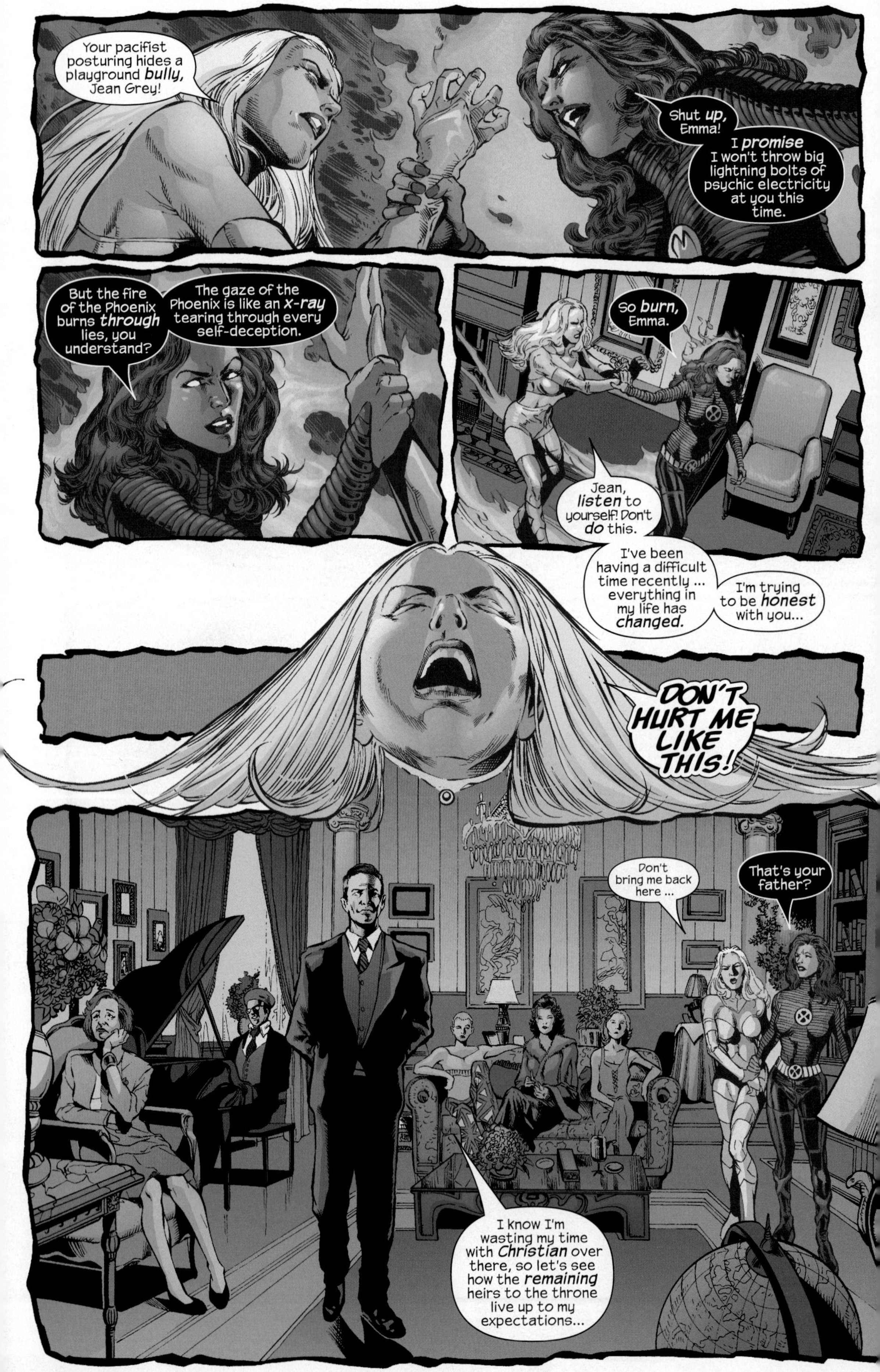
Your pacifist posturing hides a playground *bully,* Jean Grey!
Shut *up,* Emma!
I *promise* I won't throw big lightning bolts of psychic electricity at you this time.
But the fire of the Phoenix burns *through* lies, you understand?
The gaze of the Phoenix is like an *x-ray* tearing through every self-deception.
So *burn,* Emma.
Jean, *listen* to yourself! Don't *do* this.
I've been having a difficult time recently ... everything in my life has *changed.*
I'm trying to be *honest* with you...
DON'T HURT ME LIKE THIS!
Don't bring me back here ...
That's your father?
I know I'm wasting my time with *Christian* over there, so let's see how the *remaining* heirs to the throne live up to my expectations...

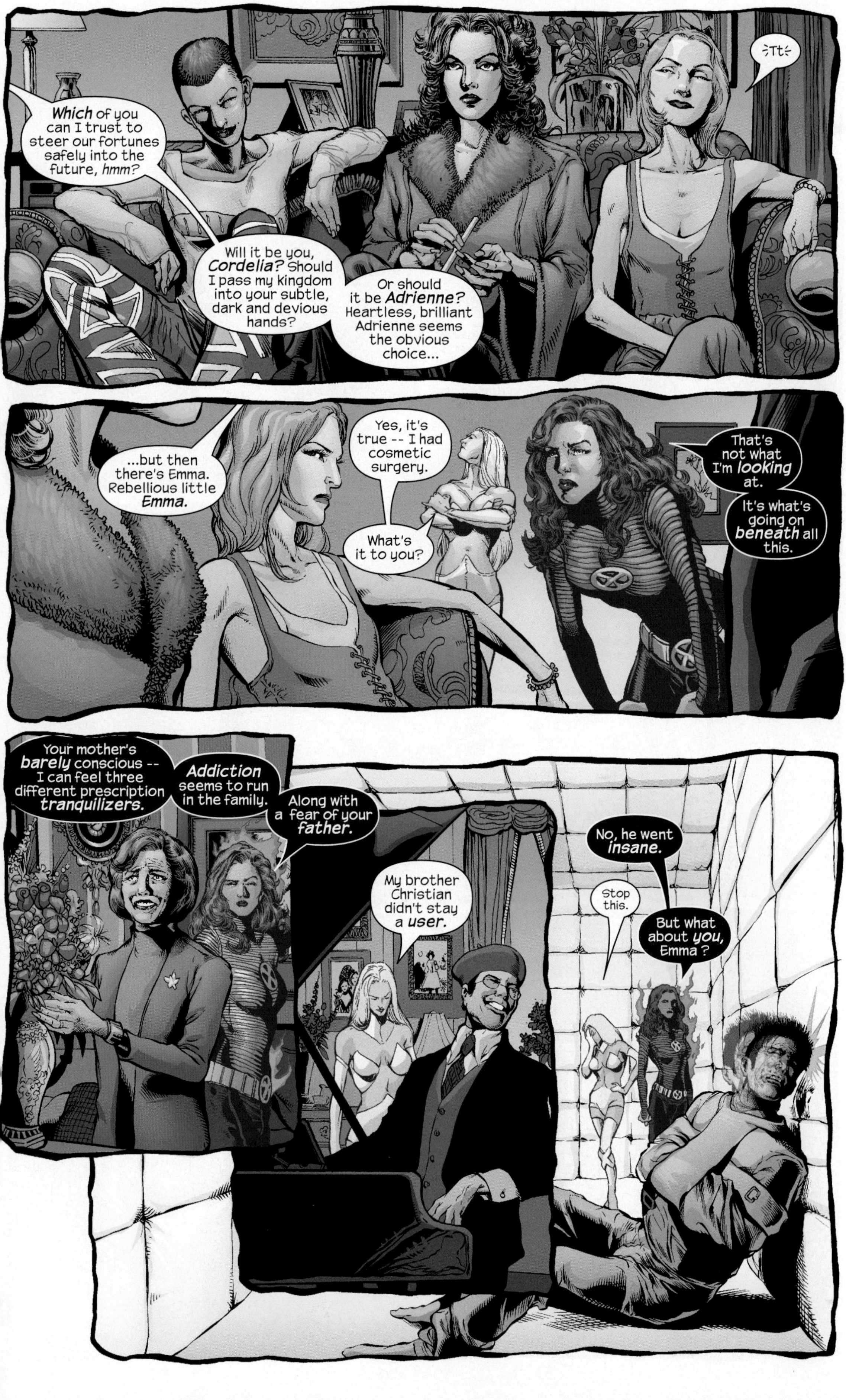
Which of you can I trust to steer our fortunes safely into the future, hmm?
Tt
Will it be you, Cordelia? Should I pass my kingdom into your subtle, dark and devious hands?
Or should it be Adrienne? Heartless, brilliant Adrienne seems the obvious choice...
...but then there's Emma. Rebellious little Emma.
Yes, it's true -- I had cosmetic surgery.
What's it to you?
That's not what I'm looking at.
It's what's going on beneath all this.
Your mother's barely conscious -- I can feel three different prescription tranquilizers.
Addiction seems to run in the family.
Along with a fear of your father.
My brother Christian didn't stay a user.
No, he went insane.
Stop this.
But what about you, Emma?

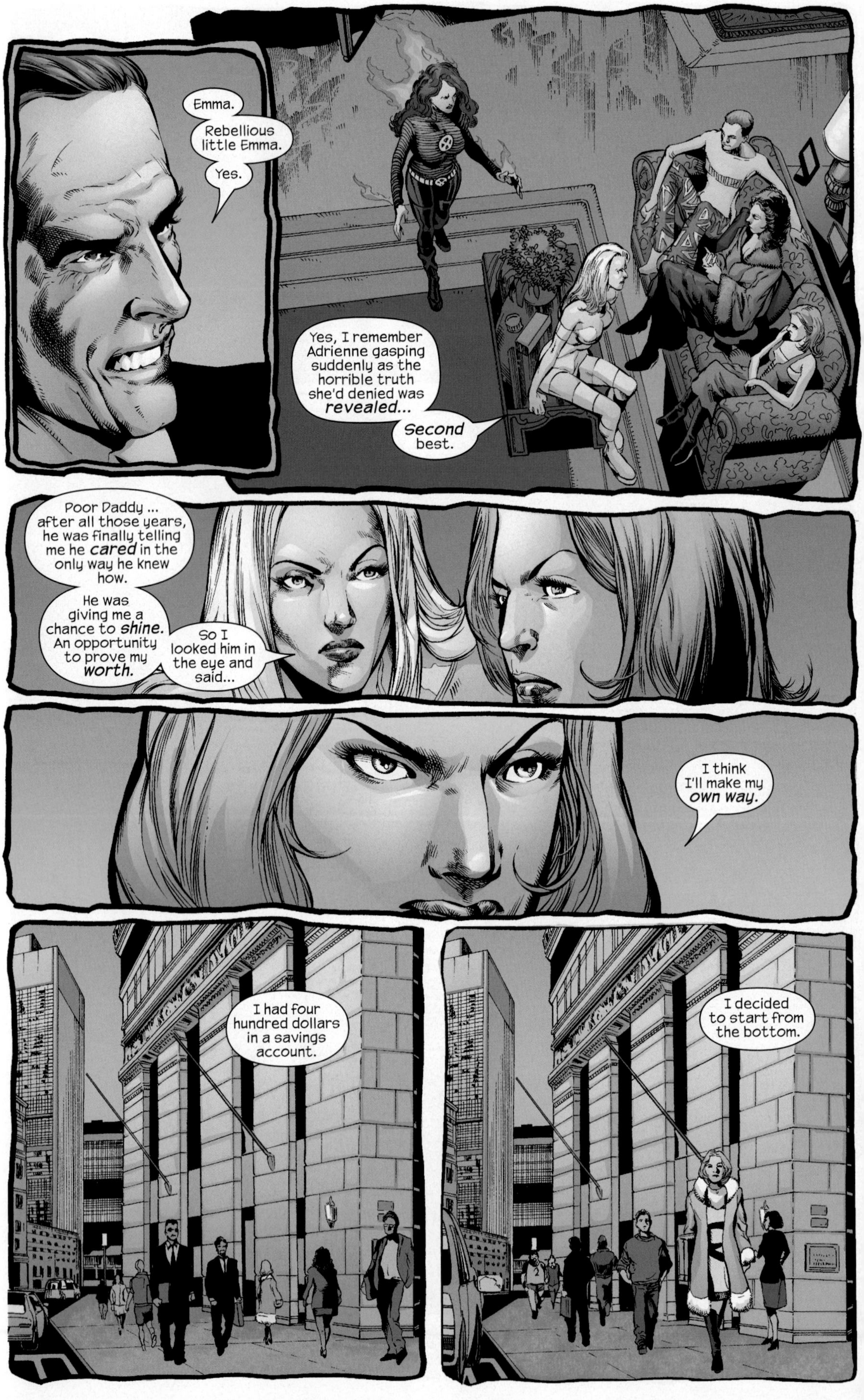
Emma.
Rebellious little Emma.
Yes.
Yes, I remember Adrienne gasping suddenly as the horrible truth she'd denied was *revealed...*
Second best.
Poor Daddy ... after all those years, he was finally telling me he *cared* in the only way he knew how.
He was giving me a chance to *shine.* An opportunity to prove my *worth.*
So I looked him in the eye and said...
I think I'll make my *own way.*
I had four hundred dollars in a savings account.
I decided to start from the bottom.

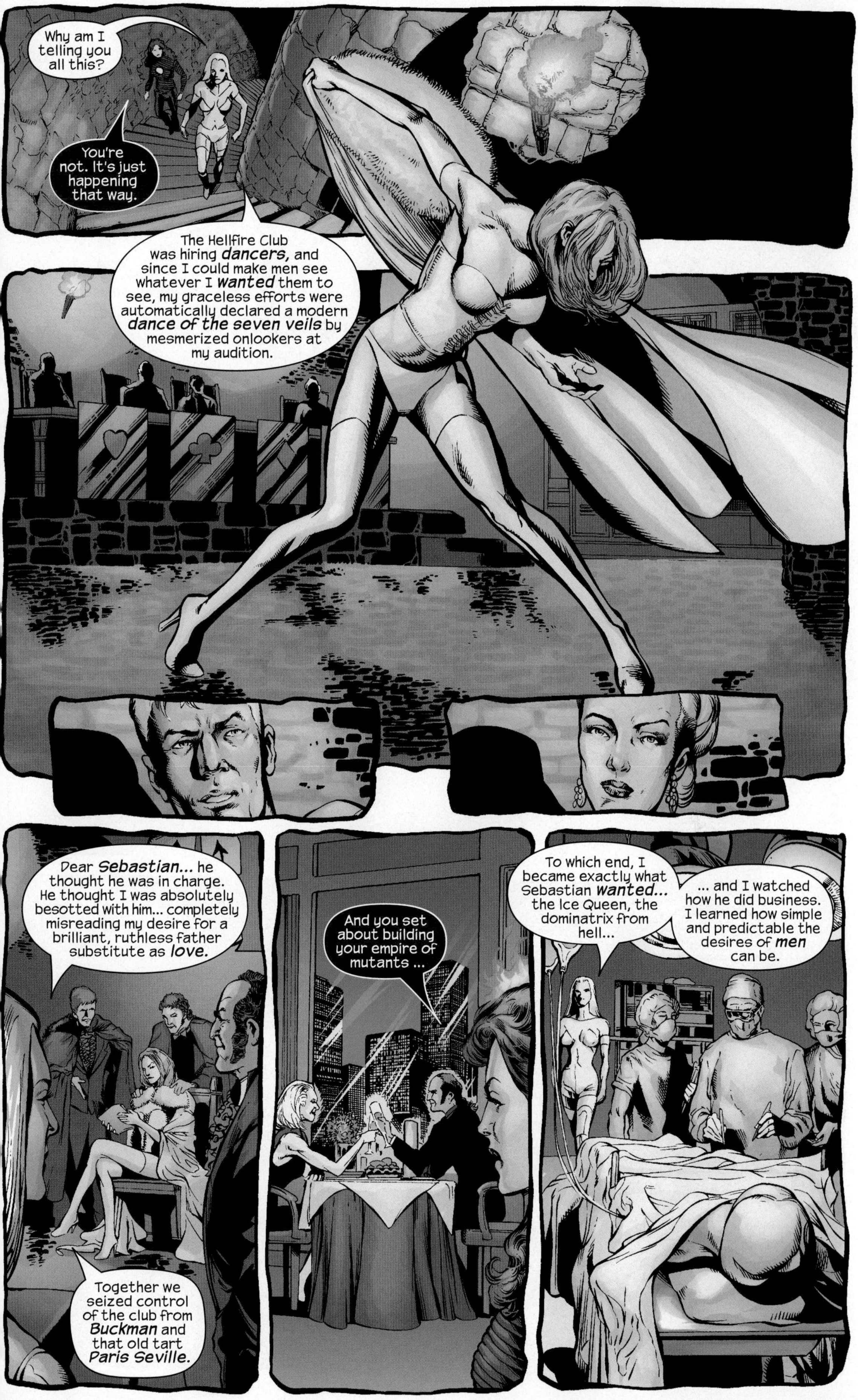
Why am I telling you all this?
You're not. It's just happening that way.
The Hellfire Club was hiring dancers, and since I could make men see whatever I wanted them to see, my graceless efforts were automatically declared a modern dance of the seven veils by mesmerized onlookers at my audition.
Dear Sebastian... he thought he was in charge. He thought I was absolutely besotted with him... completely misreading my desire for a brilliant, ruthless father substitute as love.
Together we seized control of the club from Buckman and that old tart Paris Seville.
And you set about building your empire of mutants ...
To which end, I became exactly what Sebastian wanted... the Ice Queen, the dominatrix from hell...
... and I watched how he did business. I learned how simple and predictable the desires of men can be.

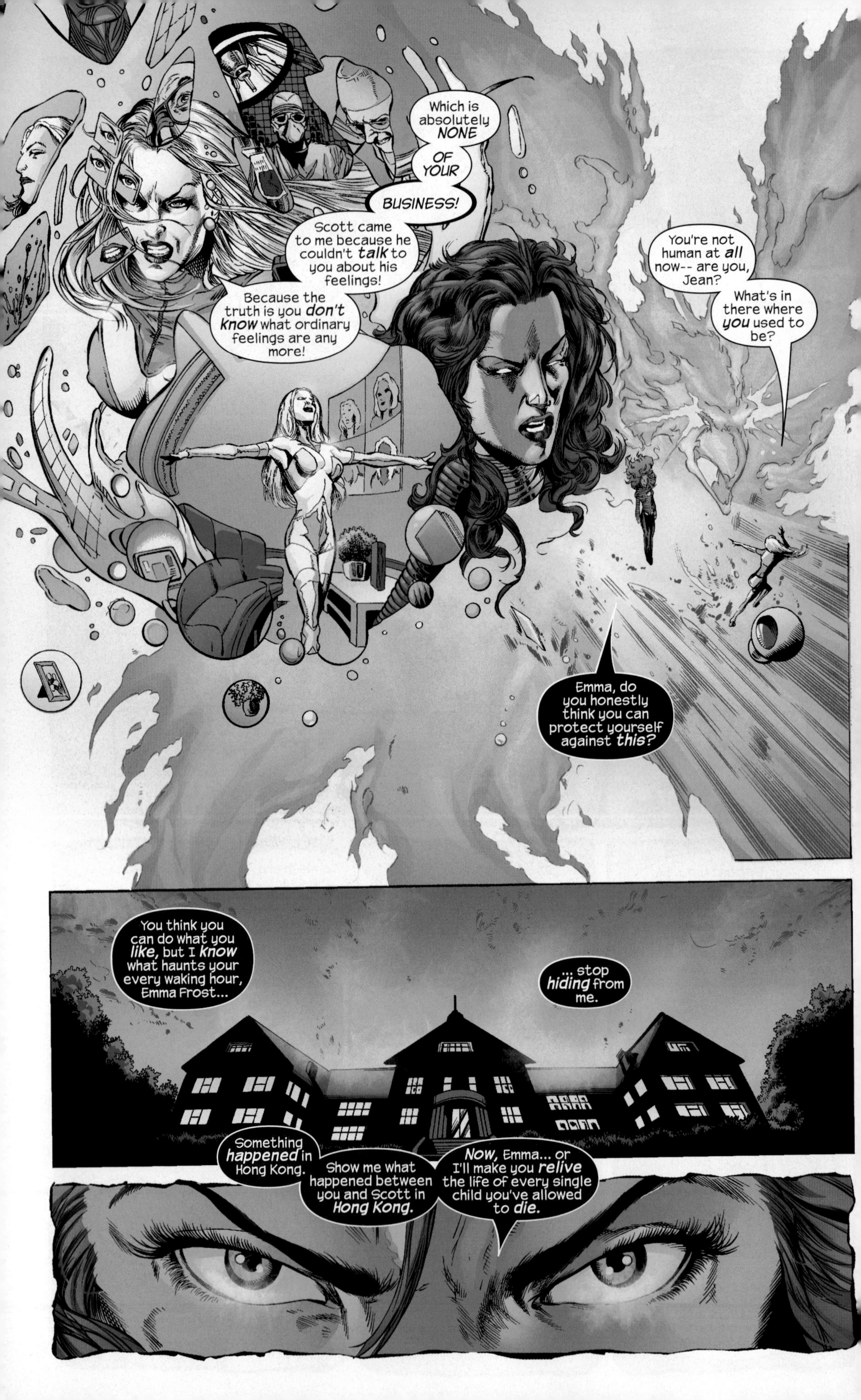
Which is absolutely NONE OF YOUR BUSINESS!
Scott came to me because he couldn't talk to you about his feelings!
Because the truth is you don't know what ordinary feelings are any more!
You're not human at all now-- are you, Jean?
What's in there where you used to be?
Emma, do you honestly think you can protect yourself against this?
You think you can do what you like, but I know what haunts your every waking hour, Emma Frost...
... stop hiding from me.
Something happened in Hong Kong.
Show me what happened between you and Scott in Hong Kong.
Now, Emma... or I'll make you relive the life of every single child you've allowed to die.

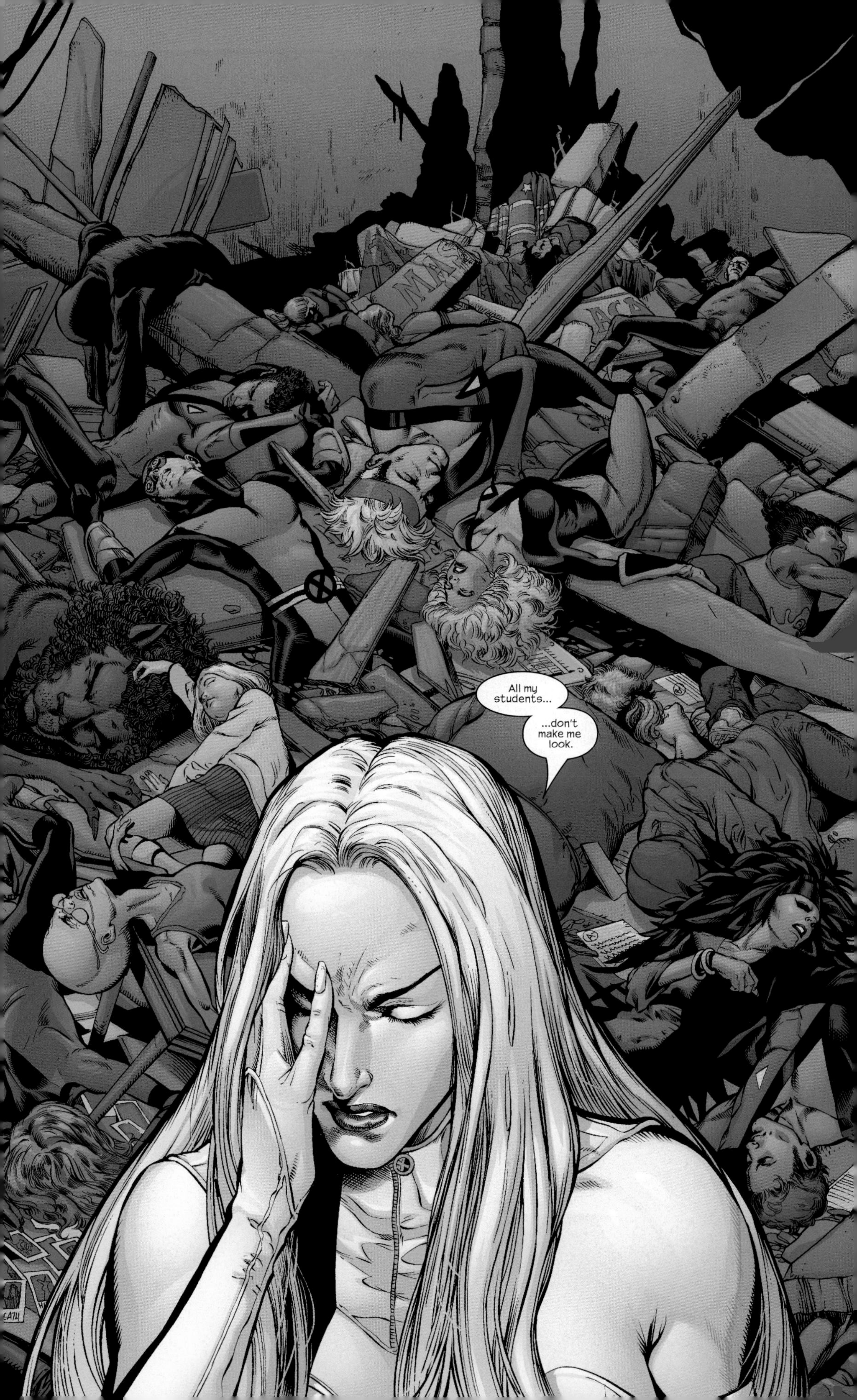
All my students...
...don't make me look.

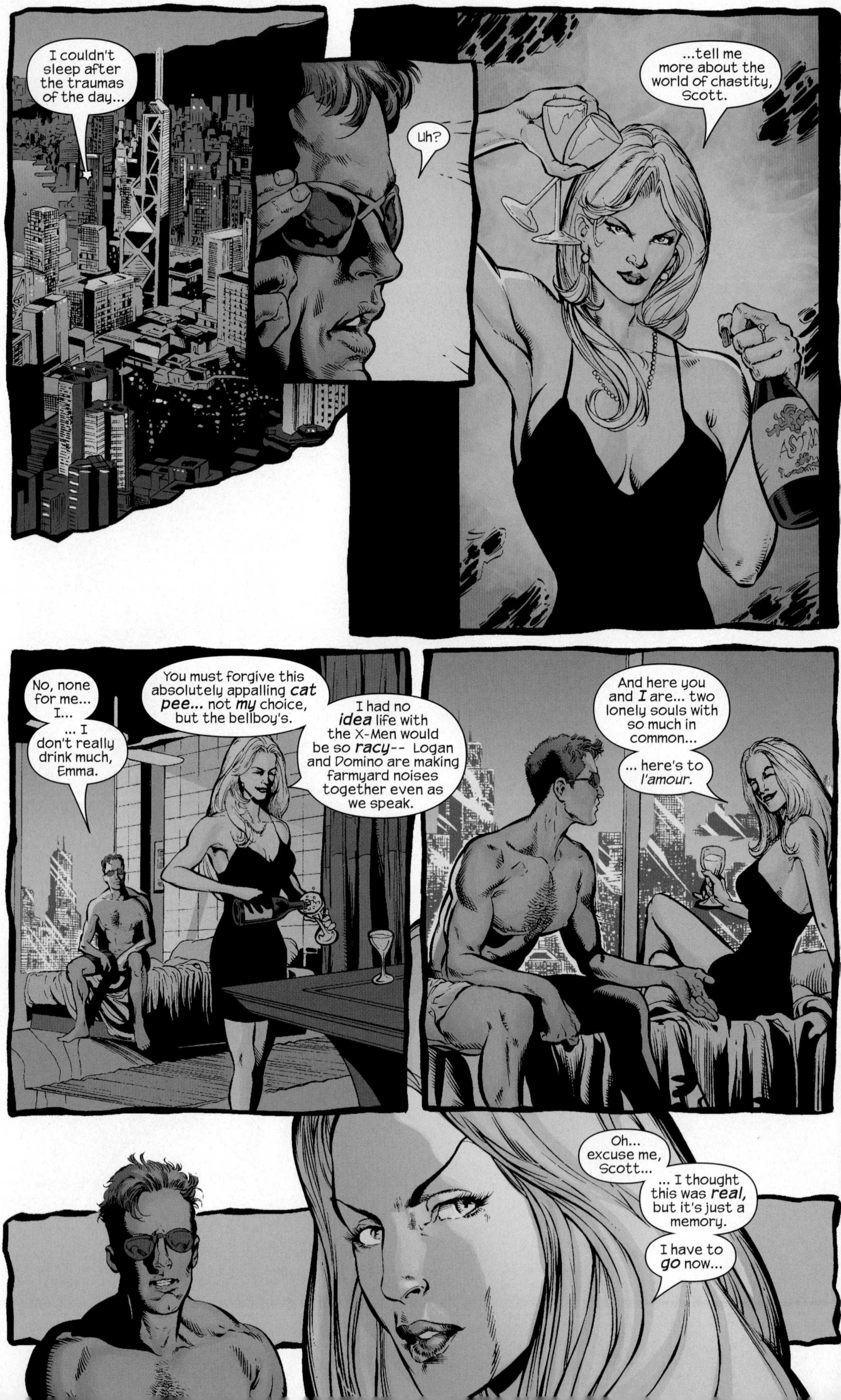
I couldn't sleep after the traumas of the day...
Uh?
...tell me more about the world of chastity, Scott.
No, none for me... I...
... I don't really drink much, Emma.
You must forgive this absolutely appalling cat pee... not my choice, but the bellboy's.
I had no idea life with the X-Men would be so racy-- Logan and Domino are making farmyard noises together even as we speak.
And here you and I are... two lonely souls with so much in common...
... here's to l'amour.
Oh... excuse me, Scott...
... I thought this was real, but it's just a memory.
I have to go now...

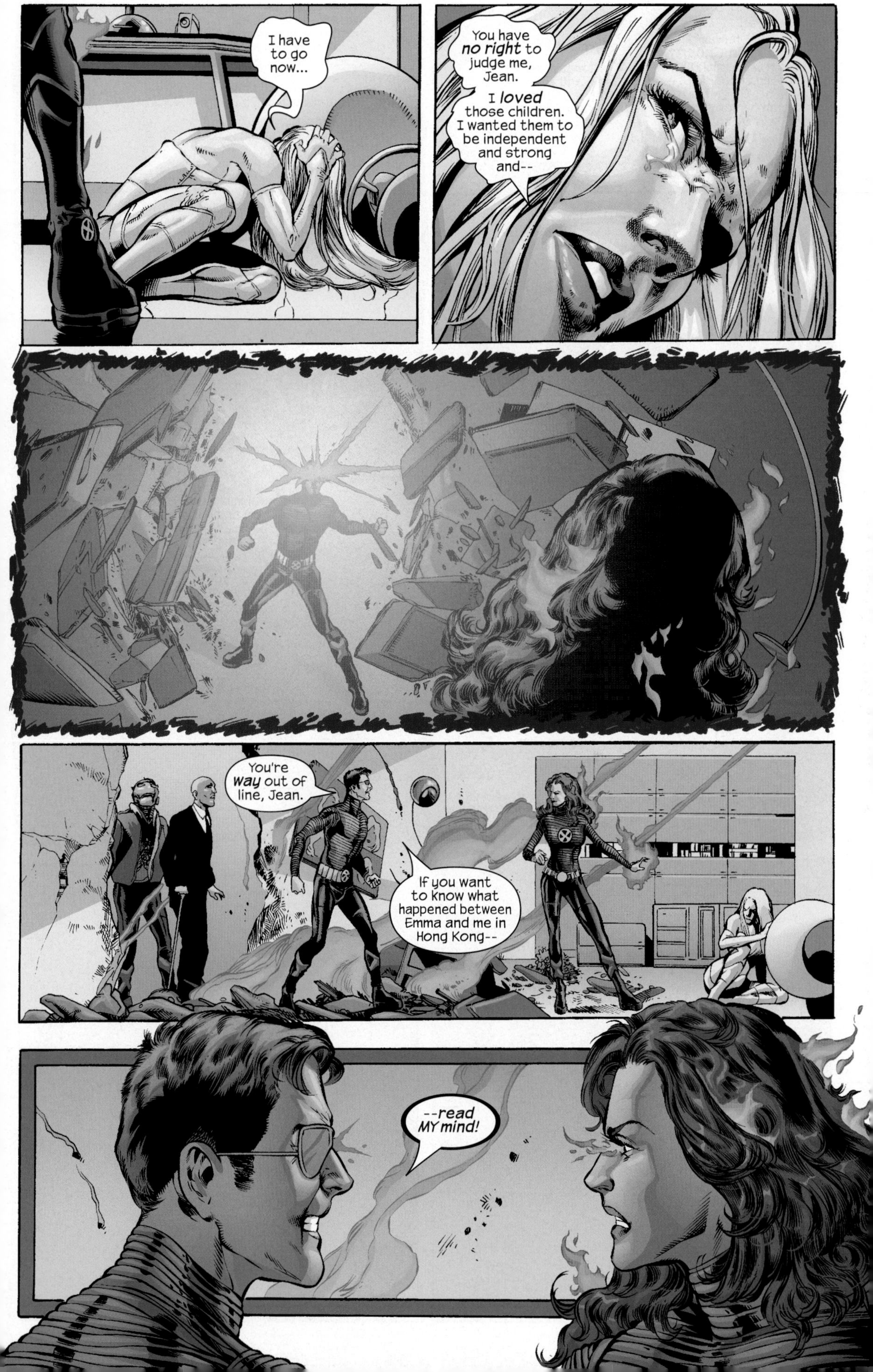

I have to go now...
You have *no right* to judge me, Jean.
I *loved* those children. I wanted them to be independent and strong and--
You're *way* out of line, Jean.
If you want to know what happened between Emma and me in Hong Kong--
--*read MY mind!*

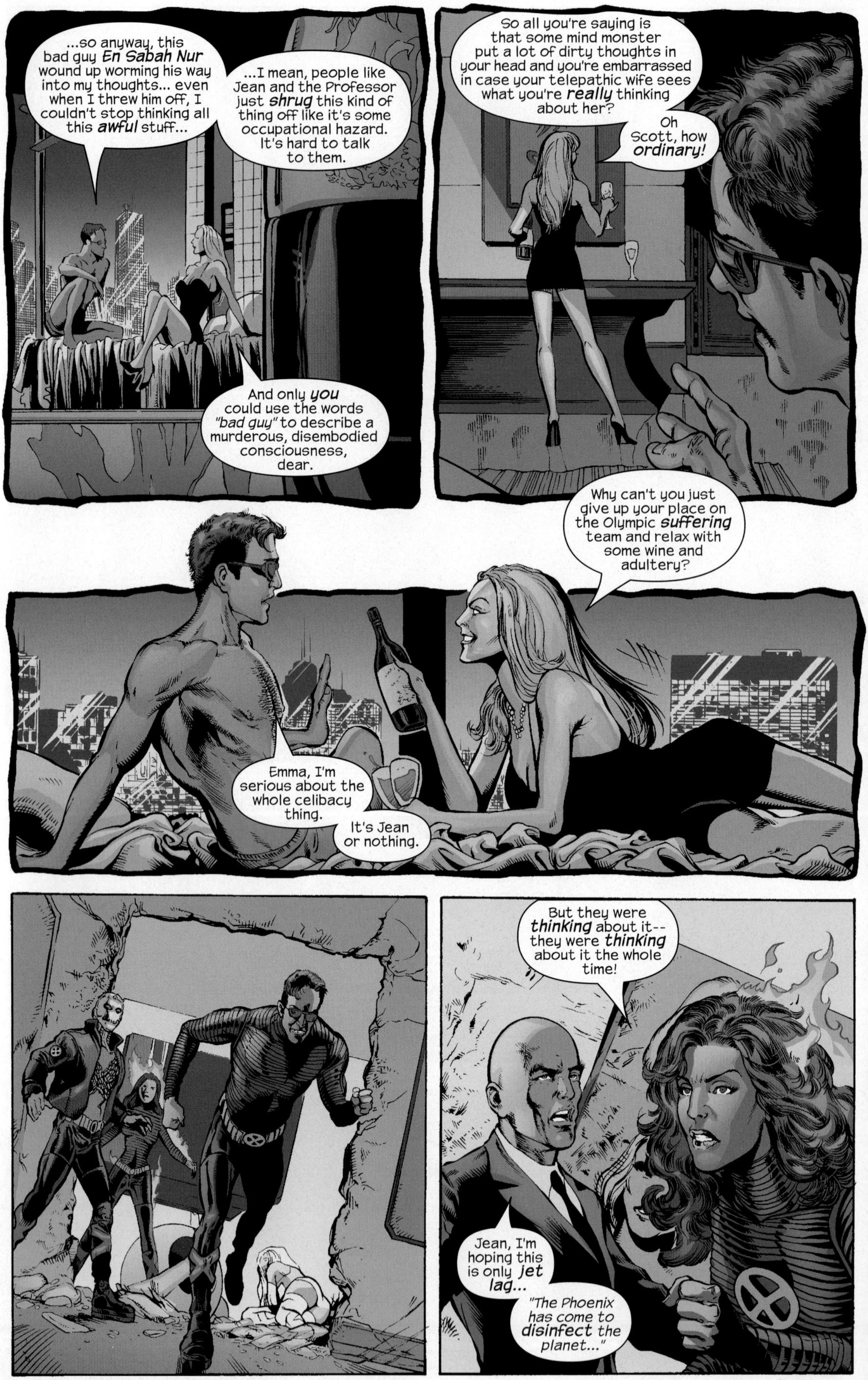

...so anyway, this bad guy En Sabah Nur wound up worming his way into my thoughts... even when I threw him off, I couldn't stop thinking all this awful stuff...
...I mean, people like Jean and the Professor just shrug this kind of thing off like it's some occupational hazard. It's hard to talk to them.
And only you could use the words "bad guy" to describe a murderous, disembodied consciousness, dear.
So all you're saying is that some mind monster put a lot of dirty thoughts in your head and you're embarrassed in case your telepathic wife sees what you're really thinking about her?
Oh Scott, how ordinary!
Why can't you just give up your place on the Olympic suffering team and relax with some wine and adultery?
Emma, I'm serious about the whole celibacy thing.
It's Jean or nothing.
But they were thinking about it-- they were thinking about it the whole time!
Jean, I'm hoping this is only jet lag...
"The Phoenix has come to disinfect the planet..."

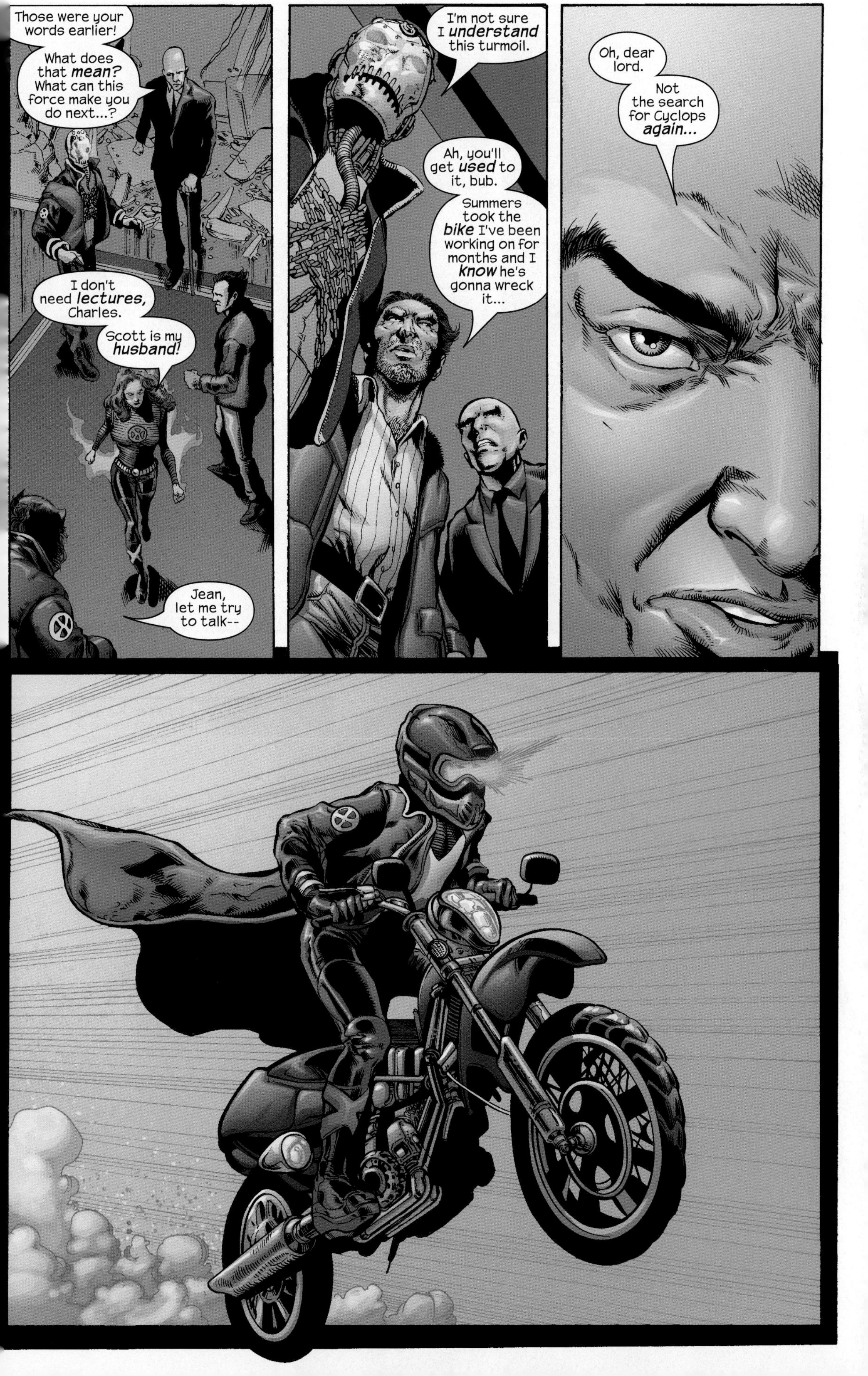
Those were your words earlier!
What does that *mean?* What can this force make you do next...?
I don't need *lectures,* Charles.
Scott is my *husband!*
Jean, let me try to talk--
I'm not sure I *understand* this turmoil.
Ah, you'll get *used* to it, bub.
Summers took the *bike* I've been working on for months and I *know* he's gonna wreck it...
Oh, dear lord.
Not the search for Cyclops *again...*

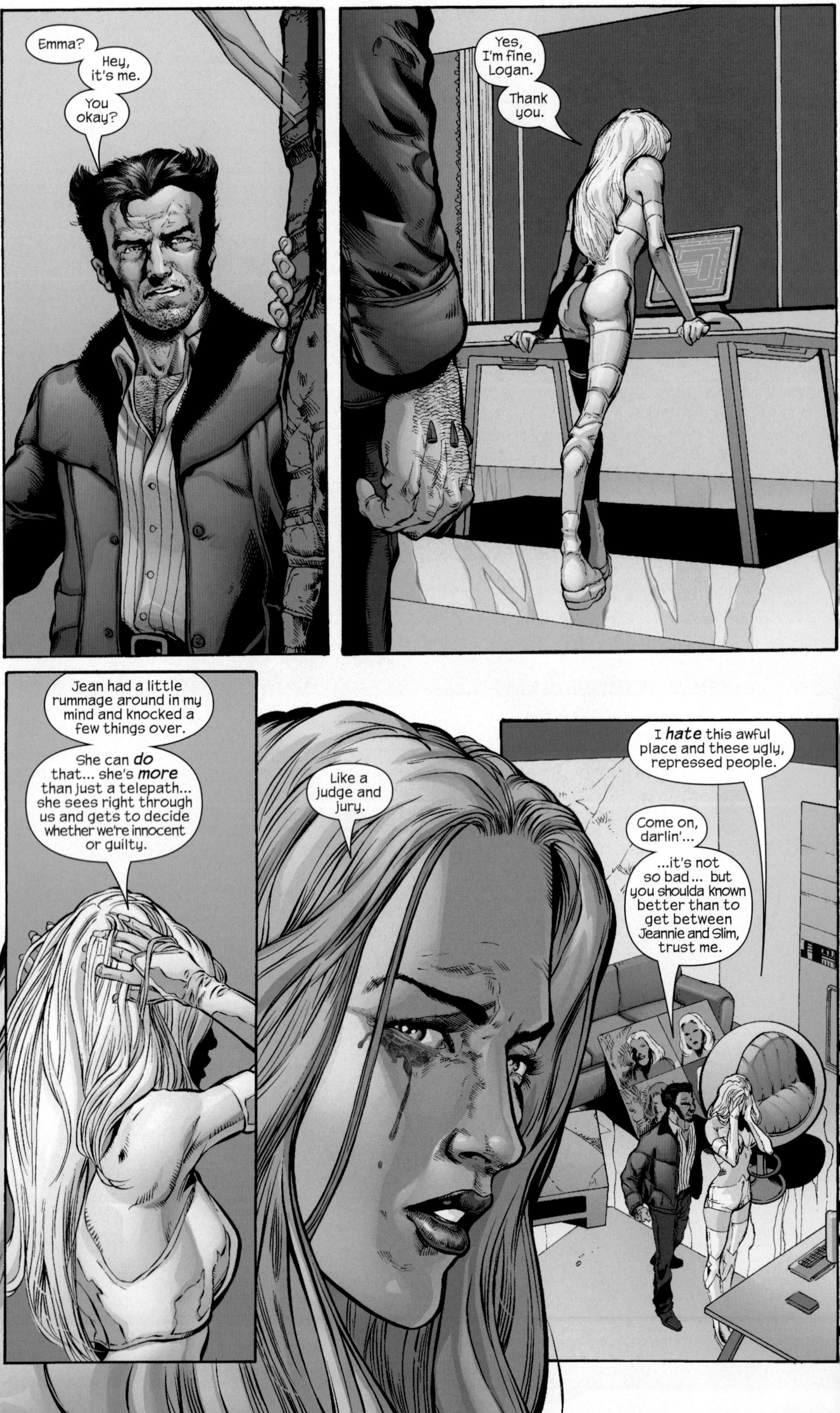

Emma?
Hey, it's me.
You okay?
Yes, I'm fine, Logan.
Thank you.
Jean had a little rummage around in my mind and knocked a few things over.
She can *do* that... she's *more* than just a telepath... she sees right through us and gets to decide whether we're innocent or guilty.
Like a judge and jury.
I *hate* this awful place and these ugly, repressed people.
Come on, darlin'...
...it's not so bad... but you shoulda known better than to get between Jeannie and Slim, trust me.

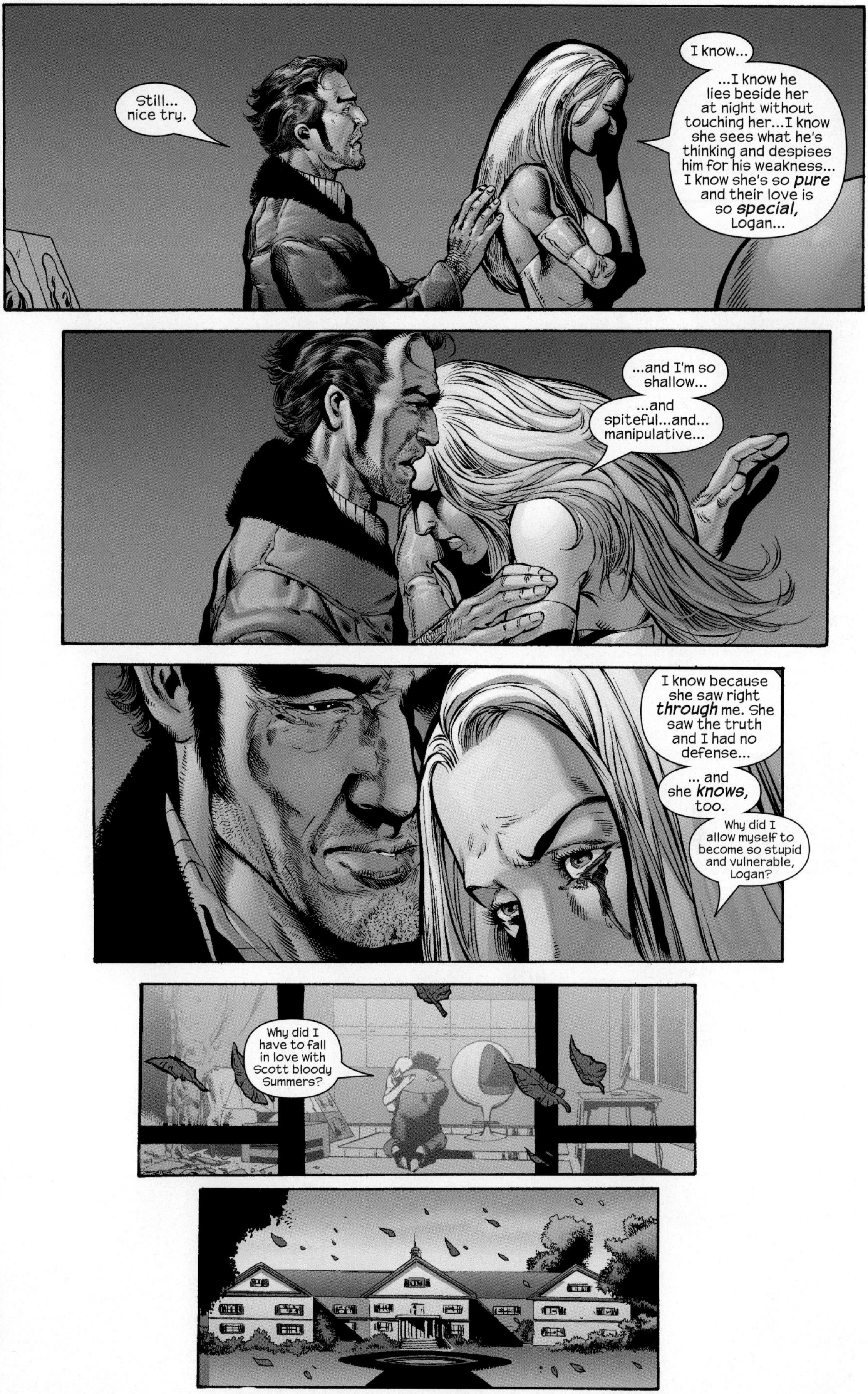
Still... nice try.
I know...
...I know he lies beside her at night without touching her...I know she sees what he's thinking and despises him for his weakness... I know she's so *pure* and their love is so *special,* Logan...
...and I'm so shallow...
...and spiteful...and... manipulative...
I know because she saw right *through* me. She saw the truth and I had no defense...
... and she *knows,* too.
Why did I allow myself to become so stupid and vulnerable, Logan?
Why did I have to fall in love with Scott bloody Summers?

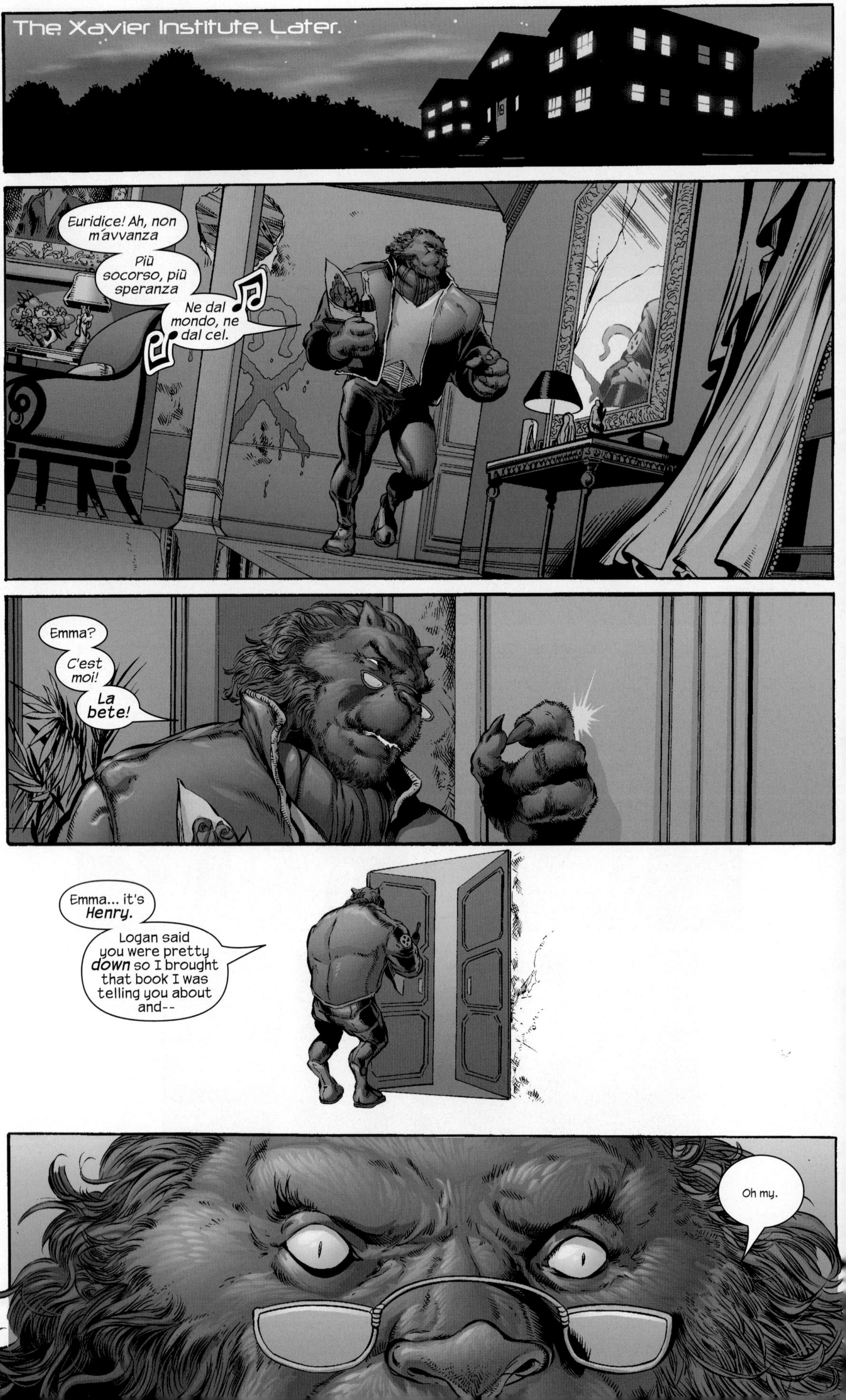

The Xavier Institute. Later.
Euridice! Ah, non m'avvanza
Più socorso, più speranza
Ne dal mondo, ne dal cel.
Emma?
C'est moi!
La bete!
Emma... it's Henry.
Logan said you were pretty down so I brought that book I was telling you about and--
Oh my.

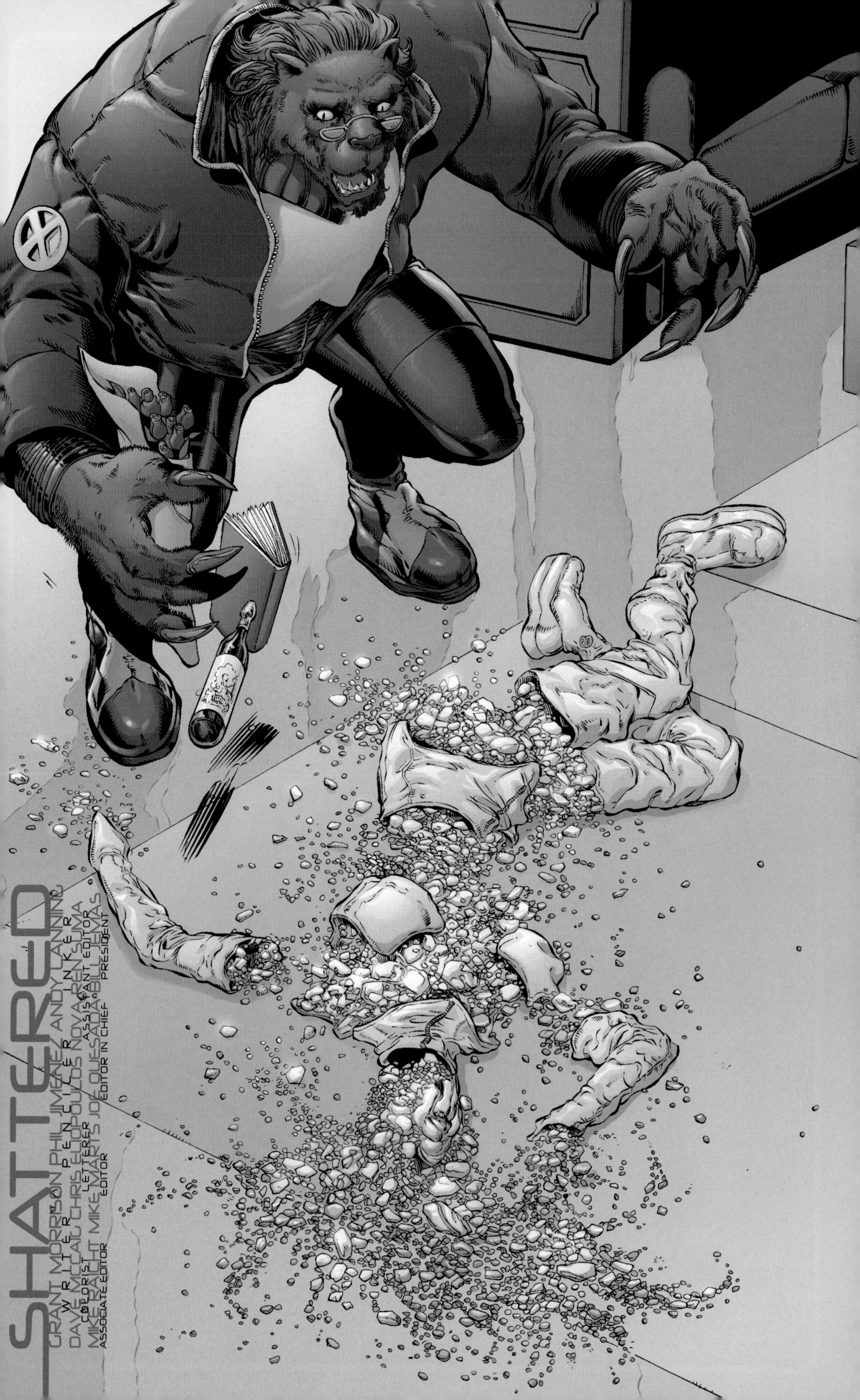

SHATTERED
GRANT MORRISON PHIL JIMENEZ ANDY LANNING
WRITER PENCILER INKER
DAVE MCCAIG CHRIS ELIOPOULOS NOVA REN SUMA
COLORIST LETTERER ASSISTANT EDITOR
MIKE RAICHT MIKE MARTS JOE QUESADA BILL JEMAS
ASSOCIATE EDITOR EDITOR EDITOR IN CHIEF PRESIDENT

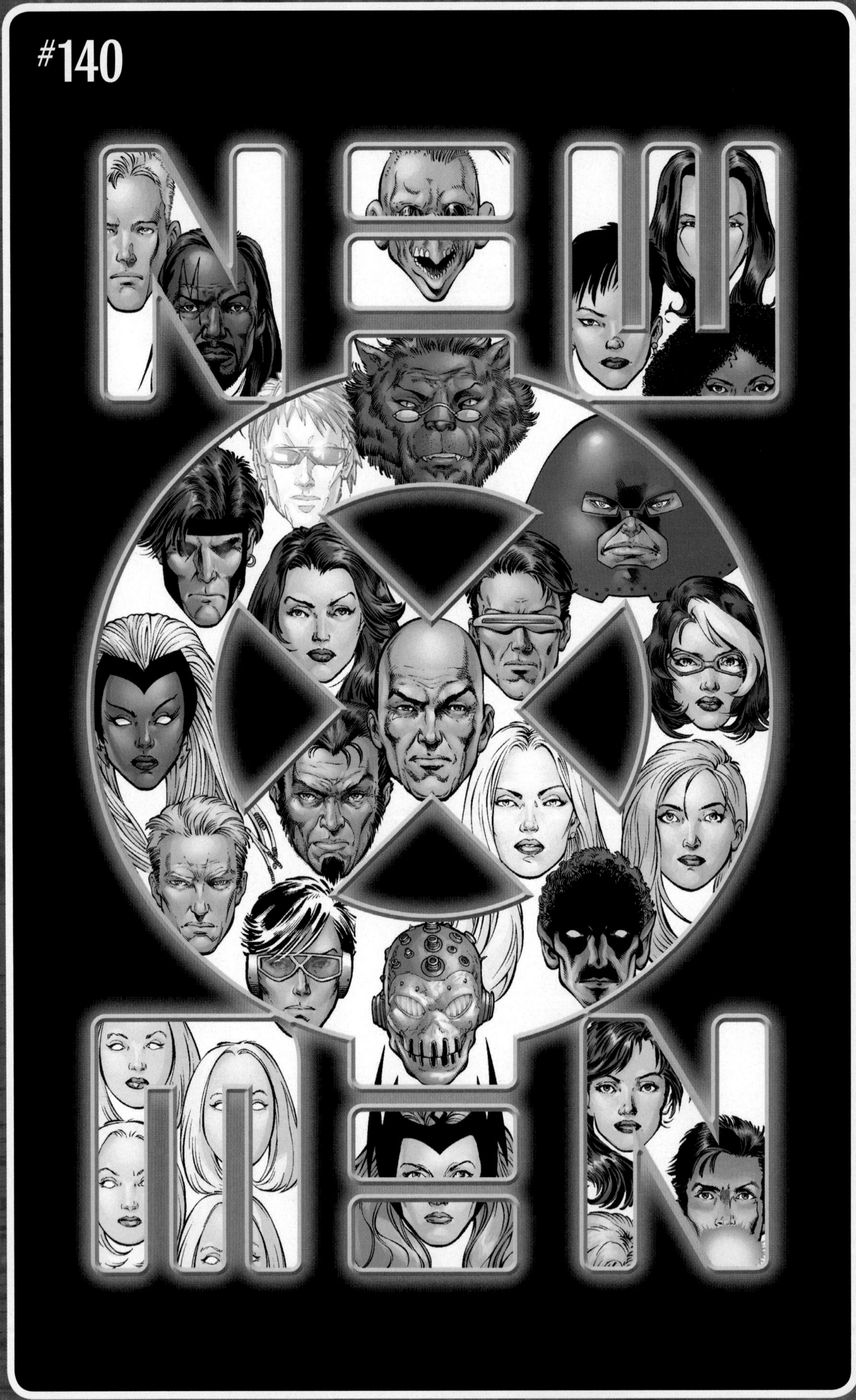
#140
NEW X-MEN

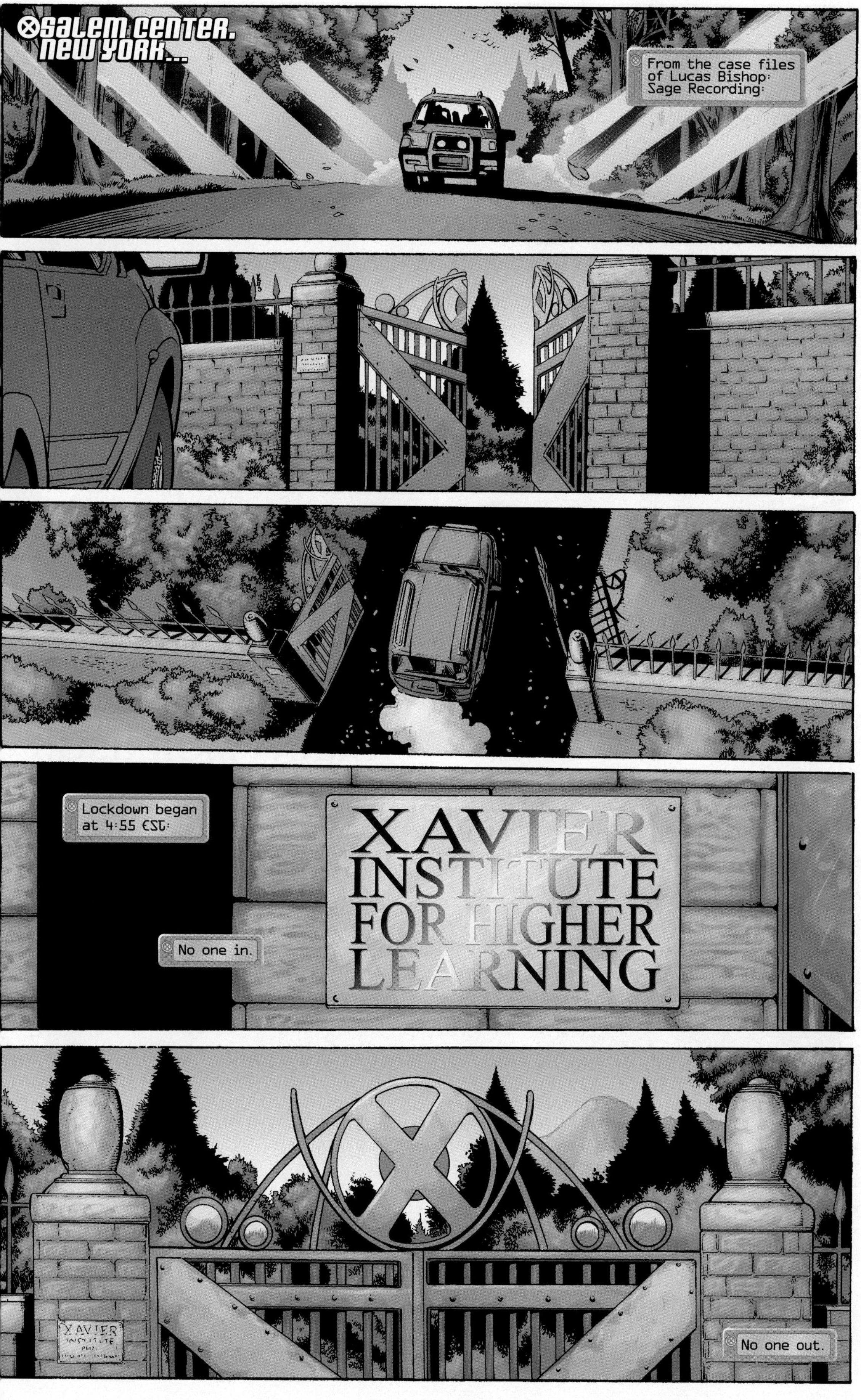
SALEM CENTER, NEW YORK...
From the case files of Lucas Bishop: Sage Recording:
Lockdown began at 4:55 EST:
XAVIER INSTITUTE FOR HIGHER LEARNING
No one in.
XAVIER INSTITUTE
No one out.

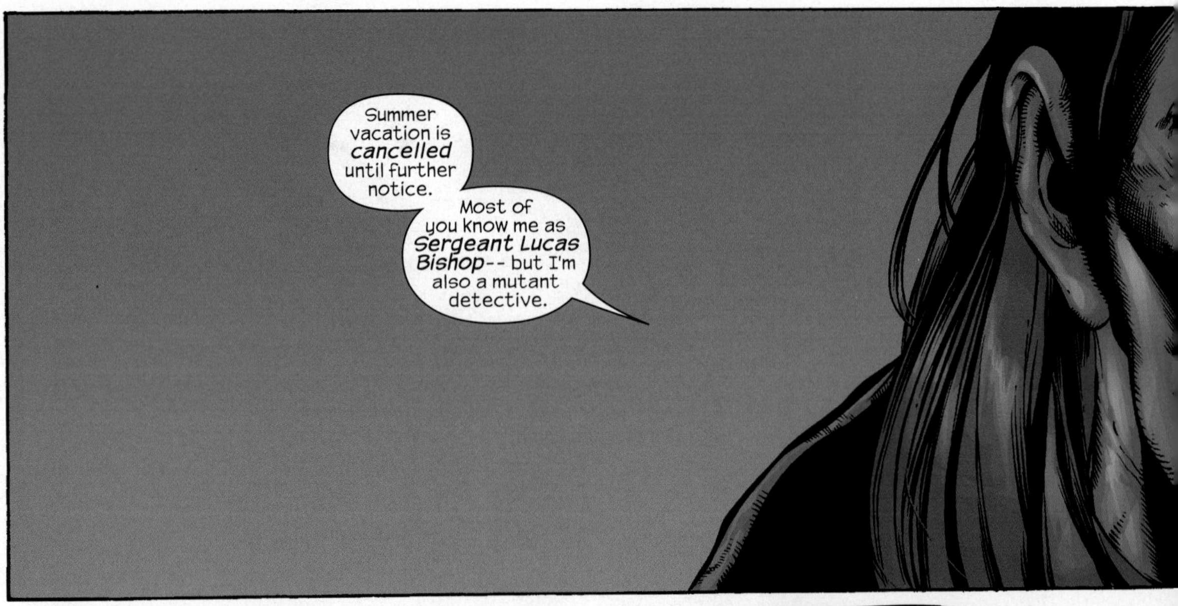
Summer vacation is *cancelled* until further notice.
Most of you know me as *Sergeant Lucas Bishop*-- but I'm also a mutant detective.

MURDER A TI

GRANT MORRISON
WRITER

CHRIS CHUCKRY
COLORIST

CHRIS ELIOPOULOS
LETTERER

MIKE RAICHT
ASSOCIATE EDITOR

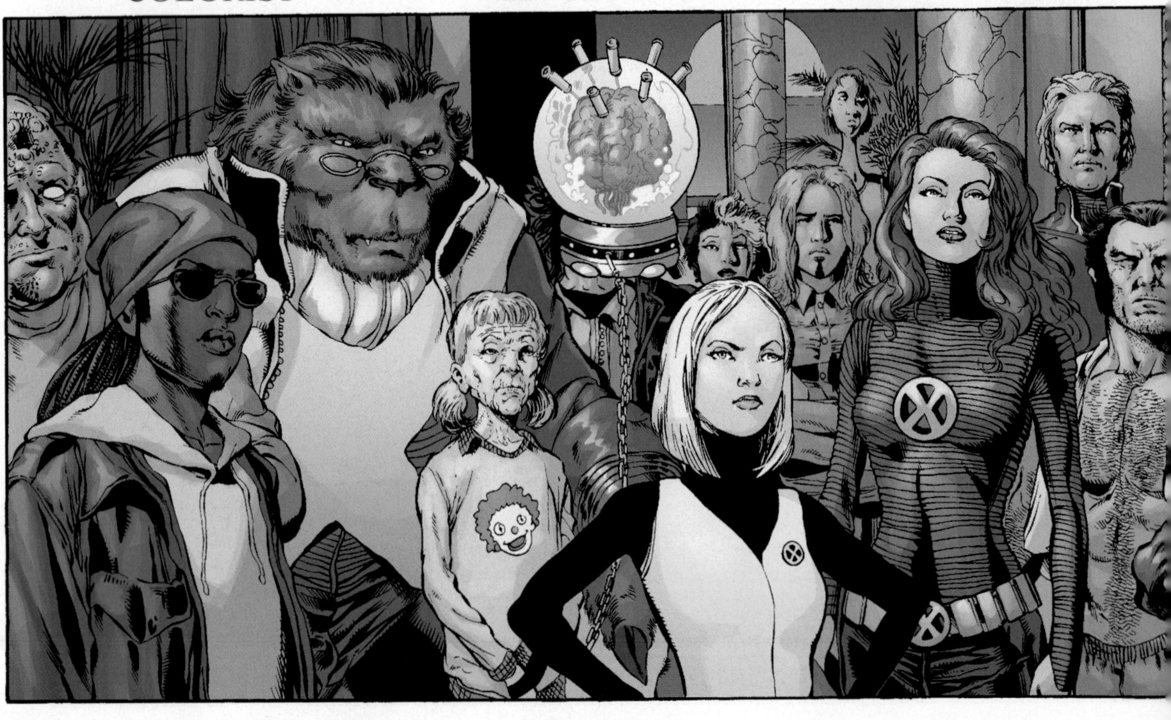

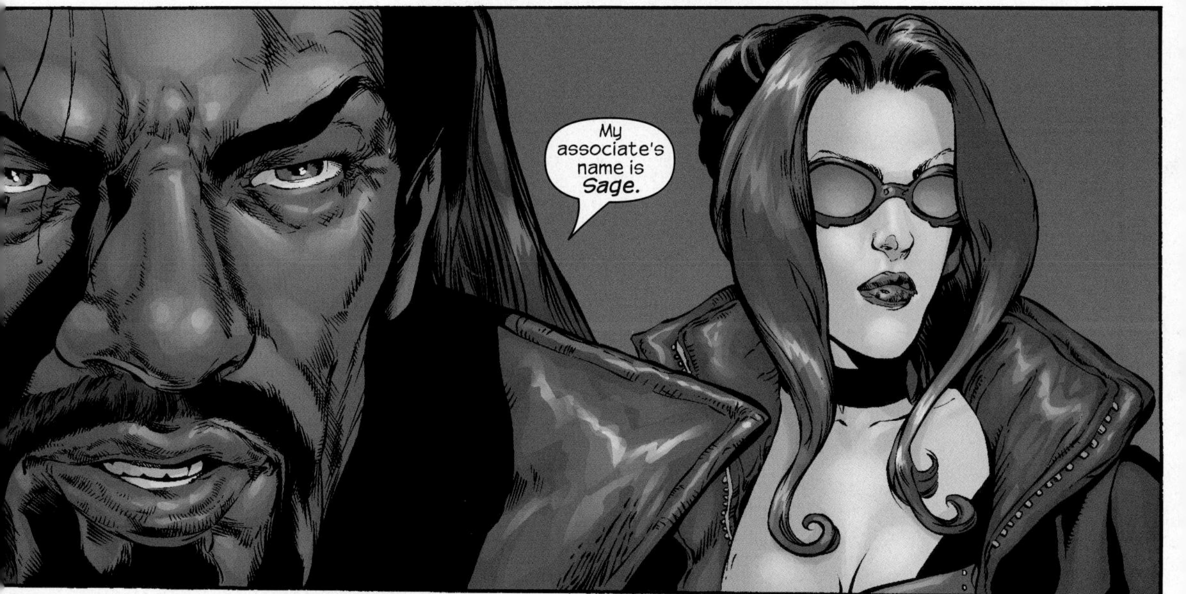
My associate's name is *Sage.*

MANSION

PHIL JIMENEZ
PENCILER

ANDY LANNING
INKER

MIKE MARTS
EDITOR

JOE QUESADA
EDITOR IN CHIEF

BILL JEMAS
PRESIDENT

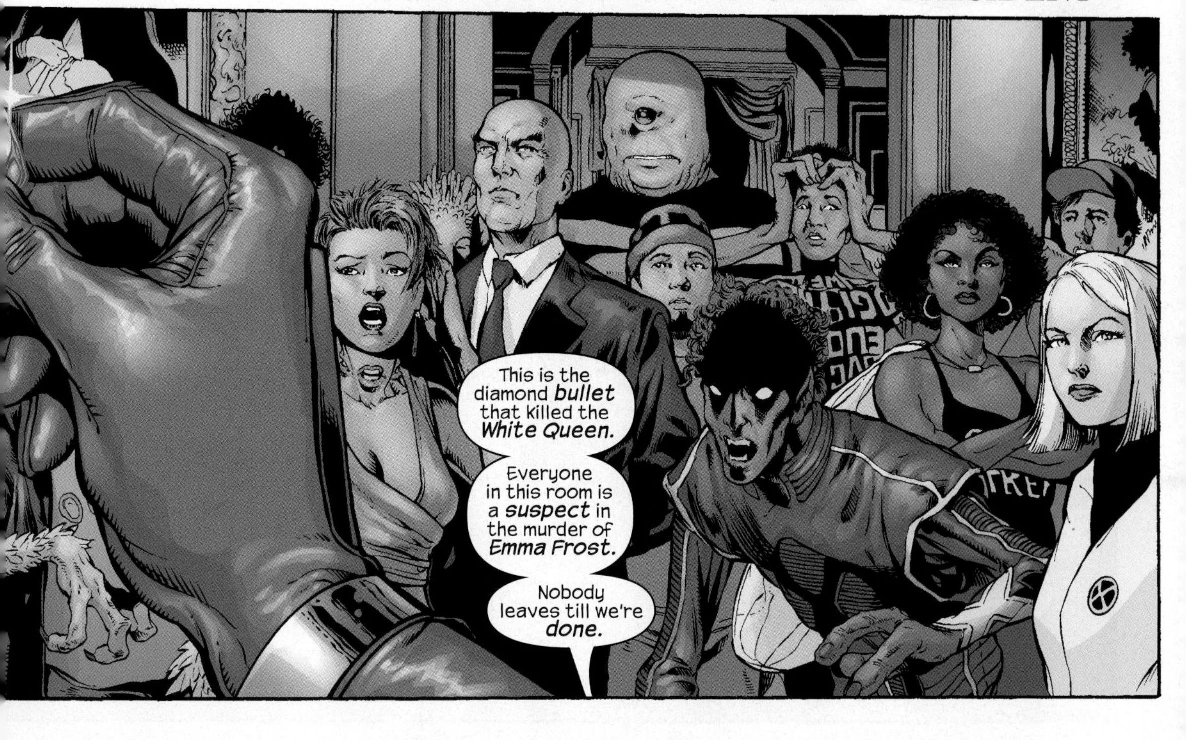
This is the diamond *bullet* that killed the *White Queen.*
Everyone in this room is a *suspect* in the murder of *Emma Frost.*
Nobody leaves till we're *done.*

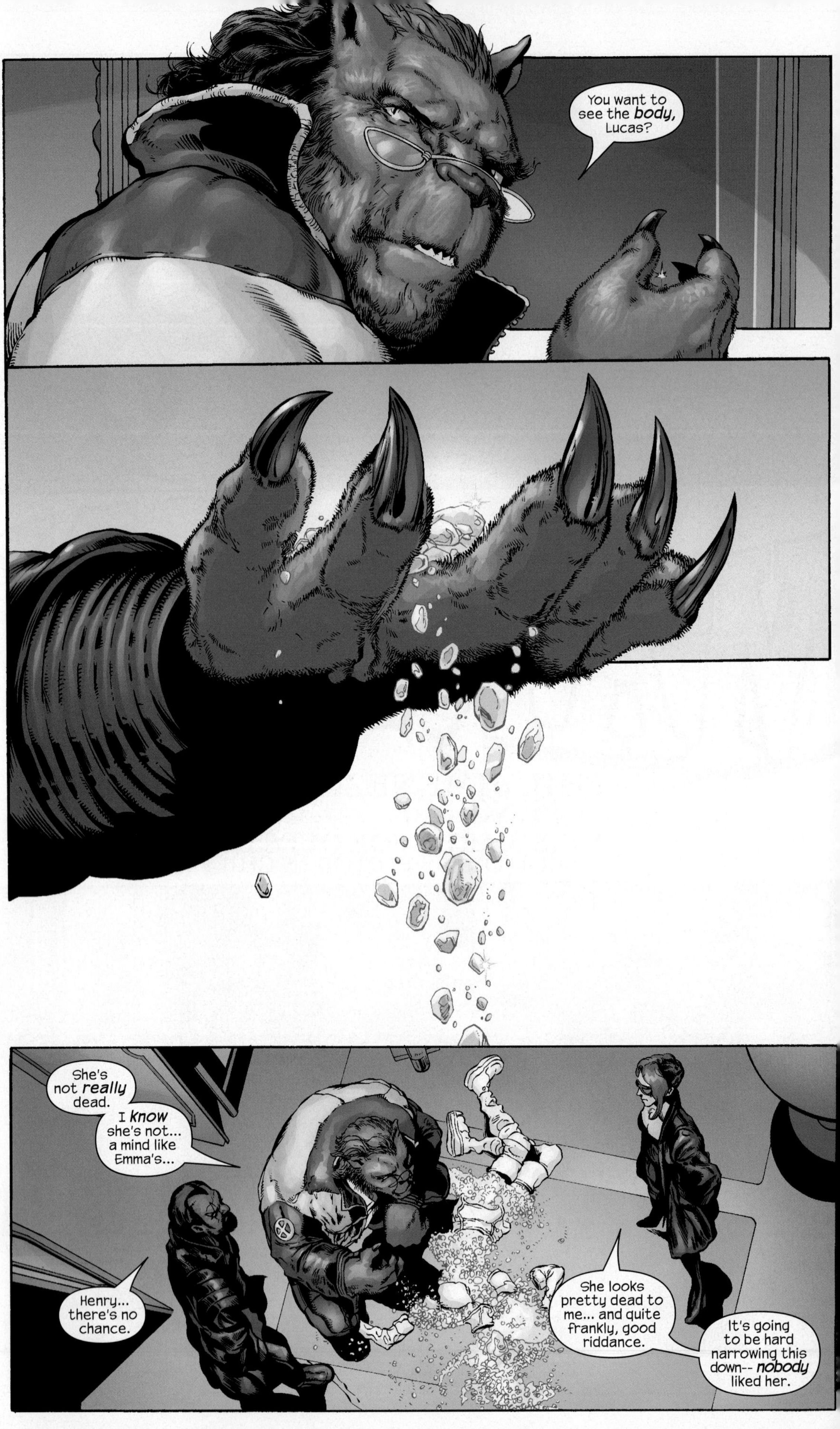
You want to see the *body,* Lucas?
She's not *really* dead.
I *know* she's not... a mind like Emma's...
Henry... there's no chance.
She looks pretty dead to me... and quite frankly, good riddance.
It's going to be hard narrowing this down-- *nobody* liked her.

Well, I did. Part 10035 -- a section of aortal valve.

She was a good listener. She laughed at my jokes. She knew every line of *Byron* by heart.

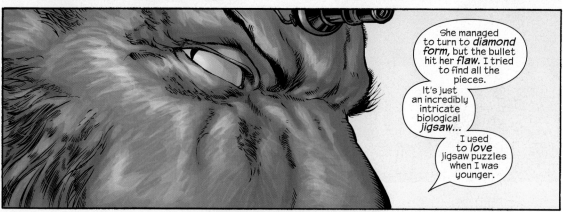

She managed to turn to *diamond form,* but the bullet hit her *flaw.* I tried to find all the pieces.

It's just an incredibly intricate biological *jigsaw...*

I used to *love* jigsaw puzzles when I was younger.

So? I'm the *least* likely and therefore *most* likely suspect?

Well, I was at the *opera-- "Orfeo"* with Emma's girls.

I do intend to put her back together, you know.

Sure, Henry.

Keep us posted.

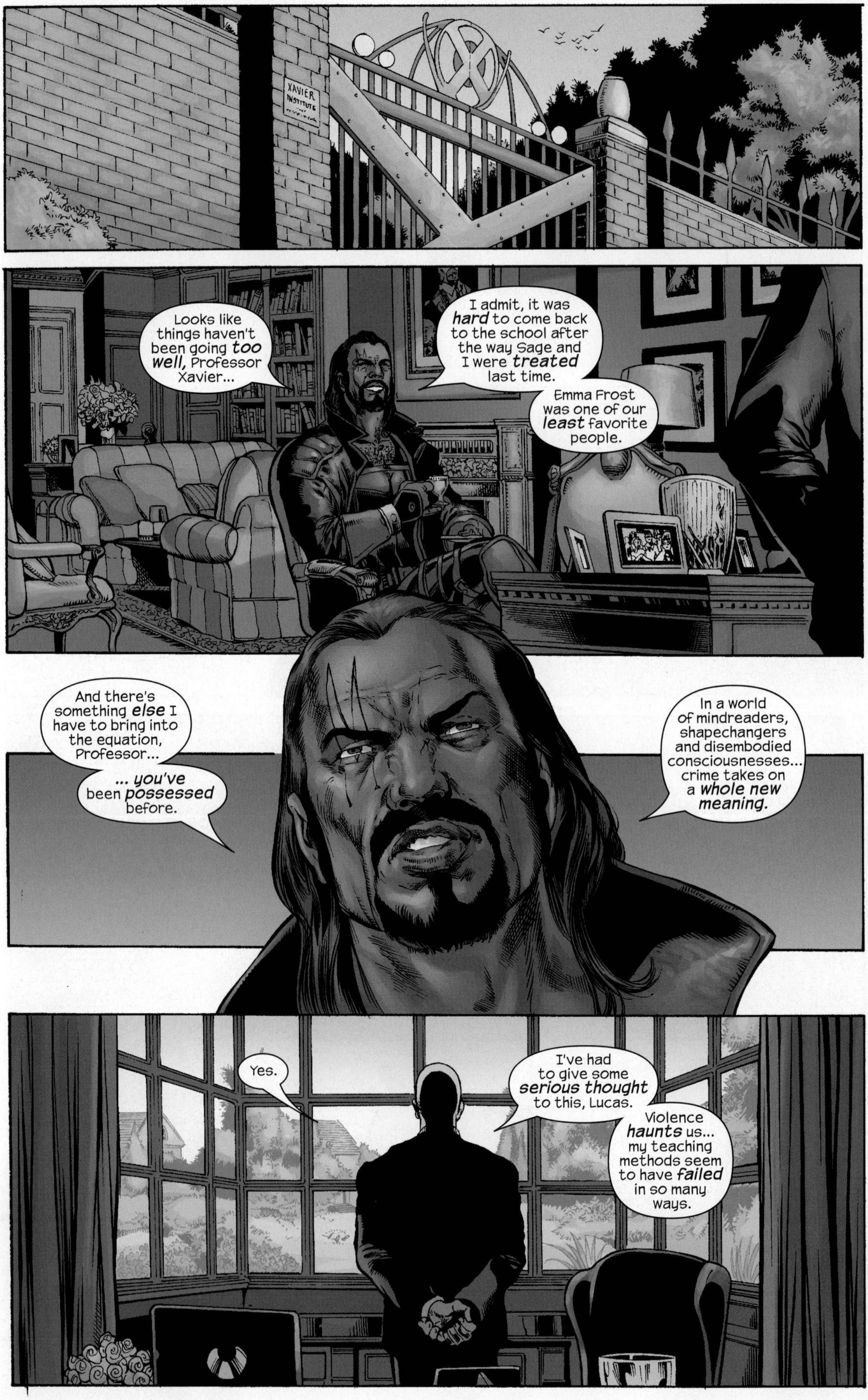
XAVIER INSTITUTE
Looks like things haven't been going too well, Professor Xavier...
I admit, it was hard to come back to the school after the way Sage and I were treated last time.
Emma Frost was one of our least favorite people.
And there's something else I have to bring into the equation, Professor...
... you've been possessed before.
In a world of mindreaders, shapechangers and disembodied consciousnesses... crime takes on a whole new meaning.
Yes.
I've had to give some serious thought to this, Lucas.
Violence haunts us... my teaching methods seem to have failed in so many ways.

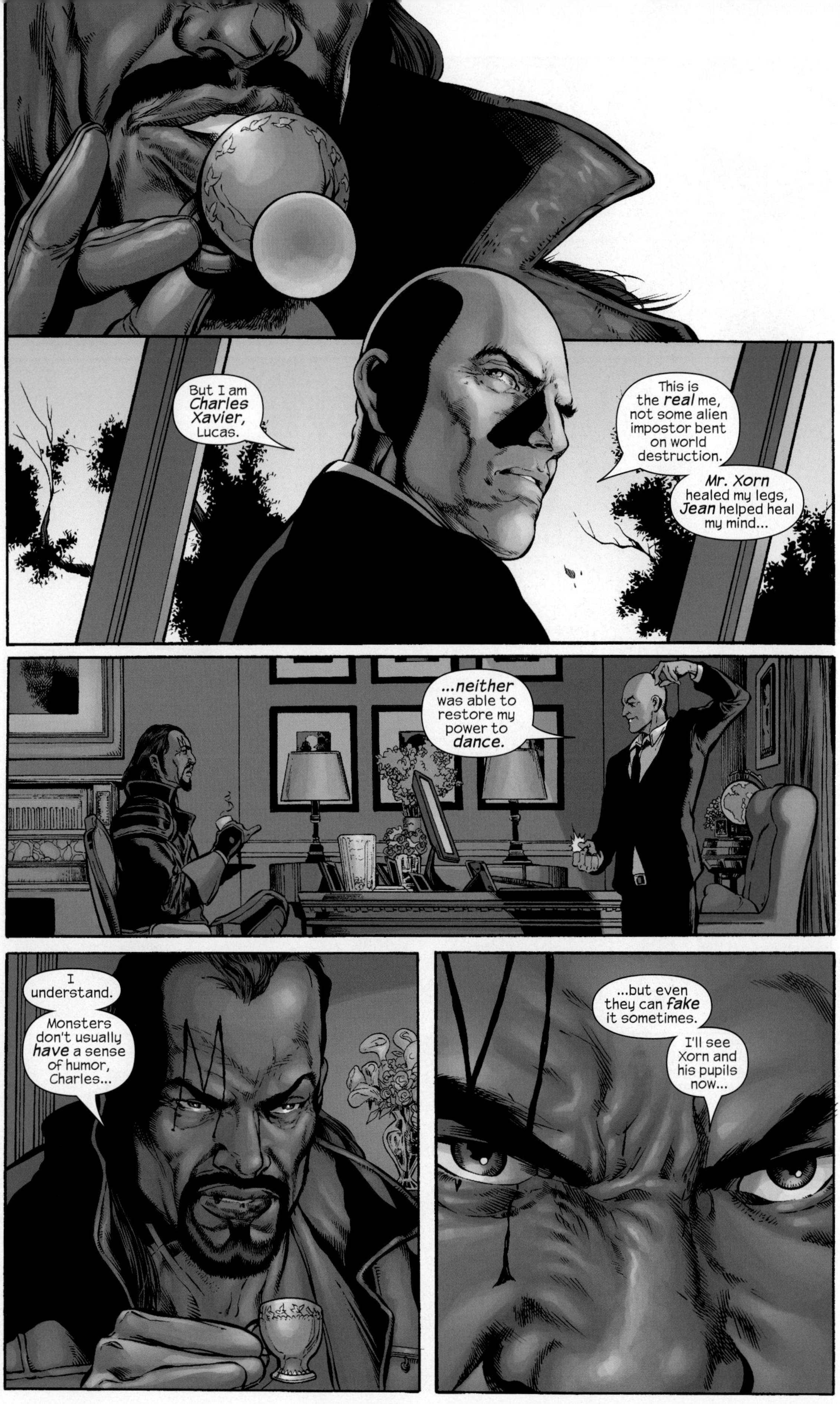
But I am Charles Xavier, Lucas.
This is the real me, not some alien impostor bent on world destruction.
Mr. Xorn healed my legs, Jean helped heal my mind...
...neither was able to restore my power to dance.
I understand.
Monsters don't usually have a sense of humor, Charles...
...but even they can fake it sometimes.
I'll see Xorn and his pupils now...

These are vulnerable children, Bishop. Please be careful with your interrogations.

All of them have been exploited and abused. They are very sensitive.

Say that again and I will have to *kill* you!

There is no such room as *"the toilet"* in *Clue!*

There is *now!* "Professor Sex in the toilet with the lawnmower"-- *that's* whodunnit!

≈Hyukk≈

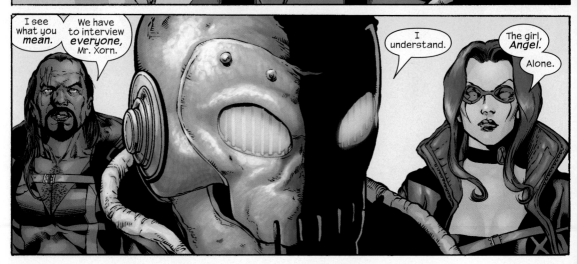

I see what you *mean.*

We have to interview *everyone,* Mr. Xorn.

I understand.

The girl, *Angel.*

Alone.

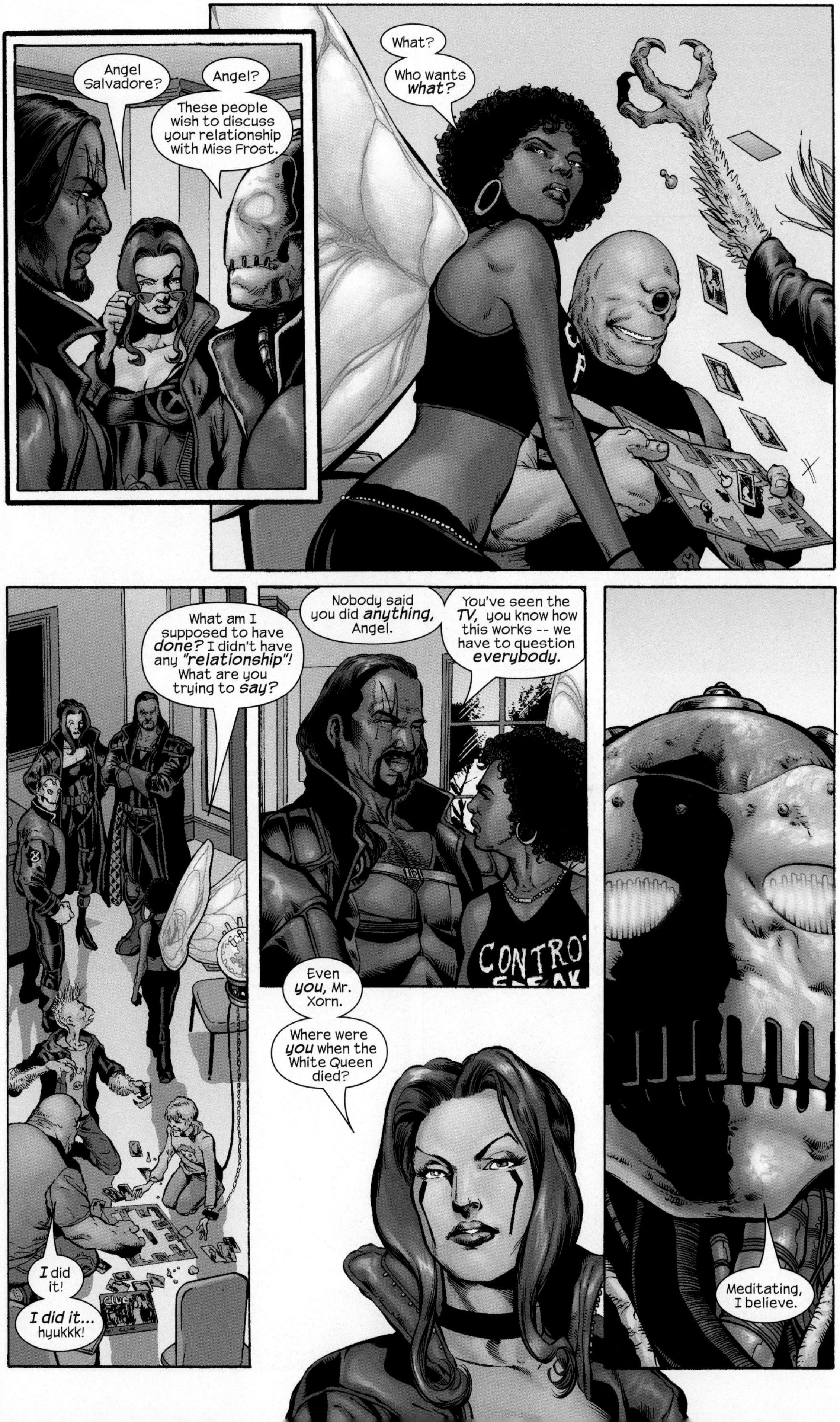
Angel Salvadore?
Angel?
These people wish to discuss your relationship with Miss Frost.
What?
Who wants *what?*
Clue
What am I supposed to have *done?* I didn't have any *"relationship"*! What are you trying to *say?*
I did it!
I did it... hyukkk!
Nobody said you did *anything,* Angel.
You've seen the *TV,* you know how this works -- we have to question *everybody.*
CONTRO
Even *you,* Mr. Xorn.
Where were *you* when the White Queen died?
Meditating, I believe.

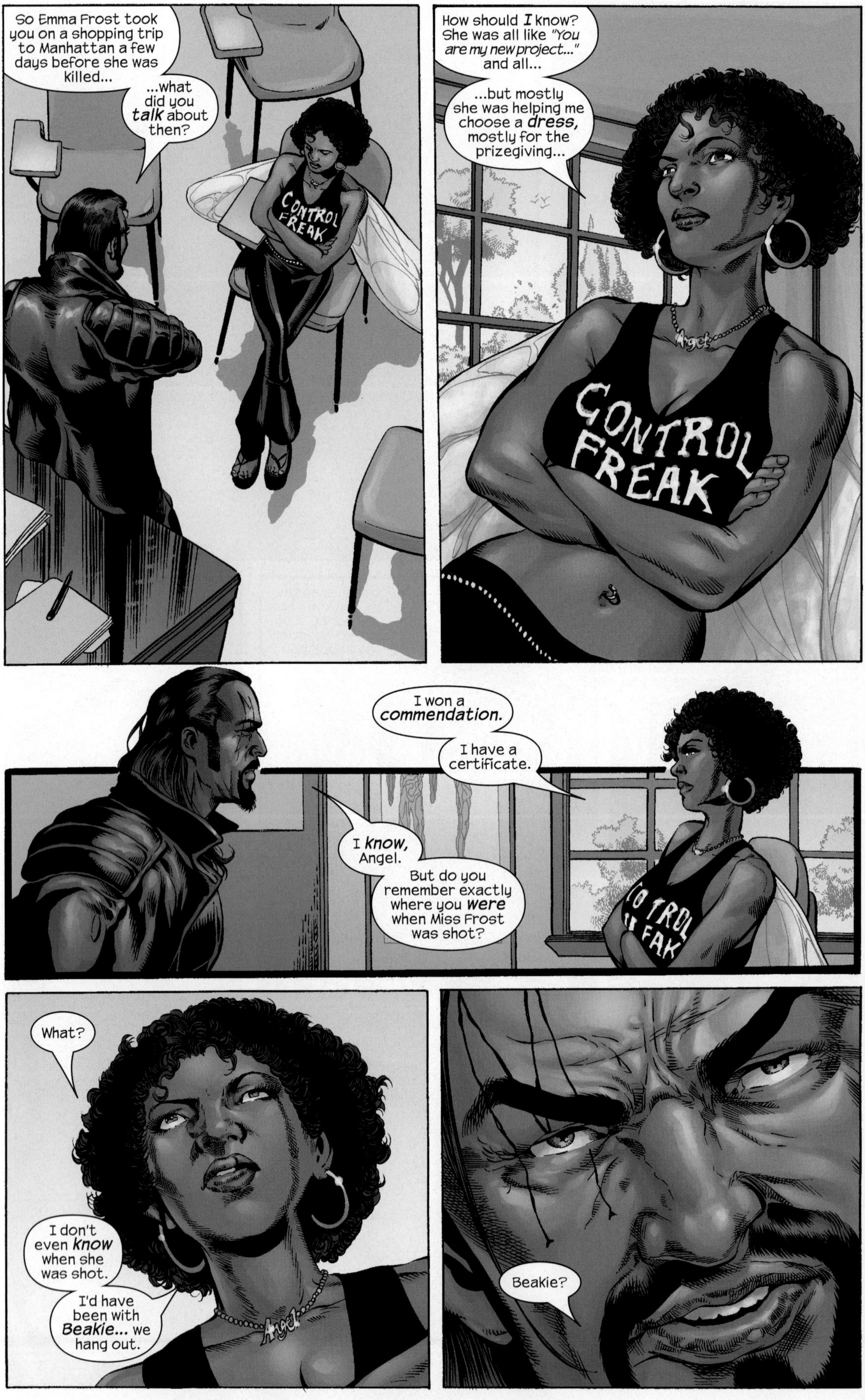
So Emma Frost took you on a shopping trip to Manhattan a few days before she was killed...
...what did you *talk* about then?
CONTROL FREAK
How should *I* know? She was all like *"You are my new project..."* and all...
...but mostly she was helping me choose a *dress,* mostly for the prizegiving...
CONTROL FREAK
I won a *commendation.*
I have a certificate.
I *know,* Angel.
But do you remember exactly where you *were* when Miss Frost was shot?
What?
I don't even *know* when she was shot.
I'd have been with *Beakie...* we hang out.
Beakie?

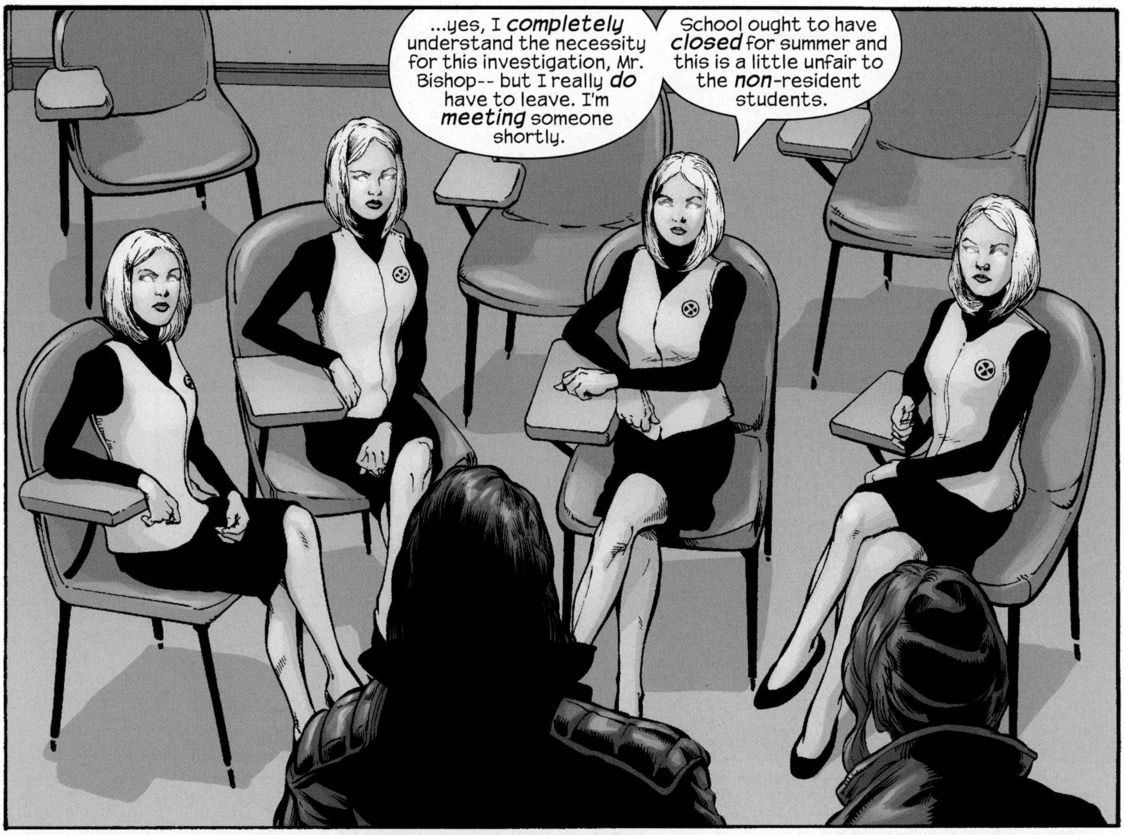
...yes, I completely understand the necessity for this investigation, Mr. Bishop-- but I really do have to leave. I'm meeting someone shortly.
School ought to have closed for summer and this is a little unfair to the non-resident students.

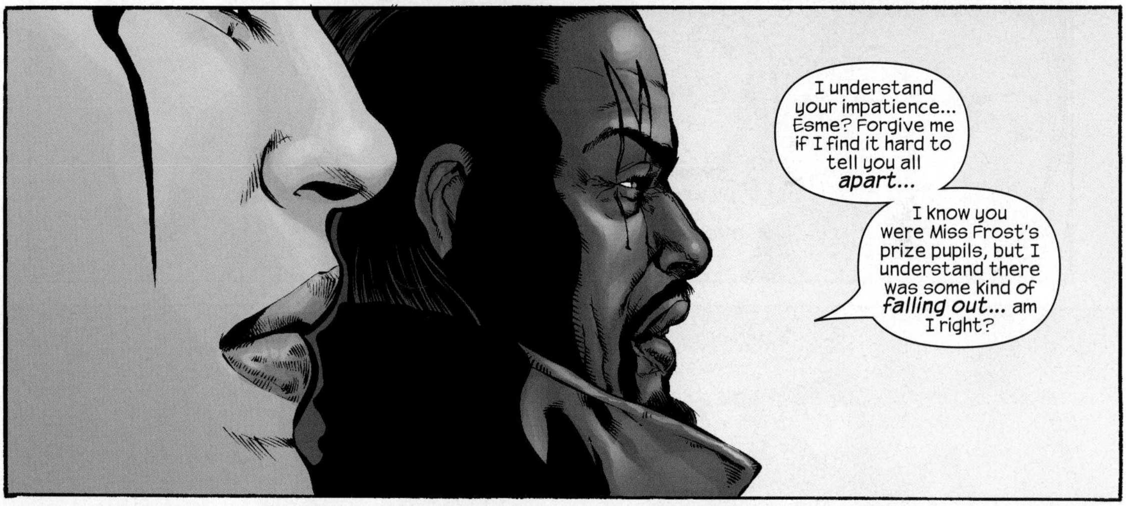
I understand your impatience... Esme? Forgive me if I find it hard to tell you all apart...
I know you were Miss Frost's prize pupils, but I understand there was some kind of falling out... am I right?

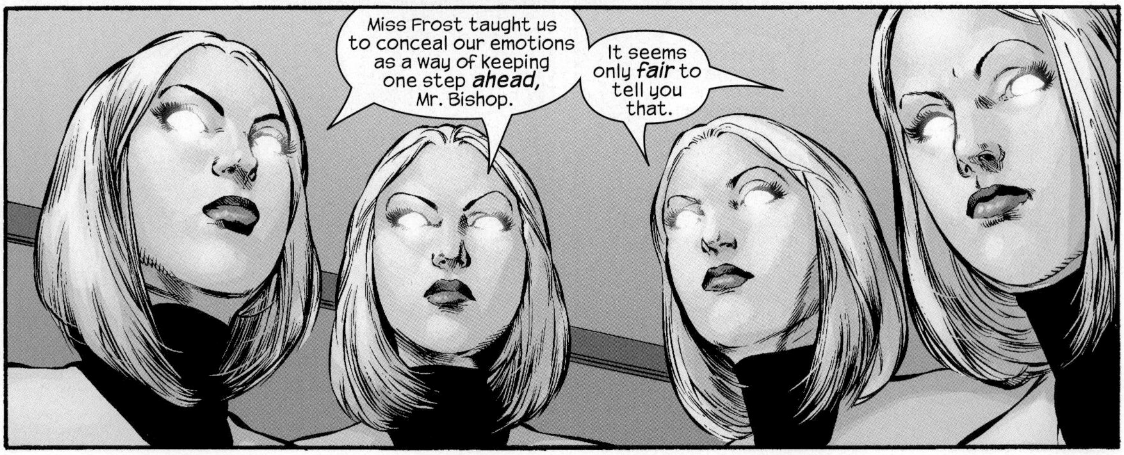
Miss Frost taught us to conceal our emotions as a way of keeping one step ahead, Mr. Bishop.
It seems only fair to tell you that.

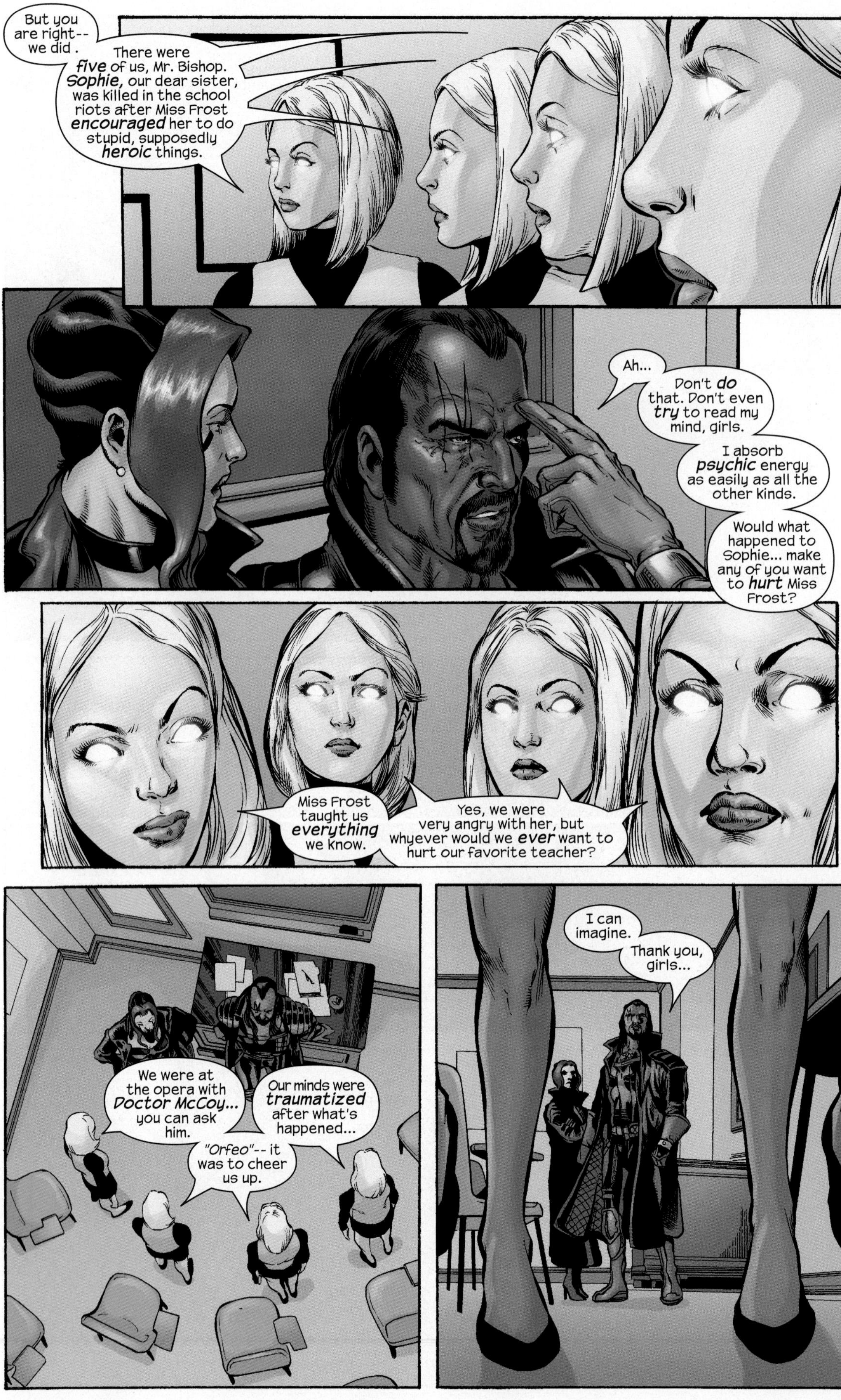
But you are right-- we did .
There were five of us, Mr. Bishop. Sophie, our dear sister, was killed in the school riots after Miss Frost encouraged her to do stupid, supposedly heroic things.
Ah...
Don't do that. Don't even try to read my mind, girls.
I absorb psychic energy as easily as all the other kinds.
Would what happened to Sophie... make any of you want to hurt Miss Frost?
Miss Frost taught us everything we know.
Yes, we were very angry with her, but whyever would we ever want to hurt our favorite teacher?
We were at the opera with Doctor McCoy... you can ask him.
Our minds were traumatized after what's happened...
"Orfeo"-- it was to cheer us up.
I can imagine.
Thank you, girls...

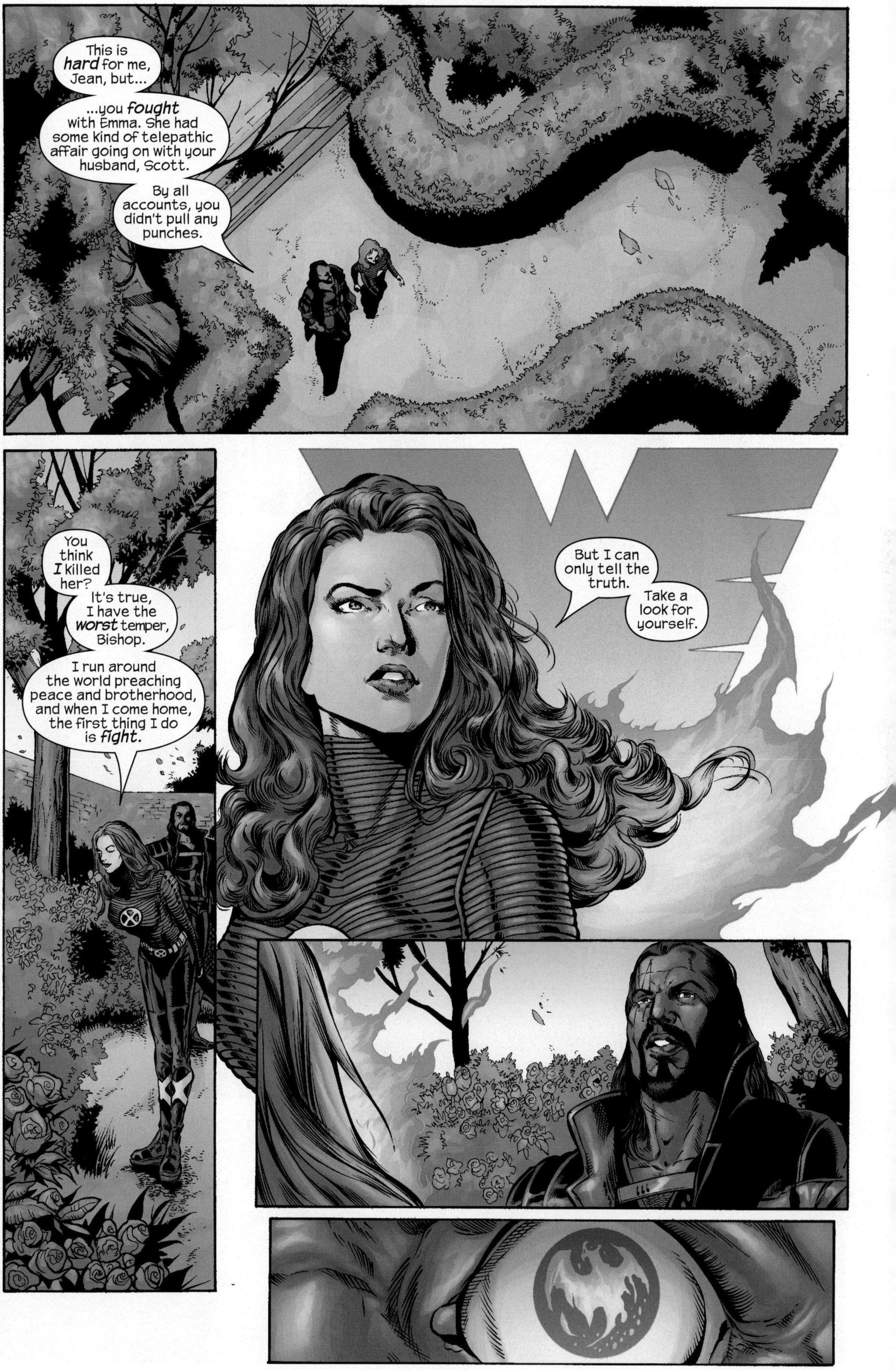
This is *hard* for me, Jean, but...
...you *fought* with Emma. She had some kind of telepathic affair going on with your husband, Scott.
By all accounts, you didn't pull any punches.
You think *I* killed her?
It's true, I have the *worst* temper, Bishop.
I run around the world preaching peace and brotherhood, and when I come home, the first thing I do is *fight.*
But I can only tell the truth.
Take a look for yourself.

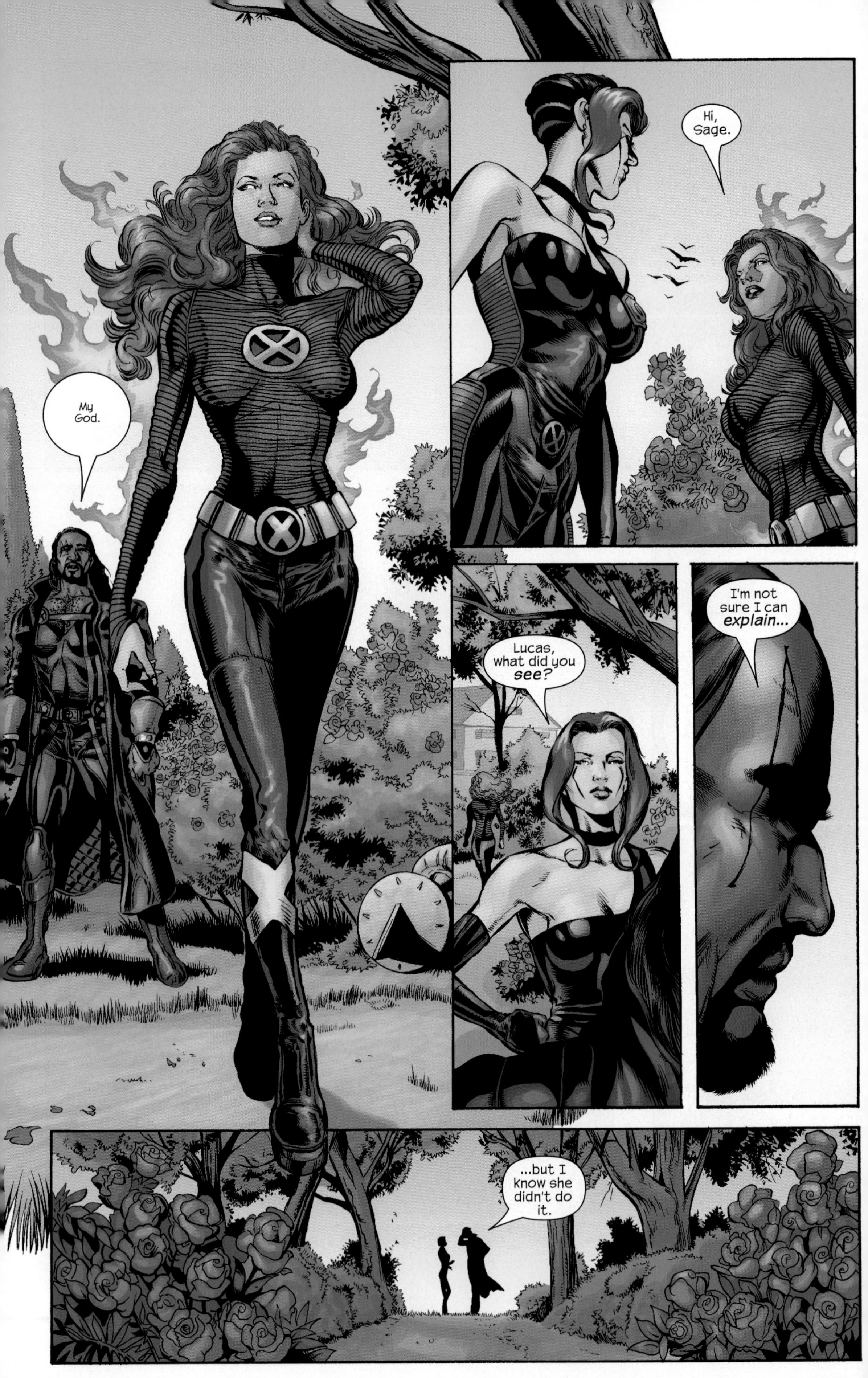
My God.
Hi, Sage.
Lucas, what did you see?
I'm not sure I can explain...
...but I know she didn't do it.

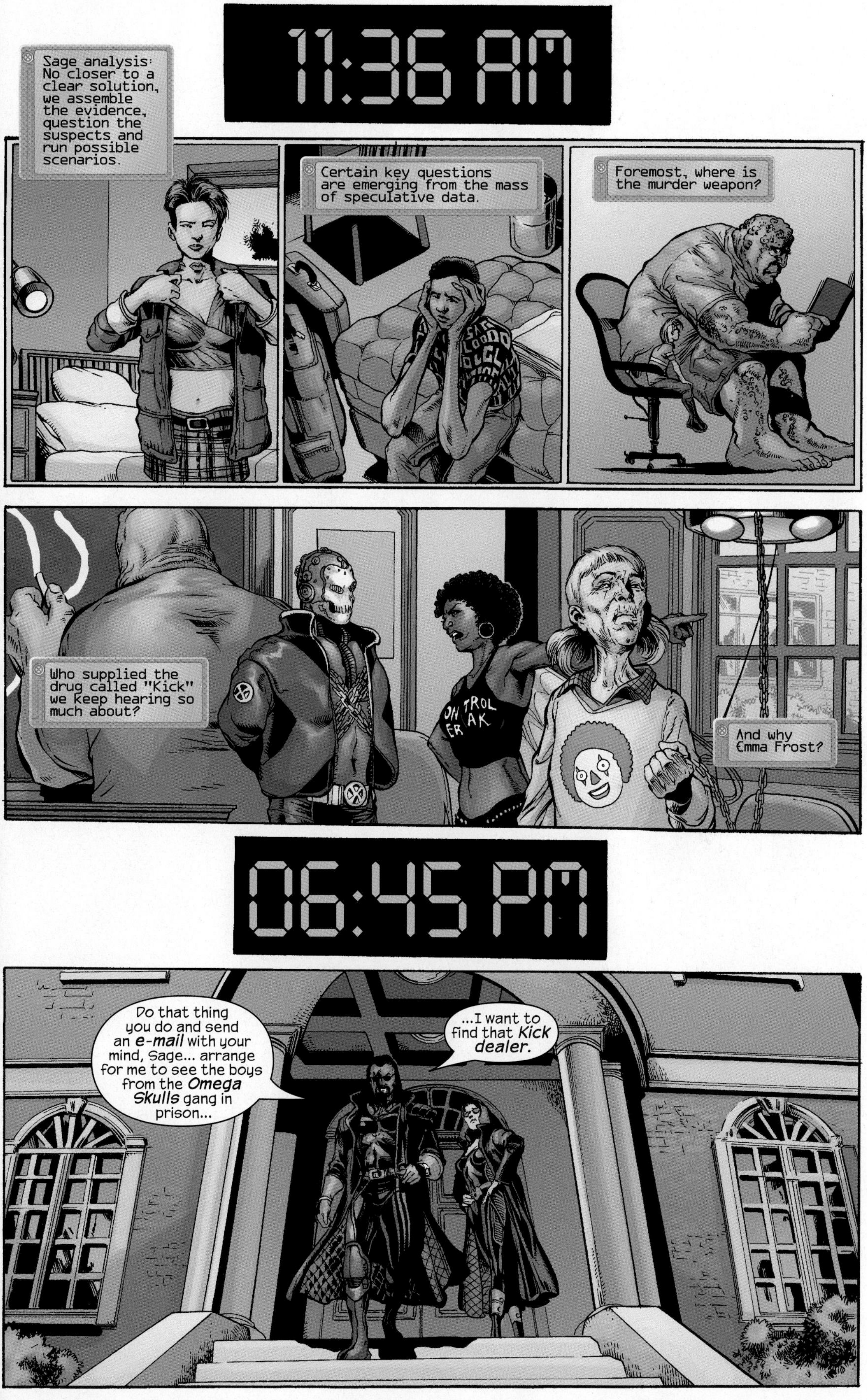
11:36 AM
Sage analysis: No closer to a clear solution, we assemble the evidence, question the suspects and run possible scenarios.
Certain key questions are emerging from the mass of speculative data.
Foremost, where is the murder weapon?
Who supplied the drug called "Kick" we keep hearing so much about?
And why Emma Frost?
06:45 PM
Do that thing you do and send an e-mail with your mind, Sage... arrange for me to see the boys from the Omega Skulls gang in prison...
...I want to find that Kick dealer.

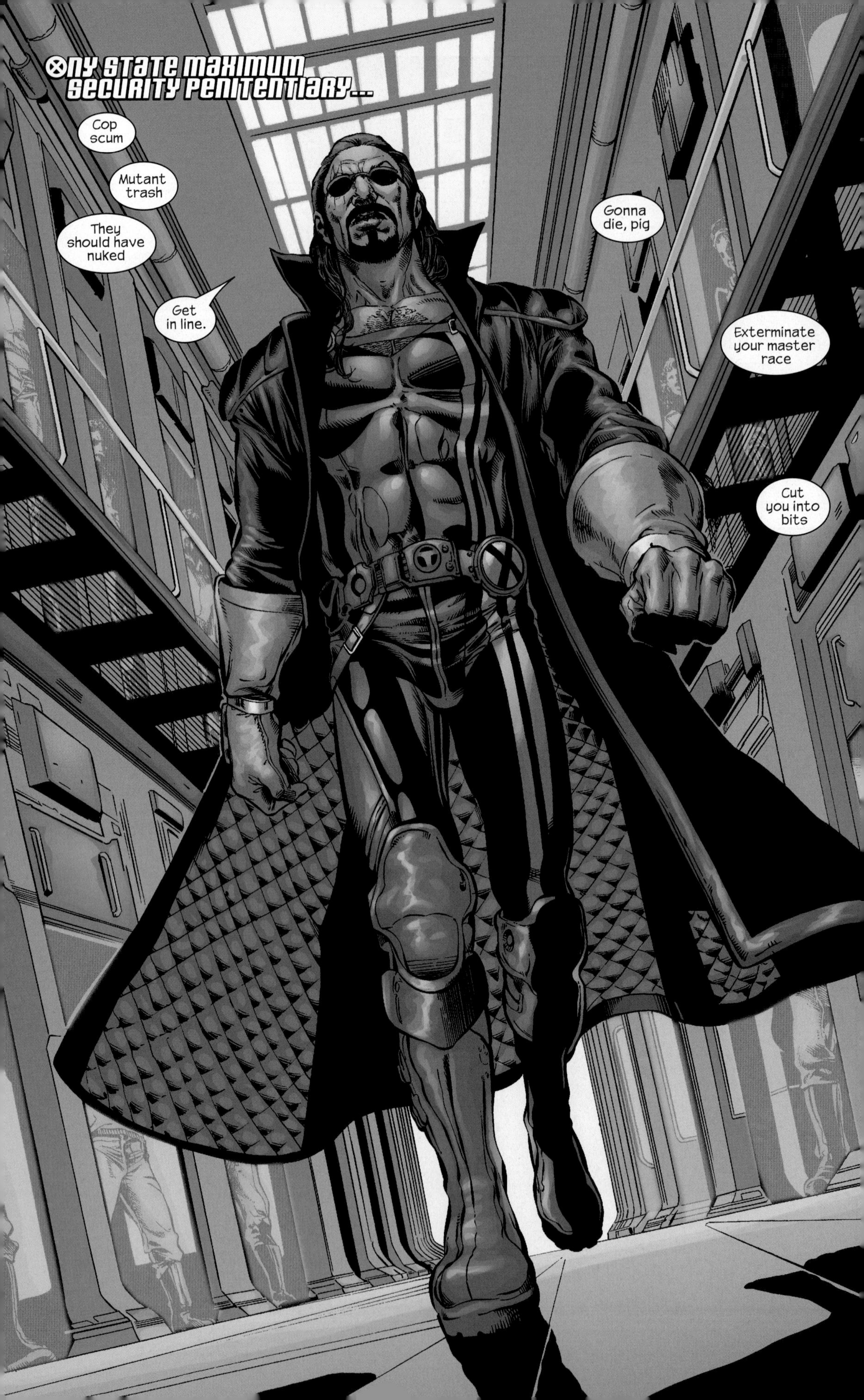
NY STATE MAXIMUM SECURITY PENITENTIARY...
Cop scum
Mutant trash
They should have nuked
Get in line.
Gonna die, pig
Exterminate your master race
Cut you into bits

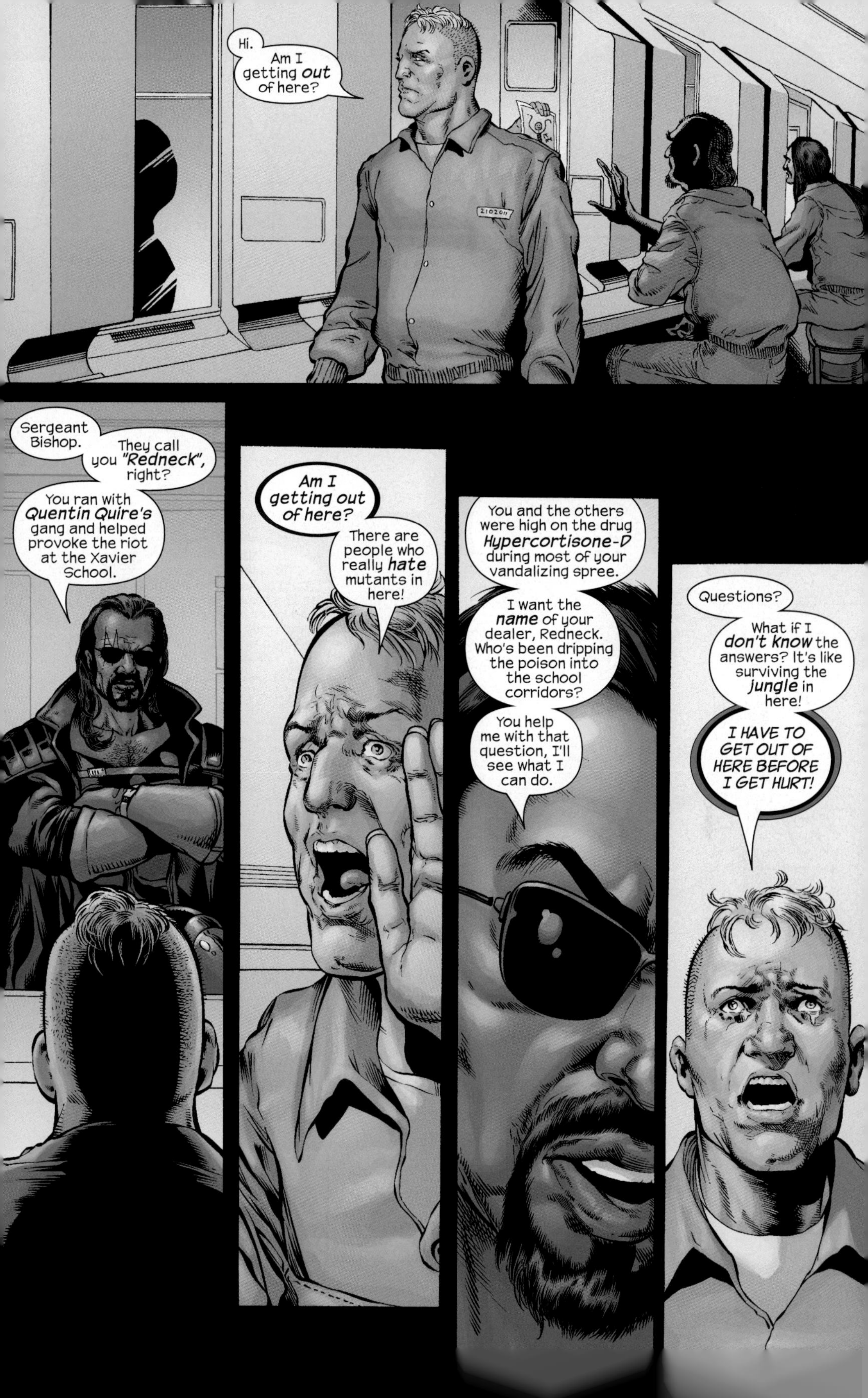

Hi.
Am I getting *out* of here?
Sergeant Bishop.
They call you *"Redneck"*, right?
You ran with *Quentin Quire's* gang and helped provoke the riot at the Xavier School.
Am I getting out of here?
There are people who really *hate* mutants in here!
You and the others were high on the drug *Hypercortisone-D* during most of your vandalizing spree.
I want the *name* of your dealer, Redneck. Who's been dripping the poison into the school corridors?
You help me with that question, I'll see what I can do.
Questions?
What if I *don't know* the answers? It's like surviving the *jungle* in here!
I HAVE TO GET OUT OF HERE BEFORE I GET HURT!

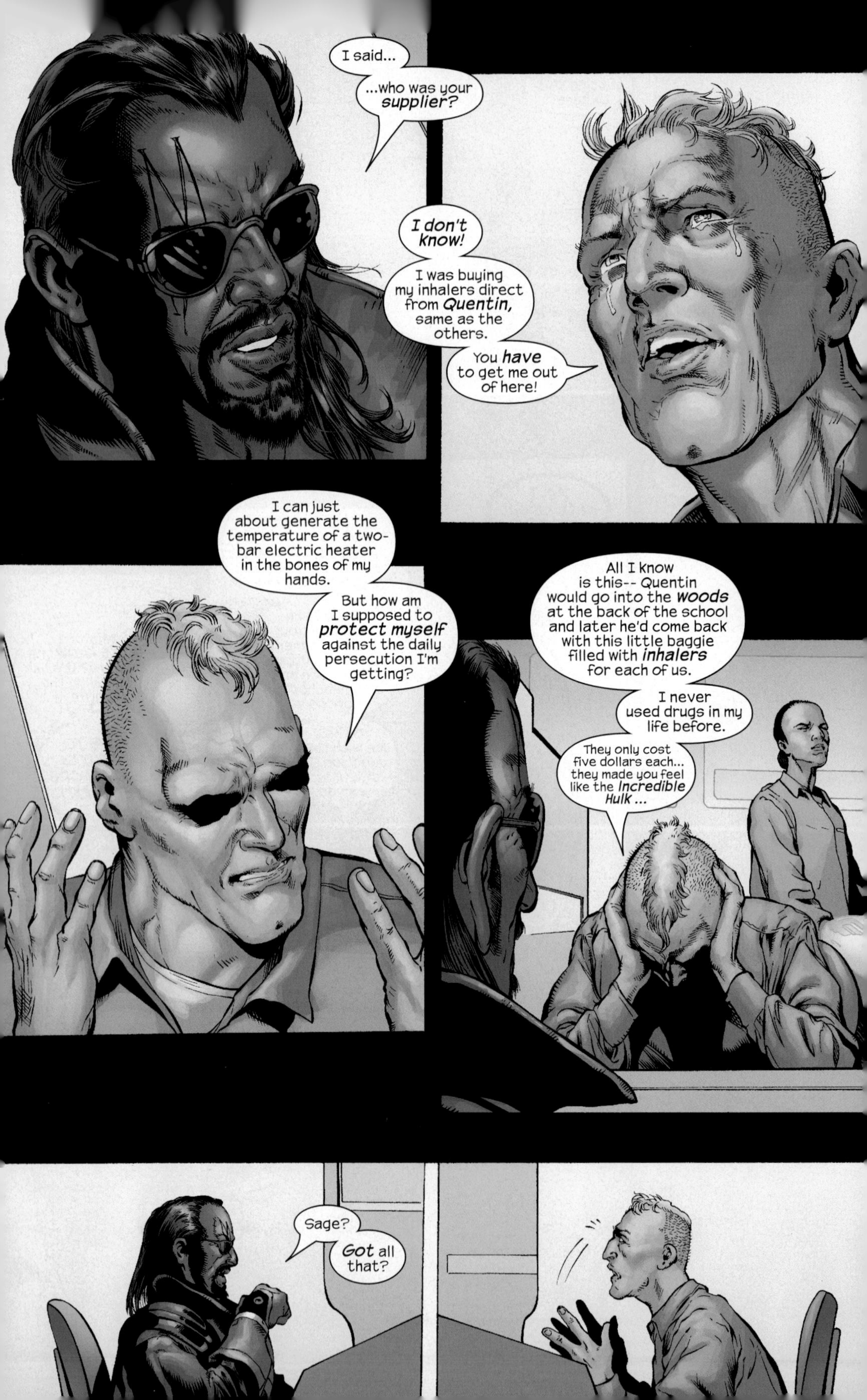
I said...
...who was your supplier?
I don't know!
I was buying my inhalers direct from Quentin, same as the others.
You have to get me out of here!
I can just about generate the temperature of a two-bar electric heater in the bones of my hands.
But how am I supposed to protect myself against the daily persecution I'm getting?
All I know is this-- Quentin would go into the woods at the back of the school and later he'd come back with this little baggie filled with inhalers for each of us.
I never used drugs in my life before.
They only cost five dollars each... they made you feel like the Incredible Hulk ...
Sage?
Got all that?

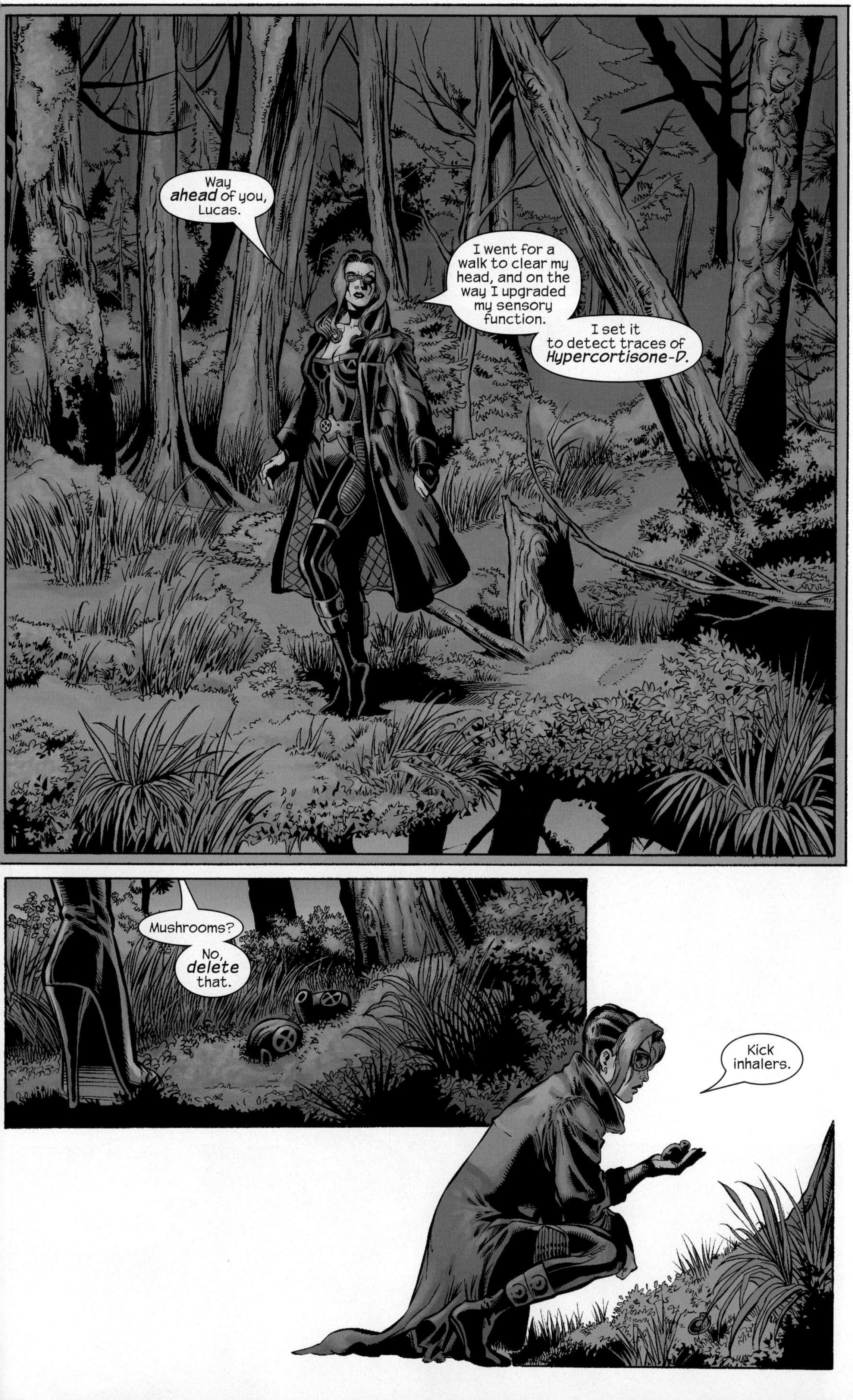
Way *ahead* of you, Lucas.
I went for a walk to clear my head, and on the way I upgraded my sensory function.
I set it to detect traces of *Hypercortisone-D.*
Mushrooms?
No, *delete* that.
Kick inhalers.

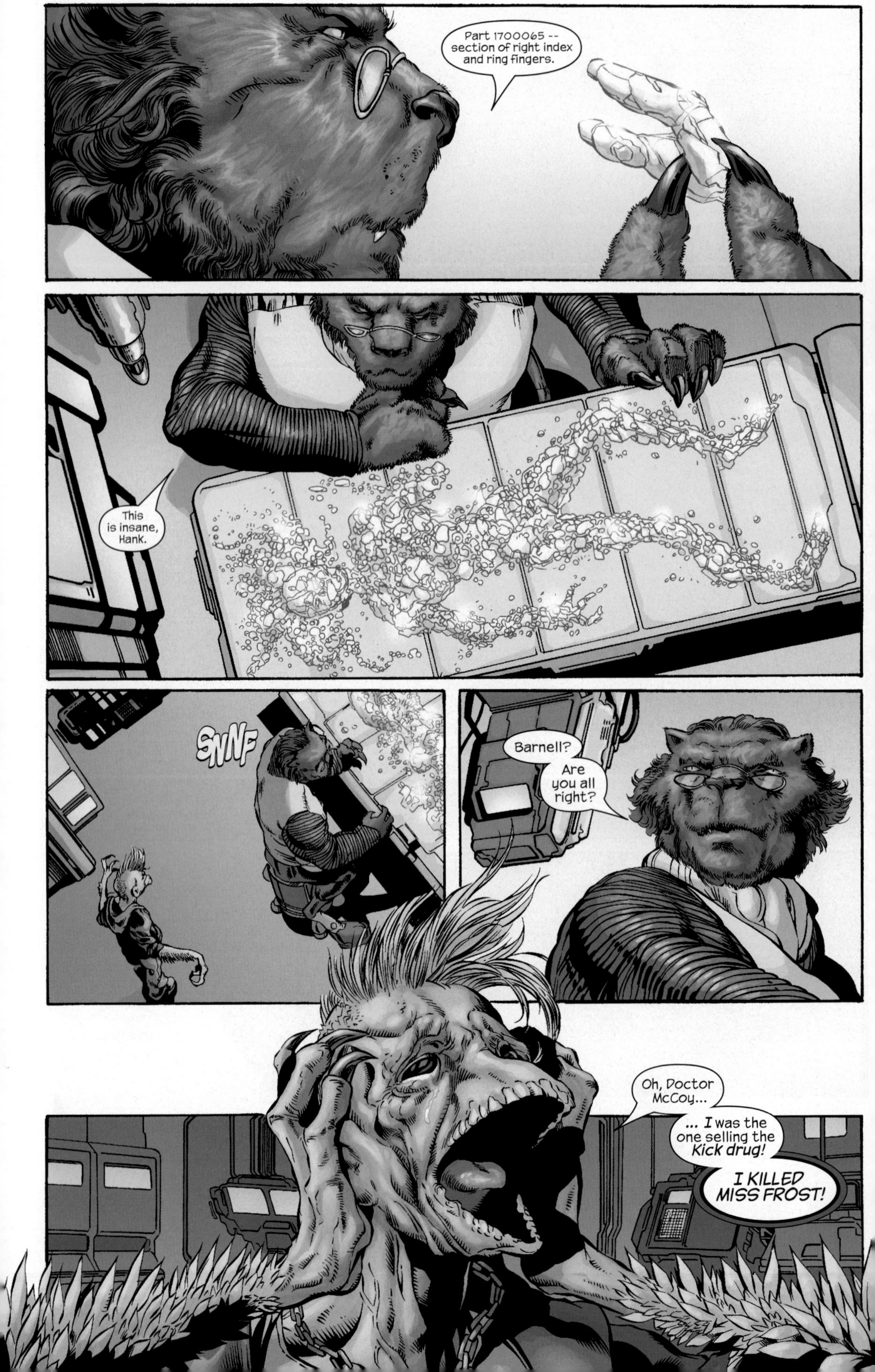
Part 1700065 -- section of right index and ring fingers.
This is insane, Hank.
SNNF
Barnell?
Are you all right?
Oh, Doctor McCoy...
... I was the one selling the Kick drug!
I KILLED MISS FROST!

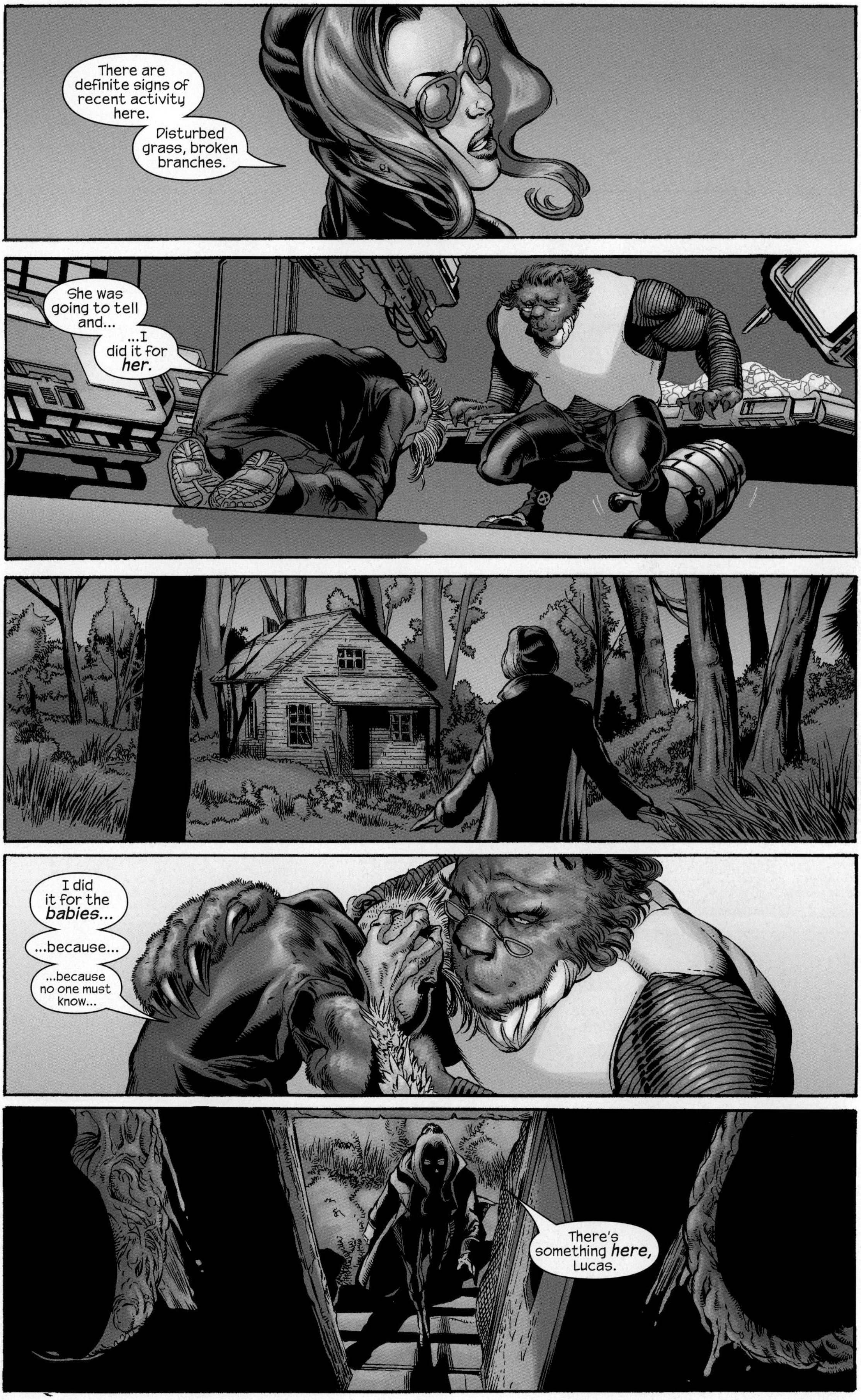
There are definite signs of recent activity here.
Disturbed grass, broken branches.
She was going to tell and...
...I did it for *her.*
I did it for the *babies...*
...because...
...because no one must know...
There's something *here,* Lucas.

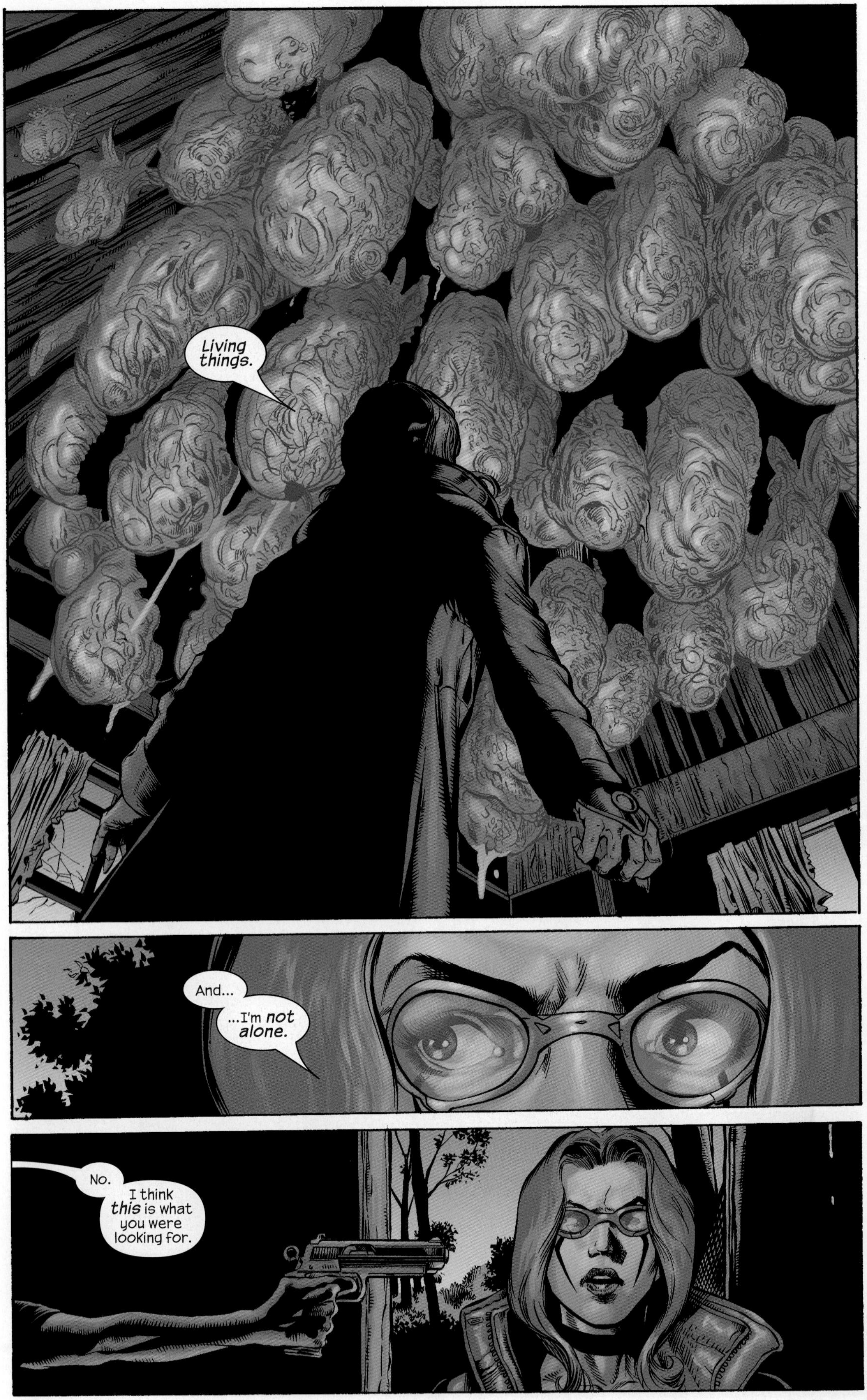
Living things.
And...
...I'm not alone.
No.
I think this is what you were looking for.

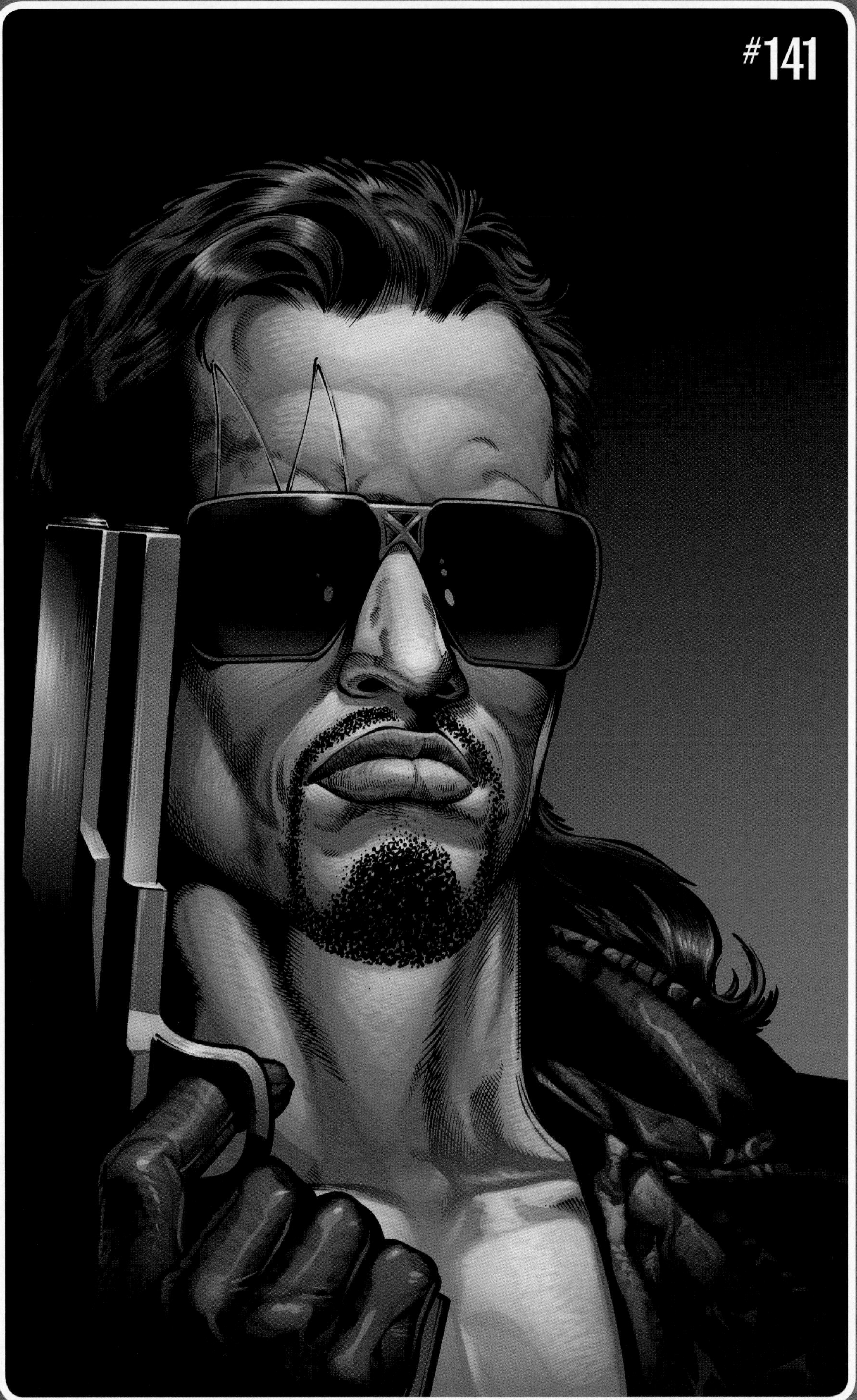
#141

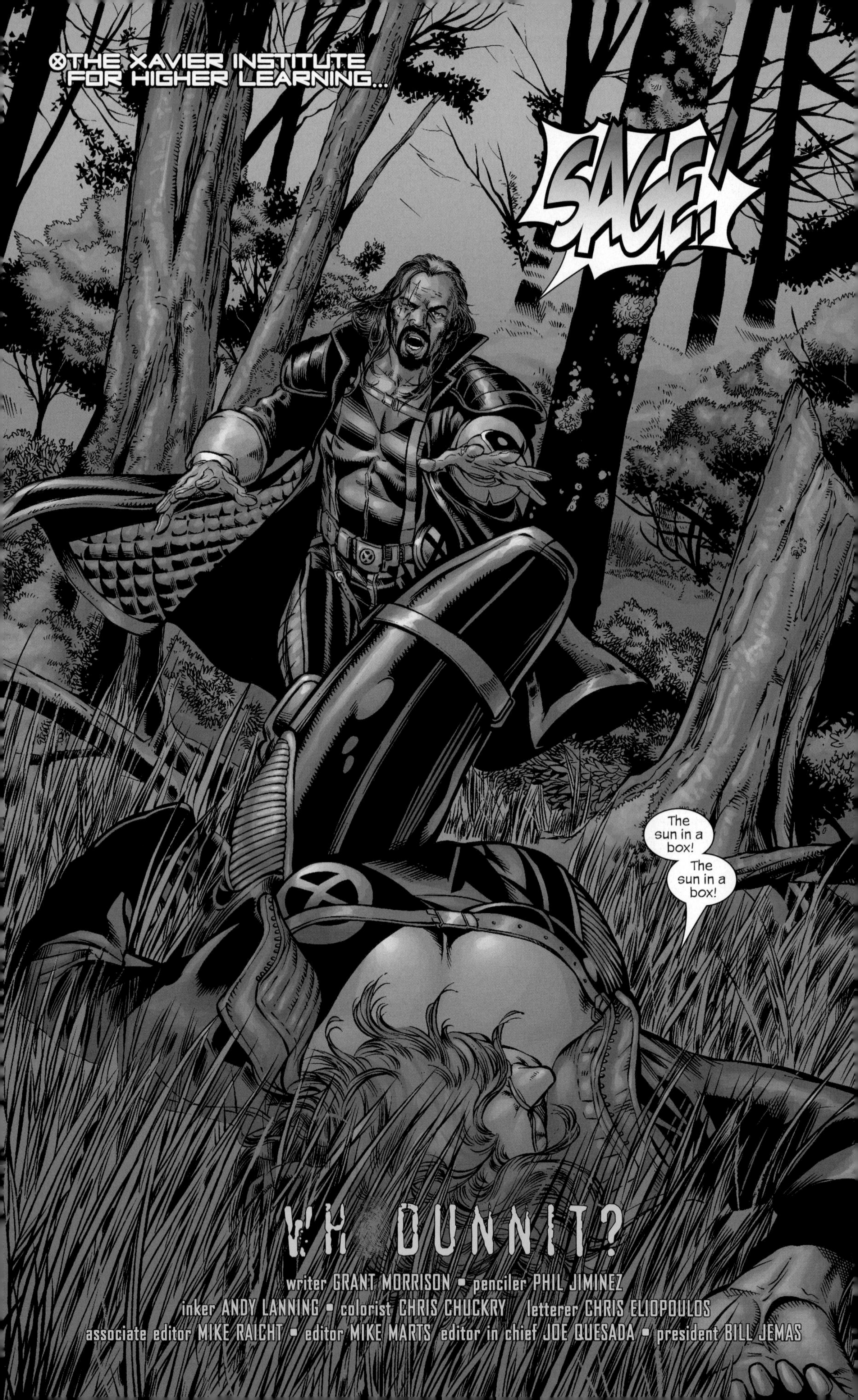
THE XAVIER INSTITUTE FOR HIGHER LEARNING...
SAGE!
The sun in a box!
The sun in a box!
WHO DUNNIT?
writer GRANT MORRISON • penciler PHIL JIMINEZ
inker ANDY LANNING • colorist CHRIS CHUCKRY letterer CHRIS ELIOPOULOS
associate editor MIKE RAICHT • editor MIKE MARTS editor in chief JOE QUESADA • president BILL JEMAS

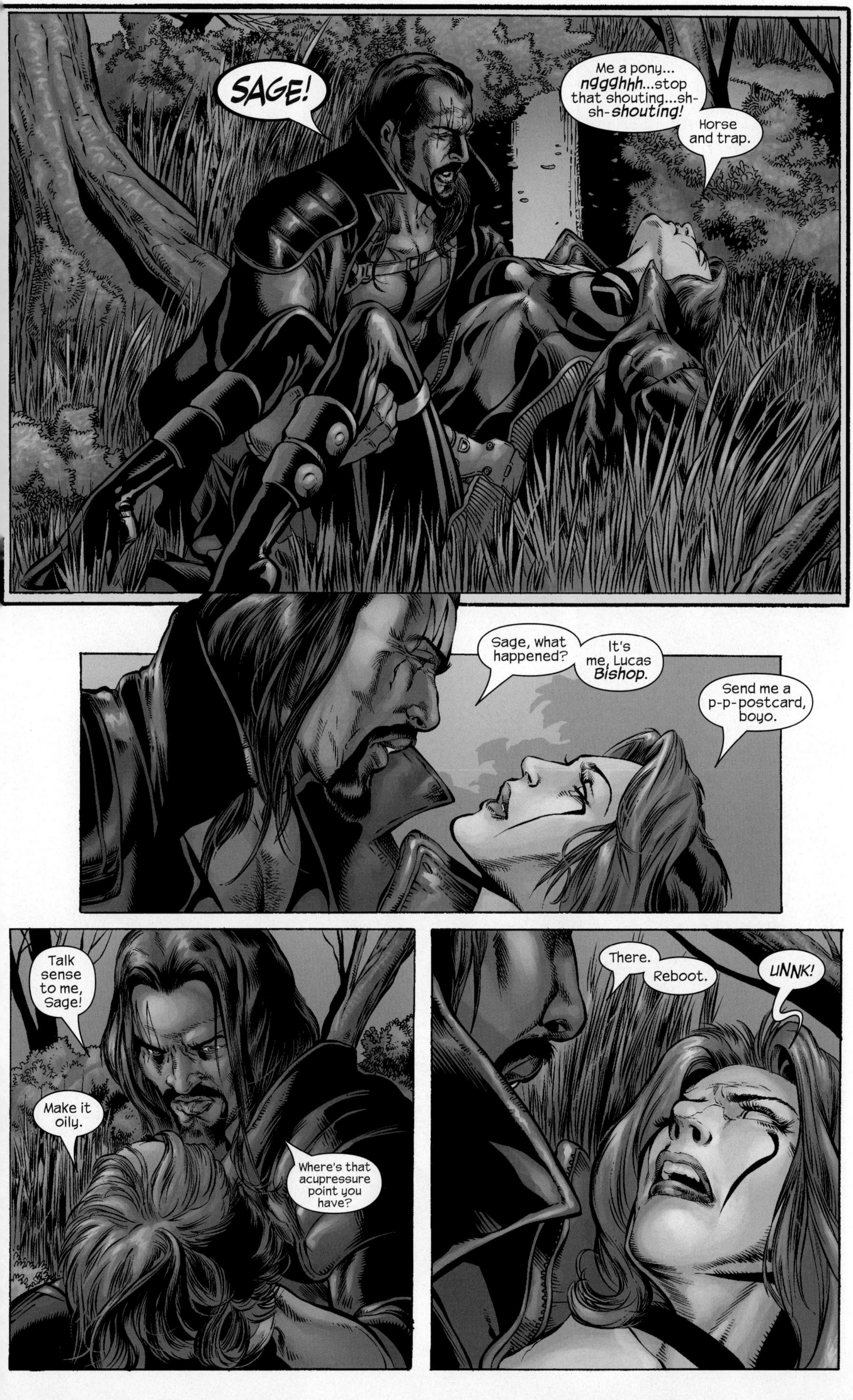
SAGE!
Me a pony... ngggghhh...stop that shouting...sh-sh-shouting!
Horse and trap.
Sage, what happened?
It's me, Lucas Bishop.
Send me a p-p-postcard, boyo.
Talk sense to me, Sage!
Make it oily.
Where's that acupressure point you have?
There.
Reboot.
UNNK!

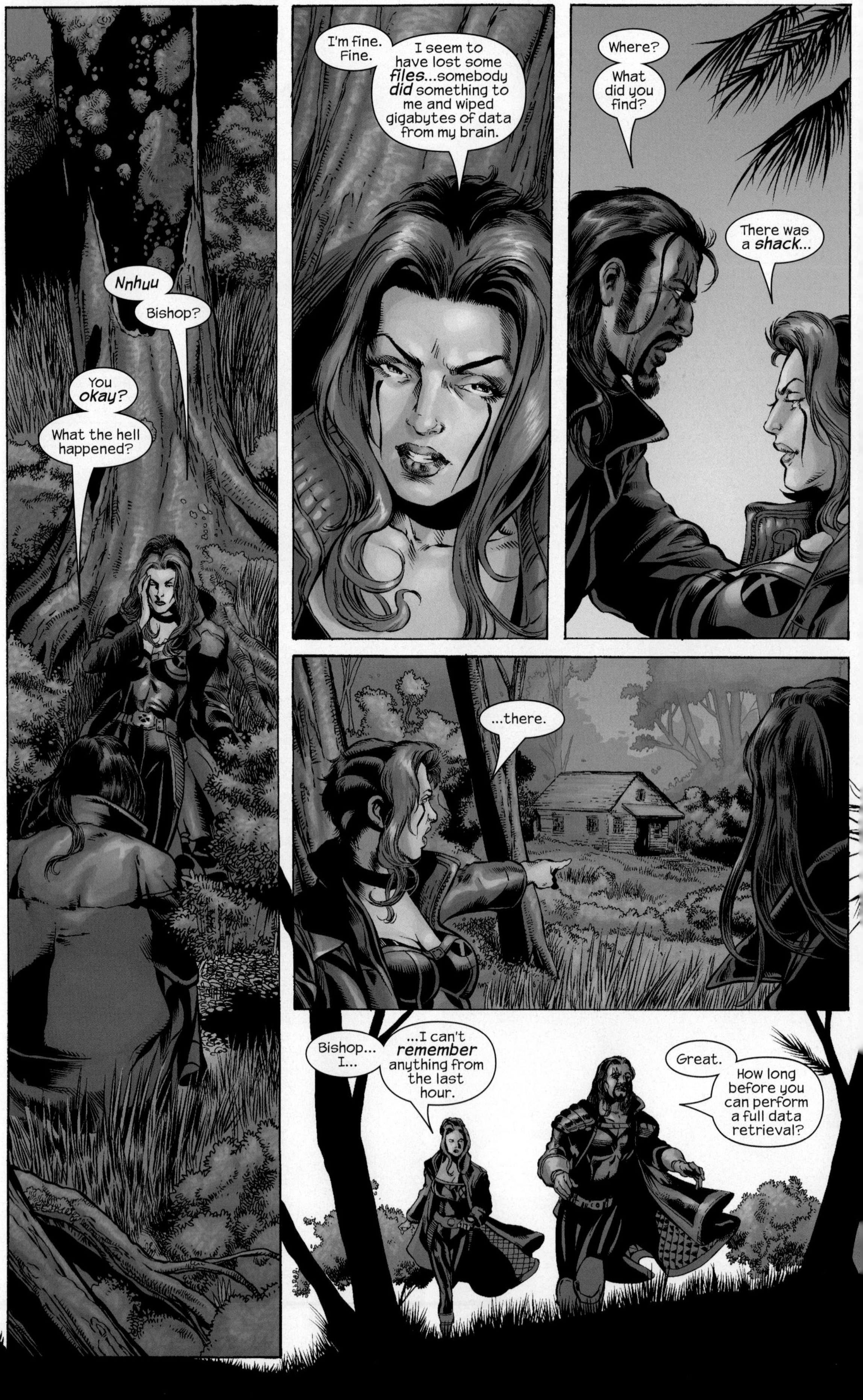

Nnhuu
Bishop?
You okay?
What the hell happened?
I'm fine. Fine.
I seem to have lost some files...somebody did something to me and wiped gigabytes of data from my brain.
Where?
What did you find?
There was a shack...
...there.
Bishop... I...
...I can't remember anything from the last hour.
Great.
How long before you can perform a full data retrieval?

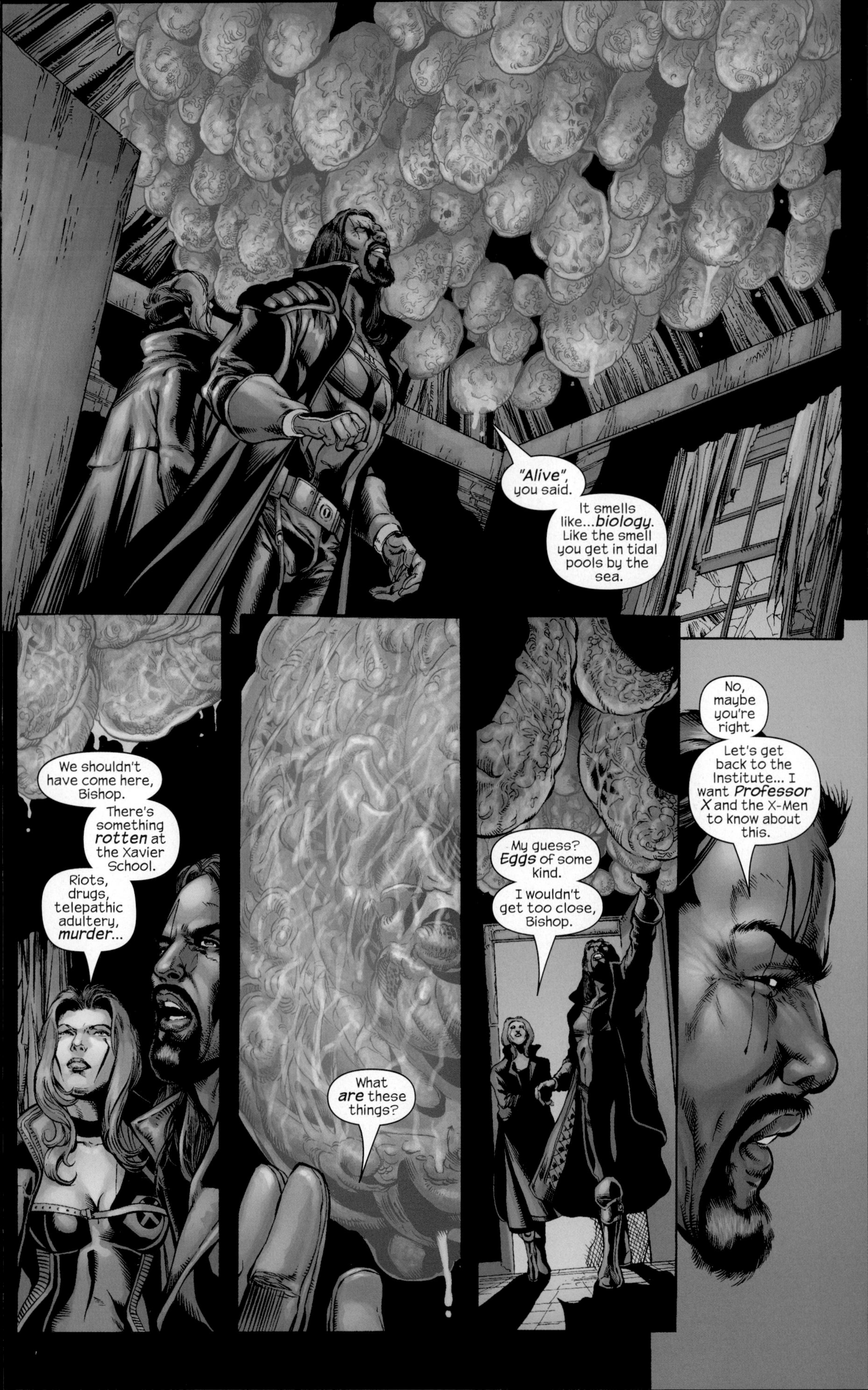
"Alive", you said.
It smells like...biology. Like the smell you get in tidal pools by the sea.
We shouldn't have come here, Bishop.
There's something rotten at the Xavier School.
Riots, drugs, telepathic adultery, murder...
What are these things?
My guess? Eggs of some kind.
I wouldn't get too close, Bishop.
No, maybe you're right.
Let's get back to the Institute... I want Professor X and the X-Men to know about this.

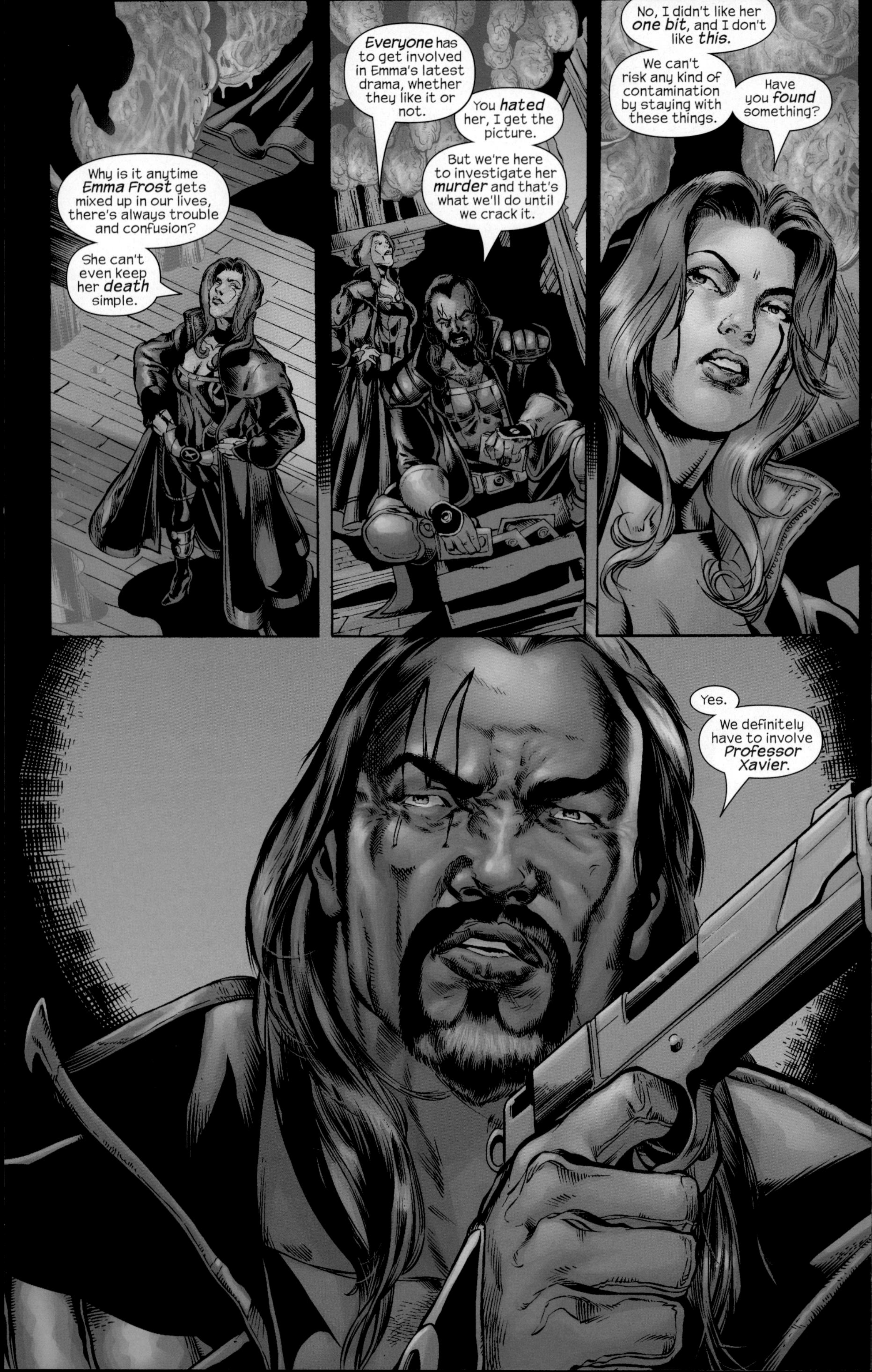
Why is it anytime Emma Frost gets mixed up in our lives, there's always trouble and confusion?
She can't even keep her death simple.
Everyone has to get involved in Emma's latest drama, whether they like it or not.
You hated her, I get the picture.
But we're here to investigate her murder and that's what we'll do until we crack it.
No, I didn't like her one bit, and I don't like this.
We can't risk any kind of contamination by staying with these things.
Have you found something?
Yes.
We definitely have to involve Professor Xavier.

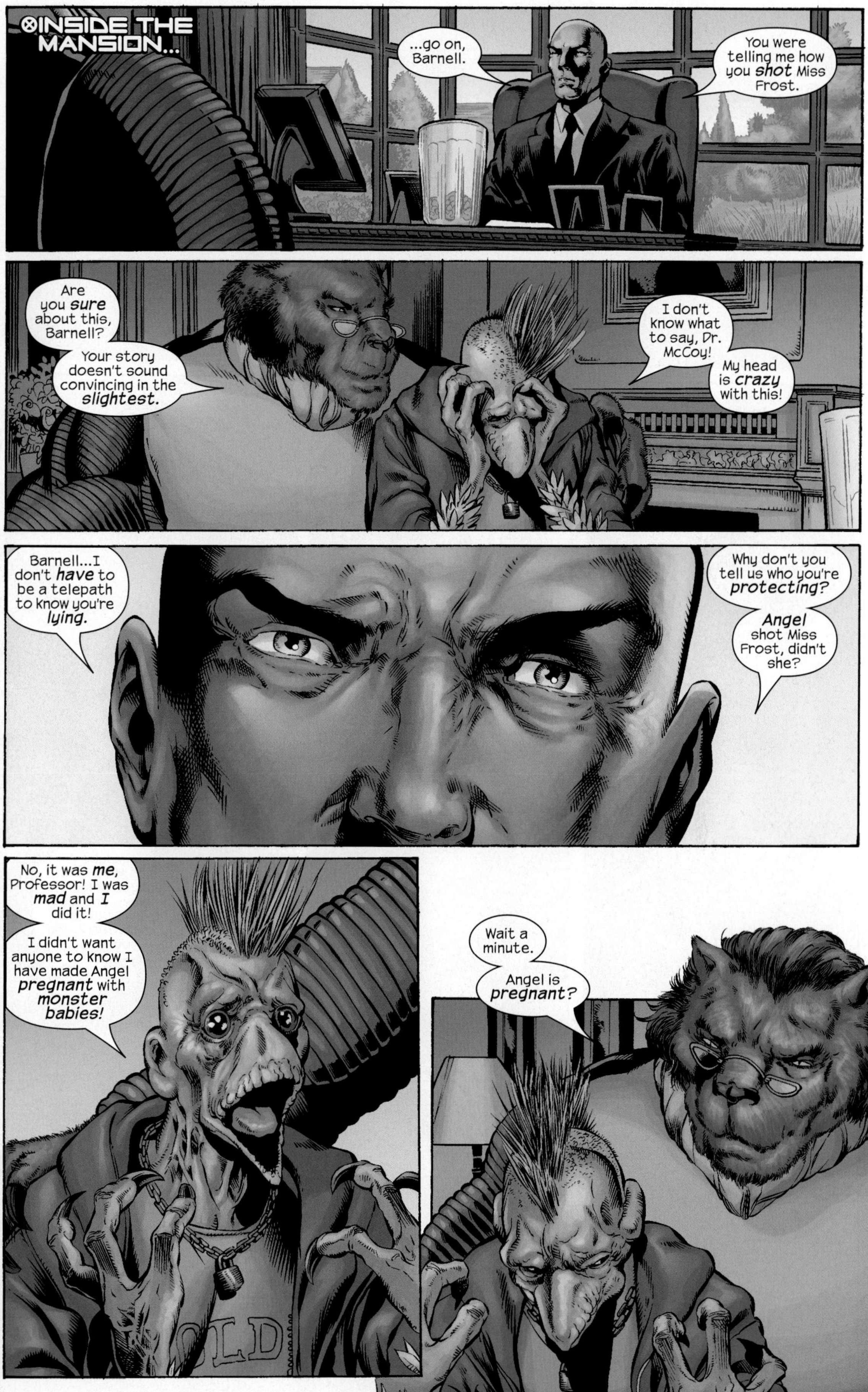
INSIDE THE MANSION...
...go on, Barnell.
You were telling me how you shot Miss Frost.
Are you sure about this, Barnell?
Your story doesn't sound convincing in the slightest.
I don't know what to say, Dr. McCoy!
My head is crazy with this!
Barnell...I don't have to be a telepath to know you're lying.
Why don't you tell us who you're protecting?
Angel shot Miss Frost, didn't she?
No, it was me, Professor! I was mad and I did it!
I didn't want anyone to know I have made Angel pregnant with monster babies!
Wait a minute.
Angel is pregnant?

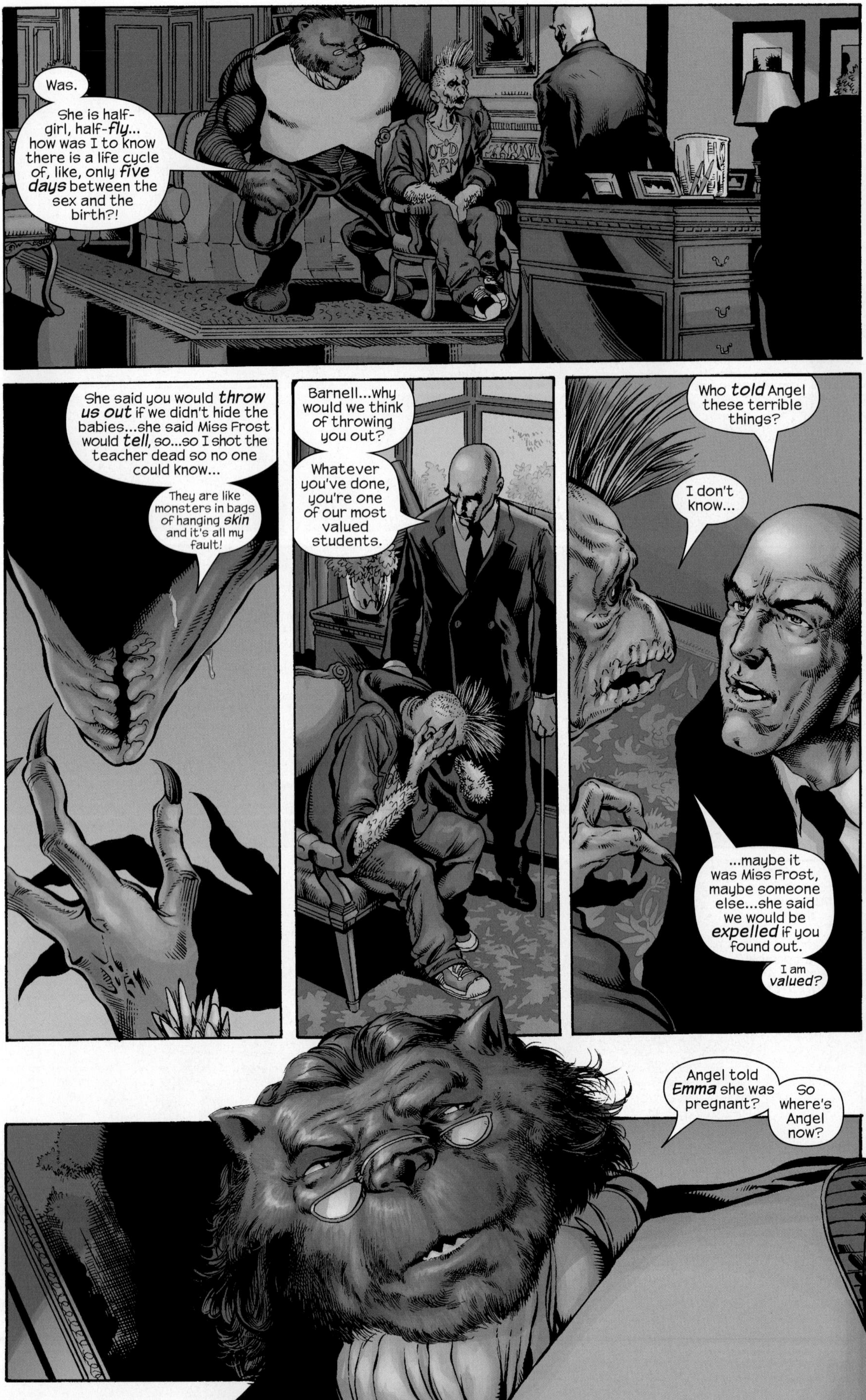
Was.
She is half-girl, half-*fly*... how was I to know there is a life cycle of, like, only *five days* between the sex and the birth?!
She said you would *throw us out* if we didn't hide the babies...she said Miss Frost would *tell*, so...so I shot the teacher dead so no one could know...
They are like monsters in bags of hanging *skin* and it's all my fault!
Barnell...why would we think of throwing you out?
Whatever you've done, you're one of our most valued students.
Who *told* Angel these terrible things?
I don't know...
...maybe it was Miss Frost, maybe someone else...she said we would be *expelled* if you found out.
I am *valued?*
Angel told *Emma* she was pregnant?
So where's Angel now?

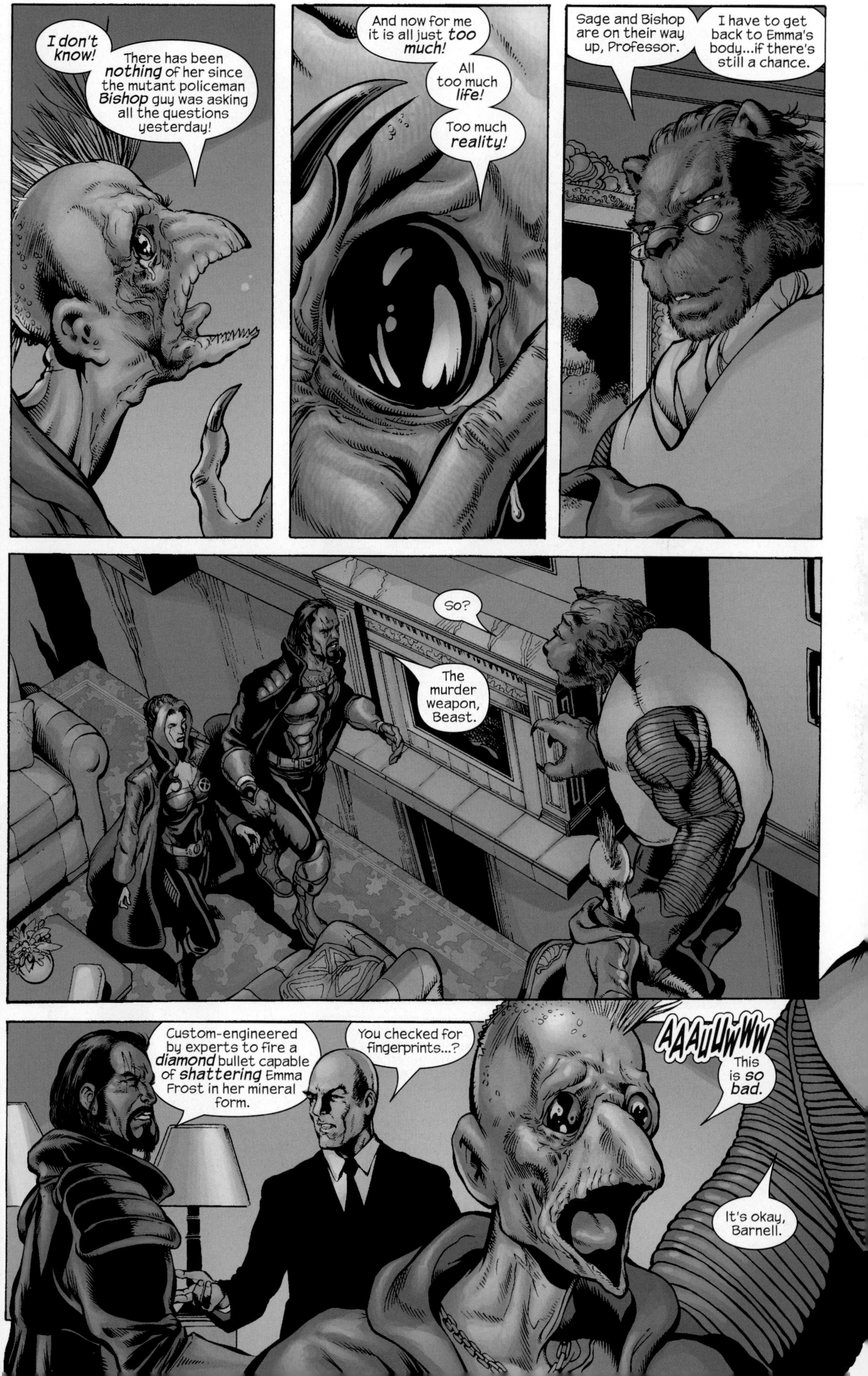
I don't know!
There has been nothing of her since the mutant policeman Bishop guy was asking all the questions yesterday!
And now for me it is all just too much!
All too much life!
Too much reality!
Sage and Bishop are on their way up, Professor.
I have to get back to Emma's body...if there's still a chance.
So?
The murder weapon, Beast.
Custom-engineered by experts to fire a diamond bullet capable of shattering Emma Frost in her mineral form.
You checked for fingerprints...?
AAAUUWWW
This is so bad.
It's okay, Barnell.

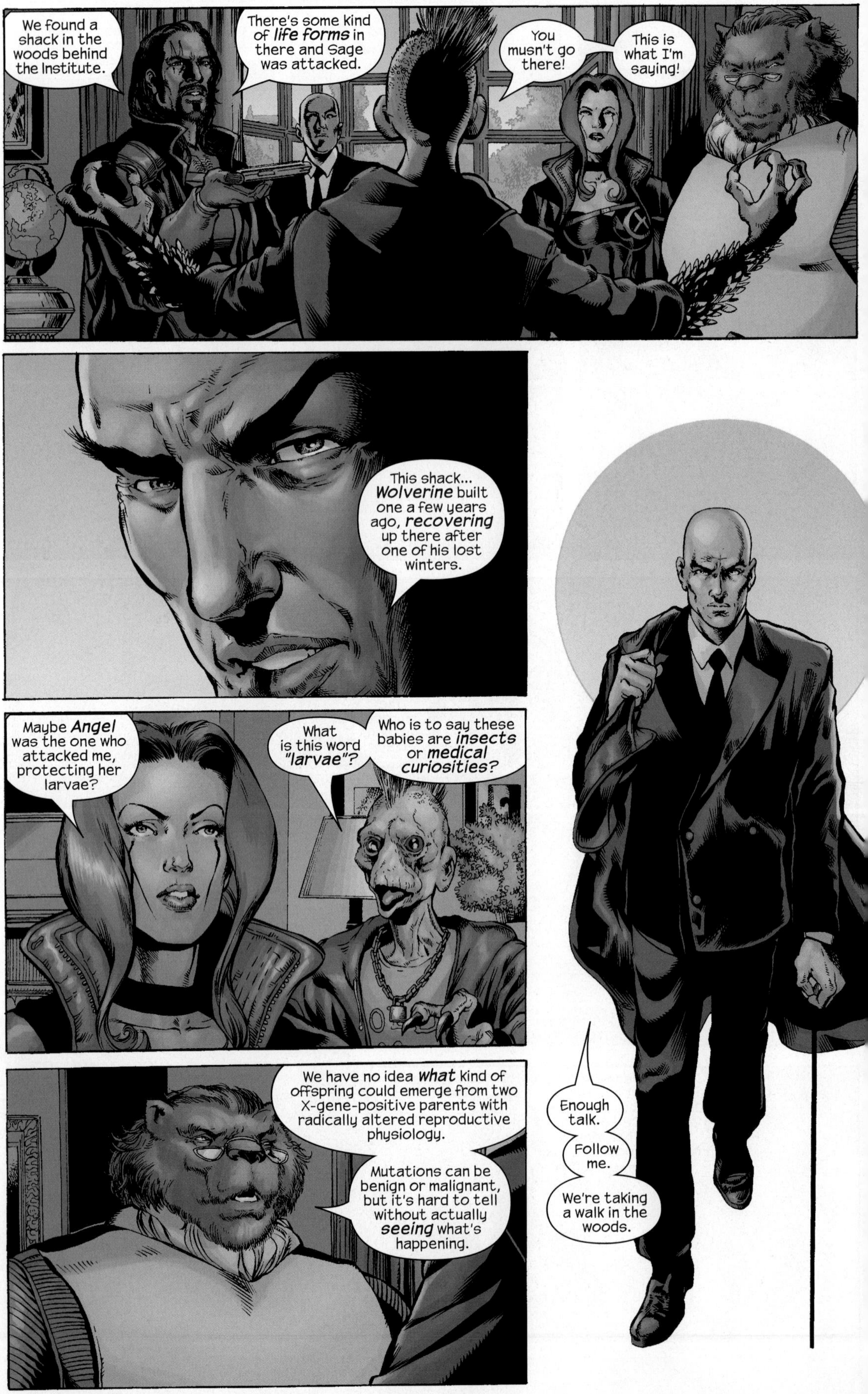
We found a shack in the woods behind the Institute.
There's some kind of life forms in there and Sage was attacked.
You musn't go there!
This is what I'm saying!
This shack... Wolverine built one a few years ago, recovering up there after one of his lost winters.
Maybe Angel was the one who attacked me, protecting her larvae?
What is this word "larvae"?
Who is to say these babies are insects or medical curiosities?
We have no idea what kind of offspring could emerge from two X-gene-positive parents with radically altered reproductive physiology.
Mutations can be benign or malignant, but it's hard to tell without actually seeing what's happening.
Enough talk.
Follow me.
We're taking a walk in the woods.

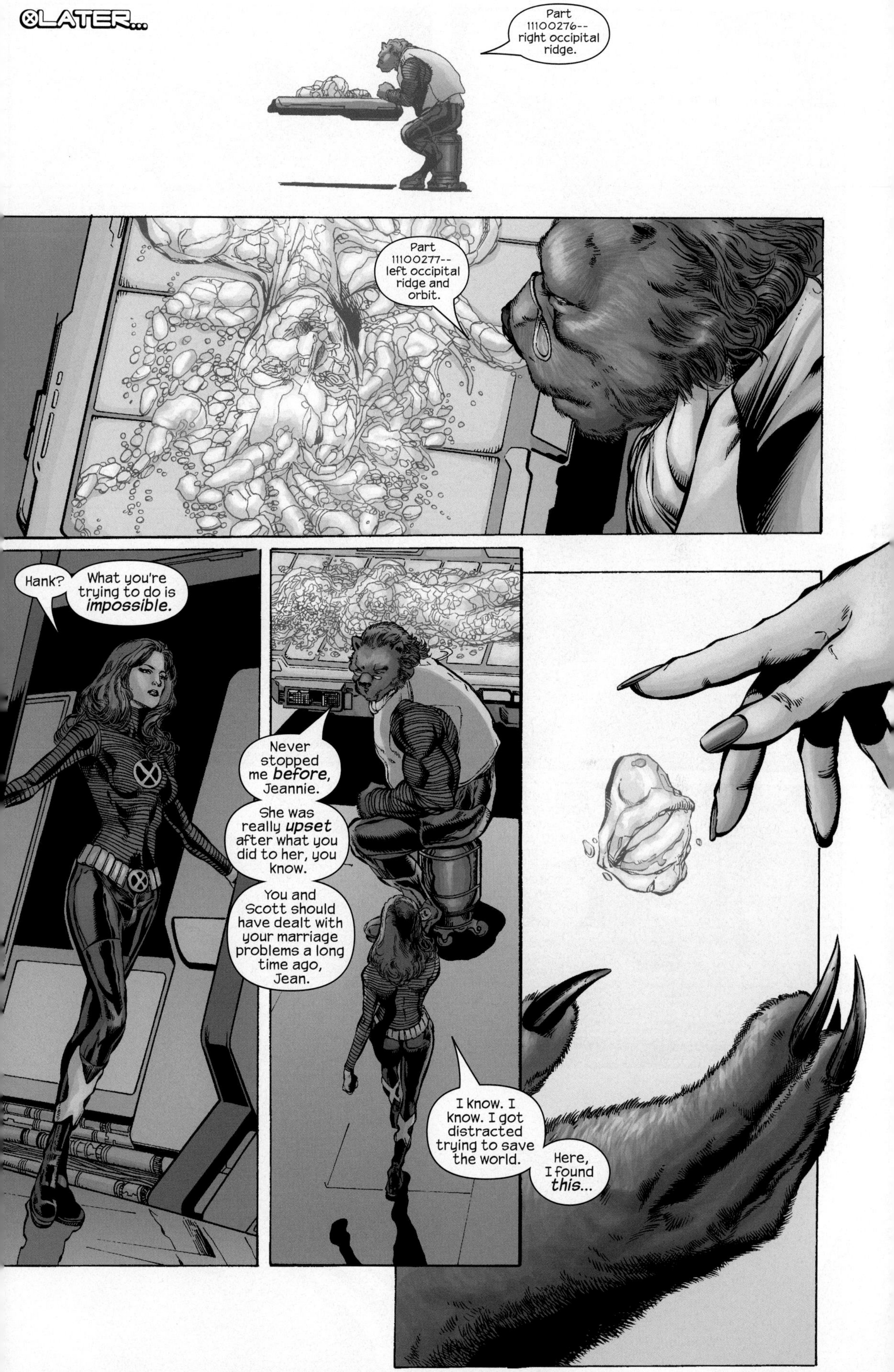
LATER...
Part 11100276-- right occipital ridge.
Part 11100277-- left occipital ridge and orbit.
Hank?
What you're trying to do is *impossible.*
Never stopped me *before,* Jeannie.
She was really *upset* after what you did to her, you know.
You and Scott should have dealt with your marriage problems a long time ago, Jean.
I know. I know. I got distracted trying to save the world.
Here, I found *this...*

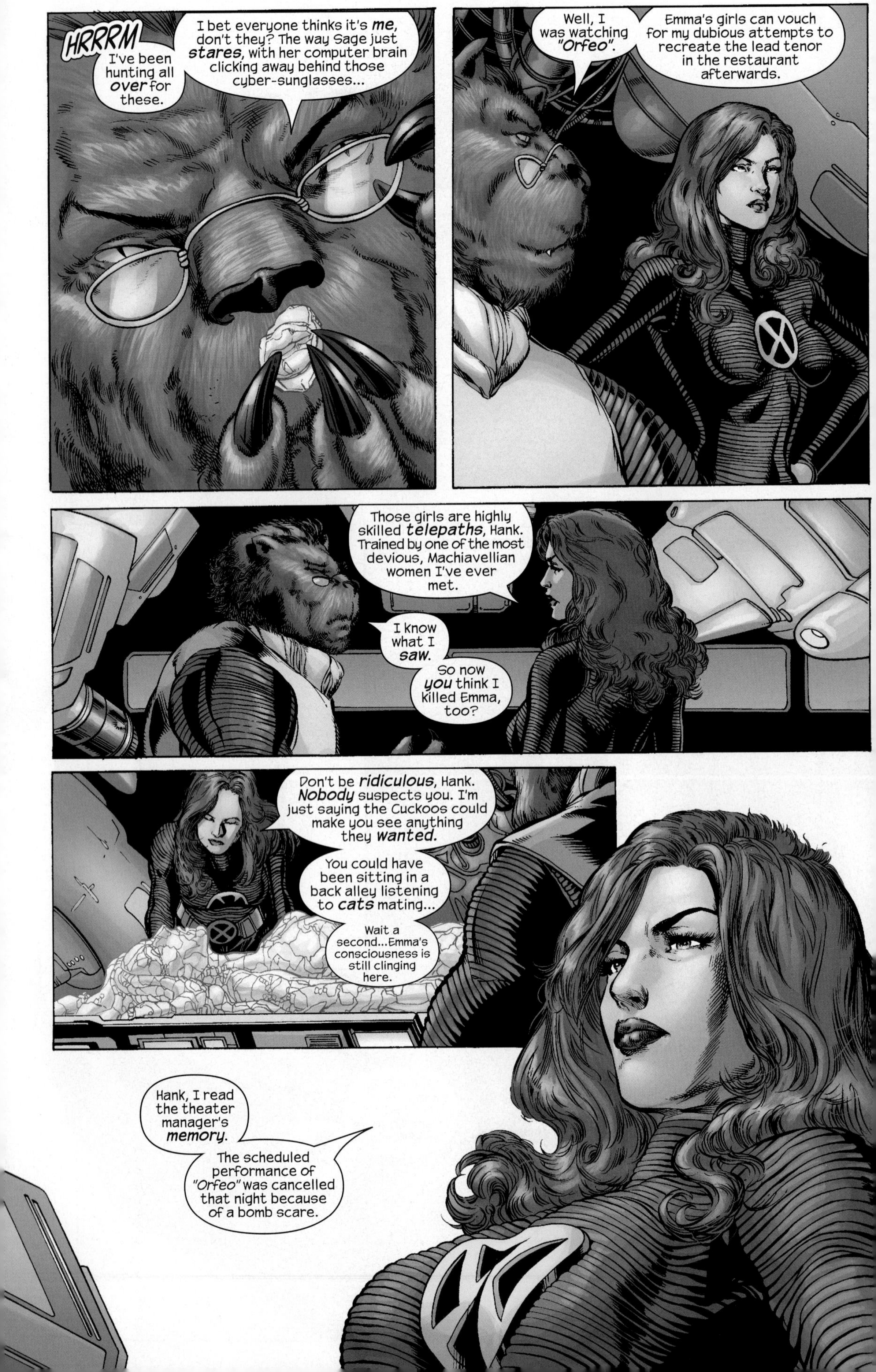
HRRRM
I've been hunting all over for these.
I bet everyone thinks it's me, don't they? The way Sage just stares, with her computer brain clicking away behind those cyber-sunglasses...
Well, I was watching "Orfeo".
Emma's girls can vouch for my dubious attempts to recreate the lead tenor in the restaurant afterwards.
Those girls are highly skilled telepaths, Hank. Trained by one of the most devious, Machiavellian women I've ever met.
I know what I saw.
So now you think I killed Emma, too?
Don't be ridiculous, Hank. Nobody suspects you. I'm just saying the Cuckoos could make you see anything they wanted.
You could have been sitting in a back alley listening to cats mating...
Wait a second...Emma's consciousness is still clinging here.
Hank, I read the theater manager's memory.
The scheduled performance of "Orfeo" was cancelled that night because of a bomb scare.

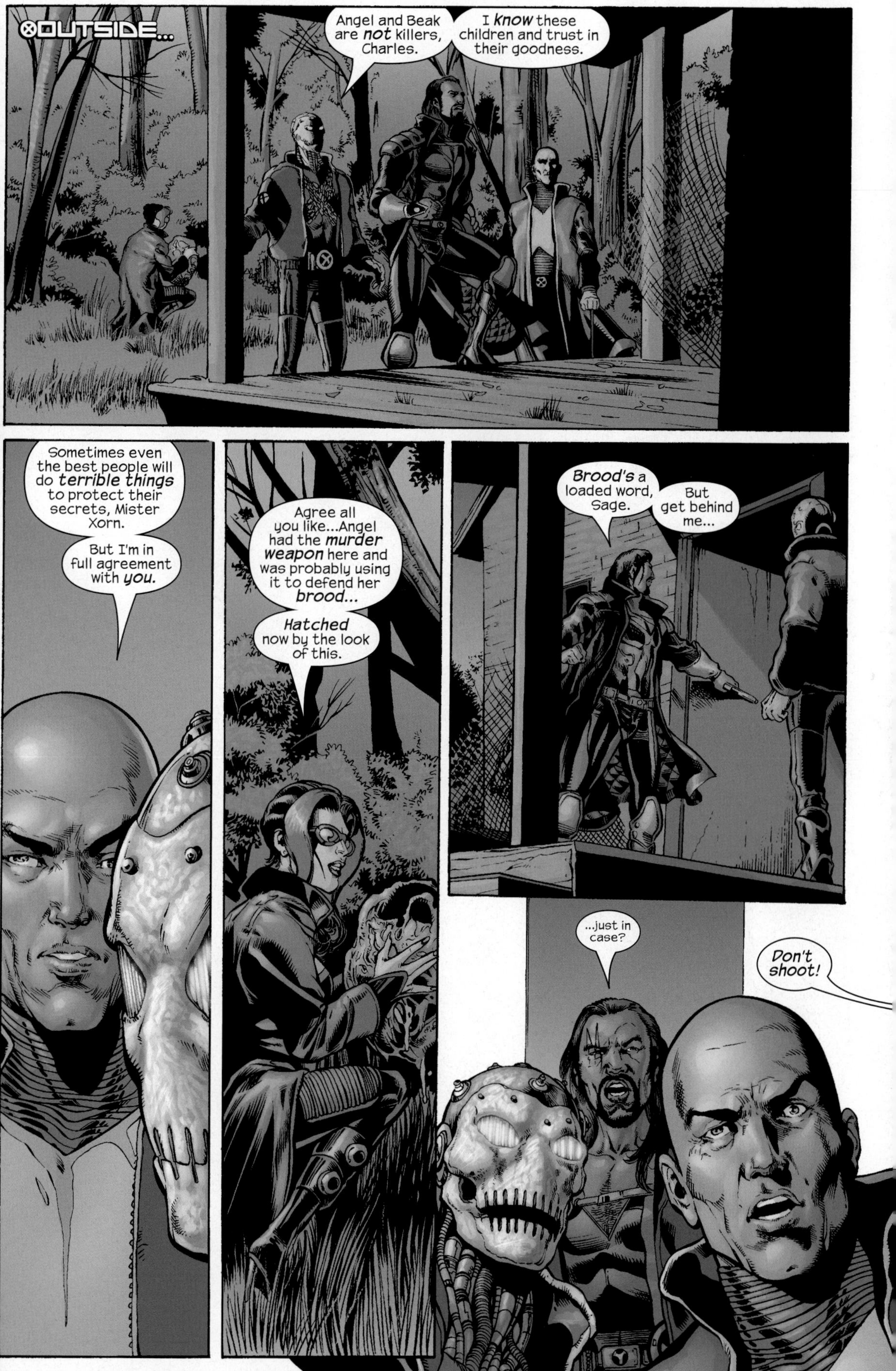

OUTSIDE...
Angel and Beak are not killers, Charles.
I know these children and trust in their goodness.
Sometimes even the best people will do terrible things to protect their secrets, Mister Xorn.
But I'm in full agreement with you.
Agree all you like...Angel had the murder weapon here and was probably using it to defend her brood...
Hatched now by the look of this.
Brood's a loaded word, Sage.
But get behind me...
...just in case?
Don't shoot!

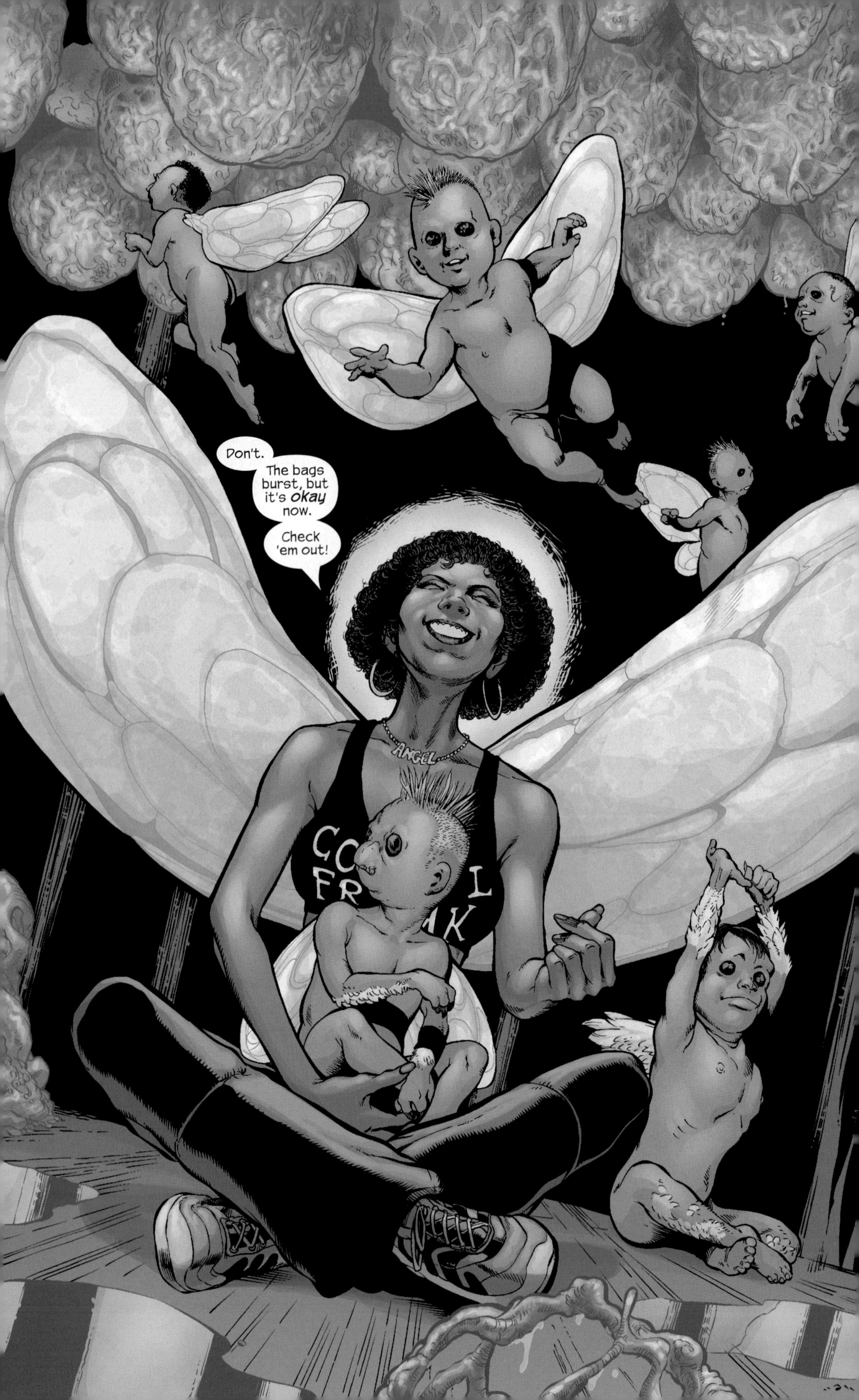
Don't.
The bags burst, but it's *okay* now.
Check 'em out!
ANGEL

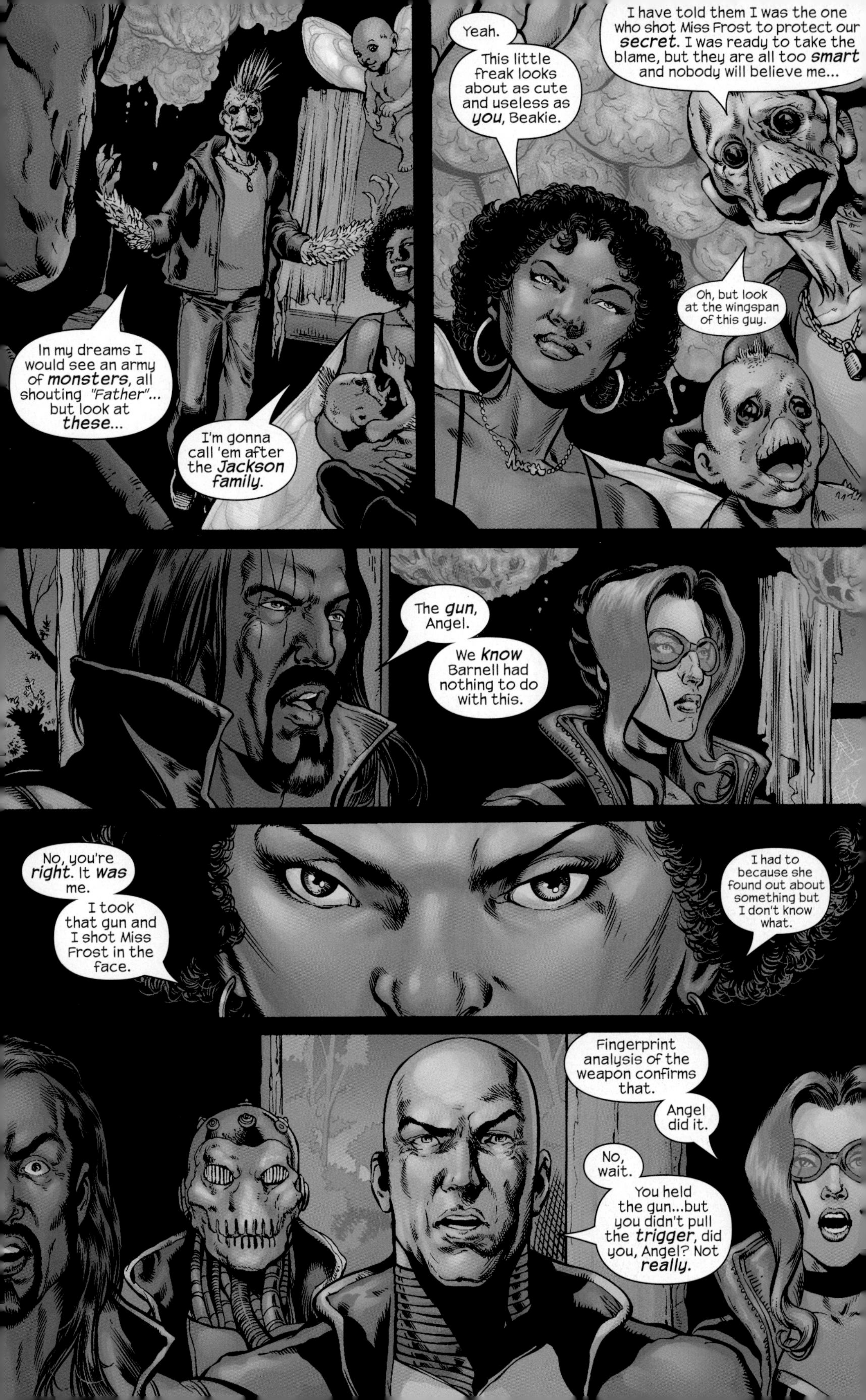
In my dreams I would see an army of *monsters*, all shouting *"Father"*... but look at *these*...
I'm gonna call 'em after the *Jackson family*.
Yeah.
This little freak looks about as cute and useless as *you*, Beakie.
I have told them I was the one who shot Miss Frost to protect our *secret*. I was ready to take the blame, but they are all too *smart* and nobody will believe me...
Oh, but look at the wingspan of this guy.
The *gun*, Angel.
We *know* Barnell had nothing to do with this.
No, you're *right*. It *was* me.
I took that gun and I shot Miss Frost in the face.
I had to because she found out about something but I don't know what.
Fingerprint analysis of the weapon confirms that.
Angel did it.
No, wait.
You held the gun...but you didn't pull the *trigger*, did you, Angel? Not *really*.

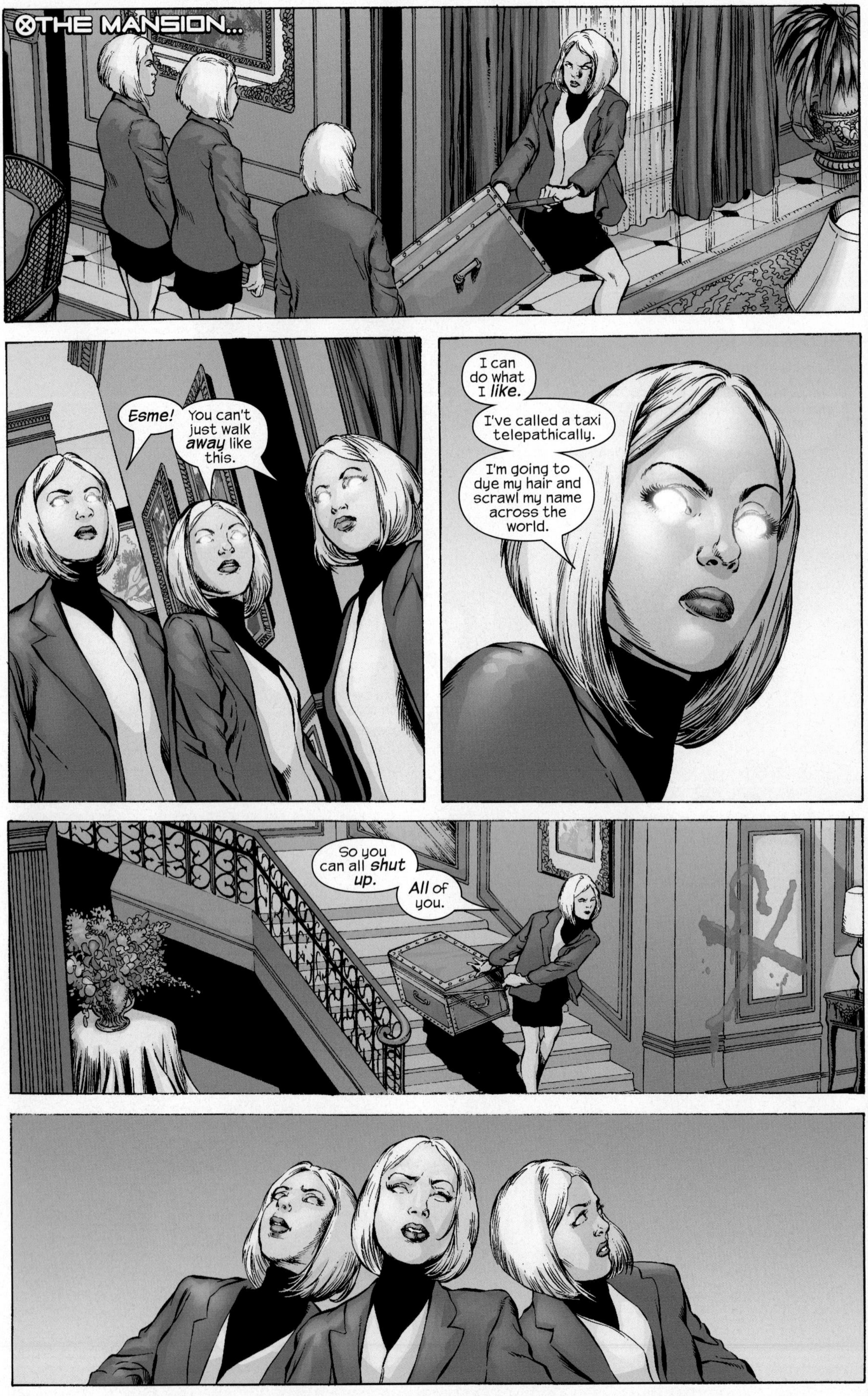
THE MANSION...
Esme!
You can't just walk away like this.
I can do what I like.
I've called a taxi telepathically.
I'm going to dye my hair and scrawl my name across the world.
So you can all shut up.
All of you.

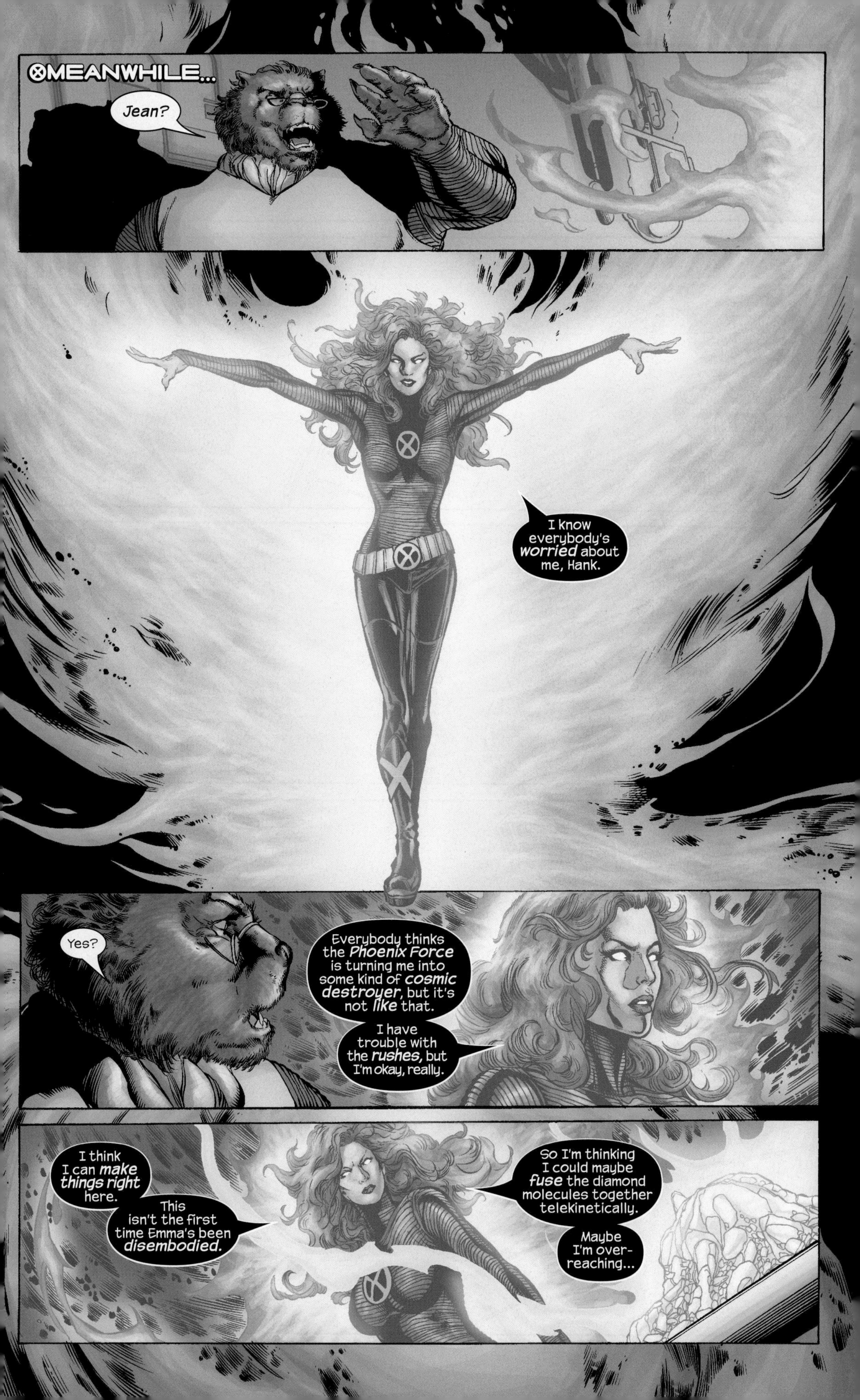
MEANWHILE...
Jean?
I know everybody's *worried* about me, Hank.
Yes?
Everybody thinks the *Phoenix Force* is turning me into some kind of *cosmic destroyer*, but it's not *like* that.
I have trouble with the *rushes*, but I'm okay, really.
I think I can *make things right* here.
This isn't the first time Emma's been *disembodied*.
So I'm thinking I could maybe *fuse* the diamond molecules together telekinetically.
Maybe I'm over-reaching...

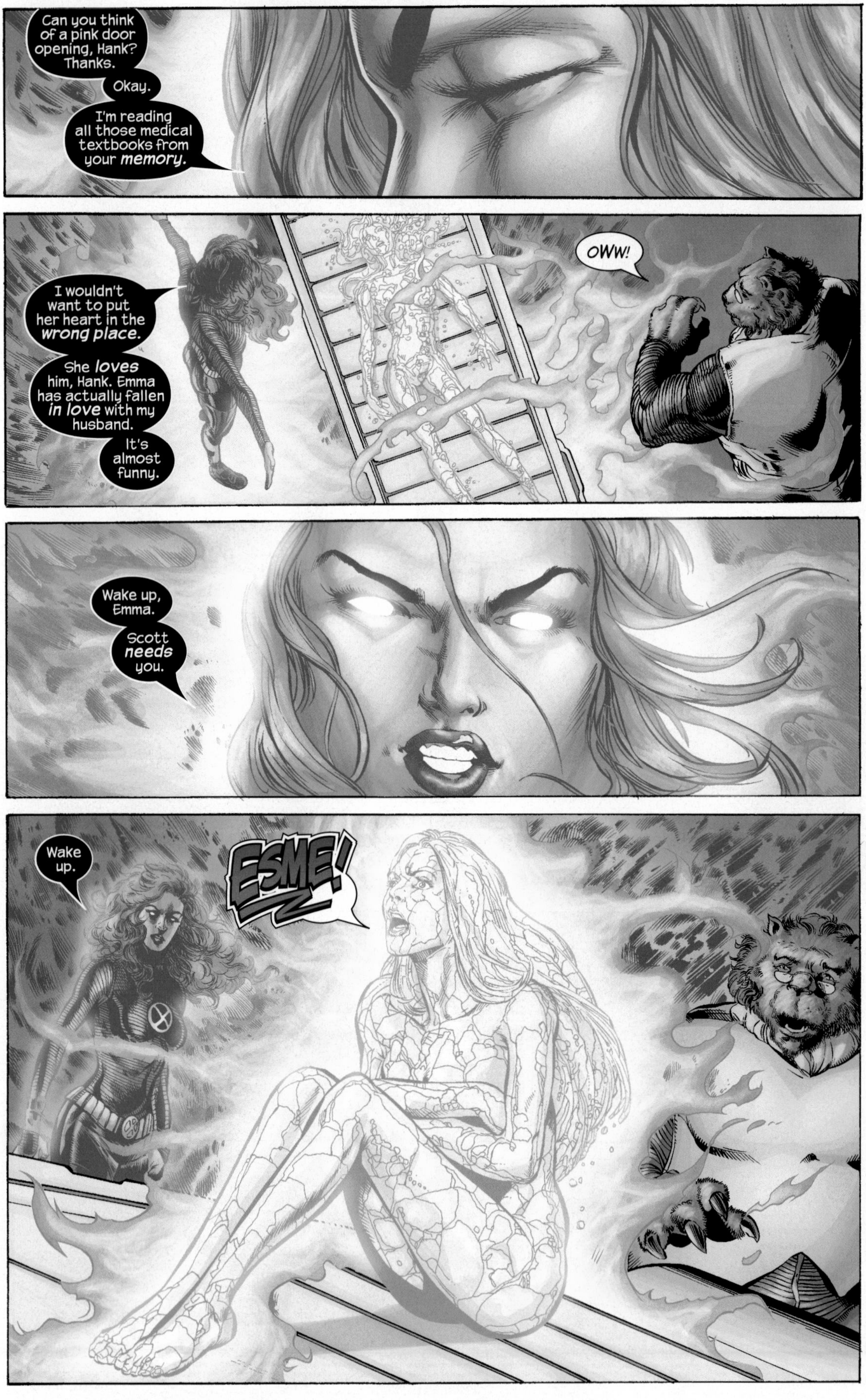

Can you think of a pink door opening, Hank? Thanks.
Okay.
I'm reading all those medical textbooks from your memory.
I wouldn't want to put her heart in the wrong place.
She loves him, Hank. Emma has actually fallen in love with my husband.
It's almost funny.
OWW!
Wake up, Emma.
Scott needs you.
Wake up.
ESME!

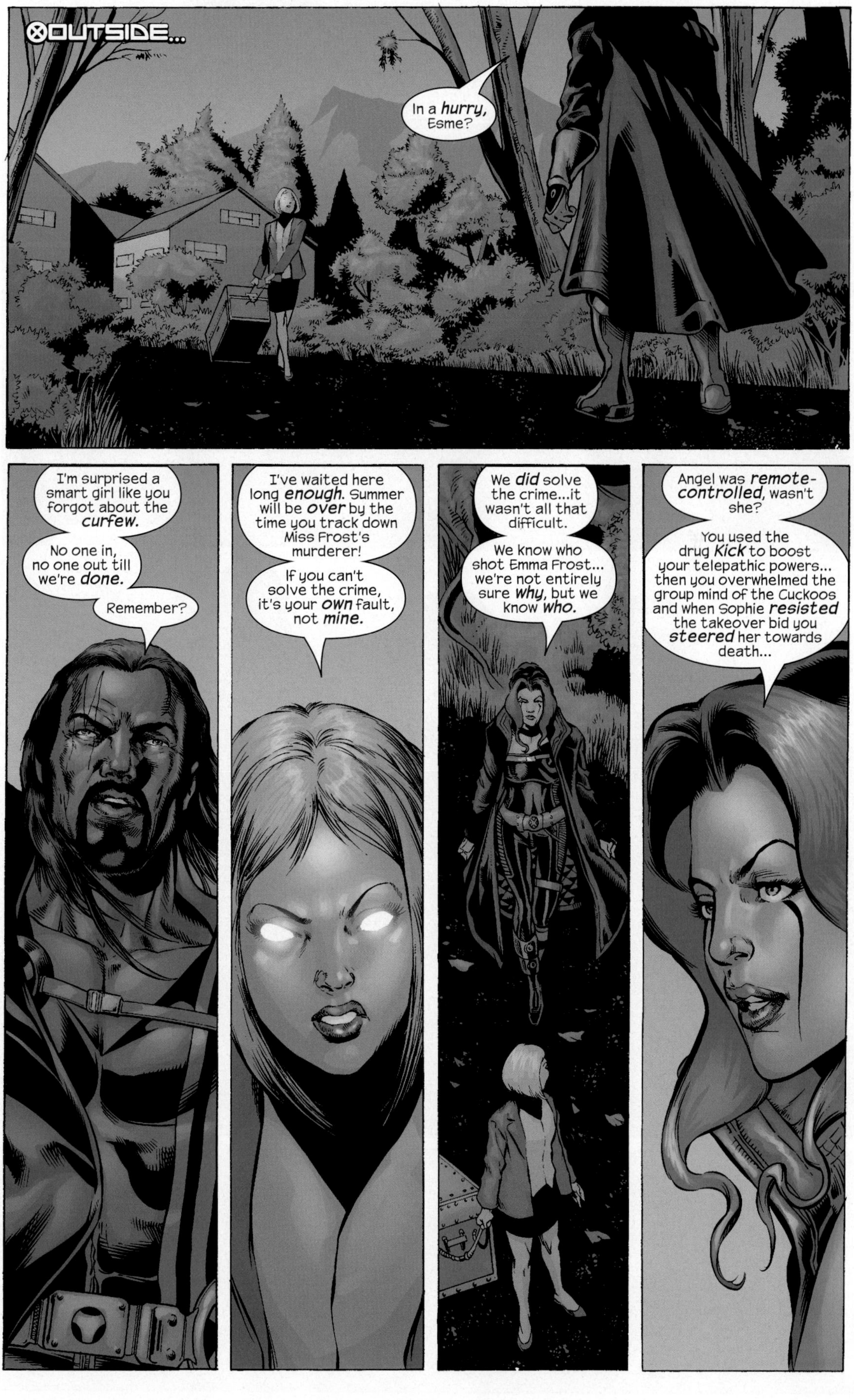
OUTSIDE...
In a hurry, Esme?
I'm surprised a smart girl like you forgot about the curfew.
No one in, no one out till we're done.
Remember?
I've waited here long enough. Summer will be over by the time you track down Miss Frost's murderer!
If you can't solve the crime, it's your own fault, not mine.
We did solve the crime...it wasn't all that difficult.
We know who shot Emma Frost... we're not entirely sure why, but we know who.
Angel was remote-controlled, wasn't she?
You used the drug Kick to boost your telepathic powers... then you overwhelmed the group mind of the Cuckoos and when Sophie resisted the takeover bid you steered her towards death...

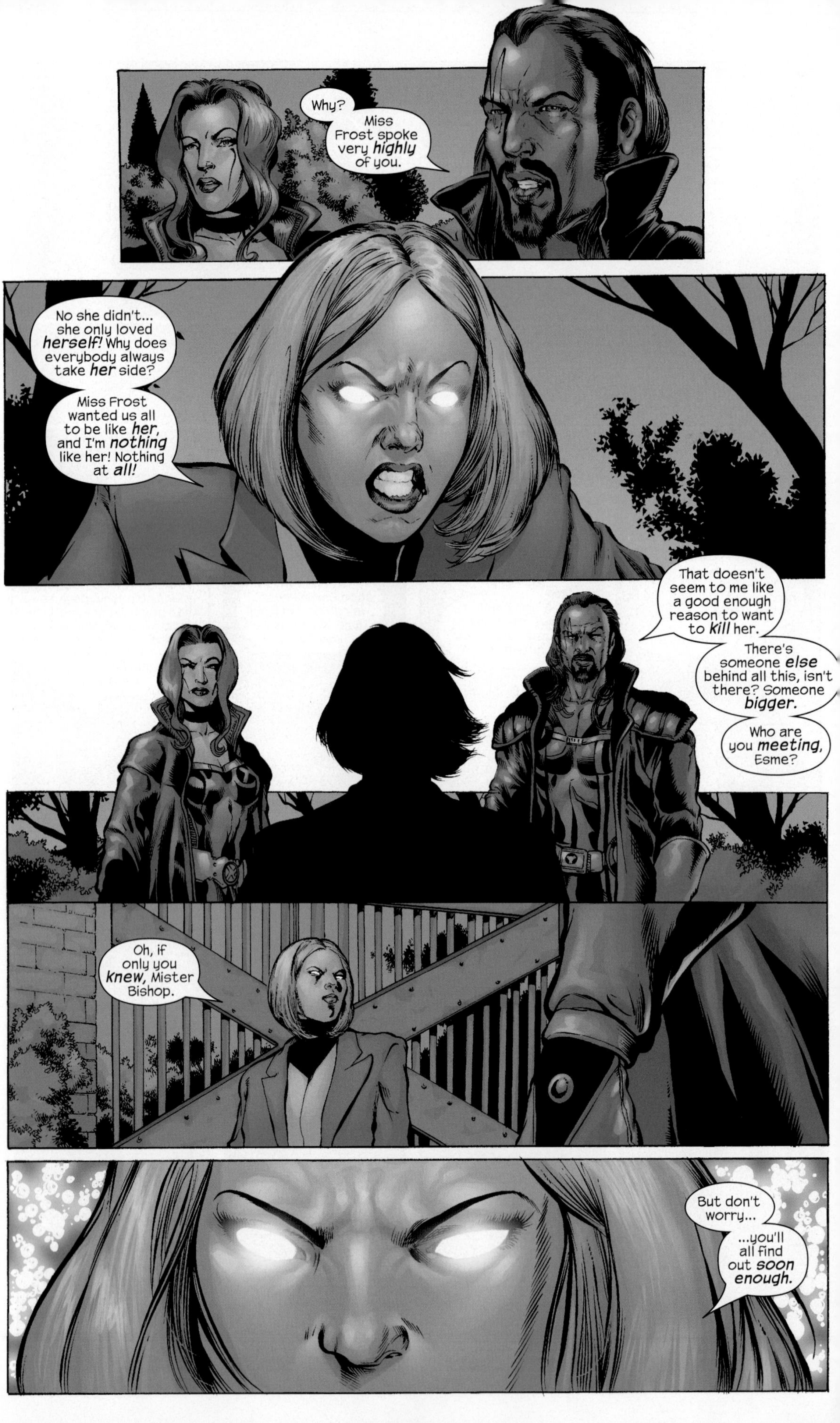
Why?
Miss Frost spoke very highly of you.
No she didn't... she only loved herself! Why does everybody always take her side?
Miss Frost wanted us all to be like her, and I'm nothing like her! Nothing at all!
That doesn't seem to me like a good enough reason to want to kill her.
There's someone else behind all this, isn't there? Someone bigger.
Who are you meeting, Esme?
Oh, if only you knew, Mister Bishop.
But don't worry...
...you'll all find out soon enough.

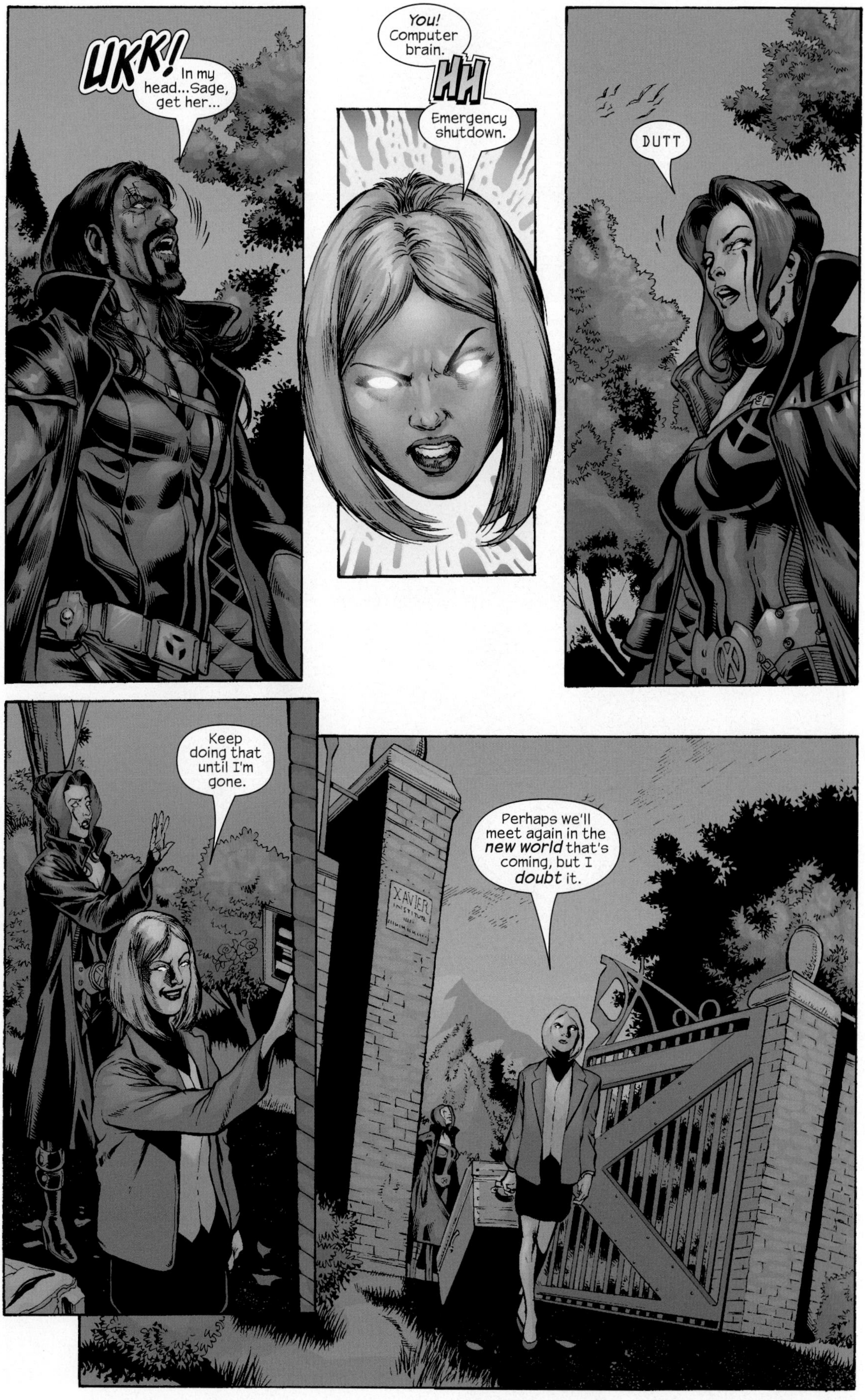
UKK!
In my head...Sage, get her...
You! Computer brain.
HH
Emergency shutdown.
DUTT
Keep doing that until I'm gone.
Perhaps we'll meet again in the *new world* that's coming, but I *doubt* it.
XAVIER INSTITUTE

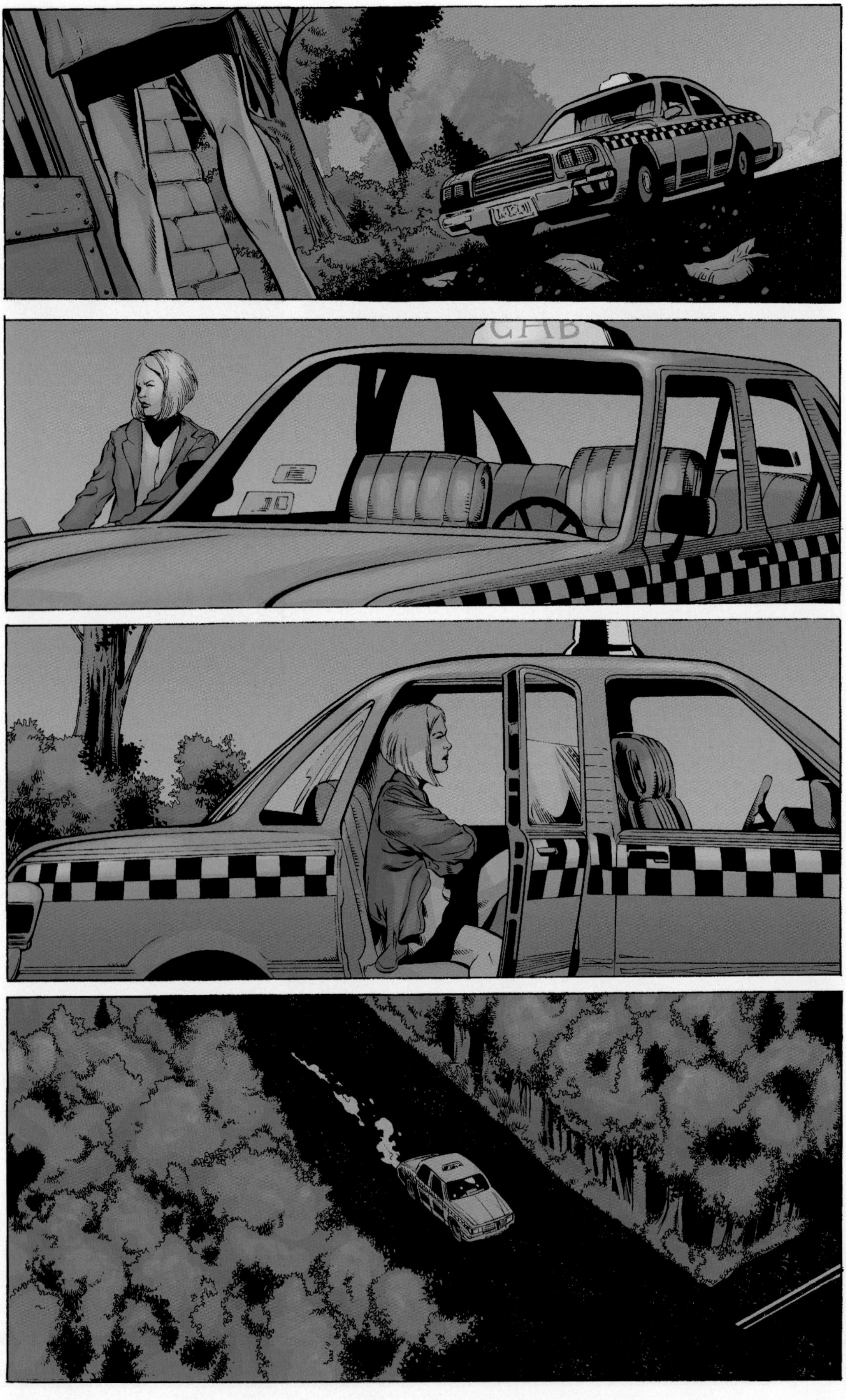

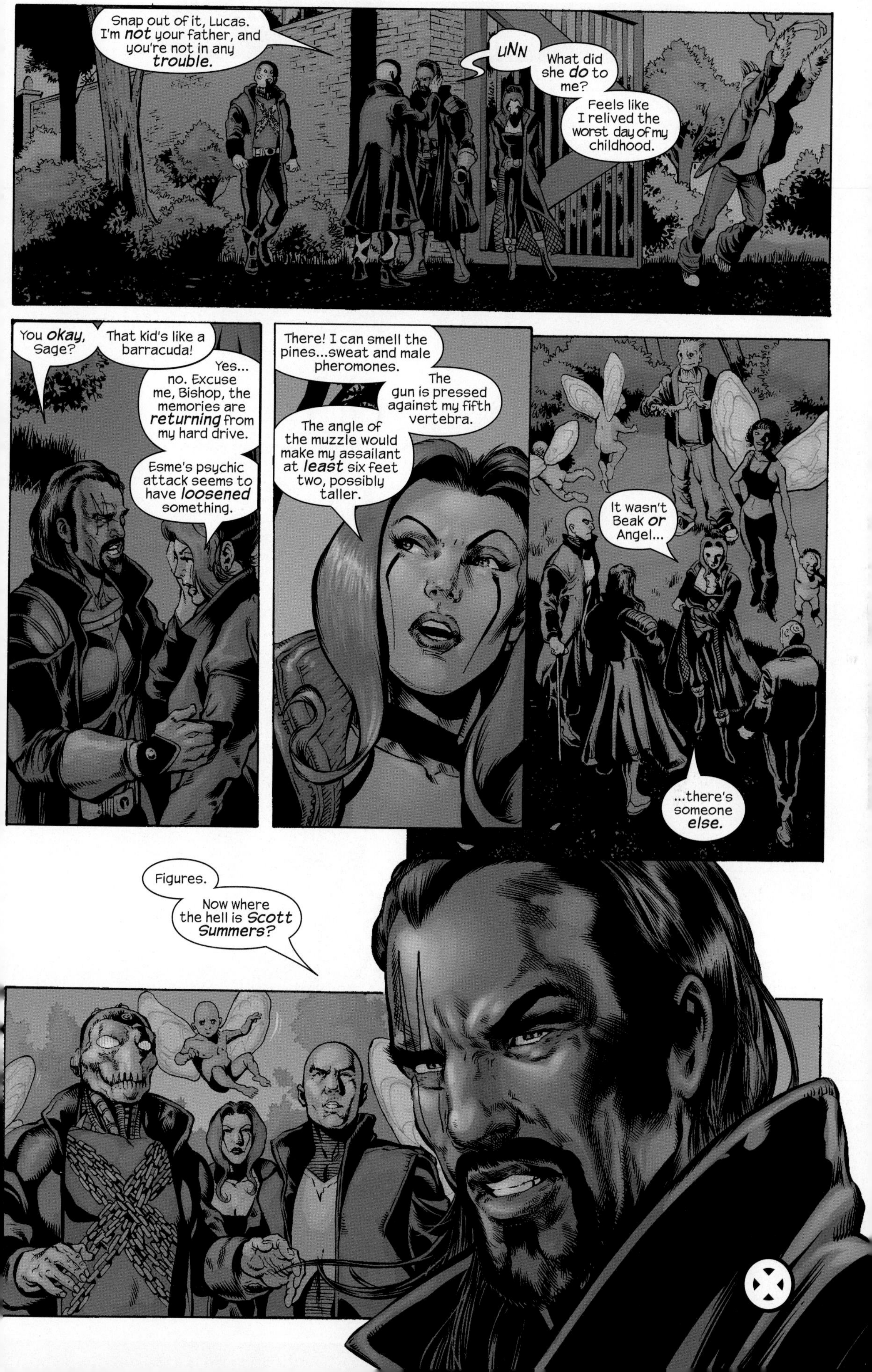

Snap out of it, Lucas. I'm not your father, and you're not in any trouble.
UNN
What did she do to me?
Feels like I relived the worst day of my childhood.
You okay, Sage?
That kid's like a barracuda!
Yes... no. Excuse me, Bishop, the memories are returning from my hard drive.
Esme's psychic attack seems to have loosened something.
There! I can smell the pines...sweat and male pheromones.
The gun is pressed against my fifth vertebra.
The angle of the muzzle would make my assailant at least six feet two, possibly taller.
It wasn't Beak or Angel...
...there's someone else.
Figures.
Now where the hell is Scott Summers?

Unused version of *New X-Men #128*, page 22
by Igor Kordey

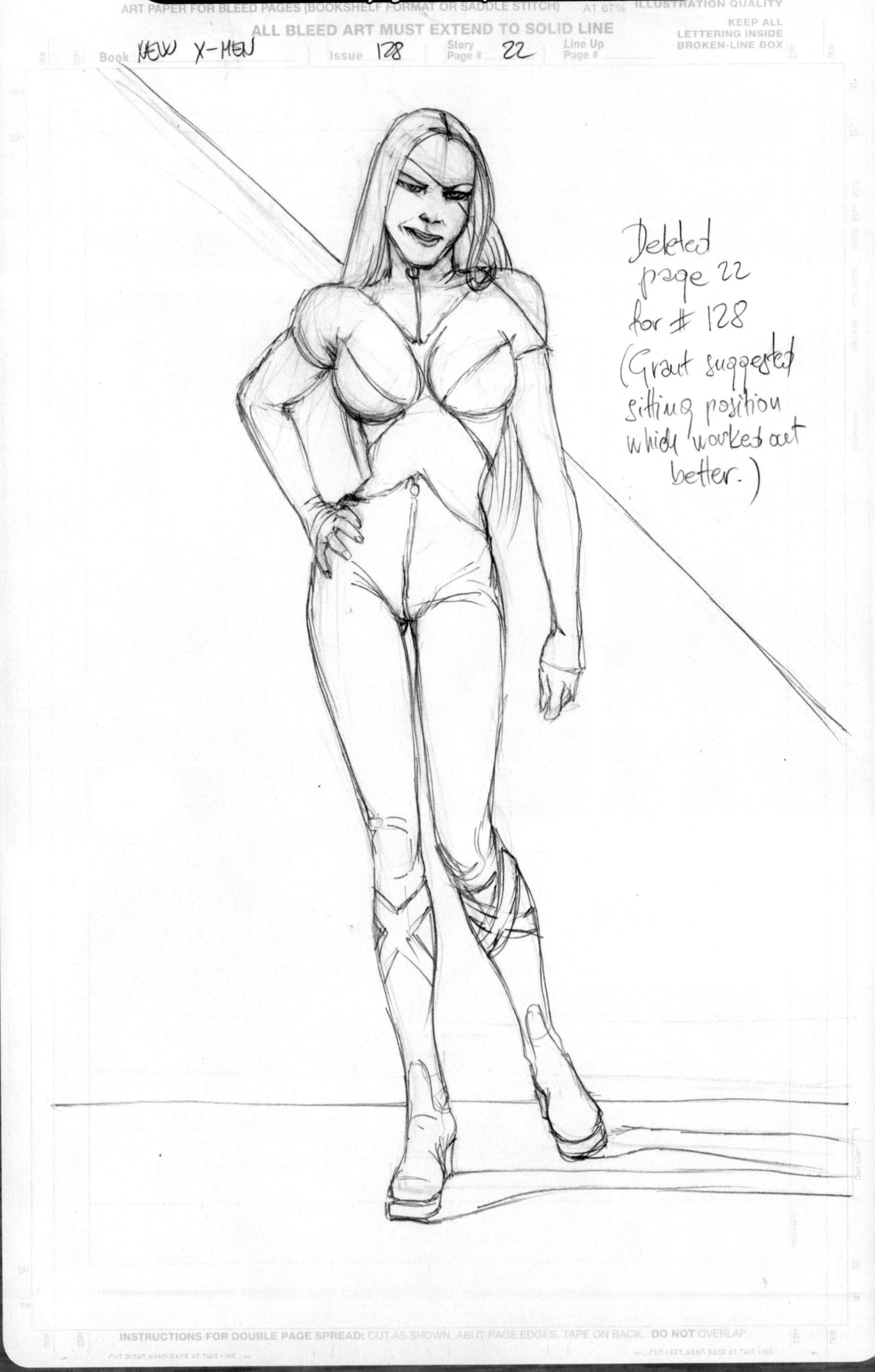
ART PAPER FOR BLEED PAGES (BOOKSHELF FORMAT OR SADDLE STITCH) AT 67% ILLUSTRATION QUALITY
ALL BLEED ART MUST EXTEND TO SOLID LINE
KEEP ALL LETTERING INSIDE BROKEN-LINE BOX
Book NEW X-MEN Issue 128 Story Page # 22 Line Up Page #
Deleted page 22 for # 128 (Grant suggested sitting position which worked out better.)
INSTRUCTIONS FOR DOUBLE PAGE SPREAD: CUT AS SHOWN. ABUT PAGE EDGES. TAPE ON BACK. DO NOT OVERLAP

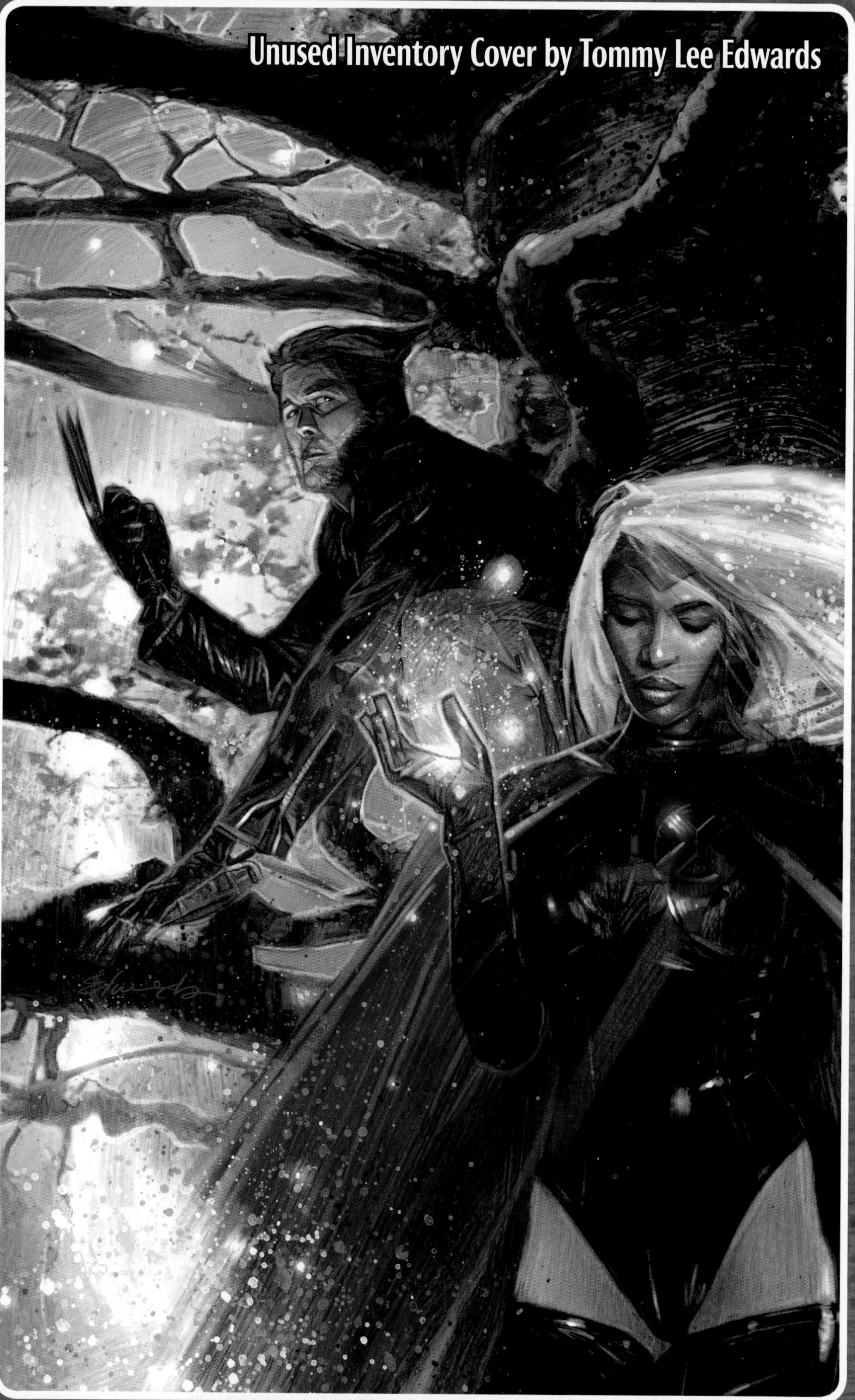

Unused Inventory Cover by Tommy Lee Edwards

Unused Inventory Cover by Tommy Lee Edwards

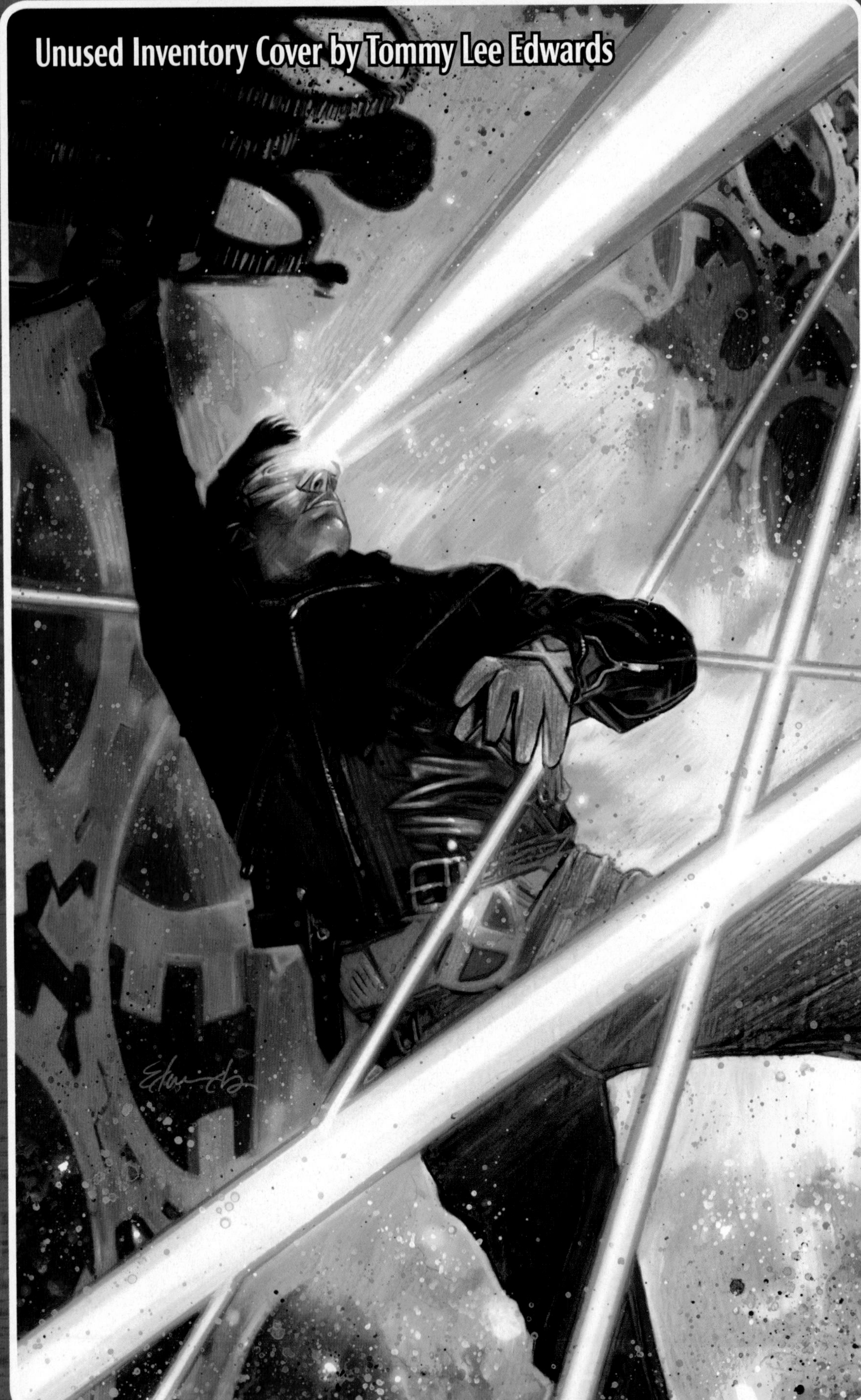

Unused Inventory Cover by Ariel Olivetti

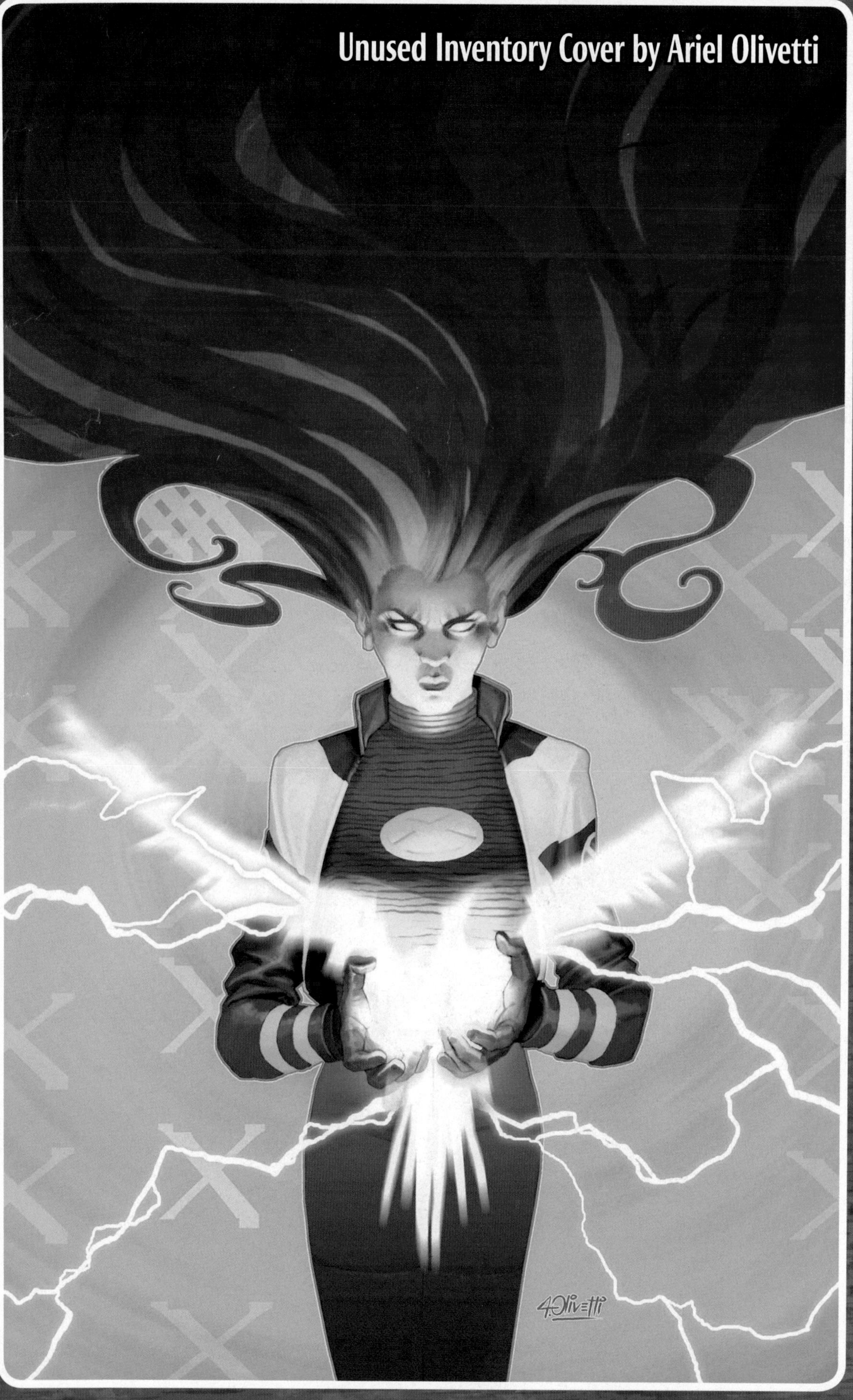

Olivetti

Wizard #147 cover by Marc Silvestri

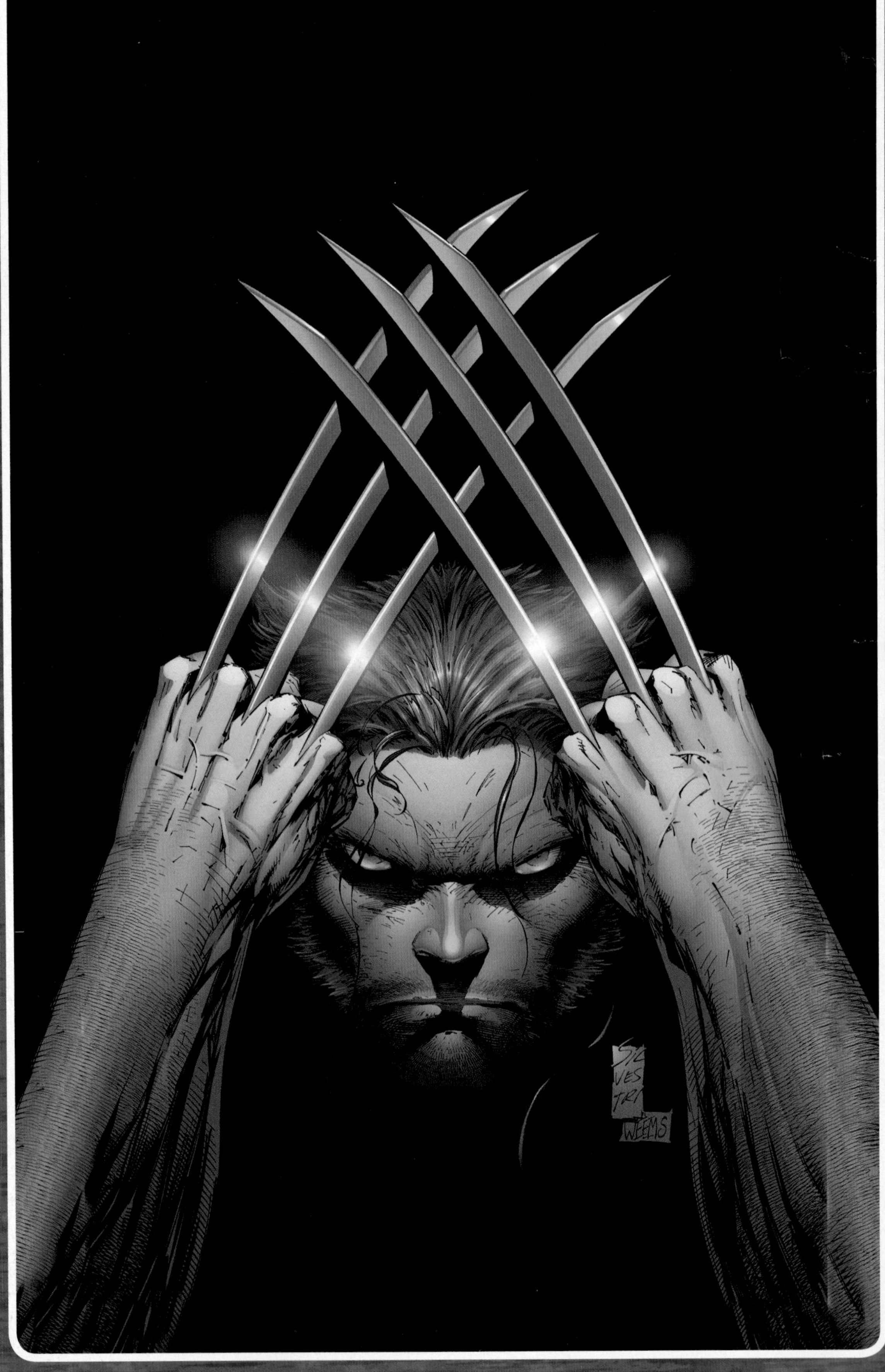